Lecture Notes in Computer Science 11265

Commenced Publication in 1973
Founding and Former Series Editors:
Gerhard Goos, Juris Hartmanis, and Jan van Leeuwen

More information about this series at http://www.springer.com/series/7409

Mitsuko Aramaki · Matthew E. P. Davies
Richard Kronland-Martinet · Sølvi Ystad (Eds.)

Music Technology with Swing

13th International Symposium, CMMR 2017
Matosinhos, Portugal, September 25–28, 2017
Revised Selected Papers

Springer

Editors
Mitsuko Aramaki
Laboratoire PRISM, AMU-CNRS
Marseille, France

Richard Kronland-Martinet ⓘ
Laboratoire PRISM, AMU-CNRS
Marseille, France

Matthew E. P. Davies ⓘ
INESC TEC
Porto, Portugal

Sølvi Ystad ⓘ
Laboratoire PRISM, AMU-CNRS
Marseille, France

ISSN 0302-9743   ISSN 1611-3349 (electronic)
Lecture Notes in Computer Science
ISBN 978-3-030-01691-3   ISBN 978-3-030-01692-0 (eBook)
https://doi.org/10.1007/978-3-030-01692-0

Library of Congress Control Number: 2018956470

LNCS Sublibrary: SL3 – Information Systems and Applications, incl. Internet/Web, and HCI

This Springer imprint is published by the registered company Springer Nature Switzerland AG
The registered company address is: Gewerbestrasse 11, 6330 Cham, Switzerland

Preface

The 13th international Symposium on Computer Music Multidisciplinary Research, CMMR 2017 "Music Technology with Swing" (http://cmmr2017.inesctec.pt/), was held in Matosinhos in Portugal during September 25–28 2017. It was organized by the Sound and Music Computing Group at INESC TEC, the Faculty of Engineering, University of Porto, Portugal, and the Orquestra Jazz de Matosinhos (OJM) in collaboration with the Laboratory PRISM ("Perception, Representations, Image, Sound, Music"), Marseilles, France.

This year's conference theme was "Music Technology with Swing" and aimed at encouraging contributions that considered the amazing ability that music has to enhance movements among people. As the local conference hosts put it:

"Music is not only about sounding, but also about moving: from the highly skilled movements of individual musicians to the involuntary foot-tapping turning into the synchronization of a thousand dancers. Technology can certainly be exciting per se, but there is nothing quite so compelling as music technology in the way it further enhances our ability to sound together, to move together, to dance together. Swing — both as in the back and forth of a pendulum and as in the surprising rhythmic event that contradicts whilst drawing from our expectations — is a word that conveys this excitement, this liveliness, and the permanent endeavor of finding new musical possibilities."

Four internationally renowned keynote speakers specialized in highly distinct domains were invited to the conference. Amílcar Cardoso from the University of Coimbra, Portugal, who is a specialist in artificial intelligence, computational creativity, programming for design gave an introduction to "Computational Creativity." Margaret Schedel from Stony Brook University, USA, who is a composer and cellist, described methods of transcribing the functions and activities of gesture for interactive performances. Peter Vuust from Aarhus University, Denmark, who is a jazz musician and neuroscientist, explained how the theory of predictive coding can be used as a framework for understanding how rhythm and rhythmic complexity are processed in the brain. Finally, Carlos Guedes from the New York University Abu Dhabi, United Arab Emirates, who is a composer, gave a talk on real-time composition and improvisation and discussed how such systems can provide interesting approaches to composition with electronic music and to music education and enculturation.

In addition to the keynote presentations, eight paper sessions, two poster sessions, and one demo session were organized, as well as three concerts representing the selected music submissions.

The CMMR 2017 proceedings volume is the 13th book published by Springer in the *Lecture Notes in Computer Science* series (LNCS 2771, LNCS 3310, LNCS 3902, LNCS 4969, LNCS 5493, LNCS 5954, LNCS 6684, LNCS 7172, LNCS 7900, LNCS 8905, LNCS 9617, LNCS 10525).

The present edition contains 44 peer-reviewed and revised papers from the conference and is divided into eight sections that reflect the wide span of subjects presented as this year's conference. Traditional CMMR topics such as automatic recognition, estimation, and classification as well as cooperative networks and tools for composing and transforming music can be found in four different sections ("Music Information Retrieval, Automatic Recognition, Estimation and Classification," "Electronic Dance Music and Rhythm," "Computational Musicology," and "Cooperative Music Networks and Musical HCIs"). One section is dedicated to the use of auditory feedback in the case of sports and remediation ("Sound in Practice: Auditory Guidance and Feedback in the Context of Motor Learning and Motor Adaptation"), while more general topics linked to new interfaces, guiding, musical interaction, and sonification strategies are presented in two different sections ("Human Perception in Multimodal Context" and "Virtual and Augmented Reality"). Finally, the last section comprises contributions from artists and musicologists and describes both installations, artistic practice and creation, philosophical viewpoints, and relations with new technologies ("Research and Creation: Spaces and Modalities").

We would like to thank all the participants of CMMR 2017 who contributed to make this symposium a remarkable event. We would also like to thank the Program and Music Committee members for their indispensable contribution to CMMR 2017. We are very grateful to the Câmara Municipal de Matosinhos and the local Organizing Committee who took care of the practical organization and insured a smooth and efficient coordination between attendees, speakers, audiences, and musicians in both the scientific and artistic programs. Finally, we would like to thank Springer for accepting to publish the CMMR 2017 proceedings in their LNCS series.

July 2018

Mitsuko Aramaki
Matthew E. P. Davies
Richard Kronland-Martinet
Sølvi Ystad

Organization

The 13th International Symposium on Computer Music Multidisciplinary Research CMMR 2017 "Music Technology with Swing" was jointly organized by the Sound and Music Computing Group at INESC TEC together with the Orquestra Jazz de Matosinhos and AMU-CNRS-PRISM, Marseilles, France.

Symposium Chairs

Matthew E. P. Davies   INESC TEC, Portugal
Rui Penha   FEUP, INESC TEC, Portugal

Program and Proceedings Chairs

Richard Kronland-Martinet   AMU-CNRS-PRISM, France
Mitsuko Aramaki   AMU-CNRS-PRISM, France
Sølvi Ystad   AMU-CNRS-PRISM, France
Matthew E. P. Davies   INESC TEC, Portugal
Marcelo Caetano   INESC TEC, Portugal

Local Organizing Committee

Matthew E. P. Davies   INESC TEC, Portugal
Rui Penha   FEUP, INESC TEC, Portugal
Jorge Coelho   OJM, Portugal
Pedro Guedes   OJM, Portugal
Miguel Carvalhais   FBAUP, INESC TEC, Portugal
Gilberto Bernardes   INESC TEC, Portugal
Marcelo Caetano   INESC TEC, Portugal
Luís Aly   FEUP, Portugal
António Sá Pinto   FEUP, INESC TEC, Portugal
Diogo Cocharro   FEUP, INESC TEC, Portugal
Eduardo Magalhães   FEUP, Portugal

Program Committee

Mitsuko Aramaki   AMU-CNRS-PRISM, France
Marta Bieńkiewicz   Aix-Marseille University, France
Lionel Bringoux   Aix-Marseille University, France
Marcelo Caetano   INESC TEC, Portugal
Amílcar Cardoso   University of Coimbra, Portugal
Roger Dannenberg   Carnegie Mellon University, USA

Matthew E. P. Davies	INESC TEC, Portugal
Joel Eaton	University of Plymouth, UK
Christine Esclapez	AMU-CNRS-PRISM, France
Georg Essl	University of Wisconsin, USA
Michele Geronazzo	University of Verona, Italy
Rolf Inge Godøy	University of Oslo, Norway
Luis Jure	Universidad de la Republica, Uruguay
Maximos Kaliakatsos-Papakostas	University of Thessaloniki, Greece
Timour Klouche	SIM Berlin, Germany
Richard Kronland-Martinet	AMU-CNRS-PRISM, France
Sylvain Marchand	University of La Rochelle, France
Jean-Arthur Micoulaud-Franchi	CNRS USR Sanpsy, France
Hélène Papadopoulos	CNRS-L2S, Paris-Sud University, France
Marcelo Queiroz	Universidade de São Paulo, Brazil
Matthew Rodger	Queen's University Belfast, UK
Charalampos Saitis	Technical University of Berlin, Germany
Flavio Schiavoni	Federal University of São João Del Rey, Brazil
Stefania Serafin	Aalborg University of Copenhagen, Denmark
Tiago Tavares	State University of Campinas, Brazil
Etienne Thoret	McGill University, Canada
Luca Turchet	Mind Music Labs, Sweden
Marcelo Wanderley	McGill University, Canada
Ian Whalley	University of Waikato, New Zealand
Duncan Williams	University of Plymouth, UK
Sølvi Ystad	AMU-CNRS-PRISM, France

Contents

Human Perception in Multimodal Context

Cooperative Music Networks and Musical HCIs

Virtual and Augmented Reality

Research and Creation: Spaces and Modalities

Music Information Retrieval, Automatic Recognition, Estimation and Classification

Automatic Recognition of Sound Categories from Their Vocal Imitation Using Audio Primitives Automatically Found by SI-PLCA and HMM

Enrico Marchetto and Geoffroy Peeters[✉]

UMR STMS 9912 (IRCAM – CNRS – Sorbonne-University), Paris, France
{marchetto,peeters}@ircam.fr

Abstract. In this paper we study the automatic recognition of sound categories (such as fridge, mixers or sawing sounds) from their vocal imitations. Vocal imitations are made of a succession over time of sounds produced using vocal mechanisms that can largely differ from the ones used in speech. We develop here a recognition approach inspired by automatic-speech-recognition systems, with an acoustic model (that maps the audio signal to a set of probability over "phonemes") and a language model (that represents the expected succession of "phonemes" for each sound category). Since we do not know what are the underlying "phonemes" of vocal imitations we propose to automatically estimate them using Shift-Invariant Probabilistic Latent Component Analysis (SI-PLCA) applied to a dataset of vocal imitations. The kernel distributions of the SI-PLCA are considered as the "phonemes" of vocal imitation and its impulse distributions are used to compute the emission probabilities of the states of a set of Hidden Markov Models (HMMs). To evaluate our proposal, we test it for a task of automatically recognizing 12 sound categories from their vocal imitations.

Keywords: Vocal imitation · Sound design · Sound recognition
Shift-invariant probabilistic-latent-component-analysis
Hidden markov model

1 Introduction

Vocal Imitations for Sound Design. In typical design approaches (whether in architecture, products, etc.), the very first step is often a "sketch", that is a simple graphical representation of the target. This initial sketch is a useful tool to enhance communications between designers and stakeholders. In the case of sound design, professionals often use vocal imitations to add more detail to the sound description [9], trying to transmit to their interlocutor the main cues of their sound idea [7]. "Vocal imitations" can therefore be considered as the sound design "sketches".

© Springer Nature Switzerland AG 2018
M. Aramaki et al. (Eds.): CMMR 2017, LNCS 11265, pp. 3–22, 2018.
https://doi.org/10.1007/978-3-030-01692-0_1

The goal of the recently achieved SkAT-VG project[1] was to develop sound design tools [3] that use voice and gesture. In SkAT-VG, each sound category (such as fridge, mixers or sawing sounds) is synthesized using a specific physical model synthesizer [1]. To select this specific synthesizer, users imitate the sound category with their voice. We therefore need to develop a system that is able to automatically recognize the sound categories from their vocal imitation. This is the goal of this paper. Once the category has been recognized the proper physical model synthesizer is launched (see Fig. 1 Left part) and users can control its parameters with their voice and gestures.

To recognize automatically the sound category, we first need to understand how people imitate each sound category. To study this, a dataset of vocal imitations has been created during the project by the Perception and Sound Design team of IRCAM. This dataset represents 26 sound categories, each represented by 2 audio examples, each imitated by 50 different users with voice and gesture (see Fig. 1 Right part). Since it was found that gesture imitations could not be used to recognize the sound category, we only consider vocal imitations here.

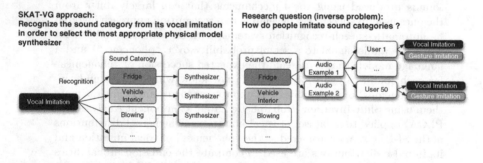

Fig. 1. [Left] SkAT-VG approach: recognizing sound category from their vocal imitation, [Right] Research question: how do people imitate each sound category?

In this paper, we consider a subset of this dataset made of 12 sound categories. Those categories were chosen as the most challenging in terms of variety of vocal imitations. They represent two super-categories: (1) sounds produced by "machines" and (2) sounds produced by "interactions" (interactions with "gases", "liquids" or "solids") (see Fig. 2).

Vocal Imitations. To better understand the characteristics of these vocal imitations, we represent in Fig. 3 the spectrogram (in log-frequency) of one of the vocal imitations of the sound category "Vehicle exterior (motorcycle engine start)". As one can see, a vocal imitation is a succession over time of sounds produced using various vocal mechanisms (such as produced by the vocal folds, the lips, the tong). We denote these sounds by "vocal primitive"s (VPs). It should be noted that these VPs can largely differ from the "phoneme" used in speech [8].

---

[1] http://skatvg.iuav.it/.

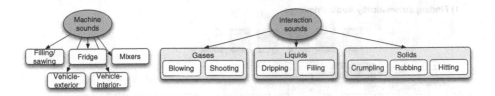

Fig. 2. The 12 sound categories of the subset of the SkAT-VG dataset.

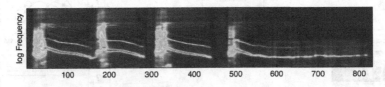

Fig. 3. Example of one of the vocal imitations belonging to the sound category "Vehicle exterior (motorcycle engine start)"(sound reference: 03AM-3V_Machine18.wav-20150114152719-0.wav)

1.1   Goal of the Paper

The goal of this paper is to automatically recognize the sound categories from their vocal imitations. In our previous work [10], we solved this problem by developing a "blind approach" that maps directly the audio signal level to the sound category level. We use here a different approach. We consider that vocal imitations use a vocabulary defined by "vocal primitive"s (VPs) and a language model (that favours the use and the temporal order of VPs) specific to each sound categories. We would like to develop an approach inspired by automatic-speech-recognition systems, in which

- an *acoustic model* first maps the audio signal to a set of probability over "phonemes",
- a *language model* then represents the expected succession of "phonemes" for a given word (or sentence).

Unfortunately, in the case of vocal imitations, we do not know what are the underlying "phonemes". Rather than defining those manually, we propose to automatically estimate them from the audio signal. We therefore denote them by "audio primitive"s (APs) rather than "vocal primitive"s (VPs). To automatically estimate the APs, we propose to use Shift-Invariant Probabilistic Latent Component Analysis (SI-PLCA). Rather than applying the SI-PLCA algorithm to a single audio file (as it is usually the case), we apply it here to the whole dataset of vocal imitations. We then consider the kernel distributions resulting from the SI-PLCA as the global set of APs used for vocal imitations (see Fig. 4 Top). For a given vocal imitation, the impulse/activation distributions of the SI-PLCA represent the succession over time (and superposition over frequency) of APs necessary to reproduce it. Using all vocal imitations of a given sound

1) Finding automatically Audio Primitives

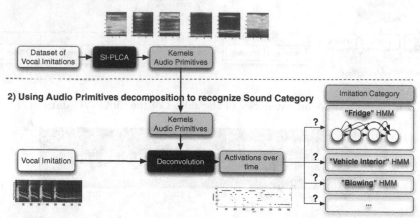

Fig. 4. [Top] Estimating the "audio primitive" (AP) using the kernels of SI-PLCA applied to the whole dataset, [Bottom] Estimating the sound category by decoding Hidden Markov Models (HMMs) using the APs to compute the emission probabilities.

category, we can then create a sequence model of this category. For each category, we train a Hidden Markov Model (HMM) which hidden states represent a specific combination of APs, the emission probability of the hidden states are computed using the impulse/activation distributions and the transition probability represent their specific temporal order for this category.

To recognize an unknown vocal imitation, we then simply chose among the set of HMMs the one that allows the most likely decoding into APs of its audio signal (see Fig. 4 Bottom).

1.2   Related Works

A well-known approach to allow time series recognition is the extraction of low level signal descriptors, which are then modelled using HMM [13]. In speech recognition [5,14], the best results are obtained combining language models (based on grammars) and acoustical models [16]. Another closely related topic is the recognition of "words for sounds", such as onomatopoeias. Proposed approaches to this problem, linked to speech recognition, still rely on phonemes [4] or lexical cues [21]. There are also examples of features clustering and modelling [22]. Description of sounds in terms of morphological profiles has been initially proposed by P. Schaeffer works [17]. The automatic estimation of these profiles for abstract sounds has been previously studied by [12,15] which propose dedicated descriptors.

1.3   Organization of the Paper

In Sect. 2, we explain how we estimate the "audio primitive"s (APs) of vocal imitations using SI-PLCA. In Sect. 3, we explain how we use this decomposition into APs to model each sound category by a HMM. In Sect. 4, we validate the fact that these APs actually correspond to significant "acoustic cue"s (ACs) and evaluate the performances of our proposed SI-PLCA/HMM system for a task of sound category recognition.

2 Using SI-PLCA to Find Audio Primitives

In the same way as speech uses "phoneme" as elementary vocabulary, we consider that vocal imitations uses "vocal primitive"s (VPs) as elementary vocabulary. Rather than defining these VPs by hand, we would like to develop a system that is able to automatically derive them by analyzing a given dataset of audio recordings. We therefore denote them by "audio primitive"s (APs) since they do not rely on any vocal production mechanism but only rely on the audio content. These APs

- should represent significant acoustic cues that arise in time and frequency
- can be super-imposed in time and/or in frequency (such as harmonics component in low-frequency superimposed to noise in high-frequency)
- can be shifted in time and/or in frequency.

The algorithm we use to derive automatically these APs is the Shift-Invariant Probabilistic Latent Component Analysis (SI-PLCA).

2.1 PLCA and SI-PLCA

Probabilistic Latent Component Analysis (PLCA) [19] can be considered as a probabilistic form of the well-known Non-negative Matrix Factorization (NMF) [6,11]. PLCA is a technique which belongs to the *latent class models* (as Probabilistic Latent Semantic Analysis or Latent Dirichlet Allocation). These models have in common:

- they are not applied directly to experimental data $\mathbf{x}$ but to their distribution $P(\mathbf{x})$,
- they are conceived to explain the distribution by means of *latent* classes z.

PLCA explains $P(\mathbf{x})$ as a mixture of latent distributions $P(\mathbf{x}|z)$ along with their mixing weights $P(z)$:

$$P(\mathbf{x}) = \sum_{z=1}^{K} P_Z(z)P(\mathbf{x}|z) \tag{1}$$

where $P(\mathbf{x})$ is the N-dimensional distribution of the random variable $\mathbf{x}$. This expresses that $P(\mathbf{x})$ is explained by several other distinct distributions $P(\mathbf{x}|z)$ which are combined using the latent variable $z \in \{1, \ldots, K\}$ whose distribution $P_Z(z)$ expresses the mixing weights among the latent classes.

The model can be fully expanded as

$$P(\mathbf{x}) = \sum_{z=1}^{K} \left[P_Z(z) \prod_{j=1}^{N} P(x_j|z) \right] \tag{2}$$

where $P(\mathbf{x}|z)$ is decomposed into its single-dimensional parts $P(x_j|z)$. By the *local independence principle*, expressing z renders independent the distributions of $\mathbf{x}$ along each of its dimensions (which otherwise could be dependent).

In order to estimate the latent components $P(\mathbf{x}|z)$ and the distribution $P_Z(z)$ it is possible to apply a standard Expectation-Maximization (EM) algorithm.

Shift-Invariant Probabilistic Latent Component Analysis (SI-PLCA) has been introduced by [20] as an extension to PLCA [19]. It adds to the former the possibility to "shift" a latent distribution over one or several dimensions. The shift invariance is obtained using a convolutive model. The model becomes:

$$P(\mathbf{x}) = \sum_{z=1}^{K} \left[P_Z(z) \underbrace{\int_{\tau} P_K(\boldsymbol{\tau}|z)P_I(\mathbf{x}-\boldsymbol{\tau}|z)d\boldsymbol{\tau}}_{P(\mathbf{x}|z)} \right] \tag{3}$$

The term $P_K(\boldsymbol{\tau}|z)P_I(\mathbf{x}-\boldsymbol{\tau}|z)$ replaces what was $P(\mathbf{x}|z)$ in the PLCA. We call **kernels** (or dictionary or bases) the "elementary" distributions $P_K(\boldsymbol{\tau}|z)$ which are latent in the input. We call **impulses** (or activations) the distributions of the shifts $P_I(\mathbf{x}-\boldsymbol{\tau}|z)$ which, when applied to the kernels, reproduce the input $P(\mathbf{x})$.

In the following we consider that $\mathbf{x}$ has 2 dimensions: time t and frequency f. We can then write

$$P(f,t) = \sum_{z=1}^{K} \left[P_Z(z) \underbrace{\int_{\tau_f} \int_{\tau_t} P_K(\tau_t,\tau_f|z)P_I(t-\tau_t,f-\tau_f|z)d\tau_t d\tau_f}_{P(t,f|z)} \right] \tag{4}$$

We also write the reconstruction obtained using a single kernel z as

$$P_z(f,t) = P_Z(z) \underbrace{\int_{\tau_f} \int_{\tau_t} P_K(\tau_t,\tau_f|z)P_I(t-\tau_t,f-\tau_f|z)d\tau_t d\tau_f}_{P(t,f|z)} \tag{5}$$

Estimation. The estimations of $P_Z(z)$, $P_K(\tau_1, \tau_2 | z)$ and $P_I(x - \tau_1, y - \tau_2 | z)$ is done using the following EM updates proposed by [20]:

$$R(x, y, \tau_1, \tau_2, z) = \frac{P_Z^{(n)}(z) P_K^{(n)}(\tau_1, \tau_2 | z) P_I^{(n)}(x - \tau_1, y - \tau_2 | z)}{\sum_{z'} P_Z(z') I_{\tau_1', \tau_2'} \{ P_K(\tau_1', \tau_2' | z) P_I(x - \tau_1', y - \tau_2' | z) \}} \quad (6)$$

$$P_Z^{(n+1)}(z) = I_{x, y, \tau_1, \tau_2} \{ P(x, y) R(x, y, \tau_1, \tau_2, z) \} \quad (7)$$

$$P_K^{(n+1)}(\tau_1, \tau_2 | z) = \frac{I_{x, y} \{ P(x, y) R(x, y, \tau_1, \tau_2, z) \}}{P_Z^{(n+1)}(z)} \quad (8)$$

$$P_I^{(n+1)}(x, y | z) = \frac{I_{\tau_1, \tau_2} \{ P(x + \tau_1, y + \tau_2) R(x + \tau_1, y + \tau_2, \tau_1, \tau_2, z) \}}{I_{x', y', \tau_1, \tau_2} \{ P(x' + \tau_1, y' + \tau_2) R(x' + \tau_1, y' + \tau_2, \tau_1, \tau_2, z) \}} \quad (9)$$

where n represents the number of iterations. We used a value of $n = 130$.

Initialization. P_Z and $P_I(x, y | z)$ are initialized according to a uniform distribution (equal values, normalized to sum to one). The kernel distributions $P_K(\tau_1, \tau_2 | z)$ are instead initialized with the realization of a uniform random variable which favours algorithm convergence.

Sparsity Constraints. In order to favour P_K to describe the "kernels/dictionary" and P_I the "impulse/activations", we should force P_I to be sparse. SI-PLCA allows a straightforward way to force this sparsity by constraining the shape of the distributions P_K and/or P_I. In this work, we used the "simulated annealing" approach proposed in [20]. After each update of P_K and P_I we apply:

$$P_K(\tau_1, \tau_2 | z) \leftarrow c_1 \cdot P_K(\tau_1, \tau_2 | z)^{\alpha(n)}, \quad \alpha(n) > 0 \quad (10)$$

$$P_I(x, y | z) \leftarrow c_2 \cdot P_I(x, y | z)^{\beta(n)}, \quad \beta(n) > 0 \quad (11)$$

where c_1 and c_2 are normalization factor to ensure that P_K and P_I remain probabilities.

- α starts in the range $[0.8, 0.9]$ and increases over iterations to 1. The exponent $\alpha < 1$ "flattens" the distributions P_k (we seek for high entropy in the kernels).
- β starts at 1 and increases over iterations to the range $[1.05, 1.1]$. The exponent $\beta > 1$ enhances the peaks of P_I, therefore increasing sparsity.

2.2 Application of SI-PLCA to Find Automatically "Audio Primitives"

To facilitate the detection of shift-invariant kernels over time and frequency, we represent the audio signal using a time and log-spaced-frequency representation. Considering that part of the sounds produced by the voice will be harmonic, we have chosen to use the Constant-Q-Transform (CQT) [2,23]: $P(f_{\log}, t)$. The

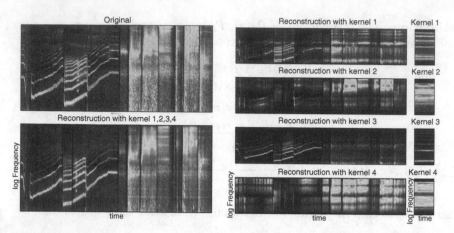

Fig. 5. [Left column] [Top]: CQT of 20 s. excerpt of the dataset, [Bottom]: reconstruction using 4 kernels of size ($f = 60 \times t = 6$). [Right column] From top to bottom: reconstruction using individual kernels (indicated on the right size of each plot).

CQT is computed using [18] Toolbox with frequencies in the range $[70, 5000]$ Hz (6.16 octaves). This leads to $6.16 \times 36 = 222$ bins and 210 frames per second.

While SI-PLCA is usually applied to a single audio file (for multi-pitch estimation or source separation), we apply it here to the whole dataset of vocal imitations with the goal of estimating "audio primitive"s (APs). To do so, we concatenate in time all the audio files of our dataset. The total duration of the dataset is 486 s. The CQT matrix resulting from this concatenation is then very large (222×102111). To reduce its size, we down-sample it by a factor of 2 on the frequency axis and of 3 on the time axis. The final input matrix for the SI-PLCA has size (111×34037).

Illustrating SI-PLCA Signal Reconstruction. In Fig. 5 we illustrate the application of the SI-PLCA to our dataset. We only represent a 20 s. excerpt of the whole dataset.

The top of the left column represents the original CQT. The bottom of the left column represents the reconstructed CQT using $K = 4$ kernels of size ($f = 60 \times t = 6$): $P(t, f)$. Each row of the right column represents the reconstructed CQT using each individual kernel z: $P_z(t, f)$ (see Eq. (5)). Along each reconstructed CQT we indicate the corresponding kernel $P_K(\tau_t, \tau_f | z)$.

We see that the reconstruction effectively highlights the main cues of the signal. 1st and 3rd kernels are clearly related to the different harmonic contents. 2nd and 4th kernels are less structured, and are activated mostly in noisy parts.

Illustrating SI-PLCA Kernels. In Fig. 6 [Left] we illustrate the kernels obtained by SI-PLCA using $K = 6$ kernels of size ($f = 30 \times t = 15$). Compare to the 4 kernels of Fig. 5, these 6 kernels are larger in time ($t = 15 > t = 6$)

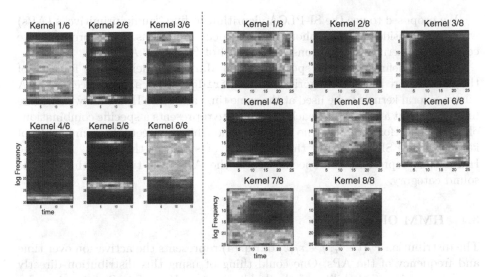

Fig. 6. SI-PLCA kernels using [Left] six kernels of size ($f = 30 \times t = 15$) [Right] Eight kernels of size ($f = 25 \times t = 25$).

and smaller in frequency ($f = 30 < f = 60$). The increase in time extent allows now to describe impulsive content: kernel 2/6 (and to a less extend kernel 5/6) appears lumped in time. The frequency extent is still enough to describe harmonic content[2]: kernels 2/6, 3/6, 4/6 and 5/6 are all oriented toward the harmonic content of the dataset. However, kernels 1/6 and 6/6 are less structured.

In Fig. 6 [Right] we illustrate the kernels obtained by SI-PLCA using [Right] $K = 8$ kernels of size ($f = 25 \times t = 25$). The kernel 4/8 correctly catches the harmonic structure. The extended time axis lets the kernels show more complex primitives in the other kernels.

Due to the memory requirements of our algorithm we cannot compute larger families of kernels (bigger cardinality and/or bigger kernels).

3 Modeling Sound Categories Using Hidden Markov Models

Our goal is to develop a system inspired by automatic-speech-recognition. In such a system,

- an *acoustic model* first maps the audio signal to a set of probability over "phonemes",
- then a *language model* represents the expected succession of "phonemes" for a given word (or sentence).

---

[2] In our CQT, harmonics are spaced by 18 bins, so the kernels size in frequency has to be at least 18 to exploit the shift-invariance.

We proposed to use the SI-PLCA algorithm to find "audio primitive"s (APs) which we consider as the "phonemes" of vocal imitations. More precisely, we consider the kernel distributions $P_K(\tau_t, \tau_f|z)$ of Eq. (4) as APs.

We then define a specific specific Hidden Markov Model (HMM) for each of the 12 considered sound categories (`sawing`, `fridge`, `mixers`, ...). Since SI-PLCA allows several kernels to be used at the same time and since HMM allows only one hidden state at a given time, each hidden state represents a specific combinations of APs. Therefore, there is no direct relationship between the number K of kernels of the SI-PLCA and the number S of states of the HMM. A specific HMM then represents the specific use of the APs over time for this specific sound category.

3.1 HMM Observations

The distribution $P_I(t - \tau_t, f - \tau_f|z)$ of Eq. (4) represents the activation over time and frequency of the APs. One could thing of using this distribution directly as the emission probability of the hidden states. However, P_I is an impulse distribution which means it only represents the starting time of the APs and not its energy contribution over time.

For this reason, instead of $P_I(t - \tau_t, f - \tau_f|z)$ we use the re-construction $P_z(t, f)$ provided by each kernel z (see Eq. (5)). Examples of these per-kernel $P_z(t, f)$ re-constructed signals are illustrated in Fig. 5 [Right]. To achieve shift-independence over frequencies, we then simply compute the marginal over frequencies: $P_z(t) = \int_f P_z(t, f)df$.

We finally consider $P_z(t)$ as our HMM observations over time. It is a K dimensional vector over time t which represents the energy contribution over time of the K kernels.

3.2 HMM Training

Each of the 12 sound categories is modelled by a specific HMM with S hidden states. Each state emits an observation (the K dimensional vector $P_z(t)$) with a probability modeled as a Gaussian Mixture Model (GMM) with G components. The training is performed using the Baum-Welch algorithm.

3.3 Recognition of the Sound Categories Using HMM

For an unknown vocal imitation, the impulse distributions $P_I(t - \tau_t, f - \tau_f|z)$ are estimated given the set of pre-computed kernels $P_K(\tau_t, \tau_f|z)$. The observations $P_z(t)$ are then computed from this. For each of the 12 HMMs, Viterbi decoding is performed. The decoding leading to the highest likelihood is chosen as the sound category to the unknown signal.

4   Evaluation

In this part, we validate our proposal using two experiments.

We first validate the fact that the "audio primitive"s (APs) automatically found by the SI-PLCA actually correspond to significant "acoustic cue"s (ACs). We do this by comparing these APs to the manual annotation of the dataset into ACs.

We then validate the use of these APs as observations of a Hidden Markov Model (HMM). We do this by using them to perform the automatic recognition of the 12 sound categories with the set of 12 HMMs.

4.1   Dataset

We have created a dataset of 115 vocal imitations corresponding to the 12 sound categories described in Fig. 2. Each sound category is represented by two referent sounds, which are each imitated by 5 subjects. The total duration of the dataset is 486.38 s. This dataset is a subset of the main SKAT-VG dataset.

4.2   Experiment 1: Comparing the "Audio Primitives" Automatically Found by SI-PLCA with "Manually Annotated Acoustic Cues"

Manual Annotation of the Dataset. We manually annotated each audio file of the dataset into a set of "acoustic cue"s (ACs). By ACs we mean salient temporal and spectral characteristics of the audio signal. We indicate in Table 1, the dictionary of ACs used for the manual annotation of the dataset.

Several elements of this dictionary can be used together to form a local annotation. We denote by *"label"* a specific combination of ACs. By "local" we mean "a specific region of the time and frequency plan". For example a region annotated with "HL" denotes that this region is both **H**armonic and has a **S**lope.

In Fig. 7, we provide an example of the manual annotation of an audio file. Each time and frequency region of the audio file has been annotated according to the aforementioned dictionary and rules. The following sequence of labels has been manually annotated over time: [HL], [RF], [HFL], [HFL], [RF], [HFL], [HFL], [HFL], [N], [HNL], [HFL], [HQS], [HS], [HL+NP].

Global Distribution of the Annotations. In order to have a better understanding of what ACs are the most used to imitate the sound categories, we represent in Fig. 8, the distribution of the annotated labels for the whole dataset. The [NP] label (Noise + Pulses) is by far the most used. Noise pulses, in fact, appear rather often in the imitations (clicks, stops, etc.), and are sometimes produced in groups (`dripping` category). The labels [N], [HL] and [NV] are then the most used, followed by [R] and [NS].

Distribution of the Annotations by Sound Category. The relationship between the sound categories and the ACs is given in Fig. 9. This distribution has been normalized by the distribution presented in Fig. 8 (each column is thus a distribution). `Fridge` category is often imitated using a static roughness [RS]. `vehicleext` category is imitated using different labels but all share the slope [L].

Distribution of the Annotations by Subjects. The relationship between the subjects and the ACs is given in Fig. 10. We can see that the majority of [RS] labels are found in imitations from the first subject, while [HRL] are mostly found in imitations by the fifth subject.

Comparing the "Audio Primitives" Automatically Found by SI-PLCA with "Manually Annotated Acoustic Cues". In this part, we validate the fact that the "audio primitive"s (APs) automatically found by the SI-PLCA actually correspond to significant "acoustic cue"s (ACs). To do this, we compare these APs with the manually annotated ACs on the same dataset.

If a kernel z of the SI-PLCA is often activated to describe regions which have been annotated with an AC l, then we conclude that z and l are linked: the kernel z successfully describes the acoustical cue l.

For each temporal segment manually labelled with l, we sum up the energy of the signal reconstruction obtained using only kernel z: $P_z(t)$. We then normalize by the segment duration and the number of segments. The co-occurrence matrix

Table 1. Dictionary of "acoustic cue"s (ACs) used for the manual annotation of the dataset.

Group	Label	Definition
Description of the content	**H**	Harmonic: clear presence of several harmonic lines
	N	Noise: region has a clear energy content, but without evident harmonics
	R	Roughness: similar to noise, but when listened there is some low-frequency repetitiveness
Description of the resonance	**F**	Presence of clearly noticeable formants/resonances
Description of the time-evolution	**S**	Static: the spectral energy distribution remains stable for more than 0.5 s
	QS	Quasi-static: long-term changes, similar to Static, but with very slow rise/fall
	V	Variable: sequence of random short-term variations in spectral energy
	L	Slope: short-term, rather fast (less than 2 s) and monotonic change in spectral distribution
	P	Pulse: very fast phenomena, with short attack and decay (clicks and similar)
Description of the time-repetition	n	A number is present if a certain pattern is clearly repeated; identical numbers identify identical patterns.

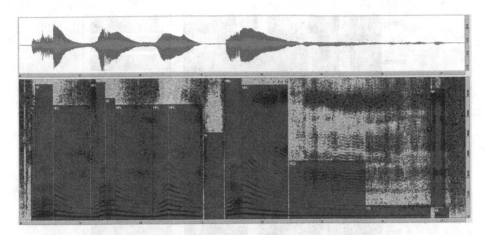

Fig. 7. Example of a manual annotation into "acoustic cue"s (ACs) of one audio file of the dataset. The following sequence of labels has been manually annotated over time: [HL], [RF], [HFL], [HFL], [RF], [HFL], [HFL], [HFL], [N], [HNL], [HFL], [HQS], [HS], [HL+NP].

$\mathcal{R}(l \in L, z \in K)$, with a row for each "acoustic cue" and a column for each kernel, indicates the average contribution of kernel z for each "acoustic cue" l.

The matrix $\mathcal{R}(l, k)$ is represented in Fig 11 [Left panel] for a decomposition using $K = 6$ kernels. We see that kernel $z = 5$ (which has an harmonic structure) is linked with "acoustic cues" H, HS, HQS and HL which are the manual labels for harmonic content. The same can be observed for kernel $z = 6$ (which has a

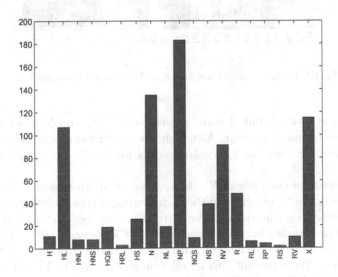

Fig. 8. Global distribution of the annotated labels for the whole dataset.

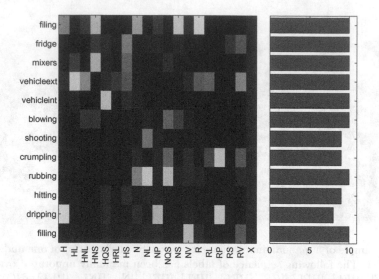

Fig. 9. Distribution of the annotated labels for each sound category.

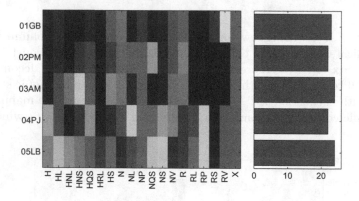

Fig. 10. Distribution of the annotated labels for each subject.

noise structure) which is linked with "acoustic cues" NS and NQS which are the manual labels for noise content. Although the correlations are less obvious for the other "acoustic cues" and kernels, there is obviously a correlation between both.

We now consider each row of $\mathcal{R}(l, k)$ as a vector of dimension K representing the lth "acoustic cue" projection in the K-dimensional space of the SI-PLCA kernels. In this space, we can compute the correlation between each pair of "acoustic cue" vectors (covariance between rows l and l' of $\mathcal{R}$, normalized by the geometrical average of two rows variances). This represents the correlation between the "acoustic cues". We represent this correlation matrix in Fig. 11 [Middle panel]. Using these correlations we then performed a hierarchical agglomerative clus-

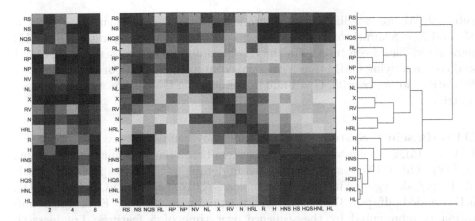

Fig. 11. Comparison between the "audio primitives"found by SI-PLCA and the "manually annotated acoustic cues". For a $K = 6$ kernels (30×15) decomposition we indicate [Left panel] the kernel activations for each "acoustic cue" l, [Middle panel] the correlation between the "acoustic cues" computed using the kernel activations [Right panel] the dendrogram resulting from this correlation.

tering (using complete linkage). The corresponding dendrogram is indicated in Fig. 11 [Right panel].

We first observe a large cluster {H, HNS, HS, HQS, HNL, HL} which groups all harmonic "acoustic cues" (H) independently of their time-evolution (static S, quasi-static QS or slope L). Actually, in our system the time-evolution is mostly represented by the impulse distribution P_I of the SI-PLCA rather than the kernel distribution P_K we consider here. Other clusters emerge such as {NS, NQS} and {NV, NL} which both group noise (N) "acoustic cues", {RL, RP, NP} which groups roughness (R) and pulse (P). Even if the other clusters cannot be explained so easily, most group similar "acoustic cues" and therefore confirms that kernels (which are used as the projection-space for clustering) are associated with these "acoustic cues" and can therefore be considered as audio primitives.

The same analysis can be done for $K = 8$ kernels.

4.3   Experiment 2: Recognition of the Sound Categories

We now validate the use of the "audio primitive"s (APs) automatically found by SI-PLCA as observations of a Hidden Markov Model (HMM). We do this by using them to perform the automatic recognition of the 12 sound categories with the set of 12 HMMs.

Evaluation Protocol. Given the reduced amount of examples in our dataset (115), we only perform a three folds cross-validation[3] applying a filter-by-

---

[3] One third of the data is used for testing, the remaining for training; each third is used in turns for testing.

subject[4]. We use two different configurations: $K = 6$ kernels of size ($f = 30 \times t = 15$) and $K = 8$ kernels of size ($f = 25 \times t = 25$). For each configuration the HMM parameters have been tuned. For the $K = 6$ configuration, we set $S = 30$, $G = 1$ and the underlying GMMs has a diagonal covariance matrix. For the $K = 8$ configuration, we set $S = 35$, $G = 1$ and the underlying GMMs has a full covariance matrix.

DTW-Baseline System. We compare the results obtained with our SI-PLCA/ HMM system with a baseline system based on Dynamic Time Warping (DTW). This DTW system is described in details in the online report available at http://skatvg.iuav.it/wp-content/uploads/2016/12/SkATVGDeliverableD5.5.1Extended.pdf pg. 31–38. We briefly summarize it here. Each vocal imitation is represented by the sequence over time of 5 features: Loudness(t), Spectral-Centroid(t), Spectral-Spread(t), Zero-Crossing-Rate(t), LPC-min(t). Each sequence is used in standard, normalized and derivative form. The comparison between two sounds is done by computing the DTW alignment between each feature sequence. For classification, K-NN is performed for each feature. The estimated class is the majority class over the classes estimated by each individual K-NN.

Results. Results are indicate in Fig. 12 for the two SI-PLCA/ HMM configurations (with $K = 6$ kernels of size f = 30 x t = 15 and with $K = 8$ kernels of size f = 25 x t = 25) and the DTW-baseline system. In the [Left] part we indicate the Recall for each of the 12 sound categories as well as the MEAN-(over-classes)-Recall. In the [Right] part we indicate the same using the Precision. It should be noted that a random classifier would give a mean-Recall of 8.33% for a 12 classes problem. Therefore all the results obtained are largely above a random classifier.

We first see that there is a slight increase of mean-Recall (but not of mean-Precision) using more kernels (8 instead of 6) and larger temporal extent (t = 25 instead of 15): 49.7% instead of 48.4%. However, this increase of performance is not homogeneous over the sound categories:

– $K = 8$ (green) works better for `fridge`, `mixers`, `filling`, `filing` and `vehicleint`,
– while $K = 6$ (blue) works better for `hitting`, `crumpling`, `dripping`, `rubbing`, and `vehiclext`.

The former categories are characterized by long-term pattern while the latter by short-term patterns. This actually makes sense since our $K = 8$ configurations uses longer kernels ($t = 25$) than the $K = 6$ configurations ($t = 15$).

However, on overall, the results provided by the SI-PLCA/HMM methods are lower (mean-Recall of 49.7%) than the ones obtained with our previous DTW-baseline system (60.6%). But here also, this trend is not homogeneous over the sound categories:

---

[4] The same subject can not appear simultaneously in the training and testing set.

- DTW-baseline (yellow) system works better for mixers, filling, dripping, vehicleint and blowing
- while SI-PLCA/HMM (with $K = 6$ or $K = 8$) works better for shooting, fridge, filing and rubbing.

The perfect system would therefore combine the three systems in a late-fusion approach and weight them appropriately depending on the considered sound category.

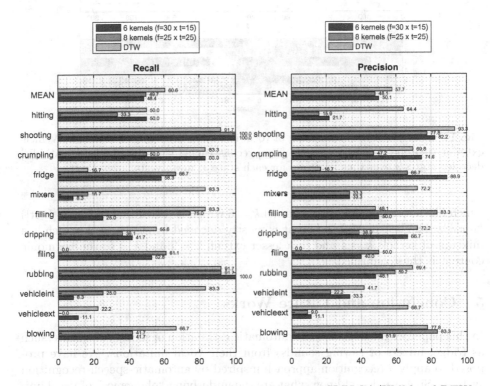

Fig. 12. Automatic recognition of sound categories using SI-PLCA/HMM and DTW.

Example. In Fig. 13 we illustrate the HMM decoding of one vocal imitation belonging to the class "Vehicle exterior (motorcycle engine start)". We used a decomposition in $K = 6$ kernels (the ones presented in Fig. 6 [Left]) and a HMM with $S = 10$ and $G = 1$. The top panel represents the CQT. The middle panel represents the decoded path through the $S = 10$ states. The bottom panel represent the centroid of each state s over the $K = 6$ kernels. We see that the vocal imitation is made alternating noisy with harmonic content. The harmonic content is mostly represented by state $s = 9$ which has a strong emphasis on kernel $k = 5$ which is (according to Fig. 6 [Left]) the most suitable to describe harmonic content. Similarly, noisy content is mostly represented by state $s = 8$

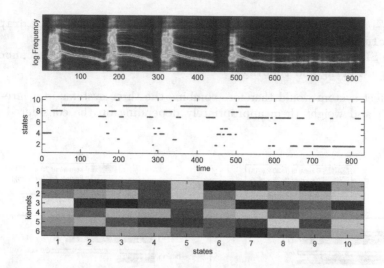

Fig. 13. Example of HMM decoding of vocal imitation belonging to the class "Vehicle exterior (motorcycle engine start)". [Top] reconstructed CQT by SI-PLCA, [Middle] decoded states s over time [Bottom] for each state s, mean vector over $P_z(t)$.

which has a strong emphasis on kernel $k = 6$ which is (according to Fig. 6 [Left]) "noisy". The last part of the input is mostly decoded by state $s = 2$, which is a mixture of kernels $k = 4$ and to a lesser extent $k = 2$ and $k = 5$; the harmonic content is thus confirmed.

5   Conclusion and Future Works

In this paper we have studied the automatic estimation of sound categories (such as fridge, mixers or sawing sounds) from their vocal imitations. We have proposed to apply a recognition approach inspired by automatic-speech-recognition systems. Since we do not know what are the underlying "phonemes" of vocal imitations we have proposed to automatically estimate them using Shift-Invariant Probabilistic Latent Component Analysis applied to a dataset of vocal imitations. The kernel distributions are considered as "audio primitives" and the impulse distributions used to derive the emission probabilities of a hidden Markov model.

To evaluate our proposal we have performed two experiments. In the first, we have compared the "audio primitives" automatically found by SI-PLCA to manual annotations into "acoustic cues" of the same dataset. We have shown that there is a strong relationship between both and that therefore the "audio primitives" automatically found by SI-PLCA represent acoustic cues.

In the second experiment, we have shown that our HMM system (based on the "audio primitives" automatically found by SI-PLCA) achieves a 49% mean-Recall recognition rate for a task of recognizing 12 sound categories. While this remains below our baseline DTW system (60%), it is largely above a random classifier (which would give 8.33). We have also analysed the HMM decoding of one vocal imitation and shown that the selected "audio primitives" were meaningful to describe vocal imitations.

One important thing to note is that the DTW baseline system has been carefully designed by hand (choice of the audio descriptor or the parameters of the model) for the specific task of sound category recognition from vocal imitation. In the opposite the SI-PLCA/HMM is completely agnostic. The system has learned by itself the audio descriptors or "audio primitives" (the kernel distributions of SI-PLCA) that allows the best re-generation of the dataset of vocal imitations. The same methodology could therefore be applied to other types of audio data to automatically find what is the best representation to describe them.

Acknowledgments. This work was supported by the 7th FP of the EU (FP7-ICT-2013-C FET-Future Emerging Technologies) under grant agreement 618067 (SkAT-VG project).

References

1. Baldan, S., Delle Monache, S., Rocchesso, D.: The sound design toolkit. Softw. X **6**, 255–260 (2017)
2. Brown, J.C.: Calculation of a constant Q spectral transform. J. Acoust. Soc. Am. **89**(1), 425–434 (1991)
3. Houix, O., Monache, S.D., Lachambre, H., Bevilacqua, F., Rocchesso, D., Lemaitre, G.: Innovative tools for sound sketching combining vocalizations and gestures. In: Proceedings of the Audio Mostly 2016, pp. 12–10. ACM (2016)
4. Ishihara, K., Nakatani, T., Ogata, T., Okuno, H.G.: Automatic sound-imitation word recognition from environmental sounds focusing on ambiguity problem in determining phonemes. In: Zhang, C., W. Guesgen, H., Yeap, W.-K. (eds.) PRICAI 2004. LNCS (LNAI), vol. 3157, pp. 909–918. Springer, Heidelberg (2004). https://doi.org/10.1007/978-3-540-28633-2_96
5. Juang, B.H., Rabiner, L.R.: Automatic speech recognition-a brief history of the technology development. Georgia Institute of Technology. Atlanta Rutgers University and the University of California 1:67 (2005)
6. Lee, D.D., Seung, H.S.: Learning the parts of objects by non-negative matrix factorization. Nature **401**(6755), 788–791 (1999)
7. Lemaitre, G., Dessein, A., Aura, K., Susini, P.: Do vocal imitations enable the identification of the imitated sounds. In: Proceedings of the 8th Annual Auditory Perception, Cognition and Action Meeting (APCAM 2009), Boston, MA (2009)
8. Lemaitre, G., Houix, O., Voisin, F., Misdariis, N., Susini, P.: Vocal imitations of non-vocal sounds. PLoS ONE **11**(12), e0168167 (2016). Public Library of Science
9. Lemaitre, G., Rocchesso, D.: On the effectiveness of vocal imitations and verbal descriptions of sounds. J. Acoust. Soc. Am. **135**(2), 862–873 (2014). http://www.ncbi.nlm.nih.gov/pubmed/25234894
10. Marchetto, E., Peeters, G.: A set of audio features for the morphological description of vocal imitations. In: Proceedings of DAFx (2015)
11. Paatero, P., Tapper, U.: Positive matrix factorization: a non-negative factor model with optimal utilization of error estimates of data values. Environmetrics **5**(2), 111–126 (1994). https://doi.org/10.1002/env.3170050203

12. Peeters, G., Deruty, E.: Sound indexing using morphological description. IEEE Trans. Audio Speech Lang. Process. **18**(3), 675–687 (2010)
13. Rabiner, L.R.: A tutorial on hidden markov models and selected applications in speech recognition. Proc. IEEE **77**(2), 257–286 (1989)
14. Rabiner, L.R., Juang, B.H.: Fundamentals of speech recognition (1993)
15. Ricard, J., Herrera, P.: Morphological sound description: computational model and usability evaluation. In: Audio Engineering Society Convention 116 (2004)
16. Saon, G., Chien, J.T.: Large-vocabulary continuous speech recognition systems: a look at some recent advances. IEEE Sig. Process. Mag. **29**(6), 18–33 (2012)
17. Schaeffer, P.: Traité des objets musicaux. Le Seuil (1966)
18. Schörkhuber, C., Klapuri, A., Holighaus, N., Dörfler, M.: A Matlab toolbox for efficient perfect reconstruction time-frequency transforms with log-frequency resolution. In: Audio Engineering Society Conference: 53rd International Conference: Semantic Audio, January 2014. http://www.aes.org/e-lib/browse.cfm?elib=17112
19. Shashanka, M., Raj, B., Smaragdis, P.: Probabilistic latent variable models as nonnegative factorizations. Comput. Intell. Neurosci. **2008**, 8 (2008). Article ID 947438. https://doi.org/10.1155/2008/947438
20. Smaragdis, P., Raj, B.: Shift-invariant probabilistic latent component analysis. Technical report, MERL (2007)
21. Sundaram, S., Narayanan, S.: Vector-based representation and clustering of audio using onomatopoeia words. In: Proceedings of AAAI (2006)
22. Sundaram, S., Narayanan, S.: Classification of sound clips by two schemes: using onomatopoeia and semantic labels. In: 2008 IEEE International Conference on Multimedia and Expo, pp. 1341–1344. IEEE (2008)
23. Velasco, G.A., Holighaus, N., Dörfler, M., Grill, T.: Constructing an invertible constant-Q transform with non-stationary Gabor frames. In: Proceedings of DAFx, Paris, pp. 93–99 (2011)

Automatic Estimation of Harmonic Tension by Distributed Representation of Chords

Ali Nikrang[1]([✉]), David R. W. Sears[2], and Gerhard Widmer[2]

[1] Ars Electronica Futurelab, Linz, Austria
an@musicresearch.eu
[2] Johannes Kepler University, Linz, Austria

Abstract. The buildup and release of a sense of tension is one of the most essential aspects of the process of listening to music. A veridical computational model of perceived musical tension would be an important ingredient for many music informatics applications [27]. The present paper presents a new approach to modelling harmonic tension based on a distributed representation of chords. The starting hypothesis is that harmonic tension as perceived by human listeners is related, among other things, to the expectedness of harmonic units (chords) in their local harmonic context. We train a *word2vec*-type neural network to learn a vector space that captures contextual similarity and expectedness, and define a quantitative measure of harmonic tension on top of this. To assess the veridicality of the model, we compare its outputs on a number of well-defined chord classes and cadential contexts to results from pertinent empirical studies in music psychology. Statistical analysis shows that the model's predictions conform very well with empirical evidence obtained from human listeners.

Keywords: Musical tension · word2vec · Musical expectations
Harmonic progression · Cadence

1 Introduction

Musical tension results from the action and interaction among numerous musical features, such as the gradual rise in loudness or pitch height at the climax of a Galant symphony (the so-called *Mannheim crescendo*), or the increase in tempo, rhythmic variability, or onset density in the development section of a classical sonata-form movement [9,13]. Indeed, even an isolated repeating tone develops a different quality and different impact on listeners after each repetition [15], thus awakening the potential for tension during music listening. However, in this study we will restrict the discussion to the *harmonic* tension resulting from simultaneously-sounding tones in a polyphonic (i.e., multi-voiced) sequence and the context in which these appear.

© Springer Nature Switzerland AG 2018
M. Aramaki et al. (Eds.): CMMR 2017, LNCS 11265, pp. 23–34, 2018.
https://doi.org/10.1007/978-3-030-01692-0_2

Among music theorists, harmonic tension is often characterized as the sense that an unstable harmonic state tends to resolve to another more calm (or relaxed) state. The resolution of a chord can occur immediately from one chord to the next, or it may be delayed via techniques of extension and prolongation, such as the pedal or organ point at the end of a Baroque fugue [17].

Psychologists have generally offered either sensory (or psychoacoustic) or cognitive explanations for the perception of harmonic tension. On the one hand, sensory accounts characterize harmonic tension as a sensory response caused by (1) the rapid beating (oscillations in amplitude) created by interactions of adjacent partials, and (2) the absence of shared partials between two or more complex tones (called *inharmonicity*) [10]. On the other hand, cognitive accounts treat tension as an emotional affect resulting from the formation, fulfilment, and violation of expectations learned from exposure to Western music [16].

This study offers a cognitive account for the experience of harmonic tension using *word2vec*, a neural network-based representation model that simulates the long-term learning of words in natural languages. Our approach is mainly motivated by two assumptions: (1) that chords—like words in a natural language corpus—are similar to each other if they occur in similar (or identical) contexts, and (2) that the ebb and flow of tension/relaxation is caused by changes in the (dis)similarity between adjacent chords. These assumptions are consistent with experimental studies in music perception and cognition that underline the role of harmonic context in the formation of expectations during music listening [3,4,23,25], in which chords that co-occur frequently in a surrounding context were found to be more expected by listeners.

We begin in Sect. 2 by reviewing chord typologies in music theory and the related evidence for harmonic tension based on sensory and cognitive accounts. Next, Sect. 3 presents a new model of harmonic tension based on word2vec and describes the datasets used in the present research. Finally, the remaining two sections present the results of two experiments designed to replicate the findings from previous studies with human participants using the word2vec model; Sect. 4 examines harmonic tension for isolated sonorities like triads and seventh chords, while Sect. 5 considers the dynamic variations of tension accompanying common chord progressions in classical music (called *cadences*).

2   Harmonic Tension in Chords and Chord Sequences

A chord is a combination of at least two simultaneously sounding tones. This paper considers two types of chords: triads and seventh chords. Depending on the interval structure, various chord qualities emerge (e.g. major, minor, diminished, augmented). Furthermore, a chord is inverted if any pitch other than the root is in the lowest (bass) voice (see Fig. 1). We will call the units of time over which these chords occur *harmonic units*.

As mentioned before, sensory models of tension investigate the effect of roughness or beating on listeners' perception of the dissonance of chords. For instance, [12] presented a sensory model that calculates the roughness of isolated

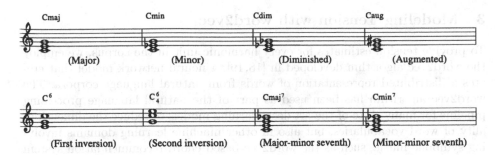

Fig. 1. Examples of different chord qualities, inversions and types (all notated with C roots).

three- or four-note chords and reported high dissonance estimates for chords that contain dissonant intervals (e.g., seconds or sevenths) and relatively low dissonance estimates for major and minor triads and their inversions. Another model in [20] computed the strength or clarity (vs. ambiguity) of the root pitch of a chord under the assumption that chords with a clear root have a strong harmonic function and are therefore more consonant. The results were consistent with music-theoretical assumptions and empirical studies [8,14]. However, these models delivered a rank ordering from the most consonant to the most dissonant triad quality (major > minor > augmented > diminished) that is only partly consistent with the responses of listeners in experimental tasks (major > minor > diminished > augmented) [1,8,14,22]. It seems that the ranks associated with diminished and augmented triads cannot be calculated by existing sensory models [8].

The effect of the musical context in which a chord occurs on listeners' perception of dissonance and consonance has been considered in [14], which showed that major and minor triads tend to be more consonant if they occur in a compatible tonal context. Furthermore, listeners judge diminished chords as less dissonant if they occur on the fourth (or *subdominant*) degree of the diatonic scale, and augmented chords as most dissonant if they occur on the first (or *tonic*) scale degree [1]. What is more, both diminished and augmented triads are less tense when they occur as part of a *cadence* [1], a melodic-harmonic formula that marks the conclusion of a musical phrase [5].

Previous studies have underlined the role of the harmonic functions of chords in a musical context for listeners' expectations [3,4,25], demonstrating that harmonic units with a strong harmonic relationship to the musical context are more expected. In [24], for example, cadences with a tonic terminal chord were found to be more expected than cadences with a non-tonic chord. Furthermore, [23] reported that listeners respond faster and more accurately to a chord at the end of a sequence if it belongs to the musical context.

Taken together, these studies suggest that harmonic tension is highly related to the musical context in which these chords occur. Chords that belong to a given harmonic context are more expected, and are therefore less tense. Thus, the present study examines whether an unsupervised learning algorithm can simulate the behavior of listeners for both isolated chords and chord progressions.

3   Modeling Tension with word2vec

To provide tension estimates for every harmonic unit in the corpus, we employ the word2vec algorithm developed in [18, 19], a neural network model that creates a distributed representation of words from natural language corpora. The word2vec algorithm has been used as part of the natural language processing pipeline for many state-of-the-art deep learning models to reduce the dimensionality of word vocabularies, but also in other machine learning domains involving symbolic music, such as the word2vec-based chord recommendation system in [11].

A formal description of word2vec can be found in [18, 19]. In short, word2vec calculates the similarity between words based on the frequency of their co-occurrence in a surrounding context. For instance the word *like* will be similar to *love*, since *like* and *love* occur frequently in the same surrounding context (e.g., I like this book vs. I love this book). This co-occurrence matrix is then used to create an embedding space of words, where each word is represented as a vector, and where the similarity between words is calculated as the cosine similarity of their vectors. In such spaces, words that appear in similar contexts therefore feature shorter cosine distances (e.g., *small* and *smaller*) compared to those in dissimilar contexts (e.g., *small* and *France*) [18].

From a music-theoretical point of view, the idea of the similarity of chords based on their surrounding context corresponds well with functional theories of tonal harmony. In [21], for example, the harmonic behaviours of chords is reduced to three functional categories—tonic, dominant and predominant. The harmonic function of a given chord therefore depends on the tonal context in which it occurs. Thus, altering a chord likely does not change its harmonic function, and so surrounding context similarity can be interpreted as similarity of harmonic function.

As an example, consider a very common chord progression in C-major: $C - F - G - C$ (i.e., $I - IV - V - I$). The surrounding context of the dominant chord G includes C and F. In practice, we might observe some alterations of the dominant chord, like G^7. Yet despite these alterations, its harmonic function remains the same: namely, dominant. In other words, in the context of C-major, G and G^7 are very similar to each other (even though they would be highly dissimilar in the context of G-major). What is more, if a new chord is inserted at the end of the sequence above, G will be less tense than Am, since our memory already contains the harmonic function of dominant (G) but not the function associated with the submediant (Am).

3.1   The Vocabulary

The word2vec algorithm requires a sequence of symbols as input, so we represent each harmonic unit as an integer ID in the model. To extract the harmonic units from each piece, we first produce a *full expansion* of the symbolic encoding [7], which duplicates overlapping note events at every unique onset time. To decrease the size of the vocabulary, the pitches in each harmonic unit are then mapped as a set of *pitch classes*, which reduces the domain of possible pitches to the twelve-tone chromatic scale (e.g., C= 0, C♯/D♭ = 1, etc.). Finally, duplicated pitch classes are removed.

3.2 The Corpus

The corpus consists of 297 string quartet movements composed during the high classical period by Josef Haydn (215; 1762–1803) and Wolfgang Amadeus Mozart (82; 1770–1790). All movements were downloaded from the KernScores database in kern format.[1] To create a dataset that equally represents all possible keys from the twelve-tone chromatic scale, all of the movements were transposed 11 times from −5 to 6 semitones. This procedure produced a vocabulary consisting of 4753 possible chord types in the corpus. The sequence of harmonic units from each piece was then converted into a sequence of integer IDs corresponding to the chord types from the vocabulary.

3.3 Training the Model

The original implementation of word2vec was used to generate a distributed representation of harmonic units.[2] The model was trained with the Continuous Bag of Words (or *cbow*) option, which predicts each word given the words in the surrounding context. The number of dimensions of the embedding space was set to 120 and the threshold for the required minimum number of word occurrences was set to 1 to consider all words. Finally, the model was trained with a window size of 6 harmonic units.

3.4 Calculating Tension

We define the tension estimate of a harmonic unit H_t as the average cosine distance between H_t and n preceding harmonic units, which was set to 24 for the experiments reported here. To simulate the decay in memory over time, each of the preceding units is multiplied by a weighting function $1 - e^{1 - \frac{1}{(i-1)/n}}$, which ensures that the cosine distances estimated from recently heard harmonic units receive higher weights than those from more remote harmonic units in the sequence.

$$tension(H_t) = -\frac{1}{n} \sum_{i=1}^{n} cos(H_{t-i}, H_t)(1 - e^{1 - \frac{1}{(i-1)/n}}) \qquad (1)$$

The output of cosine distance lies on a scale between −1 and 1, where the largest value 1 indicates minimum distance (i.e., minimum tension in our model). However, to improve the legibility of the output, we multiply the weighted output of our function with −1 so that lower values indicate less tension, and a value of 0 indicates maximum tension.

---

[1] http://kern.ccarh.org/.

[2] https://code.google.com/p/word2vec/.

4   Experiment 1

Experiment 1 examines the average tension estimates for different chord categories according to three chord conditions: *type* (triad, seventh), *quality* (major, minor, diminished, augmented), and *inversion* (root, first, second, third). Major and minor triads in root position are generally expected to be less tense than those in first or second inversion [8]. In addition, the following trend from the most consonant to most dissonant triad quality is assumed; major, minor, diminished and augmented [8,14,22]. Furthermore, seventh chords are assumed to be more tense than triads.

4.1   Analysis

To evaluate the tension estimates for all chord categories in the corpus, we applied 10-fold cross validation, in which the corpus was divided into 10 subsets and trained 10 times, each time leaving out a different subset for testing. Each condition in this experiment refers to a chord category which is defined by three chord aspects: type, quality and inversion. Due to large differences in sample size across chord conditions, the number of chords in each condition was limited to 1200 chords selected randomly from the corpus.

To examine the tension estimates of all categories, we considered the following four hypotheses:

H_1 Major triads in first inversion are more tense than those in root position or in second inversion [12].
H_2 Minor triads in root position are less tense than those in first or second inversion [22].
H_3 Regarding chord quality, the following rank for increasing tension obtains: major < minor < diminished < augmented [8,14,22].
H_4 Triads are less tense than seventh chords.

Levene's test indicated unequal variances for every between-groups factor for chord categories, so we report Type III ANOVAs with White correction [26], which is used to compute heteroscedasticity-robust covariance matrices. To examine differences between the levels of each factor, we also included four planned comparisons that do not assume homogeneity of variances. The first two comparisons examine the potential differences between the levels of inversion for major (H_1) and minor (H_2) triads. The next comparison examines the predicted trend across the levels of quality (H_3). Finally, the fourth comparison considers the potential difference between triads and seventh chords (H_4). To minimize the chance of making a Type I error, we also apply a Bonferroni correction to the planned comparisons, which divides the critical p value by the number of comparisons ($\frac{.05}{8}$, so alpha $_{crit}$= .00625). As a consequence, only p values smaller than .00625 will be significant.

4.2   Results

To examine the first two hypotheses, tension estimates for all triad categories were submitted to a two-way ANOVA with factors of *quality* (major, minor, diminished, augmented) and *inversion* (root, first, second). The interaction between quality and inversion was significant, $F(4, 10556) = 35.8, p < .001, \eta_p^2 = .01$), so we examined simple main effects of quality and inversion for the first two hypotheses.

Figure 2 presents the average tension estimates for major and minor triads for each level of inversion. Beginning with H_1, a one-way ANOVA revealed a simple main effect of inversion for major triads, $F(2, 3558) = 76.56, p < .001, \eta_p^2 = .04$. As expected, triads in first inversion elicited higher tension estimates than those either in root position, $t(3558) = -12.24, p < .001$, or in second inversion, $t(3558) = -7.56, p < .001$.

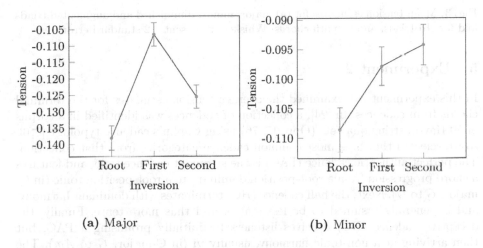

(a) Major   (b) Minor

Fig. 2. Mean tension estimates for major and minor triads in root position, and in first and second inversion. Whiskers represent ±2 standard errors.

For H_2, a one-way ANOVA carried out on minor triads also revealed a simple main effect of inversion $F(2, 3463) = 17.02, p < .001, \eta_p^2 = 0.01$. In this case, triads in root position elicited significantly lower tension estimates than those either in first inversion, $t(3463) = 4.32, p < .001$, or in second inversion $t(3463) = 5.67, p < .001$.

Figure 3a presents the average tension estimates for all triads. A reverse forward-difference contrast revealed that the mean tension estimates increased significantly for major vs. minor triads, $t(11465) = -41.2, p < .001$, minor vs. diminished triads, $t(11465) = -48.9, p < .001$, and diminished vs. augmented triads, $t(11465) = -33.15, p < .001$. Thus, the tension estimates revealed the ascending linear trend predicted in H_3 from the major to the augmented triad conditions. Finally, for H_4, triads elicited lower tension estimates than seventh chords, $t(22354) = 8.08, p < .001$.

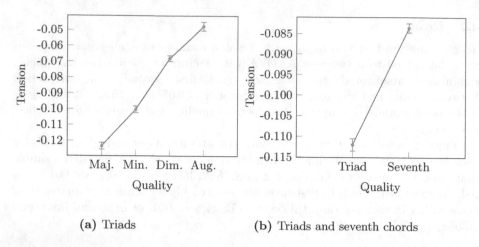

(a) Triads   (b) Triads and seventh chords

Fig. 3. Mean tension estimates for (a) major, minor, diminished and augmented triads and for (b) triads, and seventh chords. Whiskers represent ±2 standard errors.

5   Experiment 2

In this experiment, we examined the average tension estimates for the terminal chords from cadences. In [24], a collection of cadences was identified in a corpus of 50 Haydn string quartets (Opp. 17–76) using Caplin's cadence typology [5,6], so we selected the three most common cadence categories from that collection. The perfect authentic cadence (PAC) is the strongest cadence type, and features a chord progression from a root-position dominant to a root-position tonic (in C-major, G to C). Next, the half cadence (HC) terminates with dominant harmony, and is generally assumed to be less stable, and thus more tense. Finally, the deceptive cadence (DC) deceives listeners by initially promising a PAC, but then arriving at a non-tonic harmony, usually vi (in C-major, G to Am). The cadence collection consists of 122 PACs, 84, HCs, and 19 DCs, for a total of 225 example cadences.

To examine how the model calculates tension estimates for these cadence categories, we considered the following four hypotheses:

H_1 Terminal chords from PACs elicit lower tension estimates than those from non-cadential chords selected at random from the corpus ($PAC < non\text{-}cad$).
H_2 Terminal chords from HCs are more tense than those from PACs because they end with the less stable dominant harmony ($PAC < HC$).
H_3 Terminal chords from DCs are more tense than those from PACs because they end with an unexpected non-tonic harmony ($PAC < DC$).
H_4 The following rank for increasing tension obtains: $PAC < HC < DC$.

5.1   Analysis

To evaluate model performance, we again used the Haydn and Mozart string quartets corpus for training. However, since annotated movements from Haydn's

cadence collection also appear in the training set, we applied 10-fold cross validation and randomly divided movements containing the cadence collection into
10 equal disjunct groups.

5.2 Results

Figure 4 presents the average tension estimates for the terminal chords from
all three cadence categories. To calculate the average tension estimate over all
pieces (shown with the dotted blue line), we randomly selected 1200 chords
from the corpus. For H_1 ($PAC < non\text{-}cad$), Levene's test indicated unequal
variances, so we again report Bonferroni-corrected t-tests that do not assume
equal variances. In this case, the terminal chords from the PAC category elicited
significantly lower tension estimates than the non-cadencial chords that were
selected randomly from the copus: $t(1320) = 5.36, p < .001$.

For H_2 ($PAC < HC$) and H_3 ($PAC < DC$), a one-way ANOVA revealed significant differences between cadence categories, $F(2, 222) = 44.43, p < .001, \eta_p^2 =$
.28. The PAC category also elicited significantly lower tension estimates than
either the HC category, $t(204) = 7.89, p < .001$, or the DC category, $t(139) =$
$6.43, p < .001$.

Finally, the reverse forward-difference contrast to examine H_4 revealed a
significant ascending linear trend from the PAC to the DC categories: (PAC vs.
HC, $t(243) = -8.95, p < .001$; HC vs. DC $t(243) = -4.56, p < .001$), thereby
demonstrating the predicted trend, $PAC < HC < DC$.

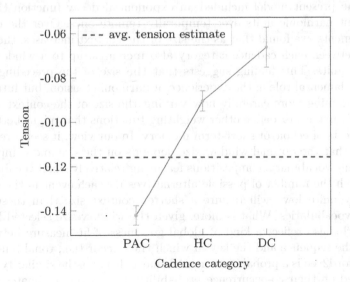

Fig. 4. Mean tension estimates for the terminal chord of the cadence categories.
Whiskers represent ±1 standard error. (Color figure online)

6 Discussion and Conclusion

This paper presented a new approach to the calculation of tension estimates of harmonic units based on a distributed representation of chords using word2vec. To obtain the reported tension estimates without requiring subjective judgments from human listeners, we conducted two computational experiments using a corpus of string quartets from the classical style. In the first experiment, word2vec provided tension estimates for different chord categories based on type (triad, seventh), quality (major, minor, diminished, augmented), and inversion (root, first, second). The results corresponded closely with previous studies in music theory and experimental psychology [1,8,12,14,22], demonstrating that an unsupervised learning algorithm can simulate the behavior of listeners in tasks related to the experience of harmonic tension.

However, the first experiment did not consider the functional context in which these chords occur. Therefore, the second experiment considered the dynamic ebb and flow of tension in tonal harmonic progressions by examining tension estimates for the terminal events from the three most common cadence categories in classical music. The model indicated that the ends of phrases (represented by terminal events in the PAC category) are less tense than non-cadential chord events selected at random from the corpus. Furthermore, the model delivered consistent results with previous research [24], which demonstrated that the terminal events from the HC and DC categories are less expected than those from the PAC category.

To examine how the preceding context influences the experience of harmonic tension, the present model included an exponential decay function that privileges recent harmonic units over temporally remote ones. Over the course of our experiments, we found that as the size of the context increases, the average distance between each cadence category also increases, up to a window size of around 24 units. This finding suggests that the size of the preceding context plays a fundamental role in the experience of harmonic tension, but future studies could examine more carefully how varying the size of the context improves model performance, or define other weighting functions that might better simulate the effects of echoic or short-term memory. In our view, it seems reasonable to suggest that the optimal window size depends on the size and complexity of the harmonic vocabulary: compositions featuring relatively small vocabularies— and in which the number of possible alternatives for each event in the sequence is generally quite low—will require a shorter context size than those featuring larger vocabularies. What is more, given the window size selected here, our results might also reflect a kind of global goodness-of-fit measure between the chords in the sequence and the key in which they occur (i.e., tonal tension).

Since word2vec is a probabilistic model that calculates the similarity between words based on their co-occurrence probability, the tension estimates reported here amount to probabilistic inferences about the co-occurrence of chords in a given harmonic context. As a consequence, this study operationalizes tension as an affective (or emotional) response to the formation, fulfillment, and violation of expectations during music listening [16,17]. However, this is not to say that tension cannot refer to other aspects of musical experience (e.g. melodic organization), or result from other (sensory or psychoacoustic) mechanisms during perception (e.g., from sensory dissonance, inharmonicity, or auditory roughness). Rather, this study simply reinforces the view that unsupervised learning algorithms can induce the statistical regularities governing complex stimulus domains like natural language and tonal music, and that aspects of emotional experience—like tonal (or harmonic) tension—might result from this learning process.

Acknowledgements. This research is supported by the European Research Council (ERC) under the EUs Horizon 2020 Framework Programme (ERC Grant Agreement number 670035, project "Con Espressione").

References

1. Arthurs, Y., Timmers, R.: Evaluating the consonance and pleasantness of triads in different musical contexts. In: Proceedings of the 3rd International Conference on Music & Emotion (ICME3), University of Jyväskylä, Department of Music, Jyväskylä (2013)
2. Bharucha, J.J., Stoeckig, K.: Reaction time and musical expectancy: priming of chords. J. Exp. Psychol. Human. **12**, 403–410 (1986)
3. Bigand, E., Pineau, M.: Global context effects on musical expectancy. Atten. Percept. Psychophys. **59**, 1098–1107 (1997)
4. Bigand, E., Madurell, F., Tillmann, B., Pineau, M.: Effect of global structure and temporal organization on chord processing. J. Exp. Psychol. Human. **25**, 184–197 (1999)
5. Caplin, W.E.: Classical Form: A Theory of Formal Functions for the Instrumental Music of Haydn, Mozart, and Beethoven. Oxford University Press, New York (1998)
6. Caplin, W.E.: The classical cadence: conceptions and misconceptions. J. Soc. Am. Music. **57**, 51–118 (2004)
7. Conklin, D.: Representation and discovery of vertical patterns in music. In: Anagnostopoulou, C., Ferrand, M., Smaill, A. (eds.) ICMAI 2002. LNCS (LNAI), vol. 2445, pp. 32–42. Springer, Heidelberg (2002). https://doi.org/10.1007/3-540-45722-4_5
8. Cook, N.D., Fujisawa, T.X.: The psychophysics of harmony perception: harmony is a three-tone phenomenon. EMR **1**, 106–126 (2006)
9. Farbood, M.M.: A parametric, temporal model of musical tension. Music. Percept. **29**, 387–428 (2012)
10. Helmholtz, H.: Die Lehre von der Tonempfindungen als physiologische Grundlage für die Theorie der Musik, zweite edn. Friedrich Vieweg & Sohn, Braunschweig (1865)
11. Huang C.A., Duvenaud D., Gajos K.Z.: ChordRipple: recommending chords to help novice composers go beyond the ordinary. In: Proceedings of the 21st International Conference on Intelligent User Interfaces (IUI 2016), pp. 241–250. ACM, New York (2016)
12. Hutchinson, W., Knopoff, L.: The significance of the acoustic component of consonance in western triads. JMR **3**, 5–22 (1979)
13. Ilie, G., Thompson, W.: Experiential and cognitive changes following seven minutes exposure to music and speech. Music. Percept. **28**, 247–264 (2011)

14. Johnson-Laird, P.N., Kang, O.E., Leong, Y.C.: On musical dissonance. Music. Percept. **30**, 19–35 (2012)
15. Margulis, E.H.: On Repeat: How Music Plays the Mind. University Press, Oxford (2016)
16. Meyer, L.B.: Emotion and Meaning in Music. University of Chicago Press, Chicago (1956)
17. Meyer, L.B.: Explaining Music: Essays and Explorations. University of California Press, Berkeley (1973)
18. Mikolov, T., Chen, K., Corrado, G., Dean, J.: Efficient estimation of word representations in vector space. arXiv preprint arXiv:1301.3781 (2013)
19. Mikolov, T., Sutskever, I., Chen, K., Corrado, G., Dean, J.: Distributed representations of words and phrases and their compositionality. Adv. Neural Inf. Process. Syst. **26** (2013)
20. Parncutt, R.: Harmony: A Psychoacoustical Approach. Springer, Berlin (1989). https://doi.org/10.1007/978-3-642-74831-8
21. Riemann, H.: Vereinfachte Harmonielehre oder die Lehre von den tonalen Funktionen der Akkorde, 2nd edn. Augener & Co., No. 9197, London (original 1893)
22. Roberts, L.: Consonant judgments of musical chords by musicians and untrained listeners. Acta. Acust. united Ac. **62**, 163–171 (1986)
23. Schmuckler, M.A., Boltz, M.G.: Harmonic and rhythmic influences on musical expectancy. Percept. Psychophys. **56**, 313–325 (1994)
24. Sears, D.: The Classical Cadence as a Closing Schema: Learning, Memory, and Perception (Unpublished doctoral dissertation). McGill University, Montreal (2016)
25. Tillmann, B., Bigand, E.: Global context effect in normal and scrambled musical sequences. J. Exp. Psychol. Human. **27**, 1185–1196 (2001)
26. White, H.: A heteroskedasticity-consistent covariance matrix estimator and a direct test for heteroskedasticity. Econometrica **48**, 817–838 (1980)
27. Widmer, G.: Getting closer to the essence of music: the Con Espressione Manifesto. ACM Trans. Intell. Syst. Technol. **8**, Article 19 (2016)

Automatic Music Genre Classification in Small and Ethnic Datasets

Tiago Fernandes Tavares[✉] and Juliano Henrique Foleiss

School of Electrical and Computer Engineering,
University of Campinas, Campinas, Brazil
tavares@dca.fee.unicamp.br

Abstract. Automatic music genre classification commonly relies on a large amount of well-recorded data for model fitting. These conditions are frequently not met in ethnic music collections due to low media availability and ill recording environments. In this paper, we propose an automatic genre classification technique especially designed for small, noisy datasets. The proposed technique uses handcrafted features and a vote-based aggregation process. Its performance was evaluated over a Brazilian ethnic music dataset, showing that using the proposed technique produces higher F1 measures than using traditional data augmentation methods and state-of-the-art, Deep Learning-based methods. Therefore, our method can be used in automatic classification processes for small datasets, which can be helpful in the organization of ethnic music collections.

Keywords: Computational ethnomusicology
Automatic music genre classification · Music information retrieval

1 Introduction

Automatic music genre classification (AMGC) is a process that associates a digitized audio signal to a label corresponding to its musical genre. This can be pursued by estimating a vector representation from each audio track and then performing a data-driven classification process. An adequate AMGC system can be helpful for the organization of musical collections.

One of the first methods for AMGC was designed by Tzanetakis and Cook [15]. It relies on the assumption that the auditory content of a recorded sound depends on its spectral shape [13], which means that features that describe the shape of short time spectra produce a vector representation of their content. In this representation, vectors that are close are related to audio excerpts that sound similar and, conversely, distant vectors are related to audio excerpts that sound very different.

The method proposed by Tzanetakis and Cook [15] begins by dividing a digital music track into short (46 ms) frames. Each frame has a set of features estimated. After that, the mean and variance of each feature in 1s-long blocks is

© Springer Nature Switzerland AG 2018
M. Aramaki et al. (Eds.): CMMR 2017, LNCS 11265, pp. 35–48, 2018.
https://doi.org/10.1007/978-3-030-01692-0_3

calculated. Last, the mean and variance of the blockwise statistics are calculated, generating a vector that describes each audio track with four dimensions (mean of means, mean of variances, variance of means, variance of variances) for each estimated feature. This vector representation yielded to further classification steps based on machine learning.

Further proposals for improvements in AMGC involved using different feature sets (such was wavelet histograms [6] estimated from the audio signal). These features were manually developed aiming at highlighting aspects of audio that are known to be relevant. For this reason, they are called *handcrafted features*.

More recently, advances in deep learning (DL) techniques enabled using deep neural networks (DNNs) [12] to perform AMGC directly using spectrograms. In this case, the neural network's hidden layers emerge adequate features during the training stage. This phenomenon has shown to be useful in optical character recognition, and work by Costa et al. [3] has shown that they can outperform other techniques in AMGC.

Both using handcrafted features and DL techniques depend on using data driven optimization processes for parameter estimation. Such data is easily available for popular music datasets, because audio files are broadly available and there are datasets [5,15] specifically aimed at research use. However, obtaining consistent data in ethnic music datasets is hard, as it often implies in performing field recordings, which are costly.

For this reason, social media networks can be a useful tool for building ethnic music datasets. However, this data can consist of low-quality recordings (using hand cameras and with a significant amount of crowd noise). Also, some genres are clearly populated by only a few artists and producers. This can become a problem because, as noted by Sturm [14], such unbalance can force classifiers to learn artist-specific features, rather than genre-specific features. Therefore, maintaining artist balance implies in building very small datasets.

As a consequence of these difficulties, ethnic music datasets can easily contain less than one hundred tracks. Such a small number of tracks implies in problems related to the dimensionality of the vectors employed to describe them (handcrafted features vectors usually contain hundreds of dimensions) and the number of parameters that must be optimized (DL models often contain thousands of parameters). Therefore, it is necessary to use adequate techniques to mitigate these problems and avoid model overfitting.

One possibility is to use data augmentation techniques. In this case, each track is digitally processed to generate a similar, yet different, track. As a consequence, the original dataset size is multiplied by the number of augmentation proposals. Data augmentation has been shown to slightly improve classification results in popular music datasets [7].

Another possibility is to use feature selection techniques. These techniques aim at reducing the dimensionality of the feature vector by removing non-informative features. Although there are many techniques for such, feature selection using a Maximum-Relevance-Minimum-Redundancy criterion [9] has shown to improve classification results in previous work [1].

Last, it is possible to employ classification models that naturally mitigate the dataset size problem. One of these models is a Hidden-Markov Model (HMM) classifier [10]. This classifier, similarly to an isolated-word recognition system, receives framewise features as inputs and models each genre as an isolated HMM. In the prediction stage, it yields the genre with a higher likelihood related to the input sequence. The HMM mitigates the dataset size problem because each track is simultaneously represented by all of its frames, instead of a single vector.

This paper proposes a bag-of-frames [2,4,16] variation to this problem. In our approach, we calculate feature tracks and aggregate them up to the texture window level, as described by Tzanetakis and Cook [15]. Then, we select a number of texture windows and use them to simultaneously represent each track. In the prediction stage, all selected texture windows are classified and the algorithm yields the most frequently predicted genre.

The proposed approach relies on the assumption that a short texture window (a few seconds long) can be representative of the whole track's content [6], as long as the track is uniform. By selecting several texture windows, we increase the amount of data related to each track, thus mitigating the problem of dimensionality. Simultaneously, we expect to prevent errors due to choosing texture windows containing crowd noise or other recording artifacts.

The algorithm is described in detail in Sect. 2. The experiments and results, discussed in Sect. 3, show that the proposed method outperforms others in a small, ethnic music dataset. This paper is concluded in Sect. 4.

2 Proposed Method

The genre classification method proposed in this paper relies on mapping each track to several points in a $\mathbb{R}^N$ vector space. Within this vector space, the similarity between two sonic textures is represented by a small Euclidean distance between their corresponding vector mappings. The mapping process, as shown in Fig. 1, consists of calculating statistics of the spectral shape descriptors described in Table 1.

The mapping process begins by dividing an audio track into short-time (46 ms) frames with 50% overlap between two consecutive frames. Then, a set of features, described in Table 1, is estimated for each frame using the methods and expressions presented by Tzanetakis and Cook [15]. The mean and variance of each feature is calculated over windows of 3 s, yielding vectors that describe texture windows.

After that, a set of K different texture windows, linearly distributed in time, are chosen to represent each track. Thus, the feature vectors representing each of the chosen windows are yielded to a classifier algorithm. This algorithm could be any vector classification algorithm, but in this work we evaluated the K Nearest Neighbors (KNN) algorithm and the Support Vector Machines (SVM), which have been successfully used in previous work [6,15].

In the training stage, all texture window representations are simultaneously yielded to the classification model. They are all labeled according to the track's genre.

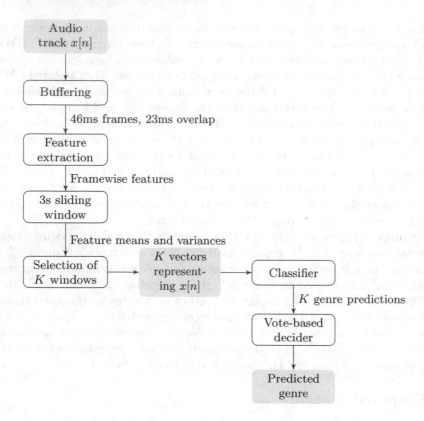

Fig. 1. Overview of the proposed method.

Table 1. Features estimated during the mapping process.

Feature	Description
Energy	Energy of a frame, that is, the squared sum of its samples
Spectral centroid	Centroid of the frame's spectrum
Spectral roll-off	Frequency under which 95% of the frame energy is located
Spectral flux	Sum of the positive difference between the spectra of two consecutive frames. Indicates percussive
Zero crossings	Number of times the time-domain signal within a frame crosses zero
MFCCs	30 mel-frequency cepstral coefficients, which provide a rough representation of the timbre within a frame

During testing, all texture windows representing a specific track are yielded to the classifier. Then, the classifier predicts genre labels for all texture tracks and the most frequent label is chosen as the track's label. This prevents errors that might occur due to localized recording problems, such as crowd noise, speech, and pauses between songs within the same track.

The proposed method was tested in two datasets: the freely-available Seyerlehner [11] dataset and a new dataset, developed for this work, comprising audio extracted from online videos of Brazilian folk music genres. Its performance was compared to previous classifier proposals. The testing procedure, the datasets and the previous classifiers are described in the next section.

3   Evaluation and Results

This section reports the experimental procedures and discussions carried out in this work. Subsect. 3.1 describes the datasets employed in evaluation. The classification process in these datasets was also evaluated using methods available in the literature, as discussed in Subsect. 3.2. Last, Subsect. 3.3 shows the results and brings further discussions.

3.1   Datasets

The proposed method had its performance evaluated over four datasets, each built under a different assumption. The first dataset, YTBR, contains ethnic music and was built using tracks extracted from online videos. The second dataset, Seynherlaner, contains popular Western music tracks. The third dataset, namely MP, contains regional and folkloric music performed in studio by professional musicians. The last dataset, Amazon, contains music recorded in riverside communities from the Amazon region.

The classification results for all datasets were generated using the proposed method and the reference methods described in the next section.

YTBR Dataset. The first dataset, YTBR, was especially built for this work and comprises 53 audio tracks extracted from online videos, divided into 7 genres of Brazilian folk music. Table 2 briefly describes this content.

The YTBR dataset was carefully built by selecting musical genres that are typically present in folk musical manifestations. Videos representing each musical genre were found online, and their audio tracks were extracted. The dataset was built taking care of not using more than one track by each artist, thus avoiding the possibility of training systems to recognize artists, instead of genres [14]. Also, it was built maintaining balance between the number of tracks representing each genre. With both of these restrictions, the resulting dataset was much smaller than the typical datasets used in Music Information Retrieval, comprising only 53 tracks, divided in 7 genres.

Seynherlaner Dataset. The second dataset, Seynherlaner [11], comprises 190 complete, studio-recorded tracks divided into 19 genres of popular Western music. It was used to further corroborate the results obtained in the YTBR dataset and evaluate their generalization in other small datasets.

Table 2. Content description of the YTBR dataset.

Genre	Tracks	Description
Capoeira	8	A dance and fighting style developed by african slaves during Brazil's colonial era. Frequently exhibited by practitioners on open streets
Fandango	7	A ballroom dance style from Southern Brazil, derived from European traditions
Forró	8	A ballroom dance style derived from both European and African music, commonly associated with the Northeast of Brazil
Frevo	7	A dance style typically present in carnival celebrations in some cities of the Brazilian North and Northeast
Maracatu	7	A rhythmic style linked to African and Portuguese musical and religious traditions, played in drum ensembles
Repente	8	A voice and guitar improvisation style in which two musicians develop a game involving rhyme and storytelling
Toada	8	A solo voice (no accompaniment) style, commonly associated to cattle farmers from semi-arid inlands
Total	53	A media collection containing Brazilian folk music genres

MP Dataset. The third dataset, MP, was extracted from the Marcus Pereira collections. These collections comprise Brazilian regional and folkloric music pieces performed in studio during the 1960's and 1970's. Since each region is related to particular musical styles, the dataset was divided so that each track's region of origin was used as a genre label.

In total, it contains 43 tracks from the South-East, 19 from the North-East, 33 from the North, and 30 from the South.

Amazon Dataset. The last dataset was extracted from the Música das Cachoeiras (*music of the waterfalls*) collection. This collection was recorded in 2013 during an expedition through Negro River (in the Amazon forest) lead by Agenor de Vasconcelos Neto. The expedition took a mobile studio and recorded musical manifestations from communities living by the margins of the river.

The dataset was divided intro three groups. The first group, with 25 tracks, contains music with high Western influence, both regarding the musical styles and the instruments. The second group contains 11 tracks of instrumental music performed using only traditional aboriginal instruments. The last group contains 50 tracks of traditional aboriginal music with vocals.

3.2   Reference Methods

The first reference method (GTZAN) is the one proposed by Tzanetakis and Cook [15]. It involves mapping tracks to a vector space short (texture-level) and long (track-level) statistics of low-level handcrafted features. After mapping, the resulting vectors are classified using a Support Vector Machine. This method was reimplemented and validated using the instructions provided in the original paper.

Using a bandpass filterbank, it is possible to build artificial variations of each track that are still recognized as belonging to the same genre. They represent audio tracks as if they were listened to through specific radio equipment. The audio bands were chosen arbitrarily, as there was no reason to choose specific bands for the filters. Dataset augmentation causes the number of samples to exceed their dimension, thus enabling the use of MRMR for feature selection. Combinations of dataset augmentation (AUG) and feature selection (MRMR) were also tested, using the method by Tzanetakis and Cook as basis. We evaluated the result variation by selecting different numbers of features with MRMR [9], and only the best results are reported.

Also, we implemented a HMM-based classifier. It works similarly to the isolated word recognition system described by Rabiner [10]. This system classifies sequences of framewise MFCCs using the Viterbi algorithm. Therefore, it takes the timewise organization of textures into account, which makes sense when classifying music. In our implementation, this classifier models each genre using an ergodic HMM with a diagonal covariance matrix and Gaussian emissions. We tested models comprising different numbers of states (6, 10, 15, 20) and only the results for the best-performing model are reported.

Last, we reimplemented the music genre classifier proposed by Nanni et al. [8]. This classifier is based on convolutional neural networks (CNNs). It interprets the track spectrogram as a sequence of images (each representing a few seconds of audio) and develops image filters that are able to highlight genre-specific characteristics of these images. The classification of each image (that is, each few seconds of audio) is decided using a SoftMax output layer, and the classification for the whole track is calculated by summing the results of all image-wise output layers. This method was reimplemented using the instructions provided in the original publication, and validated using the same datasets used by the original authors. Several variations of the training parameters were evaluated, and only the best results were reported.

The results regarding these experiments, as well as further discussions on their impact, are presented in the next section.

3.3 Results and Discussion

In all experiments, we conducted a K-fold (stratified) cross validation protocol. To evaluate each experiment, we calculated the Recall and Precision, as shown in Expressions 1 and 2, for each class. Then, we calculated the F1-score, as shown in Expression 3, for each class. The mean and standard deviation of the class-wise F1-score across the four test attempts is used as reference for evaluation and further discussion.

$$\text{Recall} = \frac{\#\text{ of correct classifications}}{\#\text{ of elements known to belong to class}}. \tag{1}$$

$$\text{Precision} = \frac{\text{\# of correct classifications}}{\text{\# of elements predicted to belong to class}}. \qquad (2)$$

$$\text{F1-Score} = 2\frac{\text{Recall} \times \text{Precision}}{\text{Recall} + \text{Precision}}. \qquad (3)$$

Our experiments were first conducted in the YTBR dataset. The experiments in this dataset used 4 folds for cross validation. This number of folds was chosen instead of the usual 10 because the number of data elements is too small.

In the first experiment, we evaluated several variations of the proposed method. This experiment allowed evaluating the impact of the number of texture windows used to represent each track, as well as the impact of using KNN and SVM as the classification model. The results for this experiment are shown in Fig. 2.

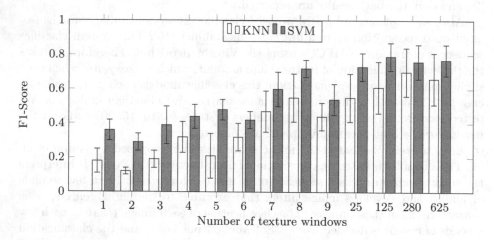

Fig. 2. Classification results in the YTBR dataset for different numbers of texture windows.

Figure 2 shows that the average F1-Score is usually higher for SVM-based classifiers than for KNN-based classifiers. Also, it is possible to see that the standard deviation for SVM-based classifiers tends to be smaller. Last, results show a tendency of increasing the average F1-score with the increase of the number of texture windows, but this increase ceases in values larger than 25. The proposed method variation using 125 texture windows and SVM classifier was used in further tests.

The same evaluation protocol was conducted using all reference methods described in Sect. 3.2. The results, shown in Fig. 3, highlight that the average F1-score achieved by the proposed method is higher than that obtained by all other methods.

The results displayed in Fig. 3 show that data augmentation generates only a small performance gain to the original GTZAN method, whereas MRMR provides a slightly higher improvement. It is evident that HMM, CNN and the

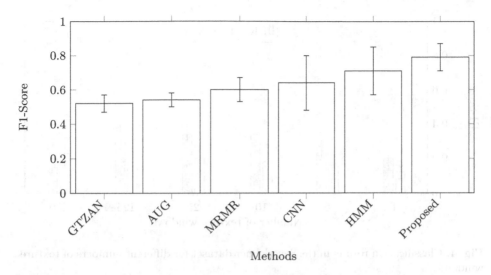

Fig. 3. Classification results in the YTBR dataset for different classification methods. Best results with MRMR were obtained using a 30 feature selection and best results with HMM were obtained using 15-state models for each genre.

proposed method outperform the other three proposals on average. Additionally, it is possible to see that the proposed method obtained a smaller standard deviation when compared to HMM and CNN.

Interestingly, the standard deviation related to both HMM and CNN results are visibly higher than the others. This can indicate insufficient or ill-conditioned data for adequate parameter fitting. However, the proposed method seems to be more resilient to that conditions, as its obtained standard deviation is smaller than the others.

These results show that the proposed AMGC outperforms the other evaluated methods in one small dataset. However, it is necessary to evaluate if these results are consistent in other datasets. For such, we conducted similar experiments in the Seyerlehner dataset [11]. In these experiments, we used a 10-fold cross validation schema. Following the same experimental procedure executed before, we first evaluated the impact of changing the number of texture windows and the classification algorithm in our method. The results are shown in Fig. 4.

Figure 4 shows some aspects that are similar to those seen in Fig. 2. SVM-based classification seems to outperform KNN-based classification, and the average performance raises with the increase of the number of analyzed texture windows. However, in this case, the best results were achieved using between 10 and 25 texture windows. This is a smaller number than that required in the YTBR dataset. In the YTBR dataset, however, there is a significant amount of audio data that contains crowd noises and speech, while this is only a minor issue in the Seyerlehner dataset. As a consequence, a smaller number of texture windows can be enough to provide a meaningful representation for such a dataset.

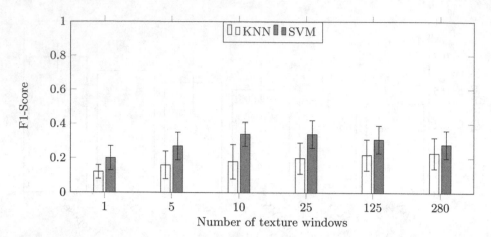

Fig. 4. Classification results in the Seyerlehner dataset for different numbers of texture windows.

The next tests were conducted using the proposed method version with a SVM classifier and 25 texture windows.

The test protocol was applied to the reference methods. GTZAN was used to provide a baseline performance measure. AUG and MRMR were not used in this setup because they were clearly less effective than the other methods. HMM and CNN were evaluated normally. Figure 5 shows the F1-Score estimated in each experiment.

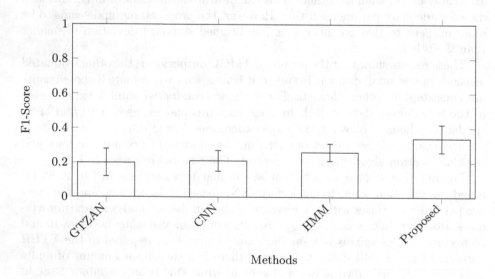

Fig. 5. Classification results in the Seyerlehner dataset for different classification methods.

As it can be seen, GTZAN and CNN had similar performances in this dataset, whereas HMM presented a small (less than one standard deviation) improvement. The best results were achieved by the proposed method.

In the MP and Amazon dataset, MRMR, data augmentation and HMM became too slow and memory-consuming. For this reason, they were not considered in the following tests. Also, only the results related to the best-performing variation of the proposed method are reported.

Figure 6 shows the classification results for the MP dataset. As it can be seen, the proposed method outperformed the two references. Interestingly, the CNN performed worse than the GTZAN method.

The results regarding the Amazon dataset are shown in Fig. 7. Again, the proposed method outperforms the references, and, as it is the case of the MP dataset, the CNN performed worse than both others.

This dataset seems to be easier to classify than the other three, as results are consistently higher. This can be due to the choice of only three labels, and to the fact that they relate to significantly different musical styles.

The results in all dataset consistently show that the proposed method outperforms the reference methods. Hence, it is possible to conclude that the proposed method is effective in small and ethnic music datasets.

Although CNNs have shown to achieve good results in larger datasets, they did not perform well in the small-data scenario. This is probably linked to their large number of parameters, which need a larger amount of data to be adequately optimized. Also, its results were worse than the GTZAN method in two of the datasets, which can be related to their unbalance. Hence, it is possible that transfer learning techniques, that is, pre-training models in larger datasets before

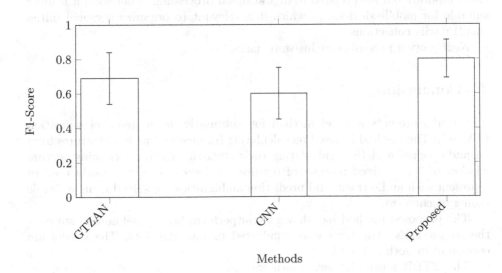

Fig. 6. Classification results in the MP dataset for different classification methods.

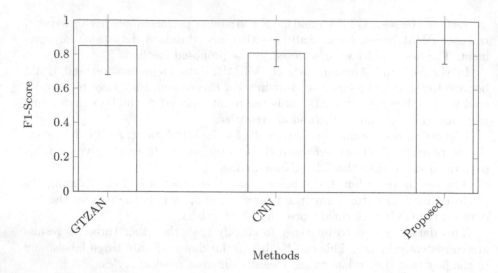

Fig. 7. Classification results in the Amazon dataset for different classification methods.

their application to the small dataset, can mitigate this issue and allow to employ the full potential of deep-learning for this scenario.

Nevertheless, our method – using handcrafted features – has outperformed other proposals for the proposed scenario. It uses algorithms that require significantly less computational power than HMMs and CNNs. Genre prediction, in special, only requires processing a fraction of the whole track, which reduces the computational load related to digital signal processing. Therefore, it is more suitable for mobile devices, in which it is relevant to organize personal (often small) media collections.

Next section presents conclusive remarks.

4   Conclusion

This works presents a novel method for automatic music genre classification (AMGC). The method is based on calculating framewise, low-level features from an audio signal and then calculating their statistics within a running texture window of 3 s. A fixed number of texture windows is simultaneously used to represent each audio track, and prediction ambiguities are solved using a simple voting mechanism.

The proposed method has shown to outperform both baseline and state-of-the-art methods. The tests were conducted in four datasets. The results are consistent in both datasets.

The YTBR music dataset, which was created for this work, can be freely downloaded. Instructions for download are available in the author's website. Therefore, it can be used in further research on AMGC.

These results show that the proposed method can be used in the organization of both ethnic music collections, which are prone to contain noisy recordings, and personal music collections, which can contain a very small amount of data. Also, the proposed method uses significantly less computational resources than deep-learning or HMM-based methods, thus being more suitable for use in mobile devices.

All results obtained in this work regard small datasets, which is a specific case for AMGC. Although the proposed method was inspired in small, ill-recorded datasets, previous work has shown that similar approaches can yield good results in larger datasets. Tests regarding such datasets comprise a clear direction for future work.

Acknowledgements. The authors thank FAPESP for financial support. The datasets and source code for the proposed method can be downloaded from the author's website (http://www.dca.fee.unicamp.br/~tavares).

References

1. Baniya, B.K., Lee, J., Li, Z.N.: Audio feature reduction and analysis for automatic music genre classification. In: 2014 IEEE International Conference on Systems, Man, and Cybernetics (SMC), pp. 457–462, October 2014
2. Barbedo, J.G.A., Lopes, A.: Automatic genre classification of musical signals. EURASIP J. Adv. Sig. Proc. (2007). https://doi.org/10.1155/2007/64960
3. Costa, Y.M., Oliveira, L.S., Silla Jr., C.N.: An evaluation of convolutional neural networks for music classification using spectrograms. Appl. Soft Comput. **52**, 28–38 (2017)
4. Jang, D., Jin, M., Yoo, C.D.: Music genre classification using novel features and a weighted voting method. In: 2008 IEEE International Conference on Multimedia and Expo, pp. 1377–1380, June 2008
5. Silla Jr., C.N., Koerich, A.L., Kaestner, C.A.A.: Feature selection in automatic music genre classification. In: 2008 Tenth IEEE International Symposium on Multimedia, pp. 39–44, December 2008
6. Li, T., Ogihara, M.: Content-based music similarity search and emotion detection, vol. 5 (2004)
7. McFee, B., Humphrey, E.J., Bello, J.P.: A software framework for musical data augmentation. In: Proceedings of the 16th International Society for Music Information Retrieval Conference, ISMIR 2015, Málaga, Spain, 26–30 October 2015, pp. 248–254 (2015)
8. Nanni, L., Costa, Y.M.G., Lumini, A., Kim, M.Y., Baek, S.: Combining visual and acoustic features for music genre classification. Expert Syst. Appl. **45**, 108–117 (2016). https://doi.org/10.1016/j.eswa.2015.09.018
9. Peng, H., Long, F., Ding, C.: Feature selection based on mutual information criteria of max-dependency, max-relevance, and min-redundancy. IEEE Trans. Pattern Anal. Mach. Intell. **27**(8), 1226–1238 (2005)
10. Rabiner, L.R.: Readings in speech recognition. In: A Tutorial on Hidden Markov Models and Selected Applications in Speech Recognition, pp. 267–296. Morgan Kaufmann Publishers Inc., San Francisco (1990). http://dl.acm.org/citation.cfm?id=108235.108253

11. Seyerlehner, K.: Annotated seyerlehner genre dataset (2012). http://www. seyerlehner.info/index.php?p=1_3_Download
12. Sigtia, S., Dixon, S.: Improved music feature learning with deep neural networks. In: 2014 IEEE International Conference on Acoustics, Speech and Signal Processing (ICASSP), pp. 6959–6963, May 2014
13. Smalley, D.: Spectromorphology: explaining sound-shapes. Org. Sound **2**(2), 107–126 (1997). https://doi.org/10.1017/S1355771897009059
14. Sturm, B.L.: Classification accuracy is not enough - on the evaluation of music genre recognition systems. J. Intell. Inf. Syst. **41**(3), 371–406 (2013). https://doi.org/10.1007/s10844-013-0250-y
15. Tzanetakis, G., Cook, P.: Musical genre classification of audio signals. IEEE Trans. Speech Audio Process. **10**(5), 293–302 (2002)
16. West, K., Cox, S.: Features and classifiers for the automatic classification of musical audio signals. In: Proceedings of ISMIR 2004 (2004)

Music Genre Classification Revisited: An In-Depth Examination Guided by Music Experts

Haukur Pálmason[1], Björn Þór Jónsson[1,2], Markus Schedl[3],
and Peter Knees[4(✉)]

[1] Reykjavik University, Reykjavík, Iceland
bjorn@ru.is
[2] IT University of Copenhagen, Copenhagen, Denmark
[3] Johannes Kepler University Linz, Linz, Austria
[4] TU Wien, Vienna, Austria
peter.knees@tuwien.ac.at

Abstract. Despite their many identified shortcomings, music genres are still often used as ground truth and as a proxy for music similarity. In this work we therefore take another in-depth look at genre classification, this time with the help of music experts. In comparison to existing work, we aim at including the viewpoint of different stakeholders to investigate *whether musicians and end-user music taxonomies agree on genre ground truth*, through a user study among 20 professional and semi-professional music protagonists. We then compare the results of their genre judgments with different commercial taxonomies and with that of computational genre classification experiments, and discuss individual cases in detail. Our findings coincide with existing work and provide further evidence that a simple classification taxonomy is insufficient.

Keywords: Music genre classification · Expert study · Ground truth

1 Introduction

In the last 20 years, almost 500 publications have dealt with the automatic recognition of musical genre [21]. However, genre is a multifaceted concept, which has caused much disagreement among musicologists, music distributors, and, not least, music information retrieval (MIR) researchers [18]. Hence, MIR research has often tried to overcome the "ill-defined" concept of genre [1,16]. Despite all the disagreement, genres are still often used as ground truth and as a proxy for music similarity and have remained important concepts in production, circulation, and reception of music in the last decades [4]. Their relevance for music perception is evidenced by studies that show the existence of common ground between individuals, e.g., [10,19], their importance in users' music similarity assessment [15], and their recognizability within fractions of seconds [6,8]. As a result, genre classification remains a relevant task in MIR research [14,17].

© Springer Nature Switzerland AG 2018
M. Aramaki et al. (Eds.): CMMR 2017, LNCS 11265, pp. 49–62, 2018.
https://doi.org/10.1007/978-3-030-01692-0_4

In comparison to work on optimising genre classification, work discussing ground truth for MIR, and in particular work discussing the viewpoint of different stakeholders, is scarce. For this reason, in this work, we investigate whether musicians and end-user music taxonomies agree on genre ground truth by comparing different commercial taxonomies and discussing individual cases in detail.

The remainder of this paper is organised as follows. We first discuss related work on defining and investigating genre ground truths (Sect. 2), then present our study involving music experts (Sect. 3). Subsequently, the results of our study are discussed in detail, including a thorough review of selected artists and songs (Sect. 4). The paper is rounded off by concluding remarks (Sect. 5).

2   Related Observations on Genre Ground Truth

The original version of [6] from 1999 is much cited although it has been unavailable in print until the re-release in 2008. The authors chose the following 10 genres: blues, classical, country, dance, jazz, latin, pop, R&B, rap and rock. 52 university students representing "ordinary undergraduate fans of music" listened to excerpts from eight songs of each genre. The excerpts varied in length from 250 ms to 3,000 ms. Genre classification was taken from CDnow, BMG and Tower Records, the leading web based music vendors of the nineties. When listening to the 3,000 ms excerpts participants agreed with the ground truth about 70% of the time. When participants were only allowed to listen to 250 ms excerpts the accuracy varied greatly with genres, with less than 20% accuracy of blues songs, but over 70% accuracy of classical songs, with the average across all genres being 44%. A study with a small group of music theory majors revealed essentially the same results as with the non-musicians in the main study.

Lippens et al. [10] compared the results of automatic genre classification and human genre classification on the MAMI dataset. The MAMI dataset consists of 160 full length songs, originally classified into 11 genres. They concluded that due to various reasons this classification was not fit for automatic genre classification and therefore conducted a user study with 27 human listeners. Each participant listened to a 30-second-excerpt from all the songs and classified each song into one of six genres. The outcome from that study was as follows: 69 pop, 25 rock, 24 classical, 18 dance, 8 rap, and 16 other, with the genre "other" being used for songs that did not fit into any of the first five genres. The next step was to compare the selected genre of each participant with this new ground truth. The accuracy of the 27 participants ranged from 57% to 86% averaging at 76%. A subset of the MAMI dataset, called MAMI2, was then created. It included songs from the first five genres mentioned above, and only songs that had received 18 or more votes for their particular genre. This resulted in 98 tracks. The average classification accuracy of the participants for this dataset was 90%.

Craft et al. [3] criticized how the MAMI2 dataset was created, and claimed that it was "not statistically well-founded". Their argument was that the meaning of the genre "other" was undefined to the participants, resulting in different ways of using that genre: should participants only use it for songs that did not find a home in any of the other genres or should they also use if a song features multiple genres? They examined the songs that did not make it into the MAMI2 dataset and found out that only one of these songs received 10 votes for "other", one song received seven votes, but the remaining songs received five or fewer votes for the "other" genre. The authors then constructed a similarity graph of all songs in the MAMI dataset, where songs with similar *distribution of genre votes* were grouped together. It turned out that there were groups of tracks that spanned multiple genres, and there were genres that spanned multiple groups of similar tracks. The main conclusion of the paper was that it is unrealistic to try to create a genre classification dataset that is entirely unambiguous, since real life datasets do not only contain unambiguous data. They proposed that all results from automatic genre classification systems should be weighted to reflect the amount of ambiguity of human classification of that same dataset.

The most commonly used dataset, GTZAN, introduced in the archetypal work in the field of genre recognition by Tzanetakis and Cook [24], contains 10 musical genres, namely: classical, country, disco, hiphop, jazz, rock, blues, reggae, pop, and metal. Despite its wide acceptance and reuse in subsequent studies, it exhibits inconsistencies, repetitions, and mislabeling as investigated in detail by Sturm [20].[1] Apart from challenging the notion of categorizing music pieces into exclusive genres, Sturm argues convincingly that the errors in the genre assignments make results stemming from different approaches non-interpretable and incomparable, as different machine learning algorithms are affected in different ways. Despite the already identified shortcomings of GTZAN, we investigated parts of this dataset with the help of musical experts to gain further insights.

3   User Study with Music Experts

For our user study, we asked music experts to classify selected tracks of the GTZAN dataset. To keep the workload low, we chose examples that were misclassified by a k-NN classifier (see below), since these seem to be difficult, mislabeled, or exhibit other particularities that justify a deeper investigation.

Using a new, very efficient k-NN classifier [7] with $k = 3$ on features consisting of MFCCs and spectral flatness measure (SFM) extracted through MARSYAS (http://marsyas.info) we reach a genre classification accuracy of 80.8% in a 10-fold cross validation setting, which closely matches the best results in the literature obtained using these particular features. That leaves 192 tracks misclassified, however, which are distributed over genres as illustrated in Fig. 1.

To analyse these tracks in more detail we set up an experiment where 20 participants listened to the 192 wrongly classified songs. The participants are all active in the Icelandic music industry, either as musicians, producers, sound engineers, or DJs, and include both semi-professionals and professionals. More precisely, among the semi-professionals we included a singer/songwriter who has

---

[1] George Tzanetakis, the author of the dataset, has repeatedly confirmed being aware of these issues, but has chosen not to correct them since the dataset has been used so many times and changing the files would render comparisons of results infeasible.

released two albums, but never received the recognition necessary to completely quit his day job, a DJ at a local club in Akureyri who also works at a computer store, a guitarist and singer in a wedding/club band who has a day job as a painter, and a music blogger who works in a factory during the day. The professionals includes a radio DJ at one of Iceland's biggest radio stations, a guitarist and guitar teacher at the Akureyri School of Music, a drummer and drum teacher at the Akureyri School of Music, and a music producer and recording engineer.

Each participant received a list of the 10 genres of the GTZAN dataset[2] and then listened to the 30-second-clips for all 192 misclassified tracks, marking each track with the genre label that they felt best described that song. The listening environment was a quiet room with a high fidelity stereo system.

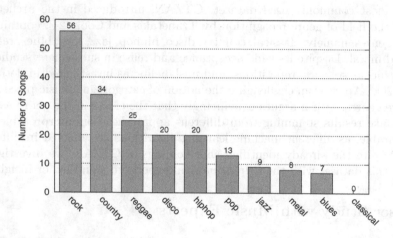

Fig. 1. Genre distribution of the 192 misclassified songs used in our user study.

While the dataset contains no information about artists or song names, listening to the songs reveals several interesting facts, including two mistakes in its creation. First, a live version of the song "Tie your mother down" by Queen is included twice, once labelled as rock and once labelled as metal. During k-NN search both versions get wrongly classified since the version labelled rock gets all its votes from the version labelled metal and vice versa. Second, one reggae sound clip is faulty, with only 6 s of music and 24 s of loud noise. It is interesting to note that the k-NN classifier labels this noise as pop.

The set often includes several songs by the same artists. Out of these 192 songs 7 songs are by Sting, 6 by Jethro Tull and 4 by Rolling Stones. Other artists that have multiple songs include Black Sabbath, Led Zeppelin, Beastie Boys, Bob Marley, Willie Nelson, Alanis Morrisette, Vince Gill and Guns'n'Roses. All Sting songs are from his first two albums "Dream of the Blue Turtles" and "Bring on

---

[2] The genre "classical" was included even though no track was classified as such.

the Night" where Sting uses famous jazz musicians including Branford Marsalis on saxophones and Kenny Kirkland on pianos. All these Sting songs are classified as rock by Tzanetakis, whereas participants were divided between pop and jazz. The Jethro Tull songs included such diverse songs as "Happy and I'm smiling", "Bungle in the Jungle" and "Life is a love song". Again were all songs considered rock by Tzanetakis. Most were also classified as rock by participants, while some were classified as pop. Many commented that "Life is a love song" is really folk or acoustic, but no such genre is included in the set.

4 Results

4.1 Comparison with GTZAN Ground Truth and k-NN Classifier

Table 1 compares the manual classification of the music experts to the ground truth of the GTZAN dataset. The table shows that the agreement between individual participants and the ground truth ranges from 52.6% to 69.8%, and is on average 59.1%. Agreement is defined as the share of songs participants annotated with the same genre as the ground truth given by the GZTAN dataset (3rd column) and as the prediction of the classifier (5th column). The table reports results at different levels of agreement/types of users, e.g., the user with the lowest agreement in row "Lowest"; analogously for the other rows. For instance, the participant (out of the 20) who agreed the least with the ground truth agreed with the classification of 101 songs (out of the 192), or 52.6%, and he agreed with the classification of k-NN on only 15 songs (out of the 192).

These numbers should not be compared with the results from [6, 10] since the dataset used for this experiment was specifically chosen because the automatic genre classifier was not able to classify the songs correctly. It is, however, interesting to note the low agreement rate on these songs. Table 1 also shows the number of tracks where the participants agreed with the results of the k-NN classifier; remember that these tracks were all wrongly classified by the automatic classification. It is interesting that for nearly 27% of the tracks, participants agreed neither with the GTZAN ground truth nor the k-NN classifier.

We then created a new ground truth using the majority vote of the 20 participants. As the last line of Table 1 shows, this new ground truth agrees with the GTZAN ground truth for 63.5% of the 192 tracks, and with the k-NN classifier for 12.5% of the 192 tracks; for 24% of the tracks the new ground truth agrees with neither. To examine closer how much the participants agreed, we used this new majority vote as ground truth. Table 2 confirms that there is considerable variation in the way our participants classified the songs, with the highest agreement with the new majority vote ground truth being 166 songs, or 86.46%. However, we also see from this table that overall there is more individual agreement with this new majority vote ground truth than the original GTZAN ground truth, so there seems to be a number of songs that everyone believes are wrongly classified in the original ground truth.

Table 1. Participants' agreement with the ground truth and the k-NN classifier. Agreement is the share of songs participants described with the same genre as the ground truth given by the GTZAN dataset (3rd column) and as the prediction of the classifier (rightmost column).

Participant agreement	GTZAN ground truth		k-NN classifier	
	Songs	Percentage	Songs	Percentage
Lowest	101	52.6%	15	7.8%
Highest	134	69.8%	34	17.7%
Median	112	58.3%	25	13.0%
Average	113.4	59.1%	24.9	13.0%
Majority vote	122	63.5%	24	12.5%

Table 2. Participants' agreement with "majority vote" ground truth. Agreement is defined as in Table 1.

Participant agreement	Songs	Percentage
Lowest	121	63.0%
Highest	166	86.5%
Median	153	79.7%
Average	150.3	78.3%

As a more detailed analysis, Table 3 shows a comparison of the majority vote for each genre to both the original ground truth and the results from our k-NN classification. As the table shows, participants agree strongly with ground truth for pop, hiphop, blues, country and jazz. Reggae and disco have moderate agreement, while rock and specially metal have very low agreement.

4.2   Comparison with the "World Out There"

In order to compare the classification of ground truth, k-NN and our participants to that of the world out there, we selected 15 songs randomly from the songs in the dataset that we recognized. We then looked at how these songs are classified on iTunes, allmusic.com and last.fm.

Apple's on-line media store, iTunes, only classifies albums so songs actually can have multiple genre classifications if they are featured on more than one album. Two songs in our set, David Bowie's "Space Oddity", and Jethro Tull's "Life is a love song" fall into this category, where both are classified as pop in one place, and rock in another place.

Allmusic.com is a music reference web page with album and artist critique. Allmusic.com classifies artists into genres and styles, where genres are usually very broad, such as "Pop-Rock" but styles are narrower. We report the genre and the two top styles of each artist.

Table 3. Majority vote agreement, by genre, with GTZAN and k-NN classifier. Agreement is defined as in Table 1.

Genre	GTZAN ground truth		k-NN classifier	
	Songs	Percentage	Songs	Percentage
Blues	6	85.7%	1	14.3%
Country	29	85.3%	1	2.9%
Disco	10	50.0%	6	30.0%
Hiphop	18	90.0%	1	5.0%
Jazz	7	77.8%	2	22.2%
Metal	1	12.5%	4	50.0%
Pop	12	92.3%	1	7.7%
Reggae	16	64.0%	4	16.0%
Rock	23	41.1%	4	7.1%
Total	122	63.5%	24	12.5%

Last.fm is an Internet radio station that allows users to tag songs. Tags can be any text that listeners use to describe songs. Most popular tags are displayed on the website. We report the three most popular tags, omitting all tags that include artists or song names.

Table 4 shows the comparison of the ground truth, k-NN classification, our participants' voting, iTunes, allmusic.com and last.fm. The table shows that iTunes agrees with the ground truth of the dataset in most cases, or 12 for out of the 15 songs, if we count the two songs that have both pop and rock classification in iTunes. The allmusic.com genre label is very broad, and in 12 out of the 15 songs this genre label is pop/rock. This goes for songs classified as pop, rock or metal by the ground truth. The table also shows that in 8 songs the k-NN classification has the correct genre in 2nd place, and in 2 songs the correct genre comes in 3rd place. From this small sample our participants only agree with the ground truth for 2 songs which is quite far from their agreement for the whole 192 songs. The participants have the correct genre in 2nd place in 6 songs, and in 3rd place in 3 songs.

4.3   Discussion of Particular Songs

We now discuss in order each of the 15 tracks from Table 4 in more detail, both the song itself as well as the various classifications.

Ani Difranco's "Cradle and all" has a very strong acoustic guitar presence and this is without a doubt the reason why our k-NN program classifies the song as country. Many country songs have this same sound character. We see folk mentioned both at allmusic.com and last.fm, which also is a genre characterized by the acoustic guitar, but our ground truth does not include this genre. iTunes uses the alternative genre for this song, but this genre is very ill-defined.

Table 4. Comparison of ground truth, iTunes, allmusic.com and last.fm, k-NN classification and participants' voting.

Artist Song	GTZAN	iTunes	allmusic.com	last.fm	k-NN genre / %		participants genre / %	
Ani Difranco Cradle and all	rock	alternative	pop/rock folk urban folk	folk female.voc indie	country jazz blues	24 22 18	pop jazz	85 15
Billy Joel Movin' out	rock	rock	pop/rock singer/songwr. soft rock	classic rock pop soft rock	disco rock country	35 21 20	pop rock	75 25
Bob Seger Against the wind	rock	rock	pop/rock rock'n'roll hard rock	classic rock rock soft rock	disco country reggae	24 23 16	pop country rock	65 25 10
David Bowie Space Oddity	rock	pop/rock	pop/rock hard rock glam rock	classic rock glam rock british rock	country disco rock	37 23 19	pop rock reggae	75 20 5
Jethro Tull Life is a love song	rock	pop/rock	progressive blues-rock hard rock	country classic rock 70s	disco rock country	43 16 15	pop rock blues	85 10 5
Led Zeppelin D'yer Mak'er	rock	rock	pop/rock blues blues-rock	classic rock rock reggae	pop disco rock	26 23 23	reggae rock pop	50 35 15
Simply Red Freedom	rock	pop	pop/rock soul adult.cont.	pop rock easy	disco rock blues	28 25 21	pop jazz disco	55 25 15
Sting Consider me gone	rock	rock	pop/rock adult cont. cont. pop/rock	rock jazz pop	pop hiphop reggae	31 15 14	jazz pop blues	50 45 5
Jimmy Cliff Many rivers to cross	reggae	reggae	reggae reggae-pop roots reggae	reggae soul jamaica	classical jazz country	26 23 22	pop classical reggae	70 25 5
Marcia Griffiths It's Electric	reggae	reggae	reggae dancehall roots reggae	funk dance party	pop disco hiphop	60 23 5	pop disco hiphop	65 30 5
Cher Believe	pop	pop	pop/rock dance-pop adult. cont.	pop dance 90s	disco pop reggae	26 24 23	disco pop hiphop	60 35 5
Madonna Music	pop	pop	pop/rock dance-pop adult.cont.	pop dance electronic	hiphop pop jazz	32 22 18	pop hiphop disco	65 25 15
Guns'n'Roses Live and let die	metal	rock	pop/rock hard rock heavy metal	rock hard rock cover	rock metal disco	54 38 4	rock metal blues	75 20 5
Living Colour Glamour Boys	metal	rock	pop/rock alt. metal alt. pop/rock	rock funk rock 80s	hiphop metal disco	34 28 22	rock pop	60 40
Willie Nelson Georgia on my mind	country	country	country trad.country progr. country	country classic country folk	blues country classical	38 29 16	country blues jazz	40 30 20
Beastie Boys Fight for your right	hiphop	hiphop/rap	rap pop/rock alt. pop/rock	hip-hop 80s rock	metal hiphop rock	59 18 17	rock metal hiphop	70 25 5

Our participants classify the song as a pop song, with several of them commenting that they would use folk, or acoustic pop, if either was available.

Billy Joel's "Movin' out" can hardly be classified as a disco song, although it has the dry 70's drum sound. Yet our k-NN classifier classifies it as disco, as too many other rock songs, with rock coming in second. 75% of our participants classify it as a pop song with the remaining votes going to rock. Both allmusic.com and last.fm use terms such as soft rock, which we believe is a synonym for pop in many people's mind.

Bob Seger's "Against the wind" is on all three websites considered a rock song. However, our solution does not have rock in the top three places, whereas 2 of our 20 participants classified the song as a rock song. The song has several elements of a classic country song including the acoustic guitar, the piano playing, and the vocal harmonies. This is one of the rock songs which our k-NN classifier classifies as a disco song, which is plainly wrong. We believe that if multiple genres were to be used, then pop, rock and country should all be used.

David Bowie's "Space Oddity" features the acoustic guitar very much, and this is without a doubt the reason in gets classified as a country song by k-NN. All websites use the rock genre, sometimes with specific sub-genres of rock for this song, although iTunes classifies it as pop when it is a part of Bowie's "Singles collection" album. Most participants in our study classified the song as a pop song, with rock coming in second. The reggae classification of one participant must be a mistake, since there is not a single reggae element in the song. Just as it is difficult to pinpoint the boundaries between rock and metal, it is also very difficult to pinpoint exactly the difference between pop and rock.

Jethro Tull's catalog of songs is extremely diverse, so classifications on artists level are not going to be very accurate. Allmusic.com classifications of blues rock or hard rock hardly describe "Life is a love song" well. Last.fm tags of progressive, classic rock and 70's are more accurate, although less popular tags, such as folk rock describe the song better, in our opinion. Our participants classified it as pop, with rock coming in second, and one participant using the blues genre. The song is very acoustic, with acoustic guitars, mandolins and a flute. As with some other acoustic songs it gets a considerable number of votes from country songs in k-NN classification.

Led Zeppelin is of course one of the greatest rock bands in history, so it does not come as a surprise that "D'yer Mak'er" is classified as a rock song by ground truth, iTunes, and two most popular last.fm tags, with allmusic.com using blues and blues rock. Blues is indeed where the roots of Led Zeppelin lie. 50% of our participants and a considerable number of last.fm users want to classify this song as a reggae song, and it cannot denied that indeed it has much more reggae feel than "Many rivers to cross". At the same time it features some pop elements, reflected for instance in its instrumentation.

Simply Red's "Freedom" is classified as rock by ground truth. This time we are not surprised with the disco classification of k-NN since the song has in our opinion more disco elements than rock elements, including the guitar sound and the prominent strings. The rhythm, although not the standard disco beat, also resembles disco, with very prominent bongo drums and tambourines. A vast majority of participants classify the song as a pop song, thereby agreeing with iTunes and the most popular last.fm tag (where rock comes in second).

Sting's "Consider me gone" is one of the songs he recorded with several famous jazz musicians. Our participants have almost the same number of votes for jazz and pop for this song, with one person considering it a blues song. None mentioned the rock genre used by the ground truth, iTunes, and last.fm. We notice, however, that last.fm also has both pop and jazz tags, while allmusic.com concentrates on the adult-contemporary label. This is one of these songs where it is very difficult to say that one particular genre is correct.

Jimmy Cliff's "Many rivers to cross" is yet another one of those difficult songs. Websites and ground truth agree on defining the song as a reggae song, but the song does not include any trademark reggae features, such as the off-beat rhythm. Instead it has some classical characteristics, such as the prominent church organ sound. Jimmy Cliff is one of those artists that has merged reggae and pop music successfully, and as with Marcia Griffiths this song is perhaps not very representative for him. Most of our participants classify this as a pop song, with classical coming in second.

Marcia Griffiths' "It's electric" is an example of a song that perhaps does not represent the artist very well, and therefore there is inconsistency between genres that are created by artist or album classifications and genres that are created by song classification. Both k-NN and our experiment participants classify this as a pop song, with disco and hip-hop coming in 2nd and 3rd, respectively. Last.fm tags include funk, dance and party which can be said to be closer to the pop, disco, hip-hop, categories than reggae assigned by both iTunes and allmusic.com. However, some of our participants commented that Marcia Griffiths is known as a reggae artist, but they still could not classify this particular song as a reggae song.

Cher's "Believe" features the infamous disco drum beat where the high-hat opens on every offbeat. Most of the instruments are obviously programmed, which makes the sound different from the classic 70's disco songs. Participants agree with k-NN in classifying this as a disco song, but both put pop in second place with the difference in votes in the k-NN classification being very low. Perhaps the style dance-pop used my allmusic.com describes it best, but what is dance-pop other than a combination of disco and pop?

Madonna's "Music" is a very electronic song. Most, if not all instruments are electronic in nature and programmed instead of being "hand-played". It has this in common with most hiphop songs, in addition to some strange vocal effects. However, in our opinion it lacks the hiphop beat to be classified as a hiphop song. We see that our participants agree with ground truth, iTunes and last.fm most popular tag, in classifying it as a pop song, and indeed pop is the genre with the second most votes in k-NN. Allmusic.com uses dance-pop which also describes the song very well.

Guns'n'Roses version of the Wings hit "Live and let die" is considered a metal song by ground truth. iTunes, k-NN, participants and last.fm all agree on rock, while the first style at allmusic.com is hard rock, with metal coming in second for both k-NN and our participants. It is difficult to say where the boundaries lie between rock and metal. This song does include a large dose of overdriven guitars, which does characterize metal, but in our opinion the overall sound and feel is much more rock.

Living Colour's "Glamour Boys" is classified as hiphop by k-NN with metal and disco in 2nd and 3rd place, respectively. Ground truth considers this a metal song, while participants, iTunes and the most popular last.fm tag agree on rock. Some participants commented that indeed the verse with its clean guitar sound of the song is a pop verse, while the chorus with its overdriven guitar and more aggressive voice is more rock oriented. This caused some of them to have problems deciding which genre to use. In the end it was 60/40 for rock against pop.

"Georgia on my mind" has been recorded by many artists. With Willie Nelson being a country icon, iTunes, which classifies albums, and allmusic.com, which classifies artists, use the country genre for his version of this song. The three most popular tags at last.fm are country, traditional country and folk. The fourth most popular tag (not counting the tag Willie Nelson) is blues. k-NN classifies the song as blues with country coming in second place, while this is reversed for our participants. The song, in our opinion, is more of a blues song than a country song, but Willie Nelson does of course bring some country flavor to it.

Beastie Boys' "Fight for your right" would probably never be classified as a hiphop song by people that heard it the first time and did not know that Beastie Boys are a hiphop/rap band. The instrumentation and rhythm are those of a typical rock/metal song, with loud overdriven guitars, and simple bass and drum beats. The vocals are the only thing that resemble rap music. k-NN strongly classifies this as metal with hiphop and rock coming in 2nd and 3rd, while 70% of our participants classify it as rock, and 25% as metal. One participant classified it as hiphop.

4.4 Impact of Ground Truth Definition on Classification Accuracy

Having seen that the participants in our ground truth experiment had in many ways different opinions on which genre songs in the GTZAN dataset should belong to, we decided to change the ground truth of the songs where the majority vote of participants differs from the ground truth. Recall from Table 1 that the majority vote results from the experiment agrees with the ground truth for 122 songs of the 192 that were incorrectly classified by the k-NN classifier, meaning that we changed the ground truth of 70 songs. Table 1 shows us that out of these 70 songs, the results of the user experiment agrees with the results from our k-NN classification for 24 songs.

After re-running k-NN classification experiments with the updated ground truth, to our surprise, the classification accuracy did not improve much: it went from 80.8% to 81.5%, meaning only 7 more songs were correctly classified, despite the ground truth for 24 songs being changed to exactly as the k-NN classifier had previously classified them. Additionally, 86 tracks had the correct genre in

2nd place, for a total of 90.1% in 1st or 2nd place. This is an increase of only one song compared with the unmodified ground truth.

The reason for this limited improvement is that in many cases the vote difference of the k-NN classifier between the genres in 1st and 2nd place is very low, so several songs that were correctly classified when using the unmodified ground truth definition changed to being incorrectly classified using the modified ground truth definition. It is also worth pointing out that we only had the participants of our experiment listen to the songs that were originally incorrectly classified. If we were to actually change the ground truth in order to make each genre more coherent we would need to perform a larger-scale study to investigate the entirety of 1,000 songs.

5   Discussion

We have seen through a number of experiments that the evaluation of the results from automatic genre classification systems is not as simple as it might seem. This confirms the findings of prior work which already took a critical view on genre classification and genre ground truth. Just because the classification of a given song does not agree with a given ground truth classification does not necessarily mean it is wrong. Given the subjective nature of genre classification, and how artists sometime merge two or multiple known genres, there are many situations where two or more prototypical genres might be appropriate for a given song.

One attempt to deal with this ambiguity and possible "intra-song genre inconsistencies" is to annotate song segments with genre rather than whole songs. However, while this strategy has shown to be advantageous when applied to the related task of *auto-tagging* [25], this might not lend itself to genre classification. Genre ambiguity is not only a matter of variation over time, but, as shown in the experimental results of this paper, a matter of mixture of elements of different genres. While individual tags are often referring to sound properties that are—in most cases—objectively either present or not, e.g., instrument playing, singing voice present, etc. [9,22,23], whether a segment belongs to a certain genre may remain as ambiguous as for a full song. The mere knowledge of the presence of certain characteristics is not informing the assignment to a specific genre either. This, again, is rooted in the general shortcoming of the way genres are defined, particularly as applied in computational settings, where *intensional* genre definitions, i.e., "what makes a genre," are subordinate to *extensional* definitions, i.e., specifying all examples that belong to the genre.

Generally, the relation of auto-tagging and genre classification is not as trivial as it is often pictured, namely that genre tags are just another subcategory of tags and that genre classification is a by-product of the more general case of semantic tagging, cf. [13]. Following the promise of the concept of genre, ideally, we would only have one true label for each song (or segment)—despite people disagreeing on which that is. For tags, every tag can apply to a song or not. Unambiguous categorization of music in any taxonomy of genres is illusive (and not even always considered necessary to fulfill the notion of genre, e.g. [5]). While strict genre classification is therefore often considered obsolete, it is the simplicity and clarity of putting a unique label onto all the complex facets of a song that makes it still a worthwhile goal on its own. However, genre classification can undoubtedly benefit from progress in auto-tagging as, e.g. contextual learning and joint prediction of tags and genre holds the potential of improving genre classification as well [2,11,12].

In terms of machine learning setup and classifier training, we have seen that changing the ground truth increased our accuracy for 7 songs out of the 1,000. We conclude that in order to create a working automatic genre classification system much more emphasis has to be put on the ground truth creation and analysis, and evaluation of the results of such systems need to be much more than simply calculating a percentage of how many of the top genres agree with a given ground truth. We agree with [3] that one good way of such evaluations could be to weight the results from such systems to reflect the amount of human classification ambiguity of the same dataset.

Acknowledgements. Supported by the Austrian Science Fund (FWF): P25655 and the Austrian FFG: BRIDGE 1 project *SmarterJam* (858514).

References

1. Aucouturier, J.J., Pachet, F.: Representing musical genre: a state of the art. J. New Music. Res. **32**(1), 83–93 (2003)
2. Aucouturier, J.J., Pachet, F., Roy, P., Beurivé, A.: Signal + context = better classification. In: Proceedings of the 8th International Conference on Music Information Retrieval (ISMIR), Vienna, Austria (2007)
3. Craft, A., Wiggins, G., Crawford, T.: How many beans make five? The consensus problem in music-genre classification and a new evaluation method for single-genre categorisation systems. In: Proceedings of the 8th International Symposium on Music Information Retrieval (ISMIR), Vienna, Austria (2007)
4. Drott, E.: The end(s) of genre. J. Music. Theory **57**(1), 1–45 (2013)
5. Fabbri, F.: A theory of musical genres: two applications. Popul. Music. Perspect. **1**, 52–81 (1981)
6. Gjerdingen, R.O., Perrott, D.: Scanning the dial: the rapid recognition of music genres. J. New Music. Res. **37**(2), 93–100 (2008)
7. Guðmundsson, G.Þ., Jónsson, B.Þ., Amsaleg, L.: A large-scale performance study of cluster-based high-dimensional indexing. In: ACM Multimedia Workshop on Very-Large-Scale Multimedia Corpus, Mining and Retrieval, Florence, Italy (2010)
8. Krumhansl, C.L.: Plink: "Thin Slices" of music. Music. Percept. Interdiscip. J. **27**(5), 337–354 (2010)
9. Lamere, P.: Social tagging and music information retrieval. J. New Music. Res. **37**(2), 101–114 (2008). Special Issue: From Genres to Tags - Music Information Retrieval in the Age of Social Tagging
10. Lippens, S., Martens, J.P., De Mulder, T., Tzanetakis, G.: A comparison of human and automatic musical genre classification. In: Proceedings of the IEEE International Conference on Acoustics, Speech and Signal Processing (ICASSP) (2004)

11. Lo, H.Y., Wang, J.C., Wang, H.M., Lin, S.D.: Cost-sensitive multi-label learning for audio tag annotation and retrieval. IEEE Trans. Multimed. **13**(3), 518–529 (2011)
12. Mandel, M.I., et al.: Contextual tag inference. ACM Trans. Multimed. Comput. Commun. Appl. **7S**(1), 32:1–32:18 (2011)
13. Marques, G., Domingues, M.A., Langlois, T., Gouyon, F.: Three current issues in music autotagging. In: Proceedings of the 12th International Society for Music Information Retrieval Conference (ISMIR), pp. 795–800 (2011)
14. McKay, C., Fujinaga, I.: Musical genre classification: is it worth pursuing and how can it be improved? In: Proceedings of the 7th International Conference on Music Information Retrieval (ISMIR), Victoria, BC, Canada (2006)
15. Novello, A., McKinney, M.F., Kohlrausch, A.: Perceptual evaluation of music similarity. In: Proceedings of the 7th International Conference on Music Information Retrieval (ISMIR), Victoria, BC, Canada (2006)
16. Pachet, F., Cazaly, D.: A taxonomy of musical genre. In: Proceedings of Content-Based Multimedia Information Access (RIAO) Conference, Paris, France (2000)
17. Scaringella, N., Zoia, G., Mlynek, D.: Automatic genre classification of music content: a survey. IEEE Signal Process. Mag. **23**(2), 133–141 (2006)
18. Schedl, M., Flexer, A., Urbano, J.: The neglected user in music information retrieval research. J. Intell. Inf. Syst. **41**, 523–539 (2013)
19. Seyerlehner, K., Widmer, G., Knees, P.: A comparison of human, automatic and collaborative music genre classification and user centric evaluation of genre classification systems. In: Detyniecki, M., Knees, P., Nürnberger, A., Schedl, M., Stober, S. (eds.) AMR 2010. LNCS, vol. 6817, pp. 118–131. Springer, Heidelberg (2012). https://doi.org/10.1007/978-3-642-27169-4_9
20. Sturm, B.L.: An analysis of the GTZAN music genre dataset. In: Proceedings of the 2nd International ACM Workshop on Music Information Retrieval with User-centered and Multimodal Strategies (MIRUM), Nara, Japan (2012)
21. Sturm, B.L.: The state of the art ten years after a state of the art: future research in music information retrieval. J. New Music. Res. **43**(2), 147–172 (2014)
22. Turnbull, D., Barrington, L., Torres, D., Lanckriet, G.: Towards musical query-by-semantic-description using the CAL500 data set. In: Proceedings of the 30th Annual International ACM SIGIR Conference on Research and Development in Information Retrieval (SIGIR), Amsterdam, the Netherlands (2007)
23. Turnbull, D., Barrington, L., Torres, D., Lanckriet, G.: Semantic annotation and retrieval of music and sound effects. IEEE Trans. Audio Speech Lang. Process. **16**(2), 467–476 (2008)
24. Tzanetakis, G., Cook, P.: Musical genre classification of audio signals. IEEE Trans. Audio, Speech, Lang. Process. **10**(5), 293–302 (2002)
25. Wang, S.Y., Wang, J.C., Yang, Y.H., Wang, H.M.: Towards time-varying music auto-tagging based on cal500 expansion. In: Proceedings of the 2014 IEEE International Conference on Multimedia and Expo (ICME) (2014)

Exploring Trends in Trinidad Steelband Music Through Computational Ethnomusicology

Elio Quinton[1(✉)], Florabelle Spielmann[2], and Bob L. Sturm[1]

[1] Centre for Digital Music, Queen Mary University of London, London, UK
{e.quinton,b.sturm}@qmul.ac.uk
[2] CREM-LESC, UMR7186, CNRS, Maison Archologie & Ethnologie Ren-Ginouvs, 92023 Nanterre, France
f.spielmann@u-paris10.fr

Abstract. We present an interdisciplinary case study combining traditional and computational methodologies to study Trinidad steelband music in a collection of recordings of the annual Panorama competition spanning over 50 years. In particular, the ethnomusicology literature identifies a number of trends and hypotheses about this practice of music involving tempo, tuning, and dynamic range. Some of these are difficult to address with traditional, manual methodologies. We investigate these through the computational lens of Music Information Retrieval (MIR) methods. We find that the tempo range measured on our corpus is consistent with values reported in ethnomusicological literature, and add further details about how tempo has changed for the best judged performances at Panorama. With respect to the use of dynamics, we find limited usefulness of a standardised measures of loudness on these recordings. When it comes to judging the tuning frequency of the acoustic recordings, we find what looks to be a narrowing of the range, but these might be unreliable given the diversity of recording media over the past decades.

Keywords: Ethnomusicology · Computational ethnomusicology
Music information retrieval · Trinidad · Steelband · Calypso · Soca
Music archive

1 Introduction

In this paper, we present a case study combining traditional and computational methodologies to study a 50-year period of Trinidad steelband music. Steelband music is a distinctive tradition in the Caribbean island of Trinidad. Its idiosyncratic musical character and its national symbol status [8,24], make it a case of particular interest for ethnomusicology, see for example [1,7,8,13]. A number of facts and trends have been identified regarding Trinidad steelband music in the ethnomusicology literature [1,7,13], while some other hypotheses formulated

© Springer Nature Switzerland AG 2018
M. Aramaki et al. (Eds.): CMMR 2017, LNCS 11265, pp. 63–75, 2018.
https://doi.org/10.1007/978-3-030-01692-0_5

have not been addressed with traditional methodologies. We use MIR techniques to facilitate the realisation of quantitative and labour intensive studies, in order to investigate these research questions and hypotheses.

The term *computational ethnomusicology* describes research that applies computational methodologies to address ethnomusicological questions. One of the first works on the subject was published as early as 1978 [12]. Collaboration across disciplines is at the heart of computational ethnomusicology. Some music studies may for instance involve the application of computational methods from other domains, e.g., population genetics [21]; computational linguistics [22]. Of particular interest in the present work is the application of methods developed in the discipline of Music Information Retrieval (MIR), which is being increasingly investigated in the recent years, e.g., [5,10,14,15,17,19,23]. In this scenario, MIR methods are applied to a corpus of audio recordings in order to gain insight into properties of the music [5,17,25]. Since MIR work has been primarily focused on Western pop music, its application to ethnomusicological material is technically challenging and is therefore a catalyst for advancing the state of the art [10].

The remainder of this paper is structured as follows. In Sect. 2 we present some background on the Trinidad steelband music tradition. We then introduce the ethnomusicological questions of interest in Sect. 3. Section 4 describes the corpus of audio recordings we use in this study as well as numerical descriptors (features) that we extract from it. The results are then presented in Sect. 5, before discussing them and concluding in Sect. 6.

2   Elements of Background on Steelband Music in Trinidad

2.1   From Steeldrum to Steelband

Steeldrums, also called steelpans or just pans, were invented in the Caribbean island of Trinidad in the 1940s out of the creative exploration of beating various steel/iron containers such as biscuit tins, old cans and dustbin lids. Since World War II, the 55-gallon oil drum has become the container of choice from which to make steeldrums.

A craftsman, called a *tuner*, is responsible for the steeldrum manufacturing process, which includes several steps, such as cutting, sinking, shaping the concave form of the drum, "grooving" the pan to separate notes, shaping the convex forms of the notes, burning and tuning the steeldrum with the use of sledgehammers and nail sets. Instruments are played with sticks tipped with rubber strips or sponge balls.

Early steelbands were marching road bands in which steeldrums were played while hung from a strap around the player's neck. In reference to the way the pans were carried, these traditional types of steelbands were called "Pan Round the Neck". The main function of these early steelbands was to accompany the street processions of the annual Carnival celebrations.

In the first steelbands, the pitch range was limited. As techniques advanced, steelbands grew into steel orchestras. Throughout the 1950s and the 1960s, ensembles became stationary and pannists started to play sets of steeldrums instead of just one pan per player. The range of the pans was extended and today each group of pans contains most if not all the notes in the equal tempered chromatic scale. As the size of the bands expanded, musical arrangements became more complex giving steelbands the possibility of playing a wider range of music.

2.2   Panorama Competition and Steelband Sound

In the newly independent republic of Trinidad and Tobago (Aug. 1962), the Panorama steelband competition was created in 1963 in the frame of a nation-building policy fostering masquerade, calypso traditional narrative ballads[1] and steelband music as carnival arts [7,11]. Through this institutional policy—interweaving cultural politics and carnival music forms [11]—the state sponsored Panorama competition has become the most prestigious steelband stage performance in Trinidad.

Every year, approximately 30 large conventional steelbands, each composed of a hundred players at the most, take part in the Panorama competition. Today, the Panorama rules require that steelbands play an arrangement of a calypso or a soca tune[2] from the current carnival season and that the duration of the arrangement should not exceed 8 min[3]. The selected tune is arranged in order to display a band's skills. The winner is proclaimed Panorama Champion for the year. Owing to both its prominent and prestigious position, the Panorama competition has had a prime influence on the development of steelband music. One of the consequences of this phenomenon has been the promotion of the arranger and the tuner as key figures of the steelband movement.

With the rising importance of the arrangers, the steelband music development incorporated elements of European repertoires, such as the symphonic sonata form, as well as adaptations of Afro-Trinidadian repertoires and musical procedures (cyclical forms, polyrhythmic texture, call-and-response) [8]. By the end of the 1960s, calypso or soca steelband arrangements displayed features that were yet to become conventions: "theme and variations" formal structure including introduction, verse, chorus, variations on the original melody (first variation, second variation), key modulations, melody in minor mode, cyclical "jam" sections and coda [8,13]. These conventions still structure today's steelband arrangements.

With the rising importance of the tuners, the manufacture of the steeldrums has evolved. Through the development of melodic steeldrums (based on diatonic

---

[1] Calypso is a style of caribbean music that originated in Trinidad and Tobago. For a more detailed description of Calypso, see for example [6].

[2] In the dictionary of the English/creole of Trinidad and Tobago edited by Lise Winer soca is defined as "a type of calypso-based music, with a fast dance beat, and party lyrics".

[3] For more details on the competition rules see http://www.panonthenet.com/tnt/2018/rules.htm.

scales) followed by the elaboration of fully chromatic ones (1950s), the unique sound of steelband was shaped over time: "compared to the early days of the steeldrum, the sound of todays instrument is far more refined, mellower in tone, and there is a much wider range of pitches utilized" [1].

3   Research Questions

We now present the research questions that we investigate in this paper. In particular, we are interested in changes in tempo, dynamic range and sonic properties of Trinidad steelband music over time. Does the tempo tend to be faster in more recent pieces? Do arrangers use increasingly large dynamic ranges? Has there been a change in the sonic properties of steelbands?

Our first research question relates to the change of tempo over time. In particular, the hypothesis suggesting that tempo has increased over time seems to emerge from ethnomusicological works. Guilbault writes that in the post-independent era: "pan calypsos were performed in an upbeat tempo in the 1960s equivalent to 112, and in the mid-1970s, reaching 126" [11]. Following a similar idea, Dudley mentions Panorama competition constraints as being responsible for "placing a premium on speed" [7]. Overall, these works suggest that the canonical tempo range may have changed over the decades and that the competitive nature of the panorama competition may be a force pushing towards ensembles to play with higher speed.

Secondly, we investigate the use of musical dynamics over time. Note that the term "dynamics" is understood in the musical sense here, that is to say to describe the loudness at which performers play music, e.g. *piano* or *forte*. More specifically, we are interested in the dynamic range used in the panorama competition, i.e. the difference between the loudest and quietest part of a given piece. Based on the premise that the tunes performed in the Panorama competition are arranged so as to display the bands' skills, and that a fine control of the musical dynamics requires a high level of musicianship, it can be hypothesised that the use of large dynamics is a valuable asset for winning the Panorama competition. Expanding on the idea that the competitive nature of the event relates to an increase in virtuosity of the performances over time, we investigate a possible change of the range of dynamics used in the panorama competition.

A final aspect of interest in our study is the sonic properties of the steelband. Aho articulates a link between the development of the Panorama competition and the change of the steelband sound [1]: "Although there is no empirical evidence to verify the observation, it seems quite likely that as the steelband began to engage in sponsored musical competition with audiences including middle-class people, they sought to maintain and increase the latter's interest and support by striving for a smoother, more refined sound, a wider range of notes". Complementary to Aho's idea, Dudley articulates a dynamic link between the change of steelband sound and the steeldrum manufacture improvements: "the transformation of the steeldrum's timbre is almost invariably portrayed as an improvement of the instrument" [8]. The emulation between tuners channeled through the Panorama competition constraints is thought to have led to a refinement of the steeldrum timbre transforming a "vulgar underclass pastime into national instrument" [8]. Building on these observations, we seek to investigate whether computational methods can help identify a change of the sound of the steelband, as a result of the improvement of the manufacture of the steeldrums.

4   Methodology

We attempt to address the ethnomusicological research questions presented in Sect. 3 with the aid of computational methods. In the remainder of this section, we describe the audio recording corpus we use for study, and then present the descriptors we automatically extract from the audio recordings.

4.1   Music Corpus

Section 2.2 highlights the prominent role played by the Panorama competition in the steelband music tradition of Trinidad. Based on this premise, we select recordings of Panorama performances as our corpus of study for its representativeness. We assume that a Panorama champions database will reflect the musical trends over the period of the competition, since these arrangements/compositions were judged as the best of the Panorama competition in their respective years.

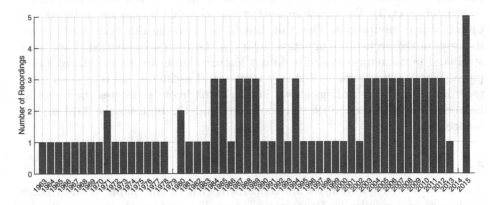

Fig. 1. The distribution of recordings over years in our collection.

All digital recordings used in this paper are part the "CNRS - Musee de l'Homme" sound archives,[4] which are accessible via the Telemeta platform [9][5]. This musical data includes field recordings as well as published recordings, which are a mixture of digitised analog recordings and digital recordings. From this

---

[4] http://archives.crem-cnrs.fr/.
[5] http://telemeta.org/.

archive, we assembled a corpus of recordings of most of the steelband calypsos/socas performed by the winners (first, second and third places) for each yearly Panorama competition between 1963 and 2015 (except for the year 1979, in which the competition was not organised). Our corpus contains 93 recordings, each one being typically 8–10 min long, totalling about 14 h of audio. Figure 1 shows the number of recordings in our collection over the years of the competition. For the competition year 2014, the archive did not have any digitised recordings at the time we compiled the dataset. Furthermore, there are five recordings for the competition year 2015 since three bands tied for third position.

Figure 2 shows the time-domain waveforms and sonograms of recordings of two championship performances of the same band, but 15 years apart. These show some peculiarities in the corpus: recording equipment with different frequency characteristics; zero-frequency (DC) bias in some recordings; spoken announcements at the beginning of some performances; and applause and other noises from the audience during and after some performances.

4.2 Tempo

In order to address the question of a change of tempo in winning Panorama pieces, we estimate the tempo value for each track using state of the art algorithms implemented in the *madmom* library [2,3]. Since the Panorama competition is restricted to steelband arrangements of soca and calypso tunes, we expect that a performance will have a tempo in the range 110–130 beats per minute (bpm) (cf. Sect. 3). We therefore restrict the possible tempo range to 80–160 bpm in our computations. The main benefit of imposing this constraint is that it prevents the occurrence of octave errors in the tempo estimation. Panorama steelband performances typically do not feature significant tempo changes in a piece. We therefore assume a steady tempo and estimate one tempo for each recording. For the recordings shown in Fig. 2, madmom estimates the tempi to be about 136 bpm for the 1988 performance, and 122 bpm for the 2013 performance.

4.3 Dynamics Range

Another research question we are concerned with in this paper is the change in the use of dynamics by Panorama winners. For each track, we compute the loudness using the ITU 1770.3 standard [16]. Following this specification, the audio recording is divided in L blocks of 40 ms length with 75% overlap. Figure 3 shows the loudness profiles for the two recordings in Fig. 2. To compute the dynamics range of a recording, we disregard its first and last 60 s since these often consist of introductory speech and applause. For the recording in Fig. 2(a), the introduction is 12 s long and the applause lasts 10 s at the end. For the recording in Fig. 2(b), the introduction lasts 15 s, and the applause lasts 30 s at the end. Some recordings have introductions that last 40 s. We define the dynamic range as the difference between the maximum and minimum of the

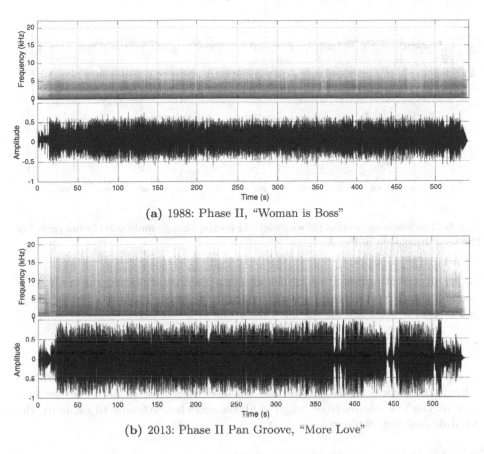

(a) 1988: Phase II, "Woman is Boss"

(b) 2013: Phase II Pan Groove, "More Love"

Fig. 2. The sonograms (top, scaled to 0–80 dB) and time-domain waveforms (bottom) of recordings of two championship performances of the band Phase II.

remaining loudness features. For the recordings in Fig. 3, these values are 11.8 dB for the 1988 performance and 30.9 dB for the 2013 performance.

4.4   Tuning Frequency

The A 440 Hz is regarded as the current Western standard diatonic tuning frequency. However, even in Western musical traditions the tuning frequency used by performers and ensembles has evolved through history and still exhibits some variability nowadays. In fact it is not unusual to encounter tuning frequencies that differ from A 440 Hz. Since the process of manufacture of steelpans has evolved in Trinidad and Tobago over the past few decades (cf. Sect. 3), we hypothesise that this may have impacted the tuning frequency used by ensembles. In order to test this hypothesis, we use the vamp plugin implementation[6]

---

[6] http://www.isophonics.net/nnls-chroma.

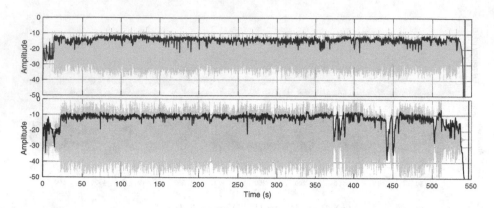

Fig. 3. The loudness profiles (black) overlaid on the time-domain waveforms (gray) of the recordings seen in Fig. 2.

of the algorithm proposed by Mauch et al. in [18] for estimating the tuning frequency of each recording. The estimated tuning frequency for the 1988 recording in Fig. 2(a) is 433.8 Hz; for the 2013 recording it is 441.1 Hz.

5   Results

In this section, we analyze the descriptors introduced in Sect. 4 to address the ethnomusicological research questions detailed in Sect. 3. In all cases, we first look at the raw results from audio analysis and then attempt to estimate the reliability of such estimates.

5.1   Tempo

Figure 4(a) shows the estimated tempo of the recordings in our dataset, sorted by competition year. We see that most of the pieces are played at a tempo in the range 110–140 bpm, consistent with observations made in the literature [13]. One may note that there are a few estimates below the 110 bpm mark, and above 140 bpm. After manual inspection, we find that several of these estimates are due to errors in the tempo estimation: the 1982 performance actually has a tempo of 137 bpm; the 100 bpm performance in 1987 is actually 136 bpm; the 102 bpm performances in 1985 and 1992 are actually about 138 bpm; and the 105 bpm performance in 1987 is actually 143 bpm. The tempi of the slow performances before 1965 are estimated correctly, as is the 1998 performance at just over 111 bpm. We find that the tempo estimate of the 1985 performance is actually 150 bpm; however, a recording of the same performance available on youtube[7] has a slower tempo, of about 140 bpm. Manual inspection of tempo estimates in the middle of the range (i.e., around 130 bpm) reveal that they are consistent with our tempo perception. These observations suggest that Madmom mostly provides reliable tempo estimates on our corpus.

---

[7] https://youtu.be/oSYpwQIXTqk.

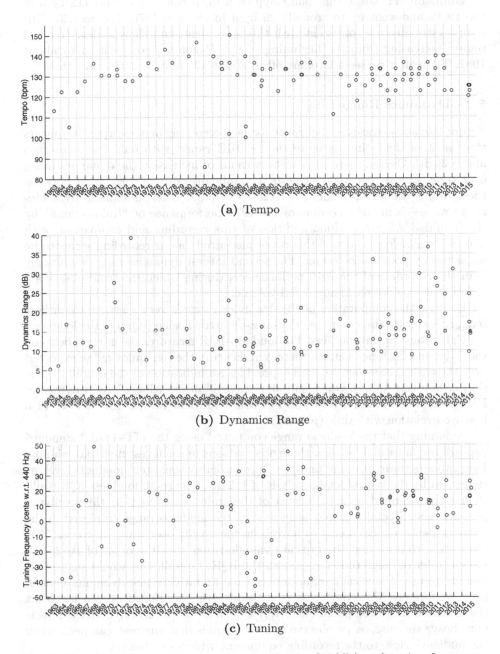

Fig. 4. The estimated tempo (top), dynamics range (middle) and tuning frequency (bottom) of each recorded Panorama performance over the time span of our collection. We have added slight jitter along the x-axis to show duplicated estimates.

Guilbault [11] wrote that pan calypsos were performed around 112 bpm in the 1960s and went up to around 126 bpm in the mid-1970s (cf. Sect. 3). Our tempo estimates are consistent with this statement, and show a clear trend of tempo increasing from the beginning of the Panorama competition to about 1981. Thereafter we see a levelling off to about 130 bpm over the time since.

5.2 Dynamics Range

Figure 4(b) shows the dynamics range for each recording in our corpus. It appears that most of the estimates lie in the 5–20 dB range, with only few recordings above 30 dB. Overall there seem to be a trend of increasing the dynamics range over time. Linear regression suggests a significant positive correlation between the dynamic range and time, $r = 0.28$ ($p = 0.007$). The maximum dynamics range we see is in the recording of the 1973 performance of "Rain-o-rama" by the Trinidad All Stars. Upon audition of this recording and comparison with another available recording,[8] this range measured on our recording seems to be impacted by poor audio coding. The second largest dynamics range we observe is in the recording of the 2010 performance, during which the band observes a grand pause before resuming at full volume.

Because the computation of the dynamics range is very sensitive to outliers (e.g., silence), we also computed the Inter-Quartile Range (IQR) of the loudness, which is robust against outliers. The loudness IQR measures the interval between the 75th and 25th percentiles, thereby indicating the dynamics range expected over the entire recording. As such it provides an indication of the overall dispersion of loudness values. Our result show nearly all recordings have a dynamics IQR of between 1 and 2 dB. The Pearson coefficient reveals the absence of a linear correlation with time ($p = 0.53$).

Assuming that the loudness range computed using the ITU-1770-3 standard capture the musical dynamics, these observations may suggest first that winning Panorama performances are played at a remarkably consistent loudness level, as suggested by the typical loudness IQR of 1–2 dB. The small loudness IQR could then be interpreted as a high level of dynamic consistency in the steelband performance. Secondly, it may suggest that the loudness range employed in the winning performances seems to have been increasing over time. Moreover, it is interesting to note that the typical dynamic range is of the order of 10–20 dB, i.e. an order of magnitude larger than the IQR. Overall, this would suggest an increasing use of musical dynamics over time and a very fine dynamics control from performers. However, these conclusions are conditioned on the fact that the loudness range computed effectively captures the musical dynamics. This is not always the case, as we observe in some signals that loudness can peak when the audience close to the recording equipment whistles or hollers.

---

[8] https://youtu.be/48jP5PYGDUY.

5.3   Tuning Frequency

Figure 4(c) shows the tuning frequency estimates for each track of the panorama winning performances corpus, computed according to the method described in Sect. 4.4. It appears that the distribution of tuning frequency seems to have narrowed around the turn of the 21st century. Indeed, in the last two decades, the tuning frequency seems to be confined in the 440–450 Hz range while it was spanning the 430–450Hz range until the late 1990's. This result may therefore suggest a homogenisation of the steelpan tuning frequency, which may be a result of a homogenisation of the steelpan manufacture specifications. However, by cross-referencing digital recordings from our archive and other versions of the same recordings available online, we have observed cases of both consistency and discrepency of tuning frequency. The origin of such discrepencies is unknown, however. Given that digital transcoding and transfer from analog to digital formats may affect the pitch of a recording, it is possible that the tuning frequency of a recording does not reflect the tuning frequency of steelpans being recorded. Unfortunately, there is no way for us to verify this. The results presented in this section are therefore to be interpreted with due caution.

6   Discussion and Conclusion

This paper presents an interdisciplinary case study of a selection of ethnomusicological hypotheses regarding musical trends in the Trinidad steelbands performances over time. Choosing the Panorama competition winners for their representativity of the musical tradition of Trinidad and Tobago, we assembled a corpus of recordings covering a period of over 50 years. Starting from research questions and hypotheses stemming from the ethnomusicological literature, we employed MIR methods to compute descriptors related to the musical properties of interest from the audio recordings. Our results show that the tempo range measured on our corpus is consistent with values reported in ethnomusicological literature but do not show any clear trend of increasing over time. On the other hand, our results suggest a possible change in the use of dynamics in the winning performances of the national Panorama competition. Finally, a possible tendency for homogenisation of the sound of the steelbands is suggested by our results. We hypothesise that this tendency may be due to the standardisation of the manufacture of the instruments.

In this paper, we propose to investigate a selection of ethnomusicological hypotheses via the use of computational methods to analyse a corpus of audio recordings of live musical performances. Music recording corpora used for ethnomusicological research typically are either ethnographic recordings or field recordings (both in our case), which are produced in very heterogeneous conditions that are mostly uncontrolled. In addition, it is often not possible to evaluate the impact of these recording conditions on the properties of the musical recordings. Though not all audio features are equally affected, the estimates produced by MIR tools on such corpora may only have limited reliability. Results of computational analyses carried out on such a corpus should therefore be interpreted with due care. In conclusion, this case study suggests some answers to our hypotheses and should therefore be regarded as a starting point from which to develop further investigations.

Acknowledgements. This work is supported by AHRC Grant No. AH/N504531/1, and the French Labex Pasts in Present http://passes-present.eu/en.

References

1. Aho, W.: Steelband music in Trinidad and Tobago: the creation of a people's music. Lat. Am. Music. Rev./Revista de Msica Latinoamericana **8**(1), 26–58 (1987)
2. Böck, S., Korzeniowski, F., Schlüter, J., Krebs, F., Widmer, G.: Madmom: a new Python audio and music signal processing library. In: Proceedings of the 24th ACM International Conference on Multimedia (2016)
3. Böck, S., Krebs, F., Widmer, G.: Accurate tempo estimation based on recurrent neural networks and resonating comb filters. In: Proceedings of the 16th International Society for Music Information Retrieval Conference (ISMIR) (2015)
4. Bogdanov, D., et al.: ESSENTIA: an audio analysis library for music information retrieval. In: International Society for Music Information Retrieval Conference (2013)
5. Bozkurt, B., Ayangil, R., Holzapfel, A.: Computational analysis of Turkish Makam music: review of state-of-the-art and challenges. J. New Music Res. **43**(1), 3–23 (2014)
6. Cowley, J.: Carnival, Canboulay, and Calypso: Traditions in the Making. Cambridge University Press, Cambridge (1996)
7. Dudley, S.: The steelband "own tune": nationalism, festivity, and musical strategies in Trinidad's panorama competition. Black Music Res. J. **22**, 13–36 (2002)
8. Dudley, S.: Music From behind the Bridge: Steelband Spirit and Politics in Trinidad and Tobago. Oxford University Press, Oxford (2008)
9. Fillon, T., Pellerin, G., Brossier, P., Simonnot, J.: An open web audio platform for ethnomusicological sound, pp. 1–8. ACM (2014)
10. Gomez, E., Herrera, P., Gomez-Martin, F.: Computational ethnomusicology: perspectives and challenges. J. New Music Res. **42**(2), 111–112 (2013)
11. Guilbault, J.: Governing Sound: The Cultural Politics of Trinidad's Carnival Musics. University of Chicago Press, Chicago (2007)
12. Hamlos, I., Koszegi, G., Madler, G.: Computational ethnomusicology in Hungary in 1978. In: Proceedings of the International Computer Music Conference (1978)
13. Helmlinger, A.: Pan jumbie: memoire sociale et musicale dans les steelbands de Trinidad et Tobago, Societe d'ethnologie (2012)
14. Holzapfel, A., Stylianou, Y.: Similarity methods for computational ethnomusicology. IEEE Trans. Audio Speech Lang. Process. (2010)
15. Huron, D.: The melodic arch in Western folksongs. Comput. Musicol. **10**, 3–23 (1996)
16. ITU Recommendation BS.1770. https://www.itu.int/rec/R-REC-BS.1770/en
17. Kroher, N., et al.: Computational ethnomusicology: a study of Flamenco and Arab-Andalusian vocal music. In: Bader, R. (ed.) Springer Handbook of Systematic Musicology. SH, pp. 885–897. Springer, Heidelberg (2018). https://doi.org/10.1007/978-3-662-55004-5_43

18. Mauch, M., Dixon, S.: Approximate note transcription for the improved identification of difficult chords. In: Proceedings of the 11th International Society for Music Information Retrieval Conference (2010)
19. Panteli, M., Benetos, E., Dixon, S.: Automatic detection of outliers in world music. In: Proceedings of the International Society for Music Information Retrieval Conference (2016)
20. Plomp, R., Levelt, W.J.M.: Tonal consonance and critical bandwidth. J. Acoust. Soc. Am. **38**(4), 548–560 (1965)
21. Savage, P.E., Brown, S.: Mapping music: cluster analysis of song-type frequencies within and between cultures. In: Ethnomusicology **58**(1), 133–155 (2014)
22. Shalit, U., Weinshall, D., Chechik, G.: Modeling musical influence with topic models. In: Proceedings of the 30th International Conference on Machine Learning (2013)
23. Shanahan, D., Neubarth, K., Conklin, D.: Mining musical traits of social functions in Native American music. In: Proceedings of the International Society for Music Information Retrieval Conference (2016)
24. Stuempfle, S.: The Steelband Movement: The Forging of a National Art in Trinidad and Tobago. University of Pennsylvania, Philadelphia (1996)
25. Tzanetakis, G., Kapur, A., Schloss, W.A., Wright, M.: Computational ethnomusicology. J. Interdiscip. Music. Stud. **1**, 1–24 (2007)
26. Voisin, F.: Musical scales in Central Africa and Java: modeling by synthesis. Leonardo Music J. **4**, 85–90 (1994)

k-Best Unit Selection Strategies
for Musical Concatenative Synthesis

Cárthach Ó Nuanáin$^{(\boxtimes)}$, Perfecto Herrera, and Sergi Jordá

Music Technology Group, Universitat Pompeu Fabra, Barcelona, Spain
carthach.onuanain@upf.edu

Abstract. Concatenative synthesis is a sample-based approach to sound creation used frequently in speech synthesis and, increasingly, in musical contexts. Unit selection, a key component, is the process by which sounds are chosen from the corpus of samples. With their ability to match target units as well as preserve continuity, Hidden Markov Models are often chosen for this task, but one common criticism is its singular path output which is considered too restrictive when variations are desired. In this article, we propose considering the problem in terms of k-Best path solving for generating alternative lists of candidate solutions and summarise our implementations along with some practical examples.

Keywords: Hidden Markov Models · Concatenative synthesis
Artificial intelligence · Musical signal processing

1 Introduction

Concatenative synthesis is a technique that generates new sounds by juxtaposing existing sounds from a large collection or 'corpus'. It was first applied in the area of speech synthesis [17], but has since been extended to musical and sound design tasks [43]. While closely related to granular synthesis, it differs in the order of scale of the length of the sounds that are used. Granular synthesis typically operates on the microscale with 'grains' of lengths 20–200 ms [33], whereas concatenative synthesis makes use of samples of unit lengths more musically related, such as a note or a phrase. An inherently Music Information Retrieval (MIR) geared approach, extraction of acoustic and musical descriptors (such as spectral, energy and timbral features) are essential for analysing and sorting existing sounds then concatenating them to create new ones according to some predefined strategy.

The unit selection procedure of concatenative synthesis is the process by which the existing sounds are selected from the corpus is named "unit selection" and is typically based on feature analysis to match the characteristics of some target sound or specification. Many algorithms have been proposed for tackling unit selection, but one of the most well-known involves the application of Hidden Markov Models (HMM) and in particular Viterbi decoding [35] of state sequences

© Springer Nature Switzerland AG 2018
M. Aramaki et al. (Eds.): CMMR 2017, LNCS 11265, pp. 76–97, 2018.
https://doi.org/10.1007/978-3-030-01692-0_6

to produce a stochastically optimal output sequence of concatenated sounds. As we will discuss in the forthcoming section, Viterbi decoding of HMMs has its limitations [35], chief of which is the fact that it outputs only the highest probable state sequence.

In many objective problem applications (such as route finding in a network) this is sufficient and objectively defined, but in sound synthesis and particularly highly subjective musical and compositional tasks we would rather produce subsequent probabilistic sequences in order to explore and evaluate alternative possibilities. To this end, we present in this article methods for reformulating and extending the well-known Viterbi decoding algorithm to handle generating the k-best candidate sequences [39], and describe how this can then be used in the practical context of musical concatenative sound synthesis.

2 Markov Chains

A Markov chain is a probabilistic system that satisfies the Markov property of memorylessness. It consists of a set of discrete states with each state having an associated probability weighting of moving to every other state in the system. At any point in discrete time, the probability of a future event is solely determined by the current state (or a few states depending on the *order*) of the system without knowledge of the preceding past events. This can be expressed more formally by Eq. 1.

$$P = (X_{t+1}|X_t = x_t, X_{t-1} = x_{t-1}, ..., X_0 = x_0)$$
$$= (X_{t+1}|X_t = x_t)$$

(1)

where X_t is the state occupied by the state machine at time t in its discrete history. To build a Markov chain, a transition matrix A is defined that determines the probability of moving from one state to each other, often by analysing or modelling some real world examples. The order (i.e. the number of states in the right hand side of the second line of Eq. 1 of this transition matrix is the number of states that are considered when determining the probability of the next state. A first order Markov chain, for example, considers the probability of jumping to the next state based on the current state, while a second order chain would use the current state and the previous state in determining where to move to next. Markov chains have enjoyed widespread application in simulating stochastic processes, and in music they are employed routinely for algorithmic composition [11,13,19]. The advantage of Markov chains in these instances is the ability for the probability distributions to be learned directly from representations of certain musical styles.

3 Hidden Markov Models

A hidden markov model $\lambda = (A, B, \pi)$ extends the concept of a Markov chain by considering the transition states as hidden [32]. The hidden states have a transition matrix A as before, but each hidden state also emits an observable symbol from a set of symbols that have a probability distribution encapsulated in an emission matrix B. Finally, to initiate the HMM there also exists the initial probability distribution π, which determines the probability of which state to commence.

The subtleties of Hidden Markov Models don't become immediately clear until we start working with some common problems and especially their role in sound and music analysis and generation, but there are three traditional problems that are usually studied, as identified by Rabiner in his tutorial [32].

1. *Evaluation* - Given an observable sequence of emissions $O = (O_1, O_2, O3, ..., O_T)$, what is the probability that the sequence was generated by a certain model λ. This is particularly useful when benchmarking or comparing different models.
2. *Decoding* - Given an observable sequence of emissions $O = (O_1, O_2, O3, ..., O_T)$, what is the most likely sequence of hidden states that produced that observation O.
3. *Learning or Training* - Given a model with its parameters $\lambda = (A, B, \pi)$ and an observable sequence of emissions $O = (O_1, O_2, O3, ..., O_T)$, how do we adjust the parameters to maximise the probability of the observable sequence O.

3.1   The Viterbi Algorithm

The Viterbi algorithm solves the decoding problem in HMMs [32], namely, for a given observation sequence $O = (O_1, O_2, O3, ..., O_T)$ we wish to determine the highest probable hidden state sequence $S = (S_1, S_2, S3, ..., S_T)$ that would produce output O given by:

$$S* = argmax(P(S|O)) \tag{2}$$

A brute force solution executed on T observations over N states would involve computing all the cartesian products of the possibilities; N^T involving exponential time complexity. Viterbi's algorithm enables us to reduce this complexity to $O(T.N^2)$, using dynamic programming techniques. Rather than exhaustively computing all the possibilities, we maintain two data structures alpha (α) and phi (ϕ). At any point t in the sequence to be decoded, we store the score of the maximum probability for emitting the observed symbol for each hidden state, along with the index or argument of the maximum probable state that led there. To get the optimal state sequence we get the index of the final highest scoring hidden state and backtrack through the ϕ structure beginning with that index, returning the accumulated list. We can express this formally in the recurrence expression 3–6.

In the initialisation of the algorithm we use the initial probabilities and the observed symbol to calculate the starting probabilities of each hidden state in α, and, as there can be no previous states, ϕ is set to 0.

The recursion step continues until T, the length of the observed sequence. We first calculate the maximum of the probability of each previous state multiplied by the transition probability to the current state. The winning maximum probability is multiplied by the emission probability of the observed symbol and stored in α while the index of that winning previous state is logged in ϕ.

The elegance of the Viterbi algorithm should be apparent here. Rather than computing the N^{t-1} possible combinations of all the previous states, dynamic programming is used to store the result of the calculations in a matrix for later retrieval.

When recursion halts, the highest final probability is computed and its index is used finally the backtrack through the state machine and thus returning S^*, the sequence of highest scoring hidden states that most likely produced the observed sequence O.

(1) Initialisation: $t = 1$

$$\alpha_1(i) = \pi_i B_i(O_1) \qquad 1 < i < N$$
$$\phi_1(i) = 0 \tag{3}$$

(2) Recursion: $t = 2, ..., t = T$

$$\alpha_t(j) = max_{i \in N}(\alpha_{t-1}(i)A_{ij}B_j(O_t)) \qquad 1 < j < N$$
$$\phi_t(j) = argmax_{i \in N}(\alpha_{t-1}(i)A_{ij}) \qquad 1 < j < N \tag{4}$$

(3) Termination:

$$p^* = max_{i \in N}(\alpha_T(i))$$
$$S_T^* = argmax_{i \in N}(\alpha_T(i)) \tag{5}$$

(4) Backtracking: $t = T - 1, ..., t = 1$

$$S_T^* = \phi_t + 1(S_{t+1}^*) \tag{6}$$

The Viterbi algorithm has been around for quite a while now [44], and implementations exist in many frameworks and programming languages [3,15]. It is a fundamental technique in bioinformatics and natural language and speech processing. Part of Speech (PoS) tagging for example, uses a HMM trained on a large corpus of text with each word labelled with its constituent part of speech (e.g. noun, verb, article etc.). It provides more robust results in identifying new samples of text, as the transition matrix helps determine the context of each word within the sequence.

Figure 1 shows a trellis diagram showing the highlighted trace of the decoded path $(S = (0, 0, 1))$, for the observed sequence $O = (0, 1, 2)$ (or 'normal', 'cold' and 'dizzy' to give it its string labels) along with its calculations, computed by our own reference implementation of the Viterbi algorithm[1], through the state

---

[1] https://github.com/carthach/kBestViterbi/blob/master/kBestViterbi.py.

Table 1. HMM parameters for Wikipedia Viterbi decoding example

O = ('normal', 'cold', 'dizzy')

S = ('Healthy', 'Fever')

π = {'Healthy': 0.5, 'Fever': 0.4}

A = {

'Healthy' : {'Healthy': 0.5, 'Fever': 0.4}

'Fever' : {'Healthy': 0.4, 'Fever': 0.6}

}

B = {

'Healthy' : {'normal': 0.5, 'cold': 0.4, 'dizzy': 0.1}

'Fever' : {'normal': 0.1, 'cold': 0.3, 'dizzy': 0.6}

}

space of the example problem in the Wikipedia article on Viterbi decoding[2]. The parameters of the model are given in Table 1. Notice how the dynamic programming stage intuitively computes and stores the necessary probabilities for each state at each time step through the trellis.

3.2 HMMs in Musical Applications

HMMs' facility for pattern recognition has been exploited for computational musical tasks. Score following, for instance, tries to consolidate the position of a live performance of a musical piece with its score representation automatically [29]. Using Viterbi decoding, an alignment can be established by extracting features for the observed live performance, and comparing them against idealised features within the model to return the expected location of the performance within the score.

HMMs also lend themselves quite naturally to the task of chord recognition [5, 30, 40]. The former demonstrate a method whereby they compare the Pitch Class Profile (PCP) representation of the signal corresponding to 24 possible chord labels (12 notes for major and minor) indicated by the emission matrix, coupled with the most probable chord sequence defined in the transition matrix, derived from prior musical knowledge or training on musical scores and transcriptions.

Compared to Markov chains, HMMs have been utilised somewhat less in generative or compositional applications (apart from concatenative synthesis, as we shall discover). Some methods however are summarised in [13,23], with the latter making the observation that "when applied to algorithmic composition, HMMs are appropriate to add elements to an existing composition."

---

[2] https://en.wikipedia.org/wiki/Viterbi_algorithm.

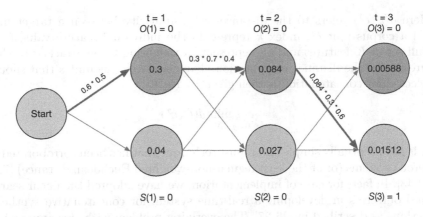

Fig. 1. Viterbi decoding of Wikipedia example using our decoder

4   Unit Selection in Concatenative Synthesis Systems

Unit selection solves the problem of determining what sounds to select from the corpus and the systematic structuring of the selected sounds for outputting logical concatenated sequences, or as Schwarz [36] defines:

> "[Concatenative sound synthesis uses] a unit selection algorithm that finds the sequence of units that match best the sound or phrase to be synthesized, called the target. The selection is performed according to the descriptors of the units, which are characteristics extracted from the source sounds, or higher level descriptors attributed to them."

Many unit selection schemata have been proposed and there exists no standard or best method. However some specific procedures have presented themselves repeatedly which we will summarise in the following subsections, including.

1. Linear Search
2. *k*-D Trees
3. HMMs and Viterbi Decoding
4. Constraint Satisfaction

4.1   Linear Search

At the most basic level a linear search criteria for unit selection simply computes the (dis)similarity of every unit in the target sequence with every possible unit in the corpus, according to some distance measure [37]. For example, a weighted variation of Euclidean could be utilised (taking care to normalise the feature vectors) that would allow the composer to place emphasis on certain features in the similarity computation as given by Eq. 7.

$$d(t^i, c^j) = \sqrt{\sum_{k=0}^{K-1} w_k (t_k^i - c_k^j)^2} \tag{7}$$

Here $d(t^i, c^j)$ refers to the distance or dissimilarity between a target unit t^i and a corpus unit c^j, index k represents the individual feature value from the full set of K features and w_k represents a weighting to be attached to that feature during the distance computation. The closest corpus unit s that should be selected for concatenation is then given by Eq. 8.

$$s = \arg\min_{0 < j < N} d(t^i, c^j) \tag{8}$$

It is a conceptually simple and robust technique that has been corroborated in numerous systems (or at the least regular non-weighted Euclidean distance) [7,8, 22,42,43]. In fact, for ease of implementation, we have adopted the linear search method ourselves in developing a real-time system for concatenative synthesis of rhythms as described in [26,27]. The overlying problem with this approach is that it only considers the disparity between the target and the corpus unit, and neglects treating the continuity or context of consecutive units within the output sequence. Depending on the size of the corpus it may also be prohibitively slow (but not in our informal usage, at least not compared to HMMs), which can be remedied by applying a structure such as a k-d Tree.

Faster Search with k-D Trees. As Collins [7] and Danneberg [8] have noted, the brute force nature of exhaustive linear search computation may not lend itself to scalability for larger datasets. The former suggests using k-D Tree structures for more strategically optimising the search process, and has also been utilised in systems by [12,21,38,42].

A k-D Tree organises points in space with a binary tree by successively cycling through each dimension of the problem space (its full name is k-Dimensional Tree), splitting the data at its median and assigning the two newly partitioned sets to the branches of the nodes at each level. The branching aspect of binary search trees allows us to eliminate vast portions of the search space when performing nearest neighbour searches.

It is important to realise that they are only approximate solutions so they may not return the actual nearest neighbour (which is an important factor to consider if it is to be used for accurate classification). A new instance may be routed down a branch too hastily, based on its proximity in a single dimension, even though the closest match based on the combined Euclidean distance may belong to a different branch. Also, as [34] stress, k-D Trees are only useful so long as the number of examples exceeds the number of dimensions in the problem space, otherwise it is no more efficient than exhaustive, linear scanning. Many k-D Tree-inspired Artificial Neural Network (ANN) algorithms exist for dealing with high dimensionality problem domains, at a possible sacrifice in accuracy (it may not return the exact nearest neighbour). For instance, in OpenCV a fast approximate k-D Tree is implemented using a Best-Bin-First algorithm [20]. In PyConcat we avail of the implementation in the SciPy scientific package for python [18].

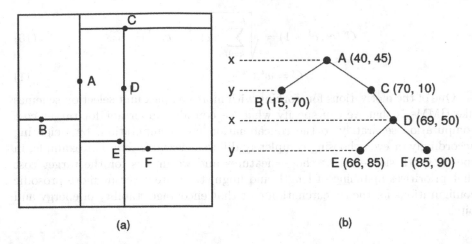

(a)   (b)

Fig. 2. Hyperplane division (left) and binary tree (right) arrangement of 2-dimensional dataset with a k-D Tree of depth 4. The origin is the top left and the size of the grid is 128×128 units. Image from Linköping University. (http://www.ida.liu.se/opendsa/ OpenDSA/Books/Everything/)

4.2 Unit Selection with Viterbi Decoding of Hidden Markov Models

The Viterbi algorithm was first applied by Hunt for the purposes of speech synthesis by performing unit selection of speech phonemes samples from a prior corpus [17]. It was then adopted for musical purposes by Schwarz in his Caterpillar System [35]. By representing a unit selection system as a Hidden Markov Model we can not only consider the disparity between the target and corpus unit (encoded in the emission matrix) but also the "best fit" of continuity between two consecutive units in the output sequence, as determined by the transition matrix of the hidden states (Fig. 2).

As with shortest path problems, unit selection requires finding the *minimisation* of a set of *costs* [17], namely the target cost C^t between target and corpus units (9, which is an identical derivation to 7 in the linear search method), and the concatenation cost C^c (10) between the consecutive concatenated units [35]. This is in contrast to the usual goal of Markov processes, which of course is concerned with *maximisation* of probabilities.

A linear combination is finally performed with weights w^t and w^c to give the total cost C (11). The constituent costs themselves are derived by computing the dissimilarity between the feature vectors of the associated units using a suitable distance metric and a set of w_k. The feature sets and accompanying weights can (and typically do) differ for the two different cost functions.

$$C^t(t^i, c^j) = \sqrt{\sum_{k=0}^{K-1} w_k (t_k^i - c_k^j)^2} \tag{9}$$

$$C^c(c^j, c^j - 1) = \sqrt{\sum_{k=0}^{K-1} w_k (c_k^j - c_k^{j-1})^2} \tag{10}$$

$$C = w^t.C^t + w^c.C^c \tag{11}$$

One of the motivations for working with more complex unit selection schemes like HMMs is that we can specify what we consider important for target cost computation separately to the concatenation cost computation, by weighting accordingly or even choosing completely different features sets. For example, in speech synthesis we might choose features and weightings for the target cost that prioritises matching of length and linguistic context versus more prosodic configurations for the concatenation cost that encourage stability of energy and pitch.

4.3   Constraint Satisfaction

Schwarz notes, however, that the HMM approach can be quite rigid for musical purposes because it produces one single optimised sequence without the ability to manipulate the individual units. To address these limitations, he reformulates the task into a constraint-satisfaction problem, which offers more flexibility for interaction. A constraint-satisfaction problem models a problem as a set of variables, values, and a set of constraints that allows us to identify which combinations of variables and values are violations of those constraints, thus allowing us to quickly reduce large portions of the search space [23].

Zils and Pachet [46] and later Aucouturier and Pachet [1] are credited with applying constraint satisfaction techniques to concatenative sound synthesis, in a procedure they refer to as musaicing (a portmanteau of music and mosaicing, acknowledging its parallels with the construction of mosaics in the visual arts). They define two categories of constraints: segment and sequence constraints. Segment constraints control aspects of individual units (much like the target cost in an HMM-like system) based on their descriptor values. Sequence constraints apply globally and affect aspects of time, continuity, and overall distributions of units. The constraints can be invoked manually by the user or learned by modelling a target. The musically tailored "adaptive search" algorithm performs a heuristic search to minimise the total global cost generated by the constraint problem. One immediate advantage of this approach over the HMM is the ability to run the algorithm several times to generate alternative sequences, whereas the Viterbi process always outputs the most optimal solution.

4.4   Adjusting Viterbi to Handle Unit Selection in Concatenative Synthesis

As already stated, Markov systems try to maximise probabilities while concatenative synthesis systems try to minimise cost. The costs should be pre-computed by calculating the target cost C^t for every target unit t_i and database unit c_j, and the concatenation cost C^c for every combination of unit c_j. These costs form the emission matrix A and transition matrix B parameters for our HMM respectively. We can then discard the initial probability matrix π and reformulate the Viterbi algorithm with the necessary changes for cost minimisation as in expression 12–15. Note that the recursion and termination steps now use the min and $argmin$ function and sum the final costs.

(1) **Initialisation:** $t = 1$

$$\alpha_1(i) = B_i(O_1) \qquad 1 < i < N$$
$$\phi_1(i) = 0 \qquad\qquad\qquad\qquad (12)$$

(2) **Recursion:** $t = 2, ..., t = T$

$$\alpha_t(j) = min_{i \in N}(\alpha_{t-1}(i) + A_{ij} + B_j(O_t)) \qquad 1 < j < N$$
$$\phi_t(j) = argmin_{i \in N}(\alpha_{t-1}(i) + A_{ij}) \qquad 1 < j < N \qquad (13)$$

(3) **Termination:**

$$p^* = min_{i \in N}(\alpha_T(i))$$
$$S_T^* = argmin_{i \in N}(\alpha_T(i)) \qquad\qquad\qquad (14)$$

(4) **Backtracking:** $t = T - 1, ..., t = 1$

$$S_T^* = \phi_t + 1(S_{t+1}^*) \qquad\qquad\qquad (15)$$

4.5 Exploring Alternatives in HMMs

The Viterbi algorithm has proved a robust and reliable solution in many problem applications. As we emphasise in this work it only outputs the maximum probability path from the model. This has been observed by other researchers as being restrictive when wanting to explore alternative paths through the system [4,35]. Rabiner and Juang also observe, in the context of dynamic time warping, that the single solution Viterbi is often too sensitive and it is desirable to produce a "multiplicity of reasonable candidate paths so that reliable decision processing can be performed" [31].

One of the most thorough and cited articles dealing with k-Best or, "List Decoding" as the author describes it, has been provided by [39] who proposes two different methods to extend the regular Viterbi algorithm to multiple output. These methods he clarifies as operating in parallel or serial modes. We summarise these methods here, and provide an implementation of the parallel approach for unit selection and concatenative synthesis.

As we were implementing the parallel decoder, we began to notice the comparisons between the search process Viterbi takes through the hidden state space in a HMM and the way that shortest path algorithms such as Dijkstra's find the path of least resistance through an acyclic directed graph. In fact there are methods in graph research that can retrieve the k-Shortest Paths sequentially. To this end, we also demonstrate a method of reformulating a cost-based HMM used in concatenative synthesis as a directed acyclic graph in order to avail of shortest path methods.

Parallel Decoder. The parallel decoder [39] or List Viterbi decoding Algorithm (LVA) is so-called because, instead of keeping track of the winning path leading into each state at time step t, it now stores the top k paths leading into the states in one pass through the state space or trellis. This is distinct from another method the authors propose and term the serial decoder, which takes several passes through the trellis in order to return multiple candidates.

To convert the regular Viterbi decoder to a k-Best parallel decoder. The following steps are required.

1. Expand the α and ϕ matrices of the HMM to account for $T * N * K$ entries that correspond to T discrete steps, N states and K sequences.
2. When computing the probabilities of the transitions from the previous states leading into the current state as per the recursion step in the equation, insert them into a continuously sorting data structure like a priority queue[3] (we use Python's *heapq*).
3. Remember that there is now the possibility of a previous state leading to the current state more than once (because that previous state now also has k previous states that are highly probable). Thus we need to another structure (such as a dictionary) to keep track of the ranking of multiple probabilities of the same previous state if it enters the current state more than once.
4. At the termination step insert the final probabilities into the queue to find the final top k scoring paths.
5. Backtrack as before while taking care to adhere to the ranking of multiple instances of the same previous state.

Curiously, we couldn't find any existing fully-formed implementations for the parallel decoder, at least not in any usable state of reproducibility, so once again we have implemented and made available ourselves a version in Python. Figure 3 shows how our newly implemented parallel decoder computes the first and second highest probability paths ($k = 2$) through the Wikipedia example previously evaluated with the regular Viterbi decoder in Fig. 1.

Serial Decoder. The Serial Decoder, also proposed by Seshadri and Sundberg [39], differs from the parallel decoder just implemented in that it first computes the single best state sequence using the regular Viterbi decoder, then returns the remaining k one by one. Despite the less efficient connotations that the serial versus parallel labelling musters up, the authors maintain it can perform less computations as "the kth best candidate is computed only when the previously found $k - 1$ candidates are determined to be in 'error' [39].

We have not implemented the Serial decoder (as of yet), as once again no reference code is available and its derivation is a bit harder to decipher from

---

[3] A heap queue is a binary tree with the special condition that every parent has a value less than or equal to that of its children (this is a minimum queue, a maximum is naturally the inverse). The important function in our case is the push function, which adds items to the tree and maintains the sorted heap property in $O(logn)$ time.

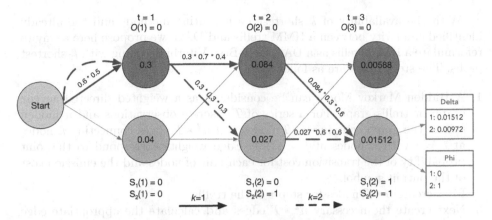

Fig. 3. Viterbi decoding of Wikipedia example using the parallel decoder. Final delta and phi matrices indicate the top *k* highest scoring probabilities and the state indices that led there. As the two previous states are different we don't need to consider the ranking here. The path is the solid line through the trellis, while *k* = 2 is indicated by the dashed line.

its scant treatment in the literature [24,31,39], than in the case of its parallel equivalent.

k-Shortest Paths. We hinted that the traversal of a state space in a HMM bears considerable resemblance to that of a Directed Acyclic Graph (DAG) of vertices, edges and a set of costs to be associated with those edges. This should also be visually apparent from the trellis diagrams presented in Figs. 1 and 3.

Shortest path algorithms aim to solve the problem of finding the path between two given vertices with the least cost. Two well-known algorithms for achieving the shortest path include [10] and Bellman-Ford [2,14]. Computing the *k*-Shortest paths then entails returning an ordered *list* of the shortest paths between the two desired vertices (from what is often called the *source* to the *sink*).

One of the first algorithms proposed for tackling *k*-Shortest path problems is known as Yen's Algorithm [45]. Yen's algorithm only operates on simple or loopless graphs (like DAGs or trellis diagram representations of a HMM) and uses a regular shortest path algorithm such as Dijkstra or Bellman-Ford in order to find the best *k* = 1 shortest path initially. Assuming the previous *k* − 1 paths have already been found, the algorithm searches the previous path for branches that deviate with higher associated cost. It is for this reason we need to have the best initial shortest path from an existing shortest path algorithm. Thankfully, many implementations exist for *k* Shortest Path routing so we don't need to worry about its inner workings too greatly and can rely on its black-box functionality in many graph-based programming libraries. We avail of Yen's Algorithm in Python using the NetworkX [16] graph library.

With the availability of k shortest path routing methods and the already identified similarity between a HMM trellis and DAG, we propose here a way to reformulate a HMM trellis as a DAG for k-Best Viterbi decoding with k-shortest paths. The steps taken are as follows:

1. A Hidden Markov Model can be considered as a weighted directed acyclic graph or trellis graph. For a series of T discrete observations and n hidden states, the graph contains $n * T$ nodes and $n^2 * T$ edges connecting n nodes at $t = i$ with n nodes at $t = i + 1$. Edge weights correspond to the joint probability of the transition cost for each pair of nodes and the emission cost of the output symbol.
2. First create $n * T$ nodes for step t of the trellis.
3. Next create the necessary $n^2 * T$ edges and calculate the appropriate edge weights as given by $A_{ij} * B_j * (O_t)$.
4. Add a start node and create edges connecting to each of the nodes at $t = 0$ with weights encapsulating the initial probabilities $\pi_i * B_i * (O_1)$.
5. Create a sink node and connect it to all the nodes at $t = T$ with a zero weighting.
6 Before we can run the shortest path algorithm we must make one final change to address the impedance mismatch between graph-based cost minimisation and Markov probability maximisation. The edge weights need to be converted by converting to negative log-space as in 16 for a probability p.

$$c = -log(p) \tag{16}$$

7. To recover the original probability just apply the inverse (17)

$$p = exp(-c) \tag{17}$$

Suffice it to say that step 6 and 7 are not required in unit selection for concatenative synthesis since the state space is already based on cost. Figure 4 shows an autogenerated trace of the k shortest paths, with $k = 2$, applied to a graph reformulation of the Wikipedia HMM example.

5   Developing a k-Best Concatenative Synthesiser

We have covered expanding HMM approaches to unit selection to enable output of multiple candidate sequences using k-Best, list decoding or graph based algorithms. Now we turn the effort to putting all these components together to actually create some sounds, coupled with some experimental evidence that exposes and confirms the validity of our contributions.

5.1   PyConcat - Python Framework for Concatenative Synthesis

PyConcat is devised in the context of this research as a framework for *research-oriented* exploration of concatenative synthesis, coalescing the state of the art

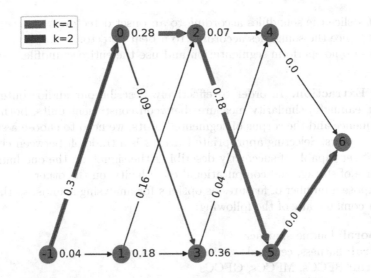

Fig. 4. Shortest Paths applied to the Wikipedia Viterbi example. The source node -1 begins on the bottom left of the graph, with 2 shortest paths computed to the sink at node 6. The second best path diverges from the best path for edges $\{0, 3\}$ and $\{3, 5\}$.

methods as well as novel ones like k-Best unit selection. We stress research-oriented as it does not address user interaction and is not suitable for real time applications. The scope of this system is also still general to all stylistic intentions. In [26, 27] a system is described that tailors such methods specifically for rhythm-centric dance production as stipulated in the introduction of the thesis.

To perform a concatenative synthesis task with PyConcat, the composer first requires a corpus of interesting sounds and a target sound they wish to emulate the sonic character of. They then provide parameters and issues instructions for performing the three key stages that are required[4]. A more detailed technical introduction to the usage of PyConcat is outside the score of this paper, but this section is intended to give a broad enough insight in order to conduct some preliminary experiments.

Onset Detection and Segmentation. The composer must choose the unit scale for segmenting sounds into their constituent units. The unit scales need not be the same for the target and the corpus. The options we provide include

- **Framewise** - slice the samples at uniform length N.
- **Framewise FFT** - slice the samples at uniform length N and convert to the frequency domain. Overlap-add IFFT is performed on selected units before final concatenation.

---

[4] In fact, the system is sufficiently decoupled that any of these logical stages can be performed separately for their own purpose. For example the tool can be used solely for slicing sounds, or performing batch feature analysis on a library for the purposes of MIR.

- **Onset** - slice the soundfiles according to an onset detector.
- **Beats** - slice the soundfiles according to a beat detector.
- **None** - do not perform segmentation and use the entire soundfile.

Feature Extraction. In order to effectively describe our audio content and produce meaningful similarity measures between constituent units, both in the target sequence and the corpus of segmented units, we need to choose a suitable set of descriptors. Selecting appropriate features is a trade-off between choosing the richest set capable of succinctly describing the signal, on the one hand, and the expense of storage and computational complexity, on the other.

We expose a number of features as options for analysing sounds, so the composer can combine any of the following:

- **Temporal:** loudness, attack
- **Spectral:** flatness, centroid
- **Timbral:** BFCCs, MFCCs, GFCCs
- **Musical:** f0, HPCPs

Unit Selection. Extracted features for the target units and corpus units and are stored in two matrices T and C. Next the distance matrices $A = T * C$ and $E = C * C$ are calculated to avoid unnecessary computation later. Beforehand, however, it is important to perform any normalisation or standardisation and weighting of individual features as required.

A unit selection procedure is engaged to return a sequence of corpus indices using the aforementioned and described methods in Sect. 4, but we reiterate them here briefly.

- **Linear Search** - return an ordered list of the closest corpus units to each target unit.
- **k-D Tree** - return the approximate nearest neighbours for each target unit.
- **Viterbi**- return the sequence with the minimised target and concatenation costs.
- **k-best Viterbi** - the top k sequences with the minimised target and concatenation costs using parallel list decoding.
- **k-shortest Paths** - return the top k sequences with the minimised target and concatenation costs using k shortest paths.

Transformation and Concatenation. The unit selection stage returns a vector of indices of length N, or a matrix of $k * N$ indices, where N is the number of target units and k is the number of sequences from the k best schemes. These indices correspond to individual sound units within our corpus. To produce the final audio representation, we simply concatenate the floating point samples uniformly back to back, but there's no reason why they can't be overlapped and crossfaded at their boundaries for further smoothing as applied by [36].

Unlike other investigators such as [6] we don't focus on complex post-selection transformations, but if there is a large discrepancy between the lengths of the target units and the corpus units or its pitch needs to be adjusted, some time compression or pitch-shifting can be applied, which we facilitate through the a transformation stage utilising the open source Rubber Band Library[5] which is also used in the systems of [9,41].

6   Analysis of the k-Best Unit Selection

In [25,28] we formulated an evaluation methodology and framework to conduct a stringent and rigorous appraisal of the more fully-formed concatenative synthesis system described in [27], which uses a type of linear search selection method coupled with a stripped-back combination of timbral, spectral and loudness features. The novel methods we propose in this paper are still in their infancy, thus we have yet to devise a formal evaluation procedure. However, in this section we give a brief analysis of the two specialised k-best and k shortest selection units for comparative reference, using our PyConcat system.

6.1   Algorithm Performance

To compare the running times of the two implemented algorithms we took a small recording of the 8 notes of the C major scale being performed on a piano and resynthesised it with itself. Figure 5 shows side by side of the running times

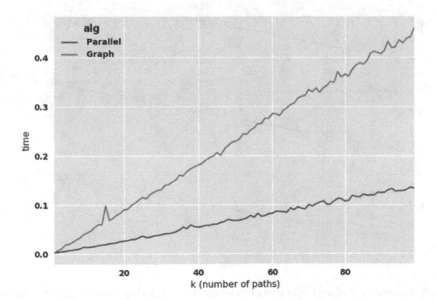

Fig. 5. Running time comparisons for both algorithms.

[5] http://www.breakfastquay.com/rubberband/.

for both algorithms based on the number of paths returned. Our implementation of the parallel decoder outperforms the NetworkX Graph approach considerably. This is mostly due to the added layer of complexity of expanding the Hidden Markov Model to a fully connected directed acyclic graph. Others have noted however that NetworkX, on account of being implemented purely in Python, performs slower than other compiled graph libraries such as *graph-tool* or *igraph*.

It will be worth benchmarking against these implementations or reimplementing completely in C/C++. In any case, it is worth bearing in mind the real culprit in these applications: audio signal processing. The segmentation and analysis of the units took 10 s for all runs.

6.2   Equivalence and Correctness

Figure 6 shows the optimal sequence generated for regular Viterbi decoding and sequences $1 \leq k \leq 4$ for the parallel decoder and graph decoder respectively. The single straight line indicates that using the chosen acoustic features and weightings, the baseline Viterbi decoder correctly reassembles its own input. The parallel and graph decoders both correctly return this sequence as the first optimal path also (obscured by the subsequent paths in the diagram). Looking at the other returned paths, we see very slight deviations of only one unit per path (k is very small relative to the total possible paths). The possible paths, and their ordering, are identical for both algorithms.

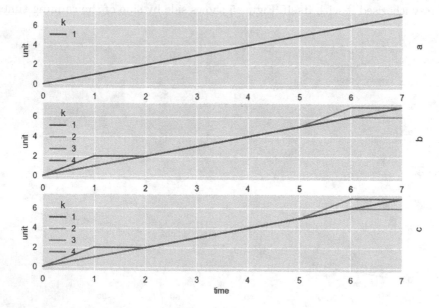

Fig. 6. Equivalency of unit selection algorithms. Graph A (top) shows correct reassembly of target units with the regular Viterbi decoder. Graph B (middle) shows the first 4 paths returned by parallel decoder. Graph C (bottom) shows the first 4 paths returned by the graph-based decoder.

6.3   Pitch and Timbre Preservation

To study the HMM's acoustical output, we selected energy, fundamental frequency ($f0$) and MFCC features, and chose a weighting scheme that gave preference to the $f0$ in the target cost while giving preference to the MFCCs in the concatenation cost. This allows us to focus on the specific ability of the target cost in preserving the pitch between each onset in the target sample and the selected units from the corpus, while the concatenation cost attempts to preserve a continuous and coherent evolution of timbre from a variety of timbres in the corpus. We used the same piano scale sample as a target, but this time using a corpus of samples from a completely different set of instruments. From a collection of orchestral samples provided freely by the London Philharmonia, 610 violin, viola, clarinet and trumpet samples were gathered with notes ranging from MIDI A3 to G7.

As we can see from Fig. 7, and after some median filtering to remove spurious spikes, the steady states of each pitch match for generated path 1 and generated path 10 taken as examples.

MFCC plots are always a bit difficult to decipher, but while it is clear that the MFCC overall profile of the target (8) contrasts with the targets, we can see the eight notes of the sequence reproduced and the difference in attacks that are also present in the plots of the fundamental frequencies. Again, notice lower values of k produce very similar results when the size of the corpus is large, differing only by a couple of units (Fig. 8).

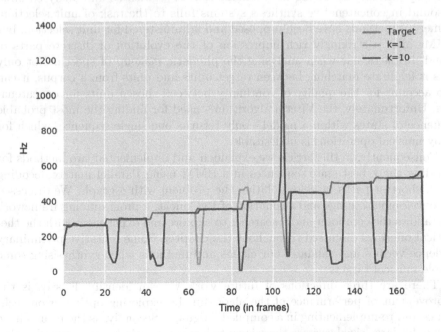

Fig. 7. Fundamental frequency of 3 different k-Best Sequences.

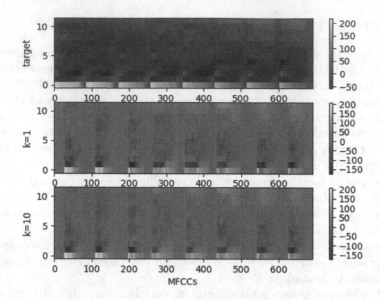

Fig. 8. MFCC plots of 3 different k-Best Sequences.

7   Conclusion

The responsibility of intelligent recombination of segmented and analysed units of sound in concatenative synthesis systems falls to the task of unit selection. Numerous methods have been proposed and administered for unit selection, but HMMs offer a strikingly rich impression of the evolution of discrete parts of sound, in particular when analysing the phonetic makeup of speech. Not only does it facilitate matching between target units and units from a corpus, it can also account for the quality of continuity between chosen units for concatenation. Unfortunately, the Viterbi algorithm - used for finding the most probable sequence of states within a model - only returns one single sequence, which for many musical operations is undesirable.

Consequently, in this article we explained and implemented two methods for decoding the k best state sequences in a HMM using Parallel matrix decoding and k shortest paths by reformulating the problem with a graph. We discussed the development, usage and evaluation of PyConcat, a programming framework that allows the composer and researcher to explore and experiment with the theoretical offerings discussed throughout the chapter. Some tentative preliminary evidence verifies and validates our claims and methods when synthesising some simple musical targets.

There are three directions of future work we can identify. Firstly, is the improvement of performance of the algorithm by exploring optimisation techniques and re-implementing in a compiled language. Secondly, as the results have shown, for large sized corpora there is quite low variance in lower values of k. One possible remedy for this is to choose a "stride" factor that skips every n items when gathering the k highest scoring paths at each state, thereby increasing novelty. Finally, an extensive evaluation of the system, preferably with listening surveys, is an important next stage for this research.

References

1. Aucouturier, J.J., Pachet, F.: Jamming with plunderphonics: interactive concatenative synthesis of music. J. New Music. Res. **35**(1), 35–50 (2006)
2. Bellman, R.: On a routing problem. Q. Appl. Math. **16**(1), 87–90 (1958)
3. Bird, S.: NLTK: The natural language toolkit NLTK: The Natural Language Toolkit. In: Proceedings of the COLING/ACL on Interactive Presentation Sessions, pp. 69–72 (2016)
4. Brown, D.G., Golod, D.: Decoding HMMs using the k best paths: algorithms and applications. BMC Bioinf. **11**(Suppl 1), S28 (2010)
5. Cho, T., Weiss, R.J., Bello, J.P.: Exploring common variations in state of the art chord recognition systems. Sound Music. Comput. **1**(January), 11–22 (2010)
6. Coleman, G., Maestre, E., Bonada, J.: Augmenting sound mosaicing with descriptor-driven transformation. In: Proceedings Digital Audio Effects (DAFx-10), pp. 1–4 (2010)
7. Collins, N.: Audiovisual concatenative synthesis. In: Proceedings of the International Computer Conference, pp. 389–392 (2007)
8. Dannenberg, R.B.: Concatenative synthesis using score-aligned transcriptions music analysis and segmentation. In: International Computer Music Conference, pp. 352–355 (2006)
9. Davies, M.E.P., Hamel, P., Yoshii, K., Goto, M.: AutoMashUpper: an automatic multi-song mashup system. In: Proceedings of the 14th International Society for Music Information Retrieval Conference, ISMIR 2013, pp. 575–580 (2013)
10. Dijkstra, E.W.: A note on two problems in connexion with graphs. Numer. Math. **1**(1), 269–271 (1959)
11. Eigenfeldt, A.: The evolution of evolutionary software: intelligent rhythm generation in kinetic engine. In: Giacobini, M., et al. (eds.) EvoWorkshops 2009. LNCS, vol. 5484, pp. 498–507. Springer, Heidelberg (2009). https://doi.org/10.1007/978-3-642-01129-0_56
12. Einbond, A., Schwarz, D.: Spatializing timbre with corpus-based concatenative synthesis. In: International Computer Music Conference, New York, USA (2010)
13. Fernández, J.D., Vico, F.: AI methods in algorithmic composition: a comprehensive survey. J. Artif. Intell. Res. **48**, 513–582 (2013)
14. Ford Jr., L.R.: Network flow theory. Technical report, RAND CORP SANTA MONICA CA (1956)
15. Guéguen, L.: Sarment: Python modules for HMM analysis and partitioning of sequences. Bioinformatics **21**(16), 3427–3428 (2005)
16. Hagberg, A.A., Schult, D.A., Swart, P.J.: Exploring network structure, dynamics, and function using NetworkX. In: Varoquaux, G., Vaught, T., Millman, J. (eds.) Proceedings of the 7th Python in Science Conference, Pasadena, CA USA, pp. 11–15 (2008)
17. Hunt, A.J., Black, A.W.: Unit selection in a concatenative speech synthesis system using a large speech database. In: 1996 IEEE International Conference on Acoustics, Speech, and Signal Processing Conference Proceedings, vol. 1, pp. 373–376 (1996)

18. Jones, E., Oliphant, T., Peterson, P.: SciPy: Open Source Scientific Tools for Python (2014)
19. Jordà, S., Gómez-Marín, D., Faraldo, Á., Herrera, P.: Drumming with style: from user needs to a working prototype. In: Proceedings of the International Conference on New Interfaces for Musical Expression, vol. 16, pp. 365–370 (2016)
20. Kaehler, A., Bradski, G.: Learning OpenCV 3: Computer Vision in C++ with the OpenCV Library. O'Reilly Media, Inc. (2016)
21. Klügel, N., Becker, T., Groh, G.: Designing sound collaboratively - perceptually motivated audio synthesis. In: New Interfaces for Musical Expression, London, UK, pp. 327–330 (2014). http://arxiv.org/abs/1406.6012
22. Maestre, E., Hazan, A., Ramirez, R., Perez, A.: Using concatenative synthesis for expressive performance in jazz saxophone. In: Proceedings of the International Computer Music Conference 2006, pp. 163–166 (2006)
23. Nierhaus, G.: Algorithmic Composition: Paradigms of Automated Music Generation. Springer, Wien (2009). https://doi.org/10.1007/978-3-211-75540-2
24. Nill, C., Sundberg, C.E.W.: List and soft symbol output viterbi algorithms: extensions and comparisons. IEEE Trans. Commun. 43(234), 277–287 (1995)
25. Nuanáin, C.Ó., Herrera, P., Jordà, S.: An evaluation framework and case study for rhythmic concatenative synthesis. In: Proceedings of the 17th International Society for Music Information Retrieval Conference, New York, USA (2016)
26. Nuanáin, C.Ó., Herrera, P., Jordà, S.: Rhythmic concatenative synthesis for electronic music: techniques, implementation, and evaluation. Comput. Music J. 41(2), 21–37 (2017)
27. Nuanáin, C.Ó., Jordà, S., Herrera, P.: An interactive software instrument for real-time rhythmic concatenative synthesis. In: New Interfaces for Musical Expression, Brisbane, Australia (2016)
28. Nuanáin, C.Ó., Jordà, S., Herrera, P.: Towards user-tailored creative applications of concatenative synthesis in electronic dance music. In: International Workshop on Musical Metacreation (MUME), Paris, France (2016)
29. Orio, N., Lemouton, S., Schwarz, D.: Score following: state of the art and new developments. In: Proceedings of the Conference on New Interfaces for Musical Expression, pp. 36–41 (2003)
30. Papadopoulos, H., Peeters, G.: Large-scale study of chord estimation algorithms based on chroma representation and HMM. In: 2007 International Workshop on Content-Based Multimedia Indexing, Proceedings, CBMI 2007, pp. 53–60 (2007)
31. Rabiner, L., Juang, B.H.: Fundamentals of Speech Recognition (1993)
32. Rabiner, L.R.: A Tutorial on Hidden Markov Models and Selected Applications in Speech Recognition (1989)
33. Roads, C.: Microsound. The MIT Press, Cambridge (2004)
34. Russell, S., Norvig, P.: Artificial Intelligence: A Modern Approach, 2nd Edn. Prentice Hall (2002)
35. Schwarz, D.: The caterpillar system for data-driven concateantive sound synthesis. In: Proceedings of the 6th International Conference on Digital Audio Effects (DAFx-03), pp. 1–6 (2003)
36. Schwarz, D.: Concatenative sound synthesis: the early years. J. New Music. Res. 35(1), 3–22 (2006)
37. Schwarz, D.: Distance mapping for corpus-based concatenative synthesis. In: Sound and Music Computing Conference (SMC), Padova, Italy (2011)
38. Schwarz, D., Schnell, N., Gulluni, S.: Scalability in content-based navigation of sound databases. In: Proceedings of the International Computer Music Conference, pp. 253–258 (2009)

39. Seshadri, N., Sundberg, C.E.: List Viterbi decoding algorithms with applications. IEEE Trans. Commun. **42**(2/3/4), 313–323 (1994)
40. Sheh, A., Ellis, D.P.W.: Chord segmentation and recognition using EM-trained hidden markov models. In: Proceedings of the International Conference on Music Information Retrieval (ISMIR), pp. 185–191 (2003)
41. Smith, J.B.L., Percival, G., Kato, J., Goto, M., Fukayama, S.: CrossSong puzzle: generating and unscrambling music mashups with real-time interactivity. In: Sound and Music Computing Conference, Maynooth, Ireland (2015)
42. Stoll, T.: CorpusDB: software for analysis, storage, and manipulation of sound corpora. In: International Workshop on Musical Metacreation (MuMe), pp. 108–113 (2013)
43. Sturm, B.L.: Adaptive concatenative sound synthesis and its application to micromontage composition. Comput. Music. J. **30**(4), 46–66 (2006)
44. Viterbi, A.J.: Error bounds for convolutional codes and an asymptotically optimum decoding algorithm. IEEE Trans. Inf. Theory **13**(2), 260–269 (1967)
45. Yen, J.Y.: Finding the K shortest loopless paths in a network. Manag. Sci. **17**(11), 712–716 (1971)
46. Zils, A., Pachet, F.: Musical mosaicing. In: Digital Audio Effects (DAFx), pp. 1–6 (2001)

Electronic Dance Music and Rhythm

Groove on the Brain

Peter Vuust[(⊠)]

Center for Music in the Brain, Department of Clinical Medicine,
The Royal Academy of Music Aarhus/Aalborg, Aarhus University,
Nørrebrogade 44, Aarhus, Denmark
pv@musikkons.dk

Abstract. A unique feature of music is its potential to make us want to move our feet and bodies to the rhythm of the musical beat. Even though the ability to synchronize our movements to music feels as a completely natural music-related behavior to most humans (but see [1, 2] for rare cases of so-called beat-deafness in humans) this ability is rarely observed in animals [3], and usually depends on specific training regimes [4]. Our brains structure the musical beat into strong and weak beats even without any such information present in the auditory stimulus [5]. Furthermore, the tendency to move to a regular beat, with isochronous intervals, may persist even if the music that we listen to emphasizes musical events that lies between these beats as for syncopated rhythms [6] or in the case of polyrhythm [7, 8]. This indicates a cognitive discrepancy between what is heard – the rhythm - and the brain's internal structuring of the beat – which in musicology is termed the meter.

In the present paper, I shall argue that this discrepancy: (1) is related to prediction as a fundamental principle of brain processing, (2) gives rise to prediction error between lower - possibly sensory - and higher levels – possibly motor networks - in the hierarchical organized brain, and that (3) perception, learning and our inclination to move to the beat depends on the right balance between predictability and surprise. This predictive coding understanding of the brain mechanisms involved in movement related musical behavior may help us understand brain processes related to aesthetic experiences in general and in designing strategies for clinical intervention for patients with movement disorders.

Keywords: Groove · Predictive coding · Neuroscience

1 Predictive Coding of Music

In recent years, there has been a consensus in cognitive neuroscience that prediction is a fundamental principle behind brain processing [9–14]. One of the most influential of these theories "the predictive coding theory" put forward by Friston and colleagues explains how specialized brain networks identify and categorize causes of their sensory inputs, integrate information with other networks, and adapt to new stimuli [13]. This theory proposes that perception, action and learning is a recursive Bayesian process by which the brain attempts to minimize the prediction error between lower-level sensory input and the brain's top-down predictions. In this way, the brain's predictive model of

© Springer Nature Switzerland AG 2018
M. Aramaki et al. (Eds.): CMMR 2017, LNCS 11265, pp. 101–110, 2018.
https://doi.org/10.1007/978-3-030-01692-0_7

the world (the prior) is constantly updated and adjusted to fit the incoming sensory input. An excellent summary of the recent advances was given by Andy Clark [13].

This idea, that cognition relies on prediction, is strikingly similar to theories holding prediction as a fundamental principle behind music perception and appreciation [15–18]. As such, prediction has for a long time been regarded as the central mechanism behind musical emotion and meaning [15]. It is also a prerequisite for joint music making [19–21] and essential for musical tension and surprise [17, 18]. Accordingly, music has been suggested to be an ideal domain for testing and further developing predictive coding theories [22–24], which again could inform our understanding of brain mechanisms in general, and perhaps even help us to understand the fundamental prediction principles of the brain.

2   Syncopation in Groove Music as an Example of How Predictive Coding Relates to Aesthetic Experiences

Syncopation in music is a particularly well-suited example of predictive coding. Studying syncopations we are able to illustrate how a particular sensory input – a syncopated rhythm - may result in prediction error against a predictive brain model, the meter. The musical meter can be defined as a hierarchically organized framework consisting of evenly spaced and differentially accented beats, providing to each metric position a timing and a metrical weight. In predictive coding terms, the meter is the brain's posterior expectations constituting its predictive model. The rhythm may, through the use of syncopation, be more or less in accordance with the meter, creating stronger or weaker prediction error between auditory input and predictive model. Depending on context (e.g. the experimental instructions), and the individual's rhythmic skills, the listener may shift the metrical framework [6] (e.g. from 4/4 to 3/4) or in predictive coding terms, infer a different metrical cause to the auditory input.

Interestingly, however, syncopations are beneficial to the pleasure that we get from listening to a particular drum rhythm excerpt, as well as to our desire to move to it. In a series of studies [25–27], we investigated the pleasurable sensation of wanting to move to highly repetitive syncopated rhythms. We used a battery of 50 groove-based drum patterns, asking participants in an online survey to rate the patterns on a 7-point Likert scale as to how much they wanted to move and the pleasure felt. We calculated the degree of syncopation in the stimuli using Witek et al.'s index of syncopation, which adds instrumental weights to the model proposed by Longuet-Higgens and Lee [28] to adjust for the polyphonic character of drum patterns. Using 50 drum patterns of which 34 we transcribed from real funk tracks, and the remaining patterns were constructed specifically for the experiment, we obtained a continuum of drum excerpts ranging from weakly syncopated to strongly syncopated rhythm patterns.

In that study, we observed an inverted U-shaped relationship between degree of syncopation and the groove ratings, suggesting that the sensation of groove is strongest at intermediate levels of discrepancy between the rhythmic (sensory) input and the metrical predictive framework. This inverted U-shape [29] has earlier been hypothesized to reflect the relationship between music complexity and liking [30–32] and perceptual complexity and arousal in art more broadly [33], although empirical studies have shown that this function largely depends on the musical style in question [32]. In a subsequent study [34] we used motion-capture to record free movements in hand and torso while participants listened to a subset of 15 of the drum patterns mentioned above, categorized into three levels of syncopation; low, medium and high. For low and medium levels of syncopation, participants synchronized their movements well to the meter, whereas for high levels of syncopation they synchronized very poorly.

Based on the predictive coding framework, we recently presented a simple, yet powerful mathematical model that accounts for these results as well as for how the brain processes rhythmic incongruity in general: *the model for predictive coding of rhythmic incongruity (PCRI)* [35]. A key concept in the later free energy formulations of the predictive coding theory is the notion of *precision*. The idea here is that the prediction error arising from a less expected event is weighed by its relative precision. Garrido and colleagues [36] convincingly demonstrated the influence of the precision. They showed that the amplitude of the mismatch negativity, a negativity observed on the averaged wave-forms measured with electroencephalography (ERPs), to a frequency outlier from randomly occurring notes within a specific spectral band, was modulated by the wideness of this band. In other words, if the brain has a precise expectation (resulting from a low variance) to a certain stimulus, a surprising event will be weighed stronger than when the expectations are less precise.

The PCRI model proposes that, in relation to rhythm, the prediction error that the lower levels in the brain feed forward depends on the synthesis of a given rhythm's *syncopation index* and its metrical uncertainty *(precision)*. For the rhythm excerpts used in our groove studies mentioned above, regularly organized rhythms with less syncopation fed forward only little prediction error, since they were relatively close to the meter. For the highest levels of syncopation the meter, however, becomes obscured, leading to less precision of the predictive model as evidenced by the lack of ability to synchronize with the meter observed in the motion capture study [26]. Here, it is difficult for the brain to detect the signal in the noise. In contrast, what the system experiences as precision-weighted prediction error is highest at intermediate levels of syncopation for which both objective prediction error and the precision of the prediction are moderate.

According to the "free energy" formulations of predictive coding, the brain can minimize prediction error through action. Moving the body in a way that changes the bottom-up proprioceptive and sensory input and thus resampling the evidence [37], the error signal will self-suppress. In the context of groove, we hence feel the urge to move our bodies to the metrical beat in order to strengthen the metric model and suppress or attenuate the precision of prediction errors. Psychologically, this corresponds to ignoring the consequences of action to discount evidence against our predictions of sensory input [38]. Hence, as long as we have a strong perception of the beat, we will try to move to it, when we encounter syncopations.

3   Brain Networks Involved in the Brain Processing of Syncopated Rhythms

The groove studies exemplify how a balance between predictability and evidence against the brain's predictive model is crucial for the experience of pleasure, wanting to move, as well as for attracting and withholding attention, which are all elements of the aesthetic experience of music. The perpetually occurring syncopations in the groovy rhythms keep the brain on its toes; feed its predictive mechanisms a constant flow of prediction error to minimize. This leads to an ongoing discrepancy between motor networks, trying to infer some kind of regularity or anchor point, and the sensory systems processing the rhythm intervals.

The sensory input from a rhythm excerpt containing rhythmic incongruity e.g. in the form of syncopation seems to lead to prediction error in the auditory cortices. Prediction error provoked by neural responses to isolated syncopations occurring in continuous rhythmic streams are thought to be marked by the deflections on the in the event-related potentials/fields, which can be measured with EEG or magneto-encephalography (MEG). Vuust and colleagues performed MEG while musicians and non-musicians were listening without attending to isolated syncopations occurring pseudo-randomly in musical drum rhythm excerpts. These syncopations elicited two prominent ERPs, the magnetic counterpart of the mismatch negativity (MMNm) and the P3am. This is consistent with the predictive coding framework in that they have properties similar to electrophysiological error signals and their subsequent evaluation [22]. The mismatch negativity seems to have the properties of an error signal arising from superficial cortical layers as posited by PC. It is in general elicited to violations of auditory expectancy and has been found in response to pattern deviations determined by physical parameters, such as frequency [39], intensity [40], spatial localization [41] and duration [42], but also to patterns with more abstract properties [43, 44].

The P3a is believed to represent a network involving both the modality/task specific areas [45] evoking the error signal and higher regions that can evaluate it [41]. This suggests that the P3am reflects a neural network that acts on the error signal of the MMN. The MMN and the P3a are generally believed to reflect different stages of processing subserving an attention switching mechanism [46, 47]. Whereas the MMN is thought to be the first stage in involuntary attention capture [48], the P3a most likely reflects the actual switch of attention [49]. The P3a response may indicate that attention should be designated to the metric violation. In terms of predictive coding, there is a close relationship between attention and precision. Prediction errors that are afforded greater precision are effectively boosted, such that they have a greater influence on higher level expectations and consequent predictions. The brain has to predict both the content of the sensorium and its precision. Simulations of predictive coding suggest that late (endogenous) responses, such as the P3a, may reflect a revision of beliefs about the precision or predictability of the sensory streams [50]. This suggests that early (i.e. mismatch negativity) violation responses correspond to a precision-weighted prediction error, while later (i.e., P300) responses reflect belief updates about precision per se [41].

In addition to the involvement of the auditory system, fMRI studies systematically show involvement of the motor system in rhythm perception, where e.g. basal ganglia structures respond more to rhythms with a clear beat, than more complex rhythms [51]. Whether there is a central clock guiding our rhythm perception is still highly debated [52] but a number of studies [53–55] relates a network comprising of auditory cortices, cortical secondary motor areas, and basal ganglia to passive listening to rhythms. Some authors also emphasize the role of the vestibular system in mediating beat induction [56]. When asked to tap to polyrhythms where the beat (the predictive model of the meter) is hard to maintain, higher level brain areas such as the inferior frontal gyrus, and the anterior cingulate cortex are needed [57, 58], indicating that these more demanding rhythmical tasks requires multi-level hierarchal processing. Importantly, inferring a meter from a given rhythm is subject to learning as shown by Philips-Silver and Trainor [59], who made children move to metrical ambiguous rhythms in different meters. Using a head-turn preference procedure the study showed that the children preferred the versions of the rhythms with accents in accordance with the meter that they were trained in, indicating that sensory-motor coupling is reciprocal and plastic.

Hence, in the hierarchically organized brain, listening to groovy syncopated rhythms leads to a perpetual state of conflict likely to occur between sensory networks processing the incoming rhythms (bottom-up) and the regular metrical prior (top-down) related to our drive to move our feet in a regular pulse [60]. Accordingly, premotor areas increase their feedback to the auditory cortices during stronger beat perception [61], indicating top-down influence from the premotor to the sensory level linking perception and action presumably as a precursor for moving to the beat.

This process can be modelled using oscillator-based network theories. Using increasingly syncopated rhythms, Large and colleagues showed [62] that participants' degree of synchronization to the meter could successfully be explained by a neuronal network model encompassing a hierarchy of only two levels; one corresponding to the sensory system, tuned to operate near a Hopf bifurcation [63] the other corresponding to the motor system tuned to operate near a double limit cycle bifurcation. Hence, the actual brain realization of predictive coding of rhythm (bottom-up) and meter (top-down) may be tightly linked to functional connectivity between auditory and motor brain networks, which at a more basic level are tuned for different tasks; listening and moving.

4   Why Do We Find Prediction Error Pleasurable?

Nevertheless, why do our subjects find the medium syncopated rhythms the more pleasurable? The involvement of the reward system in relation to pleasurable music has been known for more than a decade [64, 65]. A likely candidate for mediating the effect of musical reward is the neurotransmitter dopamine in the mesolimbic pathway [66]. Research in rodents [67, 68] has shown dopamine release to both expected and unexpected stimuli, suggesting that the complex interaction between dopamine release and predictions leads to adaptive learning in the short and long term. It is, however, important not to conflate reward prediction error (RPE) with how the term prediction error (PE) is used in the predictive coding framework. RPE pertains to expectations of how emotionally rewarding a piece of music will be evaluated, whereas PE pertains to neuronal computation of sensory input relating to the brain's predictions about music itself [69]. PE is neither positive nor negative. Furthermore, the direct neurobiological evidence for a functional link between prediction error related to music listening and activity in the reward systems is still lacking. Nevertheless, we may speculate about how prediction error and pleasure, as e.g. measured behaviorally as a U-shaped curve in relation to increasingly syncopated rhythms, are linked.

Our appreciation of music - and maybe of art more generally – is related to prediction in a special way. Music is constructed such that the brain continuously needs to resolve prediction error, even on repeated listening to the same piece of music and despite the many repetitive elements, found within the same piece of music. This perpetual need for our brains to minimize prediction error while listening to music captures and withholds our interest and may be the basis of the pleasure that we experience. In other words, it may be the process of minimizing prediction error, that we find pleasurable. To paraphrase Wolfram Schultz in his seminal Science paper by exchanging *learning* with *pleasure* [70]: no *pleasure*, without prediction error.

This may link to an evolutionary argument relating to the evident survival value of learning. Kringelbach and Berridge [71] suggested that the brain rewards prediction error since it leads to learning and thereby maximizes future prediction. Another perspective on the paradoxical attractiveness of prediction errors is that they play a central role in active inference formulations of predictive coding. In this instance, prediction errors signify an opportunity to resolve uncertainty and minimize prediction errors in the future [71]. Formally, this related to a discussion of salience or epistemic affordance. Rewarding actions minimize the brain's free energy or maximize epistemic value, thus building a more precise model of the world. In Bayesian terms, this translates into an optimization of the evidence for our models, or succinctly, self-evidencing [72]. Even, listening to a simple monophonic sequence of notes will for each new note generate a sample space such for the subsequent note, such that some notes will be more probable than others [18, 73]. Music, with its continuous stream of changing probabilities – being predictably unpredictable - may offer the brain an optimal opportunity for minimizing prediction error over time.

A predictive coding interpretation of the inverted U-shape may also help us to understand why we often like a certain piece more when we have listened to it many times [74, 75]. The prediction error that the piece generates may simply change over time. Huron [16] suggested that when we listen to a certain piece over and over again the prediction errors that it causes will persist and even grow stronger in certain memory systems such as for schematic and short term memory predictions when in the veridical memory, the uncertainty of how the specific piece of music continues decreases. The first time we listen to it, it may be too complex to our ears, the precision which we assign to the prediction error is too low. On repeated listening the precision of our veridical expectations increases such that what is left is the prediction error from schematic and short-term predictions, which are then assigned more weight. Hence, the sum of the prediction error may now reach the more optimal level for experiencing pleasure.

5 Conclusions

As pointed out in the present paper, the study of groove is an interesting probe to a predictive coding account of the brain mechanisms underlying music-related perception and action. It highlights the complex interaction between prediction error and precision, which entails an inverted U-shaped relationship between degree of syncopation and inclination to move and experience of pleasure. The prediction errors are provoked by continuous rhythmic deviations from the musical meter (syncopations) possibly creating a discrepancy between top-down predictions from motor systems and bottom-up rhythmic input to the sensory systems, providing the brain with prediction-wise balanced temporal material for minimizing prediction error. The aesthetic and emotional experience of music thus depends on the right balance between highly probable and less probable events, engaging auditory, motor, reward and attention-related networks of the brain. This novel predictive coding understanding of music in general and the predictability of rhythms in particular, may have important consequences for how we in the future design clinical interventions for patients with movement disorders, such as e.g. for patients with Parkinson's disease [76–78] or rehabilitation after stroke [79].

References

1. Palmer, C., Lidji, P., Peretz, I.: Losing the beat: deficits in temporal coordination. Phil. Trans. R. Soc. B. **369** (2014)
2. Phillips-Silver, J., Toiviainen, P., Gosselin, N., et al.: Born to dance but beat deaf: a new form of congenital amusia. Neuropsychologia **49**, 961–969 (2011)
3. Patel, A.D., Iversen, J.R., Bregman, M.R., et al.: Experimental evidence for synchronization to a musical beat in a nonhuman animal. Curr. Biol. **19**, 827–830 (2009)
4. Cook, P., Rouse, A., Wilson, M., et al.: A California sea lion (Zalophus californianus) can keep the beat: motor entrainment to rhythmic auditory stimuli in a non vocal mimic. J. Comp. Psychol. **127**, 412–427 (2013)
5. Brochard, R., Abecasis, D., Potter, D., et al.: The "ticktock" of our internal clock: direct brain evidence of subjective accents in isochronous sequences. Psychol. Sci. **14**, 362–366 (2003)
6. Fitch, W.T.: Perception and production of syncopated rhythms. Music Percept. **25**, 43–58 (2007)
7. Handel, S., Oshinsky, J.S.: The meter of syncopated auditory polyrhythms. Percept. Psychophys. **30**, 1–9 (1981)
8. Vuust, P., Roepstorff, A., Wallentin, M., et al.: It don't mean a thing… Keeping the rhythm during polyrhythmic tension, activates language areas (BA47). Neuroimage **31**, 832–841 (2006)
9. Friston, K.: A theory of cortical responses. Philos. Trans. R. Soc. Lond. B Biol. Sci. **360**, 815–836 (2005)
10. Bar, M.: Predictions: a universal principle in the operation of the human brain. Philos. T. R. Soc. B. **364**, 1181–1182 (2009)
11. Rao, R.P., Ballard, D.H.: Predictive coding in the visual cortex: a functional interpretation of some extra-classical receptive-field effects. Nat. Neurosci. **2**, 79–87 (1999)
12. llinas, R.R.: Prediction is the ultimate function of the brain. In: Llinas, R.R. (ed.) I of the Vortex, pp. 21–52. The MIT Press, Massachusetts (2001)

13. Clark, A.: Whatever next? Predictive brains, situated agents, and the future of cognitive science. Behav. Brain Sci. **36**, 181–204 (2013)
14. Friston, K.: The free-energy principle: a unified brain theory? Nat. Rev. Neurosci. **11**, 127–138 (2010)
15. Meyer, L.: Emotion and Meaning in Music. University of Chicago Press, Chicago (1956)
16. Huron, D.: Sweet Anticipation. The MIT Book, Cambridge (2006)
17. Vuust, P., Kringelbach, M.L.: The pleasure of making meaning: evidence from the neuroscience of music. Interdisc. Sci. Rev. (ISR) **35**, 166–182 (2010)
18. Rohrmeier, M.A., Koelsch, S.: Predictive information processing in music cognition. A critical review. Int. J. Psychophysiol. **83**, 164–175 (2012)
19. Keller, P.E., Knoblich, G., Repp, B.H.: Pianists duet better when they play with themselves: on the possible role of action simulation in synchronization. Conscious. Cogn. **16**, 102–111 (2007)
20. Gebauer, L., Witek, M., Hansen, N., et al.: Oxytocin improves synchronisation in leader-follower interaction. Sci. Rep. **6** (2016)
21. Konvalinka, I., Vuust, P., Roepstorff, A., et al.: Follow you, follow me: continuous mutual prediction and adaptation in joint tapping. Q. J. Exp. Psychol. (2010)
22. Vuust, P., Ostergaard, L., Pallesen, K.J., et al.: Predictive coding of music. Cortex **45**, 80–92 (2009)
23. Friston, K., Friston, D.A.: A free energy formulation of music generation and perception: Helmholtz Revisited. In: Bader, R. (ed.) Sound - Perception - Performance, vol. 1, pp. 43–69. Springer, Cham (2013). https://doi.org/10.1007/978-3-319-00107-4_2
24. Schaefer, R.S., Overy, K., Nelson, P.: Affect and non-uniform characteristics of predictive processing in musical behaviour. Behav. Brain Sci. **36**, 2 (2013)
25. Witek, M.A.G., Clarke, E.F., Wallentin, M., et al.: Syncopation, body-movement and pleasure in groove music. PLoS ONE **9**, e94446 (2014)
26. Witek, M.A., Popescu, T., Clarke, E.F., et al.: Syncopation affects free body-movement in musical groove. Exp. Brain Res. **235**, 995–1005 (2017)
27. Witek, M.A.: Filling in: syncopation, pleasure and distributed embodiment in groove. Music Analysis (2016)
28. Witek, M.A.G., Clarke, E.F., Kringelbach, M.L., Vuust, P.: Effects of polyphonic context and instrumentation on syncopation in music. Music Percept. **32**, 201–217 (2014)
29. Wundt, W.: Grundzuge der physiologischen psychologie. Englemann, Leipzig (1874)
30. North, A.C., Hargreaves, D.J.: Subjective complexity, familiarity, and liking for popular music. Psychomusicology **14**, 77–93 (1995)
31. North, A.C., Hargreaves, D.J.: Experimental aesthetics and everyday music listening. In: Hargreaves, D.J., North, A.C. (eds.) The Social Psychology of Music. Oxford University Press, Oxford (1997)
32. Orr, M.G., Ohlsson, S.: Relationship Between complexity and liking as a function of expertise. Music Percept. **22**, 583–611 (2005)
33. Berlyne, D.E.: Aesthetics and Psychobiology. Appleton-Century-Crofts, East Norwalk (1971)
34. Witek, M.A., Clarke, E.F., Wallentin, M., et al.: Correction: syncopation, body-movement and pleasure in groove music. PloS one. **10** (2015)
35. Vuust, P., Dietz, M., Witek, M., Kringelbach, M.: Now you hear it: a predictive coding model for understanding rhythmic incongruity. Ann. New York Acad. Sci. (2018, in press)
36. Garrido, M.I., Sahani, M., Dolan, R.J.: Outlier responses reflect sensitivity to statistical structure in the human brain. PLoS Comput. Biol. **9**, e1002999 (2013)
37. Friston, K.: Learning and inference in the brain. Neural Netw. **16**, 1325–1352 (2003)

38. Brown, H., Adams, R.A., Parees, I., et al.: Active inference, sensory attenuation and illusions. Cogn. Process. **14**, 411–427 (2013)
39. Sams, M., Paavilainen, P., Alho, K., et al.: Auditory frequency discrimination and event-related potentials. Electroencephalogr. Clin. Neurophysiol. **62**, 437–448 (1985)
40. Näätänen, R., Paaviliainen, P., Alho, K., et al.: The mismatch negativity to intensity changes in an auditory stimulus sequence. Electroencephalogr. Clin. Neurophysiol. **40**, 125–131 (1987)
41. Dietz, M.J., Friston, K.J., Mattingley, J.B., et al.: Effective connectivity reveals right-hemisphere dominance in audiospatial perception: implications for models of spatial neglect. J. Neurosci. **34**, 5003–5011 (2014)
42. Paavilainen, P., Karlsson, M.-L., Reinikainen, K., et al.: Mismatch negativity to change in spatial location of an auditory stimulus. Electroencephalogr. Clin. Neurophysiol. **73**, 129–141 (1989)
43. Paavilainen, P., Simola, J., Jaramillo, M., et al.: Preattentive extraction of abstract feature conjunctions from auditory stimulation as reflected by the mismatch negativity (MMN). Psychophysiology **38**, 359–365 (2001)
44. Van Zuijen, T.L., Sussman, E., Winkler, I., et al.: Grouping of sequential sounds-an event-related potential study comparing musicians and nonmusicians. J. Cogn. Neurosci. **16**, 331–338 (2004)
45. Friedman, D., Cycowicz, Y.M., Gaeta, H.: The novelty P3: an event-related brain potential (ERP) sign of the brain's evaluation of novelty. Neurosci. Biobehav. Rev. **25**, 355–373 (2001)
46. Knight, R.T., Scabini, D.: Anatomic bases of event-related potentials and their relationship to novelty detection in humans. J. Clin. Neurophysiol. **15**, 3–13 (1998)
47. Woods, D.L.: The physiological basis of selective attention: implications of event-related potential studies. In: Event-related Brain Potentials: Basic Issues and Applications, pp. 178–209 (1990)
48. Schröger, E.: A neural mechanism for involuntary attention shifts to changes in auditory stimulation. J. Cogn. Neurosci. **8**, 527–539 (1996)
49. Escera, C., Alho, K., Schröger, E., et al.: Involuntary attention and distractibility as evaluated with event-related brain potentials. Audiol. Neurootol. **5**, 151–166 (2000)
50. Feldman, H., Friston, K.J.: Attention, uncertainty, and free-energy. Front. Hum. Neurosci. **4**, 215 (2010)
51. Grahn, J.A., McAuley, J.D.: Neural bases of individual differences in beat perception. Neuroimage **47**, 1894–1903 (2009)
52. van Rijn, H., Gu, B.-M., Meck, W.H.: Dedicated clock/timing-circuit theories of time perception and timed performance. In: Merchant, H., de Lafuente, V. (eds.) Neurobiology of interval timing. AEMB, vol. 829, pp. 75–99. Springer, New York (2014). https://doi.org/10.1007/978-1-4939-1782-2_5
53. Chen, J.L., Penhune, V.B., Zatorre, R.J.: Moving on time: brain network for auditory-motor synchronization is modulated by rhythm complexity and musical training. J. Cogn. Neurosci. **20**, 226–239 (2008)
54. Kung, S.J., Chen, J.L., Zatorre, R.J., et al.: Interacting cortical and basal ganglia networks underlying finding and tapping to the musical beat. J. Cogn. Neurosci. **25**, 401–420 (2013)
55. Grahn, J.A., Brett, M.: Rhythm and beat perception in motor areas of the brain. J. Cogn. Neurosci. **19**, 893–906 (2007)
56. Todd, N.P., Lee, C.S.: The sensory-motor theory of rhythm and beat induction 20 years on: a new synthesis and future perspectives. Front. Hum. Neurosci. **9**, 444 (2015)

57. Vuust, P., Ostergaard, L., Roepstorff, A.: Polyrhythmic communicational devices appear as language in the brains of musicians. In: International Conference on Music Perception and Cognition, vol. ICMPC9, pp. 1159–1167. ESCOM, Bologna (2006)
58. Vuust, P., Wallentin, M., Mouridsen, K., et al.: Tapping polyrhythms in music activates language areas. Neurosci. Lett. (2011)
59. Phillips-Silver, J., Trainor, L.J.: Feeling the beat: movement influences infant rhythm perception. Science **308**, 1430 (2005)
60. Burger, B., London, J., Thompson, M.R., et al.: Synchronization to metrical levels in music depends on low-frequency spectral components and tempo. Psychol. Res. (2017)
61. Grahn, J.A., Rowe, J.B.: Feeling the beat: premotor and striatal interactions in musicians and nonmusicians during beat perception. J. Neurosci. **29**, 7540–7548 (2009)
62. Large, E.W., Herrera, J.A., Velasco, M.J.: Neural networks for beat perception in musical rhythm. Front. Syst. Neurosci. **9**, 159 (2015)
63. Guckenheimer, J., Labouriau, J.S.: Bifurcation of the Hodgkin and Huxley equations: a new twist. Bull. Math. Biol. **55**, 937 (1993)
64. Blood, A.J., Zatorre, R.J.: Intensely pleasurable responses to music correlate with activity in brain regions implicated in reward and emotion. Proc. Natl. Acad. Sci. U.S.A. **98**, 11818–11823 (2001)
65. Salimpoor, V.N., Benovoy, M., Longo, G., et al.: The rewarding aspects of music listening are related to degree of emotional arousal. PLoS ONE **4**, e7487 (2009)
66. Gebauer, L., Kringelbach, M.L., Vuust, P.: Ever-changing cycles of musical pleasure: the role of dopamine and anticipation. Psychomusicologys **22**, 152–167 (2012)
67. Schultz, W.: Behavioral dopamine signals. Trends Neurosci. **30**, 203–210 (2007)
68. Schultz, W., Preuschoff, K., Camerer, C., et al.: Explicit neural signals reflecting reward uncertainty. Phil. Trans. R. Soc. B Biol. Sci. **363**, 3801–3811 (2008)
69. Hansen, N.C., Dietz, M.J., Vuust, P.: Commentary: predictions and the brain: how musical sounds become rewarding. Front. Hum. Neurosci. **11** (2017)
70. Schultz, W., Dayan, P., Montague, P.R.: A neural substrate of prediction and reward. Science **275**, 1593–1599 (1997)
71. Kringelbach, M.L., Berridge, K.C.: Towards a functional neuroanatomy of pleasure and happiness. Trends Cogn. Sci. **13**, 479–487 (2009)
72. Hohwy, J.: The self-evidencing brain. Noûs **50**, 259–285 (2016)
73. Pearce, M.T., Wiggins, G.: Expectation in melody: the influence of context and learning. Music Percept. **23**, 29 (2006)
74. Green, A.C., Baerentsen, K.B., Stodkilde-Jorgensen, H., et al.: Listen, learn, like! Dorsolateral prefrontal cortex involved in the mere exposure effect in music. Neurol. Res. Int. **2012**, 846270 (2012)
75. Zajonc, R.B.: Attitudinal effects of mere exposure. J. Pers. Soc. Psychol. **9**, 1 (1968)
76. Grahn, J.A., Brett, M.: Impairment of beat-based rhythm discrimination in Parkinson's disease. Cortex. **45**, 54–61 (2009)
77. Thaut, M.H., McIntosh, G.C.: Music therapy in mobility training with the elderly: a review of current research. Care Manag. J.: Journal of Case Management; The Journal of Long Term Home Health Care **1**, 71–74 (1999)
78. Benoit, C.-E., Dalla Bella, S., Farrugia, N., et al.: Musically cued gait-training improves both perceptual and motor timing in Parkinson's disease. Front. Hum. Neurosci. **8**, 494 (2014)
79. Altenmüller, E., Marco-Pallares, J., Münte, T.F., et al.: Neural reorganization underlies improvement in stroke-induced motor dysfunction by music-supported therapy. Ann. N. Y. Acad. Sci. **1169**, 395–405 (2009)

Finding Drum Breaks in Digital Music Recordings

Patricio López-Serrano(✉), Christian Dittmar, and Meinard Müller

International Audio Laboratories Erlangen, 91058 Erlangen, Germany
patricio.lopez.serrano@audiolabs-erlangen.de

Abstract. DJs and producers of sample-based electronic dance music (EDM) use breakbeats as an essential building block and rhythmic foundation for their artistic work. The practice of reusing and resequencing sampled drum breaks critically influenced modern musical genres such as hip hop, drum'n'bass, and jungle. While EDM artists have primarily sourced drum breaks from funk, soul, and jazz recordings from the 1960s to 1980s, they can potentially be sampled from music of any genre. In this paper, we introduce and formalize the task of automatically finding suitable drum breaks in music recordings. By adapting an approach previously used for singing voice detection, we establish a first baseline for drum break detection. Besides a quantitative evaluation, we discuss benefits and limitations of our procedure by considering a number of challenging examples.

Keywords: Music information retrieval · Drum break · Breakbeat
Electronic dance music · Audio classification · Machine learning

1   Introduction

Musical structure arises through the relationships between segments in a song. For instance, a segment can be characterized as *homogeneous* with respect to instrumentation or tempo [17, p. 171]. Structure is also driven by introducing or removing certain instruments, as is the case of solo sections. Music information retrieval (MIR) research has studied these phenomena through tasks such as structure analysis [18] and singing voice detection [8,14]. In this paper we focus on finding *drum break* sections, which are homogeneous with respect to instrumentation (i. e., they only contain drums) and often contrast with neighboring segments, where additional instruments are active.

Based mainly on [20], we present the notion of *drum break*, together with its history and usage. *Drum breaks*, *breaks*, or *breakbeats* are percussion-only passages typically found in funk, soul, and jazz recordings. Breaks first came into use within early hip hop DJ practice: by taking two copies of the same record (on separate turntables) along with a mixer, DJs could isolate and loop these sections, which were particularly popular with the dancers and audience. When digital sampling technology became affordable for use at home and small studios,

© Springer Nature Switzerland AG 2018
M. Aramaki et al. (Eds.): CMMR 2017, LNCS 11265, pp. 111–122, 2018.
https://doi.org/10.1007/978-3-030-01692-0_8

Fig. 1. *Top*: Schematic illustration of a drum break on a vinyl record. *Bottom*: Location of drum break (enclosed in red) within waveform. (Color figure online)

producers started using breaks to create their own tracks by adding further musical material and rearranging the individual drum hits into new rhythms. These musical practices are a cornerstone of genres like hip hop, jungle, and drum'n'bass; they helped develop a considerable body of knowledge about the nature and location of breakbeats, fostering a culture that valued finding rare and unheard breaks.

At this point, we need to make a distinction regarding the term *break*. The sections that producers choose for looping and sampling are not always exclusively made up of percussion instruments: many famous breaks also contain non-percussion instruments, such as bass or strings. Under a broader definition, a break can be any musical segment (typically four measures or less), even if it doesn't contain percussion [20]. In this paper we use *break* to designate regions containing only percussion instruments, for two reasons. First, percussion-only breaks afford producers the greatest flexibility when incorporating their own tonal and harmonic content, thus avoiding dissonant compositions (also known as "key clash"). Second, it allows us to unambiguously define our task: given a funk, soul, or jazz recording, we wish to identify passages which only contain percussion, i.e., detect the drum breaks. In the top portion of Fig. 1 we show, in a simplified manner, the location of a drum break on a vinyl record. On the bottom we illustrate our task in this paper, which is finding percussion-only regions in digital music recordings.

Originally, vinyl records were the prime source for sampling material. When looking for rare breaks, artists visit record stores, basements and flea markets (known as "[crate] digging"). Once they acquire a record, artists carefully listen to the entire content, sometimes skipping at random with the needle on the turntable, until they find an appealing section to work with. Motivated by the current predominance and size of digital music collections, we propose a method to automate digging in the digital context.

The main contributions of this paper are as follows. In Sect. 2 we introduce the task of drum break detection and some of the difficulties that arise when trying to define it as a binary classification problem concerned with finding percussion-only passages. In Sect. 3 we present related work, the features we used, and a baseline approach adapted from a machine learning method for singing voice detection. By doing so, we explore how well machine learning techniques can be transferred to a completely different domain. In Sect. 4 we introduce our dataset and elaborate on its most important statistical properties, as well as our annotation process. The dataset represents the real-world music typically sampled in this EDM scenario. Together with a statistical overview of the results, we also go into greater detail, analyzing two difficult examples we found in our dataset. In Sect. 5 we give conclusions and future work for our paper.

2 Task Specification

In Sect. 1 we set our task as finding percussion-only passages in a given musical piece—a seemingly straightforward problem definition. Detecting breaks can thus be reduced to discriminating between percussion instruments—which contribute exclusively to rhythm—and all other instruments which contribute (mainly) to melody and harmony. We will now examine why this distinction is problematic from the perspective of prevalent music processing tasks. *Harmonic-percussive source separation* (HPSS) is a technique that aims to decompose a signal into its constituent components, according to their spectral properties [10,17]. HPSS methods usually assign sustained, pitched sounds to the harmonic component, and transient, unpitched sounds to the percussive component. From an HPSS standpoint, our class of desired instruments has both harmonic and percussive signal components: many drum kit pieces such as kicks, snares, and toms have a discernible pitch, although they are not considered to contribute to the melody or harmony. Thus, drum break retrieval is difficult because of overlapping acoustic properties between our desired and undesired instruments—in other words, it is very hard to give an intensional definition of our target set's characteristics.

Our task lies between the practical definition of *drum break* and a technical definition used for automated retrieval—with a significant gap in between. On the technical side, we have opted for the term *percussion-only passage* instead of *drum break* due to the presence of percussion instruments which are not part of a standard drum kit, such as congas, bongos, timbales, and shakers. As a final note, we also distinguish between [*drum*] *breaks* and *breakbeats*: we interpret the former as a percussion-only segment within a recording (in its "natural" or "original" state), and the latter as a [drum] break which has been spotted and potentially manipulated by the artist.

3 Baseline System and Experiments

3.1 Related Work

There are relatively few publications in the MIR field on drum breaks and breakbeats. In [2,3], the authors investigate automatic sample identification for hip hop via fingerprinting. A multifaceted study of breakbeats which covers beat tracking, tempo induction, downbeat detection, and percussion identification can be found in [11]. Furthermore, given a certain breakbeat, the authors of [12] automatically retrieve hardcore, jungle, and drum'n'bass (HJDB) tracks where it is present. On the musicological side, [19] proposes a typology of sampled material in EDM, where breakbeats are considered at fine and coarse temporal scales. Putting our paper in context, we can think of the typical artistic work-flow in two steps: drum break discovery and manipulation. To the extent of our knowledge, research has mainly focused on the second phase—after breakbeats have been extracted and manipulated. Following this analogy, our task would be at the first stage, where the artist wishes to filter useful musical material. In a fully automated pipeline, our proposed system could be inserted before any of the tasks mentioned above.

3.2 Baseline System

Our baseline system follows [14], an approach for singing voice detection (SVD). SVD is used to determine the regions of a music recording where vocal activity is present. In [14], the authors address the problem that automated techniques frequently confuse singing voice with other pitch-continuous and pitch-varying instruments. They introduce new audio features—*fluctogram*, *spectral flatness/contraction*, and *vocal variance* (VOCVAR)—which are combined with mel-frequency cepstral coefficients (MFCCs) and subjected to machine learning. VOCVAR is strongly related to MFCCs—it captures the variance in the first five MFCCs across a number of consecutive frames. Spectral contraction and spectral flatness (FLAT) are extracted in logarithmically spaced, overlapping frequency bands. The spectral contrast features OBSC [13] and SBSC [1] encode the relation of peaks to valleys of the spectral magnitude in sub-bands. In general, both variants can be interpreted as harmonicity or tonality descriptors.

In this paper we use a subset of the features from [14], along with a set of novel features derived from *harmonic-residual-percussive source separation* (HRPSS). HRPSS is a technique used to decompose signals into tonal, noise-like, and transient components [9]. The *cascaded harmonic-residual-percussive* (CHRP) feature was recently proposed in [16]; by iteratively applying HRPSS to a signal and measuring the component energies, this feature captures timbral properties along the HRP axis. We have included a seven-dimensional variant of CHRP for our experiments. Concatenating all features results in a vector with 83 entries (dimensions) per spectral frame. The set of all vectors makes up our feature matrix, which is split into training, validation, and test sets for use with machine learning.

Again following [14], we employ random forests (RF) [4] as a classification scheme. RF deliver a frame-wise score value per class that can be interpreted as a confidence measure for the classifier decision. In our binary classification scenario, the two score functions are inversely proportional. We pick the one corresponding to our target *percussion-only* class and refer to it as *decision function* in the following. A decision function value close to 1 indicates a very reliable assignment to the percussion-only class, whereas a value close to 0 points to the opposite. Only frames where the decision function value exceeds the

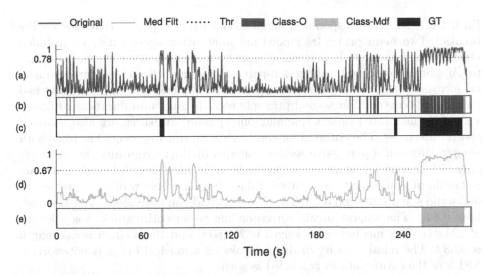

Fig. 2. (a): Original, unprocessed decision function (the output of the random forest classifier, interpreted as the confidence that a frame belongs to the *percussion-only* class, solid blue curve); optimal threshold value (0.78, dotted black line). (b): Binary classification for original decision function (blue rectangles). (c): Ground truth annotation (black rectangles). (d): Decision function after median filtering with a filter length of 2.2 s (solid red curve); optimal threshold (0.67, dotted black line). (e): Binary classification for median-filtered decision function (red rectangles). (Color figure online)

threshold will be classified as belonging to the percussion-only class. Prior to binarization, the decision function can be smoothed using a median filter, helping stabilize the detection and preventing unreasonably short spikes where the classification flips between both classes. Figure 2 illustrates the concepts mentioned above. Figure 2a (blue curve) shows the original, unprocessed decision function for *Funky Drummer* by James Brown. The ground truth (black rectangles, Fig. 2c) has three annotated breaks: shortly after 60 s, shortly before 240 s, and after 240 s (black rectangles). In Fig. 2d (red curve) we show the median-filtered decision, using a filter length of 2.2 s. In both Fig. 2a and d, the dotted black line represents the decision threshold (0.78 and 0.67, respectively). In Fig. 2b (solid blue rectangles) and Fig. 2e (solid red rectangles) we show the classification results for the original and median-filtered decision functions. In the remainder of this paper, all plots related to the original decision function are blue; the ones corresponding to median filtering are red.

4 Evaluation

4.1 Dataset

Our dataset consists of 280 full recordings, covering funk, soul, jazz, rock, and other genres. All audio files are mono and have a sampling rate of 22050 Hz.

Each track has a corresponding annotation with timepoints that enclose the breaks.[1] Two main principles guided our annotation style. First, we included regions containing strictly percussion, disregarding metrical structure. For example, if a break contained trailing non-percussive content from the previous musical measure (bar), we set the starting point after the undesirable component had reasonably decayed. Our second principle regards minimum duration: although we mostly annotated breaks spanning one or more measures, we also included shorter instances. The criterion for considering shorter fragments has to do with *sampleability*—if a percussive section contains distinct drum hits (for instance, only kick or snare), it is included. On the other hand, a short fill (such as a snare roll or flam) would not be annotated. Table 1 has an overview of the statistics for our audio and annotation data. The shortest break, an individual cymbal sound, lasts 0.84 s. The longest break, corresponding to an entire track, has a length of 224.84 s. The median track length is 251.80 s, and the median break length is 6.83 s. The relative rarity of drum breaks as a musical event is noteworthy: 5.81% of the entire dataset is labeled as such.

Table 1. Statistical overview for audio and annotation data.

Measure	Track length (s)	Break length (s)	Breaks (per track)
Min	77.00	0.84	1.00
Max	1116.00	224.84	9.00
Mean	277.11	10.23	1.55
Median	251.80	6.83	1.00
Std. dev.	128.49	17.43	1.18
Dataset total	77 600.00	4 500.00	433.00

During the annotation process, we made interesting observations on how humans treat the breakbeat retrieval problem. We used Sonic Visualiser [6] to annotate the start and end of percussion-only passages. At the dawn of EDM, when vinyl was the only medium in use, artists devotedly looking for unheard breakbeats would listen to a record by skipping with the needle through the grooves.[2] With the help of Sonic Visualiser, we found it very effective to scrub through the audio, moving the playhead forward at short, random intervals, also using visual cues from the waveform and spectrogram.

For our particular task, this fragmented, non-sequential method of seeking breaks seemed to be sufficient for listeners with enough expertise. This leads

---

[1] A complete list of track titles, artists, and YouTube™ identifiers is available at the accompanying website, along with annotations in plaintext. https://www.audiolabs-erlangen.de/resources/MIR/2017-CMMR-Breaks.

[2] In [5, p. 247], the authors relate that "[Grand Wizard] Theodore could do something amazing: he could find the beginning of a break by eye and drop the needle right on it, with no need to spin the record back."

us to believe that a frame-wise classification approach provides a satisfactory baseline model for this task. Of course, in order to refine the start and end of the percussion-only passages, we had to listen more carefully and visually inspect the waveform. As we will show, precise localization also poses a major challenge for automatic break retrieval.

4.2 Results

We now discuss the evaluation results for our experiments conducted on the entire dataset. We use the *framewise F-measure* as an evaluation strategy. Frames with a positive classification that coincide with an annotated break are counted as *true positives* (TP), frames with a negative classification that coincide with an annotated break are *false negatives* (FN), and frames with a positive classification that do not coincide with an annotated break are considered *false positives* (FP). The three quantities are represented in the F-measure by

$$F = \frac{2 \cdot \text{TP}}{2 \cdot \text{TP} + \text{FP} + \text{FN}}. \tag{1}$$

In order to reduce the *album effect*, we discarded tracks from our dataset, arriving at a subset with one track per unique artist (from 280 to 220 tracks). We performed a ten-fold cross validation: for each fold, we randomly chose 70% of the tracks for training (155 tracks), 15% (33 tracks) for validation, and 15% (34 tracks) for testing. Since the classes *percussion-only* and *not only percussion* are strongly unbalanced (see statistic in Sect. 4.1), training was done with balanced data. That means that for each track, all *percussion-only* frames are taken as positive examples, and an equal number of *not only percussion* frames are taken as negative examples. Validation and testing are done with unbalanced data [7]. During validation, we perform a parameter sweep for the decision threshold and median filter length.

Figure 3 gives an overview of experiments with threshold and median filter length. Figure 3a is a parameter sweep matrix across all folds, where each row corresponds to a certain threshold value, and each column is a median filter length. Each entry in the matrix is the mean F-measure across all ten folds, for the testing phase. Darker entries represent a higher F-measure—the colormap was shifted to enhance visibility. The red circle denotes the optimal configuration: a threshold of 0.67 and a median filter length of 4.6 s yield an F-measure of 0.79. The blue triangle at threshold value 0.78 indicates the highest F-measure (0.68) without median filtering. Figures 3c and d contain curves extracted from this matrix. In Fig. 3c, the curve corresponds to the highlighted row in the matrix (i. e., for a fixed threshold and varying median filter length). Figure 3d is the converse: we show the highlighted column of the matrix, with a fixed median filter length and varying threshold. In both Fig. 3c and d, the light red area surrounding the main curve is the standard deviation across folds. Figure 3b compares the F-measures between the original (unprocessed) binarized decision curve (blue) and after median filtering (red)—with respect to increasing thresholds (horizontal axis).

In Fig. 3a we can see that the choice of threshold has a greater effect on F-measure than the median filter length: the differences between rows are more pronounced than between columns. Indeed, Fig. 3b shows that *original* and *median filtered* have a similar dependency on the threshold. The solid red curve in Fig. 3c starts at an F-measure of 0.67 (without median filtering), reaches a peak at F-measure 0.79 (median filter length 4.6 s) and then drops to 0.76 for the longest tested median filter window (9.8 s). The standard deviation is stable across all median filter lengths, amounting to about 0.06. In Fig. 3d, the mean F-measure goes from below 0.2 (at threshold 0), through the optimal value (0.79 at threshold 0.67), and decays rapidly for the remaining higher threshold values. The standard deviation widens in proximity to the optimal F-measure. It is interesting that the optimal median filter length (4.6 s) is about half the mean annotated break length (10.23 s). This median filter length seems to offer the best trade-off between closing gaps in the detection (as seen in the last break of Fig. 2e), removing isolated false positives (seen throughout Fig. 2e), and reducing true positives (seen in the two first short breaks in Fig. 2e).

Table 2 summarizes statistics over multiple experimental configurations. Each column contains the mean, median and standard deviation (SD) for the F-measure across ten folds. The mean F-measure for the original (unprocessed) decision function is 0.68, and it corresponds to a threshold value of 0.78. Median filtering with a length of 4.6 s, together with a threshold of 0.67, yields an optimal mean F-Measure of 0.79. Generating a random decision function leads to a mean F-Measure of 0.09; labeling all frames as *purely percussive* (seen in the *biased* column) delivers 0.11.

Table 2. Evaluation results with optimal parameters. Rows are statistical measures, columns are experimental configurations.

Measure	Original	MedFilt	Random	Biased
Mean	0.6816	0.7923	0.0963	0.1170
Median	0.6636	0.7997	0.0951	0.1133
Std. dev.	0.0620	0.0636	0.0180	0.0259

The first important result from Table 2 is that variants of our approach (original and median-filtered) yield F-measures between six and seven times higher than randomly generating decision functions, or simply labeling all frames as *percussion-only* (biased). Second, we can see that median filtering increases the F-measure by about 0.11 (from 0.68 to 0.79). As seen in Fig. 2b and e, median filtering removes most false positives (boosting precision), but can also diminish (or completely remove) true positives, as is the case with the short break after 240 s. Finally, we can also be confident of the usefulness of median filtering because it increases the mean F-measure without affecting the standard deviation (0.06 in both cases).

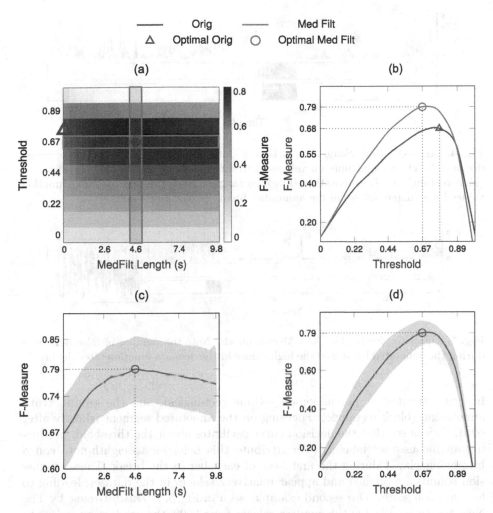

Fig. 3. (**a**): Parameter sweep for median filter length (horizontal axis) and threshold (vertical axis). Darker entries of the matrix have a higher mean F-measure. The colormap has been shifted to enhance visibility, markers denote optimal configurations. (**b**): F-measure for unprocessed (blue) and median filtered (red) decisions, depending on threshold (horizontal axis). (**c**): Highlighted row of parameter sweep matrix. (**d**): Highlighted column of parameter sweep matrix. (Color figure online)

4.3 Some Notorious Examples

Beyond the large-scale results from Sect. 4, we now show some examples that posed specific challenges to our classification scheme. The first case is *Ride, Sally, Ride* by Dennis Coffey (Fig. 4), recorded in 1972. From top to bottom, Fig. 4 shows the decision function output by the RF (solid blue curve), the threshold value optimized during validation and testing (black dotted line), the

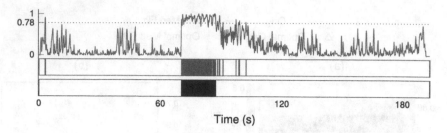

Fig. 4. Results for *Ride, Sally, Ride* by Dennis Coffey. From top to bottom: unprocessed decision function (solid blue curve) and threshold (dotted black line), classification (blue rectangles), GT annotation (black rectangle). Note the high decision function values immediately following the annotated break. (Color figure online)

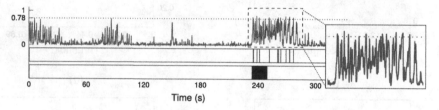

Fig. 5. *Dusty Groove* by The New Mastersounds. Note the number of false negatives during the annotated break and the high values in the decision function after the break.

frames estimated as percussion-only (blue rectangles), and the ground truth annotation (black rectangle). Focusing on the annotated segment (shortly after 60 s), we can see that the decision curve oscillates about the threshold, producing an inconsistent labeling. We attribute this behavior to eighth-note conga hits being played during the first beat of each bar in the break. These percussion sounds are pitched and appear relatively seldom in the dataset, leading to low decision scores. Our second example, seen in Fig. 5, is *Dusty Groove* by The New Mastersounds. On this modern release from 2009, the production strives to replicate the "vintage" sound found on older recordings. Around the annotated region (240 s) we highlight two issues: during the break, there are few frames classified as percussion-only, and the decision curve maintains a relatively high mean value well after the break. Again, we ascribe the misdetection during the break to the presence of drum hits with strong tonal content. Especially the snare has a distinct sound that is overtone-rich and has a longer decay than usual, almost reminiscent of timbales. After the annotated break the percussion continue, but a bass guitar playing mostly sixteenth and syncopated, staccato eighth notes appears—upon closer inspection, we observed that the onsets of the bass guitar synchronize quite well with those of the bass drum. When played simultaneously, the spectral content of both the bass drum and bass guitar overlaps considerably, creating a hybrid sound closer to percussion than a pitched instrument.

5   Conclusions and Future Work

We presented a system to find percussion-only passages (drum breaks) in digital music recordings. To establish a baseline for this binary classification task, we built our system around the work of [8,14]. With this paper we investigated to which extent binary classification methods are transferable across tasks.

Having established this baseline, in future work we wish to improve detection for difficult examples (as described in Sect. 4.3), and include genres beyond the ones studied here. When implementing machine learning techniques, it is important to address the issue of overfitting. We are aware that our dataset induces a strong genre-related bias, but it reflects the real-world bias (or practice) that EDM artists follow when selecting sampling material. Going beyond results with the F-measure, an interesting alternative to evaluate our approach would be to conduct user experience tests, measuring the potential speedup in drum break location. As for applications, DJs and producers could use our system to retrieve drum breaks from large digital collections, considerably reducing the time needed for *digging*. Our procedure can also be used as a pre-processing step for breakbeat identification tasks, as outlined in [3,12]; or for structure analysis of loop-based EDM [15]. Finally, MIR researchers could use this system to compile datasets for other tasks such as beat tracking and drum transcription.

Acknowledgments. Patricio López-Serrano is supported by a scholarship from CONACYT-DAAD. Christian Dittmar and Meinard Müller are supported by the German Research Foundation (DFG-MU 2686/10-1). The International Audio Laboratories Erlangen are a joint institution of the Friedrich-Alexander-Universität Erlangen-Nürnberg (FAU) and Fraunhofer Institute for Integrated Circuits IIS. We would like to thank the organizers of *HAMR* Hack Day at ISMIR 2016, where the core ideas of the presented work were born.

References

1. Akkermans, V., Serrá, J.: Shape-based spectral contrast descriptor. In: Proceedings of the Sound and Music Computing Conference (SMC), Porto, Portugal, pp. 143–148 (2009)
2. Van Balen, J.: Automatic recognition of samples in musical audio. Master's thesis, Universitat Pompeu Fabra, Barcelona, Spain (2011)
3. Van Balen, J., Haro, M., Serrà, J.: Automatic identification of samples in hip hop music. In: International Symposium on Computer Music Modeling and Retrieval (CMMR), London, UK, pp. 544–551 (2012)
4. Breiman, L.: Random forests. Mach. Learn. **45**(1), 5–32 (2001)
5. Brewster, B., Broughton, F.: Last Night a DJ Saved My Life: The History of the Disc Jockey. Grove Press, New York (2014)
6. Cannam, C., Landone, C., Sandler, M.B.: Sonic visualiser: an open source application for viewing, analysing, and annotating music audio files. In: Proceedings of the ACM International Conference on Multimedia, Firenze, Italy, pp. 1467–1468 (2010)
7. Chen, C., Liaw, A., Breiman, L.: Using random forest to learn imbalanced data. Technical report (2004)

8. Dittmar, C., Lehner, B., Prätzlich, T., Müller, M., Widmer, G.: Cross-version singing voice detection in classical opera recordings. In: Proceedings of the International Society for Music Information Retrieval Conference (ISMIR), Málaga, Spain, pp. 618–624 (2015)
9. Driedger, J., Müller, M., Disch, S.: Extending harmonic-percussive separation of audio signals. In: Proceedings of the International Society for Music Information Retrieval (ISMIR), Taipei, Taiwan, pp. 611–616 (2014)
10. Fitzgerald, D.: Harmonic/percussive separation using median filtering. In: Proceedings of the International Conference on Digital Audio Effects (DAFx), Graz, Austria, pp. 246–253 (2010)
11. Hockman, J.A.: An ethnographic and technological study of breakbeats in Hardcore, Jungle, and Drum & Bass. Ph.D. thesis, McGill University, Montreal, Quebec, Canada (2012)
12. Hockman, J.A., Davies, M.E.P., Fujinaga, I.: Computational strategies for breakbeat classification and resequencing in Hardcore, Jungle and Drum & Bass. In: Proceedings of the International Conference on Digital Audio Effects (DAFx), Trondheim, Norway (2015)
13. Jiang, D., Lu, L., Zhang, H.J., Tao, J.H., Cai, L.H.: Music type classification by spectral contrast feature. In: Proceedings of the IEEE International Conference on Multimedia and Expo (ICME), Lausanne, Switzerland, vol. 1, pp. 113–116 (2002)
14. Lehner, B., Widmer, G., Sonnleitner, R.: On the reduction of false positives in singing voice detection. In: Proceedings of the IEEE International Conference on Acoustics, Speech, and Signal Processing (ICASSP), Florence, Italy, pp. 7480–7484 (2014)
15. López-Serrano, P., Dittmar, C., Driedger, J., Müller, M.: Towards modeling and decomposing loop-based electronic music. In: Proceedings of the International Conference on Music Information Retrieval (ISMIR), New York, USA, pp. 502–508 (2016)
16. López-Serrano, P., Dittmar, C., Müller, M.: Mid-level audio features based on cascaded harmonic-residual-percussive separation. In: Proceedings of the Audio Engineering Society AES Conference on Semantic Audio, Erlangen, Germany (2017)
17. Müller, M.: Fundamentals of Music Processing. Springer, Cham (2015). https://doi.org/10.1007/978-3-319-21945-5
18. Paulus, J., Müller, M., Klapuri, A.P.: Audio-based music structure analysis. In: Proceedings of the International Society for Music Information Retrieval (ISMIR), Utrecht, The Netherlands, pp. 625–636 (2010)
19. Ratcliffe, R.: A proposed typology of sampled material within electronic dance music. Danc. J. Electron. Danc. Music. Cult. 6(1), 97–122 (2014)
20. Schloss, J.G.: Making Beats: The Art of Sample-Based Hip-Hop. Music Culture. Wesleyan University Press, Middletown (2014)

Drum Rhythm Spaces: From Global Models to Style-Specific Maps

Daniel Gómez-Marín$^{(\boxtimes)}$, Sergi Jordà, and Perfecto Herrera

Music Technology Group, Universitat Pompeu Fabra,
Carrer de Tànger, 122, 08018 Barcelona, Spain
daniel.gomez@upf.edu

Abstract. This paper presents two experiments carried out to find rhythm descriptors that allow the organization of drum patterns in spaces resembling subjects similarity sensations. We revisit rhythm spaces published by Alf Gabrielsson in 1973, based on subject similarity ratings of drum rhythms from an early drum machine, and construct a new rhythm space based on similarity judgments using contemporary electronic dance music (EDM) patterns. We observe how a specific set of descriptors can be used to reconstruct both Gabrielsson's and the new EDM space, suggesting the descriptors capture drum similarity sensations in very different contexts. The set of descriptors and the methods employed are explained with detail and the possibility of having method for organizing rhythm patterns automatically is discussed.

Keywords: Rhythm space · Electronic Dance Music (EDM)
Drum patterns · Rhythm representations · Music cognition
Conceptual maps

1 Introduction

Today there is an abundance of digital resources for Electronic Dance Music (EDM) composition: Gigabytes of one-shot drum sample libraries, drum loops and any other building block in the EDM production pipeline can be easily acquired and even freely downloaded from the internet. Although this proliferation can be very positive, it has an adverse effect which happens at the actual moment of starting to work and browsing (perhaps alphabetically or by date) through a collection of hundreds of poorly labeled musical files. Abundance in digital music production, and in any other context where work is based on digital media, becomes a problem. Therefore useful tools for dealing with specific information in an ordered and user centered manner must be developed. In this paper we focus on how to take advantage of abstract mappings (i.e., perceptual spaces, motivated by the specificities of human rhythm perception) to improve over the experience of organizing and retrieving audio or symbolic drum patterns.

For humans, processing and understanding a collection of items, as drum patterns, is accomplished by creating relations among those items and with other

© Springer Nature Switzerland AG 2018
M. Aramaki et al. (Eds.): CMMR 2017, LNCS 11265, pp. 123–134, 2018.
https://doi.org/10.1007/978-3-030-01692-0_9

manifestations of them that have been previously experienced [5]. In this process the notion of similarity is indispensable for dealing with perceived phenomena and linking them to past experiences in an organized manner. In our scenario, a notion of similarity must be developed in order to systematically define relations among drum patterns, so they can be connected forming a similarity-based structure. This structure can then be suited for developing knowledge about a collection, visualizing it and even interacting with what is contained in it. This has been exemplified in many domains as color [19], timbre [11] and pitch [14] representations. This structure composed of a set of drum patterns is what we define as rhythm space, a collection organized geometrically based on similarity.

Previous research on drum rhythm spaces and similarity has been carried out by different authors [3, 6, 7]. Gabrielsson [7] performed several studies with polyphonic drum patterns, and his experiments resulted in rhythm spaces obtained by applying multidimensional scaling (MDS) on subject similarity ratings of drum patterns. According to his results rhythm spaces spanned from 2 or 3 axes that were given a certain perceptual and musical meaning such as meter, pulse or syncopated accentuation, onset density and rhythm complexity. We consider this research as one of those that sewed models for polyphonic rhythm perception.

As Gabrielsson's interpretations of the axes spanning his spaces are educated guesses without strong grounding on empirical data, we approach them with the help of rhythm descriptors that capture essential aspects of rhythm patterns. By analyzing the descriptors and positions of the patterns in Gabrielsson's spaces with a Lasso regression we expect to find a set of descriptors that captures the essence of subjects ratings revealed through the structure of the spaces. We hypothesize that such a set of descriptors can be used in a new context to predict how subjects would rate the similarity between a collection of other style's drum patterns. As we said before, EDM provides a fertile ground to research on theoretical and applied aspects of rhythm representation. In order to test this idea we carry out two experiments, one to evaluate how accurately one set of descriptors predicts Gabrielsson's spaces, and a second one to evaluate how the same set of descriptors predicts the organization of EDM patterns in our new space. Our results show that a specific subset of descriptors can be used to predict human similarity ratings and construct the spaces derived from them. We discuss this relevant set of descriptors, and the possibility of using them in a general method for automatic creation of rhythm spaces.

2 Background

Rhythms are commonly described with the use of notions as syncopation and event density. Syncopation is based on the idea that different metric weights for different regions of a sequence [15, 16] are mentally constructed once subjects listen to a it and entrain with pulse and metric sensations. When a drum hit, an instrument note in a pattern, is played in a position with low metrical weight and it precedes a silence in a high metrical position we experience a tension with the pulse which is called a syncopation. Evidence of this tension has been studied from a neurological perspective observing an activation of the brain as the syncopated onset challenges the hierarchies imposed by the pulse [4,17]. These findings imply the coding of a rhythmic pattern goes deeper than the notes and silences found on its surface, so a framework based on pulse entrainment is essential for a better comprehension of rhythm cognition. Syncopation has also been found to play a fundamental role in our assessment of rhythm similarity of monophonic patterns [2,8,9,13]. Most of these research on rhythm and syncopation is based on monophonic patterns patterns but, in order to create notions of rhythm similarity useful in musical scenarios, polyphony must be addressed.

Some recent research in polyphonic syncopation [12,21] seeks to explain the effect that simultaneous layers of rhythmic patterns with different instruments have on the perceived syncopation sensation. These papers suggest that the general syncopation sensation of a polyphonic drum pattern is related to hierarchies and also timbre. Specifically, the central frequency of each individual sound present in a polyphonic percussive sequence is relevant to define the overall syncopation sensation. Experiments show how the effect of a kick drum (a low-frequency instrument) is more salient than that of a hi-hat when measuring syncopation on a polyphonic drum pattern. In these experiments patterns are segmented in three distinct layers covering different parts of the audible spectrum, which proves fundamental to compute a polyphonic syncopation value that captures the syncopation judgements of human listeners. Analyzing a percussive pattern by grouping its acoustic information, in low, mid and high bands, seems intuitively related to human perception as a mechanism perhaps to provide distinction while avoiding frequencial overlapping between instruments.

In this research we have created straightforward descriptors combining the concepts of syncopation, density, instrumentation and adapting the three frequency layers presented above. Our descriptors differ from others used in rhythm classification approaches (i.e. [10]) as ours are (i) based on notions of human rhythmic processing, and (ii) not based on audio signal analysis. Taking advantage of the typical acoustics of percussion sounds we define a mapping from the General MIDI Level 1 Percussion Key Map[1] to three insrument categories (low, mid and high) based on the spectral center of the sound (i.e. a low tom belongs to low frequency and a snare to the mid frequency instruments).

Table 1 presents the list of descriptors used in this research, where the concepts of syncopation, frequency range and density (the amount of onsets per time unit) are combined using basic algebraic formulas to define quantifiable measures that we presume can be useful when making sense of a group of patterns.

---

[1] The General MIDI standard has a list of 46 percussive instruments which are mapped one-to-one to a specific note. This is used to indicate what sort of sound will be heard when that note number is selected on a General MIDI synthesizer. https://www.midi.org/specifications/item/gm-level-1-sound-set.

Table 1. Table 1 list of used symbolic descriptors. For the detailed algorithms please visit the code repository: https://github.com/danielgomezmarin/rhythmtoolbox

Name	Description
Number of instruments (NOI)	The sum of different instruments used in a pattern
loD, midD, hiD	Sum of onsets for each different instrument group, divided by the total number of steps in the pattern
stepD	Sum of the steps in the pattern which contain at least one onset, divided by the total amount of steps
lowness, midness, hiness	Share of the total density of patterns that belongs to each of the different instrument categories. Computed as the quotient between the densities per instrument category and the total density
losync, midsync, hisync	Syncopation value computed for each instrumental group's monophonic pattern
losyness, midsyness, hisyness	Quotient of the syncopation value and the sum of onsets for each instrument group
Polysync	Polyphonic syncopation as proposed by Witek et al. [21]

3   Experiment 1: Determining Relevant Rhythm Descriptors to Build Gabrielsson's Spaces

The studies by Gabrielsson [7] on rhythm spaces bring together the theory of cognitive spaces [20] applied to rhythm perception. In experiments 1 and 2 subjects are exposed to different patterns with constant tempo and asked to rate their similarity, thus the reported distances and therefore the resulting spaces express similarity sensations based solely on the rhythmic constitution of the patterns. We want to find which descriptors are able to reproduce the spaces resulting from Gabrielsson's experiments as they are related to the mechanisms his subjects used to compare between the drum patterns. Once we achieve this goal, we further discuss that such descriptors can be used to automate rhythm classification tasks for a different collection of patterns.

3.1   Methods

Materials. The patterns used by Gabrielsson are factory presets of the Ace Tone Rhythm Ace FR-3[2] drum machine which were recorded to magnetic tape. The patterns are Foxtrot, Habanera, Rock'n'roll, Rhumba and Beguine in Gabrielsson's experiment 1 (E1) and the same patterns plus Waltz in experiment 2 (E2) (see Fig. 1). These patterns are a diverse sample of rhythms from

---

[2] https://www.gearogs.com/gear/8813-Ace-Tone-Rhythm-Ace-FR-3.

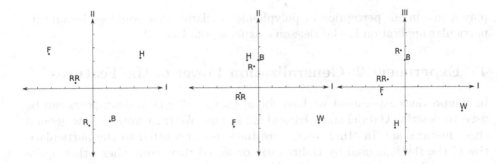

Fig. 1. Two spaces resulting from Gabrielsson's first two experiments. Space1(left) F:foxtrot, RR:rocknroll, R:rhumba, B:beguine, H:habanera. Space2 (center and right) R, B, RR, H, F and W:waltz. Gabrielson's paper is dedicated to interpreting the axes. Refer to the original paper for details.

different cultures and musical styles. The positions of the patterns we use for our analysis are extracted from Gabrielsson's paper.

Procedure. We transcribe each pattern to MIDI and extract all descriptors from them. Then we run a Multi Task Lasso regression (alpha 0.03) [18] using the positions of the patterns in each space as a target and the matrix of descriptors as variables. The Lasso regression returns a subset of descriptors and weights that maximizes correlation with the positions of the patterns in each space.

3.2 Results

The output of the Lasso analysis shows that using this set of descriptors (see Table 1) [midD, hiD, hiness, lowsync, hisyness] the results of both axes of Gabrielsson's E1 are perfectly linearly correlated. For E1 and x axis the weights -0.660, -0.86, -0.068, -0.266, 0.118 respectively present a Spearman correlation of 0.999 (p-value < 0.005). For E1 and y axis the weights respectively present a Spearman correlation of 0.999 (p-value < 0.005). For the space resulting from E2, Lasso analysis shows the descriptor set [midD, hiness, lowsync, midsync, hisync, losyness, hisyness] yields perfect correlations with its three axes. For E2 and x axis the weights 0.785, -0.073, 0.242, 0.574, -0.709, 0.044, 0.506 respectively present a Spearman correlation of 0.999 (p-value < 0.005). For E2 and y axis the weights 0.333, -0.07, 0.21, -0.032, 1, 0.002, -1.411 respectively present a Spearman correlation of 0.942 and p-value $= 0.004$. For E2 and z axis the weights 0.313, -0.032, -1.12, 0.104, 0.81, -0.053, -0.724 respectively present a spearman correlation of 0.999 (p-value < 0.005).

The sets of descriptors and weights for E1 and E2 perfectly describe the space reported by Gabrielsson and thus might be related with the overall polyphonic rhythm similarity sensations from which the spaces were created. It could be fair to presume that, if the spaces capture a similarity sensation, these descriptors play a role in our perception of polyphonic similarity that could go beyond its particular application in Gabrielsson's experiments 1 and 2.

4   Experiment 2: Generalization Power of the Features

In the previous experiment we have found that small sets of descriptors can be used to describe Gabrielsson's E1 and E2 spaces. We then wonder how general these features are. In other words, are these features fitted to the particularities of the rhythms used by Gabrielsson or would they work when other, quite different, rhythm patterns are rated? From a computational point of view, we are proposing that, if we have a new set of drum patterns location on a human-based rhythm space, we can extract only the descriptors defined on the previous experiment and by using a dimensional reduction technique as principal component analysis (PCA) or multidimensional scaling (MDS) we can predict with some accuracy the rhythm space. PCA finds a principal vector in the descriptor space in which the values of all descriptors are maximally dispersed and then additional orthogonal vectors are found to conform the predicted rhythm space. The other alternative, MDS, is based on a dissimilarity matrix of the patterns which is computed as the euclidean distance between the descriptor vectors of each pattern.

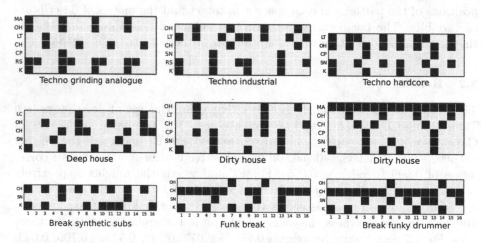

Fig. 2. Piano roll visualization of the nine EDM patterns. Steps on the x axis, onsets in dark. K: Kick Drum, S: Snare, CP: Clap, CH: Closed Hi-Hat, OH: Open Hi-Hat, LT: Low Tom, LC: Low Conga, MA: Shaker.

For this experiment we create an EDM rhythm space based on subject ratings following Gabrielsson's methodology: selecting a collection of EDM patterns and presenting pairwise combinations to subjects who report their similarity, and then, with those answers, creating a new rhythm space. An EDM drum rhythm collection is compiled specifically for this experiment.

4.1   Method

Participants. A total of 36 subjects participated in the survey, 5 females and 31 males, all had experience in music production and or musical training, according to a short survey they answered after finishing the listening task.

Materials. In order to get a subject-based rhythm space, a set of rhythm patterns is needed. In order to select EDM-representative drum patterns, we turn to the EDM production literature printed and online and collect drum patterns explicitly associated to a certain EDM style. All patterns are 16 steps long, each step lasting for a 16th note. A total of 75 different patterns were collected, 70% of them belonged to the House (28%), Breakbeat (26%), and Techno (16%) styles and the rest 30% belong to Garage, Drum n' Bass, Hip-Hop, Trance, Chillout, Dubstep, Jungle and Trip-Hop styles. We create a preliminary rhythm space of the whole 75 pattern collection by extracting the complete list of aforementioned descriptors aforementioned and then using PCA. After dividing the preliminary space in nine equal-size rectangular areas we select one pattern from each one of them. In this way, the list of 75 patterns is reduced to 9 patterns (see Table 2) intended to be representative enough of the variability of the included categories. The 9 patterns selected for the experiment are rendered to audio (in order to be played in the rating experiment) using single shot samples from the Roland 707, 808 and 909 drum machines. All selected patterns use instruments included in this set: *Low Conga, Bass Drum, Side Stick, Maracas, Hand Clap, Snare, Closed Hi-Hat, Low Tom* and *Open Hi-Hat* (Fig. 2).

Table 2. Patterns selected from the sub-regions of the preliminary space. Left, center, right and top, center bottom represent the subdivisions of the space as explained in the text.

	Left	Center	Right
Top	Techno grinding analogue	Techno industrial	Techno hardcore
Center	Deep house	Dirty house	Deep tech house
Bottom	Break synthetic subs	Funk break	Break funky drummer

Procedure. A computer program is prepared to carry out the experiment. Before the subjects start the experiment, several patterns are presented to expose the timbre range of the percussive sounds used and also examples of identical, similar and completely different pairs of patterns. To evaluate all combinations between the 9 patterns, subjects rated the existing 36 possible pattern pairs in a triangular 9 element matrix (avoiding comparing a pattern with itself or repeating any pair). Additionally, 4 randomly selected pairs are presented twice for controlling the consistency of each subject's ratings, so, in total, subjects rate 40 pairs of patterns. The pairs are presented in a random order preventing any pattern to be in consecutive pairs. Before a pair is reproduced the order of its two patterns is also randomized so the same pair is presented in the two possible directions to different subjects. Subjects could listen to the same pair as many times as they needed and the similarity value was reported in a likert scale with a range from 1 to 10 where 1 means the pair is completely dissimilar and 10 means the pair had the topmost similarity (i.e., the pair contained equal patterns). When the subjects completed the experiment they answered some questions about themselves: age, gender, years of musical training, years of musical performance training, years of percussive musical performance training, hours per week spent attentively listening to music, experience in electronic music production, experience in electronic drum programming, number times listened to the pairs before answering. Finally, the possibility to leave a comment on the experiment is available.

4.2   Results and Discussion

In order to simplify the analysis, the 10 point scale is mapped to a 5 point scale where each range of the new scale groups two values of the original scale (1 groups the results of 1 and 2, 2 groups 3 and 4 and so on). Three subjects rated different pairs as being "exactly the same", and therefore they were discarded from the experiment because there were no identical pairs. The control pairs were used to perceive distortion in the ratings of the same pairs, and the average of the maximum difference of all subjects when rating the same pair is 1.8 units. In order to approximate our analysis to that of Gabrielsson we create a subgroup of subjects compliant with the musical background reported in his experiments, which is "amateur musicians who had performed music for at least 4 years". A subset of our General Group composed of 18 subjects with at least 4 years of musical training was defined and we will refer to it as the Musicians group. For the General group, the inter quartile range (a measure of statistical dispersion) mean is 1.81 units and 1.48 units for the Musicians group suggesting more agreement in the Musicians sub-group. Pair (1, 3) presents a slight bimodal behaviour for the General Group which is reduced in the Musicians Sub group.

The observed means for each assessed pair present slight differences when both groups are compared. Only 9 pairs out of 36 differ in median value from one group to another: 6 pairs present changes in a degree of 2 units, and 3 pairs present changes in a degree of 1. Pairs that involve rhythm Deep House do not change between groups and the pairs that involve rhythm 6 Deep Tech House have 4 changes between groups.

We can observe from the MDS that the three genres from where the rhythm patterns were extracted span across three distinct regions of the space (see Fig. 3). Breakbeat patterns are located in the positive region of the X axis, while Techno and House patterns are located from the zero to the negative portion of the X axis. The X-negative quadrants of the space contain in the Y-positive region the Techno patterns and in the Y-negative region the House patterns. In EDM, rhythm and timbre are the most salient musical characteristics [1], so it is

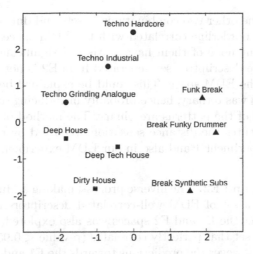

Fig. 3. Bi dimensional space obtained by using MDS on the dissimilarity matrix of subjects ratings.

relevant for EDM drum patterns to retain stylistic/similarity information that comes through when subjects compare among them by listening.

Descriptor-Based Prediction of Spaces. We extract the two descriptor sets found in the previous experiment (by adjusting E1 and E2) from the patterns in the EDM space. Using those descriptor values we compute PCA and MDS to evaluate if the locations of the EDM patterns can be predicted with any of the sets. Table 3 presents the correlations between the predicted space and the resulting EDM space.

Table 3. Spearman rank correlations between each EDM axis and the forecasts using the descriptor sets from E1 and E2 with PCA and MDS.

	X	Y
E1 set PCA	$\rho = 0.62$ p-value $= 0.076$	$\rho = 0.68$ p-value $= 0.042$
E1 set MDS	$\rho = 0.67$ p-value $= 0.049$	$\rho = -0.78$ p-value $= 0.012$
E2 set PCA	$\rho = 0.52$ p-value $= 0.154$	$\rho = 0.45$ p-value $= 0.224$
E2 set MDS	$\rho = 0.63$ p-value $= 0.067$	$\rho = 0.683$ p-value $= 0.042$
E1+E2 set PCA	$\rho = 0.466$ p-value $= 0.205$	$\rho = 0.683$ p-value $= 0.042$
E1+E2 set MDS	$\rho = 0.383$ p-value $= 0.308$	$\rho = 0.5$ p-value $= 0.17$

Using the set of descriptors E1 for analyzing the patterns of the EDM experiment and then applying MDS to those results (E1 set MDS), we observe correlations of $\rho = 0.67$ (p-value < 0.05) and $\rho = -0.78$ (p-value < 0.05) for x and y axis respectively. The other two combinations of sets and dimensional reduction techniques that are borderline correlated with the EDM space are, E1 set PCA and E2 set MDS but none of them have statistical significant correlations for any of the axes. The descriipttor set generated from E2 is not a good predictor of the patterns of the EDM space. This could be explained because in E2, one of the used patterns was ternary, hence probably introducing some "distortion", whereas in ours, all of the patterns are binary. The method of using the E1 set and then MDS captures the distance sensations reported by the subjects both in Gabrielsson's experiment 1 and also in our EDM experiment.

From EDM to E1 and E2. The inverse process, making a Multi-Output Lasso analysis to extract a set of EDM well-correlated descriptors and then finding how they can predict the E1 and E2 spaces was also explored. In this case, the resulting descriptor set that perfectly correlates (p-value < 0.05) with the EDM axes was different. However the predictions towards the E1 and E2 spaces, either by using PCA or MDS with the EDM set, were not statistically significant. This is expected as Gabrielsson's patterns are much different among them, representing six different musical styles, and thus cover a large perceptual/musical space, while the patterns used in the EDM experiment are variations of three styles which cover a small-scale rhythm space. In this case the macro scale descriptors can predict the small-scale space but not the opposite.

4.3   Relevant Set of Descriptors

The descriptors derived from the Multitask Lasso analysis that has the best fit with Gabrielson's E1 experiment and our EDM experiment using MDS are [midD, hiD, hiness, lowsync, hisyness]. These descriptors cover all frequency ranges in which the drum patterns are segmented (low, mid and high). The only low frequency descriptor present is lowsync which is expected given the crucial importance of the syncopation of the low frequencies in the overall syncopation sensation of a drum pattern, as proposed by Hove et al. [12]. The mid frequency range descriptor midD represents the normalized onset density of the mid frequency. The high frequency descriptors are hiD, hiness and hisyness, all related with teh density and the syncopation of the instruments mapped to the high frequency category (see Table 1 for details on each descriptor).

5   General Discussion

We have discovered descriptors that allow to construct very general rhythm spaces that were reported long ago but withouth such descriptors-based analysis. Then we have seen that those descriptors, based on main concepts of rhythm cognition, allow to construct spaces constrained to EDM which even have a stylistic significance. Consequently, we could use those descriptors in systems that present, visualize and manipulate pattern collections, so that users have 2D representations close to their mental representations which could be exploited for search, selection and invention tasks.

Our results show how using a reduced set of descriptors, then computing Euclidean distance between the descriptor vectors and then using MDS, a subject-based space composed of EDM patterns is reproduced with significant correlation values. Although this is a step forward towards a system capable of automatic drum pattern organization, further experiments must be carried out to evaluate its robustness in larger datasets.

Automatically visualizing in 2D a large amount of drum patterns has powerful implications in music production. The fact that a collection can be graphically explored and retrieved in a map in which similar patterns close whereas they appear far from different ones can improve the experience of music production and performance. On top of this map, we are currently developing drum pattern cross-fading algorithms adding a generative functionality to rhythm spaces. New patterns, not present in the collection, can emerge, therefore converting a discrete rhythm space into a continuous one, and expanding an original "mimetic" space into a space for discovery.

Although the reported experiments were not designed for classification, it is revealing that the concept of EDM style comes through in the space resulting from our second experiment. It can be seen as a demonstration of how musical concepts as House, Techno and Breakbeat emerge based on listening to a handful of instances, each occupying a specific region of a conceptual space. As 61% of the Musicians group reported having experience in EDM production, the distribution by styles can also represent the effect of a previous context in EDM knowledge affecting how patterns are perceived and their similarity judged.

Acknowledgments. This research has been partially supported by the EU funded GiantSteps project (http://www.giantsteps-project.eu) (FP7-ICT-2013-10 Grant agreement nr 610591).

References

1. Butler, M.J.: Unlocking the Groove: Rhythm, Meter, and Musical Design in Electronic Dance Music. Indiana University Press, Bloomington (2006)
2. Cao, E., Lotstein, M., Johnson-Laird, P.N.: Similarity and families of musical rhythms. Music. Percept. Interdiscip. J. **31**(5), 444–469 (2014)
3. Esparza, T.M., Bello, J.P., Humphrey, E.J.: From genre classification to rhythm similarity: computational and musicological insights. J. New Music. Res. **44**(1), 39–57 (2015)
4. Fujii, S., Schlaug, G.: The harvard beat assessment test (H-BAT): a battery for assessing beat perception and production and their dissociation. Front. Hum. Neurosci. **7**, 771 (2013)
5. Gärdenfors, P.: Conceptual Spaces: The Geometry of Thought, 1st edn. The MIT Press, Cambridge (2000)
6. Gabrielsson, A.: Similarity ratings and dimension analyses of auditory rhythm patterns: I. Scand. J. Psychol. **14**, 138–160 (1973)

7. Gabrielsson, A.: Similarity ratings and dimension analyses of auditory rhythm patterns: II. Scand. J. Psychol. **14**(3), 161–176 (1973)
8. Gómez-Marín, D., Jordà, S., Herrera, P.: Strictly rhythm: exploring the effects of identical regions and meter induction in rhythmic similarity perception. In: Kronland-Martinet, R., Aramaki, M., Ystad, S. (eds.) CMMR 2015. LNCS, vol. 9617, pp. 449–463. Springer, Cham (2016). https://doi.org/10.1007/978-3-319-46282-0 29
9. Gómez-Marín, D., Jordà, S., Herrera, P.: Pad and sad: two awareness-weighted rhythmic similarity distances. In: 16th International Society for Music Information Retrieval Conference ISMIR, Málaga (2015)
10. Gouyon, F., et al.: Evaluating rhythmic descriptors for musical genre classification. In: Proceedings of the AES 25th International Conference (2004)
11. Grey, J.M.: Multidimensional perceptual scaling of musical timbres. J. Acoust. Soc. Am. **61**(5), 1270–1277 (1977)
12. Hove, M.J., Marie, C., Bruce, I.C., Trainor, L.J.: Superior time perception for lower musical pitch explains why bass-ranged instruments lay down musical rhythms. Proc. Natl. Acad. Sci. **111**(28), 10383–10388 (2014)
13. Johnson-Laird, P.N.: Rhythm and meter: a theory at the computational level. Psychomusicology J. Res. Music. Cogn. **10**(2), 88–106 (1991)
14. Krumhansl, C.L.: The psychological representation of musical pitch in a tonal context. Cogn. Psychol. **11**(3), 346–374 (1979)
15. Longuet-Higgins, H.C., Lee, C.S.: The rhythmic interpretation of monophonic music. Music. Percept. Interdiscip. J. **1**(4), 424–441 (1984)
16. Palmer, C., Krumhansl, C.L.: Mental representations for musical meter. J. Exp. Psychology. Hum. Percept. Perform. **16**(4), 728–741 (1990)
17. Patel, A.D., Iversen, J.R.: The evolutionary neuroscience of musical beat perception: the action simulation for auditory prediction (ASAP) hypothesis. Front. Syst. Neurosci. **8**, 57 (2014)
18. Pedregosa, F., et al.: Scikit-learn: machine learning in python. J. Mach. Learn. Res. **12**, 2825–2830 (2011)
19. Shepard, R.N.: The analysis of proximities: Multidimensional scaling with an unknown distance function II. Psychometrika **27**(3), 219–246 (1962)
20. Shoben, E.J., Ross, B.H.: 7. Structure and process in cognitive psychology using multidimensional scaling and related techniques. In: Ronning, R.R., Glover, J.A., Conoley, J.C., Witt, J.C. (eds.) The Influence of Cognitive Psychology on Testing, Hillsdale, NJ. Lawrence Erlbaum Associates (1987)
21. Witek, M.A.G., Clarke, E.F., Wallentin, M., Kringelbach, M.L., Vuust, P.: Syncopation, body-movement and pleasure in groove music. PLoS ONE **9**(4), e94446 (2014)

Modulated Swing: Dynamic Rhythm Synthesis by Means of Frequency Modulation

Carl Haakon Waadeland[(✉)] and Sigurd Saue

Department of Music, Norwegian University of Science and Technology, NTNU,
7491 Trondheim, Norway
{carl.haakon.waadeland,sigurd.saue}@ntnu.no

Abstract. Listening to swinging music you often want to move along with the rhythm. - We pose the question: How might the production of microtiming that characterizes swing be modelled? A fundamental idea in the present paper is to apply an interaction of oscillators to achieve alterations of frequencies that create timing deviations that are typical of live performances of rhythm. - Dynamic, time-dependent features are introduced and implemented in a model based on rhythmic frequency modulation, RFM, previously developed by the authors of this paper. We here exemplify the potential of this new, extended model by simulating various performances of swing in jazz, and we also indicate how the computer implementation of the RFM model might be an interesting tool of electro-acoustic music. Moreover, we discuss our model construction within the framework of event-based and emergent timing.

Keywords: Rhythm performance · Swing · Synthesis
Frequency modulation · Computer implementation

1 Introduction: Swinging FM

'Swing' is a concept that many are likely to associate with jazz music. Indeed, one meaning of the notion "swing" is used to denote a jazz style that developed in the United States during the 1930s, see for instance [24]. Another meaning of "swing" is related to communicative qualities of a music performance (originally, a performance of jazz music). Subject to this understanding, swing is conceived as a process through which the musicians, both individually and in an interactive context of playing together, make a musical phrase, a rhythm, or a melody "come alive", by creating a performance that in varying degrees communicates *motional aspects* to the listener, thereby making the listener want to *move along with the music*. Or, as stated by the composer and jazz historian, Gunther Schuller; a rhythm is perceived as swinging when: "...a listener inadvertently starts tapping his foot, snapping his fingers, moving his body or head to the beat of the music" [24], page 223. Seen as such, the qualities characterizing a swinging performance

© Springer Nature Switzerland AG 2018
M. Aramaki et al. (Eds.): CMMR 2017, LNCS 11265, pp. 135–150, 2018.
https://doi.org/10.1007/978-3-030-01692-0_10

may be typical of musical performances belonging to other traditions than the jazz tradition, as well.

A *swing groove* is a particular rhythmic ostinato played by jazz drummers. The swing groove originated in the swing era, and has developed further in later jazz styles, like bebop and contemporary jazz. A typical swing groove is most often played on the ride cymbal. In its most basic form a swing groove may have the written representation illustrated in Fig. 1.

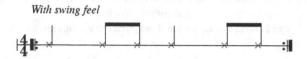

Fig. 1. An often written representation of a swing groove, commonly played on a ride cymbal.

The remark "With swing feel" in the notation in Fig. 1 indicates that the experienced jazz drummer plays this groove according to his embodied understanding of swing, where the eight notes in the swing groove are not performed with equal durations, as written in Fig. 1, but rather with characteristic long - short patterns. These patterns change the ratio between the durations of successive pairs of eight notes, often called the *swing ratio*, from 1:1 to 2:1, or around 3:1, - or somewhere in between, - dependent on, among other things, the individual drummer and the tempo of the performance. Several studies of how different performance conditions influence the swing ratio have been conducted, see e.g. [4, 9, 12, 15, 16, 21, 28]. Different performances of long - short patterns of durations subdividing the beat are also found in some Latin - American music, as well as in funk and hip-hop [6, 7, 14]. Moreover, it is interesting to know that *notes ingales* is a common practice in the performance of French baroque music, - similar to the use of swing eights in jazz, see [20].

Common to all the above mentioned examples of different swing performances is that the musician in his performance makes various deviations from exact note values. "Deviations from the exact" in music performance have been empirically investigated since the 1930s, and Seashore stated that these deviations are a *characteristic feature of artistic expression* [25]. Various such deviations have been studied in empirical rhythm research by investigating *systematic variations of durations*, SYVARD, see e.g. [5], and are also discussed and investigated as *participatory discrepancies*, PD [1, 8, 17, 21]. Deliberate discrepancies or deviations may be seen as a process by which (more or less) conceptualized structural properties of rhythm are *transformed* into live performances of rhythm. Such a process of rhythmic transformation is often denoted *expressive timing*, see [11].

One of the authors of the present paper, Waadeland, has presented a continuous model of expressive timing [27]. A basic idea in this model construction is to represent rhythmic structure (e.g. note values) by sinusoidal movements, and to apply frequency modulation to obtain movement curves that in varying ways create deviations from exact note values. A theoretical interpretation offered by this model is to view expressive timing as a result of rhythmic structure being "stretched" and "compressed" by actions of movements. Applying rhythmic frequency modulation, RFM, as suggested in the model, it is possible to simulate characteristic features of many different empirically documented examples of expressive timing. The other author of this paper, Saue, has constructed a MIDI-based computer implementation of RFM [23], and by applying this implementation we have been able to make sounding examples of the RFM syntheses.

However, even though the previously constructed RFM model is capable of constructing interesting approximations to various live performances of rhythm, an obvious limitation of the model is related to the fact that the model is *static*, meaning that the parameters in the model do not vary over time. This makes the modelled movement curves *periodic*. Live performances of rhythm, on the other hand, even different swing groove ostinatos, are *quasi-periodic*, characterized by various local and long-term fluctuations from static patterns of systematic deviations.

In this paper we present an extended version of the RFM model with a new computer implementation. A major achievement of the present model is that we now have implemented dynamic, time-dependent features in the synthesis. To demonstrate our model we present various examples of different new syntheses of swing, and we also indicate how RFM synthesis might provide an interesting compositional tool for electro-acoustic music. In the concluding section we compare our model with alternative computational models of expressive music performance, and discuss our model construction within the theoretical framework that distinguishes between two forms of timing control: emergent timing and event-based timing. Moreover, we point at some further possible extensions of our model.

2   Rhythmic Frequency Modulation

We start by briefly outlining the basic features of the formerly developed RFM model, [27], after which we present the new computer implementation of dynamic properties in the model.

2.1   A Continuous Model of Rhythmic Structure

When moving the index finger up an down in the air in such a way that the minimal points are in perfect synchronization with the clicks from a metronome, an idealized curve describing the finger movement could be something similar to what is shown in Fig. 2. To be quite explicit, this curve is given by the mathematical function:

$$y(t) = A\left[1 - \cos(2\pi ft)\right], \tag{1}$$

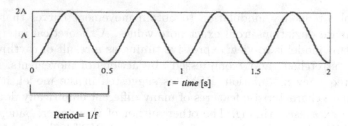

Fig. 2. Graphic illustration of an idealized performance of isochronous beats with frequency $f = 2$. Time is displayed along the horizontal axis, and the fingers vertical position is measured along the vertical axis.

where t is time, f is the frequency of the finger movement, and A is the amplitude ($2A$ is a measure of the fingers maximal distance from the minimal value, 0). In Fig. 2, $f = 2$.

Viviani [26] stated that sine waves are easy to approximate by human movements, and are among the simplest predictable motions, whereas Balasubramaniam et al. conducted an empirical experiment where they found that an unpaced oscillation of the index finger tends to create a sinusoidal, close to symmetric movement curve, - but when the finger movements were paced by clicks from a metronome, the movement curves attained different characteristic asymmetric shapes [3]. Thus, the trajectory in Fig. 2 should be seen as an illustration of a static, robot-like (unpaced) performance of isochronous beats.

If we think of the sinusoid in Eq. 1 with frequency f as a representation of (a performance of) quarter notes, a corresponding sinusoid with frequency $2f$ will represent eight notes, $3f$ corresponds to eight note triplets, whereas $(2/3)f$ represents dotted quarter notes. In other words, every note value may be represented by a sinusoid, and we have, thus, obtained a continuous representation of rhythmic structure. Figure 3 illustrates the connection between a sequence of notes, a movement curve, and a representation by sinusoidal functions. In this figure quarter notes correspond to the frequency $f = 1$ (see also [27], page 27).

2.2   A Continuous Model of "Deviations from the Exact"

In the model of rhythmic structure presented in the previous, metronomic performances of note values are represented by frequencies of sinusoidal functions. It is therefore tempting to suggest that deviations in live performances of note values should somehow correspond to some operation inducing deviations or *alterations of frequencies*. A well known technique of sound synthesis using various alterations or distortions of the frequency of an oscillator in order to achieve parameter control over the spectral richness of sound, is *frequency modulation*, FM, pioneered by Chowning [10]. The most basic FM instrument consists of two sinusoidal oscillators interacting to give the output:

$$y(t) = A \sin \left[2\pi f_c t + d \sin(2\pi f_m t) \right] \tag{2}$$

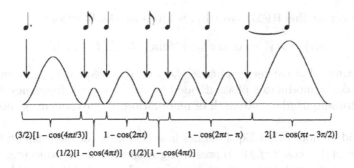

Fig. 3. An illustration showing the connections between a sequence of notes, a movement curve, and a mathematical representation of sinusoids, all related to a robot-like rhythmic performance executed in perfect synchronization with a metronome. The horizontal axis displays time, t, where the first beat occurs at time $t = 0$. In this figure we have made $A(\Delta) = \Delta = 1/frequency$, reflecting different amplitudes of finger movements related to the performance of notes with different durations (Δ).

A is the amplitude, f_c is commonly denoted *carrier frequency*, f_m is the *modulating frequency*, and d is the *peak frequency deviation*, cf. [10]. Looking at the output of the basic FM instrument, we observe that when $d = 0$, there is no modulation and the result is simply a sine wave with frequency f_c. This very situation resembles, at least *on a purely theoretical level*, the situation we are trying to establish for syntheses of rhythm: When there is no modulation, the result is a strict metronomic (i.e. sinusoidal) performance. When, on the other hand, modulation occurs, various deviations of frequency are created, resulting in different kinds of "deviations from the exact" in the modeled performance.

Motivated by this observation, the basic RFM algorithm is defined on the basis of a combination of Eqs. 1 and 2 above, and is illustrated in Fig. 4.

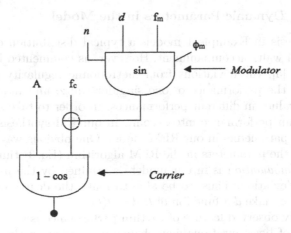

Fig. 4. Flowchart for basic rhythmic frequency modulation.

The output of this RFM algorithm is given by the function:

$$y(t) = A \left[1 - \cos \left[2\pi f_c t + d \sin^n \left[2\pi (f_m t + \phi_m) \right] \right] \right], \tag{3}$$

where t = time, A = carrier amplitude, f_c = carrier frequency, f_m = modulator frequency, ϕ_m = modulator phase divided by 2π, d = peak frequency deviation = modulator amplitude = strength of modulation, n = exponent of modulating function.

It should be noted that Eq. 3 defines how a modulator operates on the function $y(t) = A \left[1 - \cos(2\pi f_c t) \right]$, representing a specific note value (e.g., quarter note). Frequency modulation of subdivisions and ties of this sinusoid is defined accordingly, and is expressed explicitly in [27], page 29.

Example 1: Synthesis of Vienna Waltz Accompaniment. To give an example of how RFM works, we demonstrate an RFM simulation of a rhythmic characteristic documented in empirical rhythm research. As noted by Bengtsson and Gabrielsson [5], a well known feature of performances of Vienna waltzes occur at the beat level in the accompaniment; the first beat is shortened and the second beat is lengthened, whereas the third beat is close to one third of the measure length. Thus, the quarter note beats in the 3/4 meter are characterized by a cyclic pattern of durations; short (S) - long (L) - intermediate (I). By modulating a metronomic (quantized) MIDI performance of a Vienna waltz accompaniment which is played with equal durations of the quarter notes, as written in the notation of the music, we are now able to simulate the characteristic S - L - I pattern by means of the RFM algorithm in Eq. 3. We obtain this by choosing: $f_c = 3$ (3 beats to the measure), $f_m = 1$, $\phi_m = 0.25$, $n = 1$, and $d = 1$. This synthesis of Vienna waltz accompaniment is also presented in [27], pages 30–32. Figure 5 shows the movement curve of this simulation. A sounding realization of this synthesis may be heard at [2].

2.3   Including Dynamic Parameters in the Model

The RFM synthesis in Example 1 models a typical distribution of beat durations in a Vienna waltz accompaniment. However, as commented by Bengtsson and Gabrielsson [5], the deviations from metronomic regularity may, indeed, vary throughout the performance of one singular waltz, and may also change in proportional values in different performances. In order to take such dynamic features of rhythm performance into account in our FM synthesis, we need to include dynamic parameters in our RFM model. One obvious way to do this is to make some of the parameters in the RFM algorithm (Eq. 3) time-dependent. The *strength of modulation* is in our model determined by the parameter d = peak frequency deviation. Thus, to be able to make the degree of modulation vary over time, we make d a function of t: $d = d(t)$.

An empirically observed feature of rhythm performance is also that the proportional values of beat durations may change depending on the *tempo* of the performance. For instance, in the performance of swing groove in jazz the swing

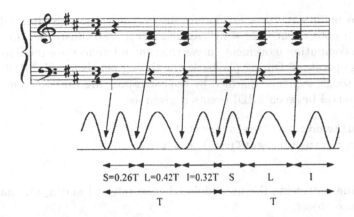

Fig. 5. Illustration of a modulated movement curve associated with a synthesis of a performance of the first two measures of a Vienna waltz accompaniment. The durations of the metronomic quarter notes are "stretched" and "compressed" by the action of the FM modulation, and the characteristic cyclic pattern of beat durations, S-L-I, is created.

ratio tends to approximate 1 at fast tempi, whereas it is often closer to 3 at slow tempi [15,16]. To include this feature in the model, we also make d a function of tempo.

3   Computer Implementation of Dynamic Features

In order to investigate the implications of the theory of rhythmic frequency modulation, we developed a computer application FMRhythm[1] which allowed interactive experimentation with modulation parameters [23]. We will now recapitulate the main ideas, before moving on to the extensions necessary to support the new dynamic features of the model.

At the core of the application are two parallel structures, labeled "MIDI song" and "FM song" respectively. "MIDI song" contains the musical material represented as sequences of MIDI events. It provides functions for handling file import/export and real-time playback based on MIDI and standard MIDI files[2]. "FM song" is an alternative view, abstracting the MIDI data into sequences of rhythmically significant temporal events (ignoring note endings and multiple notes in a chord). Each sequence is assigned a modulation operator, allowing modifications of the temporal distance between events. The "FM song" structure handles all computations and the graphical rendering of movement curves.

---

[1] *FMRhythm* is written in C++ and available as open source at https://github.com/ssaue/FMrhythm. Currently only Windows is supported, but we intend to make it platform-independent.

[2] Specifications for MIDI and the Standard MIDI File format are available from the MIDI Manufacturers Association (MMA): https://www.midi.org/specifications.

The two main structures are interconnected only through time references, one for each note in an "FM song" sequence. Figure 6 illustrates this connection. When computing movement curves the time references are modified by the modulating operators. During playback, the timing between each MIDI event in the "MIDI song" sequence is scaled by the corresponding time reference. Hence the time interval between MIDI events is given as:

```
double midiEvent::getTimeInterval() {
    return m_timeRef->getTime() * m_time;
}
```

where `m_time` represents the unmodulated time interval and `m_timeRef` is the time reference object.

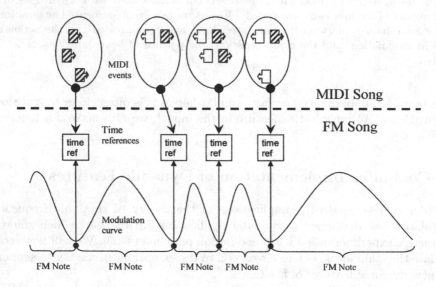

Fig. 6. A simple diagram showing the two main structures of the computer application, *MIDI song* and *FM song*, and how these are interconnected through time references. Typical MIDI events are note-on (hatched) and note-off. An *FM note* represents a single time event and the modulation curve leading up to it.

An "FM note" models the movement from one downbeat to the next as a single sinusoidal period, i.e. implementing Eq. 1. In order to achieve deviations from a strict metric timing we add a modulating operator similar to Eq. 3. The carrier frequency, f_c, is an important factor in determining the periodicity of modulation. Typically it is set equal to the number of beats per measure. The carrier amplitude, A, varies with MIDI velocity, but has no effect on the temporal behavior of the model.

The modulator part of the equation is computed as:

```
double modulator::getValue(double time) {
    expr = 2 * pi * (m_modFrequency * time + m_modPhase);
    return m_modIndex * pow(sin(expr), m_exponent);
}
```

where frequency and time are scaled according to a user-configurable temporal resolution. The modulation index m_modIndex is a static value in this implementation.

In Fig. 7, we show the basic setup of a single operator and the parameters available. The application supports a number of modulating waveforms (sine, sawtooth, triangle and square), and more complex setups with two modulating oscillators in series or in parallel.

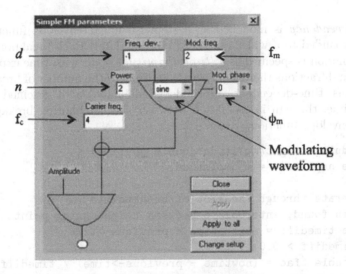

Fig. 7. A choice of parameters for swing simulation, illustrated in the basic RFM instrument.

Each sequence (i.e. voice or part) of the "FM song" refers to a single modulator throughout, but different sequences may have different modulators. In a scenario with multiple modulators synchronization between parts may become an issue. The application provides a few options, and the default is to enforce a common first downbeat in all parts. As shown in Fig. 5 the computed movement curve starts *before* the first downbeat in order to model the performers preparation of the beat. Another synchronization option is a common starting point for all movement curves.

Movement curves are calculated for every change in the modulation parameters. The computation is carried out on one "FM note" object at a time, tracking the curve from downbeat to downbeat. Due to the pre-beat preparation of the movement curve, the initial tracking progresses backwards to a starting point defined as the point where the amplitude of the function $(1 - cos x)$ crosses the value 1.0. Then the synchronization offset of each part is calculated. Finally the curve is tracked in forward direction, note by note, until the end.

Originally, the parameters were time-invariant constants, leaving no possibilities for dynamic behavior. With the current implementation, we have added two dynamic features to the modulation index: Time-dependency and tempo-dependency.

Tempo-dependency is, at this point, implemented as a simple linear function, partly inspired by the findings of Friberg and Sundström [15]. The constants of the linear function, m_a and m_b, are user configurable:

```
double modulator::getMetronomFactor() {
    return m_a * m_metronom + m_b;
}
```

Time-dependency is modelled as a stepwise linear envelope function, but could be expanded to a wider range of functions later. Each breakpoint in the envelope function is specified as a $\langle time, amplitude \rangle$-pair with time expressed in measures (and fractions thereof). There is no limit to the number of breakpoints. A continuous, time-dependent amplitude is calculated at a specified point in time, nowtime, through interpolation between the neighboring breakpoints of the linear envelope function:

```
double modulator::getAmplitude(double nowtime) {
    double amplitude = m_amplitude;
    ...
    // Iterate through the list of breakpoints
    // When found, interpolate between neighbouring points
    double timediff = next->time - previous->time;
    if (timediff > 0.0) {
        double tfac = (nowtime - previous->time) / timediff;
        amplitude += tfac * (next->amplitude - amplitude);
    }
    ...
}
```

Finally, the modulation index of the modulator that previously was a static value is now equivalent to the time-dependent amplitude multiplied with the tempo factor:

```
double modulator::getModulationIndex(double time) {
    return getAmplitude(time) * getMetronomFactor();
}
```

4   Examples of RFM Syntheses of Swing Performance

In this section we demonstrate how we can use the RFM model with its computer implementation to obtain new sounding simulations of live performances of swing. Moreover, we suggest an application of RFM which may point at some interesting possibilities for applying the RFM instrument as a tool for electro-acoustic music.

Example 2: Continuous Increase in Swing Ratio. As mentioned in the previous, jazz drummers will perform the swing groove in Fig. 1 with different swing ratios (SR), depending on the individual drummer and the tempo of the performance. We now construct a simulation of various performances of this cymbal rhythm in the following way: First, we make a MIDI recording of the cymbal ostinato where every MIDI event is quantized in eighth note triplets, i.e., $SR = 2$. Secondly, we import this recording as a MIDI file into the computer program, applying RFM with the following parameter values: $f_c = 4$, $f_m = 2$, $\phi_m = 0$, $n = 2$, d : between -1 and 1, cf. the illustration of the RFM instrument in Fig. 7.

By choosing these parameters we obtain: $d = -1$ gives $SR = 3$, whereas $d = 1$ results in $SR = 1$, see Fig. 8.

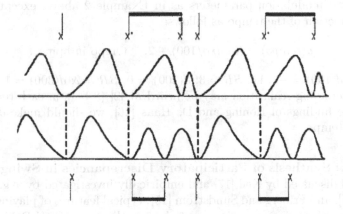

Fig. 8. Illustration of movement curves associated with two different modulations of the same rhythmic pattern. The upper corresponds to $d = -1$, in the lower $d = 1$. An amplitude adjustment, $A = (\Delta)^{1/2}$, has been made to indicate how kinesthetic considerations might be implemented in the model.

By making d a function of time, we are now able to simulate various performances of the swing groove where the subdivisions may fluctuate between sixteenth notes and eight notes, which, indeed, is the case in live performances of this rhythm in jazz [15,16]. To illustrate this, we make:

$$d(t) = 1 - (1/16)\,t, \quad t = \text{time (in seconds)}. \tag{4}$$

For this linear function $d(0) = 1$ and $d(32) = -1$, which means that the synthesized swing performance starts at $t = 0$ with $SR = 1$, and during 32 s

(= 16 bars of 4/4 swing in tempo 120 bpm) the swing ratio increases continuously, first to $SR = 2$ ($t = 16$ s), and further to $SR = 3$ ($t = 32$ s) This synthesis of continuous increase of swing ratio may be heard at the URL [2].

It should at this point be underlined that with this particular choice of $d(t)$ we do *not* try to simulate any specific live performance of the swing groove. Rather, we demonstrate how the model makes it possible to make *dynamic* syntheses of swing performances where SR varies over time. Different functions, $d(t)$, should be chosen to simulate different dynamic, live performances of swing.

Example 3: Tempo Specific Swing Ratios. Analyzing excerpts from jazz recordings, Friberg and Sundström found that a general trend in the performance of swing was an approximately linear decrease in swing ratio with increasing tempo [15]. Another study by Honing and De Haas [16] found no evidence for SR to scale linearly with tempo, but they did find that jazz experts adapt their timing to the tempo of their performance in such a way that fast tempi are performed with a smaller SR than slower tempi. To illustrate how our model may simulate the findings of Friberg and Sundström, we apply the same MIDI recording and modulation parameters as in Example 2 above, except that we make d a function of the tempo as follows:

$$d(tempo) = (tempo/100) - 2, \quad \text{tempo in bpm} \tag{5}$$

This gives: $d(100) = -1$, i.e. $SR = 3$; $d(200) = 0$, $SR = 2$; $d(300) = 1$, $SR = 1$, cf. [15]. A sounding realization may be heard at [2] (8 bars in each tempo). To simulate the findings of Honing and De Haas [16], we should make d another function of tempo.

Example 4: Synthesis of Participatory Discrepancies in Swing Performance. As discussed by Keil [17] and empirically investigated by, e.g., Prögler [21], Alén [1], and Friberg and Sundström [15], typical features of playing grooves and making music swing are various *participatory discrepancies* (PDs) in the performance of musicians playing together. For instance, in [15] we read that in a performance with The Miles Davis Quintet of the tune "My Funny Valentine", from 1964, the bass player, Ron Carter, is, in average, 30 ms behind the ride cymbal of the drummer, Tony Williams. We simulate similar PDs between bass and drums in a jazz rhythm section by means of RFM, by first making a quantized ($SR = 2$), multi-track MIDI recording of a walking bass and a cymbal swing groove, after which we apply *different* frequency modulation to the bass and drum recording. In the present example we make the cymbal perform with $SR = 3.17$, playing ahead of the bass, performing with $SR = 2$. The magnitudes of the PDs are here exaggerated compared to the findings of PDs in [15]. We do this deliberately to make the PDs in our example easy to hear, cf. a sounding realization at [2]. By making d a function of time, we are now able to make various more realistic, dynamic syntheses of PDs in rhythm performance.

Example 5: A "Weird" Two-Part Bach Invention. To give an example of how the RFM instrument might be applied to create exciting *unplayable*, rather "weird" performances, we import a metronomic, quantized MIDI recording of J. S. Bachs composition "2-Part Invention No. 13 in A Minor" as a MIDI file into the RFM program. The voices played by the right and left hand are given different rhythmic modulations, in the following way:

Right hand (1st voice): $f_c = 4$, $f_m = 0.0625 (= 1/16)$, $\phi_m = 0$, $n = 3$, $d = 16$
Left hand (2nd voice): $f_c = 4$, $f_m = 0.0625$, $\phi_m = 0$, $n = 3$, $d = -16$

Observe that the modulation parameters used for the right and left hand are the same, except for the sign ($\pm$) of d. The result of this modulation, which may be heard at [2], is that the voices played by the right and left hand are moving *out of sync* and *into sync* with each other in a somewhat "symmetric" way. Whenever the 1st voice is making an accelerando, the 2nd voice is making a ritardando, and vice versa. The two voices "meet" (i.e. are synchronized) every eight bar, and also at the end.

Rather than trying to simulate real live music performances, we have in this example created a new piece of electronic music. Seen as such, this illustrates how RFM might represent a new interesting compositional instrument for electro-acoustic music.

5   Discussion and Conclusion

In this paper we have shown how an application of dynamic frequency modulation of rhythm might be applied to obtain new syntheses of performances of swing. By introducing dynamic parameters in our RFM model we are able to simulate typical time- and tempo-dependent features of live performances of rhythm, characterized by various "deviations from the exact". As exemplified in our construction of the "weird" Bach invention, RFM synthesis may also be applied as a new compositional tool for electro-acoustic music.

Several alternative computational models of expressive music performance have, through the last 30 years or so, been developed. An overview of a large number of these models is given in [18]. An underlying assumption in the construction of these models is that there is a strong systematic link between musical structure and structure of music performances, and a common strategy in many of the model constructions has been to apply various quantitative empirical research to identify different *performance rules* by which expressive music performance can be modeled. Our present model suggests an alternative approach: Rather than applying patterns of timing deviations found through measurements and analysis of timing, we present a continuous mechanism which *models the systematic production of microtiming*. Our idea is to apply an interaction of oscillators to achieve alterations of frequencies that create timing deviations. This is an idea which can be seen as natural on the basis of the current understanding of the role of various oscillations in neural processing of timing in the brain. At this point it is interesting to know that Mcguiness has presented a model based on interactions of oscillators to reproduce the microtiming of Clyde Stubblefields drum break on James Browns track "The Funky Drummer", see [19]. The oscillators in Mcguiness' model are pulse-coupled, whereas they are continuously-coupled in our model. In addition, the oscillators in Mcguiness' model are mutually coupled, unlike our model, which utilizes one-way coupling of oscillators.

It is also interesting to discuss our model construction related to the theoretical framework within behavioural studies of movement timing that distinguishes between two forms of timing control: emergent timing and event-based timing, cf. Delignières and Torre [13], and Repp and Steinman [22]. As stated in [13], page 313, "...the essential difference between event-based and emergent timing is in the involvement or noninvolvement, respectively, of an abstract and effector independent representation of the time intervals to produce." In [13] we also read that some timing tasks tend to favour event-based timing (i.e., discrete finger tapping), some others emergent timing (i.e., continuous circle drawing or forearm oscillations), whereas other tasks appear more ambiguous. Moreover, they state: "Air tapping (in which taps are performed in the air, without contact with any surface) seems to present this ambiguity" [13], page 313. - Air tapping is the fundamental starting point of our model. - In the idealized situation this movement is represented by a symmetric, sinusoidal trajectory, mirroring a static, self-sustained oscillation. Applying different degrees of frequency modulation this sinusoidal movement curve is continuously transformed to become asymmetric, simulating various non-metronomic live performances of rhythm. Different degree of asymmetry in the movement trajectory is also a feature that is shown to reflect a distinction between emergent and event-based timing modes, - emergent timing producing more symmetric movement curves, whereas the trajectories in event-based timing have a more asymmetric shape. As stated by Delignières and Torre [13], page 315: "It is possible that during emergent epochs in air tapping the trajectory of the index finger should be smooth and harmonic, whereas during event-based epochs it should be more jagged, with the presence of systematic pauses before each downstroke." - Since asymmetry in our model is represented by the strength of modulation, determined by the peak frequency deviation, d, this might suggest that a change between the two modes of timing control, emergent vs. event-based timing, is reflected in the magnitude of the absolute value of d. A more thorough discussion of this is presented in [29].

Although we believe that dynamic rhythmic frequency modulation is shown to be an interesting tool in making syntheses of various rhythmic characteristics of live performances of music, many aspects of the model can certainly undergo further development and change. For instance, it would be nice to implement *real-time* manipulation of the modulation parameters, and to develop the RFM instrument into a MIDI plugin. It should also be noted that in this paper RFM synthesis is used to simulate *temporal* aspects of rhythm performance, whereas in [29] frequency modulation is applied to make syntheses of movement *trajectories* in rhythmic behaviour. It would be interesting to combine these approaches of FM rhythms to obtain a model by which aspects of timing, as well as characteristic gestures of live performances of rhythm could be simulated.

Acknowledgements. The authors are grateful to the anonymous reviewers for their valuable comments and suggestions.

References

1. Alén, O.: Rhythm as duration of sounds in tumba francesa. Ethnomusicology **39**, 55–71 (1995)
2. Audio Realization of FM Rhythm Synthesis. http://folk.ntnu.no/sigurds/FMrhythm.html
3. Balasubramaniam, R., Wing, A.M., Daffertshofer, A.: Keeping with the beat: movement trajectories contribute to movement timing. Exp. Brain Res. **159**, 129–134 (2004)
4. Benadon, F.: Slicing the beat: jazz eighth-notes as expressive microrhythm. Ethnomusicology **50**(1), 73–98 (2006)
5. Bengtsson, I., Gabrielsson, A.: Analysis and synthesis of musical rhythm. In: Sundberg, J. (ed.) Studies of Music Performance. Publications Issued by the Royal Swedish Academy of Music, Stockholm, vol. 39, pp. 27–59 (1983)
6. Butler, M.J.: Unlocking the Groove: Rhythm, Meter, and Musical Design in Electronic Dance Music. Indiana University Press, Bloomington and Indianapolis (2006)
7. Butterfield, M.W.: Power of anacrusis: engendered feeling in groove-based musics. Music Theory Online **12**, 4 (2006)
8. Butterfield, M.: Participatory discrepancies and the perception of beats in jazz. Music Percept. **27**(3), 157–175 (2010)
9. Butterfield, M.W.: Why do jazz musicians swing their eighth notes? Music Theory Spectr. **33**(1), 3–26 (2011)
10. Chowning, J.M.: The synthesis of complex audio spectra by means of frequency modulation. J. Audio Eng. Soc. **21**, 526–534 (1973)
11. Clarke, E.F.: Rhythm and timing in music. In: Deutsch, D. (ed.) The Psychology of Music, 2nd edn, pp. 473–500. Academic Press, San Diego (1999)
12. Collier, G., Collier, J.: The swing rhythm in jazz. In: Pennycook, B., Costa-Giomi, E. (eds.) Proceedings of the 4th International Conference on Music Perception and Cognition, pp. 477–480. McGill University, Montreal, Canada (1996)
13. Delignières, D., Torre, K.: Event-based and emergent timing: dichotomy or continuum? a reply to Repp and Steinman (2010). J. Mot. Behav. **43**(4), 311–318 (2011)
14. Frane, A.V.: Swing rhythm in classic drum breaks from hip-hop's breakbeat canon. Music. Percept.: Interdiscip. J. **34**(3), 291–302 (2017)
15. Friberg, A., Sundström, A.: Swing ratios and ensemble timing in jazz performance: evidence for a common rhythmic pattern. Music. Percept. **19**, 333–349 (2002)
16. Honing, H., Haas, W.B.De: Swing once more: relating timing and tempo in expert jazz drumming. Music Percept. **25**(5), 471–476 (2008)
17. Keil, C.: The theory of participatory discrepancies: a progress report. Ethnomusicology **39**, 1–19 (1995)
18. Kirke, A., Miranda, E.R. (eds.): Guide to Computing for Expressive Music Performance. Springer, London (2013). https://doi.org/10.1007/978-1-4471-4123-5

19. Mcguiness, A.: Modelling microtiming beat variations with pulse-coupled oscillators. Timing Time Percept. **3**(1–2), 155–171 (2015)
20. Moelants, D.: The performance of notes inégales: the influence of tempo, musical structure, and individual performance style on expressive timing. Music Percept. **28**(5), 449–460 (2011)
21. Prögler, J.A.: Searching for swing: participatory discrepancies in the jazz rhythm section. Ethnomusicology **39**, 21–54 (1995)
22. Repp, B.H., Steinman, S.R.: Event-based and emergent timing: synchronization, continuation, and phase correction. J. Mot. Behav. **42**(2), 111–126 (2010)
23. Saue, S.: Implementing rhythmic frequency modulation. In: Waadeland, C.H. Rhythmic Movements and Moveable Rhythms – Syntheses of Expressive Timing by Means of Rhythmic Frequency Modulation (Thesis), pp. 252–276. NTNU, Trondheim (2000)
24. Schuller, G.: The Swing Era: The Development of Jazz 1930–1945. Oxford University Press, New York (1989)
25. Seashore, C.E.: Psychology of Music. McGraw-Hill, New York (1938)
26. Viviani, P.: Common factors in the control of free and constrained movements. In: Jeannerod, M. (ed.) Attention and Performance XIII, 345373. Lawrence Erlbaum Associates, Publication (1990)
27. Waadeland, C.H.: "It Don't Mean a Thing If It Ain't Got That Swing" - Simulating expressive timing by modulated movements. J. New Music. Res. **30**, 23–37 (2001)
28. Waadeland, C.H.: Strategies in empirical studies of swing groove. Studia Musicologica Norvegica **32**, 169–191 (2006)
29. Waadeland, C.H.: Synthesis of asymmetric movement trajectories in timed rhythmic behaviour by means of frequency modulation. Hum. Mov. Sci. **51**, 112–124 (2017)

A Hierarchical Harmonic Mixing Method

Gilberto Bernardes[1]([✉]), Matthew E. P. Davies[1], and Carlos Guedes[1,2]

[1] INESC TEC, Sound and Music Computing Group,
Rua Dr. Roberto Frias, 378, 4200 - 465 Porto, Portugal
{gba,mdavies}@inesctec.pt
[2] New York University Abu Dhabi, PO Box 129188, Saadiyat Island,
Abu Dhabi, United Arab Emirates
carlos.guedes@nyu.edu

Abstract. We present a hierarchical harmonic mixing method for assisting users in the process of music mashup creation. Our main contributions are metrics for computing the harmonic compatibility between musical audio tracks at small- and large-scale structural levels, which combine and reassess existing perceptual relatedness (i.e., chroma vector similarity and key affinity) and dissonance-based approaches. Underpinning our harmonic compatibility metrics are harmonic indicators from the perceptually-motivated Tonal Interval Space, which we adapt to describe musical audio. An interactive visualization shows hierarchical harmonic compatibility viewpoints across all tracks in a large musical audio collection. An evaluation of our harmonic mixing method shows our adaption of the Tonal Interval Space robustly describes harmonic attributes of musical instrument sounds irrespective of timbral differences and demonstrates that the harmonic compatibility metrics comply with the principles embodied in Western tonal harmony to a greater extent than previous approaches.

Keywords: Music mashup · Digital DJ interfaces
Audio content analysis · Music information retrieval

1 Introduction

Mashup creation is a music composition practice strongly linked to the various sub-genres of Electronic Dance Music (EDM) and the role of the DJ [27]. It entails the recombination of existing (pre-recorded) musical audio as a means for creative endeavor [27]. As such, it can be seen as a byproduct of existing mass preservation mechanisms and inscribed within the artistic view of the database as a symbol of postmodern culture [20]. Mashup creation is typically confined to technology-fluent composers, as it requires expertise which extends from the understanding of musical structure to the navigation and retrieval of musical audio from large collections. Both industry and academia have been devoting efforts to enhance the experience of digital tools for mashup creation by streamlining the time-consuming search for compatible musical audio.

© Springer Nature Switzerland AG 2018
M. Aramaki et al. (Eds.): CMMR 2017, LNCS 11265, pp. 151–170, 2018.
https://doi.org/10.1007/978-3-030-01692-0_11

Early research on computational mashup creation, focused on rhythmic-only features, particularly those relevant to the temporal alignment of two or more musical tracks [13]. Recent research on this topic has expanded the range of musical attributes under consideration, notably including harmonic-driven features to identify compatible musical audio, commonly referred to as *harmonic mixing*. We can identify three major harmonic mixing methods: key affinity, chroma vectors similarity, and sensory dissonance minimization.

The affinity between musical keys is a prominent method in commercial applications. It is defined by distances across major and minor keys in a double circular representation, known within the DJ community as the *Camelot Wheel*, shown in Fig. 1. This method favors relative major-minor and intervals of fifth relations across musical keys [21] and enforces some degree of tonal stability and large-scale harmonic coherence of the mix by privileging the use of the same diatonic key pitch set. Chroma vector similarity inspects the cosine distance between chroma vector representations of pitch shifted versions of two given audio tracks as a measure of their compatibility [8,9,19]. Distances are typically computed at the beat level, thus privileging small-scale alignments over large-scale harmonic structure between audio slices with highly similar pitch class content. Sensory dissonance models have been used to search for pitch shifted versions of overlapping musical audio which minimize their combined level of roughness [12]; a motivation well rooted in the Western musical tradition by favoring a less dissonant harmonic lexicon.

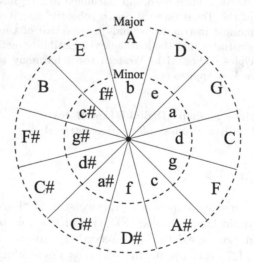

Fig. 1. Key affinity representation based on the two circles of fifths for major and minor keys aligned by relative major-minor key relationships. Enharmonic equivalence is assumed and only sharps (♯) are used.

While existing harmonic compatibility metrics have shown to correlate well with user enjoyment, we argue that they expose promising areas for investigation on harmonic compatibility. First, searching across all possible overlaps between related or in-key (i.e., diatonic) pitch sets result in highly contrasting sonorities with significant levels of enjoyment [3], thus motivating a harmonic compatibility metric below the key level. This metric is also prone to error, namely whenever processing signals with low pitch-to-noise ratio, and despite the perceptual manifestation of the key distances shown in Fig. 1 [17], it denotes temporal phenomena (i.e., key transitions). It remains unclear its validity and usefulness for mixing tracks. Second, while chroma vector distances are effective in capturing highly similar matches between any two given audio tracks, they lack a perceptually-aware basis for comparing pitch configurations [2], and can thus fail to provide an effective ranking between musical audio collections. Third, while psychoacoustic models show enhanced performance over existing approaches, they not only prove to be of limited use when the spectral content of the tracks do not overlap (i.e., when no interaction exists within each critical band), but also violate some perceptual and harmonic principles embodied in Western music, namely at the chordal level, by predicting that an augmented triad is more consonant that a diminished triad [16].

At the design level, existing software for harmonic mixing propose a ranked list of harmonically compatible tracks to a user-defined track [9,21,22]. We believe that this one-to-many mapping is reductive in offering a global view of a music collection and enabling a fluid navigation through an audio collection. Furthermore, it is computationally inefficient, as it recomputes highly intensive audio signal analysis every time a different audio track is selected as target.

In light of these limitations, we propose a new method for computing the small- and large-scale harmonic compatibility between a beat-matched collection of audio tracks, based on indicators from the perceptually-motivated Tonal Interval Space [2] and following the diagram architecture shown in Fig. 2. The proposed method has three aims: (i) to perceptually enhance the manifestation of metrics for harmonic compatibility, (ii) to inspect small- and large-scale structural levels by summarizing existing mashup creation approaches in a single framework, and (iii) to efficiently explore musical audio collections, without the need for intensive computation for each specific target, towards a more fluid user-experience which fosters experimentation.

The remainder of this paper is structured as follows. Section 2 reviews the Tonal Interval Space, which we adapt towards an enhanced representation of the harmonic content of musical audio. Section 3 presents content-driven harmonic analysis of musical audio. Section 4 introduces new metrics for computing the harmonic compatibility between audio tracks. Section 5 details an interactive visualization which exposes the compatibility of a musical audio collection. Section 6 presents an evaluation of the indicators and compatibility metrics which underpin our harmonic mixing method. Finally, Sect. 7 presents conclusions and areas for future work.

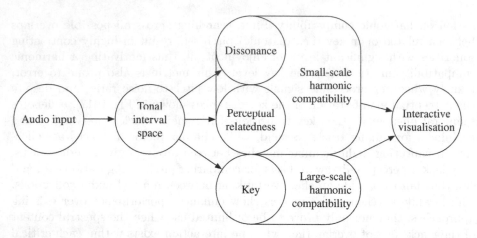

Fig. 2. Diagram of the component modules of our compatibility method for music mixing.

2   Adapting Tonal Interval Vectors for Musical Audio

We represent the harmonic content of musical audio tracks as 12-dimensional Tonal Interval Vectors (TIVs) [2]. This vector space creates an extended representation of tonal pitch in the context of the *Tonnetz* [11], named the Tonal Interval Space, where the most salient pitch levels of tonal Western music—pitch, chord, and key—exist as unique locations. TIVs, $T(k)$, are computed from an audio signal as the weighted Discrete Fourier Transform (DFT) of an L_1 normalized chroma vector, $c(n)$, such that:

$$T(k) = w_a(k) \sum_{n=0}^{N-1} \bar{c}(n) e^{\frac{-j2\pi kn}{N}}, \quad k \in \mathbb{Z}. \tag{1}$$

where $N = 12$ is the dimension of the chroma vector, each of which expresses the energy of the 12 pitch classes, and $w_a(k)$ are weights derived from empirical ratings of dyads consonance used to adjust the contribution of each dimension k (or interpreted musical interval) of the space, which we detail over the next paragraphs. We set k to $1 \leq k \leq 6$ for $T(k)$ since the remaining coefficients are symmetric. $T(k)$ uses $\bar{c}(n)$ which is $c(n)$ normalized by the DC component $T(0) = \sum_{n=0}^{N-1} c(n)$ to allow the representation and comparison of music at different hierarchical levels of tonal pitch [2]. To represent variable-length audio tracks, we accumulate chroma vectors, $c(n)$, resulting from 16384 sample windows analysis at 44.1 kHz sampling rate (≈ 372 ms) with 50% overlap across the track duration.

In [2], we used two complementary sources of empirical data—empirical ratings of dyad consonance shown in Table 1 [14] and the ranking order of triad consonance: {maj, min, sus4, dim, aug} [1,7]—to make the Tonal Interval Space perceptually relevant for symbolic music input representations (i.e., binary chroma vectors). Here, we revisit the task to comply with the timbral components of

Table 1. Composite consonance ratings of dyads consonance [14].

Interval class	m2/M7	M2/m7	m3/M6	M3/m6	P4/P5 TT
Consonance	−1.428	−.582	.594	.386	1.240 −.453

musical audio. Our goal is to find a set of weights, $w_a(k)$, which regulate the importance of the DFT coefficients k in Eq. 1, so that the space conveys a reliable consonance indicator correlated with the aforementioned empirical ratings of dyad [14] and triad consonance [7]. The applied method follows the previously used brute force approach [2], which produced a near optimal result.

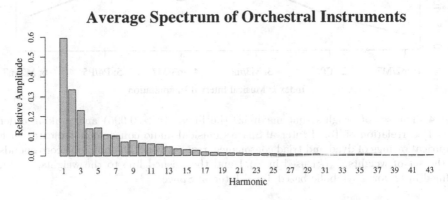

Average Spectrum of Orchestral Instruments

Fig. 3. Average harmonic spectrum of 1338 tones from orchestral instruments [23].

A major problem in defining a set of weights for robustly representing musical audio in the Tonal Interval Space is the variability of timbre across musical instruments and registers. A refined model capable of tracing the idiosyncratic timbral attributes of a particular instrument raises scalability and complexity issues which would defeat the value of the Tonal Interval Space in providing effective and, most importantly, efficient perceptual indicators of tonal pitch. To circumvent these issues, we adopt the 43-partial harmonic spectrum template shown in Fig. 3 to represent the harmonic content of musical audio. The template results from averaging 1338 recorded instrument tones from 23 Western orchestral instruments and can be understood as a time-invariant spectrum of an "average instrument" [23].

To allow a computationally tractable search for weights to represent musical audio in the Tonal Interval Space, we split the task into two steps. In the first step, we find the weights, $w_a(k)$, from all possible 6-element combinations (with repetition and order relevance), of the set $I = \{1, 19\} \in \mathbb{Z} : I = 2I + 1$ (a total of approximately one million combinations), which maintain in the Tonal Interval Space the empirical ranking order of common triads consonance [7]. Following [2], we compute the consonance of musical audio triads in the Tonal Interval Space as the norm of TIVs, $\|T(k)\|$, which we detail in Sect. 3. In the second step, from the resulting set of 111 weight vectors which preserve the ranking order of empirical triads consonance (i.e., a Spearman rank correlation $\rho = 1$), we identify those which have the highest linear correlation to the empirical dyad consonance ratings shown in Table 1.

We repeated the two aforementioned steps to further optimize the two weight vectors ($\{1, 7, 15, 11, 13, 7\}$ and $\{3, 7, 15, 11, 13, 7\}$) with the highest linear correlation ($r = .988$), below our minimal interval using 0.5 increments.

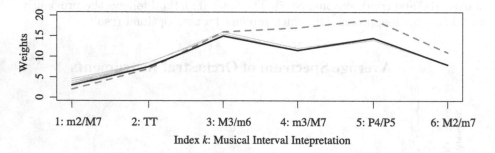

Fig. 4. The set of weights that maximize the linear ($r > 0.995$) and ranking order ($\rho = 1$) correlation of Tonal Interval Space's musical audio consonance indicator with empirical ratings of dyad and triad consonance, respectively. The bold line corresponds to the set of weights $w_a(k)$ used in Eq. 1 and the dashed line to the weights, $w_s(k)$, defined in [2] for a symbolic based Tonal Interval Space.

Figure 4 shows 11 sets of weights, $w_a(k)$, which preserve empirical triads ($\rho = 1$) and dyad ($r > .99$) consonance for musical audio. Given the inherent similarity in shape of the different sets of weights and their almost perfect linear relationship, we do not believe the choice over exactly which set of weights to be critical. Ultimately, we selected the weights with the greatest mutual separation between the triads according to consonance, thus $w_a(k) = \{3, 8, 11.5, 15, 14.5, 7.5\}$.

3   Harmonic Indicators from Musical Audio: Dissonance and Perceptual Relatedness

To provide a mathematical representation of Western tonal harmony perception as distances in the Tonal Interval Space, we distorted a DFT space according to the weights, $w_a(k)$, derived from empirical consonance ratings. In light of this design feature and following previous metrics detailed in [2], we can compute two indicators of musical audio dissonance, D, and perceptual relatedness, R, from the space as distance metrics.

$$D = 1 - \left(\frac{\|T(k)\|}{\|w_a(k)\|} \right), \tag{2}$$

$$D_{ij} = 1 - \left(\frac{\|a_i T_i(k) + a_j T_j(k)\|}{a_i + a_j \|w_a(k)\|} \right), \tag{3}$$

and

$$R_{i,j} = \sqrt{\sum_{k=1}^{M} |T_i(k) - T_j(k)|^2}. \tag{4}$$

We adapt the consonance metric presented in [2] to a musical audio dissonance metric, by subtracting the normalized norm of a TIV, $T(k)$, from one.
Drawn from the properties of the DFT at the basis of the space, the location
of multi-pitch TIVs is equal to the linear combination of its component pitch
classes [2]. Thus, we can efficiently compute the dissonance of two combined
TIVs, $T_i(k)$ and $T_j(k)$, representing two overlapping audio tracks, i and j, using
Eq. 3, where a_i and a_j are the amplitudes of $T_i(k)$ and $T_j(k)$.

Equation 4 computes the perceptual relatedness, $R_{i,j}$, as the Euclidean distance between TIVs. Small values of perceptual relatedness, R, denote voice
leading parsimony and controlled transitions of the interval content between
neighborhood TIVs, as smaller distances primarily enforce the number of shared
tones, and to a lesser degree, the interval relations imposed by the weights,
$w_a(k)$.

4   Harmonic Compatibility Metrics

Based on the two dissonance, D, and perceptual relatedness, R, indicators from
the Tonal Interval Space presented in Sect. 3, we now propose two metrics that
aim at capturing the harmonic compatibility between TIVs to be mixed. Of note
is the split between small- and large-scale harmonic compatibility, which roughly
correspond to the 'sound object' and 'meso' or 'macro' time scales of music,
respectively. In other words, the small-scale denotes the basic units of musical
structure, from notes to beats, and the large-scale inspects the structural levels
between the phrase and the overall musical piece architecture [24]. In the context
of our work, the first aims mostly at finding good harmonic matches between
the tracks in a collection, and the second in guaranteeing control over the overall
harmonic structure of a mix, i.e., the tonal changes at the key level across its
temporal dimension.

4.1   Small-Scale Harmonic Compatibility

The level of small-scale harmonic compatibility is expressed as the combination of two harmonic audio indicators from the Tonal Interval Space detailed in
Sect. 3: dissonance, D, and perceptual relatedness, R. The latter indicator finds
sonorities which have a strong perceptual affinity and thus range from a perfect
match to sonorities with different timbres and similar pitch content, to an array
of sonorities with increased levels of perceptual distance. We envisage it as an

extension of the chroma vector similarity method used as a measure of harmonic compatibility in prior studies [8,9,19], which offers a refined control over the introduction of new tones as well as its interval relations in the resulting mix between overlapped tracks.

Given the likely increase in dissonance in the mix and following some perceptual evidence from previous research [12], our small-scale harmonic compatibility also privileges the search for less dissonance mixes—a well established principle in the common syntax of Western tonal harmony [1,5,18]. Hence, our small-scale harmonic compatibility metric, H, is then computed as the product of the two indicators, such that:

$$H_{i,j} = \bar{R}_{i,j} \cdot \bar{D}_{ij}, \tag{5}$$

where $\bar{R}$ and $\bar{C}$ are R and C scaled to the range $\{0,1\} \in \mathbb{R}$ to balance the importance of both indicators in the compatibility metric. The main motivation for the simple multiplication of the two variables is rooted in the visualization method we detail in Sect. 5, notably by enforcing a small-scale harmonic compatibility, $H = 0$, when comparing the same track.

4.2 Large-scale Harmonic Compatibility

A derivation of the perceptual relatedness indicator, R, exposes an important property of the Tonal Interval Space: the formation of fuzzy key clusters of diatonic pitch class sets. Neighborhood relations between these clusters in the Tonal Interval Space result in a representation similar to Fig. 1, as a result of common-tone relations between keys. This property is adopted to estimate the global key from musical audio track, which aims to guide users in planning the large-scale harmonic structure of a mix.

We use the method reported in [4] to compute the global key estimate, Q, of an audio track in the Tonal Interval Space, as the minimum Euclidean distance of an audio input TIV, $T(k)$, from the 12 major and 12 minor key TIVs, $T_r(k)$, such that:

$$Q = \operatorname{argmin}_p \sqrt{\sum_{k=1}^{6} |T(k) \cdot \alpha - T_r(k)|^2}, \tag{6}$$

where $T_r(k)$ is derived from a collection of templates (understood here as chroma vectors) representing pitch class distributions for each of the 12 major and 12 minor keys [26]. When $r \leqslant 11$, we adopt the major profile and when $r \geqslant 12$, the minor profile. $\alpha = 0.35$ is a factor which displaces input sample TIVs to balance predictions across modes [4] (Table 2).

The estimated key, Q, ranges between $0 - 11$ for major keys and $12 - 23$ for minor keys, where 0 corresponds to C major, 1 to C# major, and so on through to 23 being B minor.

5 Interactive Visualization

We created a software prototype in Pure Data which implements the proposed hierarchical mixing method, notably the harmonic compatibility metrics. In light

Table 2. Sha'ath's [26] key profiles, p, for the C major and C minor keys.

Key	C	C#	D	D#	E	F	F#	G	G#	A	A#	B
C major	7.239	3.504	3.584	2.845	5.819	4.559	2.448	6.995	3.391	4.556	4.074	4.459
C minor	7.003	3.144	4.359	5.404	3.672	4.089	3.907	6.200	3.634	2.872	5.355	3.832

of the possibility to retrieve compatible harmonic tracks from large musical audio collections, we designed an interactive visualization which aims to (i) provide a global view of the harmonic compatibility across all audio tracks in a collection (i.e., many-to-many relationships); (ii) expose a hierarchical representation over the harmonic compatibility between tracks; and (iii) promote user experimentation and creative endeavorer.

To this end, we pursued an interface design based on crossmodal associations between sound and image, for which a screenshot is shown in Fig. 5. All audio tracks in a collection are represented graphically in a two-dimensional (2-D) space, where regular polygons denote audio tracks and grey circles key centers. Distances among polygons (i.e., audio tracks) indicate small-scale harmonic compatibility, H, and links from circles (i.e., key centers) to polygons the large-scale compatibility, Q, or, in other words, the association to its estimated key.

The computation of 2-D coordinates for each audio track from a square matrix of all pairwise tracks small-scale harmonic compatibility distances, H, is a classical problem, which can be solved by a specific class of algorithms, notably including Multidimensional Scaling (MDS). From m musical audio tracks in a collection, we compute an $H_m \cdot H_m$ harmonic compatibility square matrix, from which an MDS representation extracts two-dimensional coordinates for each sample. The resulting representation attempts to preserve the inter-sample small-scale harmonic compatibility with minimal distortion.

The computation of coordinates for each key center equals the convex combination (or the centroid, in geometric terms) of the 2-D coordinates of its estimated tracks. We adopted this efficient method for the computation of key centers based on the theoretical assumption that the diatonic set of a key is denoted in the Tonal Interval Space by the convex combination of set of diatonic note TIVs [2]. Therefore, assuming that all tracks with the same key estimate represent well its diatonic set, its corresponding key coordinates ought to be represented with minimal distortion.

Two additional rhythmic and spectral musical features of each track are represented by graphical attributes of the polygons (number of sides and color, respectively) to expand the search attributes to fit particular compositional goals. The number of sides, ranging from three to six, expose the note onset density, computed by a threefold approach. First, we extract a spectral flux onset detection function, from a windowed power spectrum representation of the audio signal (2048 analysis windows size at 44.1 kHz sampling rate with 50% overlap), using the `timbreID` [6] library within Pure Data. Second, we identify the peaks from the function above a user-defined threshold, t, whose temporal location we assume to indicate note onset times. Prior to the peak detection stage, we apply a bi-directional low-pass IIR filter, with a cutoff frequency of 5 Hz to avoid spurious detections. Finally, we compute the ratio between the number of onsets and the entire duration of the audio file in seconds and scale the values for a given audio collection to the $\{3, 6\} \in \mathbb{Z}$ range of polygon sides.

The polygons' color, ranging from continuous shades of yellow to red, represents the spectral region a sample occupies in the perceptual perceptually-motivated Bark frequency scale.[1] A threefold strategy is adopted to map these two dimensions. First, we accumulate Bark spectrum B_b, representations computed on short-time windows of 2048 samples size at 44.1 kHz sampling rate with 50% overlap across an audio track, again using the timbreID [6] library within Pure Data. Then, we extract the centroid as an indicator of its spectral region, S, using Eq. 7. Finally, we map the spectral region, S, value to the the color scheme. Bark band 1 corresponds to yellow, and bark band 24 to red. Between these values, the colors are linearly mixed.

$$S = \frac{\sum_{i=1}^{19} B_b \cdot b}{\sum_{i=1}^{19} B_b}, \tag{7}$$

where B_b is the energy of the bark band b. The S indicator can range from 1 to 24.

The user can interact with the visualization by clicking on the polygons to trigger their playback, thus promoting an intuitive search for compatible tracks as well as strategies for serendipity and experimentation, rather than a fully automatic method for mashup creation. A demo of this interactive visualization can be found online at: https://sites.google.com/site/tonalintervalspace/mixmash.

6   Evaluation

We undertake a twofold strategy to evaluate our harmonic mixing method. First, we assess the perceptual validity and degree of timbre invariance of the two dissonance, D and perceptual relatedness, R, indicators from the Tonal Interval Space, which underpin our small-scale harmonic compatibility metric. Particular emphasis is given to the implications of the newly proposed weights, $w_a(k)$, for representing musical audio. Second, we examine the level of compliance of the proposed harmonic compatibility and related metrics with Western tonal music principles.

Unless otherwise specified, across evaluation tasks the harmonic spectrum of musical audio is computed as the sum of individual notes spectra using the harmonic template of an average instrument shown in Fig. 3.

---

[1] The Bark spectrum balances the resolution across the human hearing range in comparison to the typical power spectrum representation, namely increasing the resolution in the low frequency region. It is computed by warping a power spectrum to the 24 critical bands of the human auditory system [28].

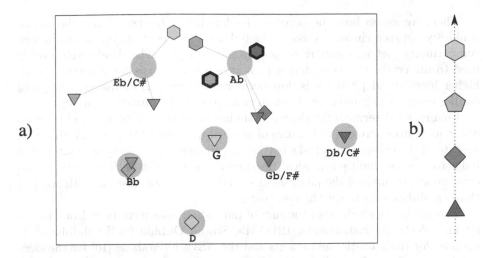

Fig. 5. (a) Interactive visualization of the hierarchical harmonic compatibility between all audio tracks in a collection. Polygons represent audio tracks and circles key centers. Polygon distances indicate small-scale harmonic compatibility and the links from circles the large-scale harmonic compatibility. The graphical attributes of the polygons show onset density (number of sides) and spectral region (color). Polygons with thick outlines indicate the selected files currently playing. (b) The ranking order of low to high onset density and spectral region.

The Spearman rank correlation, ρ, is the metric used to compare most data in our evaluation. It measures the strength and direction of the monotonic relationship between two variables. The motivation to adopt such a metric is due to the importance of the ranking order in proposing harmonic mixes rather than ensuring a linear relationship between the variables (computed, for example, by the Pearson correlation) and the prevalence of ranked data in perceptual studies. The result of the Spearman rank correlation, ρ, is expressed by a single correlation coefficient value in the $\{-1, +1\} \in \mathbb{R}$ range. Positive and negative correlation coefficients express positive and negative relationships between variables, respectively, and a correlation coefficient of $\rho = 0$ indicates that no relationship between the variables exists.

6.1   Harmonic Indicators for Musical Audio

We assess how the weights, $w_a(k)$, implemented as a design feature of the space, to provide a dissonance, D, indicator of musical audio, compare to (i) the sensory dissonance metric by Hutchinson and Knopoff [15] at the basis of Gebhardt et al. [12] mashup creation system and (ii) the previously proposed weights, $w_s(k) = \{2, 11, 17, 16, 19, 7\}$, adjusted for symbolic music representations [2], in measuring triads dissonance—the chordal level at which most mashup creation exists. All theoretical models are additionally compared to perceptual dissonance data [1, 7].

Then, we assess how the perceptual relatedness, R, metric and the cosine similarity between chroma vectors, adopted from Davies et al. [9], as a harmonic compatibility metric, compare to perceptual data [25]. The dyad pitch level is used to undertake this comparison as it lays out the basis for distances at all higher hierarchical pitch levels. Furthermore, various corroborating perceptual studies exist for this pitch level, which Schwartz et al. summarize in [25].

Finally, we determine the degree of timbre invariance of both Tonal Interval Space indicators across a wide range of musical instrument timbres. To this end, we extend the two previous tasks beyond the theoretical levels by evaluating the indicators across multiple musical instruments and registers. To constrain the experiment, we limited the pitch sets to triads in the root position with stacked thirds and dyads no larger than one octave.

The pitch sets result from the sum of individual note recordings from acoustic and electronic instruments. IRCAM's Studio OnLine (SOL) database[2] is adopted for the acoustic instruments and the NSynth database [10] for the electronic instruments. From the entire collection of acoustic instruments in the SOL database, we selected four instruments from each family, aiming to cover a wide note range: strings (violin, viola, guitar, and violoncello), woodwinds (flute, B♭ clarinet, alto saxophone, and bassoon), and brass (trumpet, trombone, horn, and bass tuba). From the NSynth database, we selected four electronic and synthetic instruments which commonly feature in EDM: electric keyboard, synth lead, and electric bass, and electric guitar.

The selected acoustic instrument samples are quasi-stationary, i.e., without any extended playing technique, and electronic and synthetic instrument samples are non-stationary, with clear temporal changes at a regular fast pace, as a result of audio effects such as tremolo, vibrato, and filtering.[3] A *mezzo-forte* dynamic was adopted in both cases. Besides the alignment of the samples on detected onsets, no further processing was applied. Due to some discrepancies in the duration of the instrument samples in both databases, we limited their duration to two seconds, thus ensuring the same duration across all pitch sets. Instrument samples are mono WAV files with 44.1 Khz sampling rate and 16 bit depth. We computed the indicators (i.e., the dissonance, D, of triads and the perceptual relatedness, R, of dyads) per instrument as the average value of overlapping 8192 sample windows at 44.1 kHz sample rate with 50% overlap.

6.2   Harmonic Compatibility Metrics

We assess the extent to which the principles embodied in Western tonal harmony, namely the prevalence of common chord sets with reduced dissonance, are promoted by our proposed small-scale harmonic compatibility metric, H, and

---

[2] We used the version 0.9 of IRCAM's SOL database, retrieved at http://forumnet.ircam.fr/product/orchids-en/ in July, 2017 as the supporting database of the Orchids software.

[3] Please refer to https://sites.google.com/site/tonalintervalspace/mixmash to listen to electronic and synthetic instrument sample examples from the NSynth database.

related approaches, namely chroma similarity [9] and sensory dissonance [12]. To this end, we inspect which pitch class sets are identified as most compatible from a total of 55 triads, which result from overlapping the pitch class C or 0 (i.e., index 0 in $c(n)$ from Eq. 1) to all remaining pitch class dyads, in each metric. All dyads resulting from the combination (without repetition and order relevance) of the $\{1 - 11\} \in \mathbb{Z}$ set are considered.

6.3 Results

Table 3 reports the perceived and computed dissonance level of common musical audio triads. The perceptual data have been corroborated by several experimental studies [1,7]. The values for sensory dissonance are taken from [15] and result from applying the metric to triads that lie within the C^4-C^5 octave. The reported Spearman rank correlations, ρ, and their significance values, p, between the perceptual data and theoretical models show that the Tonal Interval Space is more consistent in ranking the dissonance of common triads than the Hutchinson and Knopoff [15] sensory dissonance model used in related mashup literature [12]. Moreover, we demonstrate that the weights, $w_a(k)$, computed in Sect. 2 are decisive in capturing the dissonance of musical audio triads in the Tonal Interval Space, as the previously proposed weights, $w_s(k)$ for symbolic music inputs [2] fail at providing a ranking of triads consonance from musical audio in line with perceptual data.

Table 3. Ranking of triads dissonance from perceptual data [1,7] and two theoretical models: sensory dissonance [15] and the Tonal Interval Space dissonance, adopting two sets of weights adapted to symbolic representation, $w_s(k)$, and musical audio, $w_a(k)$. The Spearman rank correlations, ρ, and their significance values, p, between the perceptual data and theoretical models are reported.

Triad quality	Perceptual rank [1,7]	Sensory dissonance [15]	Tonal Interval Space (D)	
major	1	1 (.139)	1–2 (.768)	1–2 (.783)
minor	2	2 (.148)	1–2 (.768)	1–2 (.783)
sus4	3	4 (.228)	3 (.769)	3 (.784)
dim	4	5 (.230)	5 (.819)	4 (.805)
aug	5	3 (.149)	4 (.780)	5 (.806)
Correlation ρ		.700	.878	.975
Significance p		.233	.054	<.05

Table 4 reports the perceived and computed dyads relatedness, R. The perceptual data are taken from [25], which summarizes different experimental studies. The chroma similarity was computed as the cosine similarity between chroma vectors following [9]. The reported Spearman rank correlations, ρ, and their significance values, p, between the perceptual data and theoretical models show that the Tonal Interval Space is more consistent in ranking the perceptual relatedness of dyads than the chroma similarity. Moreover, the ranking order of dyad relatedness in the Tonal Interval Space is consistent with tonal harmony principles in the sense it promotes tertian harmony as a result of having fifths and thirds at a closer distance than all remaining intervals. The chroma similarity, adopted as a harmonic compatibility metric in previous computational mashup works [8,9,19], largely agrees with the dyad perceptual ranking, with the notable exception of the minor seconds and major seventh which are closer in this metric space than the major and minor thirds or their complementary minor and major sixth, thus disrupting a preference for tertian harmonies.

Table 4. Ranking of dyad relatedness from perceptual data and theoretical models. The Spearman rank correlations, ρ, and their significance values, p, between the perceptual data and theoretical models are reported.

Dyad	Perceptual rank [25]	Chroma similarity [9]	Tonal Interval Space (R)
Unison (P1)	1	1−2 (0.00)	1−2 (0.00)
Octave (P12)	2	1−2 (0.00)	1−2 (0.00)
Perfect fifth (P5)	3	3−4 (1.11)	3−4 (1.37)
Perfect fourth (P4)	4	3−4 (1.11)	3−4 (1.37)
Major third (M3)	5	7−8 (1.20)	7−8 (1.62)
Major sixth (M6)	6	10−11 (1.26)	5−6 (1.53)
Minor sixth (m6)	7	7−8 (1.20)	7−8 (1.62)
Major third (M3)	8	10−11 (1.26)	5−6 (1.53)
Tritone (TT)	9	9 (1.25)	9 (1.78)
Minor seventh (m7)	10	12−13 (1.27)	10−11 (1.79)
Major second (M2)	11	12−13 (1.27)	10−11 (1.79)
Major seventh (M7)	12	5−6 (1.16)	12−13 (1.95)
Minor second (m2)	13	5−6 (1.16)	12−13 (1.95)
Correlation ρ		.609	.956
Significance p		< .05	< .001

Table 5 shows the Spearman rank correlations between perceptual data [1, 15,25] and Tonal Interval Space indicators from musical instrument inputs. We inspected the dissonance, D, of common triads and the perceptual relatedness, R of dyads. With the sole exception of the electric bass, all instruments have a significant Spearman rank correlation between the perceptual data and their computed indicators, thus ensuring a high degree of timbral invariance in computing the harmornic indicators from the Tonal Interval Space.

These results should also be read in light of the Spearman correlation between theoretical musical audio representations and perceptual data shown in Tables 3 and 4. The triad dissonance that results from instrument recordings does not fully mirror the perfect monotonic relationship of the theoretical results. Looking across instrument families it is noticeable the optimal results across all inspected

Table 5. Spearman rank correlation, ρ, of perceptual data for triads consonance and dyads distances and dissonance, D, and perceptual relatedness, R, metrics from the Tonal Interval Space, respectively, across multiple instruments. All results are significant for $p < 0.05$, except for the electric bass dissonance, where $p = 0.233$.

	Intrument	Pitch range (MIDI)	Dissonance (D)	Perceptual relatedness (R)
Strings	Violin	55−100	1	.956
	Viola	48−96	.9	.973
	Guitar	38−83	.8	.896
	Violoncello	36−84	.9	.973
Woodwinds	Flute	59−96	.9	.945
	B♭ clarinet	50−91	1	.956
	Alto saxophone	49−81	.9	.940
	Bassoon	34−75	1	.934
Brass	Trumpet	54−86	1	.951
	Trombone	34−72	1	.951
	Horn	31−77	1	.956
	Bass tuba	30−65	1	.945
Electronic	Electric guitar	36−86	1	.951
	Synth lead	21−108	.9	.934
	Electric keyboard	21−108	.9	.912
	Electric bass	9−96	.7	.900

instruments in the brass family. The remaining families have the approximately same number of instruments which do not fully comply with the perceptual triad ranking. The small sample of observed instruments raises interesting issues which should ultimately be addressed in future adaptations of the Tonal Interval Space. The dyad perceptual relatedness that results from instrument recordings is in line with the theoretical results ($\rho = 956$).

Figure 6 shows the analysis of the electronic instruments, which the "average (acoustic) instrument" spectrum, at the basis of the adaptation of the Tonal Interval Space to musical audio, does not model. In both the triad dissonance and dyad perceptual relatedness plots, an monotonically increasing function is expected, given the order of the x-axis elements according to an ascending perceptual ranking. In the triad dissonance plot, we can observe that the perceptual ranking is not preserved by violating the order of different triads per instrument. The dyad perceptual relatedness plot questions the symmetric property of the space (as a result of the DFT) for complementary intervals (e.g., m2 and M7 or M2 and m7) whose dissonance levels are averaged, thus neglecting any distinction between them.

Figure 7 shows the seven best ranking triads resulting from the overlap of the pitch class C and all remaining 55 pitch class dyad combinations for the following five metrics: (i) sensory dissonance [15]; (ii) chroma similarity [9]; (iii) perceptual relatedness, R; (iv) dissonance, D; and (v) small-scale harmonic compatibility,

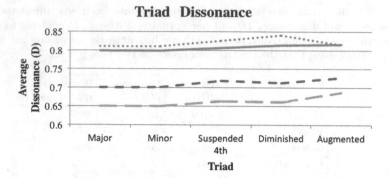

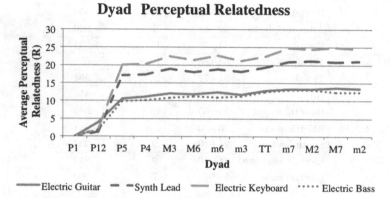

Fig. 6. Computed dyad dissonance and triad perceptual relatedness of electronic and synthetic instrument samples from the Tonal Interval Space. Pitch sets result from summing individual instrument samples. Average values across the inspected instruments' pitch range are reported for both indicators.

H. Sensory dissonance ranking order favors triads in line with the results presented in Table 3. Besides the preference for augmented over suspended 4ths and a few minor triads, to a large extent it conveys the expectancy of the Western tonal syntax. The ranking order of triads in the chroma similarity space and the perceptual relatedness, R, are aligned with the findings shown in Table 4. The chroma similarity favors chords including P4/P5 and m2/M7 intervals. Conversely, the perceptual relatedness, R, favors chords including P5/P4, m3/M6, and M3/m7 intervals. As such, combining sonorities with small R values, results in extended chords with stacked fifths and thirds. However, while the chords resulting from these vertical aggregates are building blocks of Western tonal harmony, the best ranked chords result in multiple seventh chords (with omitted notes), and not, as expected in the ideal case, triads (e.g., major, minor, and diminished).

When combining the perceptual relatedness, R, and the dissonance, D, indicators, i.e., when adopting our small-scale harmonic compatibility, H, metric, we enforce the preference for common major, minor, and suspended fourth triads—the most common building blocks of the Western tonal harmony, by favoring in the former ranking less dissonant triads. Nonetheless, the small-scale harmonic compatibility, H, ranking in Fig. 7 ignores the key level, thus promoting chromaticism (non-diatonic) progressions between neighbor sonorities. Our large-scale harmonic compatibility addresses this issue by providing in our interactive visualization a layer of information which can guide users in selecting (in-key) diatonic mixes.

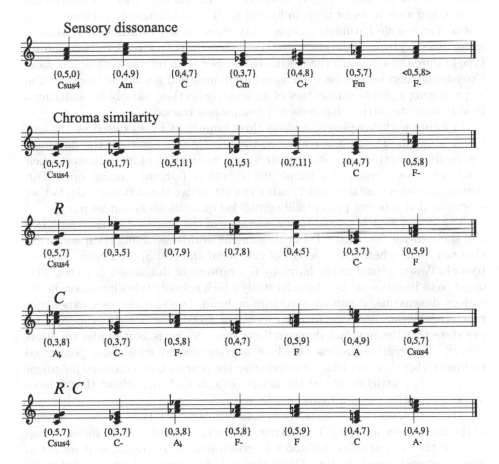

Fig. 7. Ranking order of triads resulting from overlapping the pitch class C and all remaining pitch class dyads as given by computed metrics. Apart from triad sensory dissonance, which is taken from [15], the remaining models were computed using the harmonic spectrum representation of an "average instrument" spectrum shown in Fig. 3. To the pitch class set of the resulting triads, we include the chord label whenever unambiguous and complete triads are formed. Sounding examples of the table contents are available at: https://sites.google.com/site/tonalintervalspace/mixmash.

7 Conclusion and Future Work

In this paper we have presented a hierarchical harmonic mixing method with two underlying metrics that inspect the harmonic compatibility of musical audio tracks at both small- and large-scale structural levels. Small-scale harmonic compatibility results from the combination of dissonance and perceptual relatedness indicators from the Tonal Interval Space, which we adapted to represent musical audio. Our adaptation is largely invariant to timbral differences of instrument sounds, and aims to assist users in finding good local alignments between mixed tracks. Large-scale harmonic compatibility relies on key estimates and aims to assist users in planning the global harmonic structure of a mix. A software prototype in Pure Data presents the metrics to the user in an interactive visualization. Crossmodal associations between sound attributes and geometric elements aim at promoting a global exploration of an audio collection, namely by fostering a fluid strategy to retrieve harmonically compatible tracks.

In future work, we plan to address three important issues raised by the current evaluation. The first is related to the perceptual validity of the harmonic compatibility metrics. Despite the perceptual motivation of its indicators, their combination as a result of a simple multiplicative fashion, remains open. Our evaluation shows that the model leads to an attractive theoretical result, but we speculate that a better perceptually-grounded quantification can be found.

The second issue is related to the relevancy of the proposed method for EDM and the creative flow of the DJ in meaningful world-case application scenarios. One can argue whether the design of the Tonal Interval Space design oriented towards Western tonal music harmony is a prominent dimension in EDM. This ought to be investigated by a broader study which not only takes into account the various dimensions of musical structure at hand, but also the user experience promoted by our interface in the context of EDM practice. In response, we can state that the interface design reflects these concerns as it guides the users through the creative process based on metrics aligned with some perceptual findings rather then dictating or automating the process based on some judgment about the harmonic quality of the music. To this end, we believe that a large degree of creative endeavor can be achieved.

The third aspect under consideration in future work relates to the scalability of the data under analysis. The current interactive interface is inefficient when we scale the musical collection above a certain number of tracks, as it results in dense cluttered visual clusters. Given the goal of inspecting large musical audio collections at the level of the hundreds or thousand tracks, we aim to address strategies to enhance the sparseness of the visualization.

Acknowledgments. This work is supported by national funds through the FCT - Foundation for Science and Technology, I.P., under the project IF/01566/2015.

References

1. Arthurs, Y., Beeston, A.V., Timmers, R.: Perception of isolated chords: Examining frequency of occurrence, instrumental timbre, acoustic descriptors and musical training. Psychol. Music **46**(5), 662–681 (2018). https://doi.org/10.1177/0305735617720834
2. Bernardes, G., Cocharro, D., Caetano, M., Guedes, C., Davies, M.: A multi-level tonal interval space for modelling pitch relatedness and musical consonance. J. New Music Res. **45**(4), 281–294 (2016)
3. Bernardes, G., Cocharro, D., Guedes, C., Davies, M.E.P.: Harmony generation driven by a perceptually motivated tonal interval space. ACM Comput. Entertain. **14**(2), 6 (2016)
4. Bernardes, G., Davies, M., Guedes, C.: Audio key estimation with adaptive mode bias. In: Proceedings of ICASSP, pp. 316–320 (2017)
5. Bidelman, G.M., Krishnan, A.: Brainstem correlates of behavioral and compositional preferences of musical harmony. Neuroreport **22**, 212–216 (2011)
6. Brent, W.: A timbre analysis and classification toolkit for pure data. In: Proceedings of ICMC, pp. 224–229 (2010)
7. Cook, N.: Harmony, Perspective, and Triadic Cognition. Cambridge University Press, Cambridge (2012)
8. Davies, M., Stark, A., Gouyon, F., Goto, M.: Improvasher: a real-time mashup system for live musical input. In: Proceedings of NIME, pp. 541–544 (2014)
9. Davies, M.E.P., Hamel, P., Yoshii, K., Goto, M.: Automashupper: automatic creation of multi-song music mashups. IEEE Trans. ASLP **22**(12), 1726–1737 (2014)
10. Engel, J., et al.: Neural audio synthesis of musical notes with WaveNet autoencoders. In: Proceedings of the 34th International Conference on Machine Learning, pp. 1068–1077 (2017)
11. Euler, L.: Tentamen novae theoriae musicae. Broude (1968/1739)
12. Gebhardt, R., Davies, M., Seeber, B.: Psychoacoustic approaches for harmonic music mixing. Appl. Sci. **6**(5), 123 (2016)
13. Griffin, G., Kim, Y., Turnbull, D.: Beat-sync-mash-coder: A web application for real-time creation of beat-synchronous music mashups. In: Proceedings of ICASSP, pp. 437–440 (2010)
14. Huron, D.: Interval-class content in equally tempered pitch-class sets: common scales exhibit optimum tonal consonance. Music Percept. **11**(3), 289–305 (1994)
15. Hutchinson, W., Knopoff, L.: The acoustic component of western consonance. J. New Music Res. **7**(1), 1–29 (1978)
16. Johnson-Laird, P.N., Kang, O.E., Leong, Y.C.: On musical dissonance. Music Percept. **30**(1), 19–35 (2012)
17. Krumhansl, C.L., Kessler, E.J.: Tracing the dynamic changes in perceived tonal organisation in a spatial representation of musical keys. Psychol. Rev. **89**, 334–368 (1982)
18. Lahdelma, I., Eerola, T.: Mild dissonance preferred over consonance in single chord perception. i-Perception (2016). https://doi.org/10.1177/2041669516655812
19. Lee, C.L., Lin, Y.T., Yao, Z.R., Lee, F.Y., Wu, J.L.: Automatic mashup creation by considering both vertical and horizontal mashabilities. In: Proceedings of ISMIR, pp. 399–405 (2015)
20. Manovich, L.: The Language of New Media. MIT Press, Cambridge (2001)
21. Mixed in Key: Mashup 2 [software]. http://mashup.mixedinkey.com. Accessed 28 Mar 2017

22. Native Instruments: Traktor pro 2 [software]. https://www.native-instruments. com/en/products/traktor/dj-software/traktor-pro-2/. Accessed on 1 Sep 2017
23. Plazak, J., Huron, D., Williams, B.: Fixed average spectra of orchestral instrument tones. Empirical Musicol. Rev. 5(1), 10–17 (2010)
24. Roads, C.: Microsound. MIT Press, Cambridge (2004)
25. Schwartz, D.A., Howe, C., Purves, D.: The statistical structure of human speech sounds predicts musical universals. J. Neurosci. 23(18), 7160–7168 (2003)
26. Sha'ath, I.: Estimation of key in digital music recordings. Master's thesis, Birkbeck College, University of London (2011)
27. Shiga, J.: Copy-and-persist: the logic of mash-up culture. Crit. Stud. Media Commun. 24(2), 93–114 (2007)
28. Zwicker, E., Fastl, H.: Psychoacoustics-Facts and Models. Springer, Heidelberg (1990). https://doi.org/10.1007/978-3-540-68888-4

Games Without Frontiers: Audio Games for Music Production and Performance

Jason Hockman[1,2] and Joseph Thibodeau[1,3(✉)]

[1] Detuned Transmissions (DTND), Birmingham, United Kingdom
[2] DMT Lab, Birmingham City University, Birmingham, United Kingdom
jason.hockman@bcu.ac.uk
[3] Concordia University, Montreal, Canada
joseph.thibodeau@concordia.ca

Abstract. The authors explain a method by which electronic dance music can be produced in a similar manner to producing game audio, in which the timing of sound-events is relative to the actions of the player and the state of the game environment. An interactive or live piece can be considered an audio game, in which interacting sound-machines generate patterns of sound-events that place the performer/player in a virtual space. The performer/player pursues musical goals in non-linear time while maintaining the ability to arrange pieces in a coherent mix.

Keywords: Electronic dance music · Interactive environments
Composition · Virtual spaces · Procedural audio · Sound design

1 Introduction

The emergence of the gaming industry has played a crucial role in the development of visual aesthetics and narratives in the pre-existing film and television industry. The creation of synergetic film and game releases such as *Lara Croft: Tomb Raider* and the *Resident Evil* series is indicative of the confluence of two industries that share the primarily visual perspective. A second modality—no less relevant to both industries—is that of the sonic domain.

Film sound exists mostly as a post-production process, and is intended to represent on-screen cues that exist in *linear time*—that is to say sound-events occur and vary in a predetermined sequence. Sounds are usually built up through meticulous layering of several recordings for a single event. Game sound exists in *non-linear time*, where sound-events occur and vary relative to the player's interaction with a system. Again sounds are most often the result of several layers of recordings; however, depending on the state of the game environment and the player within it, a game must deliver and modify these layered sounds appropriately. Another approach is to design sounds procedurally as in [4], which has the advantage of parametrically modelling the way a sound is generated in real-time, albeit at the expense of processing resources.

© Springer Nature Switzerland AG 2018
M. Aramaki et al. (Eds.): CMMR 2017, LNCS 11265, pp. 171–183, 2018.
https://doi.org/10.1007/978-3-030-01692-0_12

Audio games are a subset of video games that forego visual representation altogether, and focus chiefly on the auditory modality. These games have been developed for a variety of educational and entertainment uses, and are a key component in the development of an accessible gaming culture for the visually impaired [1,3]. As in audio-visual games, sound in audio games must be delivered and modified dynamically, but since sound is the sole modality for representing the game state and providing the player with feedback, audio games present a unique set of challenges in the use of sound [6].

The aim of this paper is to explain how sound design techniques used in game development may be similarly applied for the purpose of non-linear music creation. The resultant pieces can be thought of as audio games in their own right, with the performers as players who interact with a virtual space that is simultaneously an abstract musical structure with musical goals. Interactive pieces can be combined to create serial or parallel meta-structures (comparable to DJ mixing) that are navigated by nesting them within overarching interactive environments.

2   Motivation

We began our journey into electronic dance music (EDM) through the use of tools designed for linear audio playback. As with many EDM producers, our earliest releases were produced through the use of digital audio workstations (DAW) such as MOTU Digital Performer[1] and Emagic Logic (later Apple Logic[2]). Our output took the form of static compositions in vinyl records or digital sound-files intended for playback in DJ sets and so the musical structure and elements of our productions were heavily influenced by the subgenres within which we were attempting to work. Under the name *DAAT*, we began to focus on thematic concepts related to cyclic events, such as the interplay of mechanistic components (e.g., gears) within vehicles, which we implemented largely through the manipulation of field recordings. By 2014 (when we composed the album *HVAC*[3]), software sampling technology had improved sufficiently to allow for a vast amount of modulation capabilities that we used to add more and more detail to the components and to imply interactions between them. The complexity of our machine concepts grew into a film-like approach of representing the same machine from different points of view and at different points in time. As the scenes became more intricate, we needed these machines and environments to truly interact, rather than seeming to interact through clever editing. Once this motivation became apparent to us, we wanted to add more high-level control to the developed mechanisms—such as changing the speed of a vehicle and having this variable reflect upon the resultant environmental effects on the vehicle (e.g., hull vibrations).

---

[1] http://www.motu.com/products/software/dp.
[2] https://www.apple.com/logic-pro/.
[3] https://www.beatport.com/release/hvac/1320332.

We were attempting to do this in a standard DAW environment, and we began to run into problems for which programmatic solutions would be more suitable (e.g., dynamically controlling large parameter-spaces, linking events across tracks). At this point, we looked into alternative production environments such as programming languages (e.g., Max/MSP, Puredata, CSound, SuperCollider), however we found that removing the DAW from the process entirely removed many of the audio processing mechanisms and workflows that formed the basis of our existing practice, not to mention removing elements of an EDM aesthetic that stem from a basis in DAW production.

As an intermediate step, we began using Ableton Live[4] and Max for Live[5] as a way of bridging our desire for programmatic flexibility with the convenient features of a DAW. Eventually, we chose to use Max/MSP[6] as our main tool, replicating the necessary sound generation and performative functionality of Ableton and other software packages. Over the course of the past two years we have developed a method of production that is analogous to game audio production, but rooted firmly in EDM production and film sound design. In the subsequent sections, we will describe some of the techniques we have employed through providing examples from our initial work from within a DAW, along with examples from our more current methodology.

3   From Static Edits to Dynamism

In offline production with a DAW, sounds are typically fixed in time. The score progresses from left to right, triggering events until the song is finished. For electronic dance music, the events tend to reinforce metrically relevant points in time, much the same as events in a film soundtrack reinforce relevant visual cues. Shaping the form of a sound-event involves editing a potentially vast number of parameters depending on the level of detail.

One type of sound-event that we have often used is the sound of an object passing the listener, such as one vehicle passing another on a highway. It is a sound-event that we have implemented in static and dynamic forms, which we will describe to demonstrate that dynamism can both simplify a parameter-space and open up new compositional possibilities.

3.1   Apache

In *Apache* (2014)[7], a futuristic helicopter is presented from the perspective of the pilot. Air rushes past vents and windows while sensor indicators and unintelligible radio chatter infect the environment. Multiple rotor sounds emerge at different timescales, reflected off the landscape below.

---

[4] https://www.ableton.com/en/live/.
[5] https://www.ableton.com/en/live/max-for-live/.
[6] https://cycling74.com/products/max/.
[7] https://www.beatport.com/track/apache-original-mix/5509952.

Two categories of sound-events make up the soundscape of *Apache*: internal sounds associated with the helicopter's functionality (e.g., engine noises, rotor blades) and external sounds generated from the helicopter's interaction with an outside environment (e.g., wind noise, airframe stress). All of these sounds are related to the motion of the vehicle, and in particular its speed. To enhance the sense of motion, the listener passes other airborne vehicles to either side, achieved through a Doppler-like effect. Modulation envelopes control panning, filtering and amplitude across multiple field recordings for each pass. The size of each vehicle is changed by adjusting the pitch of the samples. In *Apache*, and other tracks (e.g., *Running Man* (2014)[8] and *Sixth Gear* (2014)[9]) these vehicle-passing events are laboriously hard-coded in the DAW using MIDI events and automation envelopes.

Even though the soundscape created in *Apache* successfully evokes a sense of occupying a vehicle in motion, its motion is fixed. For example, there is no practical way to explore changes to the speed of the vehicle and the resultant changes to the soundscape. There would simply be too much labour involved in re-editing every parameter. We identified this issue as a shortcoming in the affordances of traditional DAW environments, and we responded by migrating our practice to an environment in which we could programmatically generate sound-events based on high-level parameters such as speed.

3.2   11D

In *11D* (2017)[10], a similar vehicle to *Apache* is presented, however this machine also incorporates interactive user control (via game controller) for several variables, including the selected route and engine revolutions per minute (RPM).

11D depicts a scene from the vantage point of a flying vehicle travelling through airborne motorways on the periphery of a city. Cyclic mechanical sounds and combustion noise from the engines filter into a semi-permeable cabin under pressure from high-speed travel. As the vehicle accelerates onto the main route it overtakes several others. An afterburner initialises the final sequence that pushes the craft into a system malfunction, overheating the engine and ultimately leading to a fiery crash.

In a programmatic environment, the vehicle becomes a dynamic sound-machine: a virtual construction of related procedural audio generators (as in [4]) whose motion relative to its surrounding environment is indicated by generated perceptual cues (as in [5]), which carries the listener's ear. The mechanical sound of the engine is created through several short segments of field recordings of gears. A single rotation of the cylinder is achieved by cyclical switching between these recordings. The speed variable (here called RPM), which is directly controlled by the user, may then be used to adjust the cycle rate of the engine. At higher speeds, low-frequency bass tones emerge to represent sympathetic resonances of the chassis to the engine. Musical rhythm comes from the

---

[8] https://www.beatport.com/track/signs-original-mix/5509956.

[9] https://www.beatport.com/track/sixth-gear-original-mix/5509960.

[10] https://bleep.com/release/87073-daat-lvl5.

negative space achieved by interruptions of the bass resonance by external wind gusts.

Similar to *Apache*, a Doppler-like effect is used to represent passing other vehicles. The panning, filtering, and amplitude variables are still controlled by envelopes, however these are dynamically changed based on the speed of the user's vehicle and the chosen route type (see Fig. 1). The motorway vehicles are randomly generated according to four traffic densities and speeds based on (arbitrary) route types: *outskirts*, *city limits*, *main route*, *city roads*. Optionally, the speed and density of these vehicles may be driven by real-world data. Information from a traffic website (Traffic England[11]) is scraped and sent via OSC into the Max for Live object where it is combined with the user's RPM to modulate the parameters of each vehicle-passing event.

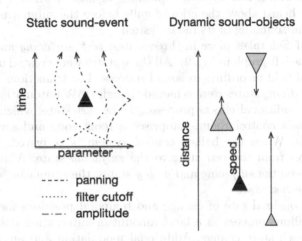

Fig. 1. A comparison between static sound-events like those used in *Apache* (2014) and dynamic sound-objects like those used in *11D* (2017). In the static example automation curves control parameters such as panning, filtering, and amplitude. In the dynamic example the size, relative position, and motion of the other vehicles is included in the resultant sound-events. In both examples the black triangle represents the listener's perspective.

4   Structural Interaction

As in other genres, musical form in EDM often comprises several sections [2]. For example, a popular structure in Drum and Bass consists of the intro (A), first drop (B), breakdown (C), second drop (B2) and outro (A2). While this form may be appropriate for many tracks, it is useful for producers to investigate a

---

[11] http://www.trafficengland.com.

variety of possibilities in the development of their tracks. Due to the difficulties in managing a large amount of hard-coded MIDI and automation data, it is not always feasible to explore these possibilities within a traditional DAW environment. However, once the various components are connected through programmatic design, it is much easier to navigate the solution space to find a time-scale and form that is optimal for a piece.

4.1 Sub

Sub (2014)[12] opens in the dormant control room of an automated warship submerged in a waterway and staged for battle. A message is received and the submarine's pressure control system is activated. The vehicle moves upwards, where it surfaces and is met by waves splashing against the hull. Distant explosions are briefly heard above the cries of gulls before the submarine dives once again with a final sounding of its radar system.

The whole of *Sub* takes place in three states: *rest, surfacing* and *diving* (as can be seen in the left graph in Fig. 2). All three states were created using a DAW with a variety of field recordings as sound sources. The transitions between the *underwater* and *diving* states were achieved though DAW automation associated with filters and additional effects processing. The *rest* state, which takes place in the submarine's control room, comprises a room tone and several display indicator sounds. When the ballast control system is activated, the state of the piece changes from the *rest* state to the *surfacing* state. After a series of transitions between the *surfacing* and *diving* states, the submarine returns from the *diving* to the *rest* state.

Selecting an optimal rate of change and temporal positions for these transitions was a tedious process as a large amount of automation data needed to be created for each state change. Additional modulation and automation was included to ensure that a listener would not hear the same events and structure upon revisiting states. The result is a track built around the idea of dynamic state transitions, but whose state transitions are fixed on a linear timeline. *010005* (2017)[13] occupies the same conceptual background as *Sub* in that it is intended to be part of the same battle scene. Using causal links between events housed on different tracks in Ableton and Max for Live, state changes are triggered that navigate the narrative of the piece.

4.2 010005

In *010005*, the slow combustion of a giant engine powers a well-seasoned warship into choppy water at the mouth of a river. The scene shifts below deck, where waves can be heard violently hitting the hull. The droning of enemy aircraft can be heard in the distance and another vessel, already involved in the fray, radios in. The ship's radar system is activated and targets the enemy. As the targets fly

---

[12] https://www.beatport.com/track/sub-original-mix/5509958.
[13] https://bleep.com/release/87073-daat-lvl5.

overhead, guided missiles are launched at them. Once the enemy aircraft have been eliminated, resounding victory music is heard all around.

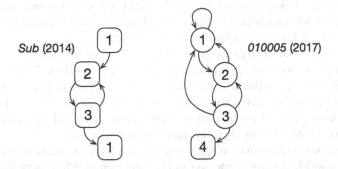

Fig. 2. State representations for the structure of *Sub* (2014) and *010005* (2017). Squares denote states that transition at precomposed time-points and circles denote states that transition according to user input. *Sub* (left) unfolds in a linear timeline and consists of three states *rest* (1), *surfacing* (2) and *diving* (3). *010005* (right) unfolds in a user-determined non-linear timeline and consists of four states: *cruise* (1), *scan* (2), *attack* (3) and *level complete* (4).

Unlike *11D*, which comprised a single state with a continuous variable associated with change in the environment, *010005* has four defined states: *cruise*, *scan*, *attack* and *level complete* (as can be seen in the right graph in Fig. 2). In addition, unlike *Sub*, *010005* exists in non-linear time, in that the unfolding of events relies on user input. In the initial *cruise* state, the sounds of waves striking the hull are randomly generated at metrically-relevant positions at the front and rear of the ship. Once the *scan* state is triggered by the user, the radar sweep sound effect is activated, and the positions of enemy aircraft populate the stereo field. Once all targets are acquired, the piece transitions to the *attack* state, during which missiles are launched from turrets. A distance model generates the duration and amplitude of the trail of each missile as it is fired, and provides an auditory indicator representing a heads-up display tracking the missile to its destination. If the missile explodes too close to the ship, its shock-wave causes powerful waves to collide with the hull. Once the enemy swarm has been defeated, the track transitions to its end state, *level complete*, during which euphoric synthesiser pads play.

Movement between these states is facilitated by message passing between Max for Live patches in each track, which trigger events without the use of hard-coded MIDI or automation. In addition, subtle variation is achieved through adding either random or probabilistic control over environmental sounds and amplitudes. The removal of deliberate control over many processes is advantageous in this sense as it allows events to be put into action without knowing the patterns that will emerge. This can result in unintended consequences, which is very useful for reducing listener fatigue and creating a space for serendipitous discovery.

5   Games Without Frontiers

A major question that began to arise in the production of these pieces is how to perform them. Since they are internally interactive (the component sound-objects interact with each other) there are plenty of ways for one to "hook in" to certain parts of the system and influence the whole.

Over the course of creating a piece such as *11D* we would determine useful high-level parameters that we would assign to a gamepad or MIDI controller, effectively allowing us to dictate the behaviour of the system on a large scale. As we became more familiar with the process of creating these pieces, we wanted to explore them as engaged participants, rather than detached empyrean figures. From this point, thinking of them as *games* arose naturally.

In simulations or first-person games, players inhabit a sensorium within virtual worlds, and ideally are immersed in the experience. They have limited freedom to navigate the space, pursue goals (whether explicit or implied) and take risks. This is similar to performers who have musical freedoms, goals, and risks according to the specifics of their selves in relation to the performance environment. By merging the relationships of music/performer and game/player, we found ourselves able to design interactions that were simultaneously audio games and musical compositions.

5.1   AC3244

AC3244 (2017)[14] tells the story of a lonely jet-gull who lives on aluminium cliffs by the sea. It is resting when it spots a predator in the distance, a gargantuan sky-whale. Taking flight, the unfortunate bird draws the predator's attention and flees as fast as its thrusters can handle. Its reactor is fundamentally unstable, and loss of focus can cause it to overload, falling to the ground to cool down. If it doesn't outrun its pursuer, it will be eaten whole and melted for scrap.

In *AC3244*, the performer takes the role of the jet-gull and must live through its life-threatening tale. The control scheme is simple yet challenging. One button ignites the power plant and starts the takeoff, after which two sliders are used to push the jet-gull to its limit. One slider controls the throttle, directing the available reactor power to the thrusters that in turn increase the speed. The other slider controls the reactant feed, increasing the available power. The state of the reactor is modeled as an inverted pendulum that the performer has to balance using the reactant feed. It becomes more unstable as the speed increases, and so becomes increasingly difficult to keep stable as the performer attempts to outfly the pursuer. If the reactor overheats, the jet-gull crashes into the soft sand by the water and daydreams about simpler times. After cooling down the player can re-ignite the engine, but by this time the sky-whale is understandably much closer and the task that much more difficult. It is worth noting that both of the flying controls are *indirectly* mapped to the higher-level parameter of speed. This serves both to mitigate the low-resolution control of MIDI messages and to create a sense of being a part of a larger system rather than its controller.

---

[14] Unreleased.

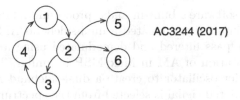

Fig. 3. State representations for the structure of the player's vehicle in *AC3244* (2017). It consists of six states: *rest* (1), *flying* (2), *overheated/crashing* (3), *cooldown* (4), *escape* (5), and *eaten* (6). The player traverses these states depending on their ability to maintain the vehicle's flight and escape their pursuer.

Much like *11D* and *010005*, this piece comprises several states through which the player can progress, illustrated in Fig. 3. The state of *flying* moves the player at a certain speed along a track, at the end of which is the reward of living another day. It includes the possibility of "losing"—being eaten by the predator before reaching the finish—and the performer has to balance these game goals with musical ones. Is it better to accept a timely death for the sake of drama? Is it possible to keep the jet-gull's reactor stable long enough to mix-in the next track?

6   Worlds Within Worlds

The previous sections have described the process by which interactive, programmatic pieces can be developed to provide a greater degree of flexibility than similar pieces constructed in a traditional DAW setting. Parallel to the development of our interactive pieces has been the development of a mixing software with which to perform them. The software, called *AH-64*, is an audio game in its own right and is an environment in which the player navigates between different musical worlds. Audio sources can be mixed by crossfading between channels, or transmitted and received from specific channels in a simulated radio spectrum using amplitude modulation (AM) and frequency modulation (FM) techniques. We can combine tracks, live broadcasts, simulated radio channels and audio effects in a modular way to suit a given set. It has streamlined our equipment needs and therefore has opened up space for exploration of interactive tracks. The first version of this software—AH-64(A)—was developed in Max for Live using the track structure of Ableton Live.

6.1   Radio Simulation

It is possible to modulate and demodulate AM and FM signals at audio rate, although typical audio bandwidth falls well below real-world radio transmission frequencies. Our first experiments in simulating AM radio were implemented in

Renoise[15] using the software's built-in audio processing modules: a ring modulator applied to an input signal created a dual-sideband AM signal at 24 kHz, which was then bandpass filtered and demodulated using another ring modulator. Our implementation of AM in Max/MSP is similar. The input signal is multiplied by a carrier oscillator to create a dual-sideband AM signal centred at 24 kHz. The modulated signal is selected from the spectrum with a bandpass filter and its amplitude contour is extracted using a Hilbert transform. Changing the center frequency of the bandpass filter and ring modulators allowed us to tune the transmission and reception of the signal during live performance.

Frequency modulation is achieved by simply scaling the input signal and using it to control the frequency of a carrier oscillator, but demodulation is a bit more complicated. We based our Max/MSP implementation on Tom Zicarelli's FM detector[16], in which the modulated signal is decomposed into amplitude and phase components using a Hilbert transform, after which the derivative of the phase reproduces the baseband signal.

The limited bandwidth of digital audio affects the number of channels that can be multiplexed onto a given spectrum, an example of which is shown in Fig. 4. To overcome this limitation we devised a method by which an arbitrary number of signals can be multiplexed without losing signal quality. Each transmission-reception chain (i.e., input signal, modulation, demodulation) is isolated within its own spectrum, modulated to a fixed center frequency, and assigned an arbitrary channel number. Then, a master tuning dial is used to move continuously along this virtual radio spectrum, and each channel is demodulated to an extent based on its proximity to the tuning channel (see Fig. 5).

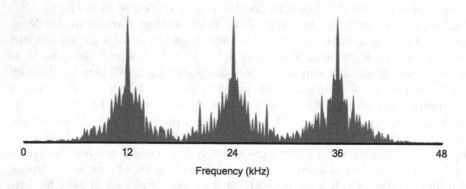

Fig. 4. FM radio simulation with three 10 kHz band-limited channels spaced 12 kHz apart ($F_s = 96$ kHz). The limited bandwidth of digital audio means that the three signals shown here take up all of the available bandwidth. More channels could be multiplexed into the spectrum but their bandwidths would have to be further limited, reducing their fidelity to the transmitted signal.

---

[15] http://renoise.com/.

[16] https://github.com/tkzic/max-projects/tree/master/demodulation/max.

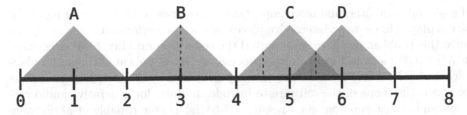

Fig. 5. Use of a virtual spectrum to overcome digital audio bandwidth limitations. Transmissions A, B, C, and D are placed on the spectrum centered at channel numbers 1, 3, 5 and 6 respectively. Each transmission has a bandwidth of 2.0. To demodulate a transmission, a master tuning ω is set to the corresponding channel number. With $\omega = 3.0$, B will be demodulated, while $\omega = 4.5$ results in C being partially demodulated (the signal will be distorted or garbled). With $\omega = 5.5$, both C and D will be partially demodulated.

6.2 Performance

A key issue we struggled with in early iterations was how to operate the controls of AH-64 while loading and performing interactive pieces—for example, creating a seamless bridge from one interactive piece to another, as one might move from track to track in an DJ set. We initially overcame this limitation with the use of multiple computers—one which would run AH-64(A) and another dedicated to interactive pieces. Clear disadvantages to this arrangement are the requirement

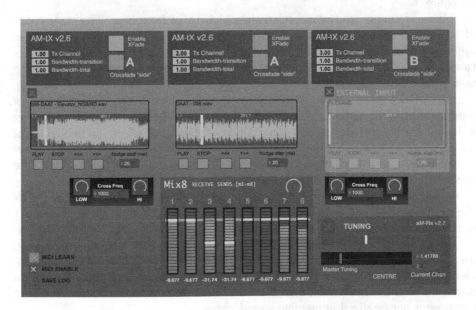

Fig. 6. AH-64(B) virtual radio. In this example, three *stations* are present, one of which has the external input enabled for performance of an interactive piece.

of a second computer, and more importantly a restriction on the ordering of the pieces played in that two interactive pieces can not be performed successively. To solve this problem, we have since ported the software into Max/MSP—resulting in AH-64(B) (seen in Fig. 6). In the process, we have replicated the audio playback and DJ mixing functionality initially provided by Ableton Live as well as extended the scope of the software to include modules for generative audio creation and transformation. As a result, AH-64(B) is now capable of performing multiple interactive pieces sequentially or in parallel within a set. In addition, the software is modular by design and may be configured in a variety of ways to suit variety of performance or compositional needs. In this way we see AH-64(B) as a meta-environment that allows us to navigate various virtual environments via radio transmission.

7   Conclusions and Future Work

Looking over the progression from detailed audio editing on a linear timeline to dynamically controlled sound-events to systems of interaction and audio games, we have described a process of identifying static, overly deterministic or linear structures of control and making them dynamic. At first the low-level parameters of a sound-event were static, so we coded models to instantiate and change them based on context. We then modified the structure of a piece to make state progression non-linear. Finally, we detached direct control over global states by placing the performer inside the piece where their global influence changed based on context.

There are many fruitful directions in which to go from here. The state-space of individual sound-machines and their causal relationships could benefit from application of machine learning and AI such that their behaviours and interactions are not fully predictable. Interactions between different pieces would bring new possibilities for performance and composition. For example, the messaging infrastructure of one could deliberately conflict with the infrastructure of another. Similarly, virtual radio techniques could be used not only for audio signals, but for control signals and other kinds of data that affect the behaviour of an interactive system. Further explorations into audio game design and immersive soundscapes will allow us to further enhance the sense of space and increase the subtleties of the game mechanics. By treating the entire performance space as an interactive installation with sensors and feedback devices, we could shift the performance away from the stage to include the immediate physical context of the concert in the game-space of a piece.

There are exciting applications to these techniques in a VR experience, and we are currently working with the National Film Board of Canada in the development of an open-ended game known as *Biocube*, in which the player's long-term interactions with the environment serve to build empathy with plant life and to compose a personalized immersive soundscape.

References

1. Archambault, D., Olivier, D.: How to make games for visually impaired children. In: Proceedings of the 2005 ACM SIGCHI International Conference on Advances in Computer Entertainment Technology, pp. 450–453 (2005)
2. Butler, M.J.: Unlocking the Groove: Rhythm, Meter, and Musical Design in Electronic Dance Music. Indiana University Press, Indiana (2006)
3. Chakraborty, J., Chakraborty, S., Dehlinger, J., Hritz, J.: Designing video games for the blind: Results of an empirical study. Univ. Access Inf. Soc., 1–10 (2016)
4. Farnell, A.: Designing Sound. MIT Press, Cambridge (2010)
5. Merer, A., Aramaki, M., Ystad, S., Kronland-Martinet, R.: Perceptual characterization of motion evoked by sounds for synthesis control purposes. ACM Trans. Appl. Percept. **10**, 1–24 (2013)
6. Röber, N., Masuch, M.: Leaving the screen: New perspectives in audio-only gaming. In: Proceedings of the 11th Meeting of the International Conference on Auditory Display, Limerick, Ireland, pp. 92–98 (2005)

Computational Musicology

Autonomous Composition as Search in a Conceptual Space: A Computational Creativity View

F. Amílcar Cardoso[(⊠)]

CISUC, Department of Informatics Engineering, DEI, University of Coimbra,
Polo 2, Pinhal de Marrocos, 3030-290 Coimbra, Portugal
amilcar@dei.uc.pt

Abstract. Computational Creativity (CC) is an emerging field of research that focuses on the study and exploitation of the computers' potential to act as autonomous creators and co-creators. The field is a confluence point for contributions from multiple disciplines, such as Artificial Intelligence, which provides most of its methodological framework, and also Cognitive Science, Psychology, Social Sciences and Philosophy, as well as creative domains like the Arts, Music, Design, Poetry, etc.

In this text, we briefly introduce some basic concepts and terminology of the field, as well as abstract models for characterising some common modes of creativity. We will illustrate how these concepts have been applied in recent times in the development of creative systems, particularly in the music domain. With this paper, we expect to contribute to facilitate communication between the CMMR and CC communities and foster synergies between them.

Keywords: Computational Creativity
Algorithmic music composition · Generative music

1 Introduction

The advent of Computation motivated from an early moment the interest in the computational reproduction of the mechanisms of the human mind. AI formally emerged as a discipline in 1956 at a meeting in Dartmouth, USA, resulting in multiple visionary proposals that would build up in the decades following some of the most fascinating research around the relationship between Man and Machine. Creativity soon emerged as one of the challenges that AI could embrace.

At that time, the study of Creativity was influenced by Guilford's work on the Structure of Intellect [14]. Creativity was acknowledged as an intrinsic facet of human intelligence and was increasingly becoming a target for scientific researchers seeking to propose explanatory models of the phenomenon, training and stimulation techniques, and measuring instruments.

AI research, however, has proliferated essentially around the paradigm of *problem solving* [21]. Although significant research on *synthesis/generation of*

© Springer Nature Switzerland AG 2018
M. Aramaki et al. (Eds.): CMMR 2017, LNCS 11265, pp. 187–198, 2018.
https://doi.org/10.1007/978-3-030-01692-0_13

artifacts, such as product design, or musical composition, has been developed, the growing success of AI on (analytical) problem solving has attracted much of the effort and resources of the AI communities during the first decades of its history, partly because of the well-defined nature of the task, in part because of the effectiveness of the early goal-oriented techniques. Successive developments of multiple search and knowledge representation techniques, as well as the diversity and importance of the problems that have arisen in the AI community, have reinforced the dominant position of that paradigm.

Only recently, in particular after the publication of Margaret Boden's book "The Creative Mind" [5], did the study of creativity begin to raise the interest of a growing community of researchers in Artificial Intelligence, who since then have been working on the study and proposal of abstract theories for characterization of the phenomenon, as well as on the experimental development and evaluation of models for computational approaches to creativity.

Computational Creativity (CC) is an emerging field that studies and exploits the potential of computers to be more interventive and autonomous in creative processes [6]. In a broader sense, CC may be seen as the Philosophy, Science and Engineering of Autonomously Creative Systems. The field has increasingly grown in the last years, and started to receive regular attention from the media, namely with the entrance of large companies like Google and IBM.

Music Composition, in particular, has been one of the most prolific focus of research in the area, not only for being a task with an inherently creative character, but also for offering a range of well studied and documented techniques that appear to be amenable for computational implementation.

This paper has a tutorial character. It intends to complement a talk with the same title in the 2017 edition of CMMR with additional material, and to provide a written account of the talk itself. For a deeper and more detailed description of the field, we forward the reader to the recent overview [29], or to books like [27], or the collection [28]. We briefly introduce some basic concepts and terminology of the field in the next section. In Sect. 3, we present abstract models for characterising different modes of creativity. We will illustrate how these concepts have been applied in recent times in the development of creative systems, particularly in the music domain. With this paper, we expect to contribute to facilitating communication between the CMMR and CC communities and fostering synergies between them.

2   Basic Concepts and Terminology

In simple terms, creativity is the ability to produce work that is both *novel* (i.e., original, unexpected) and *appropriate* (i.e., useful, adaptive concerning task constraints) [19,26]. The problem is how to assess novelty and appropriateness, as this involves social appraisal [8]. It is thus important, when studying creativity, to incorporate a multicomponential perspective and consider what is known as the *Four Components of Creativity*, or the *"four Ps"* [24], according to which creativity in an individual should be seen as the result of a complex interaction *process* between the *person* (the agent) and the environment (the *press*), which ultimately leads to some kind of *product* [4]. In music, the person may be a composer and the product a music piece, a melody, a chord sequence, etc.; the person may also be a musician, improvising or not, and the product a performance; the environment/press may be the public in a live performance, the general media audience, an offscreen studio, and so on. Any way, each of these four components play a role in the way how we perceive and assess creativity.

In this paper, for briefness, we will constrain our analysis to the *Process*, touching slightly on the *Product*, which has been the main focus of attention from most of the computer science approaches to creativity. One should stress, however, that none of the four components should be ignored when studying and developing computational approaches to creativity. Even if one acknowledges that most of the research so far focuses on only a part of the components for methodological reasons, more holistic approaches are being pursued and are object of research in the community of computational creativity (e.g., [17,25]).

The *Product* of creativity is the "observable" result of the creative process and is many times the only accessible evidence that one can have to assess creativity. It may be a concrete artifact, like a piece of music, or an idea, like a melodic phrase, or a concept, or a metaphor, etc. Besides *novelty* and *appropriateness*, it is common to also consider other attributes such as *having aesthetic value*, *being surprising*, or *revealing intentionality* when assessing the quality of a product. Actually, there is no single criterion for assessing the *creative value* of a product: a multifaceted and subjective analysis, dependent of the context, is needed to make it.

Regarding the *Process*, it is important to refer what we would call the *operational* distinction proposed by Margareth Boden, in her philosophical account of creativity [5], between three modes:

- *Exploratory Creativity*, or "e-Creativity": creativity as exploration of a conceptual space, which is said to be the most common mode in most of the creative processes;
- *Transformational Creativity*, or "t-Creativity": creativity as transformation of the conceptual space, which would correspond, according to Boden, to a superior form of creativity, associated with most of the greater achievements in many knowledge and artistic areas;
- *Combinational Creativity*, or "c-Creativity": creativity as exploring combinations of existing concepts.

We will analyze in more detail these three modes in the next section. But first, we would like to state that we can find in the literature many different computational approaches to creative processes. We can also find among them examples involving any computing and artificial intelligence technique that one can think of. This is also true for computational approaches to music composition and performance. It may be interesting, any way, to note that one can organise all these approaches according to what we may call their main *source of inspiration*. Many of them follow (more or less closely) models of creativity and cognition from *Psychology and Cognitive Science*, with the aim of reproducing/modeling –

with very different degrees of similarity – the cognitive processes behind human creativity.

Trying to imitate the real thing, however, is not always the best idea, as observed very often in the history of human invention. Following this rationale, there are many approaches that get inspiration from *Natural Evolution*, trying to reproduce the principles and mechanisms that have proved to work creatively in Nature. A third category, more radical and still very incipient, tries to find computational approaches that consider the machine itself as the source of inspiration, i.e., approaches to creativity that would only be possible with a computer machine.

It is important at this point to refer to another distinction proposed by Boden [5] between "psychological" creativity (*P-creativity* for short) and "historical" creativity (*H-creativity* for short): "P-creativity involves coming up with a surprising, valuable idea that is new to the person who comes up with it. It doesn't matter how many people have had that idea before. But if a new idea is H-creative, that means that (as far as we know) no-one else has had it before: it has arisen for the first time in human history".

3 Modes of Operation

The operational distinction proposed by Boden [5] between e-, t- and c-creativity provides useful means for better understanding the creativity process, especially to those with an artificial intelligence background, as it is based on the very familiar concept of *search in a state space*. What Boden proposes is to make a slight shift and consider search in a *space of concepts*. Then, she uses this framework to describe the distinctions between these modes in an informal way.

Taking Boden's work further, Wiggins [30] has proposed a formal distinction between e-creativity and t-creativity. In the next two subsections, we briefly try to highlight the main points of Wiggins' proposal. For detailed description, please consult Wiggin's original article, or the recent chapter [31].

As Wiggins does not consider c-creativity in his framework, we add a third subsection where we informally depict how combinational creativity could be described in such a framework.

3.1 Exploratory Creativity

Wiggins [30] assumes the existence of a Conceptual Space C, where each distinct point corresponds with a distinct concept. The space is composed by total and partially defined concepts, and may be defined in a generative way: a set of rules R determine membership of a concept c to space C. Now let us assume that one has some kind of agenda-based mechanism that allows searching in C by taking one concept c_1 and deciding which concept c_2 to visit next according to some strategy. Let us assume that one can codify such a search strategy by a set of rules T – where T is likely to be different from R. Finally, let us assume that it is possible to codify how the recipient/beholder of the creative process evaluates the quality of a found concept by a set of rules E.

Wiggins defines Exploratory Creativity as search in a conceptual space C constrained by R, using a strategy codified by T, and evaluating products with E. Figure 1 illustrates this mode.

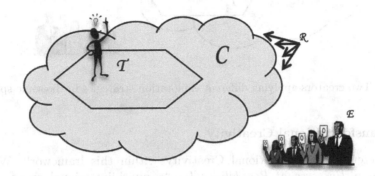

Fig. 1. Exploratory creativity.

In music, we may consider, for instance, a composer working on a new pop song as exploring the space of all the possible pop songs – the conceptual space, constrained by a set of implicit rules defining what *is* a pop song – by applying a search strategy – her own composition method – and evaluating the outputs by estimating how the public will value the artefact.

It is very important to clarify that the sets of rules R, T and E are purely abstract constructs: they are not supposed to exist explicitly. The whole model is just an abstract model that allows us interpret and characterise creative processes. It is not intended to be implemented as a computational model: it is just an analytical tool.

Figure 2 illustrates the analytical power of this model: we can see that we may represent two agents exploring the same conceptual space using different search strategies. The rules that constrain the space are the same, the evaluation rules are the same. Only the set T is different for each agent. This scenario may be seen, for instance, as describing two composers exploring the same musical genre with different styles.

This mode of operation is seen in the vast majority of generative systems documented to date, namely in those operating in musical domains. From earlier systems, like Ebcioglu' CHORAL [9] and Cope's EMI [7], for example, to more recent ones, like [10,15,16,22], despite the diversity of computing techniques used in their implementations, it is possible to frame their operation as an exploration in a given conceptual space. For other recent examples, we redirect the reader to "Musical Meta-Creation Workshop (MuMe)" [3] series of events.

Fig. 2. Two creators applying different exploration strategies in the same space.

3.2 Transformational Creativity

To characterise Transformational Creativity within this framework, Wiggins introduces a *Universe of Possibilities U*, "a multidimensional space, whose dimensions are capable of representing anything, and all possible distinct concepts correspond with distinct points in U". The Universe is the superset of all the possible conceptual spaces and provides the conceptual means to consider multiple conceptual spaces and their transformation.

To illustrate Wiggins' approach, let us consider that, starting from a situation similar to the described in Fig. 1, a creator applies a strategy T' that leads to concepts *outside* of the conceptual space in Fig. 3. If, for some reason, the creator values the results (i.e., she does not consider this exploration to be, say, a "mistake"), she will be using T' to explore a different conceptual space C'. This space should be constrained by a different set of rules. Let us call it R' (see Fig. 4). The evaluation within it should consequently be defined by a different set of rules E' (see Fig. 5). This corresponds to the notion of "t-Creativity" as proposed by Boden, which consists in changing R into R'.

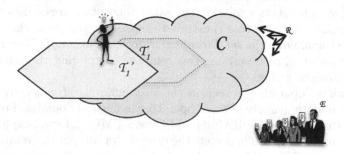

Fig. 3. Transformation (1): creator explores new space.

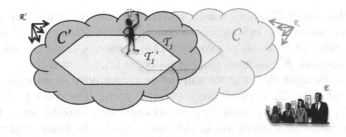

Fig. 4. Transformation (2): creator explores a different space, constrained by different rules.

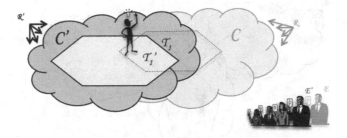

Fig. 5. Transformation (3): a new set of evaluation rules emerges, adapted to the new conceptual space.

In brief, Wiggins defines Transformational Creativity as search in a Universe of Concepts U for new conceptual spaces C', C'', ... constrained by R, R', R'', ... This leads to the definition of Transformational Creativity as *Exploratory Creativity at a meta-level*.

In music composition, this mode may be used to describe the process of a composer exploring the limits of an established set of norms. The emergence of the atonal music movement, with Alban Berg, Schoenberg and others, provides a good illustration. But much more simple examples may also be invoked, like a composer just trying to explore new genres in his repertoire.

Several consequences can be drawn from here, but a deep discussion about them would be outside the scope of this paper. It may be worthwhile, though, to highlight the demystification of transformational creativity as a kind of eldorado for computational creativity, as it could seem at first glance. Actually, Boden's suggestion that transformational creativity is innately superior to exploratory creativity is somehow questioned when one realises that the distinction between both modes resides essentially at the level at which one conceives the conceptual space that the agent is exploring.

3.3 Combinational Creativity

A third mode of creativity applies when the process seeks a novel combination of pre-existing concepts. Borrowing inspiration from Wiggins' framework, we may sketch a definition of Combinational Creativity as an exploration in a conceptual space composed by combinations of concepts from other conceptual spaces. More specifically, let us consider two conceptual spaces C_1 and C_2, and a set of combining functions K that map pairs of concepts (c_i, c_j), such that $c_i \in C_1$ and $c_j \in C_2$, into concepts $c_k \in C_b$; we will define c-creativity as an exploration in the conceptual space C_b. Figure 6 illustrates this mode. The space C_b is different from both C_1 and C_2, so it should be constrained by a specific set of rules R_b. An agent performs an exploration in this space guided by some strategy coded by a set of rules T_b, evaluating results with a set of rules E_b.

Fig. 6. Combinational creativity.

Maybe the most notable illustration of c-creativity is the mental operation known by *concept blending*, the object of the Conceptual Blending (CB) Theory [12], which we briefly describe here.

A key element in CB theory is the *mental space*, a term coined by Fauconnier to describe a partial and temporary knowledge structure created for the purpose of local understanding [11]. In the CB framework, there is a network comprising at least four connected mental spaces (Fig. 7). Two or more of them correspond to the *input spaces*, which are the initial mental spaces. Then, a partial matching between the input spaces is constructed by connecting counterparts in the input spaces (possibly resorting to analogy). This association is reflected in another mental space, the *generic space*, that contains elements common to the different input spaces, capturing the conceptual structure that is shared by them. The outcome of the blending process is the *blend space*, a mental space that maintains partial structures from the input spaces combined with an emergent structure of its own.

We give an example of conceptual blending in Fig. 8, where the concept "computer virus" results from the blending of two mental spaces: "computer" and "virus". For simplicity reasons, the generic space has been omitted. We can see the existence of an initial mapping (represented with dense dashed lines): "Computer" ↔ "Host" and "Program" ↔ "Virus". This corresponds to making the analogy of a computer with a host (and a virus with a computer program). From

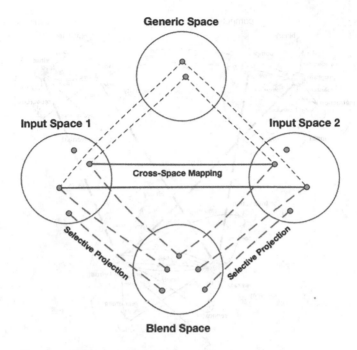

Fig. 7. The original four-space conceptual blending network [12].

these correspondences, selective projections from each input space are made into the new blended space: for example, the elements "computer", "instruction", "program" and "binary" are projected from the space "computer", while the elements "virus", "resources", "replicates", "capacity" and "unwanted" are projected from the space "virus"; relations between these elements are also selectively projected from both spaces. The result is a blended space for a new domain that describes what we know as "computer virus". The blended space borrows pieces from the two input spaces and, at the same time, has its own emerging structure. Note that a more accurate example of the "computer virus" would have included other content from background knowledge.

There are not many computational implementations of this theory. One of the first attempts was Divago [23], which recently received several expansions [20]. Although the system was conceived to work in different domains, it has essentially been used so far in linguistic conceptual spaces.

There are however reports of implementations for music in the context of the FET project COINVENT [2], which aimed to develop a computationally feasible, cognitively-inspired formal model of conceptual blending using *category theory* [13]. For instance, cadences blending is explored in [32] and generalised to chord transition blending in [18]. In the latter case, the perfect and the 15th century modal Phrygian cadences are used as input spaces. The Phrygian mode does not have an upward leading note to the tonic, but rather a downward 'leading note' from the IIb to the I. The blending mechanism creates a new harmonic 'concept'

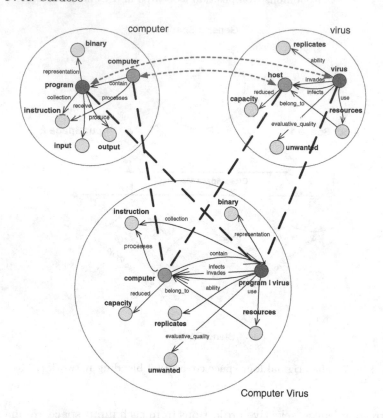

Fig. 8. The "computer virus" blend.

that was actually introduced in jazz, centuries later than the original input cadences. This mechanism was integrated in a melodic harmonisation assistant called *Chameleon* [33].

4   Conclusion

This paper aims to provide a brief introduction to the field of Computational Creativity by presenting some basic concepts and terminology of the field, as well as abstract models of three modes of creativity. We illustrate how these concepts have been applied in recent times in the development of creative systems, particularly in the music domain.

For the reader interested in deepening these and other related concepts, and get acquainted with current and past research on CC, we recommend the consultation of the proceedings of the yearly International Conference on Computational Creativity series, running yearly since 2010, available in the pages of the international Association for Computational Creativity [1]. We expect to contribute with this text to facilitate communication between the CMMR and CC communities and foster synergies between them.

References

1. Association for Computational Creativity (ACC). http://computationalcreativity. net/home/. Accessed 06 Mar 2018
2. Concept Invention Theory (CoInvent) Project. https://www.coinvent.uni-osnabrueck.de/en/home.html. Accessed 06 Mar 2018
3. International Workshop on Musical Metacreation (MuMe). http:// musicalmetacreation.org. Accessed 05 Mar 2018
4. Batey, M., Furnham, A.: Creativity, intelligence, and personality: A critical review of the scattered literature. Genet. Soc. Gen. Psychol. Monogr. **132**(4), 355–429 (2006)
5. Boden, M.: The Creative Mind: Myths and Mechanisms. Orion Publishing Co., London (1990)
6. Cardoso, A., Veale, T., Wiggins, G.: Converging on the divergent: the history (and future) of the international joint workshops on computational creativity. AI Mag. **30**(3), 15–22 (2009). http://www.aaai.org/ojs/index.php/aimagazine/article/viewArticle/2252
7. Cope, D.: An expert system for computer-assisted composition. Comput. Music J. **11**(4), 30–46 (1987)
8. Csikszentmihalyi, M.: 16 implications of a systems perspective for the study of creativity. In: Handbook of Creativity, p. 313 (1999)
9. Ebcioglu, K.: An expert system for harmonising chorales in the style of J.S. Bach. In: Balaban, M., Ebicioglu, K., Laske, O. (eds.) Understanding Music with AI: Perspectives on Music Cognition. The AAAI Press, California (1992)
10. Eigenfeldt, A., Bown, O., Brown, A.R., Gifford, T.: Flexible generation of musical form: beyond mere generation. In: Proceedings of the Seventh International Conference on Computational Creativity, ICCC 2016, Paris (2016)
11. Fauconnier, G.: Mental Spaces: Aspects of Meaning Construction in Natural Language. Cambridge University Press, New York (1994)
12. Fauconnier, G., Turner, M.: The Way We Think. Basic Books, New York (2002)
13. Goguen, J.: What is a concept? In: Dau, F., Mugnier, M.-L., Stumme, G. (eds.) ICCS-ConceptStruct 2005. LNCS (LNAI), vol. 3596, pp. 52–77. Springer, Heidelberg (2005). https://doi.org/10.1007/11524564_4
14. Guilford, J.: The Nature of Human Intelligence. McGraw-Hill, New York (1967)
15. Harmon, S.: Narrative-inspired generation of ambient music. In: Proceedings of the Eighth International Conference on Computational Creativity, ICCC 2017, Atlanta (2017)
16. Johnson, D.D., Keller, R.M., Weintraut, N.: Learning to create jazz melodies using a product of experts. In: Proceedings of the Eighth International Conference on Computational Creativity, ICCC 2017, Atlanta (2017)
17. Jordanous, A.: Evaluating evaluation: assessing progress and practices in computational creativity research. In: Veale, T., Cardoso, F.A. (eds.) Computational Creativity: The Philosophy and Engineering of Autonomously Creative Systems. Computational Synthesis and Creative Systems, pp. 209–234. Springer (2019)
18. Kaliakatsos-Papakostas, M., Queiroz, M., Tsougras, C., Cambouropoulos, E.: Conceptual blending of harmonic spaces for creative melodic harmonisation. J. New Music Res. **46**(4), 305–328 (2017)
19. Kaufman, J.C., Sternberg, R.J.: The International Handbook of Creativity. Cambridge University Press, New York (2006)

20. Martins, P., Pereira, F.C., Cardoso, F.A.: The nuts and bolts of conceptual blending: multi-domain concept creation with Divago. In: Veale, T., Cardoso, F.A. (eds.) Computational Creativity: The Philosophy and Engineering of Autonomously Creative Systems. Computational Synthesis and Creative Systems, pp. 91–118. Springer (2019)
21. Newell, A., Shaw, J.C., Simon, H.A.: The Processes of Creative Thinking. Rand Corporation, Santa Monica (1959)
22. Pachet, F.: A joyful ODE to automatic orchestration. ACM Trans. Intell. Syst. Technol. (TIST) **8**(2), 18 (2017)
23. Pereira, F.C.: Creativity and Artificial Intelligence: A Conceptual Blending Approach, vol. 4. Walter de Gruyter, Berlin (2007)
24. Rhodes, M.: An analysis of creativity. Phi Delta Kappan **42**(7), 305–310 (1961)
25. Ritchie, G.: The evaluation of creative systems. In: Veale, T., Cardoso, F.A. (eds.) Computational Creativity: The Philosophy and Engineering of Autonomously Creative Systems. Computational Synthesis and Creative Systems, pp. 157–192. Springer (2019)
26. Sternberg, R.J., Lubart, T.I.: An investment theory of creativity and its development. Hum. Dev. **34**(1), 1–31 (1991)
27. Veale, T.: Exploding the Creativity Myth: The Computational Foundations of Linguistic Creativity. A&C Black, New York (2012)
28. Veale, T., Cardoso, F.A. (eds.): Computational Creativity: The Philosophy and Engineering of Autonomously Creative Systems. Computational Synthesis and Creative Systems. Springer (2019)
29. Veale, T., Cardoso, F.A., Pérez y Pérez, R.: Systematizing creativity: the computational view. In: Veale, T., Cardoso, F.A. (eds.) Computational Creativity: The Philosophy and Engineering of Autonomously Creative Systems. Computational Synthesis and Creative Systems, pp. 1–19. Springer (2019)
30. Wiggins, G.A.: A preliminary framework for description, analysis and comparison of creative systems. Knowl. Based Syst. **19**(7), 449–458 (2006)
31. Wiggins, G.A.: A framework for the description, analysis and comparison of creative systems. In: Veale, T., Cardoso, F.A. (eds.) Computational Creativity: The Philosophy and Engineering of Autonomously Creative Systems. Computational Synthesis and Creative Systems, pp. 21–48. Springer (2019)
32. Zacharakis, A., Kalikatso-Papakostas, M., Cambouropoulos, E.: Conceptual blending in music cadences: a formal model and subjective evaluation. In: Proceedings of the 16th International Society for Music Information Retrieval (ISMIR) Conference (2015)
33. Zacharakis, A., Kaliakatsos-Papakostas, M., Tsougras, C., Cambouropoulos, E.: Musical blending and creativity: an empirical evaluation of the chameleon melodic harmonisation assistant. Musicae Scientiae **22**(1), 119–144 (2018)

On Linear Algebraic Representation of Time-span and Prolongational Trees

Satoshi Tojo[1]($\boxtimes$), Alan Marsden[2], and Keiji Hirata[3]

[1] Japan Advanced Institute of Science and Technology,
1-1 Asahidai, Nomi, Ishikawa 923-1292, Japan
tojo@jaist.ac.jp
[2] Lancaster University, Bailrigg, Lancaster LA1 4YW, UK
[3] Future University Hakodate, 116-2 Kamedanakanocho, Hakodate,
Hokkaido 041-8655, Japan

Abstract. In constructive music theory, such as Schenkerian analysis and the Generative Theory of Tonal Music (GTTM), the hierarchical importance of pitch events is conveniently represented by a tree structure. Although a tree is easy to recognize and has high visibility, such an intuitive representation can hardly be treated in mathematical formalization. Especially in GTTM, the conjunction height of two branches is often arbitrary, contrary to the notion of hierarchy. Since a tree is a kind of graph, and a graph is often represented by a matrix, we show the linear algebraic representation of trees, specifying conjunction heights. Thereafter, we explain the 'reachability' between pitch events (corresponding to information about reduction) by the multiplication of matrices. In addition we discuss multiplication with vectors representing a sequence of harmonic functions, and suggest the notion of stability. Finally, we discuss operations between matrices to model compositional processes with simple algebraic operations.

Keywords: Time-span tree · Prolongational tree
Generative Theory of Tonal Music · Matrix · Linear algebra

1 Introduction

Schenkerian analysis suggested a layered structural importance of pitch events and showed the existence of an innate skeleton of music in a hierarchical way. As a more modern theory of this structural hierarchy, the Generative Theory of Tonal Music (GTTM) [5] aims at constructing two kinds of tree: Time-span tree and Prolongational tree, and the deriving process has been automated [1,7].

The time-span tree in Fig. 1 shows that the C is more salient than the succeeding E and $F\sharp$, but surrenders to the final event G. Such a tree is roughly represented by a sequence

$$(C^\dagger(E^\dagger F\sharp))(DG^\dagger)^\dagger$$

© Springer Nature Switzerland AG 2018
M. Aramaki et al. (Eds.): CMMR 2017, LNCS 11265, pp. 199–212, 2018.
https://doi.org/10.1007/978-3-030-01692-0_14

Fig. 1. Time-span tree.

where the parentheses mean a bifurcation and the dagger '†' specifies the choice of the more salient branch between the two. Thus, the formula corresponds to the tree in Fig. 1. But, this representation with parentheses and daggers lacks information on the duration of pitch events.

Even when we add the information on duration for each pitch event, the tree cannot be fixed uniquely, as there remains the arbitrariness as to the height of junction point of branches. Matsubara et al. [8,10] have tried to fix the junction height, regarding the number of beats, e.g., 2^n beats $\leq L^n < 2^{n+1}$ beats (Fig. 2), however, when they tried to include *cadential retention* the height still remained ambiguous.

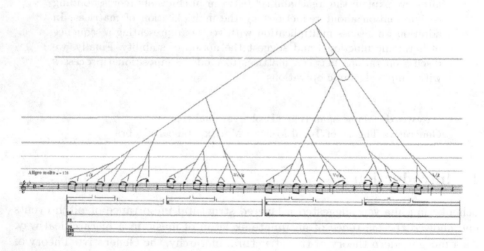

Fig. 2. Junction height by the number of beats [8].

We have proposed the notion of Maximum Time-span (MTS) of each pitch event, as the longest temporal interval during which the event is most salient [2,11]. If a pitch event does not have branching, i.e., there is no more subordinate pitch event and is a leaf of the tree, its MTS is the original pitch length. At the other extreme, the MTS of the event that reaches the top of the tree is the whole length of the music piece. Here, we can write the MTS of Fig. 1 as in Fig. 3.

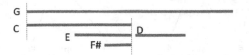

Fig. 3. MTS for the tree.

We can naively represent the tree in a matrix as in Fig. 4, left-hand side, where a pitch event in the column is connected to the one in each row with the height indicated by the matrix cell value. Or, the height is relativized if we regard the entire height should be 1, as in the right-hand side of the figure. (We arbitrarily show the top event to be connected to itself. This allows the maximum time-span for each pitch event to be read from the row of that pitch event. This choice is justified further in the representation explained in Sect. 2.)

$$
\begin{array}{c}
 \\
C \\
E \\
F\sharp \\
D \\
G
\end{array}
\begin{array}{ccccc}
C & E & F\sharp & D & G \\
\end{array}
\begin{pmatrix}
0 & 0 & 0 & 0 & 2 \\
1 & 0 & 0 & 0 & 0 \\
0 & .5 & 0 & 0 & 0 \\
0 & 0 & 0 & 0 & 1 \\
0 & 0 & 0 & 0 & 4
\end{pmatrix}
\qquad
\begin{array}{c}
 \\
C \\
E \\
F\sharp \\
D \\
G
\end{array}
\begin{array}{ccccc}
C & E & F\sharp & D & G \\
\end{array}
\begin{pmatrix}
0 & 0 & 0 & 0 & 1/2 \\
1/4 & 0 & 0 & 0 & 0 \\
0 & 1/8 & 0 & 0 & 0 \\
0 & 0 & 0 & 0 & 1/4 \\
0 & 0 & 0 & 0 & 1
\end{pmatrix}
$$

Fig. 4. Height information by MTS and its relative representation.

But, these matrices in Fig. 4 do not possess sufficient non-zero diagonal elements, *i.e.*, their rank is lower than their size, and are not regular; that is, the matrices are not algebraically tractable. In this paper, we revise the above representation and propose a musically meaningful matrix. In the following Sect. 2, we formally define a matrix for a music piece. In Sect. 3 we also introduce the multiplication by a vector of harmonic functions and in that process we discuss the notion of stability of a tree. In Sect. 4 we discuss the meaning of multiplication of matrices. In Sect. 5 we summarize our contribution and discuss the future direction, especially for new arrangement/composition methods by algebraic operations.

2   Tree Representation

In this section, we formally define the numeric values of matrices. If two consecutive pitch events have the durations d_1 and d_2, and the first one is more salient than the second (*i.e.*, more fundamental in the melodic structure, in the sense

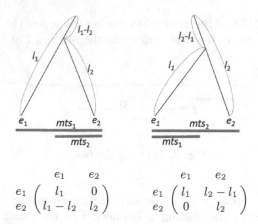

$$
\begin{array}{cc}
 & \begin{array}{cc} e_1 & e_2 \end{array} \\
\begin{array}{c} e_1 \\ e_2 \end{array} & \begin{pmatrix} l_1 & 0 \\ l_1 - l_2 & l_2 \end{pmatrix}
\end{array}
\qquad
\begin{array}{cc}
 & \begin{array}{cc} e_1 & e_2 \end{array} \\
\begin{array}{c} e_1 \\ e_2 \end{array} & \begin{pmatrix} l_1 & l_2 - l_1 \\ 0 & l_2 \end{pmatrix}
\end{array}
$$

Fig. 5. Relation between branch length and MTS.

used by Lehrdahl and Jackendoff [5]), the MTS would be $mts_1 = d_1 + d_2$ and $mts_2 = d_2$. This situation is depicted in Fig. 5.

In Fig. 5, each branch length, that is l_1 and l_2, is proportional to its MTS though the angles versus the horizontal line are not fixed and thus arbitrary. Nevertheless, notice that the junction height correctly reflects the relation of the lengths of two branches when they are mapped to a hypothetical vertical axis. The matrix below each figure in Fig. 5 represents the tree configuration. For example, the $(2,1)$-element of the left matrix shows that the second pitch event (e_2) is connected to the first (e_1) with the height relative to $l_1 - l_2$.

Let the above be the base case of recursive construction of a tree. Then, given two subtrees in matrices M_1 and M_2 we consider to connect them in one tree, as follows. First, there are the most salient pitch events p_i and p_j in M_1 and M_2, respectively, and let their branch lengths be l_i and l_j. The whole tree, consisting of the two subtrees, becomes such a disjoint union of matrices:

$$
\left(\begin{array}{c|c} M1 & 0 \\ \hline 0 & M_2 \end{array} \right) =
\left(\begin{array}{c|c} \begin{matrix} \ddots \\ & l_i \\ & & \ddots \end{matrix} & \\ \hline & \begin{matrix} \ddots \\ & l_j \end{matrix} \end{array} \right).
$$

If p_j is more salient than p_i, the branch lengths for p_i would be added to l_j as $\hat{l}_j \equiv l_i + l_j$. Thus, we revise the new matrix as in the left-hand side of Fig. 6. In the case p_i is more salient than p_j the revision would be $\hat{l}_i \equiv l_i + l_j$ and all l_i are replaced with $\hat{l}_i$ as in the right-hand side of Fig. 6.

Example. Let a sequence of two pitch events p_1 and p_2 be connected by right branching, with the branch lengths of l_1 and l_2, respectively. Also, let p_3 and p_4 be connected by left branching and have the lengths of l_3 and l_4, respectively.

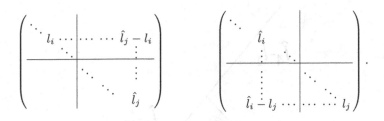

Fig. 6. The result of combining two subtrees by left branching (left) and right branching (right).

$$\begin{pmatrix} l_1 & 0 & 0 & 0 \\ l_1 - l_2 & l_2 & 0 & 0 \\ 0 & 0 & l_3 & l_4 - l_3 \\ 0 & 0 & 0 & l_4 \end{pmatrix} \qquad \begin{pmatrix} l_1 & 0 & 0 & \hat{l}_4 - l_1 \\ l_1 - l_2 & l_2 & 0 & 0 \\ 0 & 0 & l_3 & \hat{l}_4 - l_3 \\ 0 & 0 & 0 & \hat{l}_4 \end{pmatrix}.$$

Fig. 7. Example of disjoint union.

Then, the initial disjoint union becomes the left-hand side of Fig. 7. Now suppose p_4 is more salient than p_1. Then, the top of the tree becomes left branching, and thus $\hat{l}_4 = l_4 + l_1$ appears at $(1,4)$-position, and remaining l_4 are all replaced with $\hat{l}_4$, as in the right-hand side of Fig. 7. (This is equivalent to adding l_1 to all the existing non-zero elements in the column for p_4.) Note that the adequacy of $(1,4)$-element is justified as in Fig. 8. $\qquad\square$

3   Reachability and Harmonic Stability

3.1   Reachability

The matrix representation described above gives two kinds of information: the branching of the tree (*i.e.*, which time-spans are connected to which ones, and which is the dominating time-span); and the height of the branching in relation to the durations of the time-spans. In this section, we are concerned only with the connections and since this information is conveyed by whether a value is 0 or not, we simplify here by using only the values 0 and 1 in the matrix. We call

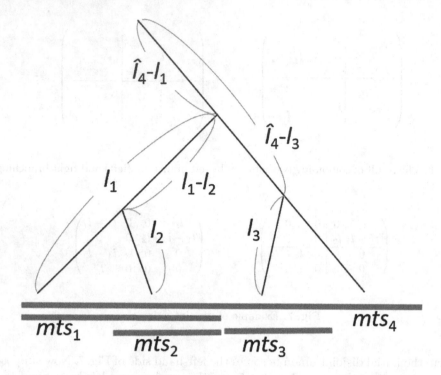

Fig. 8. Relation between four branches.

this a *topology matrix* derived from the tree representation. For example, let p_i $(i = 1, \ldots, n)$ be a sequence of the pitch events of a given piece, and then the topology corresponds to the tree in Fig. 1 is shown as follows.

$$
M = \begin{array}{c} \\ p_1 \\ p_2 \\ p_3 \\ p_4 \\ p_5 \end{array}
\begin{array}{ccccc}
p_1 & p_2 & p_3 & p_4 & p_5 \\
\left(\begin{array}{ccccc}
1 & 0 & 0 & 0 & 1 \\
1 & 1 & 0 & 0 & 0 \\
0 & 1 & 1 & 0 & 0 \\
0 & 0 & 0 & 1 & 1 \\
0 & 0 & 0 & 0 & 1
\end{array} \right)
\end{array}
$$

In the above matrix, the i-th row represents the connections from the i-th pitch event, *e.g.*, the second pitch event p_2 is attached to p_1 ((2, 1)-element) as well as p_2 itself ((2, 2)-element).

The *reduction hypothesis* in GTTM is the idea that we can retrieve the fundamental structure of a given piece of music, pruning those non-salient branches from the time-span tree; such pruning process is called *reduction* and the lineage of reduced trees is called *reduction path*. Our objective is to represent not just the connections in the matrix, but the entire reduction path for pitch events. We now consider how the reduction path for pitch events can be represented and used in a matrix.

In matrix $M = (c_{ij})$, $c_{ij} > 0$ and $c_{jk} > 0$ where $i < j < k$ imply that p_i is connected to p_j and p_j is connected to p_k. Thus, p_i can reach p_k via p_j by two steps, or equivalently, p_i is reduced to p_j and then to p_k. We can represent these remote connections explicitly in the matrix through multiplication of the matrix by itself. To ensure that the resultant matrix is also a topology matrix, using only the values 0 and 1, we use Boolean addition for '+' $(1 + 1 = 1)$ in the matrix multiplication. For example, the following M^2 indicates the reachable pitch events within 2 steps in M; the squared-1's mean the elements appear after the multiplication.

$$M^2 = \begin{pmatrix} 1\,0\,0\,0\,1 \\ 1\,1\,0\,0\,0 \\ 0\,1\,1\,0\,0 \\ 0\,0\,0\,1\,1 \\ 0\,0\,0\,0\,1 \end{pmatrix}^2 = \begin{pmatrix} 1\ 0\,0\,0\ 1 \\ 1\ 1\,0\,0\ \boxed{1} \\ \boxed{1}\ 1\,1\,0\ 0 \\ 0\ 0\,0\,1\ 1 \\ 0\ 0\,0\,0\ 1 \end{pmatrix}.$$

The *reachability* of all pitch events is shown by $\tilde{M} = M^k$ where for length n for the given piece k ($\leq n$) is the height of the tree, *i.e.*, the number of the maximum branching from the top node to a leaf, and $M^{(k+1)} = M^k$. In our current example, $\tilde{M} = M^3$ since $M^3 = M^4$, as follows

$$M^3 = \begin{pmatrix} 1\,0\,0\,0\ 1 \\ 1\,1\,0\,0\ 1 \\ 1\,1\,1\,0\ \boxed{1} \\ 0\,0\,0\,1\ 1 \\ 0\,0\,0\,0\ 1 \end{pmatrix}.$$

In a reachability matrix, the i-th row shows all the transitively accessible pitch events from the i-th pitch event. In M^3, the third pitch event p_3 can, besides reaching p_3 itself, reach p_1 ((3, 1)-element), p_2 ((3, 2)-element), and p_5 ((3, 5)-element), which are all the events above p_3 in the reduction process. On the contrary, a column indicates all the dominated pitch events. the first column vector $(1, 1, 1, 0, 0)$ of M^3 means that p_1 is reached from p_2 and p_3 as well as p_1 itself. In other words, p_1 dominates (is more salient than) p_2 and p_3.

3.2 Harmonic Stability

The reachability can help to distinguish 'stable' from 'unstable' configurations in a prolongational tree, though stableness has not been clearly defined in Lerdahl and Jackendoff's theory. We illustrate this through a discussion of two cases from GTTM.

Mozart K.331. In Fig. 9, the first part of the theme of the first movement of Mozart's piano sonata in A Major K.331, is shown.

In Lerdahl and Jackendoff's time-span reduction, the V at the end of the first phrase is connected to the opening I and the I at the beginning of the second

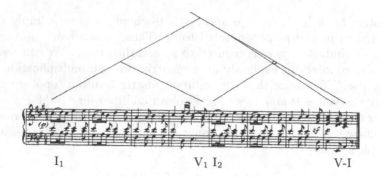

$$I_1 \qquad\qquad\qquad V_1\ I_2 \qquad\qquad\qquad V\text{-}I$$

Fig. 9. The theme of K.331 [5, p. 141].

phrase is connected to the closing cadence. In outline, the matrix representation of this is as follows.

$$
\begin{array}{c}
 \\
I_1 \\
\vdots \\
V_1 \\
I_2 \\
\vdots \\
V\text{-}I
\end{array}
\begin{array}{ccccccc}
I_1 & \cdots & V_1 & I_2 & \cdots & V\text{-}I \\
\left(\begin{array}{cccccc}
1 & \cdots & & & \cdots & 1 \\
\vdots & \ddots & & & & \vdots \\
\boxed{1} & \cdots & 1 & 0 & \cdots & 0 \\
0 & \cdots & 0 & 1 & \cdots & \boxed{1} \\
\vdots & & & & \ddots & \vdots \\
0 & \cdots & & & & 1
\end{array}\right)
\end{array}
$$

Lerdahl and Jackendoff consider the options for converting this time-span tree into a prolongational tree, as illustrated in Fig. 10. The central dominant may be attached to the cadence or the central tonic may be attached to the beginning tonic. Lerdahl and Jackendoff claim that the second is the better option. While the reasons are musically clear, they are not rigorously defined.

Here, we discuss the notion of *reachable harmonic function*. Each tonic and dominant in a piece of music is considered to play an important role in constructing a stable music structure. From the reachability matrix, we can find the sequence of harmonic functions which make up the reduction path to each pitch event. We propose that the more these sequences resemble complete and stable harmonic sequences, such as I V I, the more stable the overall structure is. For example, we can find harmonic functions in Fig. 9 as

$$(I_1, \cdots, V_1, I_2, \cdots, V\text{-}I).$$

If we multiply this vector by a reachability matrix, we can find which I's and V's reach which other I's and V's. In the matrix-vector multiplication, we take '+' to concatenate harmonic functions into harmonic sequences, indicating which other harmonic functions are reachable.

Below, we show the three reachability matrices for the K.331 example, and their multiplication by the appropriate vector of harmonic functions. (1)

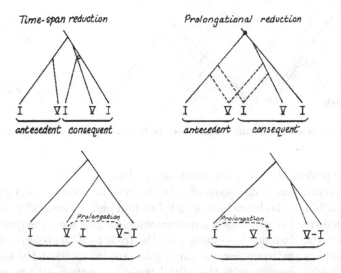

Fig. 10. Stability comparison in K.331 by Mozart [5, p. 141, 223].

corresponds to the time-span tree, (2) to the case where the central tonic is attached to the initial tonic, and (3) where the central dominant is attached to the cadence.

$$
\begin{pmatrix}
1 \cdots & & \cdots & 1 \\
\vdots & \ddots & & \vdots \\
\boxed{1} \cdots & 1\,0 & \cdots & 1 \\
0 \cdots & 0\,1 & \cdots & \boxed{1} \\
\vdots & & \ddots & \vdots \\
0 \cdots & & \cdots & 1
\end{pmatrix}
\begin{pmatrix}
I_1 \\ \vdots \\ V_1 \\ I_2 \\ \vdots \\ V\text{-}I
\end{pmatrix}
=
\begin{pmatrix}
I_1 + V\text{-}I \\ \vdots \\ I_1 + V_1 + V\text{-}I \\ I_2 + V\text{-}I \\ \vdots \\ V\text{-}I
\end{pmatrix}
\tag{1}
$$

$$
\begin{pmatrix}
1 \cdots & & \cdots & 1 \\
\vdots & \ddots & & \vdots \\
\boxed{1} \cdots & 1\,0 & \cdots & 1 \\
\boxed{1} \cdots & 0\,1 & \cdots & 1 \\
\vdots & & \ddots & \vdots \\
0 \cdots & & \cdots & 1
\end{pmatrix}
\begin{pmatrix}
I_1 \\ \vdots \\ V_1 \\ I_2 \\ \vdots \\ V\text{-}I
\end{pmatrix}
=
\begin{pmatrix}
I_1 + V\text{-}I \\ \vdots \\ I_1 + V_1 + V\text{-}I \\ I_1 + I_2 + V\text{-}I \\ \vdots \\ V\text{-}I
\end{pmatrix}
\tag{2}
$$

$$
\begin{pmatrix}
1 \cdots & & \cdots & 1 \\
\vdots & \ddots & & \vdots \\
0 \cdots & 1\,0 & \cdots & \boxed{1} \\
0 \cdots & 0\,1 & \cdots & \boxed{1} \\
\vdots & & \ddots & \vdots \\
0 \cdots & & \cdots & 1
\end{pmatrix}
\begin{pmatrix}
I_1 \\ \vdots \\ V_1 \\ I_2 \\ \vdots \\ V\text{-}I
\end{pmatrix}
=
\begin{pmatrix}
I_1 + V\text{-}I \\ \vdots \\ V_1 + V\text{-}I \\ I_2 + V\text{-}I \\ \vdots \\ V\text{-}I
\end{pmatrix}
\tag{3}
$$

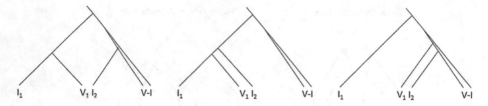

Fig. 11. All the possible prolongational trees of K.331; left (1), mid (2), and right (3).

All three prolongational trees are shown in Fig. 11.

The two central harmonic sequences in the resultant vector change with the changed branching. The branching which Lerdahl and Jackendoff reject for the prolongational tree (3) produces a sequence which begins with the dominant V_1, which is less stable than one beginning with the tonic I_2. The preferred branching (2) is the same as the result for the time-span tree except that the tonic which starts both middle sequences is the initial tonic I_1, putting all the main pitch events of the theme in the context of the overall motion from the initial to the final tonic (I_1 to V-I).

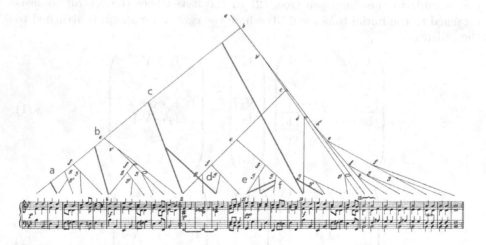

Fig. 12. The time-span tree of St. Anthony Chorale, register simplified [5, p. 205], with red lines indicating the branches in the prolongational tree which are different from the time-span tree.

St. Anthony's Chorale. In their introduction to prolongational reduction, Lerdahl and Jackendoff present both time-span and prolongational trees for the theme of Brahms' variations on the 'St. Anthony Chorale' [5, pp. 203–210] (Fig. 12). We have represented both these trees by matrices and calculated the results of multiplying them by the vector of harmonic functions, according to our own analysis of the harmony. As examples, we show the results of matrix calculations corresponding to the pitch events marked a–f in Fig. 12.

  a: I I IV I vi I becomes I IV I
  b: I I V V I becomes I I I
  c: V V I becomes I V I
  d: V V_7 I V I becomes I V V_7 I
  e: V IV_3^6 IV_3^6 V V I becomes I V IV_3^6 IV_3^6 ii_3^6 V I
  f: V IV_3^6 I_4^6 V V I becomes I V I_3^6 ii_3^6 V I

There is not space to show the complete results here, so we report only the significant differences. Of the 65 sequences in the complete resultant vector, 39 are different for the prolongational tree compared to the time-span tree. The most common change (13 cases, including two with a further change) is in sequences which, in the case of the time-span tree, began with V, corresponding to the V after the double bar. Because this is attached to the initial tonic in the prolongational tree, these sequences now begin with I. As discussed above, we believe this may be an indicator of a more stable tree. The next most common change is to replace instances of vi V I by just I (6 cases). The progression vi V is allowed by some harmonic theories (*e.g.*, [9]) but not by others (*e.g.* [4]), and in any case it is not common, so this change too could be regarded as contributing to greater stability. On the other hand, the next most common change (4 cases) replaces vi V I by vi I, which is worse. In 4 other cases V is omitted from I V I sequences to yield only repetitions of the tonic, which makes little difference to stability. In 3 cases the progression vi I is replaced by just I, counterbalancing the introduction of the questionable progression vi I in the cases referred to previously. The remaining cases are smaller in number: replacing IV^6 V by IV^6 ii^6 V, which improves stability (2 cases); replacing vii^{b7}/V V I by vii^{b7}/V I, which is worse because the diminished seventh does not resolve regularly (2 cases); replacing I_4^6 V I by I_4^6 ii^6 V I, which is irregular (2 cases); adding IV_4^6 after I V^7/IV, which is better because it gives the resolution of the applied dominant seventh V^7/IV (2 cases); replacing I V_4^6 by V IV_4^6, which is neutral (1 case); and replacing I vi I by I V vi I, which is also neutral (1 case).

In summary, a majority of the changes in harmonic sequences in the result of multiplying the reachability matrix of the preferred prolongational tree by the vector of harmonic functions can be explained as producing a harmonically more stable tree than the time-span tree in both of these examples. However, the theory of what constitutes harmonic stability, especially in this context, is not well developed and requires further research.

4   Discussion on Multiplication of Matrices

We now return to the matrix representation which gives information about the height of branching also (*i.e.*, matrices using not just 0 and 1) and consider how this kind of matrix can be multiplied to produce a kind of reachability matrix (*i.e.*, one which gives information about the entire reduction path for pitch events) which preserves information about duration and branch height. In the case of topology matrices discussed above, in order to preserve the property that matrices contained only the values 0 and 1, we modified the normal matrix multiplication operation to use Boolean addition. Similarly, in order to preserve information about duration and branch height, it is necessary to modify matrix multiplication in this case.

This can be achieved by defining the multiplication and addition operations to be used in matrix multiplication as follows. For the elements of two matrices $A = (a_{ij})$ and $B = (b_{ij})$, let $a_{ij} * b_{ij} \equiv \min(a_{ij}, b_{ij})$ and $a_{ij} \oplus b_{ij} \equiv \max(a_{ij}, b_{ij})$. Obviously, these are commutative and associative. Since all the elements in the matrices are equal to or larger than zero, $x * 0 = 0$, $x * x = x$, $y \oplus 0 = y$, and $y \oplus y = y$.

Proposition 1. $(x * (x - y)) \oplus (y * (x - y)) = x - y$ where $x \geq y$.

Proof. Since $x \geq x - y$, $x * (x - y) = x - y$. If $x - y \geq y$ then $y * (x - y) = y$ and thus $(x - y) \oplus y = x - y$. Otherwise, $x - y < y$, then $y * (x - y) = x - y$ and $(x - y) \oplus (x - y) = x - y$. $\square$

This proposition shows that in the matrix representation of a fundamental binary tree, either one of x and y is superordinate and the height information becomes $|x - y|$.

Proposition 2. *All the diagonal elements remain as the same values when a matrix is multiplied by itself.*

Proof. Let $A = (a_{ij})$ and note that $a_{ij} > 0$ $(i \neq j)$ implies $a_{ji} = 0$. Then (i, i)-element in A^2 is equal to $\sum_{j=1}^{n} a_{ij} * a_{ji} = a_{ii} * a_{ii} = a_{ii}$. $\square$

This multiplication gives information about reachability, as before. For example, in the tree represented in the matrix below, the second pitch event can reach the fourth, as non-zero $(2, 4)$-element appears by the multiplication.

$$
\begin{pmatrix}
l_1 & 0 & 0 & l_4 - l_1 \\
l_1 - l_2 & l_2 & 0 & 0 \\
0 & 0 & l_3 & l_4 - l_3 \\
0 & 0 & 0 & l_4
\end{pmatrix}^2
=
\begin{pmatrix}
l_1 & 0 & 0 & l_4 - l_1 \\
l_1 - l_2 & l_2 & 0 & (l_1 - l_2) * (l_4 - l_1) \\
0 & 0 & l_3 & l_4 - l_3 \\
0 & 0 & 0 & l_4
\end{pmatrix}
$$

However, it is not clear what the value $\min(l_1 - l_2, l_4 - l_1)$, calculated by the height times the height, means in musical terms. Also, while the result of multiplying or repeatedly multiplying a matrix by itself is always a valid reachability matrix, this is not true when multiplying two different matrices. We have examined the base cases of right- and left-branching trees of two pitch events with equal maximum time span of their heads. Multiplying two trees of this kind which have the same branching results in a copy of the left multiplicand when the duration of its first pitch event is less than or equal to the duration of the first pitch event in the other tree, and in other cases by either a copy of the right multiplicand or an invalid matrix which mixes elements from the two matrices, depending on the relation of the durations to each other and to the time-span of the head. Multiplying matrices with different branching produces an invalid matrix with non-zero values in all elements. A possible musical interpretation is that the resultant matrices indicate a distribution of possible trees resulting from the combination of the two multiplicands, but we have yet to investigate this in detail.

5   Conclusion

In this paper, we proposed a linear algebraic representation for the tree structure of music. The significance of this work is two-fold.

First, we have shown that the matrix uniquely fixes the configuration of the tree. Thus far, time-span trees and prolongational trees in GTTM include an ambiguity at conjunction heights of branches. We have revised the issue by the notion of maximum time-span (MTS), and assumed that each branch has a height relative to a virtual vertical axis in accordance with its MTS. We placed each branch height at the diagonal element and the difference of the height of two branches at the junction element in the matrix, and thus, trees have come under the rigorous mathematical domain for algebraic operations [3].

Second, rewriting those elements in matrices by Boolean values, we have defined the class of topology matrices which represent connectivity according to graph theory. Multiplying a topology matrix with itself until saturated to obtain the transitive closure results in a reachability matrix, which shows the reachability from each leaf pitch event to other higher-level pitch events. When we multiply the reachability matrix by a vector of harmonic functions, we arrive at a representation of the harmonic functions which govern each pitch event in the reduction.

We have applied this representation in an exploration of stability, hypothesizing that more stable prolongational reductions have more typical harmonic progressions in the sequence of harmonic functions which govern each pitch event. Further work is required to more rigorously define what stability means and how it can be calculated from a matrix and vector of harmonic functions. Prolongational trees are intended to represent tension and relaxation in right and left branching, respectively, so theories of harmony and tonal pitch space [6] which also include notions of distance from and to harmonies should be explored.

Future developments of our formalization are as follows. Our earlier works concerned tree operations to determine the similarity of two pieces of music and to generate new music by a tree-combination morphing process. The algebraic operations on matrix representations have the potential to lead to a new methodology for arrangement and composition. For example, join and meet of two trees are realized by addition of two matrices, where in the join operation we should redefine $a_{ij} + b_{ij} \equiv max(a_{ij}, b_{ij})$ whereas in the meet operation $a_{ij} + b_{ij} \equiv min(a_{ij}, b_{ij})$. In addition, if we would like to reverse the tree chronologically, that is, each left/right-branching is reversed, we can represent the retrograde by the transposition of the original matrix. Furthermore, as outlined above, we can consider the possibility of multiplication of two different matrices, producing a new piece from given two pieces.

Acknowledgements. This work is supported by JSPS Kaken 16H01744 and BR160304.

References

1. Hamanaka, M., Hirata, K., Tojo, S.: Implementing methods for analysing music based on Lerdahl and Jackendoff's *Generative Theory of Tonal Music*. In: Meredith, D. (ed.) Computational Music Analysis, pp. 221–249. Springer, Cham (2016). https://doi.org/10.1007/978-3-319-25931-4_9
2. Hirata, K., Tojo, S., Hamanaka, M.: Cognitive similarity grounded by tree distance from the analysis of K.265/300e. In: Aramaki, M., Derrien, O., Kronland-Martinet, R., Ystad, S. (eds.) CMMR 2013. LNCS, vol. 8905, pp. 589–605. Springer, Cham (2014). https://doi.org/10.1007/978-3-319-12976-1_36
3. Hirata, K., Tojo, S., Hamanaka, M.: An algebraic approach to time-span reduction. In: Meredith, D. (ed.) Computational Music Analysis, pp. 251–270. Springer, Cham (2016). https://doi.org/10.1007/978-3-319-25931-4_10
4. Kostka, S., Payne, D.: Tonal Harmony. Knopf, New York (2003)
5. Lehrdahl, F., Jackendoff, R.: A Generative Theory of Tonal Music. The MIT Press, Cambridge (1983)
6. Lerdhal, F.: Tonal Pitch Space. Oxford University Press, New York (2001)
7. Marsden, A., Hirata, K., Tojo, S.: Towards computable procedures for deriving tree structures in music: context dependency in GTTM and Schenkerian theory. In: Proceedings of the Sound and Music Computing Conference, pp. 360–367 (2013)
8. Matsubara, M., Kodama, and Tojo, S.: Revisiting cadential retention in GTTM. In: Proceedings of KSE/IEEE 2016 (2016)
9. Riemann, H.: Vereinfachte Harmonielehre. Augener, London (1893)
10. Sakamoto, S., Arn, S., Matsubara, M., Tojo, S.: Harmonic analysis based on Tonal Pitch Space. In: Proceedings of KSE/IEEE 2016 (2016)
11. Tojo, S., Hirata, K.: Structural similarity based on time-span tree. In: Aramaki, M., Barthet, M., Kronland-Martinet, R., Ystad, S. (eds.) CMMR 2012. LNCS, vol. 7900, pp. 400–421. Springer, Heidelberg (2013). https://doi.org/10.1007/978-3-642-41248-6_23

Four-Part Harmonization: Comparison of a Bayesian Network and a Recurrent Neural Network

Tatsuro Yamada[1], Tetsuro Kitahara[2], Hiroaki Arie[1], and Tetsuya Ogata[1(✉)]

[1] Waseda University, 1 Chome-104 Totsukamachi, Shinjuku, Tokyo 169-8050, Japan
yamadat@idr.ias.sci.waseda.ac.jp, arie@sugano.mech.waseda.ac.jp,
ogata@waseda.jp
[2] Nihon University, 4 Chome-8-24 Kudanminami, Chiyoda, Tokyo 102-0074, Japan
kitahara@chs.nihon-u.ac.jp

Abstract. In this paper, we compare four-part harmonization produced using two different machine learning models: a Bayesian network (BN) and a recurrent neural network (RNN). Four-part harmonization is widely known as a fundamental problem in harmonization, and various methods, especially based on probabilistic models such as a hidden Markov model, a weighted finite-state transducer, and a BN, have been proposed. Recently, a method using an RNN has also been proposed. In this paper, we conducted an experiment on four part harmonization using the same data with both a BN and RNN and investigated the differences in the results between the models. The results show that these models have different tendencies. For example, the BN's harmonies have less dissonance but especially the bass melodies are monotonous, while the RNN's harmonies have more dissonance but especially bass melodies are smoother.

Keywords: Machine composition · LSTM-RNN · Bayesian network Harmonization

1 Introduction

Four part harmonization, which means the generation of a harmony that consists of the soprano, alto, tenor, and bass voices, has been widely studied for many years [1–10]. Ebcioglu implemented a rule-based expert system for generating four-part harmonies using a logic programming language [4]. Pachet et al. attempted to achieve harmonization as a constraint satisfaction problem [12]. Phon-Amnuaisuk et al. compared the use of a genetic algorithm with a fitness function designed based on some harmony rules and a direct rule-based approach [13]. Phon-Amnuaisuk et al. also developed a platform for music knowledge representation that includes harmonization rules to enable users to control the system's harmonization behavior [14].

© Springer Nature Switzerland AG 2018
M. Aramaki et al. (Eds.): CMMR 2017, LNCS 11265, pp. 213–225, 2018.
https://doi.org/10.1007/978-3-030-01692-0_15

Machine learning approaches have also been applied to four-part harmonization. Hild et al. developed a J. S. Bach-style choral harmonization system using several neural networks [8]. Raczynski et al. proposed a four-part harmonization method based on a hidden Markov model (HMM) [15], while Allan et al. proposed another method using HMM [1]. Yi et al. proposed a four-part harmonization method based on a Markov decision process [19]. Buys and Merwe adopted a weighted finite-state transducer (WFST) for four-part harmonization [3].

We have also developed a four-part harmonization method using a Bayesian network (BN) [17]. In our previous paper [17], we pointed out that it is important to account for both simultaneity (i.e., vertical consistency) and sequentiality (i.e., horizontal consistency) and proposed a BN that models both these characteristics under the assumption of a limited number of training data. We obtained successful experimental results with training data taken from 254 hymn songs.

On the other hand, recurrent neural networks (RNN) [5], especially implemented with a long short-term memory (LSTM) [6], have recently shown very successful results in the field of natural language processing (NLP) [9,11,16]. Compared to Markov-based language models, LSTM models can learn long contexts involved in time-series data thanks to their memory cells' retention of past information and their gating mechanism for manipulating the information. This model can also be applied to the four-part harmonization task. In fact, Hadjeres and Pachet proposed a four-part harmonization method using LSTMs [7]. Their model called DeepBach could learn to produce chorales in the style of Bach. In the discrimination test, around 50% of the musical experts judged chorales generated by their model to be composed by Bach.

In this paper, we aim at comparing four-part harmonization using different machine learning approaches: BN and RNN. As a BN model, we use the model proposed in our previous paper [17]. This model represents sequential dependencies among three successive notes, and is repeatedly applied from the beginning to the end of a given musical piece. In contrast, an RNN based on LSTMs learns the whole sequential dependencies in a given time series of data. We investigate the differences in the harmonization results caused from the different models.

2   Problem Statement

We deal with the same problem addressed in our previous study [17]. Given a soprano melody, the melodies for the alto, tenor, and bass voices are estimated. Let $\{S_1, \cdots, S_N\}$ be the given soprano melody, where N is the number of notes, and S_i represents a pitch (specifically, a MIDI note number). For simplicity, we assume that the rhythms of all voices are identical. In other words, the number of notes and the onset and offset times for each note among all voices are identical. We adopted this assumption since this is actually assumed for exercises of harmonics at music colleges in Japan. Thus the melodies for the alto, tenor, and bass voices are represented as $\{A_1, \cdots, A_N\}$, $\{T_1, \cdots, T_N\}$, and $\{B_1, \cdots, B_N\}$, where A_i, T_i, and B_i are note numbers. To summarize, sequences of note numbers in the three voices, that is, $\{A_i\}$, $\{T_i\}$, and $\{B_i\}$, are output given a sequence of note numbers in the soprano voice $\{S_i\}$ as input.

However, musical pieces used for training models may not satisfy the mentioned assumption in that the rhythms may not be identical among the four voices. Such pieces are edited in advance by dividing notes longer than the simultaneous notes in other voices, in the same way as Suzuki and Kitahara [17].

3   Compared Models

3.1   Bayesian Network

The same BN model used in our previous study [17] is also used in the present study, as shown in Fig. 1. This model represents dependencies in three successive notes. Suppose that S_{i-1} and S_i are given from the input data and that $(A_{i-1}, T_{i-1}, B_{i-1})$ has been determined in a previous step. The BN model then infer (A_i, T_i, B_i). However, the smoothness from (A_i, T_i, B_i) to $(A_{i+1}, T_{i+1}, B_{i+1})$ should be considered in inferring (A_i, T_i, B_i). The model therefore infers $(A_{i+1}, T_{i+1}, B_{i+1})$ at the same time as (A_i, T_i, B_i) although $(A_{i+1}, T_{i+1}, Bi + 1)$ will be re-inferred in the next step. This step is repeated from the beginning to the end of a given musical piece. We assume here that every element of (S_0, A_0, T_0, B_0) and $(S_{N+1}, A_{N+1}, T_{N+1}, B_{N+1})$ is set to "0", a special symbol meaning "no note" (at the beginning or the end of the piece).

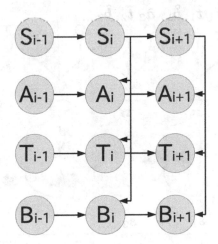

Fig. 1. A Bayesian network model for four-part harmonization.

This BN model has arcs representing both simultaneity and sequentiality. For sequentiality, A_i, T_i, and B_i are considered to be dependent on A_{i-1}, T_{i-1}, and B_{i-1}, respectively, and A_{i+1}, T_{i+1}, and B_{i+1} are considered to be dependent on A_i, T_i, and B_i. For simultaneity, A_i and T_i are considered dependent on B_i, and these three variables are dependent on S_i. A_i and T_i are actually dependent on each other, but the dependency is not considered here because we would need too much training data if the model had many arcs (which are considered dependencies). In addition, diagonal dependencies such as S_{i-1} and B_i should be considered to take into account the avoidance of the parallel 5th, one of the well-known basic harmony rules, but it is difficult due to the limited number of training data.

3.2   Recurrent Neural Network

The RNN model used here is shown in Fig. 2. The RNN was also built as a model that produces alto, tenor, and bass melodies from a soprano melody. The soprano melody $\{S_1, S_2, \cdots, S_N\}$ is encoded as a sequence of 36 dimensional one-hot vectors $\{s_1, s_2, \cdots, s_N\}$ for the model inputs, in which each vector has the value of 1 at one element and 0 at the other elements. Out of the 36 dimensions, the first 35 dimensions correspond to MIDI note numbers within a specified pitch range [50, 84]. For example, if $S_i = 70$, only the 21st element has 1. The pitch range is determined so that it covers all notes in our training data. The 36th dimension represents a piece boundary signal, in which it has 1 at the beginning and the end of a piece. The other three voices are encoded in the same way to make target data, even though their pitch ranges are [45, 79], [40, 74], [35, 69] in the order of alto, tenor, and bass.

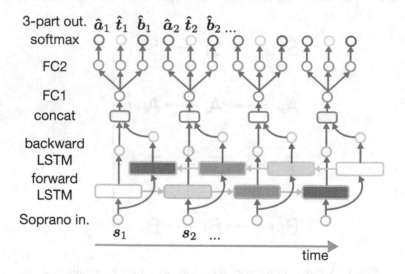

Fig. 2. An RNN model for four-part harmonization.

The model has two recurrent layers with LSTM units. For the details of the LSTM units, please refer to Gers and Schmidhuber [6]. One RNN is the forward RNN, which has recurrent connections from the beginning to the end of a piece, and the other is the backward RNN, which has inverse recurrent connections. Each RNN encodes an N step piece into N fixed dimensional vectors. After that, two paired vectors are simply concatenated.

$$\boldsymbol{f}_1, \boldsymbol{f}_2, \cdots, \boldsymbol{f}_N = ForwardRNN(\boldsymbol{s}_1, \boldsymbol{s}_2, \cdots, \boldsymbol{s}_N) \tag{1}$$

$$\boldsymbol{b}_1, \boldsymbol{b}_2, \cdots, \boldsymbol{b}_N = BackwardRNN(\boldsymbol{s}_1, \boldsymbol{s}_2, \cdots, \boldsymbol{s}_N) \tag{2}$$

$$\boldsymbol{c}_i = [\boldsymbol{f}_i; \boldsymbol{b}_i] \tag{3}$$

Here, focusing on the i-th step, $\boldsymbol{f}_i$ encodes the soprano melody from the beginning to the i-th step $\boldsymbol{s}_{1:i}$, while $\boldsymbol{b}_i$ encodes the melody from the i-th step to the end $\boldsymbol{s}_{i:N}$. Therefore, $\boldsymbol{c}_i$ encodes the information of the whole melody. This means that to estimate the other three voice notes in each time step, all the contextual information from the beginning to the end of the piece can be taken into account in contrast to the BN model. This kind of bi-directional encoding is often used in language processing tasks to encode long sentences efficiently [2]. After encoding, $\boldsymbol{c}_i$ is decoded by fully connected layers, FC1 and FC2. By applying the softmax function to the output of the FC2 layer, the three voices are predicted as a probability distribution. Learning is developed as the minimization of the cross entropy between the output and the target data. In the test phase after learning, the argmax indices are regarded as the output of the model.

The RNN was configured as follows. The numbers of units in the forward LSTM layer, backward LSTM layer, and FC1 layer were 148. The number of units in the FC2 layer was 36 for each part. The Adam algorithm [10] was used as the optimizer. The learning rate was set to 0.001, and the number of learning iterations was 10,000.

Fig. 3. An example of hymn pieces taken from a hymn book [18] for the experiment.

4   Experiment

4.1   Dataset

For training the BNs and RNNs, we use a melody corpus that consists of 124 four-part pieces taken from a hymn book [18]. Figure 3 shows an example of the four-part melodies. All the pieces are in a major key and were transposed into the C major in advance. The average length is about 15 measures. The pieces were encoded as described in Sect. 2. We also made another melody corpus consisting of 100 four-part melodies taken from the same book [18].

4.2   Evaluation Method

We compared the harmonization performance based on following criteria in accordance with Suzuki and Kitahara [17].

Criterion 1. The rate of harmonies containing dissonance intervals (the smaller, the better). The dissonance intervals are defined as minor 2nd, major 2nd, diminished 5th, minor 7th, and major 7th. The notes forming the G7 chord and Dm7 chord were excluded even though they contained diminished 5th, major 2nd or 7th.

Criterion 2. The rate of non-diatonic notes (the smaller, the better). The melodies used here are relatively orthodox. Thus, the results of harmonization should not contain non-diatonic notes.

Criterion 3. Whether the last chord is C (good if it is true). This is one of the most important rules in harmonics: ending with the tonic chord.

Criterion 4. The rate of harmonies containing the same note name in three or more voices (the smaller, the better). Allocating the same note name to simultaneous notes in different voices (e.g. Soprano: C, Alto: C, Tenor: E, Bass: C) does not cause dissonance but does make the music monotonous. Such note allocation should therefore be avoided.

Criterion 5. The rate of successive large motions (more than perfect 4th) in the bass voices (the smaller, the better). Successive large note motions will decrease the smoothness in a sequence of notes within a voice. In particular, successive large motions in the bass voice should be avoided, because a role of the bass voice is to keep the harmony stable.

Criterion 6. The number of note names appearing in each voice (the greater, the better). Musically natural melodies should consist of a number of note names. Less number makes the harmony more monotonous.

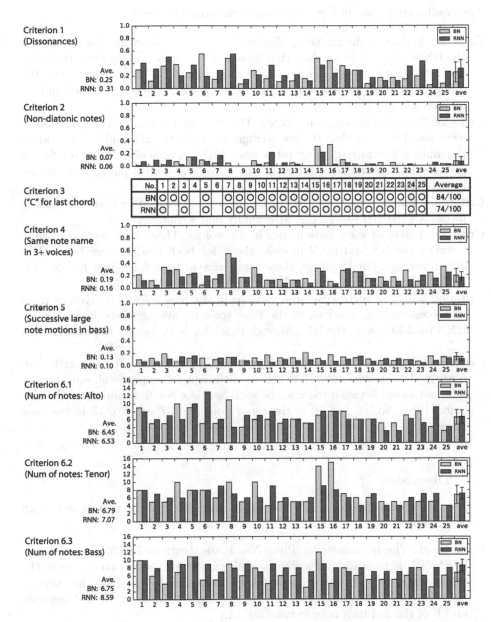

Fig. 4. Quantitative results for each criterion. The results for the only first 25 test pieces are displayed due to limitations of space. The right most bars show the average and standard deviation for the 100 test pieces.

4.3 Results

The results are shown in Fig. 4 and are summarized as follows:

Criterion 1 Rate of dissonances: The average rate of dissonant harmonies for the BN model was lower than that for the RNN model on average. However, the difference between the models is less than 0.1. For 29 pieces, the BN model showed higher scores for this criterion, while the RNN models did for 69 pieces.

Criterion 2 Rate of non-diatonic notes: The average rates of non-diatonic notes were low, i.e. lower than 0.1 on average, for both the BN and RNN models. For only a few pieces, these rates were high. Specifically, the rates for 10 pieces were higher than 0.2 for the BN while those for 6 pieces were higher than 0.2 for the RNN.

Criterion 3 Ending with C chord: Both models could end with a C chord in many pieces. Of the 100 test pieces, 91 actually end with a C chord.

Criterion 4 Rate of same note names in 3+ voices: These rates were also close between the BN and RNN models; those for both models were lower than 0.2 on average. For 18 pieces, these rates were at least 0.1 higher for the BN, while 4 pieces showed at least 0.1 higher scores for the RNN.

Criterion 5 Rate of successive large motions in the bass voice: The average rates of successive large motions in the bass voice on average were lower for the RNN model than on the BN although those for both models were lower than 0.2.

Criterion 6 Number of note names appearing for each voice: For this criterion, both models showed very close scores, although a few pieces showed largely different scores between the models, such as Piece No. 6, 8, and 24 in the alto voice, Piece No. 15 and 16 in the tenor voice, and Piece No. 15 in the bass voice.

4.4 Discussion

Here we illustrate differences in harmonies generated by the two models with some examples.

Piece No. 1: The harmonies for Piece No. 1 are shown in Fig. 5. The harmony by the BN is basically musically natural, except for the 3rd bass note in the 6th measure (F). On the other hand, the harmony by the RNN has several notes causing dissonance, such as C of the 3rd bass note in the 3rd measure and F of the 3rd bass note in measure 12.

Piece No.1

Fig. 5. Four-part harmonies generated by BN and RNN: Piece No. 1.

Piece No. 21: The harmonies for Piece No. 21 are shown in Fig. 6. The harmony by the BN is basically natural, but the bass melody is not melodious: almost all notes are C, D, G, or G. A non-diatonic note (F♯) is used in the 3rd to 4th measure in the tenor voice, but it is considered musically acceptable because it forms a very common chord, D7, with the other voices. In fact, such notes often appear also in the training data. The BN reproduced them in an appropriate context. The harmony by the RNN is also basically natural but has a different tendency from the BN. The bass melody is smoother than that by the BN, but the alto and tenor melodies are not sophisticated: almost all notes in the alto melody are C and almost all notes in the tenor melody are G.

Piece No. 25: The harmonies for Piece No. 25 are shown in Fig. 7. Similar to Piece No. 21, the harmony by the BN does not contain dissonant notes but the bass melody mostly consists of root notes and is thus less melodious. The bass melody by the RNN consists of more various notes than that by the BN. The first note in the 13rd measure in the melody, which is the C note, is not musically natural.

Piece No. 21

Fig. 6. Four-part harmonies generated by BN and RNN: Piece No. 21.

Fig. 7. Four-part harmonies generated by BN and RNN: Piece No. 25.

5   Conclusion

In this paper, we compared two four-part harmonization models based on a BN and a RNN. Various models including BNs and RNNs have been proposed for four-part harmonization, but comparison between different models had not been attempted. Our results showed different tendencies in the harmonization by the different models. For example, the BN generated basically consonant harmonies but unsmooth bass lines, while the RNN generated smooth bass lines but the alto and tenor lines tend to be monotonous.

There are many opportunities for future work. First, we should compare the characteristics of harmonization by BN and RNN with ones by other existing methods. Second, a subjective evaluation also should be conducted. Third, we should try more sophisticated models. Because the present study is a first step in making comparison, we adopted very simple models. However, the state-of-the art models, such as DeepBach [7], use more sophisticated and complicated models. We would like to try such models. Fourth, we would like to discuss the inner model parameters. Model parameters of BNs and neural networks are given as a conditional probability table and a matrix of neuron connection weights, respectively. It would be beneficial to consider differences in these parameters and in the resulting harmonization behaviors.

Acknowledgments. This work has been supported by MEXT Grant-in-Aid (No. 16H05878, 16K16180, 16H01744, 26280089, 26240025, 16KT0136, 17H00749).

References

1. Allan, M., Williams, C.K.I.: Harmonising chorales by probabilistic inference. In: Advances in Neural Information Processing Systems, vol. 17, pp. 25–31 (2005)
2. Bahdanau, D., Cho, K., Bengio, Y.: Neural machine translation by jointly learning to align and translate. In: IEEE International Conference on Learning Representations (2015). http://arxiv.org/pdf/1409.0473v6.pdf
3. Buys, J., Merwe, B.V.D.: Chorale harmonization with weighted finite-state transducers. In: Twenty-Third Annual Symposium of the Pattern Recognition Association of South Africa, pp. 95–101 (2012)
4. Ebcioglu, K.: An expert system for harmonizing chorales in the style of J. S. Bach. J. Log. Program. **8**(1–2), 145–185 (1990)
5. Elman, J.L.: Finding structure in time. Cogn. Sci. **14**(2), 179–211 (1990). http://doi.wiley.com/10.1207/s15516709cog1402_1
6. Gers, F.A., Schmidhuber, J.: Recurrent nets that time and count. In: Proceedings of the IEEE-INNS-ENNS International Joint Conference on Neural Networks, vol. 3, pp. 189–194 (2000)
7. Hadjeres, G., Pachet, F.: DeepBach: a steerable model for Bach chorales generation. arXiv:1612.01010 [cs.AI], pp. 1–20 (2016)
8. Hild, H.: HARMONET: a neural net for harmonizing chorales in the style of J. S. Bach. In: Advances in Neural Information Processing 4, pp. 267–274 (1992)
9. Johnson, M., et al.: Google's multilingual neural machine translation system: enabling zero-shot translation. arXiv preprint arXiv:1611.04558, pp. 1–16 (2016)

10. Kingma, D., Ba, J.: Adam: a method for stochastic optimization. In: International Conference on Learning Representations, December 2015. http://arxiv.org/abs/1412.6980
11. Mikolov, T., Yih, W.t., Zweig, G.: Linguistic regularities in continuous space word representations. In: Proceedings of NAACL-HLT 2013, pp. 746–751. Association for Computational Linguistics, Atlanta (2013)
12. Pachet, F., Roy, P.: Formulating constraint satisfaction problems on part-whole relations: the case of automatic musical harmonization. In: Workshop at European Conference on Artificial Intelligence 1998. Constraint Techniques for Artistic Applications (1998)
13. Phon-Amnuaisuk, S., Wiggins, G.A.: The four-part harmonisation problem: a comparison between genetic algorithms and a rule-based system. In: Proceedings of the AISB 1999 Symposium on Musical Creativity, pp. 28–34 (1999)
14. Phone-Amnuaisuk, S., Smaill, A., Wiggins, G.: Chorale harmonization: a view from a search control perspective. J. New Music. Res. **35**, 279–305 (2006)
15. Raczynski, S., Fukayama, S., Vincent, E.: Melody harmonisation with interpolated probabilistic models. Project-Team METISS (Research Report N 8110), France (2012)
16. Sutskever, I., Vinyals, O., Le, V.Q.: Sequence to sequence learning with neural networks. In: Neural Information Processing Systems 2014 (NIPS 2014) (2014)
17. Suzuki, S., Kitahara, T.: Four-part harmonization using Bayesian networks: pros and cons of introducing chord nodes. J. New Music. Res. **43**(3), 331–353 (2014). https://doi.org/10.1080/09298215.2014.911917
18. United Church of Christ in Japan Hymn Committee (ed.): Hymn: Hymn the second edition Tomoni Utaou. The Board of Publications The United of Church of Christ, Tokyo (1982). (in Japan)
19. Yi, L., Goldsmith, J.: Automatic generation of four-part harmony. In: Conference on Uncertainty in Artificial Intelligence- Applications Workshop, vol. 268 (2007)

On Hierarchical Clustering
of Spectrogram

Shun Sawada$^{(\boxtimes)}$, Yoshinari Takegawa, and Keiji Hirata

Future University Hakodate, Hokkaido 041-8655, Japan
b1012046@gmail.com

Abstract. We propose a new method of applying Generative Theory of
Tonal Music directly to a spectrogram of music to produce a time-span
segmentation as hierarchical clustering. We first consider a vertically
long rectangle in a spectrogram (bin) as a pitch event and a spectrogram
as a sequence of bins. The texture feature of a bin is extracted using a
gray level co-occurrence matrix to generate a sequence of the texture features. The proximity and change of phrases are calculated by the distance
between the adjacent bins by their texture features. The global structures
such as parallelism and repetition are detected by a self-similarity matrix
of a sequence of bins. We develop an algorithm which is given a sequence
of the boundary strength between adjacent bins, iteratively merges adjacent bins in the bottom-up manner, and finally generates a dendrogram,
which corresponds to a time-span segmentation. We conducted an experiment with inputting Mozart's K.331 and K.550 and obtained promising
results although the algorithm does not take into account almost any
musical knowledge such as pitch and harmony.

Keywords: Generative theory of tonal music
Time-span segmentation · Gray level co-occurrence matrix
Self-similarity matrix · Dendrogram

1 Introduction

A Generative Theory of Tonal Music (GTTM) is known as one of the most
reliable music theories, which proposed intuitive and effective concepts and data
structures for representing and understanding music, such as reduction, time-
span tree and prolongational tree [8]. It is, however, widely recognized that
there are intrinsic difficulties in the analysis by GTTM [5,6]; (i) although many
preference rules are specified to retrieve the information in music to generate
time-span and prolongational trees, there is not given the method to resolve the
competitive preference rules, and (ii) only a homophonic music written on a score
can be handled, but neither polyphony nor musical audio. For (i), the musical
factors that often make the preference rules competitive contain the distances
made of pitch and temporal intervals, the local structural constraint and global
dependency, and the boundaries made of harmony and metrical structure. In

M. Aramaki et al. (Eds.): CMMR 2017, LNCS 11265, pp. 226–237, 2018.
https://doi.org/10.1007/978-3-030-01692-0_16

general, it depends on cases to give priority to either of them, and the definitive rules for controlling the priority for relevant preference rules have not been found yet. For (ii), GTTM was originally developed for analyzing a homophonic music written on a score. However, in reality, there are several cases in which the music to be analyzed is given in the audio format and/or a polyphonic music.

The significance of this work is as follows. If GTTM is applicable to musical audio, any style and/or format of music could be analyzed in the musically reliable way: for example, polyphony, any genre of music, music without a score, classical music to pop music, string quartet to orchestra, and music with expression. Here, we are interested in the musical structure as the result of analyzing a spectrogram without musical knowledge and only with human's innate hearing capability, that is, gestalt.

For GTTM to be applicable directly to a musical audio, however, the following problems should be solved: (a) how to translate the GTTM preference rules into the ones applicable to a musical audio, and (b) how to integrate the results of the applications of the preference rules into a single musical structure. For (a), since we can consider a score as the 2-dimensional coordinate system of beat (x-axis) and pitch (y-axis), by translating beat into time and pitch into frequency, the preference rules may be applicable to a spectrogram. Since a spectrogram, however, contain many confusing partials, fuzzy unstable patterns, and so on, it is difficult to recognize and segregate each note in melodies and chords precisely. Hence, the straightforward way of the original GTTM preference rules being applied to the notes extracted from a musical audio or a spectrogram does not seem promising. For (b), even if the results of the original rules being applied to the notes extracted from a musical audio would be precise, the problem of integrating the results of the preference rules are not yet resolved. As long as the problem of integration is naively transformed into that of the weight adjustment for each preference rule as in the previous research [5], we might be staying far from a fundamental solution.

In the paper, we propose a new method of applying GTTM directly to a musical audio, which we think has a potential to resolve the above two difficulties. In addition, we investigate how accurate the musical structure analysis can be done from the spectrogram without using musical knowledge only with the ability of gestalt cognition which the human hearing originally possesses. We focus on the alternative features extracted from a musical audio, texture features of a spectrogram. While admitting the effectiveness of the low-level audio features such as a chromagram and the MFCC features, as a feasibility study, we would investigate a new method based on the texture features of a spectrogram to produce a time-span segmentation. A time-span segmentation is one of the basic musical structures introduced by Lerdahl and Jackedoff, which is defined as the domains over which reduction takes place. For samples, see Fig. 6.5 (p. 127) and Fig. 6.8 (p. 129) in [8]. It is constructed of the results of the grouping and metrical structure analyses so that the extracted grouping structure as the upper-level is placed on the extracted metrical structure as the lower-level.

Furthermore, a time-span tree is generated by combining the head selection within each segment with a time-span segmentation. Since we focus on the texture features of a spectrogram, not handling pitch and harmonic information, we do not handle a time-span tree but a time-span segmentation.

2   Related Work

First, let us briefly survey the typical methods employed in the previous work for detecting and extracting the musical structures, such as boundaries, repetitions, and sections within a piece of music, from low-level audio features. Chen and Li proposed a method for decomposing an audio of music into segments such as intro, verse, bridge, and outro [1]. Chen and Li used the harmonic information based on chroma features and the timbral information based on MFCC to produce segment labels, respectively. Next, a new representation *score matrix*, which serves the similar purpose of visualizing music structures as Foote's self-similarity matrix [3], were introduced for combining the two different aspects of an audio of music, harmony and timbre. Then, a score matrix was factorized into the multiplication of the templates of segment types and the activations along time by NMF. The Chen and Li's method is inspired by the observation that music structure is perceived based on various kinds of sources of sound information, among which harmony and timbre play a primary role.

McFee and Ellis proposed a compact representation for effectively encoding repetition structures within a song at multiple levels of granularity [9]. Their method begins with producing a binary recurrence matrix made of audio-level features, such as a chromagram and an MFCC sequence. Here, the two contrasting features are used: harmonic features for detecting long-term repetitions and timbral features for detecting local consistency. Then, to facilitate the discovery of repetition structures, the internal local and long-term connectivities among samples are properly developed and, finally, with balancing local and global linkages, a sequence-augmented affinity matrix that encodes repetition structures is obtained.

Ullrich, Schlüter, and Grill also tackled a similar problem of music segmentation, in which the boundaries within music such as chorus and verse are detected as humans annotate [12]. Ullrich *et al.* let a Convolutional Neural Network (CNN) directly learn the corpus of Mel-scaled magnitude spectrograms with human annotations. Then, they claimed that while many of existing music segmentation algorithms are nearly hand-designed and need much fine-tuning to optimize performance, supervised learning with CNN outperform hand-design ones without domain knowledge. CNN is advantageous for a computer because CNN can identify by itself the features relevant to music segmentation.

Next, let us briefly review the methods developed in the previous work for classifying a piece of music in terms of genre and mood. Costa *et al.* employed the gray level co-occurrence matrix (GLCM) and Local Binary Patterns (LBP) as textural features for automatic music genre classification [2]. Intuitively, GLCM provides the quantitative measures of textural properties of a picture such as smoothness, coarseness, and regularity [7] (see more in Sect. 3.1). Among the set of the 14 properties originally suggested by Haralick, Costa *et al.* used seven ones, Entropy, Correlation, Homogeneity, 3rd Order Momentum, Maximum Likelihood, Contrast, and Energy, and used SVM as the classifier with the Gaussian kernel. They considered the two different strategies of extracting features: global (holistic) and local (zoning). In the former, the features are extracted from the entire spectrogram and, then, classified by a single genre. In the latter, a spectrogram is firstly divided into several zones (bins), the bins are classified independently, and the final decision is made by combining all the partial classifications of the bins. As a result, the latter with division by 5 was better than the former and achieved the highest performance.

Nakashika, Garcia, and Takiguchi also basically employed GLCM for feature extraction and CNN for a classifier of musical genre classification [11]. Nakashika *et al.* provided multiple GLCM maps with different offset parameters (distance and angle) from a short-term Mel-scaled spectrogram. After several pre-experiments, they fixed the distance of the offset parameters as 1 and set the angle as either of $0°$, $45°$, $90°$, and $135°$. The set of GLCM maps with these different offset parameters integratively produced the input data to CNNs as a classifier. Since the set of GLCM maps cooperatively capture the local music patterns and, as a result, outperformed the cases in which a single GLCM map was only used.

3 Method for Hierarchical Clustering of Spectrogram

The method for translating the application of each GTTM preference rule into pattern recognition of a spectrogram is as follows. Grouping Preference Rule (GPR) 2 and 3 prescribe the way of forming groups and boundaries based on the proximity and change between pitch events, respectively. We first consider a spectrogram as a sequence of vertically long rectangles and a vertically long rectangle in a spectrogram as a pitch event. Using a pattern recognition technique, the distance between adjacent vertically long rectangles in a spectrogram is calculated and used for the measures of proximity and change. GPR 4 prescribes that the higher extent to which GPRs 2 and 3 hold is, the more the effects of GPRs 2 and 3 are taken into account. Thus, the measures of proximity and change are defined as real numbers. GPR 6 prescribes that if parallel (repetitive) motives or phrases are found, the endpoints of each motive or phrase work as the boundaries with the same effects. In our method, we employ the technique of a self-similarity matrix for detecting parallelism (repetition). At present, we do not take into account GPRs 1 (avoiding a group of a single pitch event), 5 (symmetry), 7 (time-span and prolongational stabilities) due to a feasibility study[1].

Figure 1 shows the overview of our method, which produces the hierarchical clustering of a spectrogram. In the top row of the figure, applying short-time fourier transform (STFT) to input audio with the window size being 1024 and

---

[1] Since the space is limited, for more detail, see literatures [8, 5, 6].

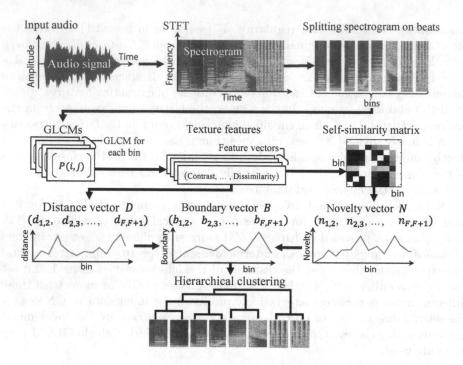

Fig. 1. Overview of our method

the hop size 256, the spectrogram is plotted in a gray scale of 256 levels. After Ullrich *et al.* [12] and Nakashika *et al.* [11], the frequency axis of the spectrogram is Mel-scaled. Then, the spectrogram is split on every beat position into the short spectrograms the length of which is a beat, called bins. We employed the same beat synchronization technique as in McFee and Ellis [10]; Costa *et al.*'s work [2] also supported the method of dividing a spectrogram into several bins outperformed the holistic processing. We used the *onset_detect* function of the librosa library for beat detection. Since the estimated onsets calculated by the *onset_detect* function may include wrong beat positions, we have selected correct ones from the calculated onsets by hand.

3.1 Gray Level Co-Occurrence Matrix and Texture Features

In the second row of Fig. 1, the texture features are extracted for each bin, using a gray level co-occurrence matrix (GLCM) [7]. GLCM is a matrix representing the frequencies of co-occurring pixel values at neighboring pixel pairs over an image (Fig. 2 (Left)). At first, the co-occurrence of the current pixel value and the value of a neighboring pixel located at a specific offset (in our model, the angles are 0°, 45°, 90°, and 135°; the distance is always 2) is taken into account. Next, for instance in Fig. 2 (Right), for the four offsets, if the co-occurrence of pixel values is (i, j), the value of GLCM at (i,j)-position is incremented. Usually,

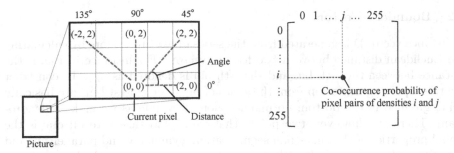

Fig. 2. (Left) Direction and distance of pixel pair; (Right) GLCM

each element of GLCM is normalized to a value from 0.0 to 1.0 so that the sum of all elements is equal to 1.0. By the definition, the GLCM is apparently invariant to the parallel transposition of patterns. Thus, if GLCM is applied to a spectrogram of a musical audio with the frequency axis plotted in the log scale, the GLCM properties are invariant to the phrases located at parallel. For the offset in our method, the same four angles and distance as Nakashika *et al.* [11] are used; the angles are 0°, 45°, 90°, and 135°; the distance is always 1.

Furthermore, Haralick proposed a method for classifying textures by calculating the secondary features from a GLCM such as contrast and dissimilarity, which represent the higher-order statistical information of an image [7]. Among the set of the 14 secondary features originally suggested by Haralick, we adopt five out of them: contrast, dissimilarity, homogeneity, angular second moment (ASM) and correlation. Contrast and dissimilarity are defined relevant to the density difference of pixel pairs. The more number of pixel pairs with a large density difference, the higher the both values of contrast and dissimilarity are. However, the value of contrast increases exponentially, yet that of dissimilarity linearly. Homogeneity is a feature indicating how close the elements in GLCM are to the diagonal line. This is because the elements on the diagonal line represent the frequency of the co-occurrence (i, i). If the number of the elements distant from the diagonal line increases, the value of homogeneity decreases exponentially. If the texture is in order, the value of ASM becomes high. In case of all the elements in GLCM having a same value, the value of ASM reaches the maximum, 1.0. Correlation is a feature indicating the degree of the linear dependency in pixel pairs over an image. For the mathematical definitions of these secondary features, see [7].

Given the GLCM for a bin, the above five secondary features are computed and standardized so that the mean of the value of each secondary feature is 0.0 and the deviation 1.0. Finally, a feature vector is constructed of these standardized values, which represents the texture feature of a bin that is a partial spectrogram.

3.2 Boundary Vector

A distance vector D is generated from the series of feature vectors by calculating the Euclidean distance between two feature vectors. For instance in Fig. 1, the distance between the i-th bin and the j-th bin is denoted as $d_{i,j}$. To construct the time-span segmentation from the series of bins, the closest bins are basically being grouped in the bottom-up manner along the time as we make a dendrogram. There are, however, two points that we should take care of; one is the global properties of the time-span segmentation, symmetry and parallelism, and the other is that a usual algorithm for making a dendrogram which may merge two bins that are close yet not next to each other.

For the former problem, the measure of novelty [4] is introduced; the novelty value is computed by correlating a (possibly Gaussian-tapered) "checkerboard" kernel matrix along the main diagonal of a self-similarity matrix made of the above feature vector; in our model, the size of a "checkerboard" kernel matrix is set 2 by 2. Since a self-similarity matrix reflects the information of relatively large structures such as repetition and section, peaks in the correlation intuitively mean the strength of structural boundaries of music, taking into account its global structure and dependency. Novelty is here represented in the form of a novelty vector of the same length as a given feature vector, N, in the middle row of Fig. 1. Finally, a boundary vector B representing the total strength of a boundary between adjacent bins are obtained by multiplying ith-elements of a distance vector D and a novelty vector N; that is, $b_{i,i+1} := d_{i,i+1} \cdot n_{i,i+1}$.

For the latter problem, we develop a new algorithm of hierarchical clustering for time-span segmentation to be described in the next section so that the adjacent bins are only merged (the bottom of Fig. 1).

3.3 Hierarchical Clustering

Figure 3 (Left) shows the algorithm for hierarchical clustering for time-span segmentation; (Right) shows the example of bins being merged into larger ones. In our method, each time two bins are merged, the GLCM features of the newly created bin are re-calculated, and accordingly the distance and the boundary vectors are also re-calculated. In (Left) of Fig. 3, the first 6 steps of the algorithm are for initialization, which have been explained in the previous section. The next 5 steps make the loop for iteratively merging bins with updating distance and boundary vectors, D and B (not novelty vector N) until all the bins are merged into a single bin (the original whole spectrogram). At step "Weighting B by number of bins", the boundary strength is augmented by the number of unit bins contained in merged bins relevant to a boundary. The weighting process is inspired by the observation that the larger a bin merged is, the stronger the effective strength of boundary is, and the harder a bin merged is further merged to adjacent one. Checking the values in the weighted boundary vector, the closest neighboring bins are identified, which have the weakest boundary, and merged into a larger bin.

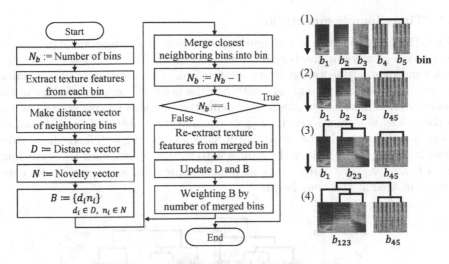

Fig. 3. (Left) Algorithm of hierarchical clustering; (Right) Iteratively merged bins

The process of merging bins is depicted as the evolution of a dendrogram as in (Right) of the figure. For instance, at stage (1), since bins b_4 and b_5 are the closest, they are merged into b_{45}[2]. The height of the line segment connecting b_4 and b_5 stands for the strength of boundary; the higher the line segment is, the stronger the strength of boundary is.

At stage (2), for the series of b_1, b_2, b_3 and b_{45}, distance and boundary vectors, D and B, are first re-calculated. Then, the boundary strength is augmented as follows; for boundary strength $b_{3,4}$, since b_3 is made of a unit bin and b_{45} two unit bins, $b_{3,4}$ is weighted by 2 ($= 1 \times 2$) to yield $b'_{3,4}$ ($= 2 \times b_{3,4}$). As a result, the boundary strength gets stronger, and it becomes hard for b_3 and b_{45} to be merged equivalently. On the other hand, for boundary strength $b_{2,3}$, since the bins on both sides, b_2 and b_3, are made of a unit bin, weighted boundary strength $b'_{2,3}$ is still the same as $b_{2,3}$. Then, $b'_{2,3}$ and $b'_{3,4}$ are compared, and b_2 and b_3 are merged because $b'_{2,3}$ is weaker than $b'_{3,4}$ in this example.

At stage (3), for the series of b_1, b_{23}, and b_{45}, distance and boundary vectors, D and B, are also first re-calculated. Then, since b_{23} and b_{45} are both made of two unit bins, boundary strength $b_{23,45}$ is weighted by 4 ($= 2 \times 2$), and $b'_{23,45}$ ($= 4 \times b_{23,45}$) is obtained. On the other hand, $b_{1,23}$ is weighted by 2 because b_1 is made of a unit bin and b_{23} two unit bins, and $b'_{1,23}$ ($= 2 \times b_{1,23}$) is obtained. Finally, $b'_{1,23}$ and $b'_{23,45}$ are compared, and b_1 and b_{23} are merged in this case.

---

[2] Note that $b_{i,i+1}$ means the strength of boundary between bins b_i and b_{i+1}, and $b_{i,i+1i+2}$ means that between b_i and b_{i+1i+2}.

3.4 Time-Span Segmentation

When the algorithm finishes merging all the bins, a dendrogram representing the process of merging the bins is obtained (Fig. 4). Translating a dendrogram to a time-span segmentation is straightforward. The resulting dendrogram is parsed in the bottom-up manner, and when the point of merging two bins in the dendrogram is met, a new group that spans the previous groups corresponding to these bins is formed. The time-span segmentation obtained in this manner is surely well-formed in the sense that it satisfies the five well-formedness rules listed in [8, pp. 37–39]. Since the groups with similar spans, such as 1 beat long and 4 beats long, are perceived as an almost same duration in reality, they are usually plotted at the same height.

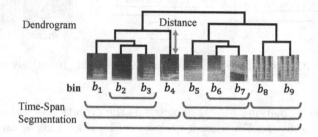

Fig. 4. Dendrogram to Time-Span Segmentation

4 Experimental Results

To demonstrate our method, we used the two themes from the opening of the Mozart's G Minor Symphony, K.550 and the first movement of Mozart's piano sonata in A major, K.331 from the RWC Music Database [13] (RWC-MDB-C-2001 Nos. 2 and 26). In addition, we used the performance of K.331 by Maria João Pires to compare the analysis results for the same piece. Here, K.550 is polyphonic music performed by a string quartet, and K.331 is homophonic music performed on a piano. For the ground truth of a time-span tree, we have referred to the literature [8]. In Figs. 5, 6 and 7, system outputs are shown upper and the ground truth lower.

4.1 Mozart's G Minor Symphony, K.550

Figure 5 shows the result of K.550 of RWC Music Database. Out method succeeded to detect the strongest boundary located between b_4 and b_5, and the analysis result of the first half of the piece was correct. However, that of the second half was wrong; when merging b_6 to either b_5 or b_{78}, the algorithm compared the boundary strengths $b_{5,6}$ and $b_{6,78}$ and made the wrong decision of merging b_6 to b_{78}. The heights of branching nodes in a dendrogram indicates the order of merging bins in reality. Firstly, b_3 and b_4 are merged, and then, so does b_7 and b_8.

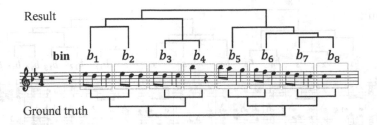

Fig. 5. Dendrogram obtained from K.550 of RWC MDB

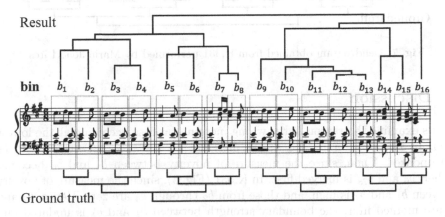

Fig. 6. Dendrogram obtained from K.331 in RWC Music Database

4.2   Mozart's Piano Sonata in a Major, K.331

Fig. 6 shows the result of K.331 of RWC Music Database, which is more problematic. Although the strongest boundary should occur between b_8 and b_9, the algorithm judged that the strongest is between b_5 and b_6. Although the pairs at the lowest level, such as b_1 and b_2, b_3 and b_4, b_9 and b_{10}, b_{11} and b_{12}, should be first merged, those pairs were all unfortunately 180°-degree shifted in the real result shown in the figure. Since those wrong pairs were formed at the early stage in generating the dendrogram, the influences of the wrong pairs were propagated up to the top.

Figure 7 shows the result of K.331 performed by Maria João Pires. In contrast, the strongest boundary between b_8 and b_9 was correctly detected, and among the pairs at the lowest level previously pointed out, the first half of them were also correctly merged, b_1 and b_2, and b_3 and b_4. As for the second half, the configuration of a dendrogram was far from the correct answer. The reason of the wrong merging process in the second half is similar to that in Fig. 5. That is, b_{12} and b_{13} were first merged, and, accordingly, b_{14} and b_{15} were merged with no choice. In this way, the influences at the early stage were propagated up to the top.

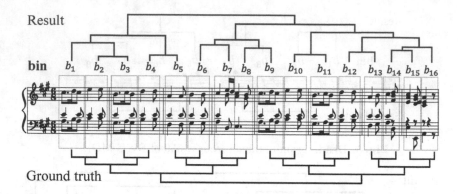

Fig. 7. Dendrogram obtained from K.331 performed by Maria João Pires

5 Discussion

Let us examine the reason of the wrong merging process occurring at the lowest level. In K.550, after b_7 and b_8 are merged, the distance between b_6 and b_7 are updated. Then, since the measure of novelty between b_5 and b_6 becomes higher, b_6 and b_{78} is merged first. In K.331 (Fig. 6), since the measure of novelty between b_1 and b_2 is high, and those from b_2 through b_4 are zero. Hence, b_2 and b_3 are merged first, the boundary strength between b_3 and b_4 is updated and becomes higher, and as a result, b_4 and b_5 are merged. As for the second half, the undesirable values of novelty are also observed where we do not suppose they are zero, for instance, b_{10} and b_{11}, b_{10} and b_{11}, b_{12} and b_{13}, and b_{14} and b_{15}.

In contrast, the result of K.331 performed by Maria João Pires in Fig. 7 is successful. This is because the correct measures of novelty are calculated here. We suppose that the size of the "checkerboard" kernel is critical. Since the size of the self-similarity matrix (SSM) in our method is 8 by 8 in K.550 and 16 by 16 in K.331, respectively, we cannot use the large size of the "checkerboard" kernel and actually use the "checkerboard" kernel of 2 by 2. However, in the original work by Foote [4], the larger size of the "checkerboard" kernel are used, for instance, 64 by 64, possibly with Gaussian taper for smoothing. Therefore, we need to develop the measure of novelty which works well to a small-sized SSM.

6 Concluding Remarks

We propose a new method of applying Generative Theory of Tonal Music directly to a spectrogram of music to produce a time-span segmentation. Although the attempt to extract a time-span segmentation almost only from the textural features of a spectrogram seemed somehow contradictory, the results shown in Figs. 5, 6, and 7 were more promising than we expected. This result suggests that the hierarchical clustering in music is not a cognitive function peculiar to music, but one of the general cognitive functions that humans are using for understanding other media. To improve the precision of our method, musical information, such as pitch, harmony, and rhythm, may be helpful.

Future work contains the following three points. The first is conducting a large-sized quantitative experiment. The next is generating the boundary vector with taking into account the musical information, such as pitch, harmony, and rhythm. The last is developing an algorithm for hierarchical clustering which employs grouping preference rule no. 7 (symmetry) that is not implemented at present as well as the other preference rules.

Acknowledgement. This work has been supported by JSPS Kakenhi 16H01744.

References

1. Chen, R., Li, M.: Music structural segmentation by combining harmonic and timbral information. In: Proceedings of ISMIR, pp. 477–482 (2011)
2. Costa, Y.M.G., Oliveira, L.S., Koerich, A.L., Gouyon, F.: Comparing textural features for music genre classification. In: Proceedings of the 2012 International Joint Conference on Neural Networks, pp. 1867–1872 (2012)
3. Foote, J.: Visualizing music and audio using self similarity. In: Proceedings of the 7th ACM international conference on Multimedia, pp. 77–80 (1999)
4. Foote, J.: Automatic audio segmentation using a measure of audio novelty. In: Proceedings of IEEE International Conference on Multimedia and Expo, vol. 1, pp. 452–455 (2000)
5. Hamanaka, M., Hirata, K., Tojo, S.: Implementing "A Generative Theory of Tonal Music". J. New Music Res. **35**(4), 249–277 (2007)
6. Hamanaka, M., Hirata, K., Tojo, S.: Implementing methods for analysing music based on Lerdahl and Jackendoff's Generative Theory of Tonal Music. Computational Music Analysis, pp. 221–249. Springer, Cham (2016). https://doi.org/10.1007/978-3-319-25931-4_9
7. Haralick, R.M.: Statistical and structural approaches to texture. Proc. IEEE **67**(5), 786–804 (1979)
8. Lerdahl, F., Jackendoff, R.: A Generative Theory of Tonal Music, The MIT Press (1983)
9. McFee, B. and Ellis, D. P. W.: Analyzing song structure with spectral clustering. In: Proceedings of ISMIR, pp. 405–410 (2014)
10. McFee, B. and Ellis, D. P. W.: Learning to segment songs with ordinal linear discriminant analysis. In: Proceedings of ICASSP (2014)
11. Nakashika, T., Garcia, C., Takiguchi, T.: Local-feature-map integration using convolutional neural networks for music genre classification. In: Proceedeings of Interspeech, ISCA, pp. 1752–1755 (2012)
12. Ullrich, K., Schlüter, J., and Grill, T.: Boundary detection in music structure analysis using convolutional neural networks. In: Proceedings of ISMIR, pp. 417–422 (2014)
13. Goto, M., Hashiguchi, H., Nishimura, T., and Oka, R.: RWC Music Database: popular, classical and jazz music databases. In: Proceedings of ISMIR, pp. 287–288 (2002)

deepGTTM-III: Multi-task Learning with Grouping and Metrical Structures

Masatoshi Hamanaka[1](✉), Keiji Hirata[2], and Satoshi Tojo[3]

[1] RIKEN, Tokyo, Japan
masatoshi.hamanaka@riken.jp
[2] Future University Hakodate, Hakodate, Japan
hirata@fun.ac.jp
[3] JAIST, Nomi, Japan
tojo@jaist.ac.jp

Abstract. This paper describes an analyzer that simultaneously learns grouping and metrical structures on the basis of the generative theory of tonal music (GTTM) by using a deep learning technique. GTTM is composed of four modules that are in series. GTTM has a feedback loop in which the former module uses the result of the latter module. However, as each module has been independent in previous GTTM analyzers, they did not form a feedback loop. For example, deepGTTM-I and deepGTTM-II independently learn grouping and metrical structures by using a deep learning technique. In light of this, we present deepGTTM-III, which is a new analyzer that includes the concept of feedback that enables simultaneous learning of grouping and metrical structures by integrating both deepGTTM-I and deepGTTM-II networks. The experimental results revealed that deepGTTM-III outperformed deepGTTM-I and had similar performance to deepGTTM-II.

Keywords: A generative theory of tonal music (GTTM)
Grouping structure · Metrical structure · Deep learning

1 Introduction

Our main goal was to develop a system that enabled a time-span tree of a melody to be automatically acquired on the basis of the generative theory of tonal music (GTTM) [1]. GTTM is composed of four modules, each of which assigns a separate structural description to a listener's understanding of a piece of music. These four modules sequentially output a grouping structure, metrical structure, time-span tree, and prolongational tree. The grouping structure is intended to formalize the intuitive belief that tonal music is organized into groups that are in turn composed of subgroups. These groups are presented graphically as several levels of arcs below a music staff. The metrical structure describes the rhythmical hierarchy of a piece of music by identifying the position of strong beats at the levels of a quarter note, half note, measure, two measures, four

© Springer Nature Switzerland AG 2018
M. Aramaki et al. (Eds.): CMMR 2017, LNCS 11265, pp. 238–251, 2018.
https://doi.org/10.1007/978-3-030-01692-0_17

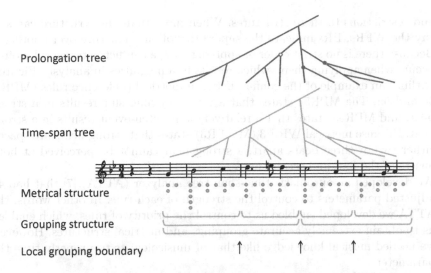

Fig. 1. Grouping structure, metrical structure, time-span tree, and prolongational tree.

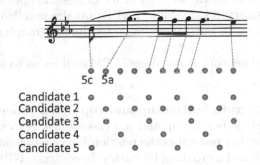

Fig. 2. Conflict between two metrical preference rules

measures, and so on. Strong beats are illustrated as several levels of dots below the music staff (Fig. 1).

The time-span tree provides performance rendering [2], music reproduction [3], and a summarization of the music [4]. This summarization can be used as a representation of a search, resulting in music retrieval systems. It can also be used for melody morphing, which generates an intermediate melody between two melodies in systematic order [5,6]. These systems presently need a time-span tree analyzed by musicologists because previous analyzers [7,8] have not performed optimally.

There are three significant problems when implementing GTTM on a computer.

- **Conflict between rules**
  There are two types of rules in GTTM: well-formedness rules (WFRs) and preference rules (PRs). WFRs are necessary conditions to assign a structure

and restrictions to these structures. When more than one structure can satisfy the WFRs, PRs indicate the superiority of one structure over another.

Because there is no strict order of applying PRs, a conflict between rules often occurs when applying them, which results in ambiguities in analysis. Figure 2 outlines an example of the conflict between metrical preference rules (MPRs) 5c and 5a. The MPR5c states that a relatively long slur results in a strong beat, and MPR5a states that a relatively long pitch-event results in a strong beat. Because metrical WRF 3 (MWFR3) states that strong beats are spaced either two or three beats apart, a strong beat cannot be perceived at both onsets of the first and second notes.

We developed an automatic time-span tree analyzer (ATTA) [7] that had 46 adjusted parameters to control the strength of each rule. In other words, the ATTA we developed enabled us to control the priority of rules, which enabled us to obtain extremely accurate groupings and metrical structures. However, we needed musical knowledge like that of musicologists to properly tune the parameters.

The full ATTA (FATTA) [8] does not have to tune the parameters because it automatically calculates the stability of structures and optimizes the parameters so that the structures are stable. FATTA obtains excellent analysis results for metrical structures but unacceptable results for grouping structures and time-span trees.

The deep layered network in our deepGTTM enables us to learn the priority of rules.

- **Difficult to integrate bottom up and top down processes**
  GTTM rules include bottom up and top down rules. For example, GPR2 is a bottom up rule that prescribes the relationship of onset (attack) and offset (release) timings, and a grouping boundary. In contrast, GPR5 is a top down rule that prefers that a group be divided into two subgroups of the same length.

  The ATTA and FATTA frequently output incorrect higher level hierarchical structures even when a low-level structure is correct because they only use a bottom up process.

  In contrast, we also developed analyzers that only use a top down process called σGTTM [9], σGTTMII [10], and σGTTMIII [11]. σGTTM and σGTTMII can detect the local grouping structure in GTTM analysis by combining the GTTM with statistical learning. However, σGTTM and σGTTMII are only suitable for grouping structures and cannot acquire time-span trees. σGTTMIII enabled us to automatically analyze time-span trees by learning with a time-span tree of 300 pieces from the GTTM database [12] on the basis of probabilistic context-free grammar (PCFG). σGTTMIII performed the best at acquiring time-span trees. However, these analyzers [7–11] do not perform sufficiently well for use in application systems [2–6].

  The deep layered network in our deepGTTM learns both top down and bottom up rules from learning data.

- **Feedback loops**
  The four modules in the GTTM are in series, i.e., the latter module uses the result from the former module. The GTTM also has a feedback loop in which the former module uses the result from the latter module. For example, GPR7 (time-span and prolongational stability) prefers a grouping structure that results in a more stable time-span and/or prolongation reduction. Another example is that MPR9 (time-span interaction) prefers metrical analysis that minimizes conflict in the time-span reduction. However, as each module has been independent in previous GTTM analyzers, they did not form a feedback loop. For example, deepGTTM-I [13] and deepGTTM-II [14] independently learned the grouping and metrical structures by using a deep learning technique.
  Figure 3 summarizes the theory reported by Lerdahl and Jakendoff [1]. The bottom right has the preference rules. If we naïvely implement this theory, the analysis process is endless looping when the output is divergence.

In light of this, we present deepGTTM-III, which is a new analyzer that solves these problems and enables simultaneous learning of grouping and metrical structures by integrating both networks of deepGTTM-I and deepGTTM-II. The deep layered network learns the priority of rules that solves the conflict between rules. The network also learns both bottom up and top down rules.

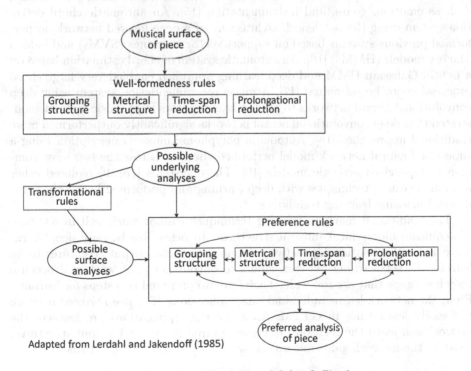

Fig. 3. Summary of Lerdahl and Jakendoff's theory.

By integrating both deepGTTM-I and deepGTTM-II networks, the integrated network possesses information to acquire the metrical structure and the grouping structure. Therefore, the information on acquiring the metrical structure can be used for acquiring the grouping structure, and vice versa. Therefore, a feedback loop is implicitly constructed inside the network.

The network was pre-trained by using 15,000 pieces of music formatted in musicXML that were acquired by Web crawling. We used 300 pieces from the GTTM database: 200 for fine-tuning and 100 for evaluation [12]. The experimental results indicated that the integrated network outperformed the independent network.

The paper is organized as follows. Section 2 describes related work, and Sect. 3 explains our GTTM analyzers: deepGTTM-I, II, and III. Section 4 explains how we evaluated the performance of deepGTTM-I, II, and III, and Sect. 5 concludes with a summary and an overview of future work.

2 Related Work

Deep learning has recently been used for tasks in the area of music information retrieval [15–19] and has demonstrated its potential to solve various kinds of tasks in the area. An automatic tagging system using a fully convolutional network was developed that predicts high-level information about a music clip, such as emotion, genre, and instrumentation [15]. An automatic chord detection system using the bottleneck architecture of a deep layered network outperformed previous systems based on support vector machines (SVMs) and hidden Markov models (HMMs) [16]. An automatic system of chord estimation based on a hybrid Gaussian HMM and deep learning approach enabled very large chord progressions to be estimated [17]. A music recommendation system using deep convolutional neural networks to predict latent factors from music audio demonstrated that deep convolutional neural networks significantly outperformed more traditional approaches [18]. Automatic polyphonic music transcription using a supervised neural network model performed the best across the two most common unsupervised acoustic models [19]. These systems [15–19] replaced other machine learning techniques with deep learning and performed better than traditional machine learning techniques.

The traditional machine learning techniques cannot work well in our task of acquiring hierarchical musical structures. In other words, only deep learning enables the relationship between input scores and output structures to be learned. Direct learning between inputs to output does not work well because they have gaps that are too wide. Therefore, we prepared two steps for learning. First, the network learns individual rule applications. The deep layered network can easily learn rules in GTTM. After the rule applications are learned, the network can learn the relationship between input scores and output structures. That is, the network gains musical knowledge by learning GTTM rules.

3   DeepGTTM-I, II, and III

deepGTTM-I, II, and III are GTTM analyzers based on deep learning. deepGTTM-I analyzes the local grouping boundaries of a grouping structure [13], and deepGTTM-II analyzes the metrical structure [14]. This paper presents deepGTTM-III, which integrates deepGTTM-I and II.

There are three main advantages of using deep learning for GTTM analysis.

- **Learning applications of both bottom up and top down rules**
  Previous analysis systems based on GTTM were constructed by human researchers or programmers. Some rules in GTTM are very ambiguous, and their implementations might differ depending on the person. However, deep-GTTM is a learning based system where the quality of the analyzer depends on the training data and trained network. The input of the network includes the score information of the whole analysis area to learn both bottom up and top down rules.
- **Learning priority of rules**
  σGTTM and σGTTMII do not work well because they only determine the priority of rules from applied rules because the priority of rules depends on the context of a piece. The input of the network in deepGTTM, on the other hand, is the score, and the network learns the priority of the rules as the weight and bias of the network on the basis of the context of the score.
- **Feedback loop in deep layered network**
  There are several kinds of feedback processes in deepGTTM-III because a deep layered network is trained by multi-task learning with grouping and metrical structures. When the grouping structure is learned, important information for acquiring grouping and metrical structures is propagated because deepGTTM-III shares hidden nodes for acquiring both grouping and metrical structures. Similarly, when the metrical structure is learned, important information on acquiring the grouping structure is also propagated.

3.1   Structure of Network

We used a deep belief network (DBN) [20] for deepGTTM-I, II, and III. Figure 4 outlines the structure for the DBN of deepGTTM-I. The input of the DBN was the onset time, offset time, pitch, and velocity of note sequences from musicXML. All inputs were normalized from zero to one. The output of DBN formed multi-tasking learning, which had 10 outputs: 9 kinds of grouping preference rules (GPR2a, 2b, 3a, 3b, 3c, 4, 5, 6, and 7) and local grouping boundary.

Figure 5 outlines the structure for deepGTTM-II. The inputs of deepGTTM-II are the onset time, offset time, pitch, velocity, and the grouping structure manually analyzed by musicologists. Each hierarchical level of the grouping structure is separately input by a note neighboring the grouping boundary as one; otherwise, it is zero. There are eight outputs of deepGTTM-II that enable multi-task learning in each hierarchical level of the metrical structure, i.e., seven MPRs

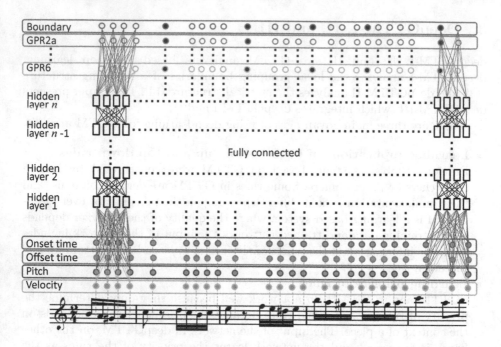

Fig. 4. DBN for deepGTTM-I.

(MPR2, 3, 4, 5a, 5b, 5c, and 5d), and one level of the metrical structure. Individual outputs have two units, e.g., rules that are not applicable (=0) and rules that are applicable (=1), or weak beats (=0) and strong beats (=1). A metrical structure consists of hierarchical levels, and we added one hidden layer to generate the next structure level. We used logistic regression to connect the final hidden layer (n,n+1,..., n+h) and outputs. All outputs shared the hidden layers from one to the final hidden layer.

Figure 6 outlines the structure for the DBN we called deepGTTM-III to generate a grouping and metrical structure. deepGTTM-III has the same input as deepGTTM-I, and its output is the same as the merged output of deepGTTM-I and II.

3.2   Learning Networks

This section describes how we learned the local grouping boundaries and metrical structure by using deep layered networks.

Pre-training. The network learned the features of the music in pre-training. As a large scale dataset with no labels was needed, we collected 15,000 pieces of music formatted in musicXML from Web pages that were linked to the musicXML page of MakeMusic Inc. [21]. The musicXMLs were downloaded in three steps.

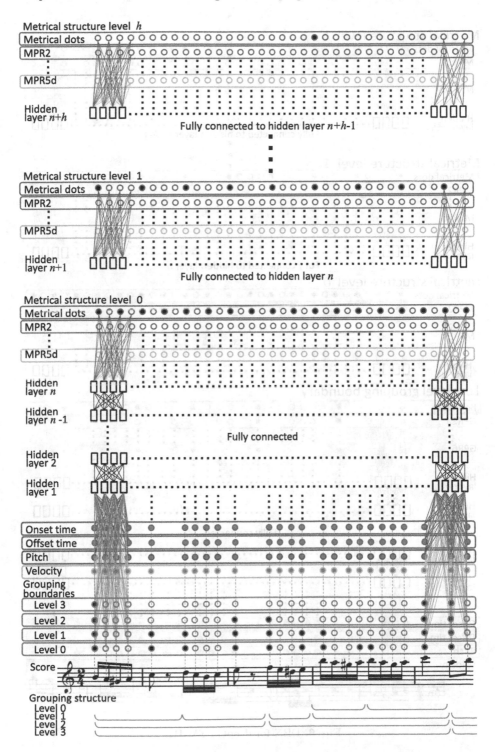

Fig. 5. DBN for deepGTTM-II.

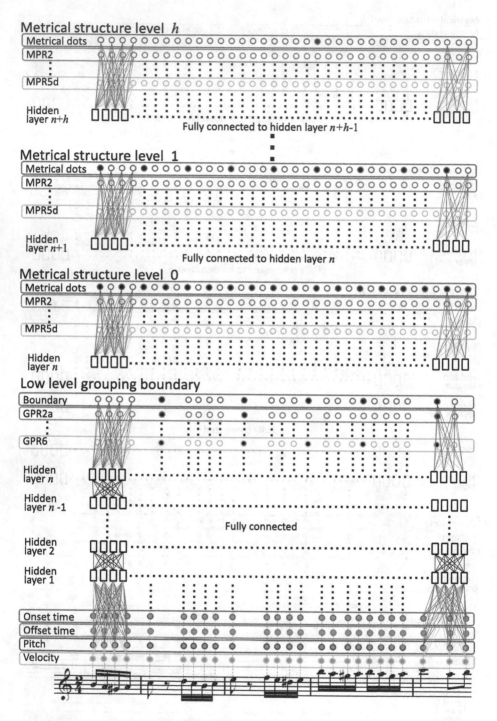

Fig. 6. DBN for deepGTTM-III.

(1) A Web autopilot script made a list of URLs that were most likely files of musicXMLs from five links on the musicXML page of MakeMusic Inc.
(2) The files in the URL list were downloaded after URLs that were clearly not musicXMLs had been omitted.
(3) All the downloaded files were opened using the script, and files that were not musicXML were deleted.

Each network of deepGTTM-I, II, and III was pre-trained by using a restricted Boltzmann machine.

Learning Rules Application and Structure. The network in fine-tuning learned with a labeled dataset. We had 300 pieces with a labeled dataset in the GTTM database, which included musicXMLs with positions of local grouping boundaries, positions of dots for each hierarchy of the metrical structure, and positions to which the grouping and metrical preference rules were applied. However, these 300 pieces were insufficient for deep learning.

Consequently, we constructed a half-labeled dataset. We automatically added the labels of six applied rules of GPR2a, 2b, 3a, 3b, 3c, and 3d, and MPR3, 5a, 5b, 5c, 5d because these rules could be uniquely applied as a score. We used our ATTA to add labels to these rules.

We also artificially increased the labeled dataset because the 300 pieces in the GTTM database were insufficient for training a deep layered network. First, we transposed the pieces for all 12 keys. We then changed the length of note values to two times, four times, eight times, a half time, a quarter time, and an eighth time. Thus, the total labeled dataset had 25, 200 ($= 300 \times 12 \times 7$) pieces.

The priority of rules and grouping and metrical structures were learned by back propagation of the deep layered network using the half-labeled dataset and labeled dataset. deepGTTM-I and II had very complex networks. The fine-tuning of local grouping boundaries and one level of the metrical structure involved multi-task learning. The fine-tuning of each PR also involved multi-task learning. Therefore, the fine-tuning of PRs involved multi-dimensional multi-task learning. The processing flow for the learning of a GPR or local grouping boundaries had four steps. The order of music pieces was changed at every epoch in all steps.

(1) The order of the pieces of training data was randomly shuffled, and a piece was selected from top to bottom.
(2) The note transition of the selected piece was randomly shuffled and a note transition was selected from top to bottom.
(3) Back propagation from output to input was carried out on the basis of whether the note transition had a boundary, or the rule was applied (=1) or not (=0).
(4) The next note transition or the next piece in steps 1 and 2 was repeated.

The processing flow for the learning of an MPR or metrical dots involved four steps.

(1) The order of the music pieces of training data was randomly shuffled, and a piece was selected from top to bottom.

(2) The beat positions of the selected piece were randomly shuffled, and a beat position was selected from top to bottom.
(3) Back propagation from output to input was carried out on the basis of whether the beat position had a strong beat, or the rule was applied (=1) or not (=0).
(4) The next piece in step 1 or the next beat position in step 2 was repeated.

The processing flow for the multidimensional multi-task learning of PRs involved three steps.

(1) The order of PRs was randomly shuffled, and a rule was selected from top to bottom.
(2) Multi-task learning of the selected PR was carried out.
(3) The next rules in step 1 were repeated.

Simultaneous Learning of Grouping and Metrical Structures in deepGTTM-III. The deep layered network of deepGTTM-III was trained by using a multi-task learning technique for the grouping and metrical structures. The main difference in learning and acquiring the metrical structure in deepGTTM-II and deepGTTM-III is that the grouping structure is needed in the input data for deepGTTM-II but not for deepGTTM-III. In other words, deepGTTM-III predicts low level grouping boundaries by itself and uses the information on predicting the low level grouping boundaries to predict the metrical structure.

The deepGTTM-I and II networks first learn individual rule applications by fixed numbers of epochs and then learn the structure on the same epochs. They then repeat learning of rule applications and structure learning. In contrast, deepGTTM-III repeats learning of GPR applications, grouping structures, MPR applications, and metrical structures by using fixed numbers of epochs. As all learning processes of grouping and metrical structures interact in the deepGTTM-III network, the feedback loop described in Sect. 3 is implicitly formed.

A GPR and an MPR are sometimes learned complementarily when the rules are learned because some GPRs and MPRs are very similar. For example, GPR6 (parallelism) prefers to form parallel parts of a group, where two or more segments of the music can be construed as parallel, and MPR1 (parallelism) prefers a parallel metrical structure, where two of more groups or parts of groups can be construed as parallel.

In another example, consider a sequence of four notes: n1, n2, n3, and n4. GPR2b (Attack-Point) states the transition n2–n3 may be heard as a group boundary if the interval between the attack points of n2 and n3 is greater than that between the attack points of n1 and n2 and that between the attack points of n3 and n4. MPR5a prefers a metrical structure in which a relatively strong beat occurs at the inception of a relatively long pitch event.

4   Experimental Results

We evaluated deepGTTM by using 100 music pieces from the GTTM database; the remaining 200 pieces were used to train the network. The F-measure was given by the weighted harmonic mean of precision P (proportion of selected dots that were correct) and recall R (proportion of correct dots that were identified).

Table 1 compares the results for deepGTTM-III with those for deepGTTM-I and deepGTTM-II for a network that had 11 layers with 3000 units. The results indicate that deepGTTM-III obtained a higher F-measure in acquiring local grouping boundaries than deepGTTM-I. However, deepGTTM-III obtained an F-measure in acquiring a metrical structure similar to that of deepGTTM-II, which was slightly higher than that of deepGTTM-III. We used the correct grouping structure in the GTTM database because deepGTTM-II needs a grouping structure for input to the network. In contrast, as deepGTTM-III does not need a grouping structure, it operates efficiently even when there is no correct grouping structure.

Table 1. Performance of deepGTTM-I, II, and III.

Melodies	Low level grouping boundary		Metrical structure	
	deepGTTM-III	deepGTTM-I	deepGTTM-III	deepGTTM-II
1. Grande Valse Brillante	0.80	0.79	0.93	0.94
2. Moments Musicaux	0.80	0.81	0.99	1.00
3. Turkish March	0.77	0.76	0.96	0.98
4. Anitras Tanz	0.78	0.76	0.90	0.90
5. Valse du Petit Chien	0.80	0.78	0.99	0.99
:	:	:	:	:
Total (100 melodies)	0.81	0.78	0.94	0.96

5   Conclusion

We presented deepGTTM-III, which integrates a grouping structure analyzer called deepGTTM-I and a metrical structure analyzer called deepGTTM-II. Whereas deepGTTM-I and deepGTTM-II have to independently learn grouping and metrical structures, deepGTTM-III learns them simultaneously. The experimental results indicated that deepGTTM-III obtained a higher F-measure in acquiring local grouping boundaries than deepGTTM-I and had a similar F-measure to deepGTTM-II in acquiring the metrical structure. This work was one step in implementing a generative theory of tonal music (GTTM) based on deep learning. We plan to implement time-span reduction analysis on the basis of deep learning in the future.

Acknowledgments. This work was supported by JSPS KAKENHI Grant Numbers 17H01847, 25700036, 16H01744, and 23500145.

References

1. Lerdahl, F., Jackendoff, R.: A Generative Theory of Tonal Music. MIT Press, Cambridge (1985)
2. Hirata, K., Hiraga, R.: Ha-Hi-Hun plays Chopin's Etude. In: Working Notes of IJCAI-03 Workshop on Methods for Automatic Music Performance and Their Applications in a Public Rendering Contest (2003)
3. Hirata, K., Matsuda, S., Kaji, K., Nagao, K.: Annotated music for retrieval, reproduction, and sharing. In: Proceedings of the 2004 International Computer Music Conference (ICMC 2004), pp. 584–587 (2004)
4. Hirata, K., Matsuda, S.: Interactive music summarization based on GTTM. In: Proceedings of the 2002 International Society for Music Information Retrieval Conference (ISMIR 2002), pp. 86–93 (2002)
5. Hamanaka, M., Hirata, K., Tojo, S.: Melody morphing method based on GTTM. In: Proceedings of the 2008 International Computer Music Conference (ICMC 2008), pp. 155–158 (2008)
6. Hamanaka, M., Hirata, K., Tojo, S.: Melody extrapolation in GTTM approach. In: Proceedings of the 2009 International Computer Music Conference (ICMC 2009), pp. 89–92 (2009)
7. Hamanaka, M., Hirata, K., Tojo, S.: Implementing 'a generative theory of tonal music'. J. New Music Res. **35**(4), 249–277 (2006)
8. Hamanaka, M., Hirata, K., Tojo, S.: FATTA: full automatic time-span tree analyzer. In: Proceedings of the 2007 International Computer Music Conference (ICMC 2007), pp. 153–156 (2007)
9. Miura, Y., Hamanaka, M., Hirata, K., Tojo, S.: Decision tree to detect GTTM group boundaries. In: Proceedings of the 2009 International Computer Music Conference (ICMC 2009), pp. 125–128 (2009)
10. Kanamori, K., Hamanaka, M.: Method to detect GTTM local grouping boundaries based on clustering and statistical learning. In: Proceedings of the 2014 International Computer Music Conference (ICMC 2014), pp. 125–128 (2014)
11. Hamanaka, M., Hirata, K., Tojo, S.: *sigma*GTTM III: learning-based time-span tree generator based on PCFG. In: Proceedings of the 11th International Symposium on Computer Music Multidisciplinary Research (CMMR 2015), pp. 303–317 (2015)
12. Hamanaka, M., Hirata, K., Tojo, S.: Musical structural analysis database based on GTTM. In: Proceedings of the 2014 International Society for Music Information Retrieval Conference (ISMIR 2014), pp. 325–330 (2014)
13. Hamanaka, M., Hirata, K., Tojo, S.: deepGTTM-I: local boundary analyzer based on a deep learning technique. In: Proceedings of the 12th International Symposium on Computer Music Multidisciplinary Research (CMMR 2016), pp. 8–20 (2016)
14. Hamanaka, M., Hirata, K., Tojo, S.: deepGTTM-II: automatic generation of metrical structure based on deep learning technique. In: Proceedings of 13th Sound and Music Computing Conference (SMC 2016), pp. 203–210 (2016)
15. Choi, K., Fazekas, G., Sandler, M.: Automatic tagging using deep convolutional neural networks. In: Proceedings of the 2016 International Society for Music Information Retrieval Conference (ISMIR 2016), pp. 805–811 (2016)
16. Zhou, X., Lerch, A.: Chord detection using deep learning. In: Proceedings of the 2015 International Society for Music Information Retrieval Conference (ISMIR 2015), pp. 52–58 (2015)

17. Deng, J., Kwok, Y.: Hybrid Gaussian-HMM-deep learning approach for automatic chord estimation with very large vocabulary. In: Proceedings of the 2016 International Society for Music Information Retrieval Conference (ISMIR 2016), pp. 812–818 (2016)
18. Oord, A., Sander, D., Benjamin, S.: Deep content-based music recommendation. In: Proceedings of the Advances in Neural Information Processing Systems 26 (NIPS 2013), pp. 2643–2651 (2013)
19. Sigtia, S., Benetos, E., Dixon, S.: An end-to-end neural network for polyphonic piano music transcription. IEEE/ACM Trans. Audio Speech Lang. Process. (TASLP) **24**(5), 927–939 (2016)
20. Hinton, G.E., Osindero, S., Teh, Y.W.: A fast learning algorithm for deep belief nets. Neural Comp. **18**, 1527–1554 (2006)
21. MakeMusic Inc., "Finale" (2018). http://www.finalemusic.com/

Analyzing Music to Music Perceptual Contagion of Emotion in Clusters of Survey-Takers, Using a Novel Contagion Interface: A Case Study of Hindustani Classical Music

Sanga Chaki[1(✉)], Sourangshu Bhattacharya[2], Raju Mullick[3], and Priyadarshi Patnaik[3]

[1] Advanced Technology Development Center, IIT, Kharagpur, India
sanga@iitkgp.ac.in
[2] Computer Science and Engineering Department, IIT, Kharagpur, India
[3] Department of Humanities and Social Sciences, IIT, Kharagpur, India

Abstract. Music has strong potential to convey and elicit emotions, which are dependent on both context and antecedent stimuli. However, there is little research available on the impact of antecedent musical stimuli on emotion perception in consequent musical pieces, when one listens to a sequence of music clips with insignificant time lag. This work attempts to (a) understand how the perception of one music clip is affected by the perception of its antecedent clip and (b) find if there are any inherent patterns in the way people respond when exposed to music in sequence, with special reference to Hindustani Classical Music (HCM). We call this phenomenon of varying perceptions, the perceptual contagion of emotion in music. Findings suggest, when happy clips are preceded by sad and calm clips, perceived happiness increases. When sad clips are preceded by happy and calm clips, perceived sadness increases. Calm clips are perceived as happy and sad when preceded by happy clips and sad clips respectively. This suggests that antecedent musical stimuli have capacity to influence the perception of music that follows. It is also found that almost 85%–95% of people on average are affected by perceptual contagion – while listening to music in sequence – with varying degrees of influence.

Keywords: Music perception · Perceptual contagion of emotion
Web based self report surveys · Hindustani Classical Music (HCM)

1 Introduction

Emotions are an integral part of life. Under different circumstances, we feel happy, excited, angry, afraid, sad and many other emotions. It has been established by researchers [2,6], that various stimuli and situations like social functions [10], interpersonal encounters [5], exposure to visual and auditory stimuli

© Springer Nature Switzerland AG 2018
M. Aramaki et al. (Eds.): CMMR 2017, LNCS 11265, pp. 252–269, 2018.
https://doi.org/10.1007/978-3-030-01692-0_18

can elicit emotional responses. Music is one such potent stimuli [7]. In this discussion, we focus on the perceptive and cognitive aspects of music listening, which form effective ways of expressing and inducing emotions [8]. The perception of emotion in the consequent musical clip might be influenced by the perception of its antecedent clip – much like the meaning of sentences are inferred with reference to the preceding words or phrases. We performed web-based surveys to track if and how such influences occur. It was found that the perception of emotional content of music is modified by preceding music and its emotional content, even when the exposure is for a short duration. Thus, emotion perception in music is a sequentially modified and complex process.

The rest of Sect. 1 documents the previous works done on emotion perception, how human emotions are captured for various studies and how emotions are represented in Indian philosophy. In Sect. 2, we describe in details of the surveys, the stimuli used for the surveys, and the methodologies followed for processing the survey results. Section 3 shows (a) the results of the context-based biases obtained in perception of music through tables and line charts and (b) the results of applying clustering algorithms on the user data obtained from the surveys using silhoutte graphs. Conclusions are drawn and future scope is discussed in Sect. 4.

1.1 Emotion Perception and Induction

There is a distinction between the perception and induction of musical emotions. In the first case, we only become aware of an emotion and in the second, we actually feel those emotions. The underlying processes might be different leading to requirement of apt representations and measurement models to study these phenomena. Juslin [8] explained how music arouses emotions by a multi-level framework, which included the phenomenon of *Contagion* among many other psychological mechanisms. In these studies by Juslin [8,9], *Emotional contagion* refers to a process whereby an emotion is induced by a piece of music because the listener perceives the emotional expression of the music, and then 'mimics' this expression internally. Egermann [4] also uses the term *Contagion* to describe an unconscious automatic mimicking of others' expressions affecting ones' own emotional state. We take this theory further and hypothesize that, as it is possible for preceding music to contagiously affect not only the listener's emotion, but also the perception of emotions, thereby resulting in modified perception of the emotions of the musical pieces or phrases that follow. This is drawn from the basic fact that emotions are contextual – thus the meaning making of one music clip might depend on the musical context it is heard in. This approach may explain why musical emotions are perceived in the way they are perceived – the same musical notes make us happy in one song and sad in another, depending on the notational and lyrical context of the musical piece.

1.2   Capturing Human Emotions

The most common method of capturing emotions is self reporting. In the context of musical emotions, the works of Egermann and Schubert ar pioneering. Egermann [4] presented the concept of web based surveys, where data regarding emotion, empathy, and preference ratings were gathered from a music-personality test, which had twenty three musical excerpts as stimuli. Schubert et al. [15,16] created an interface based on facial expressions (emoticons) "aligned in clock-like distribution", through which survey participants could quickly and easily rate emotions in music continuously. The emoticons they used depicted six emotions: Excited, Happy, Calm, Sad, Scared and Angry. We drew from these works to construct an interface that makes it possible to record people's emotions as they listen to music discretely and continuously – this is discussed in details in Sect. 2.2. Continuous emotion rating of music has resulted in better understanding and modeling of music's emotion-generating nature. This also helps in mapping musical features, structures and constructs onto emotional response data [14,17].

1.3   Emotions in HCM - Nāvā Rāsā

Our study focuses mainly on perception of Hindustani Classical Music, abbreviated as *HCM*. HCM is one of the two major branches of Indian Classical Music (*ICM*), the other being Carnatic Music. The basic melodic structure of HCM is the *Rāga*, which, according to Chordia [3] and others "is a collection of melodic atoms and a technique for developing them. These melodic atoms are sequences of notes that are inflected with various micro pitch alterations and articulated with expressive sense of timing. Longer musical phrases are built by knitting these melodic atoms together". The tempo in HCM are primarily of three types - Vilāmbit (slow), Mādhyalāyā (a little faster), and Drut (Fast). It might be noted that one significant aspect of HCM is the practitioner's freedom of improvisation, keeping the grammar of Rāgā and the tempo in mind. Many of the *Rāga*s are said to be associated with particular emotions, which are elicited through the use of different melodic constructs (or features). In Indian aesthetics, emotional responses to any art form are said to be one of nine prevalent types, or *Nāvā Rāsā*, which literally translates to Nine (= *Nāvā*) Emotions (= *Rāsā*). These are *romantic, happy, wonder, calm, anger, courage, sad, fear* and *disgust*. These are the emotions that a human perceives/shows in response to the different situations, according to Bhārāta Muni's treatise *Nātyashāsthra* [1]. The concepts of *Nāvā Rāsā* have influenced our survey interface, which is described in Sect. 2.2.

In this paper, we study the phenomenon of *perceptual contagion of perceived emotion*, in the context of music presented in sequence, using a novel contagion capturing interface – which is based on the continuous music survey framework, with the aim to understand if and how the perception of one music clip biases the perception of the next music clip. To the best of our knowledge, this study is the first of its kind, with HCM as a special case study.

2   Surveys and Data Acquisition

In this section we describe the survey structure and interface we used to capture people's emotions which were evoked when they were exposed to excerpts or clips of various music. Around 300 students belonging to different courses of IIT Kharagpur, India, took part in the surveys. The age range varied from 18 to 30 years. As part of the survey, demographic details like gender, music preference, musical training were also recorded. It might be noted here, that this is possibly the first time that such a large scale survey for understanding HCM's emotive aspects have been undertaken.

2.1   Stimuli

We used three sets of clips for the present work. The first set – called **IM1_Clips** – constituted of the six international clips used by Schubert et al. [16]. Since these clips were already annotated with their emotional content in the literature [16], we validated the correctness of our survey by comparing our ratings with Schubert's. The context-dependent biases for perception of some of these clips were also verified. The prefix *IM* in the clips' names stand for *International Music*. The number following *IM* indicates set number. The second and third sets constitute of HCM clips, called **HCM1_Clips** and **HCM2_Clips**, which were chosen by us. Each HCM clip was first annotated with the major emotion(s) it elicits by experts. These emotions depend on a number of factors like the major

Table 1. Details of Clip sets used in our surveys

Clip_Name	Origin	Clip_Emotion	Clip_Duration (Seconds)
IM1_Clips			
IM1_Exc	Toy Story: Infinity and Beyond	Exciting	16
IM1_Hap	Cars: McQueen and Sally	Happy	16
IM1_Calm	Finding Nemo: Wow	Calm	16
IM1_Sad	Toy Story 3: You Got Lucky	Sad	21
IM1_Fear	Cars: McQueen's Lost	Fear	11
IM1_Angry	Up: 52 Chachki Pickup	Angry	17
HCM1_Clips			
HCM1_Hap	Hamsadhwani	Happy	40
HCM1_Calm	Komal Rishabh Asavari	Calm	45
HCM1_Sad	Marwa	Sad	47
HCM2_Clips			
HCM2_Hap1	Desh	Happy	46
HCM2_Hap2	Desh	Happy	52
HCM2_Calm	Bhairavi	Calm	48
HCM2_Sad1	Marwa	Sad	40
HCM2_Sad2	Marwa	Sad	50

and minor note sequences of the clips and tempo. Generally, the use of major and minor notes elicit positive and negative valences respectively. Universally, high and low tempos are indication of high and low arousal respectively. The details of all the clips are provided in Table 1. It might be noted that perception of emotion is not based on familiarity of the music clip, but on intrinsic musical features.

2.2 Survey Description

The objective of our surveys was to find out – through the method of self report – how and if, the cognitive perception of one music clip gets biased due to the perception of the clip preceding it, when listeners are subjected to music clips conveying similar or radically different emotions. It might be so that a music clip elicits more than one type of emotion in the listeners. So, the interface was so designed that users may choose multiple emotions over the duration of a single clip. The survey interface consisted of a wheel structure, as seen in Fig. 1. The wheel has three distinct parts: *Central part* – which contains the play and pause buttons for the music clips. *Neutral part* – The cursor is supposed to rest here while a person decides on the emotional response. The *10 spokes* – Eight spokes represent eight emotions inspired by the *Nāvā Rāsā* concept, (a) Happy (H), (b) Calm (C), (c) Wonder (W), (d) Exciting (E), (e) Anger (A), (f) Fear (F), (g) Sad (S), (h) Romantic (R). *Other emotion* (OE) represents an emotion which is absent in the wheel and *Don't know* (DK) represents the user's indecisiveness regarding the emotional response. Each spoke is divided into 5 sub-regions, which indicate the intensity levels for each emotion. The inner-most region, which has the lightest shade of color, marks the lowest intensity. Both shade and intensity increase as we move outwards. The survey taker is expected to click on their perceived emotion intensities any number of times. The website used HTML, PHP scripts and MySQL in the back-end. The survey results stored in the database were then processed using MATLAB.

2.3 Types of Surveys

In this study two major types of surveys were used, (a) Discrete music rating (DMR) and (b) Contagion Interface Rating (CIR).

Discrete Music Rating Surveys (DMR)

In all the surveys, survey takers are subjected to more than one music clip. The idea in DMR is to present each music clip discretely, that is, with a perceptible time gap between clips. There may be questions (demographic, and/or related to the music clips) in between two music clips. This helps in removing any cognitive biases that might have been formed in the survey taker, and helps us to get the unbiased emotion ratings for each clip. The sequence of the clips were random. It might be argued that the true emotional contents of the music clips are obtained through DMR surveys. These findings are compared to the biased ratings for the same clips, to understand the extent and patterns of biases.

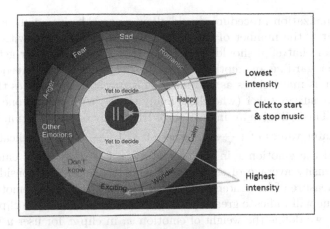

Fig. 1. The web–based survey interface

Contagion Interface Rating Surveys (CIR)

Users taking CIR surveys listen to a series of different music clips without any time gap between two consecutive clips. The music clips in the survey are of a pre-defined emotion sequence: From positive emotion generating clips to negative emotion generating clips, and vice versa. For example: The sequence of clips can be like HappyClip → CalmClip → SadClip and its opposite sequence.

2.4 Methodology of Data Normalization

For each clip, the data coming from survey has a rich temporal structure of user clicks on various emotions with different intensities. In this work, we are interested in (a) Studying effects of one clip on the perception of emotion in the next clip – **clip level analysis** and, (b) To find if there are any inherent patterns in the way users respond in this kind of surveys – **user level analysis**. These are discussed in details in Sects. 2.5 and 2.6.

For both of these, we compute a uniform representation of various emotions for each user–clip pair. We call this the normalized representation, which loses the temporal pattern of clicks, but is easily interpretable for the current study. For a clip c, a user u can click on any emotion – any number of times. Assuming he has clicked $n_x^{c,u}$ times on the emotion (x), where $x \in \{DK, OE, F, A, S, C, W, R, H, E\}$, the complete list of emotions used in survey (Sect. 2.2). Thus, the total number $N^{c,u}$ of clicks by user u for clip c is:

$$N^{c,u} = n_{DK}^{c,u} + n_{OE}^{c,u} + n_F^{c,u} + n_A^{c,u} + n_S^{c,u} + n_C^{c,u} + n_W^{c,u} + n_R^{c,u} + n_H^{c,u} + n_E^{c,u} \quad (1)$$

Let each of these $n_x^{c,u}$ responses have intensities $I_x^{c,u}(1), I_x^{c,u}(2), \ldots, I_x^{c,u}(n_x^{c,u})$, where $1 \le I_x^{c,u}(k) \le 5$ and $1 \le k \le n_x^{c,u}$. We calculate average intensity for each emotion as $\bar{I}_x^{c,u}$, as:

$$\bar{I}_x^{c,u} = \frac{\sum_{k=1}^{n_x^{c,u}} I_x^{c,u}(k)}{n_x^{c,u}}. \quad (2)$$

The normalization procedure should allow us to take into consideration two measures. First, the number of clicks on a particular emotion, with respect to total clicks for that clip, should be considered, so that each user gets one normalized vote regarding an emotion in the clip, despite using the freedom to click that emotion as many times as he wants. This measure normalizes the votes of an over-active survey taker (who clicks many times) with that of one who clicks moderately. This will give an indication of frequency of the emotion felt by the user. So, greater values of $\left(\frac{n_x^{c,u}}{N^{c,u}}\right)$ – where $0 \leq \left(\frac{n_x^{c,u}}{N^{c,u}}\right) \leq 1$ – indicate that the clip c elicited the emotion x in the user u, more than any other emotion. Second, the intensity average of a particular emotion should be considered. This provides a measure of how intensified the feeling of a particular emotion was. A high $\bar{I}_x^{c,u}$ value will indicate greater feelings of emotion x over the clip c, by user u. Therefore, we define the weight of emotion x, in clip c, for user u as:

$$Wt_x^{c,u} = \left(\frac{n_x^{c,u}}{N^{c,u}}\right) * \bar{I}_x^{c,u} = \frac{\sum_{k=1}^{n_x^{c,u}} \bar{I}_x^{c,u}}{N^{c,u}} \tag{3}$$

Thus the weight of each emotion x, for each clip c, rated by the user u can be calculated from Eq. 3.

2.5   Methodology of Clip Level Analysis

In this case, we consider entire survey results for each survey $S1$. Let survey $S1$ use C_{S1} number of clips and U_{S1} users respond to the survey. After performing the normalization procedure – as described in Sect. 2.4 – for each clip $c \in C_{S1}$, we aggregate the weights for each emotion (x), where $x \in \{DK, OE, F, A, S, C, W, R, H, E\}$, over all users U_{S1} to derive the ultimate percentage emotion contents of that clip. These percentage contents are used for clip level analysis. The results of clip level analysis are discussed in Sect. 3.2.

2.6   Methodology of User Level Analysis

In this case, we compare the response patterns of each user with the other user responses in the same survey. Let survey $S1$ use C_{S1} number of clips. Also, let the number of users taking the survey S1 be U_{S1}. For each clip $c \in C_{S1}$, each user $u \in U_{S1}$ can report maximum 10 types of emotions – DK, OE, F, A, S, C, W, R, H and E. Thus, we can represent the response of an user $u \in U_{S1}$, after being exposed to the clip $c \in C_{S1}$ as a 10 dimensional vector – called the emotion vector – where the value of each dimension equals the weighted value for each emotion, as calculated in Sect. 2.4.

Since in the CIR surveys, all C_{S1} clips are heard together one after the other, each user's response for all the clips taken together can thus be represented as a $(10 * C_{S1})$–dimensional vector. In this vector, each of the C_{S1} blocks of 10 dimensions represents normalized response of each clip $c \in C_{S1}$, for user $u \in U_{S1}$. Thus, for survey $S1$, we get U_{S1} number of such $(10 * C_{S1})$–dimensional vectors. This set of vectors is used for the user level analysis. The results of user level analysis are discussed in Sect. 3.3.

3   Results and Discussion

In this section, the results of the various surveys taken are discussed. Our work is divided into three parts – (a) Clustering the clips according to their dominant emotions, (b) Observing how the perception of the clips of different clusters are biased across the surveys and (c) Verifying any inherent patterns in the user responses of each survey. Each of these are reported in Sects. 3.1, 3.2 and 3.3 respectively.

3.1   Clustering the Clips According to Their Dominant Emotions

Table 2 gives the details of the DMR surveys, from which the dominant emotion of each clip can be identified. The *Dominant Emotion* of a clip is the emotion which has highest percentage value from the ratings across the surveys. For each clip, these are marked bold in the table. These results show that the interface is able to capture the emotional contents of the clips well. The results of DMR-1 correspond to Schubert's [16] findings of the dominant emotions for the clips. The results of DMR-2 and DMR-3 comply with the expected dominant emotions of the clips.

From the DMR surveys, we group the clips into three clusters according to their dominant emotions – (a) **Happy clips** – IM1_Hap, HCM1_Hap, HCM2_Hap1, HCM2_Hap2, (b) **Sad Clips** – IM1_Sad, HCM1_Sad, HCM2_Sad1, HCM2_Sad2 and (c) **Calm Clips** – IM1_Calm, HCM1_Calm, HCM2_Calm.

Table 2. Setwise DMR results for all the clips

Clip_Name	DK%	OE%	F%	A%	S%	C%	W%	R%	H%	E%	Dominant emotion
DMR-1											
IM1_Exc	0	0	23.03	11.60	6.46	9.08	0	0	20.92	**28.90**	Exciting
IM1_Hap	0	0	5.33	6.29	10.59	17.45	0	5.62	**29.69**	25.03	Happy
IM1_Calm	0	0	3.67	3.04	19.53	**39.94**	11.79	10.93	8.54	2.56	Calm
IM1_Sad	0	0	3.39	3.08	**29.88**	25.52	18.53	12.36	3.36	0	Sad
IM1_Fear	0	0	**30.74**	24.35	9.59	0	0	0	10.69	24.63	Fear
IM1_Angry	0	0	24.37	**31.39**	6.37	3.88	0	0	6.54	27.45	Angry
DMR-2											
HCM1_Hap	0	0	1.58	1.98	4.95	21.15	15.61	10.87	**24.3**	19.56	Happy
HCM1_Calm	0	0	5.79	2.18	23.41	**29.43**	14.09	12.94	6.52	6.04	Calm
HCM1_Sad	0	0	10.95	3.24	**38.1**	28.62	8.55	5.57	1.99	2.98	Sad
DMR-3											
HCM2_Hap1	0	0	2.02	2.23	7.59	22.99	14.51	12.73	**26.76**	18.67	Happy
HCM2_Hap2	0	0	1.05	2.06	2.49	15.98	15.15	17.84	**23.43**	14.5	Happy
HCM2_Calm	0	0	5.51	1.94	25.71	**34.15**	8.81	8.55	7.71	3.3	Calm
HCM2_Sad1	0	0	8.71	4.75	**30.03**	20.57	10.84	11.87	12.13	9.5	Sad
HCM2_Sad2	0	0	12.72	8.4	**33.33**	20.85	10.91	6.3	3.83	3.83	Sad

These clips are further used in the CIR surveys, as reported in Sect. 3.2, to observe if and how the perception of clips of each cluster are affected by the context it is heard in. The user–wise results of CIR surveys are used to perform clustering of users into similar groups. This helps in understanding how users respond in CIR surveys, as reported in Sect. 3.3.

3.2   Comparison of DMR and CIR Values

As explained earlier, the sequence of clips in the CIR surveys are predefined and fixed, which are given in Table 3.

Table 4 gives the results of all the CIR surveys. The clusters of clips with same dominant emotion are shown together so that their biases may be compared.

From the above surveys, we were able to ascertain the dominant emotion contents of each clip, from the maximum percentage values of the emotion vectors. Depending on these contents, we grouped the clips into 3 distinct categories – (a) *Happy Clips* – which express positive emotions, like happiness, excitement. (b) *Sad Clips* – which express negative emotions, like sadness. (c) *Calm Clips* – which express calmness. For each clip, 3 surveys provide data on how the perception changes under different context. This is discussed below for each group of clips.

Happy Clips. The dominant emotion for the clips of this set is Happy (H). The major observations for this set are drawn from the comparative graphs in Fig. 2, which depicts the perceptual contagion of emotion for all Happy clips, over all surveys, when they are preceded by Happy, Sad and Calm clips.

1. Depending on the survey type, significant differences in values for emotions *Happy*, *Exciting* and *Calm* were observed. The values of H and E are least in the base ratings, captured in the DMR surveys. In the CIR_PosNeg surveys, H and E increase slightly than the base values. In the CIR_NegPos surveys, H and E increase significantly than the base values. We may conclude that when happy music follows sad and calm music, it might be perceived as even more happy.

Table 3. Clip sequences for the CIR surveys

Survey name	Clip sequence
CIR-1_PosNeg	IM1_Hap → IM1_Calm → IM1_Sad
CIR-1_NegPos	IM1_Sad → IM1_Calm → IM1_Hap
CIR-2_PosNeg	HCM1_Hap → HCM1_Calm → HCM1_Sad
CIR-2_NegPos	HCM1_Sad → HCM1_Calm → HCM1_Hap
CIR-3_PosNeg	HCM2_Hap1 → HCM2_Hap2 → HCM2_Calm → HCM2_Sad1 → HCM2_Sad2
CIR-3_NegPos	HCM2_Sad2 → HCM2_Sad1 → HCM2_Calm → HCM2_Hap2 → HCM2_Hap1

Table 4. Setwise CIR survey results for the clips

Clip_Name	Survey_Type	DK%	OE%	F%	A%	S%	C%	W%	R%	H%	E%
Happy clips											
IM1_Hap	PosNeg	0	0	5.36	5.36	11.11	29.51	0	0	**34.87**	13.79
	NegPos	0	0	5.45	5.84	9.73	19.07	0	0	**37.35**	22.57
HCM1_Hap	PosNeg	0	0	1.76	2.03	4.07	22.10	4.45	9.32	**31.89**	24.38
	NegPos	0	0	0	0	1.59	4.52	4.91	10.17	**48.00**	30.81
HCM2_Hap1	PosNeg	0	0	0	0.68	0	19.37	4.33	2.28	**39.60**	33.70
	NegPos	0	0	1.40	2.72	0.49	2.12	3.28	7.22	**50.07**	32.63
HCM2_Hap2	PosNeg	0	0	1.36	4.23	2.27	19.06	7.23	8.95	**27.70**	29.20
	NegPos	0	0	0.09	0.68	0.09	1.51	3.57	14.85	**61.36**	17.86
Calm clips											
IM1_Calm	PosNeg	0	0	6.45	6.45	21.37	**36.58**	0	0	14.52	9.27
	NegPos	0	0	5.36	5.36	11.11	29.51	0	0	**34.87**	13.79
HCM1_Calm	PosNeg	0	0	1.25	0	**67.08**	19.29	2.36	8.38	1.64	0
	NegPos	0	0	1.24	0	**25.69**	**29.55**	19.33	6.22	13.82	4.15
HCM2_Calm	PosNeg	0	0	2.07	2.9	**58.68**	14.50	15.87	0	6.03	0
	NegPos	0	0	7.23	3.41	21.63	**35.96**	11.45	4.01	11.45	0.69
Sad clips											
IM1_Sad	PosNeg	0	0	9.87	8.97	**47.53**	17.94	0	0	7.62	8.07
	NegPos	0	0	9.13	6.22	**33.70**	**31.12**	0	0	14.75	8.71
HCM1_Sad	PosNeg	0	0	10.79	0	**56.63**	21.45	5.84	3.29	0	0
	NegPos	0	0	0	0	**47.73**	30.04	14.86	0.56	3.40	3.40
HCM2_Sad1	PosNeg	0	0	23.30	5.18	**44.87**	11.50	12.96	7.44	0	0.68
	NegPos	0	0	5.05	3.20	**38.90**	23.10	3.73	1.26	12.69	6.10
HCM2_Sad2	PosNeg	0	0	20.00	1.42	**42.31**	12.3	11.12	7.26	2.65	2.36
	NegPos	0	0	3.43	0.12	**45.47**	43.54	4.44	2.22	0.12	0.66

2. All happy clips have a *Calm* component. The Calm values are highest in
   CIR_PosNeg surveys. They go down significantly in the CIR_NegPos surveys,
   where the Positive clips are perceived as more positive.

Sad Clips. The dominant emotion for the clips of this set is Sad (S). The major
observations for this set are drawn from the comparative graphs in Fig. 3, which
depicts the perceptual contagion of emotion for all Sad clips, over all surveys,
when they are preceded by Sad, Happy and Calm clips.

1. Depending on the survey type, significant differences in values for emotion
   Sad was observed. The emotion values of S are least in the base ratings,
   captured in the DMR surveys. In the CIR_PosNeg surveys, S values increase
   significantly more than the base values. In the CIR_NegPos surveys, S values
   are nearer to the base values. We may conclude that when sad music follows
   happy and calm music, it might be perceived as even more sad.
2. The Calm (C) values are very low in CIR_PosNeg surveys. They are very
   high in the CIR_NegPos surveys, where the sad clips are perceived as almost
   baseline sad.
3. Fear (F) contributes in the CIR_PosNeg surveys significantly for all the clips
   in this set.

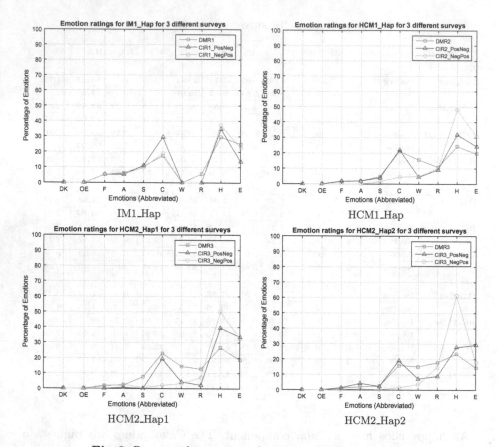

Fig. 2. Perceptual contagion of emotion for all happy clips.

Calm Clips. The dominant emotion for the clips of this set is Calm (C). The major observations for this set are drawn from the comparative graphs in Fig. 4, which depicts the perceptual contagion of emotion for all Calm clips, over all surveys, when they are preceded by Sad and Happy clips.

1. Depending on the survey type, significant differences in values for the emotion *Calm* was observed. The baseline values of (C) are captured in the DMR surveys. C values go significantly up in the CIR_NegPos surveys. In the CIR_PosNeg surveys, C decreases drastically than the baseline values. We may conclude that when calm music follows happy music, it might be perceived less calm and when it follows sad music, it might be perceived as more calm.
2. Interestingly, the calm clips are perceived as very sad in the CIR_PosNeg surveys. Sometimes, the (S) component was even higher than the (C) component in these surveys. Again, in the CIR_NegPos surveys, the (S) component were significantly low.

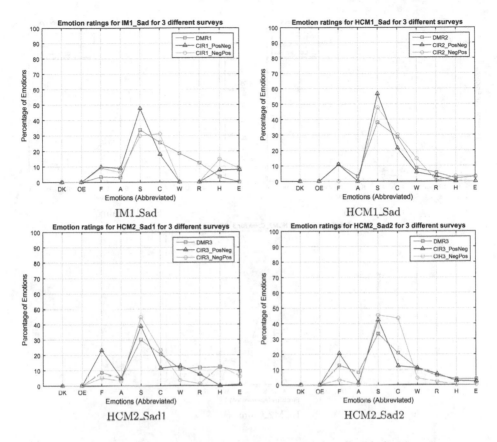

Fig. 3. Perceptual contagion of emotion for all sad clips

3. High Happy (H) component was observed for these clips in the CIR_NegPos surveys, where the (S) component was significantly low.

3.3 Verifying Patterns in the User Responses of Each Survey

Since we are primarily investigating HCM, we consider the results of the following 4 surveys here: (a) CIR-2_PosNeg, (b) CIR-2_NegPos, (c) CIR-3_PosNeg and d) CIR-3_NegPos. It might be noted here that for the first two surveys, the emotion vector for each user is of thirty dimensions – as the survey uses 3 clips. For the last two surveys, the emotion vector is of fifty dimensions each – as the survey uses 5 clips. So, from here we get four sets of user emotion vectors.

Each emotion vector is considered as a point in thirty or fifty dimensional space as applicable. To find inherent relations in users' responses, we apply the K-Means algorithm [11,12] on these 4 datasets separately. K-Means clustering is a type of unsupervised learning, which is used to find groups in unlabeled data, with the number of groups represented by the variable K. Each centroid is the mean of the points in that cluster. The distance metric is Squared Euclidean

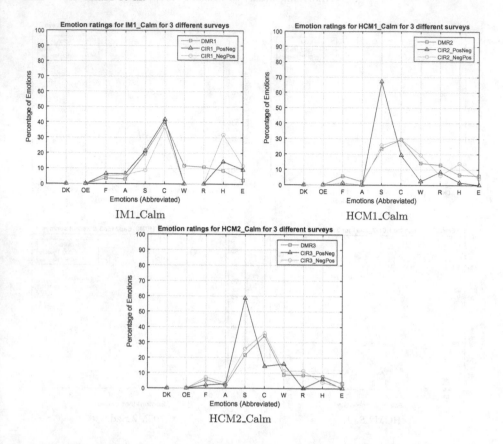

Fig. 4. Perceptual contagion of emotion for all calm clips

distance. K is varied from 2 to 10 in our experiments. The best results for all the surveys are obtained with K = 3, indicating the presence of 3 separate clusters of user responses.

Silhouette analysis [13] is used to study the separation distance between the resulting clusters in this K-Means clustering. The silhouette plot displays a measure of how close each point in one cluster is to points in the neighboring clusters and thus provides a way to assess parameters like number of clusters visually. This measure – called silhouette coefficients – has a range of [−1, 1]. Silhouette coefficients near +1 indicate that the sample is far away from the neighboring clusters. A value of 0 indicates that the sample is on or very close to the decision boundary between two neighboring clusters and negative values indicate that those samples might have been assigned to the wrong cluster. Also, from the thickness of the silhouette plot the cluster size can be visualized.

For the current datasets, the Silhouette graphs obtained are presented in Figs. 5 and 6 for the two PosNeg surveys (CIR-2_PosNeg and CIR-3_PosNeg) and the two NegPos surveys (CIR-2_NegPos and CIR-3_NegPos) respectively. The observations that can be drawn from these figures are listed in below sections.

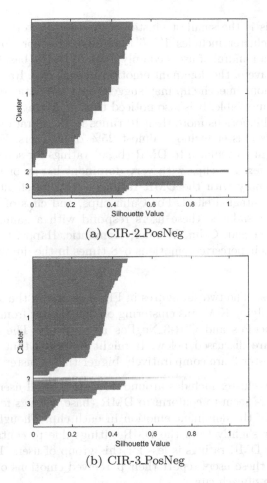

(a) CIR-2_PosNeg

(b) CIR-3_PosNeg

Fig. 5. Silhoutte plots for clusters of users in PosNeg Surveys, using K-Means algorithm with K = 3

PosNeg Surveys. The two subfigures in Fig. 5 represent the silhouette graphs obtained after applying K-Means clustering on the dataset from the two PosNeg surveys: CIR-2_PosNeg and CIR-3_PosNeg respectively. The observations for Pos-Neg surveys are discussed below. It might be noted that in both graphs, Cluster 1 is the biggest, Cluster 2 is the smallest and Cluster 3 is medium in size.

1. Cluster 1: This is the biggest cluster of emotion vectors representing user ratings. This cluster includes almost 70% of all users. For both surveys, these users seem to conform to DMR (base) ratings for each clip most – irrespective of the dominant emotion in each clip. Though the ratings for each clip differ slightly from the DMR ratings due to contagion effect, the deviation from DMR ratings is less for this group of users. It is also noticed that generally these users report their perceived emotions only 4 to 6 times in the duration of each clip.

2. Cluster 2: This is the smallest cluster of emotion vectors representing user ratings. This cluster includes 1%–5% of all users. For both surveys, it is observed that a handful of users comply least to DMR (base) ratings for each clip – irrespective of the dominant emotion in each clip. Random variation in reported emotions in each clip may suggest that the data generated by these users may be unreliable. It is also noticed that on average, these users report their perceived emotions more than 10 times in the duration of each clip.

3. Cluster 3: This cluster includes almost 25% of all users. For both surveys, these users seem to conform to DMR (base) ratings for some clips, while for others they differ. For clips with very dominant happy or sad components, these users comply with the DMR ratings – though slight variations may occur due to contagion effect. For Calm clips, and clips of lesser intensities of happiness or sadness, these users respond with a gamut of emotions – ranging between Sad, Calm, Wonder, Romantic, Happy. On average, these users report their perceived emotions 6–8 times in the duration of each clip.

NegPos Surveys. The two subfigures in Fig. 6 represent the silhouette graphs obtained after applying K-Means clustering on the dataset from the two NegPos surveys: CIR-2_NegPos and CIR-3_NegPos respectively. The observations for NegPos surveys are discussed below. It might be noted that in both graphs, Cluster 1 and Cluster 3 are comparatively bigger than Cluster 2.

1. Cluster 1: This cluster includes around 40%–45% of all users. For both surveys, these users seem to conform to DMR (base) ratings for each clip most – irrespective of the dominant emotion in each clip. Though the ratings for each clip differ slightly from the DMR ratings due to contagion effect, the deviation from DMR ratings is less for this group of users. It is also noticed that generally these users report their perceived emotions only 4 to 6 times in the duration of each clip.

2. Cluster 2: The smallest cluster of emotion vectors representing user ratings. This cluster includes around 10%–15% of all users. For both surveys, it is observed that they comply least to DMR (base) ratings for each clip – irrespective of the dominant emotion in each clip. Random variation in reported emotions in each clip may suggest that the data generated by these users may be unreliable. It is also noticed that on average, these users report their perceived emotions more than 10 times in the duration of each clip.

3. Cluster 3: This cluster includes around 40%–45% of all users. For both surveys, these users seem to conform to DMR (base) ratings for some clips, while for others they differ. For clips with very dominant happy or sad components, these users comply with the DMR ratings – though slight variations may occur due to contagion effect. For Calm clips, and clips of lesser intensities of happiness or sadness, these users respond with a gamut of emotions – ranging between Sad, Calm, Wonder, Romantic, Happy.

Thus, it is observed that some inherent pattern does exist among user responses in these surveys. There is a significant rise in Cluster 2 size in NegPos

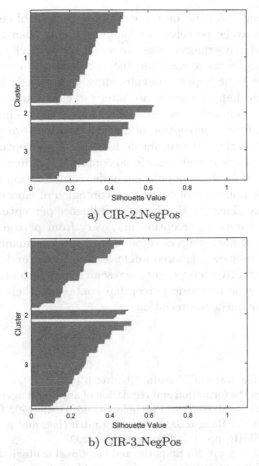

a) CIR-2_NegPos

b) CIR-3_NegPos

Fig. 6. Silhoutte plots for clusters of users in NegPos Surveys, using K-Means algorithm with K = 3

surveys over PosNeg surveys. Also, the number of users conforming to DMR ratings for all clips – as represented in Cluster 1 – goes down in NegPos surveys over PosNeg surveys, whereas the size of Cluster 3 goes up. It is interesting to note that in both kinds of surveys the contagion effect is observed in the users of both Cluster 1 and Cluster 2, amounting to almost 95% of the users in PosNeg surveys and 80%–85% of the users in NegPos surveys. This may be regarded as proof that music to music perceptual contagion of emotion in HCM is a wide-spread effect observed in majority of population under consideration in the relevant study.

4   Conclusion

Results suggest that, perceived emotions of musical clips are dependent on the emotional content of the preceding clips. Also, the type of dependence and how the perception changes depend on the emotional content of the musical clip as well. Happy clips may be perceived as far more happy than they actually are, when they are heard in a sequence, after some sad and calm clips. Again, sad clips may be perceived as far more sad than they actually are, when they are heard in a sequence, after some happy and calm clips. Calm music is perceived to be much more calm and happy, when heard after sad clips, but are perceived to be much less calm and even sad, when heard after happy clips. These trends suggest that over short durations, perception of musical emotions are modified by what we have heard just earlier. Hence, music listening is perceptually modified by earlier musical phrases and their emotional contents. Findings also suggest that a majority (almost 90%) of the population under consideration in the surveys are subjected to the phenomenon of perceptual contagion of emotion when exposed to music in sequence. Though, the degree of influence perceptual contagion may have in modifying emotion perception may vary from person to person. Also, a small percentage of survey users respond in a random manner to the survey questions. These responses if ignored might lead to better understanding of user response patterns in CIR surveys. Future research may also need to address the exact nuances of music to music perceptual contagion, their possible reasons, and implications for music appreciation.

References

1. Bharatmuni: Natyasastra of Bharata, Chapter 6
2. Berkowitz, L.: On the formation and regulation of anger and aggresion. A cognitive-neoassociationistic analysis. Am. Psychologist. **45**(4), 494–503 (1990)
3. Chordia, P., Rae, A.: Raag recognition using pitch-class and pitch-class dyad distributions. In: ISMIR, pp. 431–436, September 2007
4. Egermann, H., McAdams, S.: Empathy and emotional contagion as a link between recognized and felt emotions in music listening. Music Percept. Interdisc. J. **31**(2), 139–156 (2013)
5. Ekman, P.: An argument for basic emotions. Cogn. Emot. **6**(3–4), 169–200 (1992)
6. Frijda, N.H.: The Emotions. Cambridge University Press, New York (1986)
7. Juslin, P.N., Sloboda, J.A.: Music and emotion. Psychol. Music **3**, 583–645 (2001)
8. Juslin, P.N.: From mimesis to catharsis: expression, perception, and induction of emotion in music. Musical Commun. 85–115 (2005)
9. Juslin, P.N.: From everyday emotions to aesthetic emotions: towards a unified theory of musical emotions. Phys. Life Rev. **10**(3), 235–266 (2013)
10. Keltner, D., Buswell, B.N.: Embarrassment: its distinct form and appeasement functions. Psychol. Bull. **122**(3), 250–270 (1997)
11. Lloyd, S.: Least squares quantization in PCM. IEEE Trans. Inf. Theory **28**(2), 129–137 (1982)
12. MacQueen, J.: Some methods for classification and analysis of multivariate observations. In: Proceedings of the Fifth Berkeley Symposium on Mathematical Statistics and Probability, vol. 1, no. 14 (1967)
13. Rousseeuw, P.J.: Silhouettes: a graphical aid to the interpretation and validation of cluster analysis. J. Comput. Appl. Math. **20**, 53–65 (1987)

14. Schmidt, E.M., Turnbull, D., Kim, Y.E.: Feature selection for content-based, time-varying musical emotion regression. In: Proceedings of the International Conference on Multimedia Information Retrieval, pp. 267–274. ACM, March 2010
15. Schubert, E., Ferguson, S., Farrar, N., Taylor, D., Mcpherson, G.E.: Continuous response to music using discrete emotion faces. In: Proceedings of CMMR (2012)
16. Schubert, E., Ferguson, S., Farrar, N., Taylor, D., McPherson, G.E.: The six emotion-face clock as a tool for continuously rating discrete emotional responses to music. In: Aramaki, M., Barthet, M., Kronland-Martinet, R., Ystad, S. (eds.) CMMR 2012. LNCS, vol. 7900, pp. 1–18. Springer, Heidelberg (2013). https://doi.org/10.1007/978-3-642-41248-6_1
17. Schubert, E.: Continuous self-report methods (2011)

Sound in Practice: Auditory Guidance and Feedback in the Context of Motor Learning and Motor Adaptation

Inscribing Bodies: Notating Gesture

Emily Beattie[1] and Margaret Schedel[2(✉)]

[1] Salem State University, 352 Lafayette St, Salem, MA 01970, USA
ebeattie@salemstate.edu
[2] Stony Brook University, 100 Nicolls Rd, Stony Brook, NY 11794, USA
margaret.schedel@stonybrook.edu

Abstract. This paper focuses on methods of transcribing the functions and activities of gesture, with a specific focus on embodiment, or how the interrelated roles of environment and the body shape mental process and experience. Through a process of repeated experiments with our own custom open-source 3D printed sensors, we illuminate the complexities of tracking even a single point over time, and distinguish between casual gesture and choreographed motion.

Keywords: Gesture · Dance · Embodied cognition · Tool-making
Measurement · Expressivity

1 Introduction

Programming computers to recognize human gesture, designing prosthetics to augment human potential, building automatons to simulate human behavior, creating tools of transcription to record human kinetics, generating graphical methods to analyze human behavior, or theorizing the politics of expressive human motion, are just some of the ways in which we can notate the body using technology. While technology is a broad term encompassing tools, machines, techniques, crafts, and organizational systems, notation implies a distillation and a selection of information. As the disciplines of computer science, media studies, and the fine arts become more open to the study of works, motions, and problems whose conceptual and material conditions challenge categorization, new questions arise that complicate traditional modes of historiography and analysis of the movement of bodies in space over time. In the era of big data, the problem is no longer how to capture accurate data, instead there is a focus on how to regulate this "technological feast technological feast [which] becomes unregulated gluttony" by reducing the amount of data gathered, extracting the signal in the noise, efficiently reveal patterns, and reducing the dimensionality of the data by codifying relationships [1]. Our biological systems sift data very efficiently; "if (the eye) were sensitive to every frequency, we would find ourselves surrounded by an indistinct fog carrying too much information, it must be severely restricted. Syntaxes and rainbows are similar in this sense: they emerge from the elaboration carried by those selectional capacities that precedes experience [2]." In an era when Apple's iPhone can project and read over 30,000 infrared dots and recognize a face in less than a second, technology "allows the measurement of almost any kind of physical manifestation of corporeal

© Springer Nature Switzerland AG 2018
M. Aramaki et al. (Eds.): CMMR 2017, LNCS 11265, pp. 273–283, 2018.
https://doi.org/10.1007/978-3-030-01692-0_19

articulation ... the main problem is the theoretical approach, the experimental paradigm and the interpretation of measurements within a context of mind/body/matter relationships [3]." We challenged ourselves to track a single point over time and create an interface that could detect the difference between casual gesture and more purposeful dance motion. To develop an effective motion sensing computer system, it is crucial to understand the implications of the tool being used to capture the data. Many motion capture systems were created for scientific purposes; writing about the difference between art and science, Amy Cook and Rhonda Blair stated "In order to conduct an experiment one must reduce as much complexity (or noise) as possible; many times this squeezes the very thing we care about out of the room [4]." With our experiment in tool-building we prove that it is possible to reduce complexity of input, while still retaining the telos of measuring "the role of the human body as mediator between physical energy and meaning [5]." To understand how our work unfolded we summarize the difference between gesture and dance, give a short history of choreography and dance notation, and finally explain how embodied cognition, tool-making and material engagement theory contribute to theorizing our experiment.

2 Introducing Gesture

In this paper, we look at gesture through lenses of pedestrian uses, dance, and music. Daily movements intended to physically mark a thought or to communicate to one another are considered gestures—they can be single actions, or more complex movements made up of many sequential sections of movements. Gestures function to both fully stand in for verbal communication or present as "everyday occurrences-the spontaneous, unwitting and regular accompaniments of speech that we see in our moving fingers, hands and arms [6]." Gestures often emphasize spoken communication, and may have been a key to developing language; Mead's Loop posits that one's own gestures activate the part of the brain that responds to intentional actions, including gestures, by someone else, and thus treats one's own gesture as a social stimulus [7]." At their root, these movements are a simple chain reaction of the brain signaling to muscle and bone to flex, extend or rotate. We focus on how and why these impulses and reflexes might be constructed by the body and the mind to fulfill an intention and create meaning.

The development of our gestures into pieces of language is a highly interactive behavior that occurs over time. A gesture in one community or context does not necessarily communicate as we intend in another. Gestures cannot develop in isolated moments, but in fact, "our gestures are given meaning by their relationship to other people [8]." The social stimulus of a gesture is intertwined with intention and interaction to make gesture an effective communication device. Theoretical approaches to gesture help us look beyond the one-to-one relationship for each movement and towards a more nuanced use of how gestures are used in daily life and in performative situations. The authors are artists who come from music/composition practice and a dance/choreography practice respectively, who both integrate technology to analyze movement into our work. We refer to the role of gesture as a language in performance, a way to communicate or reinforce emotion, or even a simple trigger within interactive systems. Gesture in a music practice often refers to the performance effect of a short phrase, or a coordinating cue while gesture in a dance practices usually refers to a shape of the upper body.

This paper grows out of a pair of keynote addresses given at the Cognitive Futures Conference at Stony Brook University and the Computer Music and Multidisciplinary Research Conference in Matosinhos, Porto. Immediately when we began imagining these talks on embodied cognition and gesture, we were confronted with questions of what could be called a gesture, as studied by language experts, and what could be called a performative gesture. When Schedel talks, she constantly augments her words through gesture; drawing on the concept of mirror neurons we wondered if Beattie could imitate gesture and simultaneously make it more performative or dance-like. Then could we program a computer to understand the distinction between incidental gesture and performed gesture? While the positions of hands in space are similar, we found that gestures made while speaking have lower energy with nebulous beginnings and endings. The performative gestures had high energy and very distinct starts and stops. When reversing the roles - with Beattie gesturing, and Schedel "performing gesture" the differences were not as marked because Schedel is not a trained dancer and does not move as crisply. We quickly realized with all the pedestrian movement that is part of the canon of contemporary dance, that we needed to address dance, choreography and dance notation in our talk.

3 Introducing Dance, Choreography, Dance Notation

We look to dance as a field that is both hyperphysical and mindful but one that also carries an objective to communicate which supports our experimentation in this project. Dances have a purpose. Dances have intentional rhythm. Dances have culturally patterned sequences. Dancers have extraordinary nonverbal movement, which has value in and of itself [9]. Worldwide, the purpose of dance can be to enjoy movement of the body, to entertain, to express, to mark history, to process collectively, and to resist. Scholar Ellen Dissanayake, who argues that artmaking is a fundamental behavior, found that in evolutionary terms dance may have communicated information that increased the very survival of early humans [10]. We understand through the occurrence of dance in nearly every culture, that it is a shared phenomenon, but one that is specific to each community where it exists. In this paper and in the dance we used in our experiment, we focus on what movement expresses as well as what tools humans have developed to measure this expression. One prevalent technique to categorize dance motion is the act of choreography.

Commonly choreography is understood as a series of steps and movements that when performed together make up a dance. The term choreography derives from two Greek words, choreia and graph. In the Greek chorus, choreia is the synthesis of dance, rhythm, and vocal harmony. Graph is known as the act of writing. Dance writing is a direct, but oversimplified translation of choreography. Orches and chora are two more words that are connected to choreia that relate to the place between the stage and the audience and a general term for space. Without lighting technology to pinpoint specific moments in the dance, the location and scale in relation to the audience would have been key. These origins lead Susan Foster to conclude that choreography is the "reconciling of movement, place, and symbol [11]." Understanding what actions you are doing, where you are doing these actions, and what it might mean to you or the audience does place movement within some parameters, but for our purposes we examine what the act of choreography implies for movement.

Instead of considering choreography only as dance writing or as a way to execute a list of actionable items, we choose to focus on Andre Lepeki's concept of choreography as a function which he calls, an "apparatus of capture [12]." This viewpoint connects choreography to phenomenology, through affording particular kinds of motor and perceptual habits. In this frame we see that it is a selection of movement that reveals and conceals certain possibilities. Like the body, each of these pieces of movement can be understood as a medium for having a world or the phenomenology of embodied cognition [13]. Historically, choreography has been passed down via oral tradition across the globe. The communication of ancient forms was through direct physical mimicry, where the basic structures of dances, specificities and nuance were absorbed. As writing and tools for creating writing that endured developed, some societies began to record their dances. We are interested in how the specificities nuances were conveyed in a system that would record the movement.

Beattie is trained in western contemporary dance and dance history. We are only delving into the way that Western European dances were recorded, though incredible systems exist in many other forms of dance. Western European dance notation can be traced back to a social dance that occurred in the courts of Europe. In the 15th and 16th centuries, two monarchs, Catherine de Medici (1519–1589) and French King Louis XIV (1638–1715) adopted folk dances and theater into their court for entertainment and later as diplomacy between vying powers [14]. Dance became a social currency and courtiers rushed to learn and perfect their dance technique. The public attention and resources offered to the form created employment for dance masters who wrote dance manuals for instruction. This moment in history provided a healthy situation for early written attempts of creating a method to record movement through written manuals for instruction or dance notation.

Notation can be defined as "a system of sequential markings, usually produced by different tools, specifically conceived to store information outside the physical body [15]." The possibilities for content that can be recorded are in theory infinite, but the author or authors of the system curate the selection of what is included. How to read the notation and translate the markings into movement is specific to each system. There are four early attempts to notate dance that came from within the royal court in France. In these early texts, the arrangement of musical notes and the dance directions in text are aligned to read as one would read a musical score. There are musical notes to mark time and the written directions you are to accomplish within that time. The first example of this arrangement is from 1589, when Thoinot Arbeau wrote a treatise on dancing, swordplay, and drumming called *Orchesgraphie*. Raoul Feuillet, a French dance notator, publisher, and choreographer, in 1700, composed a book entitled *Choreographie* that explained a type of dance notation created by Pierre Beauchamp, Feuillet. This manual differs from the Arbeau text in that Feuillet includes the pathway that the dancers must progress through as they move in the specified time. The notes are more graphic, revealing an emphasis on the dimension of space. The Feuillet manual was then translated into English in 1706 by John Weaver and spread to greater England. John Essex published *For the Further Improvement of Dancing, A Treatise of Choreography* in 1710, in which he applied Feuillet's system to English country dances, which evidences a wide use of the form because the system was viewed as an efficient way to record movement [16]. Popularity moved away from Feuillet notation once facial expressions and spatial interactions onstage became more important to dance and theater forms. Rather than prioritizing the categorization of movement into an order and only thinking about location in a x and y axis, artists became interested in the ability to innovate with pantomime to forward a narrative and express emotion in the face.

Rudolph Laban is an Austrian-Hungarian who is credited with developing the widely used system for analyzing and recording movement. He entitled these systems Labanotation and Laban Movement Analysis. His interest was in democratizing dance through exploring a system that can easily be understood through creating an onto-logical system to describe the motion of bodies in space. By 1919, he created 25 schools in Germany. As opposed to the pantomime that led to a narrative in dance performance, he was interested in non-narrative content particularly in large unilateral performing groups [17]. He often worked with untrained children and men, but also included professional dancers, and thought of his work as a laboratory inside the creative process. Other artists in Germany influenced him at the time; expressionist dancers wanted to reach deep truths, not simply carry out a plot over time. Through his work with modern dance Laban added the dimension of depth and surpassed Feuillet's notation system, by observing that all movement shares the properties of "shape, rhythm, and force [18]." Laban's system of notation can also differentiate dynamic quality, the location of the movement on the body, and the direction that the pathway of movement is moving. These details that Laban notation included placed the body in three-dimensional space and offered a myriad of tactical options for movement against natural physical forces. The legacy of Laban's work is strong; many dance practitioners and educators use his Movement Analysis in their class work to help students break down how movements are performed and composed. Labanotation is still utilized, but less so since the arrival of video to capture movement. Laban's framework laid the groundwork for the integration of technology into the realm of dance notation.

We call the assemblage of technology used to collect data in order to produce a symbolic representation of movement, tracking. Tracking is the observation of point[s] over time to categorize these values. Tracking can be used to record information such as position, speed, pitch, velocity, and more. This information can then be placed on a timeline to show how all of these variables change over time, and the sum of the work of track comprises a record of the movement—a dance score. Technological devel-opments in what these sensors can track, how many points of data can be captured, and the computers used to process this information continues to escalate. A major sector of the tech industry is directed towards innovating with sensors to create a complete picture of the movement of the body so that it can be simulated in virtual space and used in video games or movies. The same technology can be used to capture dance; two choreographers of international acclaim have used the pairing of sensors and computers to process the input of the sensors.

Merce Cunningham was a dance artist focused on the architecture of the body to create expressive forms. He utilized chance procedures to create his choreographic combinations on the body as well as in space by dividing up the body into points, applying conditions of extend, flex or rotate on these points and then recombining into a whole. In later years as he suffered crippling arthritis, a computer program was developed for him to program a virtual body that allowed him to use these points and manipulations to choreograph. Programmer Tom Calvert, President of Credo Interactive Inc., worked closely with Cunningham to develop the software *Dance Forms* which can still be downloaded today at http://charactermotion.com/df-download.html. The visual language of the program consists of a symbol-based score running below a series of images that translate these symbols into the positions of the body. By untethering himself from having to physically fulfill an emotional trajectory and using the full capacity of a program that could create limitless combinations of the body Cunningham was able to create unimaginable compositions and extend his career into his nineties.

The dancer and choreographer William Forsythe is a renowned artist who developed an improvisation system that opened ballet to the world of physics and improvisation; he and his company created works that broke the rules of ballet as well as challenged the dancer to strive towards the discovering the infinite possibilities for movement within the body. As a collaborative artist, he often works with professionals in math and science. In his dance, *One Flat Thing Reproduced*, he used a computational structure to create synchronizations and diversions of groups of dancers performing specific phrases of movement. He partnered with Ohio State University to create a platform that captured the data from this dance and create" new objects - ways of visualizing dance that draw on techniques from a variety of disciplines [19]." The project can be experienced online at https://synchronousobjects.osu.edu/. By capturing information from the movement of the dancers, for instance the sweep of their legs, the data can be transcoded into design for furniture, music, or generative drawing tools. Forsythe has expanded and placed the *Synchronous Objects* under a larger project called *Motion Bank*. *Motion Bank* was a four-year project that provided a platform for choreographic research, working with several renowned artists to capture the unseen nuance in choreographies, and to translate these into information other than language so that they may be studied and preserved online. The result is a bank of data and dance scores that cover a wide a ton of information about the human body in motion as they operate within these dances.

"Like the other arts, dance frequently is said to be affecting because it expresses emotion, yet a moments reflection will make it clear that movements may be expressive without being dance. Throwing a plate against a wall because you are angry or caressing your loves cheek because you feel affectionate are both expressive gestures. It is only when these movements are controlled, however, by shaping and elaborating, that dance can be said to exist [10]." It is the shaping and elaborating that distinguishes dance from everyday gesture, a mental process that ends in physical motion, but where does the mind end and the body begin?

4 Introducing Embodied Cognition, Technology, Tool Making, and Tracking

Embodied cognition emphasizes the role one's own body and the environment play in the formation of thought. In much Western philosophy there is a false separation between body and mind, embodied cognitivists believe "the nature of what we call mind and its non-separation from body and the nature of what we call self it its non separation from others and from the surrounding embracing world out of which life and mind emerge [20]." In other words, our cognition is formed by a combination of our mind, body, physical and social environment. Frank Wilson goes so far to argue "any human intelligence which ignores the interdependence of hand and brain function, the historic origins of that relationship, or the impact of that history on developmental dynamics in modern humans, is grossly misleading and sterile [21]." Cognitive archeologist Lambros Malafouris takes this theory even further and calls for a theory of material engagement in embodied cognition. He believes that tool making is a "prototypical exemplar of material engagement [that] provides a unique way of understanding how mental events relate to matter and project to the world. (Malafouris, 113)" Dance notation is a kind of map, a "distributed hybrid network formed by the interwoven neural capacities and external memory devices [23]."

In addition to language, tool use defines us as a species. "Technologies, in short, don't just allow us to do new things, they enable us to see new things, and to become new things; we are not human without our tools, and our tools seem to always be changing, as do we [24]." In the twenty-first century the defining tool is the ubiquitous digital computer. Using a sequence of zeros and ones, we "map the world onto symbols, operate one the symbols via materialized algebra, then output back to the 'matter' at hand [25]." It is important to remember that "the world is not symbols; we turn the world into symbols for the computer [26]." How we change the world into a series symbols, and operate on them is the process of designing and interactive computer system.

In order to more fully understand and control our embodied interaction, we decided to create our own tool. We didn't take it as far as Thomas Thwaites who mined his own metal in order to make an electric toaster [27], but we decided against using a commercial sensing tool with purpose-built software and to instead built our own sensing unit—specifying the analog to digital interface, and program the interaction. Inspired by Merleau Ponty, we created a sensor that has double sensation; it is touched and measures touch, making it both subject and object, noun and verb. We wanted to create our own "intermediary between the human mental approach to music and the machine encoding of physical energy [28]." Instead of using a camera or light-based sensor we wanted to create a physical interface with its own materiality that engages with the dancer's hand—a sensor inspired by the theory of embodied cognition.

5 Building the Tool

In building the tool we leveraged the cognition of our network, working with scientists at the Center for Excellence in Wireless Technology at Stony Brook University to build an open-source 3D printed controller modeled on the Gametrak video game controller, "an increasingly popular platform for experimental musical controllers, math and science manipulatives, large scale interactive installations and as a playful tangible gaming interface that promotes inter-generational creative play and discovery … the Gametrak is attractive for music controller experiments and performance-quality instruments because of its unusually simple, cheap implementation and the ease with which it can be customized [29]. The controller features two retractable tether reels, each approximately 13.5 feet in length, set in the main body … via a ball joint and guide arm … two potentiometers measure the x and y position of the balls (and thus the guide arm), and the z position is calculated by two more potentiometers turning inside of a retractable, spring-loaded drum, wherein the number of turns each potentiometer is counted as a nylon tether is pulled … effectively providing six degrees of freedom for continuous position mapping, plus a footswitch for discrete motions (Nanou, 1)." The Gametrak is no longer in production and is also housed in an unnecessarily bulky box.

Our sensor uses a commercially available joystick component, an arduino board, an ID badge retractor, pontentiometer and custom printed 3D housing. Matthew Cordaro went through several prototypes, with much of the feedback involving the "feel" of the string pulling back on the performer. After a lot of experimentation and refinement we settled on a design that is easily modified by users depending on their needs. We have published instructions and code at: http://arts.codes/articles/vol0/article1/article.html. For our keynote address we used a shorter string so that the smaller motion of the hand produced larger input. As in embodied cognition "the rhetorical opposition of hardware and software is, on the material level, a fiction [31]." We manipulated the presets on the analog-to-digital converter used by the Arduino board to find the most effective sampling time. By making the plans for our tool open-source we are able to give back to the community, and extend the cognitive capabilities of others.

6 Using and Refining the Interactive System

We wanted to create a demo as a "temporal sequence of relationally constituted embodied processes encompassing reciprocal and culturally orchestrated interactions among humans, situated tool use, and space [32]." During the talk, Beattie imitated Schedel's gestures, first very subtly and then more and more performatively. We then moved into a live demo where we showed a Max patch where we performed the same mathematical operations on the numbers coming in from the identical sensors creating an "exchange of information and energy with the environment [33]" that we then measured to determine if we could create a tool that could distinguish between casual gesture and performed dance. Performed dance can have pedestrian movement, much contemporary dance is imbued with seemingly casual movement, but we wanted to be able to quantify the level of performative vs. pedestrian gesture.

While the sensor can track three axes of movement, we decided to track only one point over time, to provide clarity for the talk and for the challenge of creating an expressive system with only one point tracked over time. Much like the hardware, the development of the software system used a "repeated cycling of Play, Listen, Judge, Change [34]." By introducing the concept of memory we were able to track a point over time. Then using the derivative of the information coming in we could calculate velocity from position data, acceleration from the velocity, jerk from the acceleration etc. Using the same simple block of code, we created four different variables from the single point of data. Although the initial position information was very similar, the further down the derivative chain, the greater the difference between casual gesture and performed action. We sent this control data from Max to Ableton Live session to control audio, and there were sounds that only Beattie could activate; this simple system needed an expert performer to show its full potential.

7 Conclusions

The implosion of space into time, the transmutation of distance into speed, the instantaneousness of communication, the collapsing of the workspace into the home computer system, will clearly have major effects on the bodies of the city's inhabitants. The subject's body will no longer be connected to random others and objects through the city's spatiotemporal layout; it will interface with the computer forming part of an information machine in which the body's limbs and organs will become interchangeable parts. Whether this results in the 'cross-breeding' of the body and the machine—whether the machine will take on the characteristics attributed to the human body ('artificial intelligence,' automatons)—or whether the human body will take on the characteristics of the machine (the cyborg, bionics, computer prosthesis remains unclear. Yet it is certain that this will fundamentally transform the ways in which we conceive both cities and bodies and their interrelations [35].

While Grosz was writing about the relationship between cities and bodies, but her words can easily apply to artforms involving human computer interaction (HCI). We believe that toolmakers need to be aware of the theories of embodied cognition as they make device that interface with the body. Artist/programmers need to move beyond point and click, and create tools as extensions of the thought processes and bodily engagement. The digital world is a symbolic reduction; we need to consider how we reduce the messy analog world into a compact series of numbers, and what aspects of the world we want to represent in numbers. We have shown that it is possible to create an expressive system by looking at a single point of human movement over time. Adding more data points adds functionality, but it does not necessarily add more expressivity. Our embodied minds are capable of perceiving subtleties in movement that we are unable to articulate, but we can harness to create compelling interactive systems working in harmony with computational tools.

282   E. Beattie and M. Schedel

References

1. Haraway, D.: Simians, Cyborgs, and Women: The Reinvention of Nature, p. 188. Routledge, London (2013)
2. Moro, A.: Impossible Languages, p. 42. MIT Press, Cambridge (2016)
3. Leman, M.: Embodied Music Cognition and Mediation Technology, p. 132. MIT Press, Cambridge (2008)
4. Cook, A., Blair, R.: Theatre, Performance and Cognition: Languages, Bodies and Ecologies (Performance and Science: Interdisciplinary Dialogues), p. 2. Methuen Drama (2016)
5. Leman, M.: Embodied Music Cognition and Mediation Technology, p. 43. MIT Press, Cambridge (2008)
6. McNeill, D.: Gesture and Thought, p. 2. The University of Chicago Press, Chicago (2008)
7. IBID. p. 250
8. Cook, A., Blair, R.: Theatre, Performance and Cognition: Languages, Bodies and Ecologies (Performance and Science: Interdisciplinary Dialogues), p. 44. Methuen Drama (2016)
9. Hanna, J.: To Dance is Human, p. 19. The University of Chicago Press, Chicago (1996)
10. Dissanayake, E.: Homo Aestheticus Where Art Comes From and Why, p. 35. The Free Press, New York (1992)
11. Foster, S.: Choreographing Empathy, p. 16. Routledge, London (2011)
12. IBID. p. XX
13. IBID. p. 2
14. Lihs, H.: Appreciating Dance: A Guide to the World's Liveliest Art, p. 41. Princeton Book Co. Pub., Hightstown (2009)
15. Malafouris, L.: How Things Shape the Mind, p. 188. MIT Press, Cambridge (2013)
16. Foster, S.: Choreographing Empathy, p. 17. Routledge, London (2011)
17. Preston-Dunlop, V.: Rudolf Laban an Extraordinary Life, p. 1 (1998)
18. Foster, S.: Choreographing Empathy, p. 49. Routledge, London (2011)
19. https://synchronousobjects.osu.edu/
20. Varela, F., Thompson, E., Rosch, E., Kabat-Zinn, J.: The Embodied Mind, p. xiii. MIT Press, Cumberland (2017)
21. Wilson, F.R.: The Hand: How Its Use Shapes the Brain, Language, and Human Culture, p. 60. Vintage (2010)
22. Malafouris, L.: How Things Shape the Mind, p. 113. MIT Press, Cambridge (2013)
23. Penny, S.: Making Sense: Cognition, Computing, Art, and Embodiment, p. 244. MIT Press, Cambridge (2017)
24. Cook, A., Blair, R.: Theatre, Performance and Cognition: Languages, Bodies and Ecologies (Performance and Science: Interdisciplinary Dialogues), p. 159. Methuen Drama (2016)
25. Penny, S.: Making Sense: Cognition, Computing, Art, and Embodiment, p. 283. MIT Press, Cambridge (2017)
26. IBID. p. xxx
27. Thwaites, T.: The Toaster Project: Or a Heroic Attempt to Build a Simple Electric Appliance from Scratch. Chronicle Books (2011)
28. Leman, M.: Embodied Music Cognition and Mediation Technology, p. 22. MIT Press, Cambridge (2008)
29. Freed, A., et al.: Musical applications and design techniques for the gametrak tethered spatial position controller. In: Proceedings of the 6th Sound and Music Computing Conference, p. 1 (2009)

30. Huberth, M., Madeline, Nanou, C.: Notation for motion tracking controllers: a gametrak case study. In: Proceedings of the International Conference on New Interfaces for Musical Expression, p. 1 (2016)
31. Penny, S.: Making Sense: Cognition, Computing, Art, and Embodiment, p. xxvii. MIT Press, Cambridge (2017)
32. Malafouris, L.: How Things Shape the Mind, p. 78. MIT Press, Cambridge (2013)
33. Leman, L.: Embodied Music Cognition and Mediation Technology, p. 71. MIT Press, Cambridge (2008)
34. IBID. p. 54
35. Grosz, E.: Space, Time, and Perversion: Essays on the Politics of Bodies, p. 110. Routledge, London (1995)

Auditory Modulation of Multisensory Representations

Alfred O. Effenberg$^{(\boxtimes)}$, Tong-Hun Hwang, Shashank Ghai, and Gerd Schmitz

Leibniz University Hannover, 30167 Hannover, Germany
effenberg@sportwiss.uni-hannover.de

Abstract. Motor control and motor learning as well as interpersonal coordination are based on motor perception and emergent perceptuomotor representations. At least in early stages motor learning and interpersonal coordination are emerging heavily on visual information in terms of observing others and transforming the information into internal representations to guide owns behavior. With progressing learning, also other perceptual modalities are added when a new motor pattern is established by repeated physical exercises. In contrast to the vast majority of publications on motor learning and interpersonal coordination referring to a certain perceptual modality here we look at the perceptual system as a unitary system coordinating and unifying the information of all involved perceptual modalities. The relation between perceptual streams of different modalities, the intermodal processing and multisensory integration of information as a basis for motor control and learning will be the main focus of this contribution.

Multi-/intermodal processing of perceptual streams results in multimodal representations and opens up new approaches to support motor learning and interpersonal coordination: Creating an additional perceptual stream adequately auditory movement information can be generated suitable to be integrated with information of other modalities and thereby modulating the resulting perceptuomotor representations without the need of attention and higher cognition. Here, the concept of a movement defined real-time acoustics is used to serve the auditory system in terms of an additional movement-auditory stream. Before the computational approach of kinematic real-time sonification is finally described, a special focus is directed to the level of adaptation modules of the internal models. Furthermore, this concept is compared with different approaches of additional acoustic movement information. Moreover, a perspective of this approach is given in a broad spectrum of new applications of supporting motor control and learning in sports and motor rehabilitation as well as a broad spectrum of joint action and interpersonal coordination between humans but also concerning human-robot-interaction.

Keywords: Interpersonal coordination · Motor control · Motor learning
Movement sonification · Multimodal integration · Multimodal perception
Perceptuomotor representation

M. Aramaki et al. (Eds.): CMMR 2017, LNCS 11265, pp. 284–311, 2018.
https://doi.org/10.1007/978-3-030-01692-0_20

1 Introduction: The Emergence of Perceptual-Motor Representations

From different fields of research on motor behavior there is strong evidence for a comprehensive and direct impact of current perception on motor processes: Motor control is driven by perceptual information. Disturbances between perceptual information of different modalities result in earnest perturbations as demonstrated already by Kohler (1951, 1963) with prism inversion goggles. Adaption usually only takes place when a person is physically acting and is pointing out the relevance of an intermodal adjustment of simultaneous congruent perceptual streams which are configured by and allocated to the specific current motor activity. The action specific activation of efferent motor patterns triggered by the anticipation of related perceptual effects builds the key frame of the 'internal model'-theory, which has been adapted to the acquisition of motor behavior by Wolpert et al. (1995). Motor learning, resulting in long lasting changes of motor behavior, is based on the emergence of new internal models or appropriate changes of already existing ones in terms of adaptations e.g.: Changes of the inverse model as well as the forward model or the couplings of both (Wolpert et al. 2011). All three references (motor control, adaptation, motor learning) verify the importance of the anticipation of specific perceptual effects, the activation of adequate motor patterns and the emergence of according perceptual streams with close temporal relations. The structural interrelation between these patterns is a key element of motor learning, motor control and adaptation and it highlights the essential relevance of related sensory/perceptual effects - specified by the executed action pattern and configuring bottom-up the perceptual streams. The Figs. 1a and 1b below illustrate the concept of a modulation of internal representations by an artificial real-time perceptual stream, here configured as a kinematical determined acoustical stream.

Action determined perceptual streams

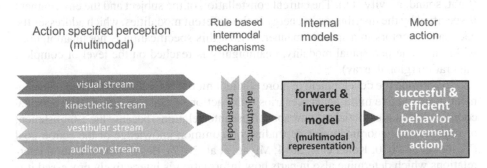

Fig. 1a. Action-specified perceptual streams of different modalities are aligned and integrated in the perceptual system (multisensory areas) configuring internal models

Action determined perceptual streams

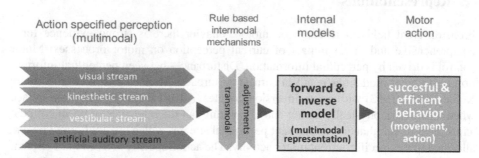

Fig. 1b. Changing one perceptual streams will change transmodal adjustments and multisensory integrations and thereon modify emergent internal models - enabling the modification of model-based movement patterns. Change of colors indicates a change within the referenced process (auditory stream, intermodal mechanisms, internal model, motor action)

With Figs. 1a and 1b the emergence of internal models based on the combined perception of different modalities is illustrated. A specifically shaped internal model can only emerge based on specifically shaped perceptual streams, which is given by the action just executed: Perceptual streams are modulated by the specific movements of the action, as described for the specification of the optical flow from the owns movement by Gibson (1966, 1979) within the visual domain. Based on the idea of direct perception and direct perception-action coupling of Gibson et al. (2001) developed the idea of a seamless unity of the different perceptual modalities into a global array postulating intensive intermodal processing of information and multimodal integration. Amodal or supramodal representations are resulting from intermodal/multisensory processing and integration. This construct is based on the idea of a unified perceptual system consisting of different channels with their sensors directed to the distribution of ambient energy (light, sound, gravity etc.). The current constellation of the subject and the environment is specified by the distribution of energy in the different modalities, which addresses the adequate receptors in a specific manner. Whilst this specification is not unambiguous within a single perceptual modality, unambiguity is reached on the level of complete integration (global array).

Concerning the development of more efficient methods for the support and enhancement of interactive multi-agent scenarios (joint action, social interaction, interpersonal coordination) it is essential to know about these interrelations, because the establishment of interpersonal coordination is depending on common knowledge of the action goal (Vesper et al. 2010; Keller et al. 2014; Miyata et al. 2017). Besides the structural interrelations which determine also in parts how information is interactively processed it is important to know what kind of information is being processed. After many decades of modality specific research within the last three decades the relevance of multisensory and intermodal mechanisms concerning the regulation of behavior has been taken into account more and more by neuroscientists (Stein and Meredith 1993; Calvert et al. 2004; Spence and Driver 2004; Baumann and Greenlee 2006; Shams and Seitz 2008;

Spence 2015). Multisensory integration and intermodal processing of sensory information are key mechanisms for an efficient use of additional auditory information which should make it possible in the future to shape internal representations and processes of motor control and motor perception directly. Some basic findings from multisensory integration research should be recalled here. To support the understanding of the observed and assumed efficiency of an anticipative auditory kinematics it is important to know that

- anticipated and perceived sensory/perceptual effects are available in different perceptual modalities during the planning and execution of action (Zmigrod and Hommel 2013),
- different perceptual streams are continuously integrated seamlessness down to the level of a single neuron (Stein and Meredith 1993; Stein and Stanford 2008), and
- that perceptuomotor internal models are consisting partially of multisensory/intermodal representations (Berthoz and Viaud-Delmon 1999; Stoffregen and Bardy 2001; Lacquaniti et al. 2014).

Based on this knowledge the configuration of an additional anticipative auditory kinematics e.g. for enhancing the perception and anticipation of movement kinematics in single as well as dual-agent scenarios is an interesting issue. Multisensory information is more effective on motor perception, motor control and motor learning (Seitz et al. 2006; Shams and Seitz 2008) as well as relearning in motor rehabilitation by (Johansson 2012; Schaefer 2014). Also from our own research group there is some evidence that individual motor behavior can be supported effectively by additional kinematic real-time sonification (motor learning: Effenberg et al. 2016, motor rehabilitation: Schmitz et al. 2014, character acquisition: Effenberg et al. 2015). Furthermore, the identification of one's own movements against others can be supported by kinematic sonification (Schmitz and Effenberg 2016) and interpersonal coordination can be enhanced (Schmitz and Effenberg 2012).

Besides, Schmitz et al. (2013) found evidence that the action observation system of humans can be addressed by additional kinematic sonification: This findings can serve as a plausible explanation for the related behavioral effects, but moreover beyond that: In future kinematic sonification if generated structurally equivalent to the visual kinematics, even the perception and interaction with artificial systems like humanoid robots might get supported. Audiovisually integrated percepts could make robots behavior easier understandable and more reliable predictable by human co-actors – even without the need of conscious cognition. Perceiving the kinematics of the co-actor audiovisually might enhance the smoothness of human-robot cooperation by supporting internal simulations as a key element of fluent interpersonal coordination (Khoramshahi et al. 2016). This idea is supported by former work of (Lahav et al. 2007; Kohler et al. 2002; Keysers et al. 2003), emphasizing the relevance of multimodal integration of the perceptual streams also via audiovisual mirror neurons as well as of intermodal binding mechanisms (Calvert et al. 2004).

Turning the focus explicitly to interactive dual-agent scenarios, additional auditory kinematics applied to both agents can enable common audiovisual perception of agents movements and thereby a more precise interpersonal temporal and spatial coordination can be expected. It is to assume that audiovisual kinematic movement information can be used to provoke an enhanced interactive temporal coupling as described by Oullier et al. (2008) for visual settings: The authors reported a relative phase and frequency overlap between movements of individuals when acting together. As a consequence, interpersonal coordination should get smoother and more reliable when interaction/ coordination is based on multisensory audiovisual information. Redirecting the gaze to the field of music as an interesting field of interpersonal sensorimotor coordination, timing, synchronization and aesthetics within an orchestra are referring to the causal relationship of the movement kinematics of violinists and conductor(s), as shown by D'Ausilio et al. (2012). Keller et al. (2007) demonstrated that sensorimotor synchronization as well as the recognition of self-played piano sequences is based on internal action simulation. Sensorimotor synchronization is a determinant of the interaction between humans as well as in human-robot interaction, as pointed out by D'Ausilio et al. (2015). Taken together results indicate that internal simulation of others actions is an important mechanism for understanding of – and the smooth participation in – cooperative actions (Bishop and Goebl 2018). Obviously internal simulation of coordinated action is not dependent on visual information and the visual mirror neuron system: Internal simulation can be also initiated by auditory information addressing auditory/ audiovisual mirror neurons, if acoustics is directly linked to the related movements. This is given when playing music instruments and it is equally given for appropriate kinds of kinematic movement sonifications.

Besides interpersonal coordination in music there is comprehensive evidence on several determinants of joint action like joint attention, action observation, task sharing, action coordination, and agency by Sebanz et al. (2006), and with reference to rocking chair movements by Goodman et al. (2005). In this field of research authors emphasize the importance of the ability to predict the actions of others (the what, when, and where of others' actions) for a smooth and successful interpersonal coordination on joint actions (Sebanz and Knoblich 2009). Referring to the concept of planned and emergent coordination from Knoblich et al. (2011) auditory information is especially suitable for the support of emergent coordination due to its fast and unconscious perceptuomotor processability. Thereby emergent auditory/intersensory coordination should support fast and precise interpersonal perception-action couplings. Demos et al. (2012) already showed that perceiving another participant moving in a rocking chair subconsciously influences one's own rocking frequency, even if both participants are instructed to ignore each other. Both modes – seeing and hearing the other person rock – elicited spontaneous coordination, but it is remarkable, that hearing amplified the visual effects. Obviously, participants unintentionally integrate the perceived movement frequency into their own movement production – a phenomenon supporting the concept of inter-corporeality. Music, in an additional condition, serves as social glue: participants, who synchronized more with music felt more connected (Demos et al. 2012).

Summing up: From a traditional point of view, perception, prediction and action referred to different phenomena guided by own rules each and based on separated functions. More current theories now state that one aspect cannot be considered without the others. For example, a key hypothesis in embodiment and joint action research is that action observation triggers an internal modelling of movements which actively involves the motor system. Therefore, during interpersonal interactions, the motor system seems to fulfill two distinct functions: one related to observing, simulating and anticipating other persons' actions and another related to planning and controlling one's own motor behavior. Some evidence was presented that auditory movement information – as on music making or movement sonification – is usable as an additional common reference framework for both interaction partners, enhancing temporal and spatial determinants of cooperative actions. Inter-corporeality, interpersonal coordination and even inter-kinesthesia in sports as well as in everyday scenarios are based on a close connection of perception and anticipation of action as well as on common motor actions of all agents being involved in interpersonal coordination such as in team-rowing. It should have become clear, that the anticipation of co-actors/co-agents actions and intentions is an essential element of smooth and successful interpersonal/inter-agent coordination.

Whilst the first section deals with the emergence of motor behavior with a focus on auditory information on a low-granular level, the 2. Section is dedicated to a finer granular level: Here adaptation modules and the references to different perceptual modalities are taken into consideration mainly. Section 3 focuses on rhythmic auditory cueing and its influence on neurophysiological activations. Furthermore, we discuss how these sensory stimulations might shape the perceptuomotor representations during rehabilitation of movement disorders. Based on the first three sections the 4. Section is dedicated to the technological side of kinematic real-time sonification as a powerful instrument to support perceptual–motor processes and modulate emergent perceptuomotor behavior specifically.

2 Sensorimotor Adaptation and Learning Aspects

Although sport scientific research predominantly focuses on the analyses of real-world like tasks, important insights into mechanisms of motor learning can be gained by fundamental research in well controllable, experimental settings with relatively simple movements. According to Haar et al. (2015), paradigms on sensorimotor adaptation belong amongst the most fundamental approaches for understanding motor control. The following section will describe adaptation mechanisms and how internal models seem to be linked to sensory modalities and effectors.

2.1 Approaches and Mechanisms

The majority of adaptation studies focuses on hand, arm or eye movements. Eye movements represent an attractive object of research, because they have only few degrees of freedom and are well describable. They are predominantly linked to visual perception, but they also exert influence on other perceptual modalities as well as movement effectors. For example, is has been shown that eye positions or eye movements affect spatial representations of sounds (Lewald and Getzmann 2006) and internal models for hand and arm movement control (Dijkerman et al. 2006; Schmitz and Grigorova 2017). Thus, they have to be considered as important for perceptions and nearly all types of movements. Accordingly, fundamental contributions to the understanding of motor learning have been achieved by research on blink conditioning and saccadic adaptation to target displacements (double-steps).

Smith et al. (2006) observed that already metrics of simple eye movements are not altered by a single adaptation mechanism, but by several mechanisms acting concurrently. A few years later the same principle was shown for hand movements (Lee and Schweighofer 2009), which helped to refine the understanding of internal models and their multiple subfunctions. An important insight was that internal models seem to be composed of further sub-units termed 'modules'. Modules specify spatial and force-related parameters of movements and can be more or less flexibly arranged during the generation of motor commands (Bock 2013; Wolpert et al. 2011). By observing that adaptation transfers between hands (Sainburg and Wang 2002), between hand pointing and walking movements (Morton and Bastian 2004) or between eye movements and hand movements (Bock et al. 2008), it was shown that internal models are rather effector-independent than effector-specific, i.e. the same internal model can by linked to different movement effectors. By showing that transfer between effectors is not obligatory but fragile as it happens in some but not other conditions, it was concluded that internal models are *flexibly* linked to effectors by a weighting or a switching function (Bock 2013).

2.2 Generalization Between Visuomotor and Audiomotor Adaptation

Whereas effector-specificity of internal models has been investigated in depth, less work has been performed with respect to the role of sensory modalities. One of the first researches who investigated whether adaptation in one modality transfers to another modality was Samuel Harris (Harris 1963, 1965). He reported that adaptation of arm movements achieved with prism glasses transfers fully to pointing movements performed with closed eyes to sound sources. The finding of fundamental transfer from the visual to the auditory modality has been confirmed several times up to now (Cohen 1974; Kagerer and Contreras-Vidal 2009; Mikaelian 1974; Michel et al. 2007) and can be regarded as validated scientifically. As Harris further found an altered position sense of the trained but not the untrained arm in the same experiments, he concluded that the position sense of the trained arm is the locus of adaptive changes. These changes would affect every arm action, independently from whether the action is performed in a visual or an auditory condition or with eyes closed.

Craske (1966) developed a simple acoustic adaptation paradigm, in which participants pressed a button below sound sources which triggered another sound from a loudspeaker 12 ° away. Repeated practice induced pre-post changes in an auditory and in a visual localization task performed with the trained arm. According to Harris (1965), the author concluded that the position sense of the trained arm had adapted. However, other results do not comply with this conclusion: Mikaelian (1972) adapted arm movements while participants continuously moved a sound source in front of the body from side to side while wearing pseudophones. These are headphones connected to rotatable microphones above the head. A rotation of the microphone axis should mimic interaural time differences with respect to the sound source in the hand. This author found audiomotor aftereffects during movements with the trained, but also with the untrained arm. Most importantly, he did not find visuomotor aftereffects, why he concluded that not the position sense but auditory perception had adapted.

Nevertheless, since then changes induced by sensorimotor adaptation have been regarded as sensory changes, and sensorimotor adaptation has been discussed in line with models on multisensory fusion and intersensory binding, accordingly (Chen and Vroomen 2013; Welch 1978). After the pioneer studies in the 60s and 70s, audiomotor paradigms had been abandoned from research on hand and arm movement adaptation for a long time or not been published, presumably until the work from Oscari et al. (2012). However, researchers broadened the overall picture by analyzing proprioceptive effects of prism adaptation. Bernier et al. (2007) let participants point to their unseen index finger of the untrained hand before and after prism adaptation. No pre-post changes became evident and these as well the authors who cited this research concluded that proprioception had not been altered by visuomotor adaptation. However, very recently another study was published, which reported significant changes of the proprioceptive position sense after adaptation to a visuomotor rotation (Flannigan et al. 2018). This suggests that proprioceptive adaptation might depend on the applied adaptation paradigm. Another possible explanation is that Bernier et al. (2007) did not test for changes in the position sense of the un-trained arm – this would have been necessary for the validity of their conclusion, because some studies indeed report this effect.

2.3   Perceptual, Motor or Sensorimotor Recalibration?

Although it seems to be plausible, several studies give rise to doubts on the hypothesis of perceptual adaptation. First of all, it seems possible to induce purely motor aftereffects (Magescas and Prablanc 2006). Second, Hatada et al. (2006) reported that visual and proprioceptive aftereffects of a single adaptation session last for several days, which is quite astonishing when participants continue their regular daily activities in the days after the experiment which should induce de-adaptation or recalibration of the perceptual changes back to normal. Furthermore, the authors observed that proprioceptive aftereffects measured during passively performed movements decayed after two days, whereas proprioceptive aftereffects persisted for seven days when movements were performed actively. Therefore, an alternative to the hypothesis of perceptual changes has to be derived: One explanation might be the adaptation of internal models that are flexibly linked to perceptual and motor processing. In the following, we describe a framework that accounts for this hypothesis.

2.3.1   Connectivity of Internal Models to Sensory Modalities

According to the MOSAIC model for sensorimotor control from Wolpert and Kawato (1998), the sensorimotor system contains of multiple parallel internal models. However, concurrent adaptations to only two sensorimotor discordances (dual adaptation) have been shown to interfere with each other, suggesting a bottle neck in the sensorimotor system during adaptation. Interference of two adaptive processes complies with the hypothesis on perceptual recalibration, because it is plausible that one sensory modality cannot have two incompatible states at the same time. Nevertheless, under some conditions, dual adaptation seems to be possible without costs. One condition is the adaptation of two arms. First Prablanc et al. (1975) and later other authors (e.g. Galea and Miall 2006; Martin and Newman 1980) showed that the left arm can adapt to one sensorimotor discordance while the right arm adapts concurrently to an opposite directed sensorimotor discordance. In such a case, it is interesting to analyze what changes occur in which sensory modality. Given the assumption that one sensory modality cannot adapt at the same time to opposite directed distortions of space, dual arm adaptation would be compatible with adaptation of the arm specific position senses, only.

Therefore, Bock and Schmitz (2013) tested, whether movements performed to visual targets with clockwise rotated visual feedback for the left arm and counterclockwise rotated feedback for the right arm transfers to movements performed to auditory targets without feedback. As shown before by other studies, both arms adapted successfully and revealed significant pre-post changes of the trajectories to visual targets. Most interestingly, adaptation transferred by 66% to the auditory modality, which is substantial but incomplete. This effect occurred in each arm. Therefore, it is not compatible with adaptation in the visual modality, but with a higher weighting of visual compared to auditory information after dual visual adaptation. Further work from the same authors (Schmitz and Bock 2014, 2017) showed that the visual modality is not per se rated higher than the auditory modality. When arm movements adapt in an audiomotor paradigm, i.e., participants perform arm movements to auditory targets with auditory real-time feedback about movement trajectories, adaptation (after-)effects are larger in the auditory compared to the visual modality. Thus, it is always the trained modality that gets larger (or similar) input weights than the untrained modality, irrespective of whether it

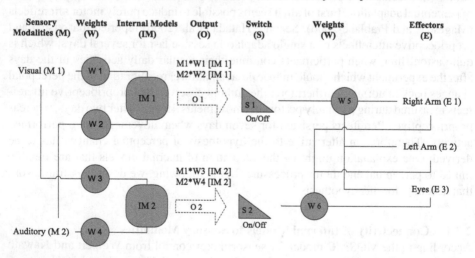

Fig. 2. Essence of the studies from Bock and Schmitz (2013), Grigorova and Schmitz (2017) and Schmitz and Bock (2014, 2017) as amendment of the model proposed by Bock (2013). Internal models are considered to be amodal and connected by weighting functions (W1-W4) to sensory modalities (M1, M2). Outputs (O1, O2) from internal models (IM1, IM2) pass two-state switches (S1, S2). If both switches are 'on', the outputs from IM1 and IM2 are added (e.g. M2*W2 [IM 1] plus M2*W4 [IM 2]). These outputs are weighted (W5, W6) before sent to different effectors. All colored components are specified during sensorimotor adaptation and learning.

is the visual or the auditory modality. This is illustrated by the schematic model in Fig. 2, whose basic features had been developed by Bock (2013) and specified in further work together with Schmitz (e.g. Schmitz and Bock 2014). Adaptation of the right arm to an audiomotor discordance recalibrates one internal model (IM 2), and specifies the weighting function W4 which gets larger than W3. At the same time, the right arm can adapt to an audiomotor discordance which recalibrates another internal model (IM 1) and enlarge W2 compared to W1 or to a visuomotor discordance which trains IM 1 with similar efficiency but enlarges W1 compared to W2 (Schmitz and Bock 2017).

2.3.2 Connectivity of Internal Models to Different Effectors

The schematic model allows to explain further phenomena related to sensorimotor adaptation and learning. Both internal models are connected to several effectors. Their outputs are weighted again (W5 and W6), which results in full or partial intermanual transfer after adaptation (Imamizu and Shimojo 1995; Michel et al. 2007). Furthermore, it accounts for transfer of adaptation from hand movements to eye movements and vice versa (Bock et al. 2008). The connection of IM 1 and IM 2 to several effectors also explains interference within hand or arm motor systems (Wigmore et al. 2002) or between hand and eye movement adaptation, when adapting to opposite directed spatial discordances (Schmitz and Grigorova 2017).

Interference between two conflicting internal models can be inhibited. Partial inhibition seems to be possible on the basis of cognitive executive inhibition. This is indicated by reports on facilitation of adaptation to two opposite directed sensorimotor discordances through explicit knowledge about these discordances (Imamizu et al. 2007) as well as by significant correlations between the amount of interference and participants' mental flexibility and cognitive inhibition abilities (Schmitz 2016). Whereas these effects occur fast and are short-term, complete inhibition seldom occurs spontaneously. Instead, it seems to be achieved through training of slow-acting mechanisms in several hundreds to thousand trials (Schmitz and Grigorova 2017). Wolpert et al. (2011) describe it as the problem to assign effectors and internal models. Bastian (2008) regards it as sensorimotor learning. In the model presented in Figs. 1a and 1b, it is a decoupling of internal model and effectors through training of the context dependent on/off-switch functions S1 and S2. As long as the switch functions have not been established, yet, the output of the two internal models is fused nearly linearly. Most interestingly, the weighting of modalities (W1-W4 in Figs. 1a and 1b) is still relevant so that adaptation transfers with these modality-specific weights between effectors (Schmitz and Bock 2017).

2.4 Conclusion

Taken together, auditory feedback of arm movements seems to address the same mechanisms for sensorimotor adaptation as visual feedback. Therefore, spatial auditory and visual feedback can substitute each other. Further data suggest that the best effect is achieved when the feedback modality corresponds to the target modality (Schmitz 2014), probably because trajectories are first specified within a modality before the trajectory specifications of different modalities are fused to achieve an optimal outcome (Oostwoud Wijdenes and Medendorp 2017; Tagliabue and McIntyre 2014).

Internal models seem to be neutral with respect to sensory modalities (amodal) and to be coupled by default with sensory and motor instances of the sensorimotor system. This becomes evident from multiple findings on intermodal as well as interlimb transfer. During sensorimotor training, the sensorimotor systems alters linkages between sensory modalities and internal models as well as between internal models and effectors (semi-)permanently by specifying weighting functions. Furthermore, extensive training is required to learn the de-coupling of an internal model and an effector, which allows efficient switching between different adaptive states subsequently. This might rather be termed sensorimotor learning than adaptation.

Adaptive changes might be less based on recalibration of sensory percepts than on recalibration of internal models. Theory states that the output from internal models is used to generate feedforward expectations about the sensory consequences of the intended actions, which are compared with the actions' actual outcome in a next step. Shadmehr et al. (2010) state that feedforward expectations are fused with sensory percepts and thereby affect the overall percept. This might explain how adaptation alters spatial perception without recalibrating sensory modalities.

3 Effects of Auditory Information on Cyclic Movements

Pre-determined auditory stimuli guiding cyclic movements have been well documented in published literature. This type of stimulation intuitively interconnects movement with rhythmic stimulations due to widespread inclination towards music. This results in influencing and coordinating movement patterns while timing the specific mechanisms and therefore initiating a common neural network. Such auditory rhythmic patterns can impart great neurophysiological and behavioral changes during motor performance. Rhythmic auditory stimulations have been reported in the published literature to allow benefits in motor execution (Ghai et al. 2017a, b; Ghai et al. 2018a, b, c), motor control (Thaut et al. 1991), interpersonal coordination (Keller et al. 2014), and breathing (Murgia et al. 2016).

Rhythmic auditory cueing exploits the intricate neuroanatomical relationship in between the auditory and motor centers especially extending towards cortical, subcortical structures, brainstem and alpha motor neurons of spinal cord (Felix et al. 2011; Thaut 2005). The auditory system is quite fast, precise and efficient in detecting anomalies in auditory stimuli, and developing stable temporal templates (Thaut 2003). Likewise, auditory cortex has been reported to perceive stimuli with shorter reaction times (20–50 ms) as compared to its visual or tactile counterparts (Nombela et al. 2013). Moreover, Fujioka et al. (2012) reported modulation of neuromagnetic β oscillations with rhythmic auditory stimuli in auditory cortex, cerebellum, inferior frontal gyrus, somatosensory area and sensorimotor cortex. The stimuli have been suggested to activate inferior colliculi (Tierney and Kraus 2013), cerebellum, brainstem (Debaere et al. 2003; Hausdorff et al. 2007), sensorimotor cortex (Asanuma and Keller 1991; Suh et al. 2014), further instigating reorganization in cortico-cerebellar circuits (Luft et al. 2004).

Rhythmic auditory stimuli have also been suggested to reap the benefits of the preserved neural centers during rehabilitation and even learning (Torres et al. 2011) (see also "kinesia paradoxica" (Rinehart et al. 2006)). Studies report that motor activities directed by external sensory cueing evoke pathways via cortical, premotor areas (Ghai et al. 2018a, b, c), effectively bypassing the affected basal ganglia region (Young et al. 2014), which usually is affected in motor dysfunctions. Studies have suggested that rhythmic sensory cues can also replace deficient pallidal-cortical projections and serve a signal to supplementary motor area, like a feed-forward input for aiding motor task, thereby reducing bradykinesia, and associated motor deficits (Cunnington et al. 1995). Similarly, the external cueing can supplement critical spatio-temporal information which is necessary for initiation or facilitating a motor activity (Nieuwboer et al. 2009; Nieuwboer et al. 2007), such as during gait or arm movements (Whitall et al. 2011). Likewise, recent research suggests that rhythmic cueing might also assist in facilitating frontal-lobe cognitive strategies (working memory) by externally cueing the motor execution (El-Tamawy et al. 2012). According to Campos-Sousa et al. (2010) frontal lobe areas can select a motor program in response to an external stimulus, and send it to the primary motor cortex, which are mainly guiding such movement patterns. External cues also contribute to sensorimotor integration that requires organizing and processing of proprioceptive inputs in working memory (Ghai et al. 2018a, b, c). In context of gait execution, the external rhythm can guide the patients to synchronize their ground contact and lift-off times (Ford et al. 2010). The patterns might also serve as a medium for assisting in planning before executing a movement (Thaut et al. 2007). Moreover, the periodicity in rhythmic auditory feedback has also demonstrated to effectively reduce variability in musculoskeletal activation patterns, thereby allowing more economical and consistent motor unit recruitment (Thaut 2005), further smoothing the velocity and acceleration profiles of joint motions by scaling movement time (Thaut 2005).

3.1 Rehabilitation Applications

Recently conducted systematic reviews and meta-analyses by our department to analyze the effects of rhythmic auditory cueing on gait performance (a cyclic task) among fall prone population groups revealed interesting findings. First and foremost, beneficial effects were reported for rhythmic auditory cueing for enhancing gait stability and performance in patients affected from parkinsonism (Ghai et al. 2018a, b, c), cerebral palsy (Ghai et al. 2018a, b, c), and in aged population groups (Ghai et al. 2017a, b). Considerable enhancements in terms of *small*-to-*large* effect sizes in spatiotemporal gait parameters were reported for all population groups. However, cadence amongst the parkinsonian patients was the only spatiotemporal parameter that saw a negligible difference. Typically, patients with parkinsonism exhibit a shuffling gait, where cadence is usually high and step length is small. Here, a reduction in cadence with the delivery of rhythmic auditory cueing suggests that the stimuli instead of increasing the gait execution, promoted more automaticity, and hence stability during its execution.

Furthermore, modulation of differential factor in rhythmic auditory stimulation have been suggested to impact different aspects of motor execution. For instance, change in tempo has been associated with various neurophysiological changes such as, increased neuronal activation in fronto-occipital networks (Thaut et al. 2009), excitability of the spinal motor neurons by reticulospinal pathways, which might possibly reduce the response time for a motor task. Likewise, variation in tempo during training is suggested to be beneficial for maintaining a healthy gait pattern, as constant rhythmic pattern for longer durations have shown to decrease fractal scaling of stride times from healthy 1/f structure, possibly because of organization of stride time variability around a single frequency (Delignières and Torre 2009; Hausdorff et al. 1996; Hove et al. 2012). Additionally, Buchecker et al. (2017) demonstrated beneficial effects of enhanced variability within training on posture and electromyographic activity. This might serve to be beneficial for parkinsonian patients to learn how to regulate gait, when passing through fall-prone environments. Moreover, the induction of variability can also be subjected subliminally (for instance changes in tempo, interstimuli interval, see also (Tecchio et al. 2000)). This might maintain variability in the rehabilitation protocol and simultaneously prevent any conscious stress to excessively speed up or slow down the gait. However, Hopkins et al. (2017) reported that cross modal cueing can avoid information overload in the native sensory modality by directing task-irrelevant information towards the underused sensory modality (Hameed et al. 2009). Here as well, the introduction of auditory feedback could have possibly allowed enhancements in repositioning accuracy by information in the sister domain (Ghai et al. 2017a, b; Lohnes and Earhart 2011).

Finally, recent research also points out the beneficial effects of engaging biologically variable rhythmic auditory cueing as compared to isosynchronous cueing. Since, patients with parkinson's, stroke, aged population groups are characterized by a higher threshold for action relevant acoustic input, therefore using ecologically valid action related sounds convening spatio-temporal information can possibly enhance saliency of sensory information, transferring spatio-temporal information effectively and therefore providing more benefits (for a detailed review see (Ghai et al. 2018a, b, c)). For instance, here timbre of an auditory input at a higher intensity merged in a broad ascending melody and a rich harmony can possibly motivate a patient to exert more power.

3.2 Referencing on the Internal Model Theory

Auditory cueing is meant to enhance and shape multisensory representations and address components of auditory motor processing. As mentioned before, this type of acoustic feedback works independently of conscious cognitive processing. This might allow an enhanced spectrum of movement information based on instructional information. Thereby, supporting the development of sensorimotor or perceptuomotor representations. According to the internal model theory of Wolpert et al. (1995) this entrainment effects might help in reducing sensory error estimation during the motor planning phase, further resulting in an efficient movement execution (Wolpert et al. 2011). Here the instructive information can be possibly used to support the development of forward models.

Rehabilitation intervention with movement sonification is still a rather unexplored territory. Concerning stroke rehabilitation there is first evidence that on hemiparesis of the upper limbs real-time kinematic movement sonification can enhance the effectiveness of a traditional method (Schmitz et al. 2014). Moreover, recent research by

Effenberg et al. (2016) has demonstrated that the effects of movement sonification extend the benefits offered by rhythmic auditory stimulations. Therefore, the current section lays possible interpretations for future studies as to how movement sonification might influence behavior and motor performance in movement disorders. The following sections explain the theoretical, experimental and technical aspects of how such online auditory feedback might shape these movement representations in real life settings.

4 Generation of Artificial Auditory Information

4.1 Digital Sound Generation

This subsection is to explain the process of generation of digital sound and its considerations. Auditory information can be generated by a speaker system connected to digital devices (e.g. computer, smartphone). A host system transmits control signals to a speaker. Referring to the control signal, an amplifier drives the mechanical vibration of the magnet and the voice coil in the speaker. The vibration is transmitted to the environment of the speaker through a speaker cone which is set into vibration, changing the pressure of the ambient air. Pressure changes between frequencies of about 20 Hz to 20 kHz are hearable for the human ear as sound. Sound can also be transmitted as waves in certain materials (e.g. air, water, metal, wood). When sound reached the human ears, vibrations are transmitted to the eardrum: Acoustic pressure changes are transformed into electrical nerve impulses and transmitted to auditory and multisensory areas in the brain. When auditory information is regarded as a perception of small movements on the eardrum, it can be compared to a perception of body movement in terms of energy transmission.

4.2 Relationship of Auditory and Movement Parameters

This subsection discusses the selection of suitable sound parameters to generate effective auditory movement information. Electronic sound synthesis offers a huge number of sound parameters and sound effects (e.g. pitch, loudness, timbre, panning effect), which can be combined to movement parameters in a certain manner. This allows a vast number of mappings between sound and movement. If the auditory information should be processed immediately, the sound should be perceivable intuitively. Natural kinetic-acoustic relationships have been taken as a base for intuitive perception (Effenberg 2005; Dubus and Bresin 2013). The pitch has been used as the most used auditory parameter in mappings such as 'kinetic energy to pitch' and 'location to pitch' (Dubus and Bresin 2013). Depending on biological and psychological factors, effects of the auditory feedback alter in different situations. For example, hearing ability, movement ability, fatigues, and mood can influence of the connection between sound and movement. Although there are a large number of possible mappings, our approach is mapping potential and kinetic energy to sound energy, which can guide at least direction and the amount of alterations in mapping. Considering the fact that human movements consist of rotational movement, the energy equation can be expressed with potential energy E_p and rotational kinetic energy E_k. The equations of total energy $E_{P.total}$ is as below:

$$E_{P.total} = E_p + E_k = mgh + \frac{1}{2}I\omega_m^2 \tag{1}$$

where m is mass, g is gravity, h is the height, I is rotations inertia (comparable to mass in linear kinetic energy equation) and ω_m is the angular velocity. In the last equation, the first term is potential energy and the second term is the kinematic energy. When potential energy is constant, the total energy is proportional to ω_m^2. In terms of the sound energy E_A, the equation is the integration of sound energy density over the volume as below:

$$E_{A.total} = E_{A.p} + E_{A.k} = \int_V \left(p^2/2\rho_0 c^2\right)dV + \int_V \left(\rho v_p^2/2\right)dV. \tag{2}$$

As shown in Eq. (2), sound energy consists of potential energy $E_{A.p}$ and kinetic energy $E_{A.k}$. The equation is expressed with given parameters (V: the volume of interest; p: sound pressure; v_p: particle velocity; ρ_0: the intrinsic density of the medium; ρ: the local density of the medium; c: the speed of sound) (Mueller and Moeser 2012). When a tiny local volume is considered because of the size of human ear, $E_{A.local}$ can be obtained from the differential of Eq. (2) about the volume as below:

$$E_{A.local} = p^2/2\rho_0 c^2 + \rho v_p^2/2. \tag{3}$$

As other parameters (ρ_0, ρ, c) are given from the environment, the parameters can be constant. Finally, the equation is become as below:

$$E_P = Ah + B\omega_m^2 = Cp^2 + Dv_p^2 = kE_{A.spot} \tag{4}$$

where, A, B, C, D, and k are coefficients. According to Eq. (4), an audio system can change the amplitude (function of p) and frequency (function of v_p) in order to control sound energy. Audio amplitude or frequency can express the movement energy change caused by the angular velocity or the height. Although personal use of movement energy determined by various factors, based on this simple equation, it is helpful to design a number of possible mapping between two auditory and two kinematic parameters. With the base design, fine tuning is possible as well as exaggerated and reduced auditory effects are also available.

Auditory Perception of Loudness. As another consideration in designing sound, this subsection deals with logarithmic human auditory perception about amplitude. In the waveform of a signal, the amplitude is defined on as the peak value in a period. Audio amplitude is regarded as loudness of sound, which is related to sound pressure. Sound pressure is defined in the international system of unit (SI unit) in Pascal (Pa), and it is the deviation between local sound pressure and atmospheric pressure without sound (equilibrium state). For express loudness, decibel (dB) is defined, which is logarithmic function of a ratio of two factors: The human ear feels loudness relatively to the equilibrium state, and human auditory perception is logarithmic. The following equation shows the relationship between decibel and the ratio of the measured power (P) and the reference power (P_0):

$$L_p = 10 \, log_{10}(P/P_0) \text{ dB} \tag{5}$$

where L_p is the ratio expressed in decibel. From Eq. (5), when P becomes ten times of P_0, L_p is 10 dB higher. Whenever loudness is 10 dB higher, the human ear perceives the same loudness difference. From Eq. (4), the sound power (derivative of energy with respect to time) is proportional to the square of sound pressure. The equation of L_p, sound pressure (p_A), and reference sound pressure ($p_{A.0}$) is as below:

$$L_p = 20 \, log_{10}(p_A/p_{A.0}) \text{ dB} \tag{6}$$

As shown Eq. (6), humans can perceive the same difference when p_A is $\sqrt{10} (=3.162)$ times more than $p_{A.0}$. For appropriate auditory feedback, loudness should be above the hearing threshold (0 dB) and clearly below the pain threshold (120 dB). An effective auditory feedback should be displayed between about 30 dB (calm room) and 80 dB (limit to avoid hearing damages under long time exposure). Though the level of decibel is affected by the basic level of amplitude, the distance from the sound source and the displayed frequencies, an effective and pleasant movement sonification should be configured carefully and the loudness should be measured just near to the ears.

4.3 Auditory Perception of Pitch

This subsection is related to the nonlinear characteristics of auditory perception concerning audio frequency and musical harmony. When mapping pitch to kinematic parameters, especially when two or more sounds are displayed simultaneously. This provides listeners with the same effect in different situations and lead them to feel pleased with auditory feedback. Human auditory perception of audio frequency is relative to a logarithmic function. An octave is defined as the interval between a musical pitch and another pitch at half or double its frequency, which means the octave is proportional to power of 2. The human brain, however, perceive the same difference when an octave changes higher or lower. For example, when an 88-key piano played the first C (C_1, 32.70 Hz) to the last C (C_8, 4186.01 Hz) [3], the frequency of the last key is 2^7 times more than that of the first key because of the seven octave difference. The human brain, however, recognize that C_8 is 7 times higher pitch than C_1. Every interval between keys are the same for human ear, whereas frequency differences between keys are different. The equation is as below:

$$f(n) = 440 \times 2^{(n-49)/12} \text{ Hz} \tag{7}$$

where f is the audio frequency and n is the number of the key. The forty-ninth piano key (major A_4, concert pitch) is 440 Hz and one octave has twelve keys. From the Eq. (7), major A_5 (the sixty-first key) is 880 Hz, major A_3 (the thirty-seventh key) is 220 Hz, and major C_4 (the fortieth key, the middle C) is 261.63 Hz.

When digital device generate sound with a single frequency, it sounds like a beep. Depending on the types of waveform (e.g. sine, square, sawtooth), different beep sounds are generated. Unlike sound with a single frequency, natural sound occurs with combinations of different waveforms and frequencies. All audio waveforms can be expressed by sine and cosine equations, which is the principle of the Fourier analysis. When most of the musical instruments are played with a fundamental frequency f, sound naturally contains multiple frequency components, such as $2f$, $3f$, $4f$, $5f$, and more (called overtones or harmonic partials). According to the nature of the harmonic feature, the perfect octave is defined as an interval between f and $2f$. As harmonic intervals, the perfect fifth ($2f$ and $3f$) and the perfect fourth ($3f$ and $4f$) are also defined in music. The combinations with harmonic partials can generate a harmony which human ear hear pleasantly. When two or more auditory feedbacks are generated, it would be better to choose the base frequencies with harmonic intervals. When start frequency is different, the range of frequency should be different for the same feedback effect.

4.4 Measurement of Acoustic Parameters

This subsection is to discuss the measurement of decibel and pitch. Before applied to auditory feedback, auditory parameters should be measured behind the audio source and before the terminal receptor—the ear of the listener. A decibel meter can measure the loudness, and spectral analysis of sound can describe the distribution of audio frequencies, supporting the estimation of pitch. If there exists a certain distance between a sound source and a listener, the physical sound is affected by the environmental temperature, the air reference pressure, and the humidity of the air. To achieve a reliable result, a microphone can be used to measure the given amplitude and frequency of the acoustic event at a certain location. Discrete-time Fourier transform (DTFT) can be used to analyze the received waveform and harmonic partials in the frequency domain (Oppenheim 1999). With the use of headphones impact of such environmental factors can be reduced.

4.5 Motion Capture: The Measurement of Movement Parameters

If the auditory information should be based on movement parameters directly, a digital motion capture system can be used to measure movement parameters. For the collection of kinematic movement data, there exists three methods of motion capture: optical, non-optical and marker-less methods. Optical methods implement cameras, markers and optic sources such as visible light and infrared ray (IR) (Kirk et al. 2005). Markers on actor's special suit reflect optical wave from the optic source, and then cameras record movement of markers. From several numbers of cameras, information of marker positions is collected, and human movement is regenerated in 3-D space by a special rendering software. Although management of hidden markers (Silaghi et al. 1998) and a high cost of multiple cameras can be problematic, optical motion capture has been matured with entertainment and computer game industry.

Non-optical methods have been developed with mechanical sensors, magnetic marker systems, and inertial sensors (Brodie et al. 2008). Mechanical methods implements banding angles of wires on human joints, whereas magnetic marker systems measure human movement considering the nearby magnetic field. The inertial sensors (accelerometers, gyroscopes) measure acceleration and angular velocity of body segments as a base for computing movement parameters (relative velocity, position) and finally, human motions and postures. Nevertheless, disadvantages of the technology have been reported. Inertial sensor systems suffer from error accumulation resulted from double integration of acceleration, which provokes position drift effects. Body mounted mechanical sensor systems can affect human motion and limit the range of measurement. Magnetic sensor systems are interfered by magnetic distortion from the ambient metal and electric field.

With cutting-edge image processing technology, marker-less systems are developed, which animates human motions with vision (Moeslund et al. 2006). Dual camera systems can estimate image depth information. The disadvantage of the technique are limitations in terms of hidden areas behind body parts or used objects. Simple markerless systems, therefore, cannot compute the human model in full 3-D space, so it is called 2.5-D motion capture. The dual camera solutions, however, can guarantee simplicity. This makes such technology applicable at home and popular in the computer game industry.

On the one hand, studies on enhancing accuracy and preciseness of IMU were conducted. Fusion of above mentioned technologies have been recently established, compensating for the disadvantages. For example, an inertial measurement units (IMU) includes not only inertial sensors (accelerometer, gyroscope), but also magnetometers (Rios and White 2002), global positioning systems (GPS) (Hellmers et al. 2013), or cameras (Hesch et al. 2014). With combined processing of the data, drift effects of inertial sensors can be reduced. Fusion technology has quickly grown in human kinematic analysis as well as in entertainment-, education- and sports-industry. On the other hand, researchers have focused on reducing the number of sensors. Depending on the particular purpose, one or more parts of the body can be measured: the lower body (Rueterbories et al. 2010), the upper body (Cromwell and Wellmon 2001), the ear (Atallah et al. 2009), and the head (Hwang et al. 2018a, b). For the generation of auditory movement information, different parts of the body have been tracked, as the feet (Reh et al. 2016), or the arms (Schmitz et al. 2018). Additionally, objects handled by humans have been sonified, as recently realized on a joint task performed with a tablet PC (Hwang et al. 2018a, b).

In real-time auditory feedback of movement, it should take less than 100 ms from the motion capture to sound generation (Stein and Meredith 1993) to achieve an integration of the auditory information with current perceptual information of other modality. In this context, IMUs are suitable for real-time movement feedback because the latency from a sensor to a host PC takes only about 30 ms.

4.6 Connecting Motion Capture with Audio Systems

This subsection is to inform about different types of interfaces between motion capture systems and audio systems, and also about the reasons of the latency of data transmission. In a motion capture system, kinematic data can be transmitted to an audio system by wired or wireless connections. When two systems or software solutions are installed on a single computer, communication between two processes can be realized through local host IP address. In this case, the delay can be ignored because both system components are internally wired, which causes only minimal delay. If the required data format (osc, json, MIDI) of the audio software is different from the data-format of the motion capture software, a managing program is needed.

When the audio system and the motion capture system are connected with an external wire, a common hardware interface is needed, such as USB or AV-cable. Concerning a common data format, a number of digital instruments communicate using the "Musical Instruments Digital Interface-Standard" (MIDI), avoiding data transmission distortion or any serious delay. For a wireless connection between two systems, the connection can be established with WiFi or Bluetooth – with a certain risk of data congestion and data loss. The audio data should be created in a common format like osc, json, or MIDI. Nowadays, a PC can be used as an audio system with free software or library, such as CSound, pureData, and a MIDI generator.

4.7 Noise Reduction

This subsection should highlight the importance of noise reduction for the creation of high quality sound. In the sonification system, noise reduction is very important because it might distort feedback effects on listeners and impact the final results. It can make listeners tired or unpleased, even up to damages of the hearing ability. To ensure a pleasant hearing experience, the maximum amplitude of sound should be limited with a proper threshold value. For preciseness of feedback, higher bit-depth is beneficial for the reduction of quantization errors, by increasing the signal-to-noise ratio (SNR) (Bialkowski 1988). In addition, a finite impulse response (FIR) digital filter aids to makes the signal smooth and to reduce noise from hardware or software systems. A digital filter can compensate for dropped sample points during wireless transmission. In conclusion, noise is reduced by higher bit-depth, higher sampling ratio, and FIR filter. In addition, sound engineer should care about the hardware noise and environmental acoustic noise.

4.8 Applications

This subsection introduces example applications that implement artificial auditory information in various situations. Real-time kinematic auditory feedback has been recently applied to enhance motor control and learning (Effenberg 2005; Effenberg et al. 2016). Additional real-time auditory feedback of movement also improves tempo and preciseness of motor learning (Effenberg et al. 2016). If kinematic real-time acoustics is integrated with other current perceptual information, it can support the development of sensorimotor representations obviously without conscious attention, as indicated by Effenberg (2005), Effenberg et al. (2016). Furthermore, auditory feedback can be divided into performance-based auditory feedback (PAF) and effect-based auditory feedback (EAF). Additional PAF supports the quality of movement, whereas the EAF indicates the result of movement (Magill and Anderson 2007; Schmidt and Wrisberg 2008). It is reported that PAF (Weeks and Kordus 1998; Nunes et al. 2014; Sharma et al. 2016) and EAF (Schmidt and Wrisberg 2008; Sharma et al. 2016; Winstein 1991) have beneficial effects on motor learning under different conditions. Artificial real-time auditory feedback can be applied to post-hospital gait rehabilitation (Reh et al. 2016), and can enhance proprioceptive repositioning accuracy of knee-angles (Ghai et al. 2018a, b, c). Above that, also the visual perception of gross-motor movement frequencies can be tuned systematically by concordant kinematic sonification in terms of acceleration or deceleration (Effenberg and Schmitz 2018). Those types of auditory feedback can also contribute to interpersonal coordination (Schmitz and Effenberg 2017, Hwang et al. 2018a, b). Further in future, we might be even able to support human-robot interactions by adding an acoustic profile to robot kinematics to address the action-observation system, as already indicated on a human avatar by Schmitz et al. 2013.

5   Conclusion

The present article describes the potential of artificially generated auditory movement information on perception and action. From different perspectives we scrutinize how auditory information addresses multisensory percepts of complex movements as well as relatively simple movements. Both frameworks refer to the internal model theory, but differ with respect to their focus: Adding artificial movement acoustics to motion perception allows to shape multisensory movement representations in order to learn, relearn or maintain movement competences (Sect. 1). Here, the key mechanisms refer to the shaping of forward models by sound for the initial learning phases. Forward models represent the prediction of sensory/perceptual consequences of actions, which are integrated with perceptual information from different sensory modalities and thereby affect overall motion percepts. The framework described in Sect. 2 predominantly explains how perceptual information is linked to internal models and how effectors can access this information. Key elements are the coupling of sensory modalities and effectors to internal models by default and the emergence of weighting and switch functions through training: Setting of weights and switches determines whether adaptation of internal models is limited to the trained task or whether it generalizes to novel situations and movements.

Whereas these behavioral frameworks refer to the mechanisms of feedback, Sect. 3 highlights the effects of external auditory information on movement competences from neurologic and neuroscientific perspectives. In this section, an emphasis has been laid to suggest the influence of rhythmic auditory cueing on cyclic tasks, for instance, gait. Here, the rhythmic auditory cueing, which is adapted according to the patients' preferred cadence, might allow the development of stable feed-forward predictive models, thereby resulting in an efficient motor planning, and execution. The section concludes that providing external auditory cueing supports the development of perceptuomotor representations, facilitating plasticity and reducing cognitive-motor overload for supporting motor recovery. The section also explains possible neurophysiological mechanisms which might underlie this effect.

Finally, Sect. 4 describes a framework for the generation of movement sounds from the perspective of an engineer. There exists a strong relationship between human perception and the physics of sound. Compared to most mechanical and electrical systems the human physics is characterized by a huge number of degrees of freedom which have to be controlled by a huge number of muscles, being innervated in an adequate way. Even with reference to the internal model-theory this is a very challenging task from the view of an engineer. Future research on computational models of the proposed internal models should be usable as a base also for research about new kinds of efficiency enhanced feedback in the auditory domain.

Acknowledgments. This research was supported by European Commission H2020-FETPROACT-2014 No. 641321.

References

Asanuma, H., Keller, A.: Neuronal mechanisms of motor learning in mammals. NeuroReport **2**(5), 217–224 (1991)

Atallah, L., Aziz, O., Lo, B., Yang, G.Z.: Detecting walking gait impairment with an ear-worn sensor. In: Sixth International Workshop on Wearable and Implantable Body Sensor Networks, BSN 2009, pp. 175–180. IEEE (2009)

Bastian, A.J.: Understanding sensorimotor adaptation and learning for rehabilitation. Curr. Opin. Neurol. **21**(6), 628–633 (2008)

Baumann, O., Greenlee, M.W.: Neural correlates of coherent audiovisual motion perception. Cereb. Cortex **17**, 1433–1443 (2006)

Bernier, P., Gauthier, G., Blouin, J.: Evidence for distinct, differentially adaptable sensorimotor transformations for reaches to visual and proprioceptive targets. J. Neurophysiol. **98**, 1815–1819 (2007)

Berthoz, A., Viaud-Delmon, I.: Multisensory integration in spatial orientation. Curr. Opin. Neurobiol. **9**(6), 708–712 (1999)

Bialkowski, S.E.: Real-time digital filters: infinite impulse response filters. Anal. Chem. **60**(6), 403A–413A (1988)

Bishop, L., Goebl, W.: Beating time: how ensemble musicians' cueing gestures communicate beat position and tempo. Psychol. Music **46**(1), 84–106 (2018). https://doi.org/10.1177/0305735617702971

Bock, O.: Basic principles of sensorimotor adaptation to different distortions with different effectors and movement types: a review and synthesis of behavioral findings. Front. Hum. Neurosci. **7**, 81 (2013)

Bock, O., Schmitz, G.: Transfer of visuomotor adaptation to unpractised hands and sensory modalities. Psychology **4**(12), 1004–1007 (2013). https://doi.org/10.4236/psych.2013.412145

Bock, O., Schmitz, G., Grigorova, V.: Transfer of adaptation between ocular saccades and arm movements. Hum. Mov. Sci. **27**, 383–395 (2008)

Brodie, M., Walmsley, A., Page, W.: Fusion motion capture: a prototype system using inertial measurement units and GPS for the biomechanical analysis of ski racing. Sports Technol. **1**(1), 17–28 (2008)

Buchecker, M., Wegenkittl, S., Stöggl, T., Müller, E.: Unstable footwear affects magnitude and structure of variability in postural control. Motor Control **22**(1), 1–35 (2017)

Calvert, G.A., Spence, C., Stein, B.E. (eds.): The Handbook of Multisensory Processes. MIT Press, Cambridge (2004)

Campos-Sousa, I.S., Campos-Sousa, R.N., Ataide Jr., L., Soares, M.M., Almeida, K.J.: Executive dysfunction and motor symptoms in Parkinson's disease. Arq. Neuropsiquiatr. **68**(2), 246–251 (2010)

Chen, L., Vroomen, Y.: Intersensory binding across space and time: a tutorial review. Atten. Percept. Psychophys. **75**, 790–811 (2013)

Cohen, M.: Changes in auditory localization following prismatic exposure under continuous and terminal visual feedback. Percept. Mot. Skills **38**, 1202 (1974)

Craske, B.: Intermodal transfer of adaptation to displacement. Nature **5037**, 765 (1966)

Cromwell, R., Wellmon, R.: Sagittal plane head stabilization during level walking and ambulation on stairs. Physiotherapy Res. Int. **6**(3), 179–192 (2001)

Cunnington, R., Iansek, R., Bradshaw, J.L., Phillips, J.G.: Movement-related potentials in Parkinson's disease. Brain **118**(4), 935–950 (1995)

D'Ausilio, A., Badino, L., Li, Y., Tokay, S., Craighero, L., Canto, R., Aloimonos, Y., Fadiga, L.: Leadership in orchestra emerges from the causal relationships of movement kinematics. PLoS ONE **7**(5), e35757 (2012)

D'Ausilio, A., Novembre, G., Fadiga, L., Keller, P.E.: What can music tell us about social interaction? Trends Cogn. Sci. **19**(3), 111–114 (2015)

Debaere, F., Wenderoth, N., Sunaert, S., Van Hecke, P., Swinnen, S.P.: Internal vs external generation of movements: differential neural pathways involved in bimanual coordination performed in the presence or absence of augmented visual feedback. Neuroimage **19**(3), 764–776 (2003)

Delignières, D., Torre, K.: Fractal dynamics of human gait: a reassessment of the 1996 data of Hausdorff et al. J. Appl. Physiol. **106**(4), 1272–1279 (2009)

Demos, A.P., Chaffin, R., Begosh, K.T., Daniels, J.R., Marsh, K.L.: Rocking to the beat: effects of music and partner's movements on spontaneous interpersonal coordination. J. Exp. Psychol. Gen. **141**(1), 49 (2012)

Dijkerman, H.C., McIntosh, R.D., Anema, H.A., de Haan, E.H., Kappelle, L.J., Milner, A.D.: Reaching errors in optic ataxia are linked to eye position rather than head or body position. Neuropsychologia **44**(13), 2766–2773 (2006)

Dubus, G., Bresin, R.: A systematic review of mapping strategies for the sonification of physical quantities. PLoS ONE **8**(12), e82491 (2013)

Effenberg, A.O.: Movement sonification: effects on perception and action. IEEE Multimedia **12**(2), 53–59 (2005)

Effenberg, A.O., Fehse, U., Schmitz, G., Krueger, B., Mechling, H.: Movement sonification: effects on motor learning beyond rhythmic adjustments. Front. Neurosci. **10** (2016). https://doi.org/10.3389/fnins.2016.00219

Effenberg, A.O., Schmitz, G., Baumann, F., Rosenhahn, B., Kroeger, D.: Soundscript–supporting the acquisition of character writing by multisensory integration. Open Psychol. J. **8**(3), 230–237 (2015). https://doi.org/10.2174/1874350101508010230

Effenberg, A.O., Schmitz, G.: Acceleration and deceleration at constant speed: systematic modulation of motion perception by kinematic sonification. Ann. N. Y. Acad. Sci. (2018). https://doi.org/10.1111/nyas.13693

El-Tamawy, M.S., Darwish, M.H., Khallaf, M.E.: Effects of augmented proprioceptive cues on the parameters of gait of individuals with Parkinson's disease. Ann. Indian Acad. Neurol. **15**(4), 267–272 (2012)

Felix, R.A., Fridberger, A., Leijon, S., Berrebi, A.S., Magnusson, A.K.: Sound rhythms are encoded by postinhibitory rebound spiking in the superior paraolivary nucleus. J. Neurosci. **31**(35), 12566–12578 (2011)

Flannigan, J.C., Posthuma, R.J., Lombardo, J.N., Murray, C., Cressmann, E.K.: Adaptation to proprioceptive targets following visuomotor adaptation. Exp. Brain Res. **236**, 419–432 (2018)

Ford, M.P., Malone, L.A., Nyikos, I., Yelisetty, R., Bickel, C.S.: Gait training with progressive external auditory cueing in persons with Parkinson's disease. Arch. Phys. Med. Rehabil. **91**(8), 1255–1261 (2010)

Fujioka, T., Trainor, L.J., Large, E.W., Ross, B.: Internalized timing of isochronous sounds is represented in neuromagnetic beta oscillations. J. Neurosci. **32**(5), 1791–1802 (2012)

Galea, J., Miall, R.: Concurrent adaptation to opposing visual displacements during an alternating movement. Exp. Brain Res. **175**, 676–688 (2006)

Ghai, S., Ghai, I., Effenberg, A.O.: Effect of rhythmic auditory cueing on aging gait: a systematic review and meta-analysis. Aging Dis. 131–200 (2017a)

Ghai, S., Ghai, I., Effenberg, A.O.: Effects of dual-task training and dual-tasks on postural stability: a systematic review and meta-analysis. Clin. Interv. Aging **12**, 557–577 (2017b)

Ghai, S., Ghai, I., Effenberg, A.O.: Effect of rhythmic auditory cueing on gait in cerebral palsy: a systematic review and meta-analysis. Neuropsychiatric Dis. Treat. **14**, 43–59 (2018a)

Ghai, S., Ghai, I., Schmitz, G., Effenberg, A.O.: Effect of rhythmic auditory cueing on Parkinsonian gait: a systematic review and meta-analysis. Sci. Rep. **8**(1), 506 (2018b)

Ghai, S., Schmitz, G., Hwang, T.-H., Effenberg, A.O.: Auditory proprioceptive integration: effects of real-time kinematic auditory feedback on knee proprioception. Front. Neurosci. **12**, 142 (2018c)

Gibson, J.J.: The Senses Considered as Perceptual Systems. Houghton-Mifflin, Boston (1966)

Gibson, J.J.: The Ecological Approach to Visual Perception. Houghton-Mifflin, Boston (1979)

Goodman, J.R., Isenhower, R.W., Marsh, K., Schmidt, R., Richardson, M.: The interpersonal phase entrainment of rocking chair movements. In: Heft, H., Marsh, K.L. (eds.) Studies in Perception and Action VIII: Thirteenth International Conference on Perception and Action (2005)

Haar, S., Donchin, O., Dinstein, I.: Dissociating visual and motor directional selectivity using visuomotor adaptation. J. Neurosci. **35**(17), 6813–6821 (2015)

Hameed, S., Ferris, T., Jayaraman, S., Sarter, N.: Using informative peripheral visual and tactile cues to support task and interruption management. Hum. Factors **51**(2), 126–135 (2009)

Harris, C.S.: Adaptation to displaced vision: visual, motor, or proprioceptive change? Science **140**, 812–813 (1963)

Harris, C.S.: Perceptual adaptation to inverted, reversed, and displaced vision. Psychol. Rev. **72**(6), 419–444 (1965)

Hatada, Y., Miall, R.C., Rossetti, Y.: Two waves of a long-lasting aftereffect of prism adaptation measured over 7 days. Exp. Brain Res. **169**(3), 417–426 (2006)

Hausdorff, J.M., Lowenthal, J., Herman, T., Gruendlinger, L., Peretz, C., Giladi, N.: Rhythmic auditory stimulation modulates gait variability in Parkinson's disease. Eur. J. Neurosci. **26**(8), 2369–2375 (2007)

Hausdorff, J.M., Purdon, P.L., Peng, C., Ladin, Z., Wei, J.Y., Goldberger, A.L.: Fractal dynamics of human gait: stability of long-range correlations in stride interval fluctuations. J. Appl. Physiol. **80**(5), 1448–1457 (1996)

Hellmers, H., Norrdine, A., Blankenbach, J., Eichhorn, A.: An IMU/magnetometer-based indoor positioning system using Kalman filtering. In: 2013 International Conference on Indoor Positioning and Indoor Navigation (IPIN), pp. 1–9. IEEE (2013)

Hesch, J.A., Kottas, D.G., Bowman, S.L., Roumeliotis, S.I.: Camera-IMU-based localization: observability analysis and consistency improvement. Int. J. Robot. Res. **33**(1), 182–201 (2014)

Hopkins, K., Kass, S.J., Blalock, L.D., Brill, J.C.: Effectiveness of auditory and tactile crossmodal cues in a dual-task visual and auditory scenario. Ergonomics **60**(5), 692–700 (2017)

Hove, M.J., Suzuki, K., Uchitomi, H., Orimo, S., Miyake, Y.: Interactive rhythmic auditory stimulation reinstates natural 1/f timing in gait of Parkinson's patients. PLoS ONE **7**(3), e32600 (2012)

Hwang, T.H., Reh, J., Effenberg, A.O., Blume, H.: Real-time gait analysis using a single head-worn inertial measurement unit. IEEE Trans. Consum. Electron. **64**(2), 240–248 (2018a). https://doi.org/10.1109/tce.2018.2843289

Hwang, T.-H., et al.: Effect and performance-based auditory feedback on interpersonal coordination. Front. Psychol. **9**, 404 (2018b). https://doi.org/10.3389/fpsyg.2018.00404

Imamizu, H., Shimojo, S.: The locus of visual-motor learning at the task or manipulator level: implications from intermanual transfer. J. Exp. Psychol. Hum. Percept. Perform. **21**, 719–733 (1995)

Imamizu, H., et al.: Explicit contextual information selectively contributes to predictive switching of internal models. Exp. Brain Res. **181**(3), 395–408 (2007)

Johansson, B.B.: Multisensory stimulation in stroke rehabilitation. Front. Hum. Neurosci. **6**, 60 (2012)

Kagerer, F.A., Contreras-Vidal, J.L.: Adaptation of sound localization induced by rotated visual feedback in reaching movements. Exp. Brain Res. **193**(2), 315–321 (2009)

Keller, P.E., Knoblich, G., Repp, B.H.: Pianists duet better when they play with themselves: on the possible role of action simulation in synchronization. Conscious. Cogn. **16**(1), 102–111 (2007)

Keller, P.E., Novembre, G., Hove, M.J.: Rhythm in joint action: psychological and neurophysiological mechanisms for real-time interpersonal coordination. Philos. Trans. Roy. Soc. B: Biol. Sci. **369**(1658), 20130394 (2014)

Keysers, C., Kohler, E., Umilta, M.A., Nanetti, L., Fogassi, L., Gallese, V.: Audiovisual mirror neurons and action recognition. Exp. Brain Res. **153**, 628–636 (2003)

Khoramshahi, M., Shukla, A., Raffard, S., Bardy, B.G., Billard, A.: Role of gaze cues in interpersonal motor coordination: towards higher affiliation in human-robot interaction. PLoS ONE **11**(6), e0156874 (2016). https://doi.org/10.1371/journal.pone.0156874

Kirk, A.G., O'Brien, J.F., Forsyth, D.A.: Skeletal parameter estimation from optical motion capture data. In: IEEE Computer Society Conference on Computer Vision and Pattern Recognition, CVPR 2005, vol. 2, pp. 782–788. IEEE (2005)

Knoblich, G., Butterfill, S., Sebanz, N.: Psychological research on joint action: theory and data. In: Psychology of Learning and Motivation-Advances in Research and Theory, vol. 54, p. 59 (2011)

Kohler, E., Keysers, C., Umilta, M.A., Fogassi, L., Gallese, V., Rizzolati, G.: Hearing sounds, understanding actions: action representation in mirror neurons. Science **297**, 846–848 (2002)

Kohler, I.: Über Aufbau und Wandlungen der Wahrnehmungswelt, insbesondere über bedingte Empfindungen.': In: Kommission bei RM Rohrer (1951)

Kohler, I.: The formation and transformation of the perceptual world. Psychological Issues (1963)

Lacquaniti, F., et al.: Multisensory integration and internal models for sensing gravity effects in primates. In: BioMed Research International (2014)

Lahav, A., Saltzman, E., Schlaug, G.: Action representation of sound: audiomotor recognition network while listening to newly acquired actions. J. Neurosci. **27**(2), 308–314 (2007)

Lee, J.Y., Schweighofer, N.: Dual adaptation supports a parallel architecture of motor memory. J. Neurosci. **29**(33), 10396–10404 (2009)

Lewald, J.M., Getzmann, S.: Horizontal and vertical effects of eye-position on sound localization. Hear. Res. **213**, 99–106 (2006)

Lohnes, C.A., Earhart, G.M.: The impact of attentional, auditory, and combined cues on walking during single and cognitive dual tasks in Parkinson disease. Gait Posture **33**(3), 478–483 (2011)

Magescas, F., Prablanc, C.: Automatic drive of limb motor plasticity. J. Cogn. Neurosci. **18**(1), 75–83 (2006)

Magill, R.A., Anderson, D.I.: Motor Learning and Control: Concepts and Applications, vol. 11. McGraw-Hill, New York (2007)

Martin, L.M., Newman, C.V.: Simultaneous right- and left-hand adaptation in opposite lateral directions following bidirectional optical displacement. Bull. Psychon. Soc. **16**(6), 432–434 (1980)

Michel, C., Pisella, L., Prablanc, C., Rode, G., Rossetti, Y.: Enhancing visuomotor adaptation by reducing error signals: single-step (Aware) versus multiplestep (Unaware) exposure to wedge prisms. J. Cogn. Neurosci. **19**(2), 341–350 (2007)

Mikaelian, H.: Lack of bilateral generalization of adaptation to auditory rearrangement. Percept. Psychophys. **11**(3), 222–224 (1972)

Mikaelian, H.: Adaptation to displaced hearing: a nonproprioceptive change. J. Exp. Psychol. **103**, 326–330 (1974)

Miyata, K., Varlet, M., Miura, A., Kudo, K., Keller, P.E.: Modulation of individual auditory-motor coordination dynamics through interpersonal visual coupling. Sci. Rep. **7**, 16220 (2017). https://doi.org/10.1038/s41598-017-16151-5

Moeslund, T.B., Hilton, A., Krueger, V.: A survey of advances in vision-based human motion capture and analysis. Comput. Vis. Image Underst. **104**(2–3), 90–126 (2006)

Morton, S.M., Bastian, A.J.: Prism adaptation during walking generalizes to reaching and requires the cerebellum. J. Neurosci. **92**, 2497–2509 (2004)

Mueller, G., Moeser, M. (eds.): Handbook of Engineering Acoustics. Springer Science and Business Media, Berlin (2012). https://doi.org/10.1007/978-3-540-69460-1

Murgia, M., et al.: Ecological sounds affect breath duration more than artificial sounds. Psychol. Res. **80**(1), 76–81 (2016)

Nieuwboer, A., et al.: The short-term effects of different cueing modalities on turn speed in people with Parkinson's disease. Neurorehabil. Neural Repair **23**(8), 831–836 (2009)

Nieuwboer, A., et al.: Cueing training in the home improves gait-related mobility in Parkinson's disease: the RESCUE trial. J. Neurol. Neurosurg. Psychiatry **78**(2), 134–140 (2007)

Nombela, C., Hughes, L.E., Owen, A.M., Grahn, J.A.: Into the groove: can rhythm influence Parkinson's disease? Neurosci. Biobehav. Rev. **37**(10), 2564–2570 (2013)

Nunes, M.E., Souza, M.G., Basso, L., Monteiro, C., Corrêa, U.C., Santos, S.: Frequency of provision of knowledge of performance on skill acquisition in older persons. Front. Psychol. **5**, 1454 (2014)

Oostwoud Wijdenes, L., Medendorp, W.P.: State estimation for early feedback responses in reaching: intramodal or multimodal? Front. Integr. Neurosci. **11**, 38 (2017). https://doi.org/10.3389/fnint.2017.00038

Oppenheim, A.V.: Discrete-Time Signal Processing. Pearson Education India, Bangalore (1999)

Oscari, F., Secoli, R., Avanzini, F., Rosati, G., Reinkensmeyer, D.J.: Substituting auditory for visual feedback to adapt to altered dynamic and kinematic environments during reaching. Exp. Brain Res. **221**, 33–41 (2012)

Oullier, O., De Guzman, G.C., Jantzen, K.J., Lagarde, J., Scott Kelso, J.: Social coordination dynamics: measuring human bonding. Soc. Neurosci. **3**(2), 178–192 (2008)

Prablanc, C., Tzavaras, A., Jeannerod, M.: Adaptation of the two arms to opposite prism displacements. Q. J. Exp. Psychol. **27**(4), 667–671 (1975)

Rinehart, N.J., Bellgrove, M.A., Tonge, B.J., Brereton, A.V., Howells-Rankin, D., Bradshaw, J.L.: An examination of movement kinematics in young people with high-functioning autism and Asperger's disorder: further evidence for a motor planning deficit. J. Autism Dev. Disord. **36**(6), 757–767 (2006)

Reh, J., Hwang, T.H., Michalke, V., Effenberg, A.O.: Instruction and real-time sonification for gait rehabilitation after unilateral hip arthroplasty. In: 11th Joint Conference on Motor Control Learning Biomechanics Training, pp. 1–2. DVS (2016)

Rios, J.A., White, E.: Fusion filter algorithm enhancements for a MEMS GPS/IMU, pp. 1–12. Crossbow Technology, Inc. (2002)

Rueterbories, J., Spaich, E.G., Larsen, B., Andersen, O.K.: Methods for gait event detection and analysis in ambulatory systems. Med. Eng. Phys. 32(6), 545–552 (2010)

Sainburg, R., Wang, J.: Interlimb transfer of visuomotor rotations: independence of direction and final position information. Exp. Brain Res. 145, 437–447 (2002)

Schaefer, R.S.: Auditory rhythmic cueing in movement rehabilitation: findings and possible mechanisms. Philos. Trans. Roy. Soc. B: Biol. Sci. 369, 20130402 (2014)

Schmitz, G., Bock, O.: Properties of intermodal transfer after dual visuo- and auditory-motor adaptation. Hum. Mov. Sci. 55, 108–120 (2017)

Schmitz, G.: Visuo- und Audiomotorische Adaptation. Hofmann-Verlag, Schorndorf (2014). ISBN 978-3-7780-4850-4

Schmitz, G.: Interference between adaptation to double steps and adaptation to rotated feedback in spite of differences in directional selectivity. Exp. Brain Res. 234, 1491–1504 (2016). https://doi.org/10.1007/s00221-016-4559-y

Schmitz, G., Effenberg, A.O.: Sound joint actions in rowing and swimming. In: Meyer, C., Wedelstaedt, U.V. (eds.) Moving Bodies in Interaction - Interacting Bodies in Motion. John Benjamins Publishing Company, Amsterdam (2016)

Schmitz, G., Bergmann, J., Effenberg, A.O., Krewer, C., Hwang, T.H., Mueller, F.: Movement sonification in stroke rehabilitation. Front. Neurol. 9, 389 (2018)

Schmitz, G., Bock, O.: A comparison of sensorimotor adaptation in the visual and in the auditory modality. PLoS ONE 9(9), e107834 (2014)

Schmitz, G., Effenberg, A.O.: Perceptual effects of auditory information about own and other movements. In: 18th International Conference on Auditory Display, Atlanta, GA, USA (2012)

Schmitz, G., Effenberg, A.O.: Schlagmann 2.0 – Bewegungsakustische Dimensionen interpersonaler Koordination im Mannschaftssport. Ger. J. Exerc. Sport Res. 47(3), 232–245 (2017)

Schmitz, G., Grigorova, V.: Alternating adaptation of eye and hand movements to opposite directed double steps. J. Mot. Behav. 49(3), 255–264 (2017). https://doi.org/10.1080/00222895.2016.1191419

Schmitz, G., Kroeger, D., Effenberg, A.O.: A mobile sonification system for stroke rehabilitation. In: The 20th International Conference on Auditory Display, New York (2014)

Schmitz, G., et al.: Observation of sonified movements engages a basal ganglia frontocortical network. BMC Neurosci. 14, 32 (2013). https://doi.org/10.1186/1471-2202-14-32

Sebanz, N., Knoblich, G.: Prediction in joint action: what, when, and where. Top. Cogn. Sci. 1(2), 353–367 (2009)

Sebanz, N., Bekkering, H., Knoblich, G.: Joint action: bodies and minds moving together. Trends Cogn. Sci. 10(2), 70–76 (2006)

Seitz, A.R., Kim, R., Shams, L.: Sound facilitates visual learning. Curr. Biol. 16(14), 1422–1427 (2006)

Sengpielaudio homepage: http://www.sengpielaudio.com/calculator-notenames.htm

Shadmehr, R., Smith, R.A., Krakauer, J.W.: Error correction, sensory prediction, and adaptation in motor control. Ann. Rev. Neurosci. 33, 89–108 (2010)

Shams, L., Seitz, A.R.: Benefits of multisensory learning. Trends Cogn. Sci. 12(11), 411–417 (2008)

Sharma, D.A., Chevidikunnan, M.F., Khan, F.R., Gaowgzeh, R.A.: Effectiveness of knowledge of result and knowledge of performance in the learning of a skilled motor activity by healthy young adults. J. Phys. Ther. Sci. **28**(5), 1482–1486 (2016)

Silaghi, M.-C., Plänkers, R., Boulic, R., Fua, P., Thalmann, D.: Local and global skeleton fitting techniques for optical motion capture. In: Magnenat-Thalmann, N., Thalmann, D. (eds.) CAPTECH 1998. LNCS (LNAI), vol. 1537, pp. 26–40. Springer, Heidelberg (1998). https://doi.org/10.1007/3-540-49384-0_3

Smith, M.A., Ghazizadeh, A., Shadmehr, R.: Interacting adaptive processes with different timescales underlie short-term motor learning. PLoS Biol. **4**(6), e179 (2006). https://doi.org/10.1371/journal.pbio.0040179

Spence, C.: Cross-modal perceptual organization. In: Wagemans, J. (ed.) The Oxford Handbook of Perceptual Organization. Oxford University Press, Oxford (2015)

Spence, C., Driver, J. (eds.): Crossmodal Space and Crossmodal Attention. Oxford University Press, Oxford (2004)

Stein, B.E., Meredith, M.A.: The Merging of the Senses. MIT Press, Cambridge (1993)

Stein, B.E., Stanford, T.R.: Multisensory integration: current issues from the perspective of the single neuron. Nat. Rev. Neurosci. **9**(4), 255–266 (2008)

Stoffregen, T.A., Bardy, B.G.: On specification and the senses. Behav. Brain Sci. **24**, 195–213 (2001). Discussion 213-161

Suh, J.H., et al.: Effect of rhythmic auditory stimulation on gait and balance in hemiplegic stroke patients. NeuroRehabilitation **34**(1), 193–199 (2014)

Tagliabue, M., McIntyre, J.: A modular theory of multisensory integration for motor control. Front. Comput. Neurosci. **8**, 1 (2014). https://doi.org/10.3389/fncom.2014.00001

Tecchio, F., Salustri, C., Thaut, M.H., Pasqualetti, P., Rossini, P.: Conscious and preconscious adaptation to rhythmic auditory stimuli: a magnetoencephalographic study of human brain responses. Exp. Brain Res. **135**(2), 222–230 (2000)

Thaut, M.H.: Neural basis of rhythmic timing networks in the human brain. Ann. N. Y. Acad. Sci. **999**(1), 364–373 (2003)

Thaut, M.H.: Rhythm, Music, and the Brain: Scientific Foundations and Clinical Applications, vol. 7. Routledge, Abingdon (2005)

Thaut, M.H., et al.: Neurologic music therapy improves executive function and emotional adjustment in traumatic brain injury rehabilitation. Ann. N. Y. Acad. Sci. **1169**(1), 406–416 (2009)

Thaut, M.H., Leins, A.K., Rice, R.R., Argstatter, H., Kenyon, G.P., McIntosh, G.C., Fetter, M., et al.: Rhythmic auditory stimulation improves gait more than NDT/Bobath training in near-ambulatory patients early poststroke: a single-blind, randomized trial. Neurorehabil. Neural Repair **21**(5), 455–459 (2007)

Thaut, M., Schleiffers, S., Davis, W.: Analysis of EMG activity in biceps and triceps muscle in an upper extremity gross motor task under the influence of auditory rhythm. J. Music Ther. **28**(2), 64–88 (1991)

Tierney, A., Kraus, N.: The ability to move to a beat is linked to the consistency of neural responses to sound. J. Neurosci. **33**(38), 14981–14988 (2013)

Torres, E.B., Heilman, K.M., Poizner, H.: Impaired endogenously evoked automated reaching in Parkinson's disease. J. Neurosci. **31**(49), 17848–17863 (2011)

Vesper, C., Butterfill, S., Knoblich, G., Sebanz, N.: A minimal architecture for joint action. Neural Netw. **23**(8), 998–1003 (2010)

Weeks, D.L., Kordus, R.N.: Relative frequency of knowledge of performance and motor skill learning. Res. Q. Exerc. Sport **69**(3), 224–230 (1998)

Welch, R.B.: Perceptual Modification. Adapting to Altered Sensory Environments. Academic Press, Cambridge (1978)

Whitall, J., et al.: Bilateral and unilateral arm training improve motor function through differing neuroplastic mechanisms a single-blinded randomized controlled trial. Neurorehabil. Neural Repair 25(2), 118–129 (2011)

Wigmore, V., Tong, C., Flanagan, J.R.: Visuomotor rotations of varying size and direction compete for single internal model in working memory. J. Exp. Psychol. Hum. Percept. Perform. 28, 447–457 (2002)

Winstein, C.J.: Knowledge of results and motor learning—implications for physical therapy. Phys. Ther. 71(2), 140–149 (1991)

Wolpert, D.M., Kawato, M.: Multiple paired forward and inverse models for motor control. Neural Netw. 11(7–8), 1317–1329 (1998)

Wolpert, D.M., Diedrichsen, J., Flanagan, J.R.: Principles of sensorimotor learning. Nat. Rev. Neurosci. 12, 739–751 (2011)

Wolpert, D.M., Ghahramani, Z., Jordan, M.I.: An internal model for sensorimotor integration. Science 269, 1880–1882 (1995)

Young, W.R., Rodger, M.W., Craig, C.M.: Auditory observation of stepping actions can cue both spatial and temporal components of gait in Parkinson's disease patients. Neuropsychologia 57, 140–153 (2014)

Zmigrod, S., Hommel, B.: Feature Integration across multimodal perception and action: a review. Multisensory Res. 26, 143–157 (2013)

Music and Musical Sonification for the Rehabilitation of Parkinsonian Dysgraphia: Conceptual Framework

Lauriane Véron-Delor[1,2], Serge Pinto[2], Alexandre Eusebio[3],
Jean-Luc Velay[1], and Jérémy Danna[1(✉)]

[1] Aix Marseille Univ, CNRS, LNC, Marseille, France
{lauriane.veron-delor,jean-luc.velay,
jeremy.danna}@univ-amu.fr
[2] Aix Marseille Univ, CNRS, LPL, Aix-en-Provence, France
serge.pinto@univ-amu.fr
[3] Aix Marseille Univ, CNRS, INT, Marseille, France
alexandre.eusebio@univ-amu.fr

Abstract. Music has been shown to enhance motor control in patients with Parkinson's disease (PD). Notably, musical rhythm is perceived as an external auditory cue that helps PD patients to better control movements. The rationale of such effects is that motor control based on auditory guidance would activate a compensatory brain network that minimizes the recruitment of the defective pathway involving the basal ganglia. Would associating music to movement improve its perception and control in PD? Musical sonification consists in modifying in real-time the playback of a preselected music according to some movement parameters. The validation of such a method is underway for handwriting in PD patients. When confirmed, this study will strengthen the clinical interest of musical sonification in motor control and (re)learning in PD.

Keywords: Movement sonification · Cueing · Feedback · Handwriting
Parkinson's disease

1 Introduction: External Cueing and Feedback as Part of Rehabilitation in Parkinson's Disease

Parkinson's disease (PD) is the second most common neurodegenerative disorder after Alzheimer's disease. It is caused by the loss of dopaminergic neurons in the *pars compacta* of the *substantia nigra* and other neurological systems, leading to a set of motor and non-motor symptoms [1]. PD symptoms are managed with medication (e.g., L-Dopa, dopaminergic agonists) and/or neurosurgical interventions, including mainly deep brain stimulation. Nevertheless, limitations of such treatments to relieve motor disturbances have led to investigate non-pharmacological additional methods based on assisted motor rehabilitation. Among the various methods of motor rehabilitation, there is a growing interest in applying external cues and/or supplementary feedback to supplement drugs-based approaches.

© Springer Nature Switzerland AG 2018
M. Aramaki et al. (Eds.): CMMR 2017, LNCS 11265, pp. 312–326, 2018.
https://doi.org/10.1007/978-3-030-01692-0_21

Gait (for reviews, see [2, 3]), and, to a lesser extent, handwriting (for a review, see [4]) were particularly brought into focus. The present chapter aims at reporting and questioning the studies carried out in the last decade and for which the effect of rehabilitation based on feedback or on auditory cueing was evaluated in Parkinsonian walking or handwriting (see Table 1).

Table 1. Auditory cueing- or feedback-based studies on gait, tapping, and writing in PD.

Ref	Subjects	Conditions	Data analysis	Main results
Auditory cueing-based rehabilitation studies				
[5]	15 PD ON & 20 CTL	*12 trainings* Individualised RAS at 3 tempos, embedded in a musical structure	BAASTA; Stride length	Improvement in synchronization and hand tapping after training
[6]	22 PD ON in 2 groups	*39 trainings* Individualised music vs. no music	Gait velocity; Stride time; Stride length; Cadence	Improvement of gait velocity, stride time and cadence following music training
[7]	12 PD OFF	*Two tasks: walking then walking + carrying a cup full of water, under 4 conditions:* No cue vs. Visual (transverse strips) vs. Auditory (metronome) vs. visual and auditory cues	Freezing number and duration; Cadence; Gait velocity; Stride length	Improvement of cadence and stride length with visual and dual cues in both tasks Improvement of FOG with all types of cues in both tasks
[8]	14 PD ON & 20 CTL	*12 trainings* - Individualised RAS at 2 tempos, embedded in a musical structure	BAASTA; Gait velocity; Stride length; Cadence; Synchronization variability	Improvement of PD gait parameters (velocity and stride length) directly and 1 month after training
[9]	15 PD ON	*Two tasks (digital tapping + foot tapping) under 2 conditions:* No cue vs. auditory cue (metronome)	Freezing duration; Tapping frequency; Tapping amplitude	Metronome decreased the frequency and the incidence of freezing, and improved both digital and foot tapping frequency
[10]	58 PD ON in 3 groups	*60 dance lessons* Tango vs. Waltz/foxtrot vs. Nothing	Balance; Gait velocity; Forward and backward walking;	Improvement in balance, gait velocity and backward walking in both dance groups Greater improvement with tango

(continued)

Table 1. (*continued*)

Ref	Subjects	Conditions	Data analysis	Main results
[11]	75 PD ON in 4 groups	*40 dance lessons* Tango vs. Waltz/foxtrot vs. Tai Chi vs. Nothing	HRQoL	Improvement in HRQoL only after tango
[12]	20 PD ON in 2 groups	*3 trainings* SDTT vs. RAC	Gait velocity; Cadence; Balance; HRQoL	RAC improved gait speed and SDTT improved balance Retention effects founded 3-month after both RAC and SDTT training
[13]	47 PD ON in 2 groups	*8 days training* RAS vs. No cue	FOG number; Gait velocity; Stride length	Improvement of all gait parameters after RAS training
[14]	25 PD ON (with vs. without FOG) & 10 CTL	*Walking session under 3 conditions*: Visual (transverse strips) vs. Auditory (metronome) vs. No cue	FOG number; Step number	Improvement in gait and FOG number with visual cue in PD FOG only No effect of auditory cue in PD FOG Better improvement in gait with auditory cues for PD without FOG than for PD FOG
[15]	10 PD OFF	*Walking session under 2 conditions*: No cue vs. RAS (metronome)	Gait velocity; Stride length; Cadence	Improvement in all gait parameters after RAS training
[16]	9 PD ON	*Walking session under 3 conditions*: No cue vs. CUET vs. CUEST	Gait velocity and variability; Stride amplitude; Cadence	Improvement of gait velocity, stride amplitude and cadence with both CUET and CUEST, the latter being the most effective
[17]	10 PD ON & 10 CTL	*3 walking sessions:* *Session 1 under 4 conditions*: Verbal instruction vs. verbal instruction + metronome vs. HFGS vs. HFGS + verbal instruction *Session 2 under 4 conditions*: HFGS vs. HFGS + verbal instruction vs. synthesized footstep sounds vs. synthesized footstep	Stride length and variability; Velocity; Cadence; Gait variability	Decrease of stride length variability in PD patients during session with HFGS and HFGS + verbal instruction Improvement in stride length in all conditions except in synthesized sounds condition PD patients fail to adapt to the synthesized footstep sounds

(*continued*)

Table 1. (*continued*)

Ref	Subjects	Conditions	Data analysis	Main results
		sounds + verbal instruction		Performances are better during cueing than during imagery
		Session 3 under 4 conditions: HFGS vs. mental imagery of HFGS vs. synthesized footstep sounds vs. mental imagery of synthesized footstep sounds		Performances are better during mental imagery of HFGS than during mental imagery of synthesized footstep sounds
[18]	19 PD OFF (with vs. without FOG)	*Walking session under 4 conditions:* Healthy footstep on a corridor sounds vs. metronome vs. healthy footstep on gravel sounds vs. synthesized footstep sound	Step time variability; Swing time variability; Rhythmicity; Asymmetry	No cueing effect in PD without FOG Improvement in temporal regularity in PD with FOG in forth conditions
Auditory feedback-based rehabilitation studies				
[19]	16 PD ON	*Walking session:* Clicking sound in response to every step	Cadence; stride length	Improvement in speed and stride length during and after training with FB
[20]	42 PD ON (with vs. without FB)	*20 trainings with visual movement FB, visual color target FB and auditory target FB*	Clinical motor evaluations	Improvement in balance during and 1 month after experimental training No change in without FB group
Auditory cueing- and feedback-based rehabilitation studies				
[21]	28 PD ON (with vs. without FOG)	*6 weeks trainings under 4 conditions:* RAS vs. IC vs. IF vs. No cue/FB	Gait deviations	Gait deviations decrease with RAS in PD with FOG
[22]	11 PD ON & 11 CTL & 11 CTL young	*Walking session under 4 conditions:* no cue vs. auditory cue vs. verbal instruction vs. COM (auditory cue and verbal instruction)	Gait velocity; Stride length; Cadence	Improvement of gait velocity and stride length with verbal feedback and COM
[23]	15 PD ON & 15 CTL & 15 CTL young	*Unimanual and bimanual drawing sessions under 3 conditions:* visual cue vs. auditory FB vs. verbal FB	Amplitude; Amplitude variability; Coordination; Precision	Improvement of coordination and amplitude variability with both auditory and verbal feedback

(*continued*)

Table 1. (*continued*)

Ref	Subjects	Conditions	Data analysis	Main results
[24]	206 PD ON	*4 weeks treadmill training with visual and auditory FB and cues*	Steps length; Cadence; Coefficient of variance of both steps	Improvement of step length and variability, and cadence

Abbreviations: PD: Individuals with PD; ON: on-medication; OFF: off-medication; CTL: Control subject; RAS: Rhythmic auditory stimulation; BAASTA: Battery for the assessment of auditory sensorimotor and timing abilities, including timing perception, discrimination and synchronization; HRQoL: Health related quality of life; SDTT: Speed-dependent treadmill training; RAC: Rhythmic auditory cue, individualised music playlist and metronome; FOG: Freezing of gait; CUET: Cue temporal, metronome with temporal instruction "As you walk try to step in time to the beat"; CUEST: Cue spatiotemporal, metronome with spatiotemporal instruction "As you walk try to take a big step in time to the beat"; HFGS: Healthy footstep on gravel sounds; IC: Intelligent cueing (auditory rhythm signal when strides deviated more than 5% from the reference cadence); IF Intelligent feedback (verbal instruction to speeding or slowing); FB: Feedback; COM: Combined information auditory cue and verbal instruction.

The organization and production of movement involves the integration of sensory information, which can be considered as basic feedback. Basic feedback informs about both the environment and the current state of the body to determine the appropriate set of muscle forces to generate the desired movement. Thus, a deficit in the processing of basic feedback affects the initiation of movements. Vision and/or audition are the most commonly used sensory modalities to support initiation and control of movement. They are differentially specialized to encode information from the environment and our body, visual information being more relevant for spatial processing, and auditory information for temporal processing [25].

On the one hand, supplementary feedback enriches the perception of self-performance during or after movement production, mainly based on internal expectations/representations. Supplementary feedback can provide information about the outcomes of an action with respect to the environmental goal or about the process, i.e. the movement produced. The terms of "knowledge of results" and "knowledge of performance" are respectively employed [26]. On the other hand, external cues yield a point of reference to guide movements execution [27]. In the field of motor rehabilitation with PD patients, the use of auditory cues has been largely preferred, especially for improving gait (e.g., [2, 28]) and speech (e.g., [29, 30]) disorders. Such enthusiasm is certainly justified by the natural and spontaneous tendency in humans to synchronize action with rhythm [31]. Very promising, and sometimes unexpected, effects have been observed with the use of rhythmic auditory stimulation (RAS; see Table 1 – e.g., [8]). PD patients are tempted to couple their steps to RAS provided by a metronome or an amplified beat of a music. Some researches reveal improvements with RAS in gait velocity and stride length, sometimes with long-term benefits [8, 13]. Music itself carries an intrinsic rhythm that plays the role of an external cue (e.g., [32]), as a metronome, guiding movements. Moreover, music contributes to something more than simple metronome rhythm: emotional aspects are conveyed with the melody, especially when the music is familiar. Music involves both cognitive and emotional processing, which can be used to carry over effects (e.g., mental singing – [33]). In healthy individuals, Wittwer and colleagues [34] have compared effects of rhythmic music and metronome as external cuing on gait. They showed that music might be more efficient than the metronome to improve the velocity and cadence of gait, due to emotional aspects and motivation ensuing by melody. In individuals with PD, it has been shown that continuous sounds, like music, lead to better gait fluency than a simple metronome (see Table 1, [18]).

2 Why Does Supplementary Feedback or External Cueing Facilitate Motor (Re)Learning for Individuals with PD?

Movement rehabilitation in PD aims at improving motor control and coordination by either strengthening pre-existing pathways [27] or creating alternative circuits bypassing the basal ganglia. Motor learning is possible in individuals with PD (for a review, see [4]). Such concept raises the question of brain neuroplasticity. Neuroplasticity encompasses the ability for healthy neural networks to form new synapses in order to bypass and reorganize the damaged network [27]. Any functional motor rehabilitation is based on this phenomenon and may facilitate neurological recovery [35]. Neuroplasticity is stimulated by frequent motor or cognitive activities. Nevertheless, it is slowed down in individuals with PD compared to healthy subjects. This must be taken into account in the rehabilitation duration [4].

Distinct phases, consolidation, automatization, and retention, are identified in the process of motor learning. Doyon and Benali [36] revisited a model describing the brain plasticity during motor learning. According to this model, a clear distinction is proposed between motor sequence learning (MSL), which characterizes the process by which practice turns a sequence of actions into a behaviour, and motor adaptation (MA), which is required in response to environmental changes. Motor learning goes along with a decrease of cortical activity, especially in prefrontal and parietal regions that are involved in attentional processing of sensory information. At the same time, the activation of the cerebellum and basal ganglia increase according to the type of motor task, MA and MSL, respectively [37].

PD affects the functioning of the striato-thalamo-cortical loop (Fig. 1, dotted arrows), particularly involved in the control of learned movements. Two possibilities can be proposed: On the one hand, the injured network (Fig. 1, black arrows) could be restored similarly as pharmacological treatments [38]. On the other hand, a compensatory neural mechanism could be used to bypass the damaged pathway: The cerebello-thalamo-cortical loop (Fig. 1, grey arrows) is involved in the control of movements in MA and seems preserved in PD, at least in the early stages of PD [4, 39].

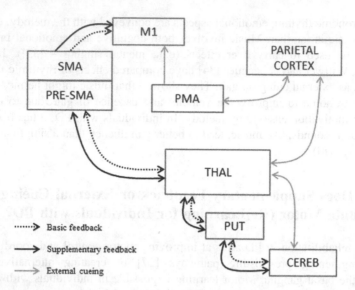

Fig. 1. Motor control loops: two options to restore efficient motor control in PD patients (adapted from [4, 39]). SMA: Supplementary motor area; PRE-SMA: Pre-supplementary motor area; M1: Primary motor area; PMA: Premotor area; THAL: Thalamus; PUT: Putamen (one of the basal ganglia); CEREB: Cerebellum.

2.1   Applying Supplementary Feedback in PD Patients "to Restore the Pathway"

A deficit of sensory integration in PD has been documented by several studies [40–42]. Regarding vision, it has been shown that visual withdrawal leads individuals with PD to increase their movement amplitude [43] and to reduce their velocity [44]. Such effects were not observed in healthy subjects. Longstaff and colleagues [45] proposed that moving slower would be a strategy of PD patients to improve online control, i.e. to be more feedback-dependent [42]. In healthy subjects, the absence of visual feedback can be compensated by kinaesthetic feedback. In PD patients, kinaesthetic feedback does not inform correctly about the hand or upper limb position and movement [42]. Therefore, the absence of visual feedback cannot be fully compensated in PD patients.

Beyond informational processing, applying supplementary feedback in a learning or rehabilitation protocol affects motivation. For example, providing learners with feedback after correct trials, compared with after incorrect trials, results in more effective learning [46]. Interestingly, basal ganglia are critical for supporting learning that is driven by feedback and is motivated by rewards [47]. Foerde and Shohamy [48] reported that the midbrain dopamine system supports feedback-dependent learning processes essential for predicting outcomes. Therefore, applying a real-time supplementary feedback would be relevant for restoring the reward network in PD patients.

2.2   Applying External Cueing in PD Patients "to Hit Another Pathway"

Motor control and coordination are managed by both basal ganglia and cerebellum. Thus, promoting the cerebellum activation to bypass the basal ganglia appears as a relevant strategy of rehabilitation. Nombela and colleagues [39] have gathered the findings of various neuroimaging studies in which the auditory external cueing on PD gait was evaluated. Their review provides an accurate description of how music influences motor mechanisms. RAS in music or metronome can act as an external "timer" guiding the execution of the movement and bypassing the dysfunction in striato-thalamo-cortical loop [39, 49]. When the movement is performed with an external cueing, the online control of movements becomes dependent to this supplementary environmental constraint: the task tends to become similar to a MA task.

3   Effects on Parkinsonian Dysgraphia

Handwriting is a complex motor activity that requires a great level of expertise. Interestingly, handwriting is particularly altered by PD [50–52]. Handwriting disorders in PD are mainly known from the observation of an abnormal reduction in writing size so-called micrographia [53]. Micrographia affects about 50% of individuals with PD. According to Van Gemmert et al. [54], micrographia would result from an inability to maintain a constant force during handwriting, as well as to synchronize wrist and finger movements. Consequently, beyond micrographia, other kinematic and dynamic variables (velocity, dysfluency, i.e. abnormal velocity fluctuations, etc.) would be more systematically altered in Parkinsonian handwriting. Therefore, the term *Parkinsonian dysgraphia* has been proposed [55, 56].

What are the causes of PD dysgraphia? On the basis of different models of handwriting, such as the kinematic model [57] or the neural model of handwriting [58], the "stroke" – the basic motor unit of handwriting – results from the coordinated activity of the muscular system coded as a velocity vector. Interestingly, in these models, only the orientation and amplitude of each velocity vector is processed in the central nervous system and this process is precisely achieved in basal ganglia that are affected in PD (e.g., [59]). Another argument concerns the nature of the task that changes in the course of learning. In beginners, handwriting is like a MA task: they must correct the ongoing movements of the pen thanks to the visual inspection of the generated written trace. Once the characters are learned, the underlying motor pattern is automatized, and handwriting becomes mainly a sequential task in which the writers must check the very rapid succession of the strokes composing a character and the correct sequences of characters composing a word. According to Doyon and Benali's model [36], this transition relative to the nature of the task would be associated with a switch from the cortico-cerebellar loop, more activated at the early stage of learning, to the cortico-striatal loop, more activated at the latest stage. This assumption was investigated and partially validated in a combined fMRI and kinematic study conducted in healthy adults during a fast-learning of a graphomotor sequence [60]. If confirmed, this may explain both why handwriting is altered in individuals with PD, and why external cueing or supplementary feedback may be particularly relevant for helping them to better control their handwriting.

3.1 The Classical Method of Handwriting Rehabilitation for PD Patients

In 1972, McLennan [53] suggested that the mere presence of parallel lines could allow individuals with PD to maintain their writing size, thus improving micrographia. This method was tested and validated several times in graphomotor tasks [23, 61]. Other visual cues, as target points [62] or grid lines [63], have been tested and the authors have shown that they improve both the writing size and width. Furthermore, these cues allow the patients to maintain a correct size during the entire task [61, 63]. Another method was tested with a graphic tablet [64]. The written trace was displayed in real-time on a screen in front of the writers and their hand and pen were hidden in such a way that participants had visual feedback about the written trace only. This feedback was either normal, smaller, or larger than the actual handwriting. The authors observed that individuals with PD succeed in the visuo-motor adaptation by changing the amplitude of their writing movement when the visual feedback was distorted. However, such effects were present when the hand was hidden only and disappeared when the hand was not hidden [65]. Beyond improvements of the spatial feature of handwriting, Nieuwboer and colleagues also demonstrated that the freezing of the upper limb was improved by visual cueing in a drawing task [61].

When comparing the effects of visual cueing and auditory feedback individuals with PD performed better in a graphomotor task when they received an auditory feedback based on verbal instructions or on a spatial sonification than when they realized the task with the presence of visual cues solely [23]. However, we cannot conclude whether the advantage of applying auditory feedback rather than visual cueing results from the use of feedback, the auditory modality, or both. Note that the positive effect of auditory cueing was not observed in a bimanual drawing task by Swinnen and colleagues [66].

3.2 Towards a New Method of Handwriting Rehabilitation with PD Patients Based on Musical Sonification

The presence of auditory feedback or cueing improves significantly the motor control of individuals with PD. On the one hand, providing a supplementary auditory feedback enriches the patients' perception of their movements and thus enhances their control. On the other hand, providing an external auditory cueing leads the patient to adapt their movements in a very promising way. Is it possible to combine the advantages of both methods?

In this international symposium on computer music multidisciplinary research (CMMR 2017), an individualized approach in the use of RAS was proposed to help PD patients to walk [8]. The principle was to adapt the RAS in real-time to patients' step times. The results revealed important individual differences among PD patients regarding their response to different cueing strategies. The strategy that we are currently evaluating differs from that: we are assessing the effect of abrupt changes of music linked to kinematic thresholds. This method of *musical sonification* consists of modifying a preselected music according to movement variables: music is distorted when the movement is dysfluent and too slow. The aim is both to improve the perception of movement irregularities (when music changes) and to provide an auditory guidance (when music does not change).

The melodious music associated to a correct movement supplies the writer with an auditory cueing based on musical rhythm. Moreover, melody is also a reward motivating the patients, provided that it is pleasant. This strategy of musical sonification allows patients:

(a) To use music as an external cue, considering the advantages of musical rhythm and RAS effects on motor control in PD patients that we have previously described (e.g. [31, 35]).

(b) To use music as an auditory feedback informing about the movement correctness if s/he has some difficulties in synchronizing his/her movements with the musical rhythm. Indeed, the ability to synchronize movements with an external rhythm requires a temporal processing on both the metronome and the movement itself. This concomitant processing is potentially affected in PD because it involves the cortico-striatal loop [8]. In the present strategy, writing becomes a pseudo-musical practice. The presence of kinematic thresholds, which can be individualized, leads the writer to manage music with the pen like an orchestra conductor with the baton. The writer can stop and start music when s/he decides to. The pen shapes and reshapes music. Consequently, music can be considered as an external goal on which the patients pay attention. Actually, it has been shown that the external focus of attention enhances motor control in PD patients (e.g., [67]).

(c) To integrate music as auditory feedback *and* auditory guidance if they succeed in taking advantage of both supports.

We are currently evaluating this strategy of musical sonification with PD patients and healthy controls. The experiment is designed as a "pre-test/training/post-test" with three different training sessions: one with music, one with musical sonification, and one in silence. During the tests (all in silence), participants were asked to draw loops, write the French word "*cellule*" (cell) in cursive, and make their own signature (for an illustration, see Fig. 2).

During the training phases, the participants were required to achieve graphomotor exercises under one of the three conditions (music vs. musical sonification vs. silence). The conditions' order was counterbalanced between participants and all participants were tested just before and after each training. When the performance of both groups during each training session (in silence, music or musical sonification) was compared, the very preliminary results (on nine PD patients and nine controls) revealed that writing speed was much higher in both groups under musical sonification. When the differences of performance between post- and pre-test were compared for each training session, both PD patients and controls were faster after musical sonification, both in drawing loops and word writing. These preliminary findings must be interpreted with many cautions. If confirmed, they show that PD patients better perform the task under musical sonification and maintain these improvements at short term. Therefore, musical sonification would be a very promising rehabilitation method for individuals with PD.

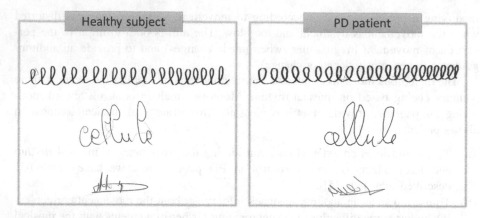

Fig. 2. Handwriting tasks produced during the pre-test by a healthy subject (left) and an individual with PD (right).

4   Conclusions

In the digital age, the interest of handwriting rehabilitation in PD may be limited, although writing a short message on a sticky note or a shopping list is still very useful in the daily life. The advantage for the patient lies rather in the possible transfer of the effects to fine motor rehabilitation. Beyond handwriting, the rehabilitation of the "clumsy hands" that hampers the activities of daily life [68] significantly improves the patients' quality of life, in eating, getting dressed, washing *etc.* [23, 27]. Furthermore, motor rehabilitation also slows down the degenerative processes related to PD. The positive effects of external cueing seem to persist over time as if it remains present "inside the head" whereas it is not physically present [4], similarly as basic auditory feedback when playing piano or when producing other audible motor activities [17, 69]. However, a definite conclusion will be reached when the neural changes underlying the motor improvements following a rehabilitation based on musical sonification will be observed.

Acknowledgments. This research was supported by Grants ANR-16-CONV-0002 (ILCB), ANR-11-LABX-0036 (BLRI), and ANR-11-IDEX-0001-02 (AMIDEX) the Excellence Initiative of Aix-Marseille University. We want to thank Richard Kronland-Martinet, Sølvi Ystad and Mitsuko Aramaki (laboratory PRISM), as well as Charles Gondre for the technical development related to the musical sonification.

References

1. Jankovic, J.: Parkinson's disease: clinical features and diagnosis. J. Neurol. Neurosurg. Psychiatry **79**, 368–376 (2008)
2. Dalla Bella, S., Benoit, C.-E., Farrugia, N., Schwartze, M., Kotz, S.A.: Effects of musically cued gait training in Parkinson's disease: beyond a motor benefit: auditory cueing in Parkinson's disease. Ann. N. Y. Acad. Sci. **1337**, 77–85 (2015)

3. Rodger, M.W.M., Craig, C.M.: Beyond the metronome: auditory events and music may afford more than just interval durations as gait cues in Parkinson's disease. Front. Neurosci. **10**, 272 (2016)

4. Nieuwboer, A., Rochester, L., Müncks, L., Swinnen, S.P.: Motor learning in Parkinson's disease: limitations and potential for rehabilitation. Parkinsonism Relat. Disord. **15**, S53–S58 (2009)

5. Benoit, C.-E., Dalla Bella, S., Farrugia, N., Obrig, H., Mainka, S., Kotz, S.A.: Musically cued gait-training improves both perceptual and motor timing in Parkinson's disease. Front. Hum. Neurosci. **8**, 494 (2014)

6. de Bruin, N., Doan, J.B., Turnbull, G., Suchowersky, O., Bonfield, S., Hu, B., Brown, L.A.: Walking with music is a safe and viable tool for gait training in Parkinson's disease: the effect of a 13-week feasibility study on single and dual task walking. Park. Dis. **2010**, 1–9 (2010)

7. Chen, P.-H., Liou, D.-J., Liou, K.-C., Liang, J.-L., Cheng, S.-J., Shaw, J.-S.: Walking turns in Parkinson's disease patients with freezing of gait: the short-term effects of different cueing strategies. Int. J. Gerontol. **10**, 71–75 (2016)

8. Dalla Bella, S., Benoit, C.-E., Farrugia, N., Keller, P.E., Obrig, H., Mainka, S., Kotz, S.A.: Gait improvement via rhythmic stimulation in Parkinson's disease is linked to rhythmic skills. Sci. Rep. **7**, 42005 (2017)

9. Delval, A., Defebvre, L., Tard, C.: Freezing during tapping tasks in patients with advanced Parkinson's disease and freezing of gait. PLoS ONE **12**, e0181973 (2017)

10. Hackney, M., Earhart, G.: Effects of dance on movement control in Parkinson's disease: a comparison of Argentine tango and American ballroom. J. Rehabil. Med. **41**, 475–481 (2009)

11. Hackney, M.E., Earhart, G.M.: Health-related quality of life and alternative forms of exercise in Parkinson disease. Parkinsonism Relat. Disord. **15**, 644–648 (2009)

12. Harro, C., et al.: The effects of speed-dependent treadmill training and rhythmic auditory-cued overground walking on gait function and fall risk in individuals with idiopathic Parkinson's disease: a randomized controlled trial. NeuroRehabilitation 557–572 (2014)

13. Ledger, S., Galvin, R., Lynch, D., Stokes, E.K.: A randomised controlled trial evaluating the effect of an individual auditory cueing device on freezing and gait speed in people with Parkinson's disease. BMC Neurol. **8**, 46 (2008)

14. Lee, S.J., Yoo, J.Y., Ryu, J.S., Park, H.K., Chung, S.J.: The effects of visual and auditory cues on freezing of gait in patients with Parkinson disease. Am. J. Phys. Med. Rehabil. **91**, 2–11 (2012)

15. Lopez, W.O.C., Higuera, C.A.E., Fonoff, E.T., de Oliveira Souza, C., Albicker, U., Martinez, J.A.E.: Listenmee and Listenmee smartphone application: Synchronizing walking to rhythmic auditory cues to improve gait in Parkinson's disease. Hum. Mov. Sci. **37**, 147–156 (2014)

16. Rochester, L., Burn, D.J., Woods, G., Godwin, J., Nieuwboer, A.: Does auditory rhythmical cueing improve gait in people with Parkinson's disease and cognitive impairment? A feasibility study. Mov. Disord. **24**, 839–845 (2009)

17. Young, W.R., Rodger, M.W., Craig, C.M.: Auditory observation of stepping actions can cue both spatial and temporal components of gait in Parkinson's disease patients. Neuropsychologia **57**, 140–153 (2014)

18. Young, W.R., Shreve, L., Quinn, E.J., Craig, C., Bronte-Stewart, H.: Auditory cueing in Parkinson's patients with freezing of gait. What matters most: action-relevance or cue-continuity? Neuropsychologia **87**, 54–62 (2016)

19. Baram, Y., Aharon-Peretz, J., Badarny, S., Susel, Z., Schlesinger, I.: Closed-loop auditory feedback for the improvement of gait in patients with Parkinson's disease. J. Neurol. Sci. 363, 104–106 (2016)
20. Carpinella, I., et al.: Wearable sensor-based biofeedback training for balance and gait in Parkinson disease: a pilot randomized controlled trial. Arch. Phys. Med. Rehabil. 98, 622–630.e3 (2017)
21. Ginis, P., et al.: External input for gait in people with Parkinson's disease with and without freezing of gait: one size does not fit all. J. Neurol. 264, 1488–1496 (2017)
22. Lohnes, C.A., Earhart, G.M.: The impact of attentional, auditory, and combined cues on walking during single and cognitive dual tasks in Parkinson disease. Gait Posture 33, 478–483 (2011)
23. Ringenbach, S.D.R., van Gemmert, A.W.A., Shill, H.A., Stelmach, G.E.: Auditory instructional cues benefit unimanual and bimanual drawing in Parkinson's disease patients. Hum. Mov. Sci. 30, 770–782 (2011)
24. Studer, V., et al.: Treadmill training with cues and feedback improves gait in people with more advanced Parkinson's disease. J. Park. Dis. 7, 729–739 (2017)
25. Welch, R.B., Warren, D.H.: Immediate perceptual response to intersensory discrepancy. Psychol. Bull. 88, 638 (1980)
26. Schmidt, R., Lee, T.: Motor Learning and performance, 5E with web study guide: from principles to application. Human Kinetics (2013)
27. Nackaerts, E., Vervoort, G., Heremans, E., Smits-Engelsman, B.C.M., Swinnen, S.P., Nieuwboer, A.: Relearning of writing skills in Parkinson's disease: a literature review on influential factors and optimal strategies. Neurosci. Biobehav. Rev. 37, 349–357 (2013)
28. McIntosh, G.C., Brown, S.H., Rice, R.R., Thaut, M.H.: Rhythmic auditory-motor facilitation of gait patterns in patients with Parkinson's disease. J. Neurol. Neurosurg. Psychiatry 62, 22–26 (1997)
29. Atkinson-Clement, C., Sadat, J., Pinto, S.: Behavioral treatments for speech in Parkinson's disease: meta-analyses and review of the literature. Neurodegener. Dis. Manag. 5, 233–248 (2015)
30. Fujii, S., Wan, C.Y.: The role of rhythm in speech and language rehabilitation: the SEP hypothesis. Front. Hum. Neurosci. 8, 777 (2014)
31. Zatorre, R.J., Chen, J.L., Penhune, V.B.: When the brain plays music: auditory–motor interactions in music perception and production. Nat. Rev. Neurosci. 8, 547–558 (2007)
32. Mainka, S.: Music stimulates muscles, mind, and feelings in one go. Front. Psychol. 6, 1547 (2015)
33. Satoh, M., Kuzuhara, S.: Training in mental singing while walking improves gait disturbance in Parkinson's disease patients. Eur. Neurol. 60, 237–243 (2008)
34. Wittwer, J.E., Webster, K.E., Hill, K.: Music and metronome cues produce different effects on gait spatiotemporal measures but not gait variability in healthy older adults. Gait Posture 37, 219–222 (2013)
35. Sihvonen, A.J., Särkämö, T., Leo, V., Tervaniemi, M., Altenmüller, E., Soinila, S.: Music-based interventions in neurological rehabilitation. Lancet Neurol. 16, 648–660 (2017)
36. Doyon, J., Benali, H.: Reorganization and plasticity in the adult brain during learning of motor skills. Curr. Opin. Neurobiol. 15, 161–167 (2005)
37. Doyon, J., et al.: Contributions of the basal ganglia and functionally related brain structures to motor learning. Behav. Brain Res. 199, 61–75 (2009)
38. Pinto, S., et al.: Functional magnetic resonance imaging exploration of combined hand and speech movements in Parkinson's disease. Mov. Disord. 26, 2212–2219 (2011)
39. Nombela, C., Hughes, L.E., Owen, A.M., Grahn, J.A.: Into the groove: can rhythm influence Parkinson's disease? Neurosci. Biobehav. Rev. 37, 2564–2570 (2013)

40. Berardelli, A., Rothwell, J.C., Thompson, P.D., Hallett, M.: Pathophysiology of bradyki- nesia in Parkinson's disease. Brain **124**, 2131–2146 (2001)
41. Schneider, J.S., Diamond, S.G., Markham, C.H.: Parkinson's disease: sensory and motor problems in arms and hands. Neurology **37**, 951 (1987)
42. Klockgether, T., Borutta, M., Rapp, H., Spieker, S., Dichgans, J.: A defect of kinesthesia in Parkinson's disease. Mov. Disord. **10**, 460–465 (1995)
43. Ondo, W.G., Satija, P.: Withdrawal of visual feedback improves micrographia in Parkinson's disease. Mov. Disord. **22**, 2130–2131 (2007)
44. Klockgether, T., Dichgans, J.: Visual control of arm movement in Parkinson's disease. Mov. Disord. **9**, 48–56 (1994)
45. Longstaff, M.G., Mahant, P.R., Stacy, M.A., Van Gemmert, A.W., Leis, B.C., Stelmach, G. E.: Discrete and dynamic scaling of the size of continuous graphic movements of parkinsonian patients and elderly controls. J. Neurol. Neurosurg. Psychiatry **74**, 299–304 (2003)
46. Chiviacowsky, S., Wulf, G.: Feedback after good trials enhances learning. Res. Q. Exerc. Sport **78**, 40–47 (2007)
47. Turner, R.S., Desmurget, M.: Basal ganglia contributions to motor control: a vigorous tutor. Curr. Opin. Neurobiol. **20**, 704–716 (2010)
48. Foerde, K., Shohamy, D.: The role of the basal ganglia in learning and memory: insight from Parkinson's disease. Neurobiol. Learn. Mem. **96**, 624–636 (2011)
49. Nombela, C., Rae, C.L., Grahn, J.A., Barker, R.A., Owen, A.M., Rowe, J.B.: How often does music and rhythm improve patients' perception of motor symptoms in Parkinson's disease? J. Neurol. **260**, 1404–1405 (2013)
50. Margolin, D.I., Wing, A.M.: Agraphia and micrographia: clinical manifestations of motor programming and performance disorders. Acta Psychol. (Amst.) **54**, 263–283 (1983)
51. Lewitt, P.A.: Micrographia as a focal sign of neurological disease. J. Neurol. Neurosurg. Psychiatry **46**, 1152 (1983)
52. Phillips, J.G., Stelmach, G.E., Teasdale, N.: What can indices of handwriting quality tell us about Parkinsonian handwriting? Hum. Mov. Sci. **10**, 301–314 (1991)
53. McLennan, J.E., Nakano, K., Tyler, H.R., Schwab, R.S.: Micrographia in Parkinson's disease. J. Neurol. Sci. **15**, 141–152 (1972)
54. Van Gemmert, A.W.A., Teulings, H.-L., Contreras-Vidal, J.L., Stelmach, G.E.: Parkinsons disease and the control of size and speed in handwriting. Neuropsychologia **37**, 685–694 (1999)
55. Letanneux, A., Danna, J., Velay, J.-L., Viallet, F., Pinto, S.: From micrographia to Parkinson's disease dysgraphia: Parkinson's disease dysgraphia. Mov. Disord. **29**, 1467–1475 (2014)
56. Pinto, S., Velay, J.-L.: Handwriting as a marker for PD progression: a shift in paradigm. Neurodegener. Dis. Manag. **5**, 367–369 (2015)
57. Plamondon, R.: A kinematic theory of rapid human movements, Part I. Biol. Cybern. **73**, 295–307 (1995)
58. Grossberg, S., Paine, R.W.: A neural model of cortico-cerebellar interactions during attentive imitation and predictive learning of sequential handwriting movements. Neural Netw. **13**, 999–1046 (2000)
59. Berardelli, A., et al.: Single–joint rapid arm movements in normal subjects and in patients with motor disorders. Brain **119**, 661–674 (1996)
60. Swett, B.A., et al.: Neural substrates of graphomotor sequence learning: a combined fMRI and kinematic study. J. Neurophysiol. **103**, 3366–3377 (2010)

61. Nieuwboer, A., Vercruysse, S., Feys, P., Levin, O., Spildooren, J., Swinnen, S.: Upper limb movement interruptions are correlated to freezing of gait in Parkinson's disease. Eur. J. Neurosci. **29**, 1422–1430 (2009)
62. Oliveira, R.M., Gurd, J.M., Nixon, P., Marshall, J.C., Passingham, R.E.: Micrographia in Parkinson's disease: the effect of providing external cues. J. Neurol. Neurosurg. Psychiatry **63**, 429–433 (1997)
63. Bryant, M., Rintala, D., Lai, E., Protas, E.: An investigation of two interventions for micrographia in individuals with Parkinson's disease. Clin. Rehabil. **24**, 1021–1026 (2010)
64. Contreras-Vidal, J.L., Teulings, H.-L., Stelmach, G.E., Adler, C.H.: Adaptation to changes in vertical display gain during handwriting in Parkinson's disease patients, elderly and young controls. Parkinsonism Relat. Disord. **9**, 77–84 (2002)
65. Teulings, H.L., Contreras-Vidal, J.L., Stelmach, G.E., Adler, C.H.: Adaptation of handwriting size under distorted visual feedback in patients with Parkinson's disease and elderly and young controls. J. Neurol. Neurosurg. Psychiatry **72**, 315–324 (2002)
66. Swinnen, S.P., Steyvers, M., Van Den Bergh, L., Stelmach, G.E.: Motor learning and Parkinson's disease: refinement of within-limb and between-limb coordination as a result of practice. Behav. Brain Res. **111**, 45–59 (2000)
67. Wulf, G., Landers, M., Lewthwaite, R., Toöllner, T.: External focus instructions reduce postural instability in individuals with Parkinson disease. Phys. Ther. **89**, 162–168 (2016)
68. Jankovic, J.: Pathophysiology and clinical assessment of motor symptoms in Parkinson's disease. Handb. Park, Dis (1987)
69. Bangert, M., et al.: Shared networks for auditory and motor processing in professional pianists: Evidence from fMRI conjunction. NeuroImage **30**, 917–926 (2006)

Investigating the Role of Auditory Feedback in a Multimodal Biking Experience

Jon Ram Bruun Pedersen[1(✉)], Stefania Serafin[1], and Francesco Grani[2]

[1] Multisensory Experience Lab, Aalborg University Copenhagen,
Copenhagen, Denmark
{jpe,sts}@create.aau.dk
[2] Here Technologies, Berlin, Germany

Abstract. In this paper, we investigate the role of auditory feedback in affecting perception of effort while biking in a virtual environment. Subjects were biking on a stationary chair bike, while exposed to 3D renditions of a recumbent bike inside a virtual environment (VE). The VE simulated a park and was created in the Unity5 engine. While biking, subjects were exposed to 9 kinds of auditory feedback (3 amplitude levels with three different filters) which were continuously triggered corresponding to pedal speed, representing the sound of the wheels and bike/chain mechanics. Subjects were asked to rate the perception of exertion using the Borg RPE scale. Results of the experiment showed that most subjects perceived a difference in mechanical resistance from the bike between conditions, but did not consciously notice the variations of the auditory feedback, although these were significantly varied. This points towards interesting perspectives for subliminal perception potential for auditory feedback for VR exercise purposes.

Keywords: Auditory feedback · Proprioceptive feedback · Training
Healthcare · Virtual environment · Virtual reality

1 Introduction

Auditory feedback is known to affect the perception of a multimodal experience. A classic example is the parchment skin illusion, where the interactive variation of auditory feedback affects subjects' perception of hand dryness when performing the action of rubbing hands in front of a microphone [8].

Previous research has also shown how sound, specifically music, can affect the perception of effort during exercise. In [9], using the Borg scale of perceived exertion, [2], it was shown how music versus non music affects perception of effort in aerobic training. Most of the studies present in the literature consider auditory feedback in the form of music. In this paper we are interested to investigate whether auditory feedback in the form of everyday sound effects affects perception of effort. In previous research, we showed that altering the frequency

M. Aramaki et al. (Eds.): CMMR 2017, LNCS 11265, pp. 327–337, 2018.
https://doi.org/10.1007/978-3-030-01692-0_22

and amplitude of the friction sound produced by a pulley machine affects perception of effort [1]. The experiment was conducted placing a microphone attached to the string connected to the pulley machine, and manipulating in realtime the pulling sound while playing it back to the subjects through headphones.

In this paper we want to investigate whether perception of effort is affected by auditory feedback. Specifically, we used a virtual reality (VR) biking experience originally developed for elderly users, to motivate regular exercise [3]. Many elderly users who have very little strength, have experienced increased motivation to keep going, or to push harder, if their exercise environment affords the motivation increase [4]. Specific for these type VR bike rides were their foundation on nature experiences, which showed to redirect attention from pain and boredom, onto experiencing something beautiful in VR instead [4]. This paper wants to keep investigating methods to further manipulate the user perception of exercise; this time how auditory feedback augmentation can possibly affect the perception of exertion.

2   Design

The system used to display the VR exercise setup had three main components; a visual display (custom-made park VE), bike interface (a consumer product chair bike and a wireless gyroscope-based microcontroller for the pedal arm), and two auditory displays (soundscape and auditory feedback from biking).

2.1   Visual Display

Visuals of the park VE was a created using the Unity 5 engine. Figure 1 shows an overview screenshot of the park VE.

During active usage (biking), the user drives along a brick path, at a fixed route, through the park. No steering was needed for this experiment, as the VR camera was set to simply follow the path, using a pathfinding algorithm. The visual artistic direction of the park VE is directed toward a lush nature representation, targeting a 'restorative' experience of this type milieu [5].

Throughout any part of the VE, the path is surrounded by various types of flora (flowers, trees, rocks, a lake, waterfalls, plants), fauna (birds) and human construction (benches, small bridges, lamp posts, small fences).

To support the auditory display of biking, we wanted a visually explicit existence of a bike-type object in the VE. One concern, however, was issues developing kinematics and embodiment aspects related to the mapping the users' real world movements onto the biking and avatar behaviour in VR. Another concern was the chair bike used for the experiment; chosen for being a dominant bike-type for elderly rehabilitation, but with a specific biking-position (posture and seating position, seating height, etc.) to mimic in VR. The solution was to introduce a cabin-based recumbent bike to the VE (as seen in Fig. 2, left). A 3D model was created for Unity5, and attached to the VE camera in the park VE (as seen in Fig. 2, right). While driving the path, users would be able to see the front

Fig. 1. The park virtual environment

Fig. 2. Left: A cabin-based recumbent bike. Right: A 3D model of the bike in Unity5.

of the cabin of the recumbent bike, as seen in Fig. 3. The visualization of the cabin would follow the path while the user would pedal, simulating recumbent bike actively steering itself along the trail.

The speed of the forward going motion for the visual display was controlled by the users' pedal action. Faster pedaling resulted in higher biking speed. The pedal speed was translated to Unity through a set of UDP and acceleration oriented scripts, controlling the VE camera forward.

2.2 Bike Interface

The bike interface part of the setup consisted of a normal chair, a DeskCycle (a commercial chair bike), and a wireless microcontroller attached to the pedal arm of the DeskCycle. The DeskCycle features a knob on front of the pedals, which can regulate pedaling resistance (see Fig. 4).

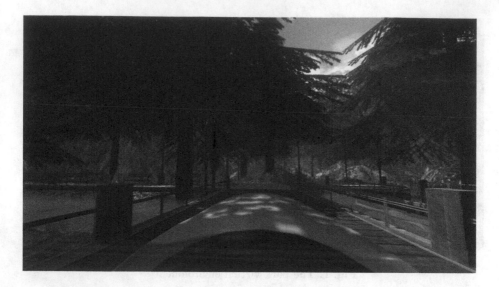

Fig. 3. View of the VR recumbent bike, as seen by participants.

Fig. 4. The mini stationary exercise bike used in the experiment.

Attached to one pedal is a small and compact wireless device built by our group which has been deployed successfully also in previous studies, see: [7]. The device contains an Adafruit Feather HUZZAH microcontroller board equipped with the ESP8266 WiFi chip, an ITG-3200 high precision gyroscope, and a 3.7 V 1200 mAh lithium polymer battery. The pedaling movement is sampled and transmitted at 20 Hz resolution rate, which is enough to let the study participants perceive a consistent real-time synchronization between their pedaling gesture and the advancement of the VE visualization. The rotational speed of the bike pedal (radians-per-second) is sent via a WiFi UDP stream (UDP protocol is used - instead of TCP/IP - to achieve lower latency) to Unity5 and to MaxMSP, respectively for the control of visuals and sound.

2.3   Auditory Feedback

The auditory feedback consisted of two different parts: the soundscape of the VE, and the auditory feedback of the VR recumbent bike. The VE soundscape was handled by Unity5, and comprised of natural soundscape elements such as the sounds of wind, birds, waterfall, etc. and delivered through a frontal stereo loudspeaker setup (Logitech 2.1 Z623). The design of the soundscape followed the design direction found in [6].

The second audio element; the auditory feedback of the recumbent bike, was synthesized in MaxMSP according to the measured pedaling speed rate and delivered through one single Dynaudio BM5 MKIII studio monitor. Three elements took part in creating the recumbent bike sound:

- a "chassis sound": a white noise signal passed through three resonant band-pass filters (at frequencies: 220, 500 and 730 Hz, Q = 10, Gain = 1)
- a "chain sound": short bursts of white noise whose interval time and amplitude envelope was related to the pedaling speed
- one 60 Hz humming sound which becomes more audible at high speed (simulating the typical bicycle hub noise) At different pedaling speed these elements are crossfaded to hear a natural transition from a predominant chassis sound at lower speeds to a predominant combination of chain and hub sound at higher speeds

3   Method

The test setup combined two computers (Dell PC and a 13″ Macbook Pro), the two sound systems, the DeskCycle chair bike, the microcontroller interface and wireless router, and a Philips 55 in. LED TV. The desktop PC was running the Unity5 build, and connected to the 55″ LED TV to display the Park VE. It was also connected to the Logitech 2.1 system for the Park VE soundscape. The Macbook Pro running MaxMSP was connected to the Dynaudio speaker through RCA, and to the microcontroller through the wireless router.

The experiment was performed in an office space, in a specific office with sound-isolation treatment, able to block sounds from surrounding spaces. The soundscape and the bike-specific sound outputs were fitted in the room to blend seamlessly into each other. This was done primarily through volume settings, and acoustics, according to the listener position. Speaker placement proved important for a convincing blend of the bike-specific and soundscape sound output. Ultimately, the Logitech speakers were placed next to the LED TV pointing towards the user. The Dynaudio monitor was placed on top of a cardboard box on the floor, underneath a desk, with the speaker baffle/woofers pointing upwards. The listener position was placed against the wall opposing the LED TV. The sub-woofer was placed behind the furniture holding the LED TV, playing into the back of the office room.

With the chair properly placed, the sound from the Dynaudio monitor bounced off office surfaces and the back wall, to make the sound appear as if it was surrounding a seated user. This emulated very well the sensation of being very close to a sound emitting recumbent bike cabin. The final setup (here, with participant 21) can be seen in Fig. 5.

Fig. 5. Experiment setup.

The 3 amplitude levels and 3 filters gave 9 conditions, which was repeated twice for each participant, in a randomized order. During the experiment, the Macbook Pro was used as the test conductor's user interface, to select the appropriate condition.

3.1 Participants

21 participants performed the experiment (10 female). The average age was 32 (stdev 10.3). No participants had impaired hearing. 16 had performed exercise regularly within the past 2 months, where 7 of exercise routines included biking. Other frequent routines included running (6), and fitness (6).

3.2 Procedure

The experiment procedure had participants enter the office room, and sit on the specifically placed chair. From there, they were introduced to the test procedure; how they would experience a display of a virtual environment park, and drive through it using a virtual cabin-based recumbent bike (participants were shown an image of one). Hereafter, participants were then introduced to the Deskcycle, and its resistance wheel. They were informed how they would need to perform 18 quick trials of 5 pedal pushes (2.5 rounds). After each trial, participants should stop pedaling immediately and rate their perceived exertion, using the Borg scale. All participants were presented with a printout of the Borg scale (Fig. 6) which they were always free to turn at any time during the experiment. Lastly, they were informed how the resistance wheel of the DeskCycle would be turned between each trial, and that they would not be allowed to look at- or know the resistance position. While logging demographics (gender, age, occupation), participants were also asked to report if they had performed regular exercise during the past two months, as well as which exercise type they had most often performed in their overall lifetime. After each concluded trial, the experimenter would note the participant's Borg RPE rating on a piece of paper, set the next condition using MaxMSP, and lean forward to turn the resistance wheel on the DeskCycle. The wheel would always end in the same position, but the wheel-turning was consciously exaggerated in terms of back and forth turning, so that participants would not be able to hear where it ended. During trials, volunteer responses from participants were noted by the experimenter, for instance if they stated that they believed the mechanical resistance had changed, or if they indicated notice to the auditory feedback changing. Comments or statements about the experience post-trial were also noted to the extent possible.

Borg	Rating Perceived Exertion Scale
0	Nothing at all
0.5	Very, very weak (just noticeable)
1	Very weak
2	Weak (light)
3	Moderate
4	Somewhat strong
5	Strong (heavy)
6	.
7	Very Strong
8	.
9	.
10	Maximal

Fig. 6. The Borg scale print-out given to participants during the experiment

4   Results

When analyzed the reported Borg scale, no significant difference could be measured among the conditions. Figure 7 shows the mean (circle) and standard deviation for all participants for the different conditions. As can be seen in Fig. 7, the differences among conditions are minimal, and the standard deviation is consistent. Between participants, the Borg scale was used quite differently, despite the chair bike resistance being equal in every session. Perceptions of how exerted they were, were quite different, with some participants stating that there was almost no resistance, and others perceiving the resistance to be heavy.

The qualitative responses gave interesting insights to participants rating tendencies. Qualitative responses from participants, both during and after the experiment were voluntary. But anything stated was noted by the experimenter, both during and after the participant session.

Using basic coding, responses were categorized related to participants statements on the audio feedback, perceived exertion change, whether they believed it to be resistance changing, or whether they perceived a big exertion change. 15 participants hinted to a belief in mechanical change on the bike, during the

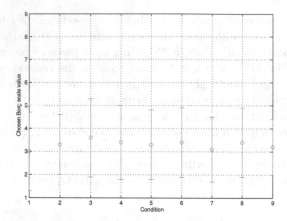

Fig. 7. Results from the experiment: the horizontal axes represent the condition, while vertical axes the value chosen in the Borg scale.

experiment. Of these, 7 suggested small changes, 6 suggested medium changes, and 2 felt a large variation. Participant statements also suggested that at least 14 participants did not notice sound changes at all, where 3 participants reported to have indeed noticed changes in audio. The last 4 participants remained unclear in this regard. Meanwhile none of the participants linked the audio to the sensations of exertion change during the experiment.

The most frequently mentioned aspects to the experiment from participants were (a) how the differences were too small for ratings to differ more than one or two steps on the scale *"Hard to tell the difference, but the last ones were clearly geared higher than the previous"*; (b) how 5 pedal pushes (2.5 full pedal rounds) were too short a while to manage to get a sense of the resistance properly (more time pedaling would produce more accurate results, according to these participants); and (c) how some participants afterwards reported that they simply chose their ratings in small increments up or down, more so than really looking at their Borg RPE scale printout for the rating most representative of their perceived exertion: *"Hard to feel. I was measuring the resistance based on the previously given rating, perhaps more than the scale. The differences always came in small increments, up and down. Never in 'jumps"*.

Also interesting were the participants who found the resistance to have changed noticeably, based on their perceived exertion during trials; *"Felt like it went down hill sometimes. Sometimes visually too. Made pedaling easier."*, indicating how they sometimes felt that the perceived exertion change transposed itself onto the perception of other aspects of the biking experience, despite the participant well knowing that e.g. the visual change did not in fact happen. A follow-up question from the experimenter confirmed that participant did not notice the change in auditory feedback. One participant noticed that the sound changed, but had the experience that the sound feedback was faulty, as (paraphrasing) *"the audio did not at all correspond to the changes in resistance from the pedals"*. This indicates that while this specific participant noticed the auditory feedback, consciously interpreted it, and still thought a mechanical resistance was in fact changing.

After the experiment was completed, out of curiosity from the experimenter, the three subjects who noticed sound change were asked to listen to it again while biking, and give their interpretation of the audio effect, in relation to the perception of exertion. One participant commented that the high pass sound felt 'rusty' and made the bike feel as if resistance was higher. The low-passed condition was considered 'smooth', and thus signaling less resistance. Another participant highlighted how low pass filtering indicated low speed, whereas the amplitude represented friction.

5   Discussion

Results of the experiment showed that most subjects perceived a difference in mechanical resistance from the bike between conditions, but did not notice the variations of the auditory feedback, although these were significantly varied. And that most of those who noticed the variance, did not manage to understand its purpose in the experiment design.

This might be due to several factors. First of all the experience of the visual feedback might have been dominant, preventing subjects to focus on the auditory feedback. Moreover the variations in auditory feedback might have been too subtle in order to be perceived as significant. Looking a bit into the details; seeing as only a few participants noticed sounds to change, but must have noticed the biking sounds due to their sheer volume from the setup, the audio must have been perceived as simply a natural part of the biking experience/display. This credits the sound design of the bike feedback.

However, it does pose questions about (a) the dampened role and perception of audio under heavy visual circumstances, or (b) how sound experiments should be designed to both disguise its purpose, but still be sufficiently obvious to make a measurable difference. Investigations into prior work on these questions could direct the coming experiments. There is no doubt that seeing a participant majority rate their perception of exertion to change is interesting - but also useless unless we become more informed on the rationale behind it.

Parts of the experiment design that could have hindered the consistency of the results are the soundscape from the VE, the inconsistency in the route through the park between participants, the fake position change of the resistance wheel on the DeskCycle between trials, the free interpretation of the Borg scale between participants, the relative strength difference between participants (which there inevitably was), and the length of each trial with only 5 pedaling pushes for each trial.

The VE soundscape had its specific traits depending on where in the VE a user ventures. Some spots include lots of sounds from various birds, and a few spots include waterfalls. There is a risk that certain participants' perception of the biking sounds, could be cluttered from certain types of noises throughout the VE. For future studies, a more consistent soundscape should be prioritized.

A different VE design should also be considered for a future experiment. The park VE contains some sharp corners. The visual speed is very different in sharp corners, compared to going straight ahead. This is because the forward speed inside the VE is lowered in sharp corners, to ensure smooth turns and pleasant direction transitions. If the participant is placed next to a corner before commencing a given trial, and has 5 pedal pushes to get around the corner, the turn itself is the only motion gained, which becomes too different from a straight ahead experience to be categorized as mutually consistent. Therefore, a VE with consistent speeds in which ever position should be a priority.

Another potentially most influential factors in the experiment could be the turning of the resistance wheel. During the experiment, it acted both as a rhythm breaker between trials, but also as a 'suggestive black box', which constantly reminded participants of the possibility of resistance changing.

Participants' autonomous interpretation of exertion should also be controlled (or guided) more, given a follow-up study. Participants' interpretation of the scale varied a lot. Examples of how well-known physical activities would reflect a given rating could make the scale less abstract.

The strength between individual participants could have made a difference. Meanwhile, it is not obvious to these authors how to overcome that type of unknown variable.

The pedaling length of each trial could be extremely interesting to change for a future experiment. Many participants mentioned the 5 pedal pushes as a problem with the current method. The rationale from the experiment design was to avoid giving them too long to adjust to the resistance, between trials. Meanwhile, this rather poorly reflects an exercise run, so extending the trials could be both interesting and more validating of the concept, should it keep providing perceived differences with participants.

6 Conclusion

In this paper we presented an experiment whose goal is to investigate the role of interactive auditory feedback in affecting perception of effort during a biking experience in VR. Subjects were asked to bike in a simulated park, while exposed to varying auditory feedback where the frequency content and amplitude was varied. Quantitative results measure using the Borg scale showed that the perception of effort did not significantly increase when varying the auditory feedback. However, subjects reported a perceived change in mechanical resistance from the bike. These results provided some insights into the potential of interactive auditory feedback in exercise. Further investigations are needed in order to better understand if sound can significantly affect perception of effort.

References

1. Bordegoni, M., Ferrise, F., Grani, F., Bruun-Pedersen, J.R., Serafin, S.: Auditory feedback affects perception of effort when exercising with a pulley machine. In: Online Proceedings From the International Conference on Multisensory Motor Behavior: Impact of Sound (2013)
2. Borg, G., Linderholm, H.: Perceived exertion and pulse rate during graded exercise in various age groups. J. Intern. Med. **181**(S472), 194–206 (1967)
3. Bruun-Pedersen, J.R., Pedersen, K.S., Serafin, S., Kofoed, L.B.: Augmented exercise biking with virtual environments for elderly users: a preliminary study for retirement home physical therapy. In: 2nd Workshop on Virtual and Augmented Assistive Technology (VAAT), pp. 23–27. IEEE (2014)
4. Bruun-Pedersen, J.R., Serafin, S., Kofoed, L.B.: Motivating elderly to exercise-recreational virtual environment for indoor biking. In: IEEE International Conference on Serious Games and Applications for Health (SeGAH), pp. 1–9. IEEE (2016)
5. Bruun-Pedersen, J.R., Serafin, S., Kofoed, L.B.: Restorative virtual environment design for augmenting nursing home rehabilitation. J. Virtual Worlds Res. **9**(3), 1–24 (2016)
6. Bruun-Pedersen, J.R., Serafin, S., Maculewicz, J., Kofoed, L.B.: Designing recreational virtual environments for older adult nursing home residents: how nature and content matter for improving augmented exercise experiences. In: Proceedings of the Audio Mostly 2016, pp. 222–228. ACM (2016)
7. Grani, F., Bruun-Pedersen, J.R.: Giro: better biking in virtual reality. In: IEEE 3rd Workshop on Everyday Virtual Reality (WEVR), pp. 1–5. IEEE (2017)
8. Jousmäki, V., Hari, R.: Parchment skin illusion: sound-biased touch. Curr. Biol. **8**(6), R190–R191 (1998)
9. Seath, L., Thow, M.: The effect of music on the perception of effort and mood during aerobic type exercise. Physiotherapy **81**(10), 592–596 (1995)

Considerations for Developing Sound in Golf Putting Experiments

Benjamin O'Brien[1(✉)], Brett Juhas[1], Marta Bieńkiewicz[1], Laurent Pruvost[2], Frank Buloup[1], Lionel Bringnoux[1], and Christophe Bourdin[1]

[1] Aix Marseille Univ, CNRS, ISM, Marseille, France
`benjamin.O-BRIEN@univ-amu.fr`
[2] Aix Marseille Univ, CNRS,
PRISM (Perception, Representations, Image, Sound and Music),
31 Chemin J. Aiguier, CS 70071, 13402 Marseille cedex 09, France

Abstract. This chapter presents the core interests and challenges of using sound for learning motor skills and describes the development of sonification techniques for three separate golf-putting experiments. These studies are part of the ANR SoniMove project, which aims to develop new Human Machine Interfaces (HMI) that provide gestural control of sound in the areas of sports and music. After a brief introduction to sonification and sound-movement studies, the following addresses the ideas and sound synthesis techniques developed for each experiment.

Keywords: Sonification · Auditory feedback · Biomechanics
Kinematics · Motor-coordination · Golf

1 Introduction

This chapter describes the development of sonification techniques for three separate golf-putting experiments. These studies are part of the ANR SoniMove project, which aims to develop new Human Machine Interfaces (HMI) that provide gestural control of sound in the areas of sports and music. The SoniMove project poses how an intimate manipulation of sound, which is based on morphological invariants that bear meaning, is not only capable of informing, but also guiding or possibly modifying the motor behaviour of people in a given cognitive context. The SoniMove project is based on the collaboration between three partners: Institute of Movement Sciences (ISM) and Perception, Representation, Image, Sound, Music (PRISM) academic laboratories and Société Peugeot-Citroën Automobiles (PSA).

While the objectives of each golf-putting study differ, they all focus on studying the effects of sound on novice golfers. Each experiment involves the process of synthesising sound from data collected from participants or expert players performing the golf-putting gesture. This process of converting data into sound is commonly known as *sonification*. The following offers a brief overview of sonification and sound-movement studies.

© Springer Nature Switzerland AG 2018
M. Aramaki et al. (Eds.): CMMR 2017, LNCS 11265, pp. 338–358, 2018.
https://doi.org/10.1007/978-3-030-01692-0_23

1.1   Sonification Definition

In general, sonification is the use of sound to represent data.[1] Sonification requires a fundamental understanding of the data being used. The context of its collection, scale, and properties are significant for development. Carla Scaletti defines sonification as "a mapping of numerically represented relations in some domain under study to relations in an acoustic domain for the purpose of interpreting, understanding, or communicating relations in the domain under study" [48]. One might view the goal of sonification as reflexive, where the data used for sound synthesis is capable of delivering, conveying, or relaying information about itself [3].

Natural sonification of course happens all the time in our daily lives, [23] which is typically understood as acoustic feedback generated by the contact of two surfaces, for example, dropping a ball onto a surface. Research has shown healthy people can perceive and extract from environmental sound characteristics, such as an object's size [31] or material [60].

But what makes people want to extract information from the sounds they hear? Is it because they are able to identify characteristics of the sound and associate them with a specific source? If a natural or artificial sonification is supposed to convey the data used for its synthesis, which characteristics of the data, if any, are significant? What sound criteria are necessary to make the data perceptible? These questions are at the center of developing artificial sonifications for studying its effect on subjects exposed to augmented realities.

Of course there are many ways to develop data-to-sound mapping schemes. Several papers discuss the data-to-sound development process, which can be categorised as one-to-one, one-to-many, many-to-one, and many-to-many mappings [16,25]. If someone wants to model a golf swing, for example, they could measure club head position, velocity, and acceleration, which - all or some - could then be mapped to different sound synthesis parameters, such as amplitude or brightness. This categorisation illustrates the numerous ways to map data-to-sound, so justifying the selection of mapping criteria and parameters are significant. However, when developing a mapping scheme for scientific study, not only is a mastery the data properties required, but also a clear direction as to the hypothetical subject responses one wants to elicit for examination, which, in this case, involve subject motor behaviour.

1.2   Sound and Movement

A recent research focus has been on the relationships between sound and its affect on human motion. Several studies have found that people are able to utilise

---

[1] In this context sound is defined as any non-verbal audio. Defining sonification is a bit of a controversial topic, especially in recent years, as some composers and sound artists make sound through the manipulation of values from data streams and large databases. What makes this process different from sonification is a matter of intention and interpretation: How *well* does the sound represent the data used for sonification? An overview of this problem is addressed by Hermann [27].

acoustic information for guiding their movement when reaching and grasping objects [10,62]. The study conducted by Castiello et al. (2010) suggests that, when trying to make contact with an object, the contact sound with a material is as significant as its perceived center of mass. These studies show that "auditory information affects grasping kinematics...when vision is present," which suggests the strong relationship between hearing and seeing when completing physical tasks.

Several studies propose that one possible reason sound has a capacity to influence or affect one's perception of motion or moving forms and multisensory nature of motor representations is due to the close-proximity between the auditory and multi-sensory motor areas in the brain [5,30,46]. A sonification of movement study found that when subjects viewed congruent audiovisual movement as opposed to incongruent movement, there was an increase in the brain activity in the human action observation system [49]. A summary of psychophysical studies also suggest sound has a capacity to prompt dynamic cues that are beyond the field of vision, which are the result of handicapping visual cues or strengthening auditory ones [22,40]. Research on the impact of sound in nonvisual learning situations is particularly convincing when tests focus on learning different motor skills. A major study by Danna et al. (2014) showed "sonifying handwriting during the learning of unknown characters improved the fluency and speed of their production" [14]. Thus, there is scientific precedence that the audio-motor coupling has benefits for learning a new skill.

Hebbian theory implies that experience gives rise to a pattern of coupling neural activity, which, through repetition, becomes entrained and more easily repeatable [26]. Of course an excellent example of this are skilled pianists, who create sound-patterns through the careful manipulation of their hands. They experience *auditory feedback* where their movement maps to sound, which, in turn, can help influence or guide their process of learning a particular task involving motion [17]. Numerous studies have traced this relationship, examining the activity of the motor cortex of professional pianists and non-musicians who listen to piano music [6,33,38].

Like musicians, most athletes use their hands in a manner that requires high degree of fine motor control. Over the last decade, several research projects have been dedicated to developing audio-motor feedback schemes for the purposes of informing or aiding athletes about their physical actions. Effenberg et al. (2016) found an increase in the mean boat velocity for the elite rowing subjects who experienced acoustic feedback, where four movement parameters were mapped to modulations in frequency and amplitude [18]. A study by Brown et al. (2008) showed an inverse relationship between a sprinter's reaction time and the intensity of a starter signal [9]. A similar study was conducted in sports involving hurdling or hammer throwing [2]. There is growing scientific evidence that athletes use the sound of ball impact as acoustic feedback in ball sports to adjust their behaviour accordingly [54]. Specific to golf, Roberts et al. looked at the relationships between the subjective responses of elite golfers and the objective (acoustic) measurements of ball impact sounds [45]. In particular, the study found a strong and positive correlation between the 'pleasant' feel of a shot and the impact having a 'loud, crisp, sharp sound.'

1.3 Why Sonify Golf-Putting?

The physical fitness required to play and succeed in golf is unlike most other sports. The physical stature of expert and professional golfers is quite vast. However, successful golfers require, among other things, expert concentration, precision, and force management in order to swing a golf-club. In addition, golf requires players to keep their eyes on the ball before making contact, which stresses the importance of other sensory cues for guiding the gesture. These prerequisites make golf an ideal candidate for studying whether sound can be used as an affective tool for novice golfers.

The decision to use the putter, as opposed to other golf clubs (driver, iron, sand wedge), concerns the force and aim of its use. The general goal for using other clubs is to maximise the distance the ball travels, which requires a careful management of different forces. However, the aim of using the putter is to get the ball to a specified target by controlling club head motion at impact [12]. Moreover, there are many ways to swing the putter, for example, increasing movement in the wrist or elbow, each of which can effectively get the ball to the target. This variability is particularly interesting when considering how the sound could be used in real-time situations to give subject immediate auditory-feedback. This chapter describes the development of different sonification strategies based on the golf putting gesture.

2 Sonifying the Expert

The first experiment proposed whether sound could be an affective tool for guidance in a golf putting setting. Over the course of an eight-week training period, participants were divided into control, audio, and visual groups. During each session, all subjects putted balls over three distances (3 m, 6 m, 9 m), where their movement was recorded using the CodaMotion data acquisition system.[2] The subjects in the experimental groups were guided by auditory or visual stimuli, respectfully, which was based on professional golfer data. Prior to testing, a professional golfer's movement was recorded while successfully completing putts over the three distances. The data collected and used for the experiment was based on kinematic smoothness and personal feedback from the professional. The following describes the development of sound for the experiment.

2.1 Parameter Selection

Before developing strategies for sound synthesis, a movement parameter needs to be determined. Given certain ecological observations based on aerodynamics and

---

[2] Two markers were placed near the putter hand grip and the top of the club head. The data acquisition sampling rate was 200 Hz.

mechanical noise, velocity was an intuitive choice for sonification [23, 42]. After classifying the general trajectory of the club head as quasi-circular, the club head angular velocity was selected. In order to calculate the angular velocity of the club head, a center of rotation, which can be imagined to be at the shoulder, was estimated from club head and handgrip expert position data. Following this estimation, the club head angular velocity of the expert was calculated offline.

The other candidate variable was 'time-to-arrival' (τ) [34], which was selected because of its use in a study involving golf and the rate of 'gap closures' [12]. The study found a strong relationship between the perceived distance between the golf club and the ball and the rate in which golfers arrive at impact with the ball. In addition, as of the date of the pretest, studies had yet to use the τ-variable for sonification, all of which made it worthy of further examination.

A 15-person survey was conducted to determine whether participants could discriminate sounds based on the two candidate variables. Subjects listened[3] to a series of sound pairs and were told to imagine that the sound corresponded with the golf putting movement. They were asked whether the sounds were the same, and, if different, which (imagined) ball went further. To make the sounds used for testing, the professional putting data at all three distances was mapped to sound synthesis parameters of a custom synthesiser written in Matlab. In general, the synthesiser maps and scales data to a user-specified frequency range. In this manner, data drives the center frequency of a band-pass filter (BPF) with white noise input. Nicknamed the 'whoosh' synthesiser, it was designed to create a sound that resembles the aural consequence of metal passing through the air. For this pretest, a Bark scale[4] (range 5) was used with center frequencies ranging from 150 to 700 Hz.

For each distance the candidate data was linearly mapped in two ways: to frequency (Hz) and to mels, where the Bark scale is first transformed into a Mel scale [41]. This second mapping is known as *psychometric*, which was selected because it has been proven to be more indicative of how humans perceive pitch [55].

The results of the survey (Fig. 1) showed participants were unable to distinguish sounds based on the τ-variable. In addition, participants were better at discriminating sounds that were psychometrically (Mel scale) mapped as opposed to those that were frequency mapped. Thus velocity was selected for sonification with psychometric mapping.

2.2   Mapping Velocity to Sound Synthesis Parameters

As stated in the introduction and alluded above, there are many ways to map and scale velocity. It was important to create a sound that might evoke for the

---

[3] For this pretest and all experiments described throughout the chapter, subjects wore Sennheiser headphones.

[4] A Bark scale is a psychoacoustic scale developed by Edward Zwicker in 1961 [64]. It can be defined as a scale in which equal distances between frequencies correspond with equal distances in perception. The scale ranges from 1 to 24, which corresponds with the first 24 critical bands of hearing.

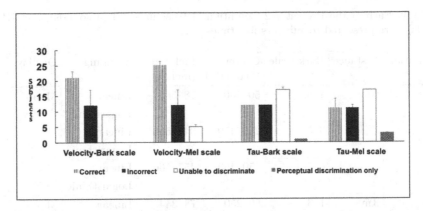

Fig. 1. Summary of discrimination rates in pretest, which tested the different combinations of parameters (velocity, τ) and mappings (Hz, mels) used for sonification

subjects the sound associated with the golf putting gesture and the parameter being sonified (club head angular velocity) and not just some metal object passing through the air at any velocity. Thus, as a way of learning about its spectral content, the sound of the experimental putter passing through the air was recorded with a semi-circular microphone consisting of 32 captors in the anechoic laboratory at PRISM. After reviewing the spectrogram of the recording, a maximum frequency of 450 Hz was determined.

Next a 20-person pretest was designed to examine the behavioural effects of subjects performing the golf putting task while listening to sound. Subjects were asked to perform a putting-like motion without actually making impact with the ball, and their only instruction was to return to their starting position whenever they heard ball impact through their headphones. Three different synthesis conditions were developed: center frequency range (I), mapping function (II), and display (III). As a way of observing whether the frequency content of the sounds had any effect on subjects, Condition I shifted the range of the center frequency used for the BPF with white noise input. Condition II was developed to similarly examine the effects, if any, of using different functions (linear, logarithmic) to map velocity to sound. Finally Condition III was developed to see whether display (monophonic, stereophonic[5]) had any significant effect on subjects. In all cases, a Bark scale was selected and transformed into a Mel scale, which velocity was then mapped onto. The specifics of each condition are outlined in Table 1. Each sound was preceded by three metronome beeps (60 bpm), as a way of preparing the subject, and concluded with a recording of ball impact. Each condition was presented five times (70 trials per participant) in random order.

Pretest Root-Square-Mean Error (RSME) analysis showed that, for Condition I, the best match for sound had a center frequency range of 250–450 Hz. A similar assessment was determined for Conditions II and III with center

---

[5] Club head position was used to map sound to stereo.

Table 1. Each of the Pretest #2 Conditions I (6 sounds), II (4 sounds), and III (4 sounds) were presented to subjects five times.

Condition	Distance	Bark scale	Center Freq. (Hz)	Mel scale (mels)	Mapping	Display
I	9 m	1–5	50–450	78–560	Linear	Mono
					Logarithmic	
		3–5	250–450	344–560	Linear	
					Logarithmic	
		4–5	350–450	457–560	Linear	
					Logarithmic	
II	3 m	1–3	50–250	78–344	Linear	Mono
					Logarithmic	
		2–4	150–350	219–457	Linear	
					Logarithmic	
III	9 m	1–5	50–450	78–560	Linear	Mono
					Logarithmic	
					Linear	Stereo
					Logarithmic	

Note: All logarithmic mappings are base 10.

frequency ranges of 0–253 Hz and 0–450 Hz, respectfully. With regards to Condition III analysis showed that a stereophonic display diminished the RSME.

2.3   Experiment #1 Sounds

Following the analyses of the pretests, it was decided to linearly map velocity to mels with a stereo display. However, given the three distances being tested, different sounds should be developed, such that the center frequency range of each reflects these differences in distance. In general, to transfer energy from the putter to the ball over a greater distance, there needs to be an increase in velocity. Thus, given our analysis of Condition I, which showed that mapping the velocity of 9 m putts to sounds with a center frequency range of 250–450 Hz (Barks 3–5) worked best, it was decided to scale the velocity of the 3 m and 6 m putts in proportion to Barks 1–3 and 2–4, respectively. Table 2 outlines the sounds used in the experiment.

In general, the study showed that, in comparison with the control group, subjects in the auditory and visual groups benefited from the augmented sensory information. Our analysis of the retention tests, however, suggested sensory dependence, which is inline with the 'guidance hypothesis' [1, 47]. One possible way of enhancing learning while diminishing the guiding effect of concurrent augmented sensory feedback is to introduce online feedback, which is an approach that has been shown to be successful [18].

Table 2. The following outlines the relationship between target distance and sounds developed for the auditory group in Experiment #1.

Distance	Barks	Center Freq. (Hz)	Mel scale (mels)	Mapping	Display
3 m	1–3	50–250	78–344	Linear	Stereo
6 m	2–4	150–350	219–457	Linear	Stereo
9 m	3–5	250–450	344–560	Linear	Stereo

3   The Effects of Different Real-Time Sonifications

Unlike the previous study, the second experiment sonified subject movement in real-time. It was believed that if subjects could perceive their near-immediate[6] movement as affecting the synthesis of the sounds they heard, then their motor behaviour might change or become exaggerated [57]. To make this movement-sound connection obvious for subjects, velocity was mapped to the amplitude of the synthesiser, such that when there was no movement, there was no sound.

But because of the physiological differences between listeners, sound affects and is perceived differently, and thus any one strategy for sound synthesis does not guarantee subject engagement or interest. Thus, a first step was to develop different ways of mapping velocity[7] to sound. Instead of using Matlab, all sounds were developed using the audio programming language Max/MSP. The following briefly describes this initial research and outlines the sounds used in the experiment and their construction from different combinations of synthesisers, modulations, scaling sizes, and mappings.

3.1   Synthesiser Development

Three categories of synthesisers were developed to explore different ways velocity could be mapped to synthesis parameters. The first two concerned the *timbre* of the synthesised sound. Although a complex and much discussed topic, [19, 37] timbre is what makes one sound different from another despite having the same pitch and loudness. This distinction is a combination of a sound's spectrum, the energy of vibrations at each frequency, and its amplitude envelope over time.

As a way of getting subjects to engage with the sounds they heard, the last category sought to create sounds that (possibly) carried images or associations with the golf-putting gesture. This category follows closely to the *action-object* paradigm, which describes sound as a auditory consequence of some action on an object [23]. In this way, listeners can perceive or imagine the properties of the object or the morphologies that carry information about the action.

---

[6] During pretesting, a 25–27 ms latency was measured.

[7] To calculate angular velocity in real-time, additional markers would be required and placed near the subject's shoulder. Moreover, variance in the amount of wrist rotation can greatly affect the club head's angular velocity. Thus linear velocity across the x-z plane was selected for sonification.

The goal was to make the relationship between movement and sound perceptible for subjects so as to entice them to play, experiment, and reflect on the sound they affected through their movement.

Frequency and Brightness. Research on timbre spaces [24,44,59] illustrates a strong correlation between a sound's *onset transients*[8] and its *brightness*, the weighted-mean of frequencies present in a signal, which can be calculated by taking its *spectral centroid*. As a first step, two simple synthesisers were developed that scale and map velocity to the frequency parameter of sine and sawtooth wave oscillators. Because the waveforms of the oscillators differ,[9] despite having the same frequency, each synthesiser generates a distinctly different sound. As expected the synthesiser with the sine wave oscillator has a smoother sound, whereas the one with the sawtooth wave oscillator has a rougher sound.

Following this initial work, a subtractive-synthesis synthesiser was developed that maps and scales velocity to the center frequency of a second-order IIR digital resonator filter[10] with white noise input. Because decay rate, or *damping*, is proportional to the width of the filter, increasing it also increases the presence of previous input values, yielding a richer output signal with a more robust frequency spectrum. Fixing the decay rate to 30 ms creates, like the synthesiser used in the first experiment, a 'whoosh' sound, which (to some) evokes the sound of an object passing through the air.

Developing the previous synthesis model a bit further, another synthesiser first maps and scales velocity to a (low) frequency between 20 and 160 Hz that serves as the fundamental frequency of a collection of 50 harmonics. Each harmonic is set to the center frequency of a BPF with white noise input. In addition, velocity is also mapped and scaled to the BPF gain and bandwidth. The filtered white noise then serves as the input for a second-order IIR digital resonator filter with a center frequency set to the harmonic frequency. These 50 synthesisers then sum together to create a rich, but sharp sound.

Rhythmicity. Rather than modulate the (spectral) content of synthesised sound, this category seeks to modulate its form by employing different enveloping techniques. Studies show that altering a sound's natural amplitude envelope, which can be described in terms of attack, sustain, decay, and release (ASDR) times, makes identifying it more difficult [13,35]. Moreover, given a continuous sound, envelopes with different durations can be applied to create impulses and, subsequently, a sense of rhythm.

---

[8] A *transient* is a sound at the beginning of a waveform that has a very short duration and high amplitude. It typically has non-periodic components.

[9] A sine wave is continuous and periodic and has as smooth form due to its fundamental relationship to the circle. This differs from the sawtooth wave, which is also continuous, but has the conventional form of ramping up and then dropping sharply.

[10] For the second-order IIR filter, the s2m.resFS1~ Max/MSP object was used and is available at https://metason.prism.cnrs.fr//Resultats/MaxMSP/.

This interest in rhythmicity follows studies that propose a strong correlation between body movement and auditory rhythm [43,56,61]. In order to examine these timbral changes as a result of impulse density and rhythmicity, it was important to develop synthesisers whose frequency parameters were not dramatically altered by changes in velocity. Thus, a method was developed that maps velocity to envelope duration, such that as velocity increases, the envelope duration decreases, which effectively maps velocity in proportion to the rate of impulses.

Two simple synthesisers were developed to test this mapping. Adopting a basic tubular bell model the first synthesiser uses a two-pole resonant filter with a fixed collection of frequency, gain, and decay rate values. For the second synthesiser, a simple frequency modulation synthesis instrument was developed. During preliminary pretests, several team researchers mentioned that they noticed their 'natural' swing changed or was 'disrupted,' which they attributed to variations in the sound's rhythm.

Sounds and Their Associations. Finally a more creative category of synthesisers was developed, where velocity was mapped to parameters that modulated particular settings of physical-model synthesisers. These models were selected and developed so that might inspire imagery of things relating to the task of golf putting.

Wristwatch: Several golf studies have examined the effects of pre- and post-training with metronomes and timing devices [32,53]. Coupling this research with the comments regarding the mapping of velocity to sound rhythmicity, a synthesiser was developed that employs a wristwatch synthesis model. In this case, velocity maps and scales to an impulse rate of between 50 and 125 ms. Because of the inverse relationship between them, as velocity increases, so too does the duration between impulses, which increases a sense of regularity. Alternatively, as velocity decreases, there is an increase in impulse rate and, subsequently, sound density.

Vowel Synthesis: Like most sporting events, crowds of supporters often congregate and voice their support for athletes. With this observation, a synthesiser was developed that simulates a virtual crowd. Following a similar development by Kleiman-Weiner and Berger, [29] a vowel synthesis synthesiser was developed that, depending on the velocity along the x-axis, selects the center frequencies, gains, and bandwidths of four *formants*[11] for BPFs with a shared sawtooth oscillator input. Using the sign function, when the velocity is negative (backswing), a method selects, synthesises, and sums together the first four formant values for the U ("oh") vowel. Alternatively, when velocity is positive (downswing), the method does the same process for the a ("ah") vowel. To simulate a crowd, ten different voices were created, where, for each one, a random frequency, between 60 and 300 Hz, is selected and set to the frequency parameter of the sawtooth oscillator. This range was selected because the fundamental frequency of an

---

[11] *Formants* are amplitude peaks in the frequency spectrum of a sound.

adult male is between 85 and 180 Hz and, for an adult female, the range is 165 to 255 Hz. Depending on the selected vowel, the velocity scales the sawtooth oscillator frequencies up and down an octave, respectfully.[12]

Jet Engine: Another way to develop sounds that might bring attention to the putting gesture is to design a synthesiser that exaggerates the speed of swinging the putter. Studies have shown that acoustic feedback has an effect on a person's ability to perceive speed, [15] and, more specifically, the relationship between vehicle speed and engine rotations-per-minute [58]. Bringoux et al. (2017) examined the role of auditory feedback in scenarios involving continuous speed, and found significance with regards to acoustic content and its dynamics for car speed control [8]. All of these points are inline with a study on the effect of sound on elite rowing subjects, where acceleration data was mapped to the "brightness of the sound of a car engine when pressing the gas pedal for accelerating" [16].

With these points in mind, a synthesiser was developed that adapts a jet engine model developed by Andy Farnell [20]. Unlike the previous synthesisers, this one introduces the concept of *inertia*. Farnell writes, "Mechanical systems can speed up and slow down at a limited rate, and can sound wrong if you change speed too quickly" (Farnell 2010: 511–512). First velocity maps and scales to a range of 0.0 ('engine off') and 1.0 ('engine maximum speed'), where it is then converted into a signal that is filtered by a single-pole low-pass filter (LPF) with a 0.2 Hz center frequency. With a sampling rate of 44.1 kHz, this center frequency creates a 5 s roll-off, which creates the effect of a mechanical system "speed[ing] up" or "slow[ing] down" at a "limited rate." Thus, velocity maps to the *speed scalar* of the synthesiser, which affects the overall brightness of the synthesised sound in two ways.

This change in brightness mainly happens in the synthesis model of the engine's "turbine," which is composed of five fixed-frequency sine wave oscillators,[13] whose sounding *partials*[14] change depending on the value of speed scalar signal. This is summed together with filtered noise, whose amplitude is also modulated by the speed scalar, and filtered with a cutoff frequency of 11 kHz. During pretests, multiple researchers made comments that the synthesised sound "pumped [them] up" and that they "felt the inertia" while swinging the putter.

3.2   Experiment #2 Sounds

Following a demonstration of the synthesisers developed, a study was proposed by SoniMove researchers to examine whether sounds synthesised from particular

---

[12] This scaling choice was purely intuitive. One might imagine a crowd's "excitement" and frequency as proportional.

[13] To better explain how the speed scalar affects brightness, consider when the value of the speed scalar is 0.5, a 1000 Hz fixed-frequency, for example, sine wave oscillator is halved (500 Hz). Thus, velocity, as mapped to the speed scalar, affects the frequencies of the five sine wave oscillators. The following are the frequencies (in Hz) of the five oscillators: 3097, 4495, 5588, 7471, and 11100.

[14] A *partial* is any tone composed in a complex sound.

combinations of synthesisers, timbral modulations, scaling ranges, or mapping functions have any effect on the behaviour of novice golf putting subjects. Unlike the previous experiment, subjects would only have one target distance (3.5 m). The following describes the development of sounds used in the experiment by selecting these synthesis factors.

Synthesiser Selection. Based on comments regarding the noticeable perceptual differences between their sounds, the 'whoosh' and 'jet' synthesisers were selected. In general, the former creates a softer, gentler sound and the latter creates a more acute and sharp sound. In general, the 'whoosh' synthesiser follows a subtractive synthesis model, whereas the 'jet' adopts a (mostly) additive synthesis model.

Timbral Modulations. Given these two synthesisers, a first point of study was to examine the effects of mapping velocity to parameters that modulate sound brightness or rhythmicity. Of course to study one parameter, the other must remain fixed. Thus, to study the effects of modulating brightness, the parameter controlling rhythmicity needs to be set to zero - in other words, continuous. Alternatively, to examine the effects of modulating rhythmicity, the brightness parameter needs to be fixed.

Scaling Ranges. Similar to pretesting in the first experiment, two scaling ranges were developed for each synthesiser and modulation. But, when considering brightness, because of the differences in synthesiser design, the range of acceptable minimum and maximum values for which to scale velocity differ. Thus, it was necessary to develop a robust method, such that a change in range reflects a proportional change in brightness for both synthesisers.

As previously discussed the 'jet' synthesiser maps velocity to the speed scalar with a fixed-range of 0.0 to 1.0. Considering this limited range, one might imagine the two states of the jet engine as starting off (0.0) or resting at a certain speed (0.5) and then shifting to maximum speed (1.0). Thus, the two ranges selected were 0.5–1.0 (1:1) and 0.0–1.0 (1:2).

Considering the 'whoosh' synthesiser, because subjects would be wearing headphones during the experiment, it was necessary to select a frequency range that minimised discomfort and not require amplitude adjustments for each subject. Equal-contour loudness curves show that the lower limit of human hearing is around 20 Hz, and that there is a relative flatness - a continuous number of phons - between 300 and 1000 Hz. Following the work conducted in the previous experiment, where there was a decision to select frequencies in the low-mid range, a minimum frequency of 80 Hz and a maximum of 1000 Hz were selected. Thus the two ranges selected were 540–1000 Hz (1:1) and 80–1000 Hz (1:2).

Fortunately, the parameters affecting rhythmicity are the same for both synthesisers. To create a sense of rhythmicity, a simple method was developed that continuously sends an attack-decay-release (ADR) amplitude envelope to the signal generated by a synthesiser. The attack duration was fixed with a duration of 5 ms, whereas the decay duration was variable and controlled by the scaled velocity. Once the envelope is released, the method retrieves a decay duration value from the scaled velocity and repeats the process. A minimum of 20 ms and maximum of 200 ms were selected - between a fifth and a fiftieth of a second. Unlike the relationship with brightness, velocity and decay length are inversely proportional, so that velocity and impulse rate are proportional. Thus, the two ranges, for both synthesisers, are 110–20 ms (1:1) and 200–20 ms (1:2).

Mapping Functions. Three different types of mapping functions were used: linear, exponential (coefficient 2), and logarithmic (base 2). Because the human ear can detect pressure changes from micro- to kilo-pascals, sound pressure levels are typically measured in dB, a logarithmic unit. This justifies studying any effects of logarithmic mapping, which might yield, for subjects, a better relationship between their movement and the sound they hear. It was also decided that its inverse, exponential mapping, might yield interesting comparative results. Finally, linear mapping provides a baseline.

Calibration and Experimental Trials. To test the effects of sound, during the experiment, at the moment of impact with the ball, subject vision would be eliminated. This being based on the assumption that if subjects could see how far the ball travelled and its distance from a target 3.5 m away, they might make adjustments to their swing. However, it was also important that subjects had an opportunity to assess their progress. Thus, during this calibration period subjects would hear pink noise through their headphones. Reasons for this decision are twofold. First, it is common in psychometric experiments to use noise as a way of attenuating feedback sound to enhance proprioception. In this case, pink noise is used to minimise or mask the effects of the impact sound with the ball. Second, the use of pink noise is to match exposure to sound sources in other auditory conditions in the experiment - the experimental trials. The experimental trials test 25 different sounds, which are outlined in Fig. 2. The 25 sounds include static pink noise and 24 sounds synthesised by mapping velocity to unique combinations of synthesisers ('whoosh', 'jet'), modulations (brightness, rhythmicity), scale sizes (1:1, 1:2), and mappings (linear, exponential, logarithmic).

After several pretests, where subjects began with 10 calibrations followed by 40 experimental trials, we found a noticeable drift, as subjects increasingly overshot the target. To adjust for this drift, following a sequence of 25 experimental trials, subjects would have 5 calibration trials. These calibrations provide subjects with a period to reassess their swing and re-familiarise themselves with their distance from the target. Additionally, in order to see if the experimental trials have any overall affect on performance, a final round of calibrations concludes experiment.

Because each experimental trial consists of 25 different sounds, it is important to develop a method that does not bias any one sound over another. Thus, the sequence of sounds in each experimental trial is pseudo-randomised. Each

Synthesis parameters :
Synthesiser : {Jet, Whoosh}
Modulation : {Brightness, Rhythmicity}
Scale : {1:1, 1:2}
Mapping : {Linear, Exponential, Logarithmic}

Combinations : Synthesiser * Modulation * Scale * Mapping = 24 combinations
Sounds : 24 combinations + 1 pink noise = 25 sounds

Fig. 2. Shows the different synthesis parameters, combinations, and sounds developed for the second experiment

sequence is composed of five bins that contain five different sounds. For each repetition, each sound is randomly distributed into a different bin. In total, the experiment consists of 185 trials, divided into several sections. It begins and ends with calibration trials, 20 and 15, respectfully. The remaining 150 trials are organised into five repetitions of 30, which divide into 25 experimental and 5 calibration trials.

3.3   Preliminary Results

While analysis is ongoing, we found great variability between subjects. After normalising subject ball distance by each round, a Repeated Measures (RM) ANOVA analysis was conducted, which found significance ($p < 0.05$) with sounds synthesised from combinations of modulation and mapping. Given a target distance of 350 cm, Table 3 compares the mean ball distance for sonified putts as grouped by the different combinations of modulation (brightness, rhythmicity) and mapping (linear, exponential, logarithmic). While there is little difference between the exponentially mapped sounds, there are differences of around 10 cm for linearly and logarithmically mapped sounds.

Table 3. Shows the mean ball distance for the different combinations of modulation (brightness, rhythmicity) and mapping (linear, exponential, logarithmic).

	Brightness	Rhythmicity
Linear	344.47 cm	353.51 cm
Exponential	350.15 cm	352.26 cm
Logarithmic	354.84 cm	344.57 cm

Looking closer at the effects of mapping, we calculated each subjects skill level by taking their average distance away from the target during the calibration trials (60). Given their skill level, the mean standard deviation distance from the target was calculated for each mapping (linear, exponential, logarithmic) and fitted regression lines were added (Fig. 3). While the type of mapping seemed

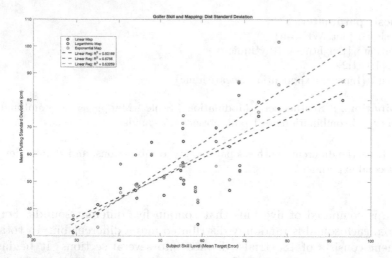

Fig. 3. Shows the relationship between subject skill level and mean standard deviation distance from target for sonified putts. For each subject, sonified putts were grouped by the mapping functions used. Fitted regression lines were then added: linear ($R^2 = 0.50169$), exponential ($R^2 = 0.63269$), and logarithmic ($R^2 = 0.6756$).

to have little effect on the more skilled subjects, logarithmically mapped sounds seemed to exacerbate the effects of the poorly-skilled subjects ($R^2 = 0.6756$).

In addition to ball distance, we also wanted to see whether certain sounds would produce variations in velocity. Each subject's Mean-Velocity Profile (MVP) was calculated by lining up all sonified putts at the time of impact and then averaging them. A RM ANOVA analysis was then conducted with subject MVP as the response variable, which showed significance ($p = 0.008$, effect size 0.3) between both synthesisers and pink noise. A pairwise post-hoc comparison was then applied which found the pink noise case to be most significant ($p <= 0.05$). It was while developing this form of analysis that we began thinking about our third experiment and the possibility of developing sound that reflects each subject's average velocity while completing the golf-putting task.

4   Sonification for Consistency

Following observations from the previous study, the third experiment was designed to study whether sound could be used as a tool for creating swing consistency [46, 50]. After a period of measuring movement during 20 putts at 2 m and 4 m, each subject's MVP was calculated for successful[15] trials at both distances. After dividing subjects into different groups (5), they completed a number trials at both distances where club head speed was mapped to parameters controlling the sonification of their unique MVP data. In some groups, the

---

[15] Trials were considered successful if they measured within a distance of 25 cm from the target.

sounds subjects heard were modulated by real-time deviations from their MVP. In other words, changes to the sound were because they were too 'fast' or 'slow' in comparison to their MVP.[16] The following describes the sounds developed for the experiment.

4.1   MVP Sound

The purpose of sonifying the MVP is to transform the average speed of movement necessary for a successful putt (at the same distance) into sound, so that it might be more palpable, accessible, and, through repetition, familiar for subjects. Following discussions with golf professionals, who, to describe the golf-putting swing, often whistled in an upwards-downwards direction, a simple sinusoidal oscillator was selected to sonify the MVP. For each distance, the absolute value of the MVP is first taken, linearly mapped, and scaled to a frequency range of 80 to 2000 Hz, which is further transformed to a Mel scale (122 to 1521 mels). For each distance, the glissando profile is the same. For subjects in this group, the MVP sound was consistent and complete. Any deviation between a subject's real-time speed and MVP was not sonified.

4.2   Modulations

Two different synthesis strategies were developed to provide subjects with immediate auditory feedback based on real-time deviations from their MVPs. Both take the MVP sound signal and modulate it in different ways. Because of this, it was important to develop synthesis strategies that did not ask too much more of the subjects, who are already given the arduous task of simultaneously completing a putt and listening to sound through their headphones. Before the experimental trials, subjects in each group were instructed on how to interpret the modulations relative to their speed.

Modulation 1: Directivity. In an effort to extend previous research involving golf training and sound directivity, [32] the first synthesis technique modulates the MVP sound signal by panning it in real-time. The percentage of this stereo panning is based on error intensity. For example, if a subject begins slow and then speeds up, she hears the MVP sound shift from right to left. It was important to let subjects know that the stereo panning corresponded to differences in speed and not club head position.

Modulation 2: Roughness. To develop a second method for conveying the error between real-time and MVP speeds, an amplitude modulation model was

---

[16] A method was developed that takes a subject's real-time club head speed and position and, using her MVP and mean-acceleration profile (MAP), calculates a real-time error. The error corresponds to the difference between the current estimation time of impact and that of the MVP.

developed. The error is mapped and scaled to the frequency of a sinusoidal oscillator (modulator signal), which modulates the MVP sound (carrier signal). Like before, error intensity affects the modulation frequency. Many sonification studies have used amplitude modulation to test our ability to perceive changes, such as *tremolo* or *roughness*, to a carrier sound signal [4,21]. Tremolo is a variation in amplitude, which is caused by a modulator signal with a low frequency, which is typically between 0 and 16 Hz. Roughness is a multimodal descriptor of texture, which can be applied in visual, haptic, and auditory modalities. In the auditory domain, it can be simulating when the modulator has a frequency between 15 and 70 Hz [63].

For this experiment, if subjects are too slow, sound is modulated in a way that creates a tremolo effect, where error is mapped to a frequency range of 0 to 4 Hz. However, if the subject is too fast, a sense of roughness is synthesised, where error is mapped to a frequency range of 16 to 70 Hz.

4.3 Musical Sonification

Some sonification studies note subjects have difficulty interpreting synthesised sound and have found success when musical material is used [17,51]. These studies suggest subjects find musical sonifications to be more intuitive. With these observations in mind, a sound was developed that maps the error between real-time and MVP speeds to the playback of a popular music excerpt. Michael Jackson's *Billie Jean* (1983) was selected, as it is popular and has tempo of 117 beats-per-minute (bpm). The tempo is close to 120 bpm, which some movement and music studies have shown is the 'spontaneous tempo of locomotion' for humans [36,39]. The real-time error is scaled in a way that limits speed playback to half and twice speed.

4.4 Experiment #3 Groups

As previously discussed, the third experiment tested five groups, including a control group. Subjects in the control group heard static pink noise for the duration of their swing for both distances. Table 4 outlines the sounds used in each group. Testing began February 2018 and analysis has yet to be conducted.

Table 4. Experiment #3 Groups. 'X' constitutes auditory condition and text, if any, specifies modulation type.

Groups	Pink noise	MVP	Music	Error
1. Control	X			
2. MVP		X		
3. Mod. 1		X		Directivity
4. Mod. 2		X		Roughness
3. Playback			X	Speed

5   Discussion

This chapters outlined different strategies for developing sound to study its affect on novice golf-putting subjects. The first experiment proposed to sonify professional golf data and used it to study the effectiveness of sound as a guidance tool. The second experiment looked at the effects of different real-time sound synthesis strategies on subjects. Combining many of the themes in the previous two experiments, the third experiment involved the development of sound based on averaging subject speed during golf-putting swings in an effort to create more consistent motor behaviour.

There are still many pending questions on how sonification could yield optimal effects on golf putting improvement. Among them, future research may consider the availability of auditory feedback during execution. Indeed, several studies emphasised the powerful influence of a concurrent sensory feedback that was displayed on demand by observers or actors during motor execution, as compared to sustained feedback [28,52]. Such active or transient use of sensory-available cues may decrease the well-known dependence upon artificial feedback during learning, [1,47] hence avoiding learning transfer to ecological conditions of practice.

In closing, the way sound can be used to complement or invite engagement with other sensory information, such as haptic or visual feedback, is of great interest for the upcoming challenges to be tackled around multi-sensory-based learning. Of course the manner of its use invites many questions. For example, does congruent multimodal information always lead to an improvement of gesture control and learning, especially in terms of precision and accuracy? [7] Or does one sensory channel mask or override the others, yielding no benefits from multi-sensory feedback enhancement? These are some of the question to consider moving forward in developing sound for future golf-related studies.

Acknowledgements. Many thanks to PRISM researchers Richard Kronland-Martinent, Mitsuko Aramaki, and Sølvi Ystad for their guidance and help developing materials that were used in the first two experiments. In addition to Mario LaFortune for his expertise and enthusiasm. This work was funded by the French National Research Agency (ANR) under the SoniMove: Inform, Guide and Learn Actions by Sounds project (ANR-14-CE24-0018-01).

References

1. Adams, J.: A closed-loop theory of motor learning. J. Mot. Behav. **3**(2), 111–149 (1971)
2. Agostini, T., Righi, G., Galmonte, A., Bruno, P.: The relevance of auditory information in optimizing hammer throwers performance. In: Pascolo, P.B. (ed.) Biomechanics and Sports. CCL, vol. 473, pp. 67–74. Springer, Vienna (2004). https://doi.org/10.1007/978-3-7091-2760-5_9
3. Altavilla, A., Caramiaux, B., Tanaka, A.: Towards gestural sonic affordances (2013)

4. Altinsoy, M.E.: The effect of auditory cues on the audiotactile roughness perception: modulation frequency and sound pressure level. In: Pirhonen, A., Brewster, S. (eds.) HAID 2008. LNCS, vol. 5270, pp. 120–129. Springer, Heidelberg (2008). https://doi.org/10.1007/978-3-540-87883-4_13
5. Arnott, S., Alain, C.: The auditory dorsal pathway: orienting vision. Neurosci. Biobehav. Rev. **35**(10), 2162–2173 (2011)
6. Baumann, S., Koeneke, S., Schmidt, C., Meyer, M., Lutz, K., Jancke, L.: A network for audio-motor coordination in skilled pianists and non-musicians. Brain Res. **1161**, 65–78 (2007)
7. Besson, P., Richiardi, J., Bourdin, C., Bringoux, L., Mestre, D., Vercher, J.: Bayesian networks and information theory for audio-visual perception modeling. Biol. Cybern. **103**, 213–226 (2010)
8. Bringoux, L., et al.: Influence of speed-related auditory feedback on braking in a 3D-driving simulator. Transp. Res. Part F Traffic Psychol. Behav. **44**, 76–89 (2017)
9. Brown, A., Kenwell, Z., Maraj, B., Collins, D.: "Go" signal intensity influences the sprint start. Med. Sci. Sports Exerc. **40**, 1142–1148 (2008)
10. Castiello, U., Giordano, B., Begliomini, C., Ansuini, C., Grassi, M.: When ears drive hands: the influence of contact sound on reaching to grasp. PLoS ONE **5**(8), e12240 (2010)
11. Conan, S., et al.: An intuitive synthesiser of continuous-interaction sounds: rubbing, scratching, and rolling. Comput. Music J. **38**(4), 24–27 (2014)
12. Craig, C.M., Delay, D., Grealy, M.A., Lee, D.N.: Guiding the swing in golf putting. Nature **405**(6784), 295–296 (2000)
13. Corso, J., Saldanha, E.: Timbre cues and the identification of musical instruments. J. Acoust. Soc. Am. **36**, 2021–2026 (1964)
14. Danna, J., et al.: The effect of real-time auditory feedback on learning new characters. Hum. Mov. Sci. **43**, 216–228 (2014)
15. Denjean, S., Roussarie, V., Kronland-Martinet, R., Ystad, S., Velay, J.-L.: How does interior car noise alter driver's perception of motion, Multisensory integration in speed perception. In: Proceedings of the Acoustics 2012 Nantes Conference (2012)
16. Dubus, G., Bresin, R.: Exploration and evaluation of a system for interactive sonification of elite rowing. Sports Eng. **18**, 29–41 (2014)
17. Dyer, J., Rodger, M., Stapleton, P.: Transposing musical skill: sonification of movement as concurrent augmented feedback enhances learning in a bimanual task. Psychol. Res. **81**, 850–862 (2017)
18. Effenberg, A., Ursula, F., Schmitz, G., Krueger, B., Mechling, H.: Movement sonification: effects on motor learning beyond rhythmic adjustments. Front. Neurosci. **10**, 219 (2016)
19. Erickson, R.: Sound Structure in Music. University of California Press, Berkeley and Los Angeles (1975)
20. Farnell, A.: Designing Sound, pp. 491–497. The MIT Press, London (2010)
21. Ferguson, J., Brewster, S.: Evaluation of psychoacoustic sound parameters for sonification. In: Proceedings of 19th ACM International Conference on Multimodal Interaction, pp. 120–127 (2017)
22. Fitch, W.T., Kramer, G.: Sonifying the body electric: superiority of an auditory over a visual display in a complex, multivariate system. In: Kramer G. (ed.) Auditory Display: Sonification, Audification and Auditory Interfaces, pp. 307–325. Addison-Wesley, Reading (1994)
23. Gaver, W.: What in the world do we hear?: An ecological approach to auditory event perception. Ecol. Psychol. **5**, 1–29 (1993)

24. Grey, J.: Exploration of musical timbre. Stanford University Department of Music, Technical report, STAN-M-2 (1975)
25. Grond, F., Berger, J.: Parameter mapping sonification. In: Hermann, T., Hunt, A., Neuhoff, J.G. (eds.) The Sonification Handbook, pp. 363–397. Logos Publishing House, Berlin (2011)
26. Hebb, D.: The Organization of Behavior. Wiley & Sons, New York (1949)
27. Hermann, T.: Taxonomy and definitions for sonification and auditory display. In: Proceedings of the 14th International Conference on Auditory Display, Paris, France (2008)
28. Huet, M., Camachon, C., Fernadez, L., Jacobs, D., Montage, G.: Self-controlled concurrent feedback and the education of attention towards perceptual invariants. Hum. Mov. Sci. **28**(4), 450–467 (2009)
29. Kleiman-Weiner, M., Berger, J.: The sound of one arm swinging: a model for multidimensional auditory display of physical motion. In: Proceedings of the 12th International Conference on Auditory Display (2006)
30. Kohler, E., Keysers, C., Umilta, A., Fogassi, L., Gallese, V., Rizzolatti, G.: Hearing sounds, understanding actions: action representation in mirror neurons. Science **297**(5582), 846–848 (2002)
31. Lakatos, S., McAdams, S., Causse, R.: The representation of auditory source characteristics: simple geometric form. Percept. Psychophys. **59**, 1180–1190 (1997)
32. Libkum, T., Otani, H., Steger, N.: Training in timing improves accuracy in golf. J. Gen. Psychol. **129**(1), 77–96 (2002)
33. Lotze, M., Scheler, G., Tan, H.R.M., Braun, C., Birbaumer, N.: The musician's brain: functional imaging of amateurs and professionals during performance and imagery. Neuroimage **20**, 1817–1829 (2003)
34. Lee, D., Georgopoulos, P., Clark, M., Craig, C., Port, N.: Guiding contact by coupling the taus of gaps. Exp. Brain Res. **139**(2), 151–159 (1999)
35. Luce, D.: Physical correlates of non-percussive musical instruments, Ph.D. dissertation, Massachusetts Institute of Technology, Cambridge, MA (1963)
36. MacDougall, H., Moore, S.: Marching to the beat of the same drummer: the spontaneous tempo of human locomotion. J. Appl. Physiol. **99**(3), 1164–1173 (2005)
37. McAdams, S., Bregman, A.: Hearing musical streams. Comput. Music J. **3**(4), 26–43 (1979)
38. Meister, I., et al.: Playing piano in the mind - an fMRI study on music imagery and performance in pianists. Cogn. Brain Res. **19**, 219–228 (2004)
39. Moelants, D.: Preferred tempo reconsidered. In: Proceedings of the 7th International Conference on Music Perception and Cognition, Causal Production, Adelaide (2002)
40. Newton, P.: The learning styles myth is thriving in higher education. Front. Psychol. **6**, 1908 (2015)
41. O'Shaughnessy, D.: Speech Communication: Human and Machine, p. 150. Addison-Wesley, Reading (1987)
42. Parseihian, G., Ystad, S., Aramaki, M., Kronland-Martinet, R.: The process of sonification design for guidance tasks. Wi J. Mob. Media **9**(2) (2015)
43. Phillips-Silver, J., Trainor, L.: Feeling the beat: movement influences infant rhythm perception. Science **308**(5727), 1430 (2005)
44. Risset, J., Mathews, M.: Analysis of musical instrument tones. Phys. Today **22**, 23–30 (1969)
45. Roberts, J., Jones, R., Mansfield, N., Mansfield, S.: Evaluation of impact sound on the 'feel' of a golf shot. J. Sound Vib. **287**(4–5), 651–666 (2005)

46. Ronsse, R., et al.: Motor learning with augmented feedback: modality-dependent behavioural and neural consequences. Cereb. Cortex **21**(6), 1283–1294 (2011)
47. Salmoni, A., Schmidt, R., Walter, C.: Knowledge of results and motor learning: a review and critical reappraisal. Psychol. Bull. **95**(3), 355–386 (1984)
48. Scaletti, C.: Sound synthesis algorithms for auditory data representation. In: Kramer, G. (ed.) Auditory Display (XVIII) of Santa Fe Institute. Studies in the Science of Complexity Proceedings, pp. 223–252. Addison-Wesley, Reading (1994)
49. Schmitz, G., et al.: Observation of sonified movements engages a basal ganglia frontocortical network. BMC Neurosci. **14**, 32 (2013)
50. Shea, C., Wulf, G., Park, J.-H., Gaunt, B.: Effects of an auditory model on the learning of relative and absolute timing. J. Mot. behav. **33**(2), 127–138 (2001)
51. Sigrist, R., Rauter, G., Riener, R., Wolf, P.: Augmented visual, auditory, haptic, and multimodal feedback in motor learning: a review. Psychon. Bull. Rev. **20**(1), 21–53 (2013)
52. Sigrist, R., Schellenberg, J., Rauter, G., Broggi, S., Riener, R., Wolf, P.: Visual and auditory augmented concurrent feedback in a complex motor task. Presence Teleop. Virtual Environ. **20**(1), 15–32 (2011)
53. Sommer, M., Rønnqvist, L.: Improved motor-timing: effects of synchronized metronom training on golf shot accuracy. J. Sports Sci. Med. **8**(4), 648–656 (2009)
54. Sors, F., Murgia, M., Santoro, I., Prpic, V., Galmonte, A., Agostini, T.: The contribution of early auditory and visual information to the discrimination of shot power in ball sports. Psychol. Sport Exer. **31**, 44–51 (2017)
55. Stevens, S., Volkmann, J.: A scale for the measurement of the pscyhological magnitude pitch. J. Acoust. Soc. Am. **8**(3), 185–190 (1937)
56. Su, Y., Salazar-López, E.: Visual timing of structured dance movements resembles auditory rhythm perception. Neural Plast. **2016**, 1–17 (2016)
57. Thoret, E., Aramaki, M., Kronland-Martinet, R., Velay, J.-L., Ystad, S.: From sound to shape: auditory perception of drawing movements. J. Exp. Psychol. Hum. Percept. Perform. Am. Psychol. Assoc. **40**(3), 983–994 (2014)
58. Taschuk, E., Kavarana, F., DeYoung, J.: Acceleration Noise Metric for Vehicles with CVT Transmission. SAE Technical Paper (2011)
59. Wessel, D.: Timbre space as a musical control structure. Comput. Music J. **3**(2), 45–52 (1979)
60. Wildes, R.P., Richards, W.: "Recovering Material Properties from Sound," Natural Computation, pp. 356–363. MIT Press, Cambridge (1988)
61. Witek, M., Clarke, E., Wallentin, M., Kringelbach, M., Vuust, P.: Syncopation, body-movement and pleasure in groove music. PLoS ONE **9**(4), e94446 (2014)
62. Zahariev, M., MacKenzie, C.: Auditory, graphical and haptic contact cues for a reach, grasp, and place task in an augmented environment (2003)
63. Zwicker, E., Fastl, H.: Psychoacoustics: Facts and Models, vol. 22. Springer, Heidelberg (2013)
64. Zwicker, E.: Subdivision of the audible frequency range into critical bands. J. Acoust. Soc. Am. **33**(2), 248 (1961)

Human Perception in Multimodal Context

Feel It in My Bones: Composing Multimodal Experience Through Tissue Conduction

Peter Lennox[✉], Ian McKenzie, and Michael Brown

University of Derby, Derby, UK
{p.lennox, i.mckenzie1, m.brown2}@derby.ac.uk

Abstract. We outline here the feasibility of coherently utilising tissue conduction for spatial audio and tactile input. Tissue conduction display-specific compositional concerns are discussed; it is hypothesised that the qualia available through this medium substantively differ from those for conventional artificial means of appealing to auditory spatial perception. The implications include that spatial music experienced in this manner constitutes a new kind of experience, and that the ground rules of composition are yet to be established. We refer to results from listening experiences with one hundred listeners in an unstructured attribute elicitation exercise, where prominent themes such as "strange", "weird", "positive", "spatial" and "vibrations" emerged. We speculate on future directions aimed at taking maximal advantage of the principle of multimodal perception to broaden the informational bandwidth of the display system. Some implications for composition for hearing-impaired are elucidated.

Keywords: Bone conduction · Tissue conduction · Multimodal perception
Multimodal composition · Pallesthesia

1 Introduction

We describe listening experiments to elicit descriptive terms of the experience of tissue-conducted (often referred to as "bone-conducted") multichannel sound. The aim here is to explore the dimensionality of the subjective experiences, and whilst we expect significant inter-participant differences in reporting (since uninstructed listeners are unlikely to report in the precise terminology used in a quantitative psychophysical study), we would like to understand to what extent these are merely semantic differences or whether there are substantive differences in qualia.

As we are interested in reports suggesting spatial impressions of some sort, such differences are interesting in as much as it is likely that there are significant variances in conceptualisations of "space". This follows from the observation that spatial perception is neither functionally monolithic, nor independent of the perception of other attributes (see Sect. 1 below). In allowing participants to choose what they wish to comment on about the experience, we avoid imposing rigorous experimental constraints that could result in reductionism. This approach has the advantage of avoiding 'leading the witness' and can elicit observations of qualia that we (the experimenters) might not anticipate. The disadvantage is that precision is compromised and quantitative data

© Springer Nature Switzerland AG 2018
M. Aramaki et al. (Eds.): CMMR 2017, LNCS 11265, pp. 361–386, 2018.
https://doi.org/10.1007/978-3-030-01692-0_24

cannot be obtained. Our objective at this stage is to identify emergent themes that can be the targets of future, quantitative investigations.

We observed that many respondents described the experience with extra-auditory terms such as *vibration* and *feeling*, and some remarked that the experience was markedly different from other modes of listening. We take the implicature that they may be experiencing the sensory input multimodally, leading us to investigate the possibility of deliberately composing multimodal experiences using this technique.

2 Auditory Spatial Perception

Space is a multifarious term that includes shape, size, texture, location, distance and movement, all of which can be described in terms of Euclidean geometry and the temporal dimension. Additionally, beyond Euclidean geometry is 'spatial meaning', which, for an ambulant individual organism, is of primary importance.

Spatial perception is a fundamental ingredient of perception in general. From an evolutionary perspective, it is how we understand our relationships with our heterogeneous environment, locating and evaluating threats and opportunities. Navigating and acting in complex environments requires competence in real-time cognitive representation of spatial relationships, and unsurprisingly, large volumes of the brain are involved. From another perspective, few perceiver-environment interactions *do not* involve spatial responses.

Understanding the nature of an item (in the environment), its proximity, direction, movement (including acceleration), the opportunities for avoiding (or facilitating) confrontations and the affordances [13] the local environment offers (escape routes, hiding places, vantage points etc.) all require different types of computation. Hence, we might expect multitudinous specialised computational resources in the brain. Advances in neuroscience indicate distinct neural processing pathways for 'what' and 'where' [30, 33].

Brain-region specialisation in spatial cognition has been observed for task-specific processing of understanding the position of one's own body parts in space [16], motor planning for action through space and even, at the level of individual neurons, for planning different types of action [32].

In terms of spatial meaning, the region of space directly surrounding a perceiver and within reach (the peripersonal space) is intrinsically more meaningful (because of the imminence of interaction-opportunities) than the extrapersonal space (in the locale, but beyond immediate reach). Similarly, items moving toward the perceiver are potentially more urgent than those departing. Consequently, spatial challenges in these cases differ, entailing different patterns of neural excitation [38] and are likely to be reported differently. Effectively, spatial perception is deeply biased toward survival, and this bias is structurally instantiated in the individual.

Auditory-specific spatial representation clearly involves, at some stages of processing, signals derived from the reception of audible signals. However, at higher, more abstract levels of representation of space in the posterior parietal cortex, representation is multimodal [10]; there is no distinct, autonomous 'auditory space' [32]. A consequence of this is that, even in the case of single-sense spatial audio presentation, the evoked impressions of spatiality are derived from multimodal thinking about space and listeners are unlikely to describe qualia in audio-only terms.

3 Tissue Conducted Sound

The source of a sound is something we might usually think of as external to one's body, our own voice, although originating from within might easily be perceived as exclusively peripheral. Listening to a play-back of our voice may sound strange to us as it is not in agreement with the sound heard while recording it; a percentage of the sounds heard whilst talking propagates internally and is not recorded, this part is tissue conducted sound. As a means of propagation it has been known and used for centuries and is historically known as bone-conduction (BC); 16th century to assess ear pathology, early assisted hearing devices late 18th century and tuning fork tests (TFT) evaluating hearing and ear pathology 20th century to present day. As bone is only one of several transmission pathways the term "tissue conduction" is preferred as a more comprehensive description.

During vibro-tactile stimulation, skin, bone, fluids, soft tissue and the cranium contents are all transmission pathways to various extents. Pathways are frequency dependant contributing forces that act on parts of the hearing system; inertial forces on the ossicular chain and cochlear fluids, distortion of the temporal bone and cochlear shell, occluded ear canal resonance and fluid pressures [17, 21, 42, 44]. While the importance of each pathways contribution remains in debate there is general agreement that their summed contribution result in passive travelling wave motion along the basilar membrane leading to auditory perception. Cancellation experiments suggest basilar wave motion to be similar whether elicited through air-conducted, bone-conducted or tissue-conducted sound [5, 7, 44]. In spite of the similarity in basilar motion, it was long believed that cues available for sound localisation in air, interaural time difference (ITD), interaural level difference (ILD) and spectral cues would not be available during tissue conduction. Recent TC research reports some success in lateralisation when appealing to interaural level and time differences [26, 43, 45]. The outer ear is not subject to stimulation during tissue conducted sound and in the absence of spectral cues provided by the pinnae, localisation of sound sources should remain 'in the head' on the horizontal plane. We note interesting anomalies while using a multiple vibro-tactile transducer array; in the absence of spectral cues from their pinnae listeners nevertheless continued to experience elevation and varying degrees of externalisation.

4 Spatial Tissue Conducted Sound: One Hundred Listeners

One hundred volunteers (24 female 16–60 yrs. 76 male 16–62 yrs.) were invited to take part in a listening experiment; participants received no prior instruction on any target attributes. Participants were invited to take part then offer any observations they may have on the experience in the form of written comments [1, 56], participants were also asked to record their age, sex, occupation and whether or not they were musicians (details are being used in ongoing correlative analysis). Audition elicited during the experiment was through a multi-channel vibro-tactile transducer array; five BCT-1 8Ω 90 dB 1 W/1 m tactile transducers held in a tensioned framework exerting contact force with skull were used to elicit auditory spatial impressions through tissue conduction.

The significant differences here lie in the use of a distributed array of transducers to carry programme content, and the deployment of ambisonically encoded signals to that array. In proper usages of ambisonics, multiple transducers (loudspeakers) are arranged around a volume of space (the listening area). Signals are encoded to this array so as to manage the interaural differences at the ears of an ideally placed listener, evincing spatial impressions of location, movement, image size, distance (actually, *range* from the listener) and spaciousness of the depicted environment. For a discussion of ambisonics, see [54].

In our usage, whilst the aim is to manipulate interaural signal differences, in practice this is somewhat indeterministic, since suppose that signal path length and speed (from each transducer, through soft tissue and bone, to each cochlea) is currently unknown. Therefore, this randomisation of arrival times (at the cochleae) interferes with the theoretical basis of ambisonics and we would not expect to coherently manage perceptual impressions of detailed three-dimensional sound fields. Nevertheless, ambisonics encoding remains a useful panning method, not least because spatial impression always relies on multiple transducers; that is to say, for a given auditory image, in a given direction, multiple transducers contribute to the impinging waves (normally at the outer ears). This is convenient because, physical impedance matching problems (between transducer and bone-and-soft-tissue) normally constrain dynamic range and frequency balance (of signals arriving at the cochleae). Use of multiple transducers can, to some extent, offset such constraints.

4.1 Equipment

A prototype transducer array using five tactile transducers was used to display a range of spatial soundscapes and music. Discrete signal sets were constructed in Reaper DAW running on MAC and routed to five individual 1 W amplifiers via fire-wire connection through a Focusrite PRO 26 i/o interface. Each transducer receives a unique set as a channel, channel 1 - left mastoid process, channel 2-25 mm above left temple, channel 3 - midway between forehead and vertex, channel 4 - 25 mm above right temple, channel 5 - right mastoid process. Banded style 3 M Ear Plugs were available for listeners to experience any perceived differences between plugs in vs out.

Dayton Audio BCT-1 tactile transducers were used for the array, specifications according to manufacturer: Power handling: 1 W RMS/2 W max • Le: 1.26 mH • Impedance: 8 ohm • Re: 5.8 ohms • Frequency response: 300-19,000 Hz • Weight: 0.02 lbs. • Fs: 1,600 Hz • SPL: 90.1 dB 1 W/1 m • Xmax: 5.5 mm • Dimensions (L x W x H): 0.85" x 0.57" x 0.31" (Fig. 1).

The contact exerted by the framework was originally designed to apply 300–350 g of force whilst holding the transducers in place against a participant's skull; contact force was based on average head diameters of 18 cm for Male and 17 cm for Female. Improvements in transmission gain related to contact force are known; considerable variance observed in head size and shape across the 100 participants introduced a wider

Fig. 1. Dayton Audio BCT-1 tactile transducer.

margin than expected, the implications and limitations of this are discussed in section (see Sect. 3.3). In spite of the sizeable differences in size and shape the transducer locations remained achievable across participants by virtue of the adjustment built into the framework.

Transducer location has reported differences in threshold, frequency range and transmission pathway stimulation, locations were selected based on previous research [28]. The mastoid process is a traditional bone conduction stimulation site; lateralisation performance equivalent to binaural lateralisation during bilateral stimulation of the mastoids is feasible. The 'ultrasound' window just above the zygomatic arch provides a sensitive stimulation point; this region is the thinnest area of the skull allowing useful stimulation of the cranial contents. Transcranial attenuation has been reported as higher than at the mastoid when stimulation occurs at the ultrasound window, notably at higher frequencies. The forehead, notwithstanding lower sensitivity and higher thresholds than the mastoid and temporal region, is at an equidistant point to the cochleae. Stimulation of a single point at the forehead may be used to process signals against at other locations to realise externalised phantom imagery; this hypothesis continues to be a subject of research (Fig. 2).

4.2 Listening Materials and Conditions

Auditory stimuli was signal processed through a variety of FX plugins and routed simultaneously in different formats; stereo, modified stereo, ambisonics and direct feed. An ambient background was provided by a B format 1st order ambisonic recording of a country park captured using a Soundfield ™ microphone; stereo recordings of bird sounds, a steam train and music alongside mono FX clips were used to create the soundscape. Signal sets were spatially encoded using WigWare [54] 1st order ambisonic panning and decoded through a Wig-Ware 1st order periphonic ambisonic decoder patched to the transducer array.

Listening tests took place across three days as part of the Exploratorium exhibit during PLASA London 2017 on the upper level of a large exhibition hall; a less than ideal high level noise floor was maintained throughout the day by sounds from other exhibitors and a large footfall. Attendees of the event who expressed any interest in our exhibit were immediately invited to take part in the listening test before any further discussion could take place. Participants were seated and the headset placed on their head, comfortable amplitude levels were arrived at during a short piece of music after

Fig. 2. Prototype five transducer headset array, PLASA London 2017.

which the five minute audition began. Upon completion participants were asked to record their comments on prepared forms.

4.3   Limitations

The method of recording data proved to be suboptimal in that many of the participants described their experience in far greater detail during post-test discussions than in writing. The high percentage of positive comments should be cautiously assimilated, since participants were self-selecting. The generic headset, being based on average head size does not actually suit all participants equally; with consequent variations in contact force at each transducer for each participant, affecting efficiency of energy transfer between transducer and cranial tissue [28].

4.4   Comments

The written comments of the one hundred participants were collated into a word document and then into a spreadsheet for analysis, below are few sample comments and associated themes (see appendix A for complete list).

Male, 23, DJ, Musician.

"Very interesting, new experience of sound. Vibrations feel slightly unusual but also add a new dimension to the sound experience. Very cool."
(Themes: positive, interesting, vibrations, weird)

Male, 28, Theatre Tech, Non-Musician.

"Loved the vibrations of the aeroplane flying over and in general how the sound felt all around."
(Themes: positive, spatial, surround, vibrations, external)

Male, 37, Equipment Sales, Musician.

"I enjoyed the vibrations on the pressure points. Sound has remarkable stereo/surround perception. With ear plugs in, it felt like listening to headphones. A pleasant experience."
(Themes: positive, surround, vibrations, feel, external, headphones)

Female, 18, Student, Musician.

"Occasionally you could feel the deeper sounds as physical vibrations especially in the front central point. The higher sounds like bird song were easier to pick up what direction it was coming from. The music sounded better than it would through regular headphones as you felt surrounded by the sound as you would in a realistic setting of an orchestra."
(Themes: positive, spatial, surround, clarity, vibrations, feel, external, headphones)

4.5   Emergent Themes

The written comments were aggregated and analysed for emergent themes, primarily our interest lay in the arrays ability to convey auditory spatial information; 38% of the recorded comments were indicative of participants experiencing a 'sense of space' during the experiment. Other interesting themes include 'positive experience', 'interesting', 'spatial', 'vibration', 'weird' and 'clarity', Fig. 3 shows results correlated to 'positive' (Table 1).

4.6   Discussion

In the absence of pinnae related spectral cues, we hypothesise in respect to comments indicating spatial impressions that while presenting signal sets via multiple pathways we may achieve a degree of perceptual equivalence through more abstract relationships. Propagation through tissue conduction by means of multiple, frequency dependant transmission pathways may be responsible for differences in frequency component arrival times within grouped and segregated sensory data [3, 17, 21, 42, 44]. There is also an intriguing notion that plausible interaural time difference fluctuations are created as complex sounds interact during transmission to the cochleae, eliciting a sense of spacious envelopment [34]. Due to the complex nature of propagation during multiple-location tissue conduction it is not yet possible to model the signal arriving at the cochleae; methods by which we may examine this remain in development and will feature in future papers.

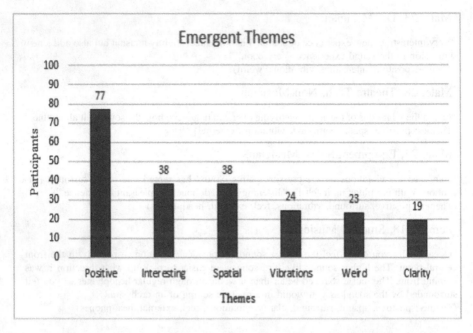

Fig. 3. Emergent themes from aggregated comments of 100 listeners correlated with comments of a 'positive' experience.

Table 1. Emergent themes and descriptors

Theme	Grouped characteristics
Positive	Nice, incredible, amazing, awesome, excellent, loved, good, enjoyed, cool, wonderful, extraordinary, impressive, effective
Negative	Muddy, muffled, lacking, limited, quiet, dull, distortion
Hearing loss	Hearing loss
Spatial	Spatial, surround, 3D, virtual reality, image location, movement, image positioning, 360 sound-field, external
Clarity	Clarity, clear, crisp, pure
Interesting	Interesting, fascinating
Weird	Weird, unusual, surreal, strange, uncanny, ethereal, eerie, bizarre
Vibrations	Vibrations, tickling, tickling
Feel	Feel, felt, feeling, natural, sensorial
External	Distant, immersive, overhead, above, around, spacious, outside
Headphones	Headphones

4.7 Vibration

An unexpected result emerged from the aggregated comments, 24% referred to vibration in a neutral or positive context; 12% of these where positively associated with comments on spatial impression. The result was unexpected as we had assumed that any vibration from the array would generate negative terms, this was only the case in 3% of the responses. We note that in addition to audition, the disturbance of mechanoreceptors in the body can give rise to a range of perceptions. What is normally meant by 'sense of touch' can be either passive *receptive* touch or active, exploratory *haptic* touch. The former refers to stimuli detected by mechanoreceptors (usually near the skin surface) whereas the latter incorporates proprioceptive mechanisms; we manipulate, pick up, detect weight and so on. In sensory psychophysics the work of Weber and Fechner discovered that despite the diversity of sensations, all sensory systems convey four basic types of information, modality, location, intensity, and timing [11]. In our context, using vibrotactile transducers, tactition is the appropriate term, and this has dimensions of frequency, intensity, spatial location and direction.

There is another important aspect to touch in the form of *pallesthesia* (sensitivity to vibration). This can take place at the surface of the body, but can also be detected internally in skeletal structure, balance organs (in mammals: the otoliths) and soft tissues such as the abdomen and eyeballs. The contributions of pallesthesia to everyday perception are not well understood; it is normally studied within the context of high-energy low frequency vibration in conjunction with health and safety concerns and annoyance factors. As a potential information-channel, pallesthesia is often overlooked, but *might* play a significant role in multimodal perception; the current broad consensus is that most, if not all, higher, as well as lower level neural processes are in some form multisensory [18, 50].

5 Multimodal Perception

Multimodal perception refers to percepts formed of combined information from two or more sense-modes, involving multisensory integration. In the past four decades there has been a burgeoning of interest in the subject, often framed in the context of the binding problem, which is related to understanding how multitudinous sensory qualia (within particular sense modes, or across several sense modes) are combined into unitary perceptions of objects and events [36].

At a philosophical level, the difficulties in precisely defining, individuating and counting discrete senses are well known [27]. Nevertheless, study of perception has tended to be specialised in particular sense modes. Vision scientists have had only passing acquaintance with theories of auditory perception and vice versa [9]. Haptic, olfactory, gustatory and somatosensory sciences have traditionally had similarly little intercourse. This conceptual reification also tends to affect art forms, so that pictures and music are produced by different people and often enjoyed in separate places.

At the level of real world experience, unimodal sense-perception is a peculiarity, rarely occurring in real-environment perception; real events naturally produce information that is potentially available to two or more sense-modes.

Characterising multimodal perception in terms of performance, variance and neural mechanisms is therefore a central challenge in the study of perception.

Evidence from neuroscience indicates that multisensory neurons are ubiquitous in the central nervous system, at peripheral as well as central levels [4], suggesting that perception is intrinsically multimodal. Multimodality can be examined in terms of cross-modal effects, wherein information from one modality is modified by the influence of information in another. The McGurk effect typifies this; a unimodal auditory stimulus of repeated spoken syllables: "ba, ba, ba" is perceived accurately, but the addition of incongruent visual stimuli – a video of a speaker mouthing: "ga, ga, ga" produces reports of hearing "da, da, da" [29]. The interaction produces an intermediate perceptual conclusion that minimises incongruity, indicating that congruity is an important underlying principle in multimodal processing. For a discussion of cross-modal effects, [20].

Additive effects occur when the perceptual conclusions via a single modality might be weak, but the addition of other-mode information provides more robust perceptual conclusions – this might be typified in the problem of discerning the contents of speech in a noisy environment; if we can see the talker, we can *hear* the talker better [46]. Sometimes *supra-additive* effects can occur, whereby each unimodal stimulus is weak, but in combination add up to more than the simple sum of the two or more stimulus components [52].

In theory, at least, the addition of tactile stimulus elements to auditory stimulus material can be *sub-additive* (a multisensory neuron might show a given response to input from a single sense-mode input, and greater response for signals from two or more modes, but not a proportionate summing of unimodal response), additive, or even super additive. Another way to consider this is to say that, in conditions where the unimodal signals capture sufficient complexity of information, multimodal input provides less additional information than where unimodal signals are comparatively weak. So, in conditions of unimodal impairment (hearing deficits or high noise-floor, or combinations of both), multimodal additions can provide more robust perceptual conclusions.

In the principle of psychophysical complementarity [40], we might assume that, since events in the world often or usually stimulate multiple sense-modes, integration of disparate information-streams should proceed according to evolved heuristics. That is, some form of "multimodal scene analysis" might be postulated, and this will take information from prior experience as well as on-going sensation; we are always contextually aware.

The key features of such multimodal scene analysis appear to be congruence and concomitance; synchronicity and spatial co-location would promote perception of concomitance, repetition of synchronicity (of stimuli) would reinforce it. Congruence might have higher-order implications; if an item in the environment visibly moves as though it has considerable inertial mass, and makes sounds with considerable (in amplitude) low frequency content, these would be congruent with the impression that the item is massive. Congruence-comprehension, the major component of *cognitive causal mapping* [23] must, in order to function in timely fashion, feature some efficient and rapid heuristics. Wilson and Sperber [55] in discussing Relevance Theory propose heuristics for comprehension:

a. Follow a path of least effort in computing cognitive effects: Test interpretive hypotheses (disambiguations, reference resolutions, implicatures, etc.) in order of accessibility.

b. Stop when your expectations of relevance are satisfied.

Although they are thinking specifically of language communication and comprehension, in theory a similar parsimonious approach might be appropriate for comprehension of other types of signal in the environment. Their use of "...interpretive hypotheses" and "...expectations" suggests that higher-order comprehension of context probably influences more peripheral neuronal responses, and by extension this could explain differences in multimodal processing. If unimodal information is incomplete, information from other modes can be recruited, whereas if the former is sufficient, the latter is redundant.

6 Compositional Use of Congruent Auditory and Tactile Spatial Signals

Music is inherently a multi-sensory experience; we *hear* in space, we may *see* or associate in our imagination a causal source, we may *feel* objective resonance and create internal narratives to support emotional constructs, guided by expressed extra-musical identities. A typical dictionary definition of music offers:

> *"the art and science of combining vocal or instrumental sounds or tones in varying melody, harmony, rhythm, and timbre, esp. so as to form structurally complete and emotionally expressive compositions"*[52]

This presents the dominant characteristic and compositional preoccupation as *sound*; regular patterns which ideally result in listener coherence and sustained interest.

We might reasonably define music as simply *'organised sound'*; which, though seemingly superficial is satisfying since it is open and all-embracing of musical space. Edgard Varése similarly expressed it [14] when discussing his own aesthetic sensibilities in relation to his recent excursion into multi-speaker tape composition: Poème électronique (1957-58). What is composition? A sonorous creative act, idea, performance or recording that might be considered new and valuable. This could involve a transformation in an existing stylistic domain or the establishment of a new one that achieves cultural recognition. Alternative organisational designs in music we will call *style*, to mean the accepted *norms* of a musical period or individual. *Style* refers to the common attributes and behaviours within a musical form; in any given *style*, certain features are considered normal and others anomalous.

All sound may be considered *musical*, which is the virtue of the above definition, but in each culture musicians tend to admit only a subset of acceptable sounds, frequency arrangements, combinations and temporal patterns, into sonic expression. Given the self-imposed limitations, music remains a system of sufficient complexity to allow for combinatory and sequential variation accommodating novelty, identity and meaning. Innovation in music however, requires more than mere *novelty*; the newness must have a context for it to be validated by the domain gatekeepers, as Frank Zappa said [57]: "Without deviation (from the norm), 'progress' is not possible...In order for one to *deviate successfully*, one has to have at least a passing acquaintance with whatever *norm* one expects to deviate from".

There may be no single intercultural definition of music and the boundary between musical sounds and noise may be culturally blurred. Varése speculated [14] upon the future of music *"the score of the future would need to be seismographic in order to illustrate their full potential"*, citing the definition of music given by Józef Maria Hoene-Wroński: "the corporealization of the intelligence that is in sound", as being particularly influential in shaping his musical imagination. Music could dispassionately be regarded as an abstract sonic temporal construction, constrained by pre-formed elements organised in predefined relationships; a product perhaps more of *discovery* than invention, that might conceivably be determined or computed; the permutations and combinations of acceptable outcomes calculated and selected according to stochastic design. From this perspective, mechanised musical culturally-verified arte-facts might be fabricated according to audience requirements for expectation, consis-tency, coherence and originality.

Educationally it is not uncommon to study the *craft* of composition by learning the characteristics of archetypal work, through systematic analysis codifying behaviours tested through re-creation; creative motivation and method is somewhat less often addressed and there are other important peripheral attributes of musical expression and experience missing (from the analysis) that may offer new perspectives and valuable insights such as:

- The creative process: which is very likely non-linear; does music have to be experienced along a fixed timeline?
- The communication and expression of emotive design through dynamic physio-logical gestures in performance; music has at times been considered a language with linguistic syntactical structure [30]. The imprecision within the symbolic repre-sentation (notation) is also profitable for performers, allowing for expressive indi-vidual interpretation.
- The tactile sensations of performing/composing upon instrument, sensing and responding to the resonant vibrations within a space. Each performer has individual muscle memories and patterns of behaviour that may be meaningfully codified outside of sound.

If we could transform and translate our perspective, music might be qualified in another way; Varése experienced such an epiphany when listening to a Beethoven symphony:

"I became conscious of an entirely new effect produced by this familiar music. I seemed to feel the music detaching itself and projecting itself in space. I became conscious of a third dimension in the music" [31]

We consider here the translation of compositional patterns into a tactile domain; exploring the challenges of *sound* being the only medium within which musical intelligence might be conveyed and appreciated. Music could be considered, as Clifton [6] suggests, in terms of its inherent expressive qualities alone, conveyed as ordered events within which meaning and significance might be inferred.

For a performer of music, a significant tactile dimension is present; the vibration of the instrument against the body and muscular tensions are important extensions of expressive intent that are ordinarily absent in musical *reception*. In application, musical designs realised through tissue conduction alone offer constrained frequency and dynamic space (previously inaccessible to the composer) in which to convey a hitherto missing dynamism in musical design. There are implications for the hearing impaired in providing unique spatial insights and the potential for composers to explore new musical domains composed explicitly for a tissue conduction system.

6.1 Spatial Composition

Whilst it might not be aesthetically imperative to adhere to strict Euclidian representations, *spatial* parameters can be useful adjuncts to *musical* parameters, since they introduce dimensions of blending/separability, ensemble depth [35] and motion. For a discussion see [24].

In the case of blending/separability, it may be that, at times the desired percept is of a harmonious whole, even if formed by distinct elements; much classical orchestration is of this nature. On other occasions, the composer may be desirous of the ability for individual elements to perceptually break away from the whole, becoming individually distinct. Utilising this dimension can produce effects of swarming, dispersing and coalescing musical elements. Manipulation of perceived spatial location, including position-within-ensemble-depth (where some sources are apparently nearer to the perceiver than are others) can be effective in controlling blended/separate percepts. Perceived motion can include literal trajectories through three dimensions, with concomitant parameters of speed, change of loudness, Doppler effects, and changes in simulated early reflections. A particularly perceptually impressive parameter is that of auditory looming [38, 39], humans are intrinsically inclined to pay increased attention to items in the environment that are approaching, and this is exacerbated if the items are fast, unfamiliar or even unpleasant-sounding [47]. Musically, this could be used to surprise, generate anticipation or divert attention.

The more interesting compositional domain lies perhaps in the metaphorical mappings between space and musical parameters such as loudness, frequency, tempo, movement and acceleration. Here, it is relatively unexplored what might be perceived as congruent; temporal congruence (items that start together and modulate together are probably part of the same causal stream, or 'event') and spatial congruence (items that spatially coincide are probably related) seem reasonable first principles. More complex principles might stem from observation of relationships between items in environments; items in environments affect each other. Antiphony, or "Call-and-response" exemplifies the notion of musical elements interacting, giving the impression of communication; this can be very effective when combined with spatial separation of instruments.

6.2 Spatial Qualia for Different Displays

Whilst potentially exciting, there are some limitations that are intrinsic to the display methods for music; the range of perceptual significance [22] is constrained. For instance, loudspeaker presentations cannot simulate distances from horizon to the peripersonal (within-reach) space of the listener; on the other hand, headphone presentations can produce 'in the head' soundstage at the expense of externalisation and precision of ensemble depth.

Another, sometimes-overlooked deficit refers to vibration. In real environments, many events are accompanied by very low frequency sound and ground or structure-borne vibrations and these can be used to detect the approach of some items before their audible output reaches supraliminal proportions. Indeed, snakes rely on this type of information exclusively, as they lack air-conduction hearing apparatus [19]. There is evidence that the saccule in the vestibular system is sensitive to low frequencies [8] and can be recruited to a compensatory role in deaf [51]. It may even contribute to enjoyment in traditionally-loud music genres [48, 49]. As the saccule is involved in the detection of self-movement in the vertical plane, it could be that "being moved by the music" is more than a figure of speech.

It could be that finer control of stimuli that engage the saccule can grant us finer control of the 'in-head/externalised' axis of experience, since the saccule is normally stimulated by a person's own speech, as Trivelli *et al.* note [51]. It might also be used to govern the perception of size of objects independently of range; very large events (such as distant thunder) may be only marginally louder than the local noise-floor, yet can rattle the windows.

So whilst it is a convention to refer to "sound" as those airborne vibrations with frequencies of between 20 Hz and 20 kHz, there is potential information available to perception below the lower frequency. In artificial presentations using loudspeakers, for practical purposes, the frequency range of 20 Hz to 40 Hz is problematic as it is expensive to convey, similarly expensive to arrest, and tends to comprise noise to neighbours. Extending signal content down to 1 Hz would exacerbate such problems. However, using direct injection techniques such as vibrotactile transducers might allow us to explore the information-terrain that is normally inaccessible to composers and listeners.

An important caveat is that (at this stage of our research) we are largely considering passive tactile sensation, as distinct from active tactile sensation. For a discussion of the distinction, see [12]. That is, we are limited to stimulation of the somatosensory system in respect of tactile sensation through the activity of vibrotactile transducers. Tactile discrimination of frequency can be learned [15] and spatial location of stimulus can be finely identified (we know where on our body a stimulus is occurring). However, interactions between temporal and spatial characteristics of tactile perception require further study.

Interoception of vibrotactile stimuli is even less well understood; anecdotal evidence suggests that people can feel high amplitude low frequency sound in various parts of the body, varying with frequency. This could be caused by different internal structures of the body having different resonant frequencies, in which case internal spatial perception would be governed by frequency (rather than the actual position of actuators).

Given that hearing impairment clearly does not entail insensitivity to vibration, and may indeed be associated with increased discrimination of vibration [25, 37, 41], multimodal composition for hearing-impaired is theoretically feasible; experiences thereof may qualitatively differ from the normal experiencing of music.

7   Conclusion

Originally, we had embarked on an exploration to facilitate auditory spatial perception through tissue-conducted sound. Incidental input to the saccula notwithstanding, we thought of this as essentially an equivalent means to stimulate auditory perception. The reactions of one hundred listeners in our unstructured elicitation listening tests lead us to suspect some qualitative differences; we now think that the vibrotactile input amounts to something distinct from, and possibly additive to, audition.

The rules of congruence of concomitant multimodal stimuli await explication. Largely, this is because the relative contributions of low frequency vibrations (apprehended through the saccula and through the resonances in the body's internal structure) to ostensible auditory perceptions are not thoroughly understood. We suppose that some model of "multimodal scene analysis" (equivalent to Bregman's auditory scene analysis [3]) could be developed. This would include heuristics that describe how inputs are bound together in perception on the basis of synchronous onsets, offsets and modulations, or separated due to asynchronicity along certain dimensions. It should also account for cross-modal effects, where the conclusions in one modality are modified by input in another and especially where particular signal-features in one modality are additive (in perception) to concomitant features in another (such as the exaggeration of transients)

Composing for amodal spatial perception, and utilising cross-modal effects via multimodal inputs is at a comparatively immature stage; parameters of the target qualia await elucidation.

Appendix A. – Transcribed Comments of 100 Participants

Comments	Age	Sex	Mus.	Occupation
Works better than expected, what about VR/AR	40	M	N	Engineer
Very faint, weird sensation, especially with sensor under chin, crazy sensation after removal of head gear	26	F	N	Lecturer
Was an interesting experience, as someone with moderate hearing loss I could hear quite clearly. I was surprised how much conduction through the chin helped to amplify the sound	27	M	Y	Lecturer
Muddy sound, was the music recording professional quality? Difficult to get into it in current surroundings, fun though	39	M	Y	Tech
Absolutely amazing!	46	M	N	Send. Eng.
A bit band limited but still pretty good, very immersive, localisation a bit smeared, needed to close my eyes	56	M	Y	Snd. Eng.

(continued)

(continued)

Comments	Age	Sex	Mus.	Occupation
Doesn't surprise me in concept but surreal and interesting to use plus clarity of sound and positioning was interesting	31	F	Y	Studio Eng.
Subtle... interesting to see better coupling and more volume	37	M	N	Programmer
Uncanny, ethereal	39	F	Y	Comms.
Very surprised by HF extension plus "large soundstage". Easy to forget you're not listening to headphones, especially with the ear plugs installed	32	M	Y	Aud. Eng.
Spatial feel without traditional 'stereo' L/R fatigue. Felt as inner-head frontal image, not to external. Could clearly hear 'wet' recording, wanted to hear clean ones to see what it could do	37	M	Y	IT Dir.
This is something I am recently aware of. I look forward to exploring more. I'm interested in products that use this methodology. More awareness of the phenomena would be helpful to my industry and its products	42	M	U	Audio
Found this really affective, for localising sounds in a multi-channel (surround) experience. the extra conductor was especially effective at the back of the head and enhanced low frequency content substantially	25	M	U	Audio Eng.
Amazing!! Also the fact that you interact using the extra conductor. Please get my contact for further info. I want to explore this to add to the VR experience I plan to develop	41	M	U	Student
Very interesting research project, demo quite effective – much to my surprise! Keep up the good work	64	M	U	Audio Eng.
More higher quality than expected. Felt tightness of headset could be improved. Would love to try to image in a quiet room	27	M	Y	Audio Sales
Immersive experience. New way of listening. If somehow could be integrated with VR it would be cool	U	U	U	U
Enjoyed it a lot. Would have been nice if musical part went on longer or an orchestra would play to "show" that you can feel like you're in the concert hall	U	U	U	U
Did not realise sound was not coming through Ears!. Eerie sound, first thoughts remind you of the sound of a gramophone	27	M	Y	Comms Eng. Drummer

(continued)

(*continued*)

Comments	Age	Sex	Mus.	Occupation
Variety of sounds, running water, children playing, oriental female voice, cello, propeller aeroplane, running water etc. etc. Very clearly definable sounds, even at low level. Having suffered with temporary hearing-loss as a child, no surprise to "hear" via the skull – but very interesting to experience the clarity	57	M	N	Tech solutions
Good to give life to older gritty credibility to the pre-digital finds "Olderworldie". Good to know that not relying on air-borne sound via the ears is not the only methodology that will be condoned; a more "even" field in my perception (which is the "reality" for me – a very subjective thing is aural perception even if it is sent by digital accuracy and time line-up displays) Good to know that neck-transducers could be hidden from view under a shirt collar. (the "pride" factor of the hearing impaired person is still a very reluctant factor – people don't want others treating them as 2nd class citizens because of an impairment. "I know its only rock an roll, but I liked it" (I just didn't like being deaf!!)	60	M	Y	Mentor coach
Fascinating – would be better in a quiet environment but impressive	53	M	N	Lecturer
Unusual sensation of vibration on head. Sound is lacking in HF detail. Got clearer toward the end of recordings/	30	M	N	Lecturer
Visceral; immersive "sound" experience. Dull with not much LF either but the vibrations making/shift the experience to something "other" than typical listening. Hand on ear plugs – altered negatively	38	M	Y	Sound
Very surreal distant sounding. Passing sounds such as the train and plane felt closer and move forward. The higher sounds such as water (?) felt harder to make out. Fidelity sometimes felt lost when many sounds were overlapped. As strange as it sounds it was like a memory or dream of a sound	30	M	N	Snd. Eng.
Immersive. Almost noises in your head as you were aware your ears were covered, but as you still "heard" the sounds, you were aware your ears were still in use. The true source was only made aware at loud points when you felt the transducers vibrate, not totally dissimilar to the Jecklin float "no contact" headphones	41	M	N	Snd. Eng.

(*continued*)

(continued)

Comments	Age	Sex	Mus.	Occupation
Could be louder. Sounded good. I would like to try quieter environment to see how good the quality is	55	M	N	Snd. Eng.
A unique experience – almost like the audio version VR. It provides a more intimate experience than headset	59	M	Y	Editor
Very interesting like nothing I've ever tried before, amazing	18	M	Y	Apprentice
It felt really strange and when the headset vibrated on my head	20	M	Y	Student
Very spatial experience. Far more effective than '3D' stereo headphones etc. Lacking low frequency depth somewhat. Surprisingly clear and loud given ambient noise	33	M	N	Draftsman
Occasionally you could feel the deeper sounds as physical vibrations especially in the front central point. The higher sounds like bird song were easier to pick up what direction it was coming from. The music sounded better than it would through regular headphones as you felt surrounded by the sound as you would in a realistic setting of an orchestra	18	F	Y	Student
Unusual feeling. Almost feels like it's coming through your ears due to ear plugs. Vibrations felt for higher pitches – front and back left during train whistle and plane. When plane flies overhead the vibration moves from front to back as though flying over	24	F	Y	LAMDA student
Very interesting! Doesn't really feel like it came from the skull. But the sound was very clear. Guess it would be awesome for listening to psychedelic music	24	F	Y	Student
A completely bizarre experience, so glad I did it! Its extraordinary technology and so impressive. It's definitely not what I was expecting. It really is technology of the future and I wish you the best of luck with future development	19	M	Y	Student
It's actually 3D sound, from all around and above. It felt like it was coming from my ears but more pure	18	M	Y	Student
Literally burst out laughing out of the fact this is truly incredible!	25	M	N	Snd. Eng.
Like nothing I've ever experienced before! Absolutely incredible!!!	16	F	N	Student
So amazing, deeper sounds had more clarity	16	F	N	Student

(continued)

(continued)

Comments	Age	Sex	Mus.	Occupation
Sound was very clear and you could even feel some of the lesser bass sounds	16	M	Y	Student
Very unusual sonic experience. It felt like a mono soundscape but with a strange depth, a "spatial-mono" (I know it doesn't make much sense, but it was that unusual!!) Frequency range was not very wide. Dynamic range not that wide either	50	M	Y	Composer
Sounded slightly "muffled" some spatial "separation" but not dramatic	62	M	Y	Con. Producer
Would have been good to compare with the same source through ears! Interesting though – just hope I'm never deaf	61	F	N	Accounts
Very quiet, the low flying sound was clearest. The vibrations were quite strange and difficult to get used to. Very cool though!	22	F	N	Marketing
Very strange as I could feel vibrating on the back of my head, plus the fact I could hear without my ears	21	M	N	Student
I enjoyed the vibrations on the pressure points. Sound has remarkable stereo/surround perception. With ear plugs in, it felt like listening to headphones. A pleasant experience	37	M	Y	Equipment sales
Very left heavy, generally inside head, a little outside	36	M	Y	Rec. Eng.
Loved the vibrations of the aeroplane flying over. and in general how the sound felt all around. Thanks!	28	M	N	Theatre
Soft bird sounds – different birds getting slowly louder. Move onto classical music- very clear sound. Next train/train whistle, was there a voice to? Some vibration felt – bit weird. Sound quietening down like how it started	46	F	N	Administrator
Feels slightly odd at first but great idea and execution	16	M	N	U
Music feels a lot more comfortable than sound FX. dramatic increases in volume can be quite surprising but I got used to it	16	M	Y	U
Surprised at the definition, clarity plus frequency range – very "natural" feeling	44	M	N	Editor
Very clear and crisp sound. it felt like was immersed within the sound field	36	M	Y	Snd. Eng.
Great adventure, very interesting work, can see it in VR as having future. Would be delighted to hear about it more and be connected	25	F	U	Designer

(continued)

(continued)

Comments	Age	Sex	Mus.	Occupation
Mind-blowing and confusing… felt like I was there	46	M	N	Design Eng.
Great sensorial experience. Interesting concept especially for the 3D audio image	24	M	Y	Snd. Eng.
Interesting idea. Not very comfortable after a while. Little bit distortion on high volumes	22	M	Y	Snd. Eng.
Amazing the way it works. Inspired thinking of ways to implement technology. (good dynamics) Sounded like coming from ears, not full range spectrum. (Could hear heartbeat because of the ear plugs)	50	M	U	Snd. Eng.
Amazing technology	27	F	Y	Student
Very interesting, new experience of sound. Vibrations feel slightly unusual but also add a new dimension to the sound experience. Very cool	23	M	Y	DJ
I can feel it tingling in a pleasant way when the train sounded particularly vibrated to my head. I read about a Neuro-phone many years ago and imagine sound is conducted that method? The rain forest, birds, foreign landscape all felt vey spacious, the piano felt lonely and shrill	40+	F	U	Artist
Pretty impressed. At the beginning I heard the 'noises' in a park etc. and I could not feel any vibrations until the cello in 'Nothing else Matters'. Felt the vibrations the most when the women talked	34	M	Y	Event manager
I felt good surround feeling. Sounds were quite clear. I did not realise where the sound came from. So quiet hard to describe where the sound source is. At some point where the music got loud, you feel the vibration when the level is low, I felt like hearing with my ears	34	M	Y	Event manager
Incredible new way of listening, great clarity. Felt strange. Vibration with the plane recording. Sometimes quiet	22	M	Y	Snd Tech
Audio panorama seemed interesting. Was a little faint with background noise from show. Was curious as to what was actually happening with head sensors	66	M	Y	Music educator
Weird but interesting	U	M	U	Student
A surreal auditory experience with lots of depth	28	M	N	Manager
Much improved HF response compared to other systems. Would like to hear in a quieter environment	48	M	Y	Acoustic engineer

(continued)

(continued)

Comments	Age	Sex	Mus.	Occupation
Incredible feeling, not sure how this would work in a commercial environment but in education/or therapy could be a very intuitive tool. It all sounds a bit 'tinny' but heard the different sounds/effects	51	M	Y	Pro audio sales
Very curious experience, can't understand the meaning of it	U	U	U	U
I found this experiment very interesting as musician. I been always thought ears are the only source to hear, but this test shows we hear even by our head. All the best	42	M	Y	Music producer
Really impressed by the current frequency response that already existing, will be very original with the advances	28	M	U	Electronic engineer
Good idea, find uses for it. Good luck	51	M	U	Electronic engineer
'Therapy'	U	U	U	U
I felt rippling nerve? Effects over my scalp (random from playback). Sample piece was very quiet and almost non present in right ear until gain was adjusted. I noticed 'FX' send had a high pass effect	50	M	U	Sound composer
I want one! Maybe adding a subwoofer to the experience would be interesting	25	M	N	Sound design
Very strange experience, almost like you are in a dream state	19	M	N	Tech director
Very weird sensation	17	M	N	Student
Interesting, different experience. Sound quality?	36	M	Y	U
It's a wonderful experience, really like the sound technique. Excellent	33	M	Y	Business
Sounds like audio coming from inside head rather than ears. Slight tickling on head, very pleasurable. A little bass light	43	M	Y	U
Very interesting, I could hear the music clearly enough. I hope this gets developed for the people who might need it	33	M	N	AV Tech
Extremely interesting! Thanks for the demo!	31	M	Y	U
Really interesting, I look forward to using it in a few years. Thanks	51	M	U	Sound engineer
A new way of surround. It feels like surround sound is nothing compared to this. You can also feel the vibrations from the surroundings	31	M	N	Sound engineer
Strange, but a real new experience. Very nice, clear sound	38	M	N	Audio rental

(continued)

(*continued*)

Comments	Age	Sex	Mus.	Occupation
Amazing technology. I can imagine it could be used in covert ops, e.g. SAS. Would be nice not to hear others music on the train too!	27	M	N	Importer
Very interesting. Quite relaxing as the sound is heard first and then you get a head massage! Similar to airborne sound but lacking high frequency content. Very good ambient sound	45	M	Y	Dpt. Engineer
Really amazing to feel and sense the music and sounds around you without actual sound 'in ears'. The spikes, high levels vibrate against your skull and this gives sense, but interesting to hear without your ears!!	40	M	Y	Music manager
Very interesting concept- would like to use it in conjunction with IEMs. Good luck with the project	62	M	Y	Company manager
Very different from normal hearing, but very audible, 'sounds inside my head '. Very little treble and low bass	U	U	U	U
Great bit of research.. Very surreal	37	M	U	Operations director
Felt/sounded just like it would if wearing headphones. Had to remind myself that sound was actually coming through my head, because the experience was so similar	34	F	U	Actress
Incredibly odd. Felt both normal but not at the same time. Very relaxing	16	F	U	Student
Awesome trip. Great experience. I hope to see more about this tech	U	U	U	U
Although the sound was still 'one sided ' to a certain degree I felt for the first time that I was immersed in a soundscape and that my hearing loss was not making me lose out on part of the effect. The train in particular really felt 360, especially with the chin transducer on my right cheek bone	36	F	U	Stage manager
Felt physical vibrations from head contacts. Would like to have heard headphone comparison. Range seemed to be around 900 hz–4000 kh, but experience was from ear canal directly. Also feel slightly nauseous?	45	M	Y	Sound engineer

(*continued*)

(continued)

Comments	Age	Sex	Mus.	Occupation
It is quite an interesting if somewhat confusing sensation. Hearing without hearing. I had not expected the level of clarity achieved, being able to pick out changes in the soundscape and individual notes in the Chopin piece	28	M	U	Production manager
In the beginning I felt it's going to fall off my head until I made myself sure it's the vibrations only. Also at some point I was trying to locate the sound in using my ears, and it was confusing. It's quite interesting experience, the sound felt quite natural. Wasn't sure how very reproduced it felt	21	F	N	Student
An amazing experience, hope it can help deaf people	44	F	N	Interior designer

References

1. Berg, J., Rumsey, F.: Spatial attribute identification and scaling by repertory grid technique and other methods. In: Proceedings of the Audio Engineering Society International Conference on Spatial Sound Reproduction (AES16), Rovaniemi, Finland 10–12 April 1999
2. Bernstein, L.: The Unanswered Question: Six Talks at Harvard (Charles Eliot Norton Lectures). Harvard University Press, Cambridge, USA (1990)
3. Bregman, A.S.S.: Auditory Scene Analysis. MIT Press, Cambridge, MA (1990)
4. Cappe, C., Thut, G., Romei, V., Murray, M.M.: Auditory–visual multisensory interactions in humans: timing, topography, directionality, and sources. J. Neurosci. **30**(38), 12572–12580 (2010). https://doi.org/10.1523/JNEUROSCI.1099-10.2010
5. Chordekar, S., Kriksunov, L., Kishon-Rabin, L., Adelman, C., Sohmer, H.: Mutual cancellation between tones presented by air conduction, by bone conduction and by non-osseous (soft tissue) bone conduction. Hear. Res. **283**(1–2), 180–184 (2012). https://doi.org/10.1016/j.heares.2011.10.004
6. Clifton, T.: Music as Heard: A Study in Applied Phenomenology. Yale University Press, New Haven and London (1983)
7. Dietz, A.J., May, B.S., Knaus, D.A., Greeley, H.P.: Hearing protection for bone-conducted sound. In: New Directions for Improving Audio Effectiveness, Meeting Proceedings RTO-MP-HFM-123, Paper 14. Neuilly-sur-Seine, France: RTO, pp. 1–18 (2005)
8. Emami, S.F., Pourbakht, A., Daneshi, A., Sheykholeslami, K., Emamjome, H., Kamali, M.: Sound sensitivity of the saccule for low frequencies in healthy adults. ISRN Otolaryngol. **2013**, Article ID 429680 (2013). http://dx.doi.org/10.1155/2013/429680
9. Fodor, J.A.: Modularity of Mind: An Essay on Faculty Psychology. MIT Press, Cambridge (1983)
10. Gallese, V., Lakoff, G.: The brain's concepts: the role of the sensory-motor system in conceptual knowledge. Cogn. Neuropsychol. **22**(3/4), 455–479 (2005)
11. Gardner, E., Martin, J.: Coding of Sensory Information. Princ. Neural Sci. **21**, 411–429 (2000)

12. Gibson, J.J.: Observations on active touch. Psychol. Rev. **69**(6), 477–491 (1962). https://doi.org/10.1037/h0046962

13. Gibson, J.J.: The Senses Considered as Perceptual Systems. Allen and Unwin, London (1966)

14. Goldman, R.F.: "Varèse: Ionisation; Density 21.5; Intégrales; Octandre; Hyperprism; Poème Electronique. Instrumentalists, cond. Robert Craft. Columbia MS 6146 (stereo)" (in Reviews of Records). Musical Quarterly 47, no. 1. (January), pp. 133–34 (1961)

15. Imai, T., Kamping, S., Breitenstein, C., Pantev, C., Lutkenhoner, B., Knecht, S.: Learning of tactile frequency discrimination in humans. Hum. Brain Mapp. **18**(4), 260–271 (2003)

16. Jäncke, L.: neuroanatomy of the parietal cortex. In: Mast, F.W., Jäncke, L. (eds.) Spatial Processing in Navigation, Imagery and Perception, pp. 135–145. Springer, New York (2007)

17. Jun, K.C.: Objective measurements of skull vibration during bone conduction audiometry [thesis]. Medical Faculty, Zürich University (2009)

18. Klemen, J., Chambers, C.D.: Current perspectives and methods in studying neural mechanisms of multisensory interactions. Neuroscience Biobehaviour Review **36**, 111–133 (2012). https://doi.org/10.1016/j.neubiorev.2011.04.015

19. Knight, K.: Snakes hear through skull vibration. J. Exp. Biol. 215, ii (2012). https://doi.org/10.1242/jeb.069104

20. Landry, S.P., Guillemot, J.P., Champoux, F.: Audiotactile interaction can change over time in cochlear implant users. Front. Hum. Neurosci. (2014). https://doi.org/10.3389/fnhum.2014.00316

21. Lenhardt, M.L., Shulman, A., Goldstein, B.A.: Bone-conduction propagation in the human body: implications for high-frequency therapy. Int. Tinnitus J. **13**(2), 81–86 (2007)

22. Lennox, P.P., Myatt, A., Vaughan, J.M.: From surround to true 3-D. In: Proceedings Audio Engineering Society's 16th International Conference: Spatial Sound Reproduction. AES (1999)

23. Lennox, P.P.: Cognitive maps in spatial sound. In: Proceedings Audio Engineering Society's 52nd International Conference: Sound Field Control- Engineering and Perception. AES (2013)

24. Lennox, P.P.: Music as artificial environment: spatial, embodied multimodal experience. In: Wöllner, C. (ed.) Body, Sound and Space in Music and Beyond: Multimodal Explorations. Routledge, Oxford (2016)

25. Levanen, S., Hamdorf, D.: Feeling vibrations: enhanced tactile sensitivity in congenitally deaf adults. Neurosci. Lett. **301**, 75–77 (2001)

26. MacDonald, J.A., Henry, P.P., Letowski, T.R.: Spatial audio through a bone conduction interface. Int. J. Audiol. **45**, 595–599 (2006)

27. Macpherson, F.: Taxonomising the senses. Philos. Stud. **153**, 123–142 (2011). https://doi.org/10.1007/s11098-010-9643-8

28. McBride, M., Letowski, T., Tran, P.: Bone Conduction Head Sensitivity Mapping: Bone Vibrator. ARL-TR-3556. Army Research Laboratory: Aberdeen Proving Ground, MD, July 2005

29. McGurk, H., MacDonald, J.: Hearing lips and seeing voices. Nature **264**(5588), 746–748 (1976)

30. Mishkin, M., Ungerleider, L.G., Macko, K.: Object vision and spatial vision: two cortical pathways. Trends Neurosci. **6**, 414–417 (1983)

31. Music and The Drama, Varese, Ultra-Modernist Composer, Prophesies Symphonies in "Space", The Lewiston Daily Sun, 8 December (1936)

32. Neuhaus, C.: 'Music as fluid architecture': investigating core regions of the spatial brain. In: Wöllner, C. (ed.) Body, Sound and Space in Music and Beyond: Multimodal Explorations, pp. 168–188. Routledge, Abingdon (2017)

33. Rauschecker, J.P., Tian, B.: Mechanisms and streams for processing of 'what' and 'where' in auditory cortex. PNAS **97**(22), 11800–11806 (2000)

34. Rumsey, F., Mason, R.: Interaural time difference fluctuations: their measurement, subjective perceptual effect, and application in sound reproduction. In: Proceedings of the Audio Engineering Society Conference: 19th International Conference: Surround Sound-Techniques, Technology, and Perception (AES19), Schloss Elmau, Germany, 21–24 June (2001)

35. Rumsey, F.: Spatial quality evaluation for reproduced sound: terminology, meaning and a scene-based paradigm. J. Audio Eng. Soc. **50**(9), 651–666 (2002)

36. Schnupp, J.W., Dawe, K.L., Pollack, G.L.: The detection of multisensory stimuli in an orthogonal sensory space. Exp. Brain Res. **162**(2), 181–190 (2005). https://doi.org/10.1007/s00221-004-2136-2

37. Schürmann, M., Caetano, G., Hlushchuk, Y., Jousmäki, V., Hari, R.: Touch activates human auditory cortex. NeuroImage **30**(4), 1325–1331 (2006) (2006). http://doi.org/10.1016/j.neuroimage.2005.11.020

38. Seifritz, E., et al.: Neural processing of auditory looming in the human brain. Curr. Biol. **23**, 2147–2151 (2002)

39. Seifritz, E., et al.: Spatiotemporal pattern of neural processing in the human auditory cortex. Science **297**, 1706–1708 (2002)

40. Shepard, R.N.: Psychophysical complementarity. In: Kubovy, M., Pomerantz, J.R. (eds.) Perceptual Organisation, pp. 279–341. Erlbaum, Hillsdale, N.J. (1981)

41. Shibata, D.K., Zhong J.: Tactile vibrations are heard in auditory cortex in the deaf: study with FMRI. In: Annual Meeting of the Radiological Society of North America; Chicago, Ill, p. 259 (2001)

42. Sohmer, H.: Reflections on the role of a traveling wave along the basilar membrane in view of clinical and experimental findings. Eur. Arch. Otorhinolaryngol. **272**, 531 (2015)

43. Stanley, R., Walker, B.N.: Lateralization of sounds using bone-conduction headsets. In: Proceedings of the Annual Meeting of the Human Factors and Ergonomics Society, San Francisco, CA, pp. 1571–1575, 16–20 October (2006)

44. Stenfelt, S., Goode, R.L.: Transmission properties of bone conducted sound: measurements in cadaver heads. The J. Acoust. Soc. Am. **118**, 2373–2391 (2005). https://doi.org/10.1121/1.2005847

45. Stenfelt, S., Zeitooni, M.: Binaural hearing ability with mastoid applied bilateral bone conduction stimulation in normal hearing subjects. The J. Acoust. Soc. Am. **134**(1), 481–493 (2013). https://doi.org/10.1121/1.4807637

46. Sumby, W.H., Pollack, I.: Visual contribution to speech intelligibility in noise. J. Acoust. Soc. Am. **26**, 212–215 (1954)

47. Tajadura-Jiménez, A., Väljamäe, A., Asutay, E., Västfjäll, D.: Embodied auditory perception: the emotional impact of approaching and receding sound sources. Emotion **10**(2), 216–229 (2010)

48. Todd, N.: Evidence for a behavioral significance of saccular acoustic sensitivity in humans. J. Acoust. Soc. Am. **110**(1), 380–390 (2001)

49. Todd, N.P.M., Cody, F.W.: Vestibular responses to loud dance music: a physiological basis of the rock and roll threshold? J. Acoust. Soc. Am. **107**(1), 496–500 (2000)

50. Tozzi, A., Peters, J.F.: A symmetric approach elucidates multisensory information integration. Information **8**(1), 4 (2017). https://doi.org/10.3390/info8010004

51. Trivelli, M., Potena, M., Frari, V., Petitti, T., Deidda, V., Salvinelli, F.: Compensatory role of saccule in deaf children and adults: novel hypotheses. Med. Hypotheses **80**(1), 43–46 (2013)

52. Websters New World College Dictionary. http://websters.yourdictionary.com/

53. Werner, S., Noppeney. U.: Superadditive Responses in Superior Temporal Sulcus Predict Audiovisual Benefits in Object Categorization. Cerebral Cortex (2009). https://doi.org/10.1093/cercor/bhp248

54. Wiggins, B.: An Investigation into the real-time manipulation and control of three-dimensional sound fields. Ph.D. thesis, University of Derby (2004)

55. Wilson, D., Sperber, D.: Relevance theory. In: Horn, L., Ward, G. (eds.) The Handbook of Pragmatics. Wiley-Blackwell, Oxford (2005)

56. Zacharov, N., Koivuniemi, K.: Audio descriptive analysis and mapping of spatial sound displays. In: Proceedings of the 7th International Conference on Auditory Display, Helsinki, Finland, pp. 95–104, 29 July–1st August (2001)

57. Zappa, F., Occhiogrosso, P.: The Real Frank Zappa Book. Picador, London (1989)

Enriching Musical Interaction on Tactile Feedback Surfaces with Programmable Friction

Farzan Kalantari$^{(\boxtimes)}$, Florent Berthaut, and Laurent Grisoni

University of Lille - Science and Technology, CNRS, Lille, France
{farzan.kalantari,florent.berthaut,laurent.grisoni}@ed.univ-lille1.fr

Abstract. In the recent years, a great interest has emerged to utilize tactile interfaces for musical interactions. These interfaces can be enhanced with tactile feedback on the user's fingertip through various technologies, including programmable friction techniques. In this study, we use a qualitative approach to investigate the potential influence of these tactile feedback interfaces on user's musical interaction. We have experimented three different mappings between the sound parameters and the tactile feedback in order to study the users' experiences of a given task. Our preliminary findings suggest that friction-based tactile feedback is a useful tool to enrich musical interactions and learning.

Keywords: Tactile musical interface · Haptic rendering
Frequency modulation · Programmable friction · Musical perception
User experience

1 Introduction

Touch interactions with tactile interfaces such as smart-phones and tablets, have become more and more ubiquitous in our daily life. However, there is still a lack of dynamic haptic feedback on these tactile interfaces to the user's finger. Buxton et al. [6] showed that flat touchscreens need haptic feedback in order to ease the users' various interaction tasks, to enhance the efficiency of the interfaces and to increase the feeling of realism in visual environments. Accordingly, researchers have explored different technologies to generate dynamic haptic feedback to enhance input on tactile displays.

Tactile feedback technologies are mostly based on the modulation of the friction between the user's fingertip and the tactile interface. Different types of vibrotactile actuators such as solenoids, vibrotactile coils, and ERM motors can be used for tactile rendering as described in [10]. These actuators are used presently on smart phones and tablets, by typically providing on-or-off sensation. Alongside vibrotactile actuation, two technologies called electrovibration [4,21] and electroadhesion [29], use electrostatic force generated, respectively, by applying a voltage to the screen surface or by applying DC excitation of the tactile

© Springer Nature Switzerland AG 2018
M. Aramaki et al. (Eds.): CMMR 2017, LNCS 11265, pp. 387–401, 2018.
https://doi.org/10.1007/978-3-030-01692-0_25

display. Both of these techniques increase the friction between the finger and the interaction surface when activated. Another technology is based on friction reduction using ultrasonic vibrations via the "squeeze film effect" [1,15,32]. In the remainder of this paper, we are particularly interested in the latter technology.

It has been shown that programmable friction feedback on tactile displays improves performances on different interaction tasks [7,19,33]. Therefore, several studies and guidelines proposed in [18,22] to assist designers to find out how users feel and manipulate tactile elements on haptic feedback displays for touch interactions.

On the other hand, numerous studies investigated the use of tactile interfaces with haptic feedback for sound synthesis and musical productions. The first investigation to add haptic feedback to tactile musical interface proposed by Chafe in [8], by leveraging vibration modulations to design two vibro-tactile audio cues. Chu [12] reported that there is a close relationship between haptic feedback and sound production in computer music performances. The author also demonstrated that the lack of haptic feedback sensation is a major concern in computer music performances between a musical performer and the sound being produced. Serafin and Young [28] investigated the role of friction modulation for musical interactions by proposing several musical instruments that operate by means of a friction-based excitation. Chang and O'Sullivan [9] proposed a novel design of audio-haptic effects to enhance the user interface on mobile phones. Birnbaum and Wanderley [5] described a new approach for the design and integration of vibrotactile feedback into digital musical instruments (DMIs). Menelas et al. [23] showed that the combination of audio and haptic cues improve the acquisition of a desired targeting task within virtual environments. Huang et al. [16] investigated the contribution of haptic information in *feeling* musical rhythm by evaluating how the auditory and tactile inputs were integrated in humans for performing a musical meter recognition task.

Furthermore, Beamish et al. [17] developed "D'GROOVE", an intelligent Disc Jockey (DJ) tactile interface by using a haptic turntable for controlling the playback of digital audio effects. Baillie et al. [2] proposed a mobile music player, enhanced with haptic feedback to generate novel method of audio playback on a mobile device. Lim et al. [20] developed a haptic library that created tactile feedback by converting an audio source to tactile output through analyzing its audio data that may be utilized in various musical applications. Papetti et al. [26] designed a novel hardware/software system for rendering multi-point, localized vibrotactile feedback in a multi-touch musical interface by leveraging piezoelectric actuators. The development of different haptic interfaces for the purpose of granular sound synthesis technique for musical performances can be found in [25,27]. Researchers have also explored in [24,30] how haptic feedback may be a useful tool for visually impaired musicians and sound producers in order to improve their different musical interactions.

However, there is still no studies as far as we aware for the explanation of how the musical interaction on tactile displays can be enriched with programmable friction and haptic feedback. In this context, we discuss how haptic feedback by means of programmable friction on tactile interfaces might influence and enrich musical interaction. In particular, we explore different mappings between sound synthesis parameters and haptic feedback, and evaluate the impact of these mappings on user experience when performing a given musical task.

2 Exploring Mappings Between Sound and Haptic Rendering

The mapping between different sensory stimuli is one of the key issue when considering the relevance of haptic feedback interfaces in a multimodal context and particularly in audio-haptic DMIs, i.e. our case in the present study.

In this section we discuss mapping opportunities for tactile feedback with programmable friction. In fact, the control of the parameters of the sound is considered to be an important factor which defines the relationship between gesture and music (also called mapping) in DMIs. As Doornbusch reported in [13], *mapping* concerns the connection between structures, or gestures and audible results in a musical performance or composition. In our study we notice that, due to the nature of the technology used for the tactile feedback i.e. ultrasonic lubrication, haptic feedback occurs only when sliding the finger on the surface. Therefore musical gesture which can be augmented correspond to fingers displacements on the surface, i.e. not tapping. Usable musical gesture parameters, which can be mapped to sound parameters, therefore include speed, curvature, shape, direction and so on.

We propose to classify feedback according to its relation with both sound parameters and gestural parameters. We define four categories, labelled C1 to C4.

Table 1. Classification of tactile feedback with programmable friction

	Distinct from audio	Linked to audio
Distinct from gesture	C1	C2
Linked to gesture	C4	C3

- In category **C1**, the feedback is separated from both input gestures and audio feedback, which means it can change and provide information without changes in the sound perceived or in the gestural parameters. This can be used to provide information on current gesture to sound mappings before their results are heard, as a sort of feed-forward that guides the musicians' interactions.
- In category **C2**, the tactile feedback amplifies audio feedback but is still separated from input gestures. This can be used to provide feedback on sound parameters which are mapped to non-gestural parameter (e.g. position) while the sound is heard.

- In category **C3**, the tactile feedback is combined with both audio and gestures, and might amplify both of them. It can be used as in [26] to amplify both or either of the gesture and audio feedback, for example increasing self-agency of the musician with the instrument, i.e. provide a better sensation of control over the instrument.
- Finally, in **C4** the feedback is combined with the gesture but separated from the audio, which can be used for preparation gestures. For example it may provide information on gestural parameters before reaching a zone where the gesture will actually trigger sound, allowing the musician to anticipate the sonic result of their actions.

3 Experiment

We carried out an experiment to find out how the ultrasonic based haptic interface with programmable friction might influence and enrich the interaction with Digital Music Instruments (DMIs). To do so, we tested the effect of added tactile feedback, and three mappings that follow the categories C1–C3, in a musical phrase replication task.

3.1 Apparatus

We used an enhanced visual-tactile actuator (E-$ViTa$), a tactile feedback display based on ultrasonic vibrations for haptic rendering [31]. E-ViTa is developed on a Banana Pi, a single-board computer (Shenzhen LeMaker Technology Co. Ltd., China) with a 1 GHz ARM Cortex-A7, dual-core CPU and 1 GB of RAM working in parallel with STM32f4 microcontroller (STMicroelectronics, France). The communication between the microcontroller and the single board computer is provided via the Serial Peripheral Interface (SPI) bus at 10 kHz. This single-board computer is connected to a 12.5 cm capacitive touchscreen (Banana-LCD 5"-TS, MAREL, China) for detecting the user's finger position on the display with a sampling frequency of 62 Hz.

Ten $14 \times 6 \times 0.5$ mm piezoelectric cells actuate a $154 \times 81 \times 1.6$ mm fixed glass plate, resonating at 60750 Hz with a half wavelength of 8 mm. A power electronic circuit converts a 12V DC voltage source into an AC voltage, controlled in amplitude and frequency and supplied to the piezoelectric cells. The microcontroller synthesizes a pulse-width modulation (PWM) signal to drive a voltage inverter that actuates the piezoceramics. The E-$ViTa$ tablet has a resolution of 800 * 480 pixels. The detailed structure of E-$ViTa$ haptic tablet is shown in the Fig. 1.

3.2 Participants

Six volunteers (4 male and 2 female) from the age of 27 to 33 with a mean age of 29.14 (SD = 1.95) took part in our experiment. They were all regular users of at least one tactile display (i.e. smart-phone or tablet) during their daily life. The experiment took on average approximately 35 min for each participant.

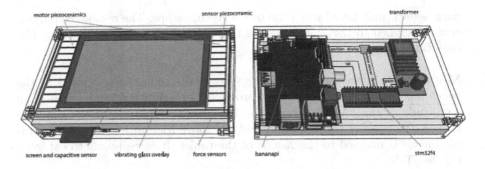

Fig. 1. The structure of *E-ViTa* haptic feedback tablet [31]

All participants used an active noise-cancelling headphone (Panasonic RP-DJS200, Japan) in order to prevent the influence of the little noises produced by the haptic tablet in their performances.

3.3   Design

We used a basic form of FM synthesis with only two oscillators using *Pure Data* to generate the auditory signals. In FM synthesis [11], the timbre of a simple waveform is changed by modulating its frequency in the audio range which leads to a more complex waveform with a different-sounding tone. In our case we have two sine waves: modulating wave and carrier wave in which the modulating wave changes the frequency of the carrier wave. The communication between the PC (which generates the FM synthesis) and the haptic feedback tablet is done using the OpenSoundControl protocol. We have to note that in the *E-ViTa* haptic feedback tablet, the generated tactile feedback (with a specific spatial frequency and amplitude) is always proportional to the user's finger velocity as explained in [31]. In other words, there is a linear transfer function between the tactile signal's spatial frequency (μm) and the sound signal frequency (Hz) which is proportional to the user's finger velocity (mm/s) at each moment. This relationship can be expressed with the following equation:

$$Sound\ Signal\ Frequency\ (Hz) = \frac{Tactile\ Signal\ Spatial\ Frequency\ (\mu m)}{Finger\ Velocity\ (mm/s)}$$

(1)

In all mappings, the volume of the sound is mapped to the speed of the gesture, i.e. the speed at which the user's finger moves on the surface, and the pitch of the sound is mapped to the Y axis of the tablet. We then defined 3 different mappings between the auditory and tactile signals as following. The order of three tested mappings was counterbalanced among participants.

- **Mapping 1**: In the first mapping, the tactile signal is associated to the *resonance* of the produced sound, i.e. the time it takes for the sound to fade out. The more resonance there is, the less friction can be felt. However this parameter is only heard when the user's gesture stops. The resonance parameter is mapped to the X axis on the tablet. It corresponds to category C1. (see Table 1)

- **Mapping 2**: In the second mapping, the tactile signal is associated to the *roughness* of the sound, which is produced by modifying the modulation amplitude of the FM synthesis. The higher the amplitude of the modulation is, the rougher the sound is, and the more friction felt by finger. This parameter is mapped to the X axis of the tablet. It corresponds to category C2 (see Table 1)

- **Mapping 3**: In the third mapping, the friction is only mapped to the gesture speed and therefore to the *volume* of the sound signal. It corresponds to category C3 of classification provided in Table 1.

3.4 Task and Procedure

First of all a brief description of our task as well as all the necessary instructions for interacting with our audio/haptic tactile interface were given to each participant. We asked participants to do a *replication task* of previously recorded sounds with a duration of few seconds for each of the 3 provided mappings (Fig. 2). There were two pre-recorded sounds for each of the mappings and thus

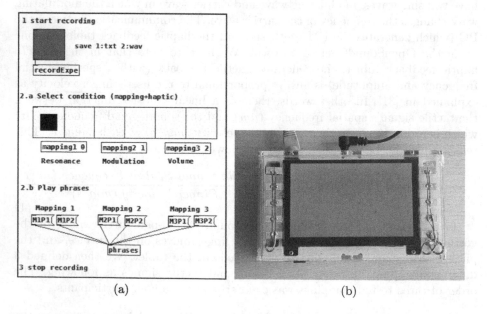

(a)   (b)

Fig. 2. (a) The setup of our experimental procedure using *Pure Data*. (b) The E-ViTa haptic display used in our experiment for tactile feedback perception. No visual feedback was shown to participants during the experiment.

12 total trial for each of the participant (3 mappings × 2 pre-recorded sounds × 2 feedback condition = 12 total trials). In order to prevent any influence on the participants' performances of the given task, the order of three tested mappings was randomized. The participants were free to explore the surface as long as they wanted and then replicated the provided sounds. We have also saved the gesture trajectory of finger movements of each participant for the further analysis in our study. The setup of our experimental procedure and the *E-ViTa* haptic display used in our experiment are illustrated in Fig. 2.

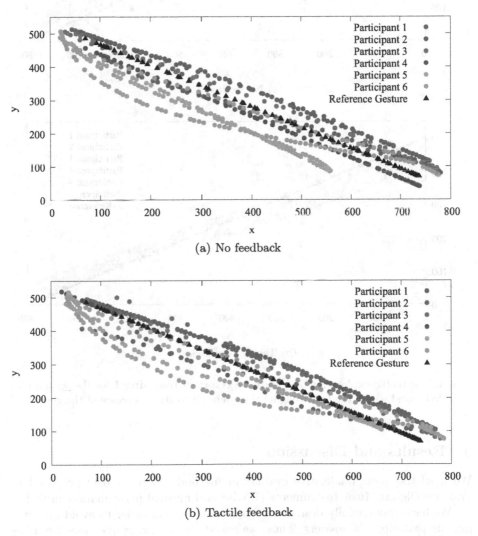

Fig. 3. The tactile exploration of gesture trajectory of **mapping 1** for the <u>first</u> pre-recorded sound where the tactile signal is associated to the resonance of the generated sound.

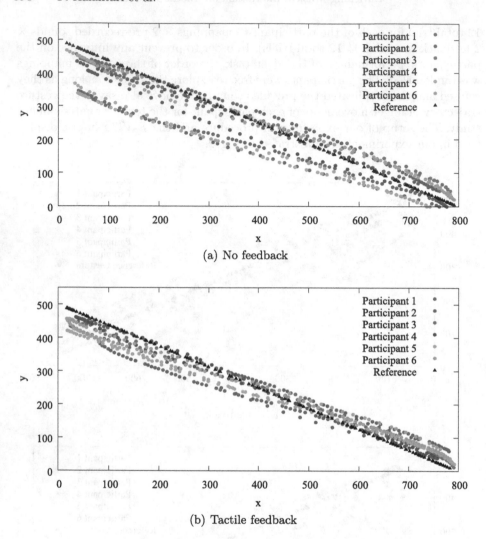

(a) No feedback

(b) Tactile feedback

Fig. 4. The tactile exploration of gesture trajectory of **mapping 1** for the <u>second</u> pre-recorded sound where the tactile signal is associated to the resonance of the generated sound.

4   Results and Discussion

We used the same qualitative evaluation methods as previously proposed to evaluate Digital Music Instruments (DMIs) and musical performances in [3,14].

We have thoughtfully designed our questionnaire in order to avoid influencing the participant's answers. Thus, we asked the following questions from the participants:

1. How do you feel about the sound you created?
2. How do you describe your experiment with our audio/haptic interface?

3. Can you identify and distinguish each of the 3 mappings?
4. How do you compare the 3 mappings and which one you preferred most?
5. Do you consider haptic feedback as a useful tool for sound synthesis and musical performances?

In summary, all the participants declared that the audio/haptic interface was very useful and interesting to enrich their musical perception. In particular, they expressed that the provided friction-based haptic feedback allowed them to feel the interaction with the real instruments as well as feeling what they hear simultaneously. They were all able to correctly identify and distinguish the three

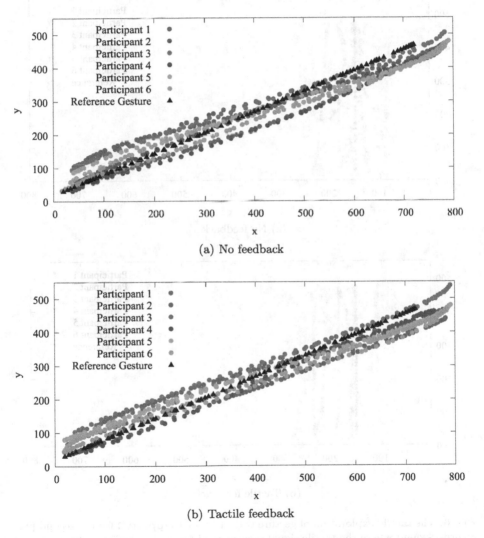

(a) No feedback

(b) Tactile feedback

Fig. 5. The tactile exploration of gesture trajectory for **mapping 2** for the <u>first</u> prerecorded sound where the tactile signal is associated to the roughness of the generated sound.

provided mappings. This means that they were all capable to detect which sound parameters in the 3 cases were associated to the corresponding tactile feedback.

50% of the participants preferred *mapping 1* in which the tactile signal was mapped to the resonance of the sound. Followed by *mapping 1*, the rest 50% of the participants preferred *mapping 3*, in which the generated sound was correlated with the gesture speed. This does make sense, taking into account that by principle; our audio/haptic interface exploit user's gesture velocity for tactile feedback rendering.

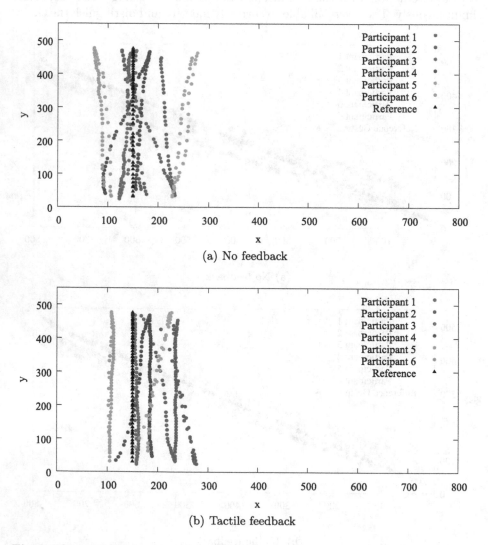

(a) No feedback

(b) Tactile feedback

Fig. 6. The tactile exploration of gesture trajectory of **mapping 2** for the <u>second</u> prerecorded sound where the tactile signal is associated to the roughness of the generated sound.

We also analyzed the gesture trajectories for each of the 3 provided mappings in order to study the influence of tactile feedback for users' performances of each musical gesture. The trajectories of participants when replicating a reference sound, illustrated in Figs. 3, 4, 5, 6, 7 and 8, suggest that the tactile feedback has an slight effect on the trajectory accuracy of the performed gestures compared to the reference one, since some variations can be seen for several participants. However, further experiments and investigations by means of a quantitative approach seems to be required to better evaluate the tactile feedback effect on musical gestures, with more participants as well. In all the figures

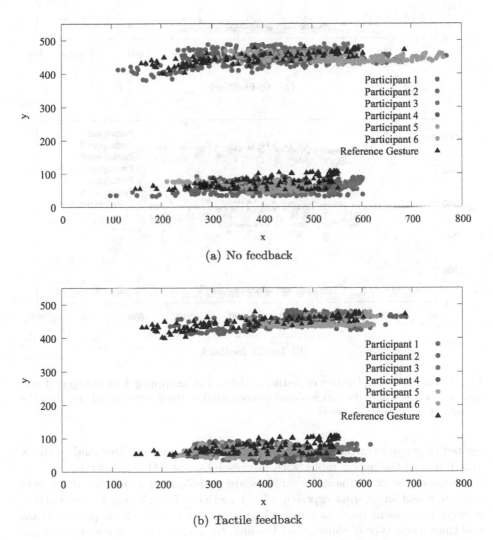

(a) No feedback

(b) Tactile feedback

Fig. 7. The tactile exploration of gesture trajectory of **mapping 3** for the <u>first</u> prerecorded sound where the tactile signal is associated to the gesture speed and thus the volume of the generated sound.

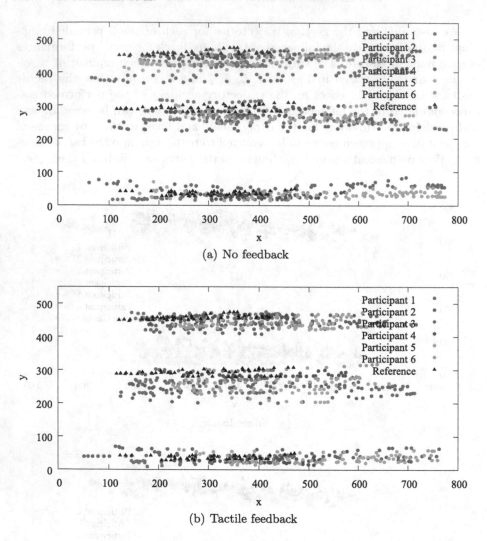

(a) No feedback

(b) Tactile feedback

Fig. 8. The tactile exploration of gesture trajectory of **mapping 3** for the <u>second</u> pre-recorded sound where the tactile signal is associated to the gesture speed and thus the volume of the generated sound.

related to gesture trajectory of different mappings, x and y correspond to the X and Y axis of the haptic tablet with the resolution of 800 * 480 pixels.

Some of the participants' comments are as follow: *"I think that it's a very enjoyable and interesting experience"*. "I feel that I'm playing the real string musical instrument (such as a guitar), taking into account the haptic feedback and the various type of sounds that I'm able to create." Or, *"I have never played a DMI before, however this interface may considerably facilitate the process of learning the sound synthesis and musical productions for me. The haptic feedback also help me to have a better feeling of the sounds that I create."*

Also, *"As a musician I believe this audio/haptic tactile display, enables us to enhance our perception of the basic principles of theory and harmony in music productions. It may also be useful to teach basic musical performances to beginner users as they are capable of hearing and feeling the sounds simultaneously."* Or *"The provided haptic feedback permits me to perform the appropriate gesture faster and easier for each mapping (specially for mapping 3), even without looking at the device."* Or *"The tactile feedback gives me an extra dimension to the music which I have never experienced before. In fact it provides a novel sensational feeling to the music that I used to only hear it."*

5 Conclusions and Perspectives

In the present paper we reported our preliminary investigations regarding to the potential influences of tactile feedback displays with programmable friction on users' musical interactions by means of a qualitative approach. We proposed four categories of mappings between the sound parameters and tactile feedback and analyzed user's experiences with three mapping conditions and two repetitions concerning to two pre-recorded sounds. Our preliminary results suggest that all the users consider the friction-based tactile feedback as a useful and interesting phenomenon for enhancing musical interactions, performances and learning. For the future works, we aim to investigate the tapping gesture with our audio/haptic interface which could allow us to simulate a wide range of instruments (e.g. touching the piano keyboard). We may also leverage other sound synthesis techniques in our future study (such as: granular synthesis, amplitude modulation etc.) rather than FM synthesis. Furthermore, it will be interesting to use quantitative approach for data analysis in terms of future lines of research, for instance using psychophysics for estimating discrimination thresholds between two sounds within a given mapping. The study of perceptual sensory discrimination may be of value to determine the best mapping to be used, and/or establish whether the subjects' preferences are linked to their actual perceptual abilities in DMIs.

Acknowledgments. The authors would like to appreciate Babak Rabbanipour for his useful help in our study. This work is partially funded by European ERDF grants (IRCICA, CPER MAUVE) and ANR funding agency (equipex IRDIVE).

References

1. Amberg, M., Giraud, F., Semail, B., Olivo, P., Casiez, G., Roussel, N.: STIMTAC: a tactile input device with programmable friction. In: UIST 2011 Adjunct Proceedings of the 24th Annual ACM Symposium Adjunct on User Interface Software and Technology, pp. 7–8. ACM (2011)
2. Baillie, L., Beattie, D., Morton, L.: Feel what you hear: haptic feedback as an accompaniment to mobile music playback. In: Proceedings of Interacting with Sound Workshop: Exploring Context-Aware, Local and Social Audio Applications, IwS 2011, pp. 1–6. ACM (2011)

3. Barbosa, J., Malloch, J., Wanderley, M.M., Huot, S.: What does "Evaluation" mean for the NIME community? In: 15th International Conference on New Interfaces for Musical Expression, NIME 2015, pp. 156–161. Louisiana State University, Baton Rouge, United States, May 2015
4. Bau, O., Poupyrev, I., Israr, A., Harrison, C.: TeslaTouch: electrovibration for touch surfaces. In: Proceedings of the 23rd Annual ACM Symposium on User Interface Software and Technology, UIST 2010, pp. 283–292. ACM (2010)
5. Birnbaum, D.M., Wanderley, M.M.: A systematic approach to musical vibrotactile feedback. In: Proceedings of International Computer Music Conference (ICMC 2007), pp. 397–404 (2007)
6. Buxton, W., Hill, R., Rowley, P.: Issues and techniques in touch sensitive tablet input. In: Proceedings of the 12th Annual Conference on Computer Graphics and Interactive Techniques, SIGGRAPH 1985, pp. 215–224. ACM (1985)
7. Casiez, G., Roussel, N., Vanbelleghem, R., Giraud, F.: Surfpad: riding towards targets on a squeeze film effect. In: Proceedings of the SIGCHI Conference on Human Factors in Computing Systems, CHI 2011, pp. 2491–2500. ACM (2011)
8. Chafe, C.: Tactile audio feedback. In: Proceedings of International Computer Music Conference (ICMC 1993), pp. 76–79 (1993)
9. Chang, A., O'Sullivan, C.: Audio-haptic feedback in mobile phones. In: CHI 2005 Extended Abstracts on Human Factors in Computing Systems, CHI EA 2005, pp. 1264–1267. ACM (2005)
10. Choi, S., Kuchenbecker, K.J.: Vibrotactile display: perception, technology, and applications. Proc. IEEE 101(9), 2093–2104 (2013)
11. Chowning, J., Bristow, D.: Fm Theory and Applications: By Musicians for Musicians. Hal Leonard Corp, New York (1987)
12. Chu, L.L.: Haptic feedback in computer music performance. In: Proceedings of International Computer Music Conference (ICMC 1996), pp. 57–58 (1996)
13. Doornbusch, P.: A brief survey of mapping in algorithmic composition. In: Proceedings of International Computer Music Conference (ICMC 2002) (2002)
14. Ghamsari, M., Pras, A., Wanderley, M.: Combining musical tasks and improvisation in evaluating novel digital musical instruments. In: Proceedings of the 10th International Symposium on Computer Music Multidisciplinary Research, CMMR 2013. Springer (2013)
15. Giraud, F., Amberg, M., Lemaire-Semail, B., Casiez, G.: Design of a transparent tactile stimulator. In: 2012 IEEE Haptics Symposium (HAPTICS), pp. 485–489, March 2012
16. Huang, J., Gamble, D., Sarnlertsophon, K., Wang, X., Hsiao, S.: Feeling music: integration of auditory and tactile inputs in musical meter perception. PLOS ONE 7(10), 1–11 (2012)
17. Beamish, T., van de Doel, K., MacLean, K., Fels, S.: D'groove: a haptic turntable for digital audio control. In: Proceedings of the International Conference on Auditory Display (ICAD 2003), July 2003
18. Kalantari, F., Grisoni, L., Giraud, F., Rekik, Y.: Finding the minimum perceivable size of a tactile element on an ultrasonic based haptic tablet. In: Proceedings of the 2016 ACM on Interactive Surfaces and Spaces, pp. 379–384. ISS 2016. ACM (2016)
19. Levesque, V., et al.: Enhancing physicality in touch interaction with programmable friction. In: Proceedings of the SIGCHI Conference on Human Factors in Computing Systems, CHI 2011, pp. 2481–2490. ACM (2011)

20. Lim, J.M., Lee, J.U., Kyung, K.U., Ryou, J.C.: An audio-haptic feedbacks for enhancing user experience in mobile devices. In: 2013 IEEE International Conference on Consumer Electronics (ICCE 2013), pp. 49–50, January 2013
21. Linjama, J., Makinen, V.: E-sense screen: novel haptic display with capacitive electrosensory interface. In: International Workshop on Haptic and Audio Interaction Design (HAID 2009). Springer (2009)
22. MacLean, K.E.: Haptic interaction design for everyday interfaces. Rev. Hum. Factors Ergon. 4(1), 149–194 (2008)
23. Menelas, B., Picinalli, L., Katz, B.F.G., Bourdot, P.: Audio haptic feedbacks for an acquisition task in a multi-target context. In: 2010 IEEE Symposium on 3D User Interfaces (3DUI), pp. 51–54, March 2010
24. Metatla, O., Martin, F., Parkinson, A., Bryan-Kinns, N., Stockman, T., Tanaka, A.: Audio-haptic interfaces for digital audio workstations. J. Multimodal User Interfaces 10(3), 247–258 (2016)
25. O'Modhrain, S., Essl, G.: PebbleBox and CrumbleBag: tactile interfaces for granular synthesis. In: Proceedings of the International Conference on New Interfaces for Musical Expression, NIME 2004, pp. 74–79. National University of Singapore (2004)
26. Papetti, S., Schiesser, S., Fröhlich, M.: Multi-point vibrotactile feedback for an expressive musical interface. In: Proceedings of the International Conference on New Interfaces for Musical Expression, NIME (2015)
27. Sanganeria, M., Werner, K.: GrainProc: a real-time granular synthesis interface for live performance. In: Proceedings of the International Conference on New Interfaces for Musical Expression, NIME 2013, pp. 223–226 (2013)
28. Serafin, S., Young, D.: Toward a generalized friction controller: from the bowed string to unusual musical instruments. In: Proceedings of International Conference on New Interfaces for Musical Expression (NIME 2004), pp. 181–191. Springer (2004)
29. Shultz, C.D., Peshkin, M.A., Colgate, J.E.: Surface haptics via electroadhesion: expanding electrovibration with Johnsen and Rahbek. In: 2015 IEEE World Haptics Conference (WHC), pp. 57–62, June 2015
30. Tanaka, A., Parkinson, A.: Haptic wave: a cross-modal interface for visually impaired audio producers. In: Proceedings of the 2016 CHI Conference on Human Factors in Computing Systems, CHI 2016, pp. 2150–2161. ACM (2016)
31. Vezzoli, E., Sednaoui, T., Amberg, M., Giraud, F., Lemaire-Semail, B.: Texture rendering strategies with a high fidelity - capacitive visual-haptic friction control device. In: Bello, F., Kajimoto, H., Visell, Y. (eds.) EuroHaptics 2016. LNCS, vol. 9774, pp. 251–260. Springer, Cham (2016). https://doi.org/10.1007/978-3-319-42321-0_23
32. Winfield, L., Glassmire, J., Colgate, J.E., Peshkin, M.: T-PaD: tactile pattern display through variable friction reduction. In: Second Joint EuroHaptics Conference and Symposium on Haptic Interfaces for Virtual Environment and Teleoperator Systems (WHC 2007), pp. 421–426, March 2007
33. Zhang, Y., Harrison, C.: Quantifying the targeting performance benefit of electrostatic haptic feedback on touchscreens. In: Proceedings of the 2015 International Conference on Interactive Tabletops & Surfaces, ITS 2015, pp. 43–46. ACM (2015)

Assessing Sound Perception Through Vocal Imitations of Sounds that Evoke Movements and Materials

Thomas Bordonné[1]([✉]), Manuel Dias-Alves[1,2], Mitsuko Aramaki[1],
Sølvi Ystad[1], and Richard Kronland-Martinet[1]

[1] Aix Marseille Univ, CNRS, PRISM, Perception, Representations, Image, Sound,
Music, 31 Chemin J. Aiguier, CS 70071, 13402 Marseille Cedex 09, France
{bordonne,aramaki,ystad,kronland}@prism.cnrs.fr,
manuel.diasalves@gmail.com
[2] Service Psychiatrie Centre Hospitalier de Toulon, Toulon, France

Abstract. In this paper we studied a new approach to investigate sound perception. Assuming that a sound contains specific morphologies that convey perceptually relevant information responsible for its recognition, called *invariants*, we explored the possibility of a new method to determine such invariants, using vocal imitation. We conducted an experiment asking participants to imitate sounds evoking movements and materials generated through a sound synthesizer. Given that the sounds produced by the synthesizer were based on invariant structures, we aimed at retrieving this information from the imitations. Results showed that the participants were able to correctly imitate the dynamics of the sounds, i.e. the action-related information evoked by the sound, whereas texture-related information evoking the material of the sound source was less easily imitated.

Keywords: Perception · Voice · Imitation · Invariant · LPC

1 Introduction

Here we suggest a new method to investigate auditory perception. As a starting point we based our study on the ecological approach to perception proposed by Gibson [7] in the visual domain, which considers that invariant structures that carry meaning are contained in a perceived stimulus. This approach was later extended by [15], who assumed that these *invariants* are divided in two categories: *structural invariants* characterizing the physical properties of a sound object, and *transformational invariants*, describing the action exerted on the object.

The main goal of our study is to identify such invariants. Several methods already exist, for example in [1] or [4], but our approach is different. While traditional approaches usually use intermediates to study perception, our approach

M. Aramaki et al. (Eds.): CMMR 2017, LNCS 11265, pp. 402–412, 2018.
https://doi.org/10.1007/978-3-030-01692-0_26

allow us to directly question our perception through vocal imitations. We suppose that the vocal imitation will sort of summarise ones perception of a sound. In fact, it has been shown that vocal imitation is more efficient to describe a sound than words [9]. In order to validate the fact that invariants can be retrieved from vocal imitations, we developed a preliminary experiment, which is presented in this paper. We posed two main questions: Which characteristics of a sound do we use when we imitate sounds? How are they transmitted by the voice?

In this study we used synthesized sounds based on invariant structures identified previously. Hence a transformational invariant responsible for the evocation of elliptic movements [13] was combined with 3 structural invariants responsible for the evocation of 3 different material categories, i.e. wood, metal and liquid [3]. We asked participants to vocally imitate sounds that evoked the elliptic movement on one of these three materials. To analyze the vocal imitations, we decided to use a conventional method based on linear predictive coding (LPC), like the one proposed in [10]. We assume for the moment, and for simplicity reasons, that a pole estimation will fit the spectral envelope of a vocal imitation. In order to avoid errors in the formant estimation, we still apply a sorting method based on quality factors over the poles to determine the formants. The general method is detailed later in the paper.

2 Method

In this section we describe the perception of invariants through a movement sonified thanks to a perceptually-validated synthesizer.

2.1 Creation of the Referent Sounds

In this experiment, the referent sounds are composed of synthetic rubbing sounds generated from a velocity profile, derived from an elliptic movement made by an experimenter.

In practice, an experimenter drew an ellipse on a WACOM INTUOS PRO graphic tablet. He was asked to reproduce the same shape 10 times. We asked the experimenter to draw the ellipse "in the most natural way", using the most available space. No instructions were given concerning the eccentricity nor orientation either. We used a 60 bpm metronome while the experimenter was drawing to help him being periodic. The position of the stylus was recorded by a Max/MSP interface at a sampling rate of 129 Hz. We then derived the position to get the velocity profile and kept the one that best corresponded to the initial 60 bpm rhythm. For technical reasons, we then duplicated the chosen velocity profile three times. The total duration of the drawing was 604,5 ms. It has been shown in [13] that an ellipse can be recognized when a blindfolded subject listens to the sound of the pencil or to the sonified trajectory. We therefore chose this shape for the vocal imitations to check the perceptual importance of the dynamics of this movement.

Then, we used the sound synthesizer described in [1] and [4] to generate the sounds textures that evoked different material categories. The elliptic movement was then combined with the three materials: wood, metal and liquid, to evaluate the subjects' capacity to imitate the perceived timbre. The advantage of using this synthesizer is that the acoustic descriptors of the materials have already been perceptually validated in previous studies meaning for example, that no preliminary study needed to be conducted to check whether subjects recognized the material.

We finally obtained the following three referent sounds: rubbing on wood, rubbing on metal, and rubbing on a liquid.

2.2   Experimental Setup

All participants provided written consent to participate in this study.

Stimuli. We used the 3 referent sounds. Each sound was presented only once in a random order. The order of presentation was different for each subject. The volume of the sounds was equalized.

Participants. A total of 31 French speaking persons volunteered as participants in the experiment (21 male, 10 female), between 20 and 62 years old (median 26 years old). Each participant performed an audiogram before participating in the experience. We reported no hearing impairments.

Apparatus. The sounds were played with an Apple Macintosh MacBookPro 9.1 (Mac OS X 10.9.5) with a MOTU UltraLite mk3 over a single Yamaha HS5 studio speaker facing them. The vocal imitations were recorded by a SMK4060 DPA microphone at a 44100 Hz sampling rate. The participants were also facing an interface displayed on a screen. They could interact with the interface and control the microphone with a mouse and a keyboard left at their disposal. This interface was developed with Max/MSP software. Participants were seated in a in a quiet room, acoustically isolated from the outside.

Procedure. The participants with a normal audiogram were introduced to the experience. They were first introduced to a preliminary experiment aiming at familiarizing the subject with thee experimental setup. It also enabled to create a small database for later use. The preliminary experience was performed in three steps: A recording aiming at ensuring the effective comprehension of the instructions. Then, the subjects pronounced five French vowels [a ø i o y] (in phonetical alphabet), that were recorded. Finally, an additional recording of two French sentences containing all the French phonemes was effectuated.

Sentence 1: "Au loin, un gosse trouve, dans la belle nuit complice, une merveilleuse et fraîche jeune campagne."

Sentence 2: "Il faut déjà que vous sachiez que les bords de telles rues ne sont qu'un peu glissants le matin à Zermatt."

The participants then began the experience. The instruction was: "You will hear sounds produced by movements on different materials. You will have to record one or two vocal imitations that describe at best the sound you heard." The participants first accessed an interface where they were allowed to record two imitations. The participants were informed that they had to record at least one imitation and listen to it before continuing. The participants secondly accessed another interface were they were allowed to evaluate their vocal imitations. The evaluation was done on a scale from 1 to 5, from "Not satisfied at all" to "Very satisfied". Finally, they had to answer the following questions: "What did you try to imitate? Which elements of the sounds did you based your imitation on?". The participants could write their answers in a designed location.

Analysis. For each referent sound, we gathered one or two vocal imitations per subjects. Depending on the participant, we obtained whether conventional voices, easy to modelise with a linear predictive model, or more complicated, like nasal vowels (the [ɔ̃] in "Bonjour" in french for example).

We began by segmenting the signal using a Pitch Synchronous OverLap-Add (PSOLA) [11] inspired algorithm. The pitch was calculated the YIN algorithm [5]. We then analyzed the segments with a simple LPC AR algorithm proposed in [10], which gave us an estimation of the positions of the poles of the estimated spectral envelope. We chose to estimate the spectral envelope with 12 coefficients.

We also filtered and sorted the formants by quality factors Q[1], keeping only the ones above $Q = 0.02$ (empirically determined threshold), in order to avoid wrong estimations of formants (detecting a formant that is not a formant), and to minimize formant jumps from one frame to another. In addition, and when all frames were calculated, we chose to mark as outliers and to remove the formants' frequencies that were superior to three times the median absolute deviation.

We finally calculated the prediction gain Pg for each frame, to quantify the voicing level. The higher the prediction gain is, the more periodic the signal is. It is based on the mean of the ratio between the energy in frames and the variance of the prediction error. Pg is given by the formula (1). This gives us an indication of how much did the subjects used voice or noise in their imitations.

$$Pg = \frac{1}{n} \sum_{k=1}^{n} \frac{E_k}{\sigma_k} \tag{1}$$

With n the number of frames, E_k the energy of the kth frame and σ_k the variance of the prediction error of the kth frame.

---

[1] A1 As a reminder, a pole z can be decomposed in a complex root pair as $z = r_0 e^{\pm \theta_0}$ ffrom which can be deduced the formant frequency $F = f_s/2\pi\theta_0$ and the -3dB bandwidth $B = -f_s/\pi \log |r_0|$ with f_s the sampling frequency. We easily deduce $Q = F/B$.

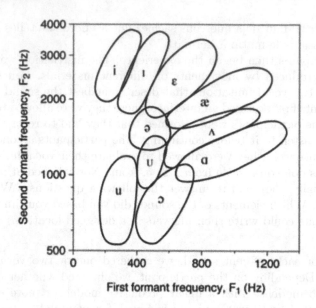

Fig. 1. Formant space between the first formant frequency and the second formant frequency. Here the different vowels corresponding to a couple of F1, F2 are represented. Source: [12]

We chose to look at the results in the space formed by the first formant frequency (F1), and the second formant frequency (F2) (See Fig. 1). We extracted the values of F1 and F2 from the previously cited method, and plotted them in an F1F2 space. We then studied the shape of the trajectory of the formants by calculating the centre and fitting an ellipse to 95% of the trajectory with a method derived from postural analysis which can be found in [6]. We then extracted the trajectory's barycentre, but also the phase, the surface and the orientation of the fitted ellipse. The phase is related to the eccentricity by the following relation:

$$\phi = 2 * \arctan \sqrt{1 - e^2} \tag{2}$$

With e the eccentricity of an ellipse. We chose to look at the phase instead of the eccentricity because the range of variations is larger. It allows us to study smaller variations of the eccentricity. It is important not to confuse the fitted ellipse and the drawn ellipse, used in the stimuli. They are two completely different variables, and their characteristics are independent. A representation of the different extracted parameters is given Fig. 2.

We performed an analysis of variance (ANOVA) using STATISTICA, on all of these variables, except on the range of the fundamental frequency, due to a lack of data. A Tukey's HSD test was used in order to specify significant effects. Results are presented and discussed in the next section.

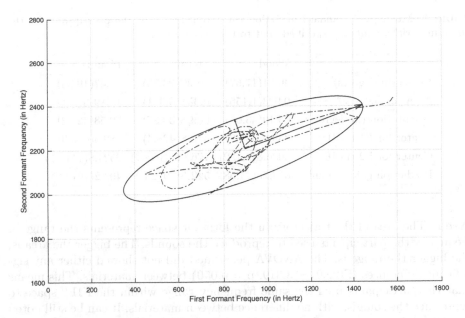

Fig. 2. Formant trajectory drawn in the F1F2 space. The trajectory is represented by the dashed line. The fitted ellipse is represented in black. The angle is calculated between the major half axe, represented here by the small arrow in black, and the horizontal level. We can see here that the center of the ellipse (F1 − 890,6 Hz, F2 − 2206 Hz) is situated at the limit of the known vowels

3 Results

One of the main goals of this study was to determine the characteristics of the sounds chosen by the subjects during imitation, and to figure out in which case voicing was used. We identified five possible indices. Studying the trajectory of the first two formants, we fitted an ellipse, allowing us to identify 4 indices: the trajectory's center, the phase, derived from the eccentricity, the surface and the orientation of this ellipse. The fifth indice, the prediction gain, is based on the mean of ratio between the energy in frames and the variance of the prediction error. Means and standard deviations of these four indices are presented in Table 1.

Phase. The flatter the trajectory, i.e. the closer the phase is to 0, the more selective between the formants the participant is. In other words, if the phase is small, the participant varies over one formant or the other, but not both. The ANOVA performed over the phase between materials did not showed any significant differences ($F(2,60) = 0.668$, $p = 0.516$). This means that independently of the materials, there is a preferred use of F1 or F2.

Table 1. Means and standard deviation (in parenthesis) for the descriptors, for the three materials. Units are specified next to the descriptors.

	Wood	Metal	Liquid
Phase (in degrees)	40.31(17.67)	36.20(23.33)	41.47(19.34)
Area (in $Hz^2 * 10^6$)	0.923(1.156)	0.351(0.371)	1.519(3.111)
Orientation (in degrees)	65.19(43.05)	80.98(39.87)	70.58(42.12)
Center for F1 (in Hz)	839.9(335.2)	616.8(428.4)	989.5(480.9)
Center for F2 (in Hz)	2036.8(990.2)	1762.6(1058.7)	2524.8(1113.3)
Prediction gain (no unit)	61.67(124.58)	522.58(922.69)	40.22(107.02)

Area. The area of the trajectory in the formant space represents the range of frequency the participants used to reproduce the sounds. The bigger the area is, the bigger the range is. The ANOVA performed did not showed either any significant differences ($F(2,60) = 3.319$, $p = 0.050$) between materials. This means that the participants used the same frequency range within the F1F2 space to reproduce the sounds, with no difference between materials. It can be still noted that the difference are nearly significative ($p = 0.0504$), showing a tendency for a bigger area for the liquid, which would mean a wider range of use of the formants for this material.

Orientation. The orientation of the formants' trajectory tells us which formant is used during imitation. If the orientation is vertical, close to $90°$, it means that only F1 is used. On the contrary, if the orientation is close to 0, it means that only F2 is used. Here again, the ANOVA did not show any significant differences ($F(2,60) = 1.135$, $p = 0.328$) between materials meaning that there is a preferred orientation during imitation. Looking at the values of the orientation, there is a covariation between F1 and F2.

Center. The centers of the formants' trajectory represent a preferred location in the F1F2 space, that is to say, a preferred configuration of the vocal tract. It appears from the ANOVA that there is a significant difference between materials ($F(2,60) = 6.219$, $p = 0.003$ for the center over F1 and $F(2,60) = 4.776$, $p = 0.011$ for the center over F2). Results can be seen in Table 1 and in Fig. 3. A Tukey's HSD test showed us that the center for metal was significantly different from the center for liquid for both F1 and F2 ($p = 0.002$ and $p = 0.009$ respectively). This means that different vocal tract configurations were used for the metal and for the liquid. The wood is still undistinguishable from the other two regarding this cue.

Prediction Gain. The higher the prediction gain is, the more periodic the signal is. In other words, it means that it indicates whether the subject used its voice, with fundamental frequency, or used only noise while imitating. It

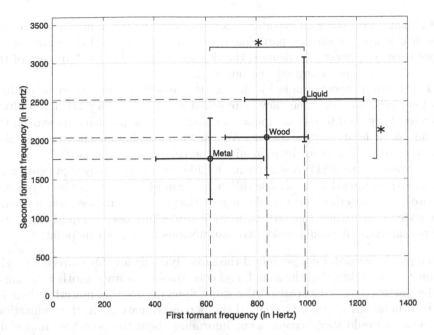

Fig. 3. Center of the ellipses following the three materials in the (F1, F2) space. Horizontal and vertical plain bars represent the standard deviation. Stars signals the significant differences

appeared from the ANOVA that there is also a significant difference between materials ($F(2,60) = 7.912$, $p = 0.00089$). A Tukey's HSD test showed that the prediction gain for the metal was different from the wood's prediction gain ($p = 0.003$) and from the liquid's prediction gain ($p = 0.002$).

4   Discussion and Further Work

Here we discuss several points raised by the previous results. The initial questions were related to the characteristics of the sound used by the participants during their imitation, and, consequently, how did they expressed it. Given the previous results, dynamics and the material are the two characteristics the participants chose. They transmitted it through replicating the dynamic and voicing or not their imitation.

4.1   Participants Imitate the Dynamics Similarly

One initial hypothesis was that the participants could retrieve the dynamics of the movement independently from the three materials. Results show that participants in majority perceived the same dynamics of the sound. The three chosen descriptors of the trajectory in the formant space (Phase, Area and Orientation) are not significantly different across materials. Results also show that the participants used the same strategy to reproduce the dynamics of the sound. Even if it is unsure whether participants specifically perceived the shape of the ellipse used to generate the sounds, the rhythm induced by the dynamics of the elliptical shape was recognized and imitated.

The written reports made by the participants themselves tend to confirm this tendency. Indeed, when they were asked about what they tried to imitate and what they used to imitate the sound, nearly all the participants evoked the rhythm, or at least, a cyclic aspect. We can therefore assume that the morphological invariant linked to the dynamics is perceived and expressed.

However, as the ANOVA suggest it, the differences are nearly significative for the area ($p = 0.0504$). In fact the differences would be between the liquid and the two other materials. This would suggest that participants use their formants in a wider range when they try to imitate something over a liquid than over others materials. We could make two assumptions to clarify this point:

- the participants did not perceived the same dynamic for this material, maybe due to the "fluidity" of the sound, and consequently imitate another dynamic.
- the participants did perceived the same dynamic for this material than for the others, but also tried to embed the perceived material in their imitation. The area would then become a cue informing about the perceived material

One way to check which assumption is right would be to ask participants to imitate sounds with different dynamics. It has been shown in [13] that a biological movement following the 1/3 power law[2] can be recognized through timbre variations by the velocity profiles and that drawn shapes also can be distinguished through the different velocity profiles produced during the drawing process. It would be interesting to study the influence of changing the dynamics of the sound. First, simply by changing the shape from which the velocity profile is taken. And second, by making the velocity profile following another law. This would maybe allow us to retrieve, the already known dynamical invariant in relation with the shape, by looking at the dynamic evolution of the imitation.

4.2 The Metal Clearly Recognized and Highlighted

Our hypothesis was that the participants would make a difference between materials during their imitations by changing the timbre. What can be seen is that only the metal induced a significant change in timbre. The "metallic" aspect, which can sound like more "resonant" or more "harmonic", convinced the participants to voice their imitation more than for the other materials as reflected in the prediction gain.

The position of the centers of the formant's trajectories also informs us about the metallic aspect of the sound, or at least allow us to differentiate metal from liquid (which is quite reassuring!). An analysis of the fundamental frequency range may complete the distinction between material but unfortunately, too few participants used it in their imitation strategy to make significant statistics.

---

[2] For documentation about 1/3 power law, see [14].

Still, the hypothesis that different materials induce different imitations is again comforted by the reports of the participants. The participants reported a perceptual difference of perception between the three materials. In addition, as mentioned before, the area of the formant trajectory may be an indicator of the material, allowing the distinction between liquid and other materials. Again, an experiment containing other dynamics with the same materials should reinforce the data yet extracted and confirm our hypotheses.

4.3 Further Work

In addition to the previous propositions, the excitation is an object of importance. For the moment, all the descriptors we studied, except the fundamental frequency to a certain extent, were extracted from the spectrum. The excitation has to be taken into account when analyzing and describing complex sounds. For example, in the case of liquid sounds, the information included in the spectrum or the fundamental frequency is not sufficient. Imitations can be half-voiced half-unvoiced, for example like in the French pronunciations of "r" or "j", like in "rouler" or "jouer". Using inverse filtering in LPC to retrieve information about the excitation can easily be made, but modeling complex sounds like the previously cited ones is more complicated. The next field of investigation will surely focus on extracting information from the residual from linear prediction.

More broadly, assessing the sound perception through vocal imitations opens a wider perspectives for sound synthesis. In [2], the authors proposed an approach based on a Brain-Computer Interface (BCI) to highlight and extract the aforementioned invariants. The questions we may ask are, how does the human brain reacts when one hears a sound that evoke a known movement and material? And does the brain reacts equally when one imitates the evoking a movement and a material. There is already existing studies studying and measuring the reaction of the brain when hearing a sound evoking a movement, for example in [8]. In fact, it has been shown directly that the area involved in speech is also involved in motor functions [3] so it would normally be a good track to follow to search for relations between an movement evoked by hearing and the way we imitate it, in order to find the aforementioned invariants.

5 Conclusion

In this experiment, we aimed at determining the main characteristics of sounds used by participants during vocal imitations. We also wanted to determine how the participants translated these characteristics using their own vocal apparel. For that, we extracted several descriptors from the F1, F2 space: The phase, the area and the orientation of an ellipse fitting the trajectory of the formants along with the centers of these trajectory. We also extracted the prediction gain to characterize the usage of the voice. The dynamics of the sound turned out to be well recognized and well imitated by all the participants. In addition, the fundamental frequency is used by participants as a tool to complete the missing information given by the formants concerning the material. Further work is planned to deepen these two assumptions. Vocal imitation seem to be a good tool to access the perception and determine which aspects of the sounds are relevant. The next goal is to validate its use in the search of invariants.

Acknowledgments. This work was financed by the National Research Agency (ANR) within the SoniMove project (ANR-14-CE24-0018).

References

1. Aramaki, M., Besson, M., Kronland-Martinet, R., Ystad, S.: Controlling the perceived material in an impact sound synthesizer. IEEE Trans. Audio Speech Lang. Process. **19**(2), 301–314 (2011)
2. Aramaki, M., Kronland-Martinet, R., Ystad, S., Micoulaud-Franchi, J.-A., Vion-Dury, J.: Prospective view on sound synthesis BCI control in light of two paradigms of cognitive neuroscience. In: Miranda, E.R., Castet, J. (eds.) Guide to Brain-Computer Music Interfacing, pp. 61–87. Springer, London (2014). https://doi.org/10.1007/978-1-4471-6584-2_4
3. Buccino, G., et al.: Neural circuits involved in the recognition of actions performed by nonconspecifics: an fMRI study. J. Cogn. Neurosci. **16**(1), 114–126 (2004)
4. Conan, S., et al.: An intuitive synthesizer of continuous-interaction sounds: rubbing, scratching, and rolling. Comput. Music. J. **38**(4), 24–37 (2014)
5. De Cheveigné, A., Kawahara, H.: YIN, a fundamental frequency estimator for speech and music. J. Acoust. Soc. Am. **111**(4), 1917–1930 (2002)
6. Duarte, M., Zatsiorsky, V.M.: Effects of body lean and visual information on the equilibrium maintenance during stance. Exp. Brain Res. **146**(1), 60–69 (2002)
7. Gibson, J.J.: The Ecological Approach to Visual Perception: Classic Edition. Psychology Press, New York (2014)
8. Kohler, E., Keysers, C., Umilta, M.A., Fogassi, L., Gallese, V., Rizzolatti, G.: Hearing sounds, understanding actions: action representation in mirror neurons. Science **297**(5582), 846–848 (2002)
9. Lemaitre, G., Rocchesso, D.: On the effectiveness of vocal imitations and verbal descriptions of sounds. J. Acoust. Soc. Am. **135**(2), 862–873 (2014)
10. Makhoul, J.: Linear prediction: a tutorial review. Proc. IEEE **63**(4), 561–580 (1975)
11. Peeters, G.: Analyse et synthèse des sons musicaux par la méthode psola. In: JIM98-Workshop, Agelonde, France (1998)
12. Peterson, G.E., Barney, H.L.: Control methods used in a study of the vowels. J. Acoust. Soc. Am. **24**(2), 175–184 (1952)
13. Thoret, E., Aramaki, M., Kronland-Martinet, R., Velay, J.L., Ystad, S.: From sound to shape: auditory perception of drawing movements. J. Exp. Psychol. Hum. Percept. Perform. **40**(3), 983 (2014)
14. Viviani, P., Flash, T.: Minimum-jerk, two-thirds power law, and isochrony: converging approaches to movement planning. J. Exp. Psychol. Hum. Percept. Perform. **21**(1), 32 (1995)
15. Warren, W.H., Verbrugge, R.R.: Auditory perception of breaking and bouncing events: a case study in ecological acoustics. J. Exp. Psychol. Hum. Percept. Perform. **10**(5), 704 (1984)

Exploration of Sonification Strategies for Guidance in a Blind Driving Game

Gaëtan Parseihian[(⊠)], Mitsuko Aramaki, Sølvi Ystad,
and Richard Kronland-Martinet

Aix Marseille Univ, CNRS, PRISM (Perception, Representation, Image, Sound,
Music), 31 Chemin J. Aiguier, CS 70071, 13402 Marseille, Cedex 09, France
{parseihian,aramaki,ystad,kronland}@prism.cnrs.fr

Abstract. This paper explores the use of continuous auditory display for
a dynamic guidance task. Through a driving game with blindfolded players, the success and the efficiency of a lane-keeping task in which no visual
feedback is provided is observed. The results highlight the importance of
the display information and reveal that a task-related rather than an error-
related feedback should be used to enable the driver to finish the circuit.
In terms of sound strategies, a first experiment explores the effect of two
complex strategies (pitch and modulations) combined with a basic stereo
strategy that informs the user about the distance and the direction to the
target. The second experiment examines the influence of morphological
sound attributes on the performance compared to the use of the spatial
sound attributes alone. The results reveal the advantage of using morphological sound attributes for such kinds of applications.

Keywords: Auditory display · Sound guidance · Blind driving
Sonification

1 Introduction

During the last decade, a growing number of applications involving the auditory modality to inform or guide users has been developed in a large number
of domains ranging from guidance for visually impaired [11,13], positional guidance in surgery [2], rehabilitation for patients with disabilities [5,16], learning
of handwriting movements [4], or gesture guidance [17]. These applications are
based on the sonification concept which is defined as "the use of non-speech
audio to convey information or perceptual data" [1,10]. Despite an increasing
development of studies based on sonification for auditory guidance, there is a
lack of fundamental studies aiming at evaluating the efficiency of specific sound
attributes to guide a user towards a target.

This work aims at evaluating the efficiency of specific morphological sound
attributes to guide a user towards a target without focusing on a specific application using parameter mapping sonification [8]. It follows a former study which
aimed at comparing and evaluating sonification strategies in order to propose

© Springer Nature Switzerland AG 2018
M. Aramaki et al. (Eds.): CMMR 2017, LNCS 11265, pp. 413–428, 2018.
https://doi.org/10.1007/978-3-030-01692-0_27

new guidelines for one-dimensional guidance tasks [14]. This study introduced a method that aimed at identifying and comparing sound attributes for precise, rapid and direct (no overshooting) auditory guidance. This first study provided relevant information for predicting the user performance with a chosen sonification strategy and constituted a first step toward general guidelines for mapping data onto auditory display dimensions and towards the identification of efficient perceptual sound structures for guidance tasks. The proposed categorization was constructed for one-dimensional cases and the results of this study are therefore mainly of interest for such kinds of tasks (e.g., detection of distances to obstacles, representation of the distance between the tip of the needle and an organ in surgery, etc.).

However, depending on the application, the audio feedback should guide the user according to one or several variables and/or in one or several spatial dimensions (1D, 2D, 3D in Cartesian or spherical coordinates). Depending on the context, guidance may also be either directed toward a static (e.g., guiding the user's hand to grasp an object) or a dynamic target (e.g., a pursuit-tracking task). All these considerations strongly influence the choice of the mapping between the data and the sound and require different approaches. In [14], one-dimensional guidance toward a static target case was considered. The present study aims to go further by considering one dimensional guidance toward a dynamic target.

Compared to the static case, guidance toward a dynamic target (where the target evolves over time), forces the subject to continuously pursue a moving target. In this particular context, the target might follow either a periodic (predictable) or noisy (unpredictable) trajectory and the gap between the current (user) and the desired state (target) of the system will evolve as a function of this trajectory. In this particular case both the sound parameter and the data to sonify will be decisive for the success of the sonification. Indeed, the perceptual information that enables the guidance should allow the user to anticipate his/her movements. In a tracking task, two behavioural strategies might be used to perform the task [6]: the first is the pursuit strategy that informs the user about the target's current position, the second is the interception strategy, that informs the user about the angle between his/her position and the target. Several studies have explored the use of continuous auditory feedback to complement visual feedback in a manual tracking task. In [15], Rosati et al. indicate that auditory biofeedback can improve patients' tracking movements and that task-related information leads to better performances than error-related information. To go further, Boyer et al. [3] explored the contribution of task-, error-, and user-related sonification in the same kind of task in the context of sensorimotor learning. Their results highlight a significant effect on performance and learning of the three types of auditory feedback and an increased motor learning retention in user-related feedback.

Similarly to these studies, this article explores the use of continuous auditory feedback in tracking tasks. However, the present case study tackles the situation in which sounds are used to replace vision in a highly visual dynamic tracking task. The idea here is to explore the potential of sonification to resolve a tracking task for blindfolded subjects, and to explore the influence of sonification strategies and the choice of information to provide. Such situations can be encountered for example in movement rehabilitation, in sport training, or in medicine. Keeping in mind that this study must treat a sufficiently general situation while being sufficiently realistic, we chose to work on an ordinary situation that consists in driving.

Driving is a task that predominantly relies on vision [7]. Although lane-keeping is a relatively simple task, steering with only auditory cues might be complicated as the sound cannot display specific, complex information such as the shape or the curvature of a road. However, through a driving game with blindfolded players, this article aims at exploring the effect of sound strategies and displayed information on lane-keeping with auditory cues in absence of visual information.

The article first describes the implemented model for the driving game. Second it presents the two morphological sound attributes and the spatial sound attribute used to guide the participants during the driving task. Then two experiments based on a blind driving game are described. The first one is designed to evaluate the influence of the information to display and compares the efficiency of the two morphological sound attributes. The second experiment is designed to compare the performance using a morphological sound attribute (e.g. the pitch) and a basic spatial sound attribute (e.g. the stereo).

2 The Driving Simulator

2.1 A Simple Vehicle Model

This study is based on a simple approach that consists in considering the driver?s steering behavior as essentially independent from the underlying vehicle locomotion scheme. The driving simulator is implemented with a locomotion model based on a simple vehicle simplified by the point source approximation (one-wheel model). Such an approximation leads to a very simple and computationally cheap model although it is far from being a physically realistic vehicle model.

The vehicle is represented by its position and its direction. In order to join or to keep the lane, the algorithm computes for each iteration:

- the vehicle position with respect to the trajectory,
- a target on the trajectory that must be reached by the vehicle,
- the steering angle allowing to reach the target.

The target on the trajectory is calculated by defining an anticipation distance. Indeed, during a standard lane keeping task, the driver uses a visual target defined by the road center at "n" meters to correctly steer the vehicle. The position of this target depends of the vehicle speed, and can be considered as the position on the trajectory that will be reached in "x" seconds. The lane keeping task strongly relies on the anticipation time. Figure 1 represent two computer simulations of lane keeping at a constant speed with two different anticipation

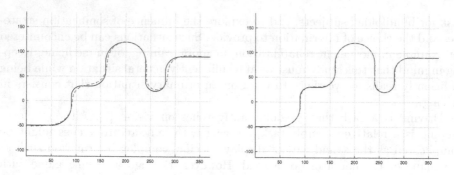

Fig. 1. Computer simulation of path tracking with two anticipation distance: 30 m (left) and 20 m (right). The black line corresponds to the theoretical trajectory. The red lines represent the vehicle trajectory and headings at each iteration. (Color figure online)

distances. This highlights the effect of the anticipation time. Indeed with an oversized anticipation time, the vehicle tends to ignore strong curvatures whereas an insufficient anticipation time provokes oscillations around the trajectory.

2.2   The Information to Display

With visual feedback, a wealth of information is available to the driver. With only auditory feedback, the challenge consists in providing the driver with the information needed to keep the lane and anticipate trajectory turns. As in Rosati et al. [15], the study explores the influence of two feedback categories. The first corresponds to the error-related feedback which informs about the user's actual performance, whereas the second corresponds to the task-related feedback which informs the user on the action required to track the path.

Based on these two categories, four different types of information to display were explored:

- Distance Error (DE): The first feedback condition corresponds to the distance error. It is defined by the lateral difference between the vehicle and the desired position on the road (e.g., the vehicle's projection on the road). It corresponds to an error-related feedback. This condition is represented in Fig. 2 (left).
- Anticipated Distance Error (ADE): The second feedback condition corresponds to the distance error, but with an anticipation distance. The idea here, is to inform the driver about the error with respect to the position to be attained in X meters. It is defined by the difference between the vehicle and its projection on the road X meters from the vehicle. It corresponds to an error-related feedback. This condition is represented in Fig. 2 (middle).
- Angular Distance Anticipation (ADA): The third condition is based on task-related feedback. It corresponds to steering wheel rotation needed to attain the target position in X meters. The ADA is defined by the angle between the front of the car and the target on the trajectory. This condition is represented in Fig. 2 (right).

- Angular Time Anticipation (ATA): The last feedback condition corresponds to an extension of the ADA. When driving, the distance anticipation might vary according to the speed of the vehicle. Indeed the faster the vehicle, the larger the anticipation distance. In this condition, the target is not calculated as a function of an anticipated distance, but as a function of an anticipated time. The resulting action corresponds to the steering wheel rotation that needs to be done to be on the trajectory in N seconds. This condition is represented in Fig. 2 (right).

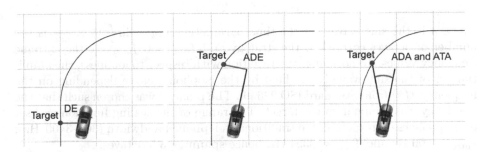

Fig. 2. Representation of the displayed information: Distance Error (DE) on the left; Anticipated Distance Error (ADE) in middle; Angular Distance or Time Anticipation (ADA or ATA) on the right.

As a first hypothesis, the DE may not be able to guide the driver correctly as the information needed to help the driver get back on the track arrives too late. This condition may lead to oscillations around the trajectory and lane departure in the first turn. The addition of a distance that enables anticipation (ADE) should stabilize the guidance and reduce the oscillations whereas task-related feedback (ADA and ATA) is likely to be even more appropriate [15] and should lead to more efficient guidance especially when taking into account the vehicle speed (ATA).

3   Sound Strategies

In order to explore the influence of the sound parameter on the tracking task, two of the nine sound strategies presented in [14] were selected. As the driving task requires high rapidity, the strategies were chosen to allow for precise and rapid guidance. [14] suggests that certain strategies such as the Multi-Band Frequency Modulation/Multi Scale Beating/pitch/tempo would produce good performances independently of the type of the task, whereas performances obtained with "strategies with reference" might be highly task dependent. Therefore, in order to explore a potential effect of the strategy type, a basic strategy (e.g., the pitch) and a strategy with reference and zoom effect (e.g., the multi-band frequency modulation) were chosen. The implementation of these two sonification strategies are described in this section.

3.1 Pitch

The pitch strategy consists of mapping the normalized distance onto the frequency of a pure tone. This strategy is implemented using a sine wave of varying frequency $f(x)$ based on the normalized distance to the target $0 \leq x \leq 1$:

$$s(t) = A(f(x)) \cos(2\pi f(x)t)$$

As human perception of frequency varies logarithmically, we chose the following scaling function $f(x)$:

$$f(x) = f_{min}.2^{x.n_{oct}}$$

where s is the sine wave, t is the time parameter, $n_{oct} = \ln \frac{f_{max}}{f_{min}} \times \frac{1}{\ln 2}$ is the number of octaves covered by the strategy and f_{min} and f_{max} are the extreme frequency values. To normalize the variation with respect to loudness, the amplitude A of the sine wave is weighted by the isophonic curve depending on the frequency $f(x)$ from Standard ISO 226 [9]. The polarity was chosen such that the frequency was minimal on the target. The range of the scaling function was set to frequencies corresponding to traditional telephone bandwidth (300–3400 Hz): $f_{min} = 300$ Hz and $f_{max} = 3394$ Hz, hence spanning 3.5 octaves.

3.2 Multi-band Frequency Modulation (MBFM)

This strategy is based on frequency modulation of a harmonic sound with fundamental frequency $f_0 = 200$ Hz. Here, each harmonic is frequency modulated in a different way: the modulation frequency of the kth component is $f_m(x) = 10k.x$ and depends on the normalized distance x such that the frequency of the modulation signal increases with the frequency of the component. When the user approaches the target, the modulation frequency decreases (there is no modulation when the target is reached). The farther the target, the higher the modulation frequency and the more complex the sound:

$$s(t) = \sum_{k=1}^{N} sin(2\pi f_k t + Ik.sin(2\pi f_m(x)t))$$

where f_k is the frequency of the kth harmonic, $I = 50$ is the modulation index, and $f_m(x)$ is the modulation frequency.

By using a harmonic sound an "auditory zoom" can be constructed. The concept is simple: frequency modulation affects all harmonics but with different temporalities. For a fixed distance, the higher the frequency, the faster the modulation. Near the target, the modulation frequency of the first harmonic is too small to rapidly grasp the target, but the modulations from the second harmonic, which are twice as fast, and then from the third harmonic (three times faster) enables faster and more precise location of the target.

3.3   Target Direction

The presented sonification strategies provide information concerning the distance to the target. However, for the present task the user should also be informed about the direction towards the target. Indeed, during the tracking task, the target might be on the left or on the right. This information is provided by sound spatialisation. When the target is on the left, the user needs to rotate the steering wheel toward the left and therefore the sound is heard on the left ear. When the target is on the right, the sound is heard on the right ear. To provide directional information, the gap between left and right ears is tightened close to the target and the transition is very sharp.

4   Experiment 1

This experiment aims first at evaluating the influence of the information displayed with sounds in the case of a driving task without visual information and second at assessing the effect of the type of morphological sound attribute on the guidance.

4.1   Method

Subjects. Twenty subjects participated in the experiment [5 women and 15 men; age: min. 20; max. 50 years]. All were naive regarding the purpose of the experiment and none of the subjects reported any hearing losses. All of them participated on a volunteer basis; they signed an informed consent form prior to the testing. This study was performed in accordance with the ethical standards of the Declaration of Helsinki (revised Edinburgh, 2000).

Stimuli and Apparatus. The subjects were placed in a quiet room wearing closed-ear stereo headphones (model Sennheiser HD280). They sat in front of a steering wheel (model Driving Force GT) and a computer screen. The experiment ran on an interactive interface implemented using the Max programming environment[1] and the instructions were automatically displayed on the screen in the beginning of each session.

The sound stimuli were synthesized in real-time using the two strategies defined in the previous section. In each strategy, the given sound parameter changed as function of the normalized distance between the steering wheel and the target. The overall sound level was fixed at a comfortable level at the beginning of the experiment and subjects were not able to modify it during the experiment.

The car speed was kept constant throughout the experiment and the participant had no possibility to use the gas-pedal or to brake.

---

[1] Available: http://cycling74.com/downloads/.

Procedure. The participants were instructed to drive without visual information and with the aid of two different sound strategies. The experiment was divided in two sessions (one for the Pitch strategy and one for the MBFM strategy).

Before each session, a familiarization step of 75 s was proposed to the participants to help them identify and understand the sound strategies. This step consisted in turning the steering wheel while listening to the sound variations associated with its angle. A visual display allowed the participant to view a representation of the angle on a line. This representation consisted of a black dot moving with respect to a red dot (corresponding to the central position of the steering wheel). For each session, the variations of the sound attribute were explain with simple words (as describe in [14]).

After the familiarization test, the subjects were told how many trials they needed to do (12 trials per session), the maximum duration of each trial (75 s), and the commands for triggering the trial and proceed to the next trial. They were asked to follow the trajectory by tracking the auditory signal as precisely as possible. They were told that the gas pedal was not functional. There was no visual feedback during the test. At the end of each trial, participants were informed about their success (or failure) with an applause (or a voice pronouncing "you loose!").

The session order was counterbalanced across the subjects. Each session was composed of 12 trials for three different race tours by four display conditions (DE, ADE, ADA, and ATA). Each tour was composed of the same number of turns with an equal number of left turns and right turns.

The experiment lasted between 30 and 40 min.

4.2   Results

For each subject and each trial, the success/failure, the total time, and the accumulated error were computed. Figure 3 represents typical trajectories obtained for each display condition. When the subject managed to finish the tour, the trial was considered a success. For example, in the DE condition, the subject failed to keep track of the lane and got lost in the first turn. This resulted in a total time of 75 s. In the other cases, the total time depended on the error and the number of turns performed by the subject. The accumulated error corresponds to the sum of differences between the theoretical trajectory and the user trajectory.

These descriptors were averaged across the three trials for each subject and analyzed in a two-way repeated measures analysis of variance (ANOVA) with "sound strategy" (2 levels) and "display condition" (4 levels) as within-subject factors. For all statistical analyses, effects were considered significant if the p-value was less than or equal .05. Significant differences were analyzed with LSD Fisher post-hoc tests.

Success Rate. For the DE condition, no trials were successful, resulting in a 0% success rate. This condition was therefore excluded from the followings analyses. The ADE condition led to 58.3 ± 42.7% with the Pitch strategy and 28.3 ± 36.3%

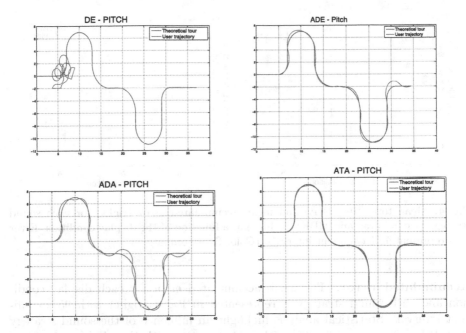

Fig. 3. Examples of results for one typical subject for the *Pitch* session for each display condition. DE top left; ADE top right; ADA bottom left; and ATA bottom right.

with the MBFM strategy. The ADA condition led to 86.7 ± 27.4% with the Pitch strategy and 78.3 ± 34.7% with the MBFM strategy. The ATA condition led to 75.0 ± 37.3% with the Pitch strategy and 58.3 ± 40.3% with the MBFM strategy. Statistical analyses show a significant effect of the sound strategies $[F(1, 19) = 23.22, p < 0.0005]$ with higher success with the Pitch strategy; a significant effect of the display conditions $[F(2, 38) = 36.91, p < 0.0001]$ and a quasi significant interaction between sound strategies and display conditions $[F(2, 38) = 2.75, p = 0.076]$. Considering the display condition, the post-hoc test highlights a significant superiority of the ADA condition over other conditions $(p > 0.05)$.

Total Time. The mean total time for each display condition and each sound strategy is represented in Fig. 4 (left) with 95% confident intervals. Statistical analyses highlight an influence of the sound strategy $[F(1, 19) = 27.81, p < 0.0001]$, an influence of the display condition $[F(2, 28) = 30.65, p < 0.0001]$ and a quasi-significant interaction between sound strategy and display condition $[F(2, 38) = 3.18, p = 0.053]$. The Pitch condition generally allows for a faster guidance (total time of 47 ± 13 s) than the MBFM strategy (total time of 55 ± 12 s). Post-hoc analyses highlight a significant difference between ADE and, ADA and ATA. The ADE condition conducts to longer guidance than the ADA and ATA conditions.

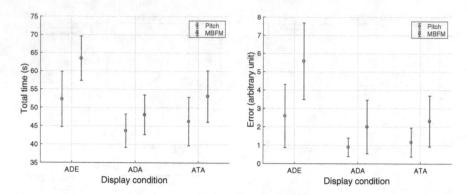

Fig. 4. Mean total time (left) and mean accumulated error (right) for each sound strategy (Pitch in red and MBFM in blue) as a function of the display condition. Error bars represent 95% confident intervals. (Color figure online)

Accumulated Error. The mean accumulated error for each display condition and each sound strategy is represented in Fig. 4 (right) with 95% confident intervals. Statistical analysis highlight an influence of the sound strategy $[F(1, 19) = 20.54, p < 0.0005]$ with better results with the pitch strategy; an effect of the display condition $[F(2, 38) = 16.73, p < 0.0001]$ with a significant difference between ADE and ATA $(p < 0.0001)$ and between ATA and ADA $(p < 0.0001)$; and no significant interaction $[F(2, 38) = 1.19, p = 0.314]$.

4.3   Discussion

The aim of the present experiment was first to evaluate the influence of the information displayed with sounds in the case of a driving task without visual information and second to evaluate the effect of the sound strategy on the guidance. Four types of display information were tested with two types of sound strategies.

Considering the display information, the results show that an anticipation distance (or time) is absolutely required to achieve the task, meaning that a simple *Distance Error* information doesn't allow to dynamically follow the target and to achieve the task. In contrast, the use of a display information based on anticipation reduces oscillations around the trajectory and introduces a stability in the control loop.

Analyses of the total time and accumulated error highlight the advantage of task-related information compared to error-related information. The *Anticipated Distance Error* enables dynamic guidance, but with more failures and with longer duration and greater errors. This result confirms the findings on task-related information reported in [15] in the absence of visual information. Considering the task-related information, the steering wheel angle allows the participant to easily follow the trajectory and leads to a greater number of successful trials. There are no differences between the distance-related (*Angular Distance Anticipation*) and the time-related anticipation (*Angular Time Anticipation*), although there is a slight superiority in the distance-related anticipation in terms of success rate. This absence of differences is probably due the absence of speed control by the participants. Indeed, the aim of the driving task was to follow the lane and the speed of the vehicle was not controlled by the participants. This might have reduced the advantage of a time anticipation over the distance anticipation.

Considering the sound strategies, the results highlight a significant superiority of the *pitch* strategy over the *multi band frequency modulation* strategy in terms of success, rapidity and task precision. This can be explained by the structure of the sound signal which is simpler for the pitch than for the MBFM strategy. Furthermore, in [14] the *pitch* was the best strategy for rapid guidance tasks whereas *MBFM* was the best strategy when high precision was required. In the case of a dynamic guidance task, it seems that rapidity is more important than efficiency.

To go further, it would be of interest to explore the specific role of the stereo feedback to inform the user on the position of the target. Indeed, in the present experiment, the spatial sound attribute informed the user on the direction of the target (right or left), while the morphological sound attribute informed on the distance to the target. Since the present experiment doesn't allow to conclude on the contribution of the morphological sound attribute with respect to the spatial sound attribute, an additional experiment comparing the basic stereo feedback with the pitch strategy was performed.

5   Experiment 2

This experiment aimed at measuring the importance of the two different sound attributes used in the dynamic guidance task. The first experiment highlighted an influence of the morphological sound attributes with a significant superiority of the *pitch* strategy, but didn't allow to evaluate this contribution alone, since the directional information provided by the stereo spatialisation described in Sect. 3.3 was not tested separately.

5.1   Method

Subjects. 18 participants that didn't take part in the first experiment [7 women and 11 men; age: min. 25; max. 41 years] participated in the experiment. All were naive regarding the purpose of the experiment and none of the subjects reported any hearing losses. All of them participated on a volunteer basis; they signed an informed consent form prior to testing. This study was performed in accordance with the ethical standards of the Declaration of Helsinki (revised Edinburgh, 2000).

Stimuli and Apparatus. The setup of Experiment 2 was the same as the setup used in Experiment 1.

The sound stimuli were synthesized in real-time using the Pitch strategy defined in Sect. 3.1 and a stereo strategy corresponding to the target's direction described in Sect. 3.3. In each strategy, the given sound parameter changed as function of the normalized distance between the steering wheel and the target. The overall sound level was fixed at a comfortable level at the beginning of the experiment and subjects were not able to modify it during the experiment.

The car speed was kept constant throughout the experiment and the participant had no possibility to use the gas-pedal or to brake.

Procedure. The participants were instructed to drive without visual information and with the aid of two different sound strategies. The experiment was divided in two sessions (one for the Pitch strategy and one for the Stereo strategy). The session order was counterbalanced across the subject.

Before each session, a familiarization step was proposed to help the participants identify and understand the sound strategies. This step first consisted in turning the steering wheel while listening to the sound variations associated with its angle. Then it consisted in following a simple circuit with four straight lines and three turns (45° right, 90° left, and 45° right). During this step the participants were instructed to perform the circuit with an audiovisual feedback in order to link the sound variations associated to the steering wheel angle to a visual representation of the task. The visual display consisted in a red spot that responded to the user movement of the steering wheel and a green spot that correspond to the target angle. For each session, the variations of the sound attribute were explained with simple words (as described in [14]).

After the familiarization test, the subjects were told how many trials they needed to do (4 trials per session), and how to trigger the trial and proceed to the next trial. They were asked to follow the trajectory by tracking the auditory signal as precisely as possible. They were also told that the gas pedal was not functional and that there would be no visual feedback during the test.

In order to avoid unsuccessful trials, participants were automatically replaced on the trajectory when leaving it for more than X meters. This was notified by a specific sound followed by the extinction of the guidance sound. Participants restarted from the nearest position on the circuit by pushing the start button. Participants were informed that the trial was finished by another specific sound.

Each session was composed of 4 trials for four different race tours with only one display conditions (ADA). Each tour was composed of the same number of turns with an equal number of left turns and right turns. These tours were different from the three tours used in the first experiment. The experiment lasted between 15 and 25 min.

5.2   Results

For each subject and each trial, the total time, the accumulated error, and the number of oscillations around the path were computed. The number of times the participants were automatically replaced on the trajectory when leaving it for more than X meters was considered as the number of restarts.

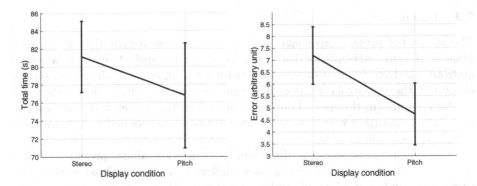

Fig. 5. Mean total time (left) and mean accumulated error (right) for the stereo and the pitch strategy. Error bars represent 95% confident intervals.

Total Time. The mean total time for the stereo condition and the pitch strategy is represented in Fig. 5 (left) with 95% confident intervals. Statistical analyses show a quasi significant effect of the sound strategy [$F(1, 17) = 3.72$, $p = 0.07$] with a mean total time of 76.8 ± 5.8 s per trials, the use of the pitch strategy induced a slightly faster guidance than the stereo strategy (mean total time: 81.1 ± 4.0 s).

Accumulated Error. The mean accumulated error for the stereo condition and the pitch strategy is represented in Fig. 5 (right) with 95% confident intervals. Statistical analyses highlight an influence of the sound morphology [$F(1, 17) = 19.02$, $p < 0.0005$] with better results with the pitch strategy. Indeed the mean accumulated error computed across the mean errors of each subject is 7.19 ± 1.21 (arbitrary unit) when guiding with the directional information only, whereas it is 4.74 ± 1.28 when adding the sound morphology in order to provide information about the distance (e.g. the pitch strategy).

Number of Oscillations. The number of oscillations around the trajectory highlight the participants' difficulty to achieve the correct steering-wheel angle and their tendency to overestimate it. Statistical analyses show a non significant effect of the sound strategy [$F(1, 17) = 3.57$, $p = 0.08$] on the number of oscillations, but a slight diminution of these oscillations with the pitch strategy. The mean number of oscillation is 25.5 ± 2.9 with the stereo strategy whereas it is 22.7 ± 3.2 with the pitch strategy.

Number of Restart. The mean number of restart is 0.17 ± 0.10 for the stereo condition and 0.056 ± 0.11 for the pitch condition. Statistical analyses highlight a statistical difference between the two strategies [$F(1, 17) = 7.16$, $p < 0.05$].

5.3 Discussion

The aim of the present experiment was to measure the contribution of the morphological sound attribute for distance guidance with respect to the spatial sound attribute. Indeed, the first experiment highlighted an effect of the sound strategies but without control condition. In the present experiment, the use of the pitch strategy to inform the user about the distance of the target was compared to the control condition where the only information corresponded to the direction of the target (right or left).

The results show that the directional information alone, provided with a spatial sound attribute (the stereo), is sufficient to achieve the task with a relatively low number of failures (number of restarts). However, the addition of the morphological sound attribute (e.g. the pitch) that adds information about the target's distance significantly reduces the accumulated error and the number of failures and slightly reduces the guidance time and the number of oscillations.

6 Conclusion

This study aimed at exploring the use of sonification in the case of dynamic guidance task. It investigated the use of continuous auditory feedback in a tracking task across a driving game with blindfold players. An experiment was designed to evaluate the importance of the information to display and the influence of the chosen sound strategy. It consisted in driving without visual cues, guided with auditory cues. An additional experiment was designed in order to quantify the contribution of the morphological sound attribute (providing distance information) with respect to the spatial sound attribute (providing directional information).

The results of the first experiment show that the information provided by sonification makes it possible to guide a subject without visual feedback along a curved road. Second it points out the information to be displayed in such cases. Indeed, it is possible to drive with auditory information only, but this requires information that enables the subject to anticipate and a task-related feedback. The results of the experiment show the superiority of the display information related to what the driver needs to do compared to the information related to the driver's error. The experiment highlights the influence of the sound strategy. The driving task requires a high reactivity and rapid reactions from the driver. The results show that a sound strategy allowing rapidity is more important than a strategy allowing high precision in a dynamic guidance case for the speed chosen in this experiment.

The second experiment highlights the benefit of using a morphological sound attribute in order to provide distance information with respect to the use of a spatial sound attribute that provides only directional information. If the spatial sound attribute alone enabled to achieve the guidance task, it led to lower precision, longer guidance with more oscillations around the trajectory and more failures. In line with [12], this result draw attention to the interest of combining morphological sound attributes to spatial sound attributes in sonification.

Furthermore, this study highlights the importance of the choice of the sound strategy in the case of dynamic guidance task. To go further, it will be of interest to investigate the dynamic guidance with morphological sound attributes alone without the use of spatial sound attributes. This can be achieved with combined strategies (with several auditory cues) and might be more appropriate in situations where spatial sound attributes cannot be used. This will be investigating in future experiments.

Acknowledgements. This work was supported by the French National Research Agency (ANR) under the SoniMove: Inform, Guide, and Learn Actions by Sounds project ANR-14-CE24-0018-01.

References

1. Barrass, S.: Auditory Information Design. Ph.D. thesis (1998)
2. Black, D., Hansen, C., Nabavi, A., Kikinis, R., Hahn, H.: A survey of auditory display in image-guided interventions. Int. J. Comput. Assist. Radiol. Surg. **12**, 1665–1676 (2017). https://doi.org/10.1007/s11548-017-1547-z
3. Boyer, É.O., Bevilacqua, F., Susini, P., Hanneton, S.: Investigating three types of continuous auditory feedback in visuo-manual tracking. Exp. Brain Res. pp. 1–11 (2016)
4. Danna, J., Velay, J.L.: Handwriting movement sonification: Why and how? IEEE Trans. Hum.-Mach. Syst. **47**(2), 299–303 (2017)
5. Danna, J., Velay, J.L.: On the auditory-proprioception substitution hypothesis: movement sonification in two deafferented subjects learning to write new characters. Front. Neurosci. **11**, 137 (2017)
6. Fajen, B.R., Warren, W.H.: Visual guidance of intercepting a moving target on foot. Perception **33**(6), 689–715 (2004). https://doi.org/10.1068/p5236. pMID: 15330365
7. Groeger, J.A.: Understanding Driving: Applying Cognitive Psychology to a Complex Everyday Task. Psychology Press, New York (2000)
8. Grond, F., Berger, J.: Parameter mapping sonification. In: Hermann, T., Hunt, A., Neuhoff, J.G. (eds.) The Sonification Handbook. Logos Publishing House, Berlin (2011)
9. Normal equal-loudness level contours - Acoustics International Organization for Standardization (2003)
10. Kramer, K., et al.: Sonification report: Status of the field and research agenda. Faculty Publications, Department of Psychology (1999)
11. Loomis, J., Golledge, R., Klatzky, R.: Navigation system for the blind: auditory display modes and guidance. Presence: Teleoper. Virtual Environ. **7**, 193–203 (1998)
12. Parseihian, G., Conan, S., Katz, B.: Sound effect metaphors for near field distance sonification. In: Proceedings of the 18th International Conference on Auditory Display (ICAD 2012) (2012)
13. Parseihian, G., Jouffrais, C., Katz, B.F.: Reaching nearby sources: comparison between real and virtual sound and visual targets. Front. Neurosci. **8**, 269 (2014)
14. Parseihian, G., Gondre, C., Aramaki, M., Ystad, S., Kronland-Martinet, R.: Comparison and evaluation of sonification strategies for guidance tasks. IEEE Trans. Multimed. **18**(4), 674–686 (2016)

15. Rosati, G., Oscari, F., Spagnol, S., Avanzini, F., Masiero, S.: Effect of task-related continuous auditory feedback during learning of tracking motion exercises. J. Neuroeng. Rehabil. **9**(1), 79 (2012)
16. Scholz, D.S., et al.: Sonification as a possible stroke rehabilitation strategy. Front. Neurosci. **8**, 332 (2014)
17. Thoret, E., Aramaki, M., Gondre, C., Ystad, S., Kronland-Martinet, R.: Eluding the physical constraints in a nonlinear interaction sound synthesis model for gesture guidance. Appl. Sci. **6**(7), 192 (2016)

DIGIT: A Digital Foley System
to Generate Footstep Sounds

Luis Aly[1,2]([✉]), Rui Penha[1,2], and Gilberto Bernardes[2]

[1] Faculty of Engineering, University of Porto, Porto, Portugal
up200203376@fe.up.pt
[2] INESC TEC, Sound and Music Computing,
Rua Dr. Roberto Frias, 378, 4200-465 Porto, Portugal

Abstract. We present DIGItal sTeps (DIGIT), a system for assisting
in the creation of footstep sounds in a post-production foley context—
a practice that recreates all diegetic sounds for a moving image. The
novelty behind DIGIT is the use of the acoustic (haptic) response of a
gesture on a tangible interface as means for navigating and retrieving
similar matches from a large database of annotated footstep sounds.
While capturing the tactile expressiveness of the traditional sound foley
practice in the exploration of physical objects, DIGIT streamlines the
workflow of the audio post production environment for film or games by
reducing its costly and time-consuming requirements.

Keywords: Sound design · Foley · Footsteps · Haptic
Tangible control

1 Introduction

Foley is a sound design practice in the film industry that aims to recreate all the
diegetic sounds for a moving image [18]. Foley adopts an experimental design
approach, which merges multiple areas of knowledge such as aesthetics, cognition, and emotion on the idea of *found object* [4] to enhance the visual narrative
with synchronized sonic events. The re-creation of footsteps sound is one of the
main tasks of a foley artist. Footstep sounds represent important elements to the
narrative because they provide the concreteness, embodiment and materiality to
what is on-screen [5]. Contrary to the recent audiovisual industry trend in promoting technology which can assist in audio post production tasks, and despite
its time-consuming and costly requirements, the practice of footstep foley has
remained a manual task with deep roots in the traditions of its pioneers [1].

However, recent efforts have been made to promote digital tools to assist
in the practice of foley, particularly in the creation of footstep sounds, due to
their primacy across the task, and the inherent difficulty to record these types
of sounds on location due to the normal noisy conditions of a crowded film
set [7]. Several experimental studies can be found on designing a system that is

© Springer Nature Switzerland AG 2018
M. Aramaki et al. (Eds.): CMMR 2017, LNCS 11265, pp. 429–441, 2018.
https://doi.org/10.1007/978-3-030-01692-0_28

able to afford real-time sound synthesis of footsteps sounds taking into account: different surface materials [13,19], audio haptic physically-based simulation of walking [21], the multimodality between induced haptics on the feet and footstep sounds [12] and between auditory cues and locomotion patterns [20], and on the evaluation of whether foley sounds, real recordings and low quality synthetic sounds can be distinguished, and their level of expressiveness, when used to sonify a video [6]. Also studies on auditory recognition focusing on the discrimination of walks on hybrid formulations of different materials/surfaces modeled by temporal and spectral cues of walking [9].

Current industrial standards for footstep sound creation, can be split into two categories. The first category consists of large sound libraries, annotated by experts into broad labels (e.g., Sound Ideas's *Foley Footsteps Sound Effect Library*[1]). These sound libraries can significantly reduce the time-consuming and costly requirements for recording and performing sounds in sync with a moving image. Yet, they typically lack efficient strategies for navigation and retrieval of content. The second category includes applications such as *Audio Steps Pro*[2] and *Virtual Foley Artist*[3] that make use of MIDI controllers to drive the search parameters of expert-annotated sound databases.

This latter category presents a significant addition to the widespread footstep sounds databases on the market. However, we argue that they lack the necessary suitability and flexible control for navigating and experimenting with sound databases. First, in order to promote variation, these tools require heavy and constant parametrization over time. Second, they exclude any sensible know-how from the sound foley practice in the interaction loop between user and system; for example, tactile exploration as a control strategy.

In light of these limitations, we present DIGIT, a system whose driving principle is the exploration of the acoustic (haptic) response of gestures performed on a tangible control surface to automatically navigate and retrieve footstep sounds from an annotated database. In redefining the control, navigation, and retrieval of digital foley systems, we frame our research within the traditional sound foley practice.

The remainder of this paper is organized as follows. Section 2 details the DIGIT system components. In Sect. 3, we present both an objective and subjective evaluation of our system. In Sect. 4, we report the results of our evaluation. Finally, in Sect. 5, we draw our conclusions.

---

[1] https://www.sound-ideas.com/Product/442/Foley-Footsteps-Sound-Effects-Library (accessed January 12, 2018).

[2] https://lesound.io (accessed January 12, 2018).

[3] https://www.boomlibrary.com/sound-effects/virtual-foley-artist-footsteps/ (accessed January 12, 2018).

2   Methods

2.1   Overview of the System

DIGIT consists of a system composed of a tangible control surface and a software tool developed in the Max programming environment.[4] The system architecture, shown in Fig. 1, includes four top-level modules, grounded in concepts from concatenative synthesis—in the sense it retrieves good matches of footstep sounds from large audio databases for the selection of a given target criteria [2,17].

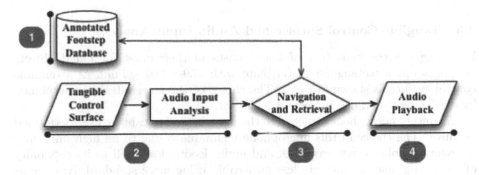

Fig. 1. Overview of the DIGIT system.

The first module consists of a database of annotated footstep sounds. The second module analyzes input gestures performed on a tangible control surface. A contact microphone captures the gesture's acoustic profile which is then used to represent the gesture on the remaining modules of the DIGIT system. The third module navigates in a collection of feature annotated footstep sounds to find the most similar match to an input gesture acoustic profile. Finally, the fourth module synthesizes selected footstep sounds using a granular sound synthesis engine, to which some post processing effects can be applied in the context of *brassage* techniques [16].

2.2   Footstep Sounds Database

Footstep sounds have a vast array of perceptual differences that can range from character attributes such as gender, speed, and type of shoe, to environmental aspects such as the type of floor materials. To this end, a footstep sound database must necessarily be constrained to, and labeled by, high-level features.

The footstep database of DIGIT includes a unique type of shoe: the business shoe, on four different types of floor: wood, gravel, cement, and water (i.e. wet ground). For each floor: slow, average, and fast speeds were considered, with 300 footstep sounds each. The footstep sounds, ranging between 250 ms and 1 s,

---

[4] https://cycling74.com (accessed January 12, 2018).

were collected from the *AudioStepsPro* database, sampled at 44.1 kHz with 16-bit precision. The relatively high number of sounds included in each floor aims at minimizing the need to repeat a footstep sound, as well as allowing subtle nuances in the input gestures to be recognized in the system's output.

Each footstep sound, s, included in the database was then annotated by a set of low-level audio descriptors using Max's `descriptors~` object.[5] The adopted descriptors characterize relevant temporal and spectral attributes of footstep sounds, selected on a threefold criteria basis, which we discuss at length in Sects. 3.2 and 4.2. In all remaining components of the system, a feature vector, F_s, represents the attributes extracted from database footstep sound, s.

2.3   Tangible Control Surface and Audio Input Analysis

Following the the know-how of foley artists in their quest for found objects [4], we adopt a rectangular metal plate with $750 \times 300 \times 1\,mm$ as a tangible control surface as shown in Fig. 2. The choice of the material was underpinned by experiments detailed in Sects. 3.1 and 4.1.

A contact microphone attached to the plate is used to capture user-performed gestures. The choice of this microphone technique is due to its high immunity to external noise, room acoustics, and audio feedback as well as its capability of capturing nuances that are less noticeable using more standard dynamic or condenser microphones.

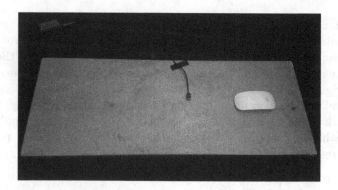

Fig. 2. The metal plate used as a tangible control surface in DIGIT. A computer mouse is used in the image as a guiding reference for the plate dimensions.

To extract an input feature vector, I_s, representing a gesture's acoustic profile, we first apply dynamics processing by way of peak limiting and a noise gate to avoid level distortion and eliminate floor noise. We then detect the onset of user-performed gestures in the tangible control surface, using the Max object `bonk~` [15], to trigger the real-time extraction of the gesture's acoustic profile

---

[5] http://www.alexanderjharker.co.uk/Software.html (accessed January 10, 2017).

using the Max object `descriptorsrt˜`. Analysis is performed on 2048 sample windows, with 25% of overlap across the duration of the attack transient of each gesture (the initial 250 ms).

2.4   Navigation and Retrieval

At the core of the sound foley task is the problem of mapping between visual stimuli and the sonic properties of physical objects. We transpose this analogy to DIGIT as a strategy to navigate a database of descriptor-based footstep sound annotations to find good matches to a given image on screen. To this end, we adopt a twofold operation chain: (i) a visual stimulus drives a user to perform an input gesture on the tangible control surface, (ii) its feature vector is then used to browse the footstep database to retrieve a similar match.

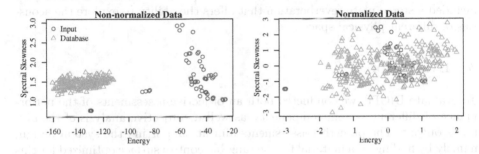

Fig. 3. Descriptor data space for input gestures and database footstep sounds before and after normalization.

An effective exploration of database sounds entails an overlap between the descriptor space of input, I_s, and database sounds, D_s. However, the timbral differences between input and database sounds do not guarantee this overlap. Thus, following previous research [10], we normalize the input, $\hat{I}(k)$ and database, $\hat{D}_s(k)$, feature vector data to zero mean and unit variance. To comply with the real-time nature of the system's input, a calibration step is then necessary to perform the input normalization.

After ensuring a consistent exploitation of database sounds via input and database feature data normalization, we browse the footstep database feature vectors $\hat{D}_s(k)$ to find the closet match, M, to an input feature vector, $\hat{I}(k)$, in the Euclidean space, so as to retrieve the footstep sound s that most closely resembles our input sound:

$$M = \operatorname{argmin}_s \sqrt{\sum_{k=1}^{K} (\hat{I}(k) - \hat{D}_s(k))^2}, \tag{1}$$

where K is the number of elements (i.e., sound attributes) of the input, $\hat{I}(k)$, and database, $\hat{D}_s(k)$, feature vectors, which we detail at length in Sect. 4.2.

Prior to the selection process, we introduce two algorithms that prevent the most recent units to be selected in sequence. To this end we store the four last played units and exclude them from the distance computation. In this way, we prevent repetition and promote (timbral) variation in the system's output.

2.5 Audio Playback

Selected footstep sounds, M, are reproduced by a granular sound engine [16], which enables polyphony (up to 16 simultaneous voices)—for the creation of composite sounds (e.g., layering footsteps from two different gravel and cement databases)—and sound transformations per voice, such as playback speed and duration—relevant to the realization of less realistic footstep sounds of animated characters.

To enhance DIGIT's expressiveness and adaption to different scenarios, we included a stereo plate reverberation that offers the ability to explore the acoustics of different physical spaces.

3 Evaluation

To evaluate DIGIT, we conducted both an objective assessments of the performance of different system components, as well a subjective analysis of the system's output. The objective assessments aim at supporting the system design, namely by finding (i) a material for the tangible control surface optimized for this foley task – the navigation and retrieval of footstep sounds from the database and (ii) a set of descriptors which are not only aligned to perceptual and haptic acoustic responses, but also are the most relevant for the characterization of footstep sounds. The subjective analysis consists of a user interaction experiment which aims to assess the expressiveness of the system output, as well as the usability of the software.

3.1 Tangible Control Surface Selection

We designed an experiment to identify a tangible control surface to be adopted in DIGIT. We restricted our selection to the following six surfaces: wooden box, wood kalimba, wooden table top, metal plate, metal box and a glass jar as shown in Fig. 4.

We further identified a set of seven gestures: (i) one finger touch (OF), (ii) knocking (KNO), (iii) nails scratching (NS), (iv) thin metal strip scratching (MSS), (v) thick metal strip scratching (TMS), (vi) multiple finger touch (MF) and (vii) muffled touch with the palm of the hand (MPT).

From an unlimited pool of gestures available for interaction with solid surfaces the rationale behind the choice of hand gesture taxonomy is due to its wide adoption in the foley practice, as well as the distinct acoustic responses that can be representative of the interaction with the various surfaces, which we perform with hands on the surface or with the use of props.

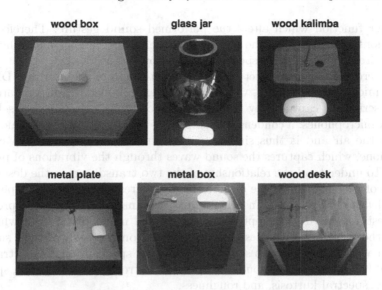

Fig. 4. The set of the six surfaces selected for experimenting taking into account the different materials, dimensions and shapes.

The aim behind this experiment is to find a control surface in which performed gestures with similar attributes are related to a confined descriptor space, and perceptually different gestures are spread in the descriptor space. To this end, we first analyzed eight repetitions of each gesture per surface, using the acoustic (haptic) response analysis strategy described in Sect. 3. Then, we computed the intra-feature vector distances between repeated gestures and the inter-feature vector distances between different gestures. Ideally, an optimal DIGIT surface confines gestures repetitions to a small descriptor space and spreads different gestures in the space.

We inspected the surfaces' performance using two analysis data collections. The first includes the entire descriptor data resulting from the analysis of the seven gestures on different surfaces. The second includes the six principal components of the descriptor data for each individual surface using Principal Component Analysis (PCA). The use of Principal Component Analysis (PCA) to reduce the data collection aims to capture the most relevant dimensions (or descriptors) for each surface. In greater detail, the use of PCA on the descriptor data aims at minimizing redundant information and favoring those dimensions which provide most discrimination on the selected gestures.

3.2   Haptic and Perceptually-Based Descriptions

The exploration of a tangible control surface in DIGIT is driven by a perceptual exploration. Yet, while the adoption of a contact microphone to capture the acoustic profile of performed gestures is ideal from an audio signal quality standpoint, the material over which the contact microphone is placed acts as a transfer function which alters the performed sound gesture. Therefore, the descriptions gathered from the haptic response of the contact microphone are different from the acoustic response perceived by the user.

To overcome the disconnect between the intention of the user and DIGIT's contact microphone response, we have set an experiment which compares gestures descriptions captured by two different techniques or, more precisely, two different microphones: a condenser microphone, which captures the sound waves through the air and is thus similar to the human perception; and a contact microphone, which captures the sound waves through the vibrations of physical bodies. To understand the relationship of the two transducers in the description analysis of the acoustic profile of performed gestures, we follow the experiment design detailed in Sect. 3.1. In other words, we analyze the acoustic profile of seven gestures (with eight repetitions each) on a metal plate, from which we extract the following set of descriptors—selected on the basis of their suitability for characterizing footstep sounds [11]: energy, spectral rolloff, spectral flux, Modified Kullback-Leibler,[6] loudness, spectral centroid, spectral spread, spectral skewness, spectral kurtosis, and roughness.

The aim of the experiment is to find a set of descriptors that exhibit a similar behavior in their haptic and perceptual responses to guarantee that the driving perception of the user is mirrored in the haptic response.

3.3 Usability and Expressiveness

A pilot user interaction experiment was conducted to make initial observations about the usability of DIGIT's interface as well as the expressiveness of its output. The experiment was run individually for each participant according to the four following stages. (i) A training period of about 2 min during which the participant was informed about the principles for operating DIGIT. (ii) Performing the core task (which simulates real foley) of the experiment in which participants synchronize sound with a pre-recorded motion sequence of images consisting of two scenarios (footsteps on cement and gravel) at three different speeds (slow, medium and fast). Participants were asked to pay particular attention to the character's movement speeds and simulate the change of direction of the character's movement. (iii) A questionnaire on the usability of the system using the standard System Usability Scale (SUS) [3]. Finally, (iv) a qualitative questionnaire for assessing the expressiveness of the system output, with a particular focus on a comparison to prior experiences of the participants in the sound foley domain (e.g., by assessing "how [they] compare DIGIT to other foley experiences with respect to its type of control, output expressiveness, and requirements").

The goals of this experiment are (i) to gauge the possibilities of introducing a system like DIGIT in a sound foley practice, (ii) to assess the degree of expressiveness of the system output, and (iii) to explore its effectiveness in the relationship between the effect achieved and the intended objectives.

---

[6] MKL stands for Modified Kullback-Leibler, a descriptor that measures the difference between two probability distributions as defined in [14].

4   Results

4.1   Tangible Control Surface Selection

To evaluate the performance of the tangible interfaces under consideration in our experiment, we adopted the Dunn index [8] to analyze the descriptor data resulting from each interface. The Dunn index is a metric used to evaluate clustering algorithms, by identifying sets of well separated clusters with compact intra-cluster members. A higher Dunn index indicates better clustering. Since, to the best of our knowledge, no standard test exists for the comparison of different descriptor data compactness for a given gesture and high discrimination between different gestures, we argue that this widely study clustering validation statistic is suitable for the task under study. To this end, we treat each gesture as a cluster, and each gesture repetition as a cluster member.

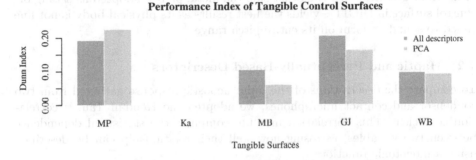

Fig. 5. Dunn Index performance of the following five tangible control surfaces: metal plate (MP), wooden kalimba (Ka), metal box (MB), glass jar (GJ), and wooden box (WB). A higher Dunn index indicates better performance.

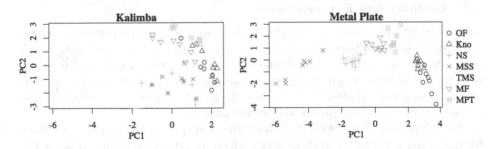

Fig. 6. Visualization of the descriptor data for two tangible control surfaces with low (Kalimba) and high (Metal Plate) clustering quality indexes, using the two principal components for each surface

Figure 5 shows the Dunn index for each tangible control surface and over two data collections: the entire descriptor data collection and a reduced set including only six principal components. The wooden kalimba shows the poorest results. The metal and wooden boxes slightly enhance the performance, and finally the glass jar and metal plate surfaces show the best performances. Figure 6 shows 2-dimensional plots of the two principal components of the lowest and highest ranked performance surface. Each gesture is indicated by a specific color.

The highest ranked performance indices differ in relation to the data collection adopted. The metal plate provides better results for the data collection adopting only the six principal components and the glass jar performs best for the entire collection of descriptor data. While these top ranked results show that a careful selection of the descriptors for each surface is important for enhancing the results of the system, no significant difference appears to exist between the two surfaces under consideration.

Not surprisingly, musical instruments such as the kalimba perform worst, as its physical body is fine tuned to sound uniform on its entire pitch range (or in different gestures). On the other side the metal plate—adopted as a tangible control surface in DIGIT—yields the best results as its physical body is not fine tuned to sound uniform on its entire pitch range.

4.2 Haptic and Perceptually-Based Descriptors

To compare the descriptions of the input acoustic response gathered from two condenser and contact microphones, we adopted the Kendall Tau, τ correlation coefficient. This correlation measure computes the statistical dependence between two variables, assessing how well their relationship can be described using a monotonic function.

Figure 7 shows the τ correlation rank between the descriptor data collected from the condenser and contact microphones. The results guided the selection of a set of features for describing the audio input, from the collection of pre-selected features for the characterization of footstep database sounds.

4.3 Usability and Expressiveness

In total, eight participants took the pilot user interaction experiment, of whom six were experienced foley artists, and the remaining two were acquainted with sound design. All participants volunteered to take the experiment and were not paid. After the experiment, participants completed a SUS test, which consisted of a 10 item questionnaire. Table 1 shows the SUS test questions along with the participants' mean score (and standard deviations).

We adopted a 10-question SUS test with five qualitative response options, from *strongly disagree* to *strongly agree*, which we report in Table 1 using a 1–5 scale correspondence.

Adopting the strategy reported in [3], we computed a final (weighted) SUS test score, which should be considered in terms of their percentile ranking, between 0 and 100.[7] A final SUS test score of **81.5** was obtained for DIGIT,

[7] A SUS score above a 68 should be considered above average and anything below 68 is below average [3].

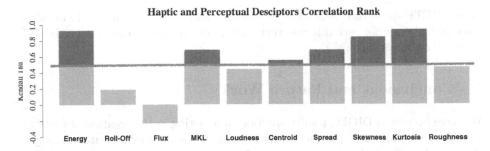

Fig. 7. Kendall's Tau correlation rank for gesture analysis on a metal plate captured by a condenser vs. contact microphone for the following set of audio descriptors: energy (Ene), spectral rollOff (Rol), spectral flux (Flu), Modified Kullback-Leibler (MKL), loudness (Lou), spectral centroid (Cen), spectral spread (Spr), spectral skewness (Ske), spectral kurtosis (Kur), and roughness (Rou). Features with statistical significance value $p < 0.001$ were used as an input attribute in DIGIT, thus forming the following collection: energy, MKL, spectral centroid, spectral spread, spectral skewness and spectral kurtosis.

Table 1. System Usability Test used to evaluate the effectiveness, efficiency and satisfaction to evaluate a wide variety of products and services, including hardware, software, mobile devices, websites and applications in general.

Question	Mean	Std
I would like to use this system frequently	3.4	0.5
The system is not complex	3.9	0.3
The system was easy to use	3.3	0.7
I do not need technical support to use this system	3.1	1
The various functions in this system are well integrated	2.7	1
There wasn't inconsistency in the system	2.9	0.6
Most people would learn to use this system very quickly	3	0.9
The system very easy to use	3.7	0.4
I felt very confident using the system	2.9	0.6
I didn't need to learn a lot before using the system	3.9	0.3

i.e. a, classification of **A**, which enforced the effectiveness and user satisfaction of the system usability.

The qualitative questionnaire assessing the efficacy and expressiveness of the DIGIT system in view of the past experience of the participants in sound foley and sound design resulted in a common view of the system as responsive ("DIGIT facilitates a foley task because of its immediacy") and expressive ("In DIGIT, it is very easy to create footstep sounds in sync with the moving image"). Particular attention was given to the consistent mappings between input gestures and output footstep sounds ("I feel more limited in other non-conventional foley practices. DIGIT's interface it is more interactive and feels more natural" or "after some initial training period it was very easy to obtain good results using DIGIT due to its control surface").

5   Conclusions and Future Work

We have presented DIGIT, a software tool for assisting in the creation of footstep sounds in an audio post production foley context. Inspired by concatenative synthesis techniques and in the know-how of expert foley artists, we have expanded current research in digital foley tools with gestural control on tangible surfaces to drive the search for footstep sounds from expert-annotated databases.

Although the collected data came from a small sample of users (only 8 participants) who were not given any actual comparative hands-on task that could generate more objective results, the evaluation of the system demonstrated that our proposed approach has the potential for real-world use in a foley context. The ability to use the acoustic profile of a gesture performed on a tangible surface proved to be the most relevant element in DIGIT and, according to the test and questionnaire results, it was the uniqueness of the system that created the most impact on the participants. Furthermore, the use of control gestures on a surface, has enabled DIGIT to overcome the established limitations identified in existing systems by providing more expressiveness than traditional MIDI controllers.

In future work, we aim to address the exploration of *time delay of arrival* techniques to use the spatial location in the touch surface as a control parameters and the use of audio fingerprinting techniques as a strategy to enhance the robustness of the haptical signal detection.

Acknowledgements. Project TEC4Growth - Pervasive Intelligence, Enhancers and Proofs of Concept with Industrial Impact/NORTE-01-0145-FEDER-000020 is financed by the North Portugal Regional Operational Programme (NORTE 2020), under the PORTUGAL 2020 Partnership Agreement, and through the European Regional Development Fund (ERDF).

This work was also supported by a doctoral scholarship from the Portuguese Foundation of Science and Technology (FCT) which sponsors the Collaboratory for Emerging Technologies (CoLab) initiative as part of the UT Austin|Portugal Program.

References

1. Ament, V.T.: The Foley Grail: The Art of Performing Sound for Film, Games, and Animation. CRC Press, Abingdon (2014)
2. Bernardes, G., Guedes, C., Pennycook, B.: EarGram: an application for interactive exploration of concatenative sound synthesis in pure data. In: Aramaki, M., Barthet, M., Kronland-Martinet, R., Ystad, S. (eds.) CMMR 2012. LNCS, vol. 7900, pp. 110–129. Springer, Heidelberg (2013). https://doi.org/10.1007/978-3-642-41248-6_7

3. Brooke, J., et al.: SUS - a quick and dirty usability scale. Usability Eval. Ind. **189**(194), 4–7 (1996)

4. Camic, P.: From trashed to treasured: a grounded theory analysis of the found object. Psychol. Aesthetics Creativity Arts **4**(2), 81 (2010)

5. Chion, M., Murch, W.: Audio-Vision: Sound on Screen. Columbia University Press, New York (1994)

6. De Götzen, A., Sikström, E., Grani, F., Serafin, S.: Real, foley or synthetic? An evaluation of everyday walking sounds. In: Proceedings of SMC (2013)

7. Doyle, J.: Subtlety of sound: a study of foley art. Senior honors projects, University of Rhode Island (2013). http://digitalcommons.uri.edu/srhonorsprog/333/

8. Dunn, J.C.: A fuzzy relative of the isodata process and its use in detecting compact well-separated clusters. J. Cybern. **3**(3), 32–57 (1973)

9. Fontana, F., Morreale, F., Regia-Corte, T., Lécuyer, A., Marchal, M.: Auditory recognition of floor surfaces by temporal and spectral cues of walking. International Community for Auditory Display (2011)

10. Hackbarth, B., Schnell, N., Schwarz, D.: Audioguide: a framework for creative exploration of concatenative sound synthesis. Technical report, IRCAM (2010). http://articles.ircam.fr/textes/Hackbarth10a/index.pdf

11. Mitrovic, D., Zeppelzauer, M., Eidenberger, H.: Analysis of the data quality of audio descriptions of environmental sounds. J. Digital Inf. Manag. **5**(2), 48 (2007)

12. Nordahl, R., Berrezag, A., Dimitrov, S., Turchet, L., Hayward, V., Serafin, S.: Preliminary experiment combining virtual reality haptic shoes and audio synthesis. In: Kappers, A.M.L., van Erp, J.B.F., Bergmann Tiest, W.M., van der Helm, F.C.T. (eds.) EuroHaptics 2010. LNCS, vol. 6192, pp. 123–129. Springer, Heidelberg (2010). https://doi.org/10.1007/978-3-642-14075-4_18

13. Nordahl, R., Turchet, L., Serafin, S.: Sound synthesis and evaluation of interactive footsteps and environmental sounds rendering for virtual reality applications. IEEE Trans. Vis. Comput. Graph. **17**(9), 1234–1244 (2011)

14. Peeters, G., Giordano, B.L., Susini, P., Misdariis, N., McAdams, S.: The timbre toolbox: extracting audio descriptors from musical signals. J. Acoust. Soc. Am. **130**(5), 2902–2916 (2011)

15. Puckette, M.S., Apel, T., Zicarelli, D.D.: Real-time audio analysis tools for Pd and MSP. Analysis **74**, 109–112 (1998). http://citeseerx.ist.psu.edu/viewdoc/summary?doi=10.1.1.40.6961

16. Roads, C.: Microsound. MIT Press, Cambridge (2004)

17. Schwarz, D., Beller, G., Verbrugghe, B., Britton, S.: Real-time corpus-based concatenative synthesis with cataRT. In: 9th International Conference on Digital Audio Effects (DAFx), pp. 279–282 (2006)

18. Sonnenschein, D.: Sound Design: The Expressive Power of Music, Voice, and Sound Effects in Cinema. Michael Wiese Productions, Studio City (2001)

19. Turchet, L., Nordahl, R., Serafin, S., Berrezag, A., Dimitrov, S., Hayward, V.: Audio-haptic physically-based simulation of walking on different grounds. In: 2010 IEEE International Workshop on Multimedia Signal Processing (MMSP), pp. 269–273. IEEE (2010)

20. Turchet, L., Serafin, S., Cesari, P.: Walking pace affected by interactive sounds simulating stepping on different terrains. ACM Trans. Appl. Percept. (TAP) **10**(4), 23 (2013)

21. Turchet, L., Serafin, S., Dimitrov, S., Nordahl, R.: Physically based sound synthesis and control of footsteps sounds. In: Proceedings of Digital Audio Effects Conference, vol. 11 (2010)

Cooperative Music Networks and Musical HCIs

Composing and Improvising. In Real Time

Carlos Guedes[✉]

New York University Abu Dhabi, PO Box 129188 Saadiyat Island,
Abu Dhabi, United Arab Emirates
carlos.guedes@nyu.edu

Abstract. This paper presents a summary of my keynote address discussing the differences between real-time composition (RTC) and improvisation. A definition of real-time composition is presented, as well as a summary discussion of its theoretical framework. Finally, a comparison between RTC and improvisation is done taking into account Richard Ashley's discussion of improvisation from a psychological perspective [1], which provides an interesting insight in this distinction. RTC is then redefined as *improvised composition with computers,* and the possibilities of RTC existing outside of computer music are also briefly addressed.

Keywords: Composition · Improvisation · Real-time composition

1 Introduction

I define real-time composition (RTC) as a *"Compositional practice* utilizing *interactive* music systems in which *generative* algorithms with a *non-deterministic* behavior are manipulated by a user during *performance"* [14]. The terms in italic also define important keywords about RTC: it is a performative practice, it is interactive, it is generative, and non-deterministic. In a recent paper [16] I provide a more detailed contextualization and framework of RTC in the context of my work. This short paper summarizes my recent keynote at the 13th Symposium on Computer Music Multidisciplinary Research where I addressed the differences between RTC and Improvisation.

RTC is a practice made possible by computers and has become increasingly present in music making. This is due to the progressive shift from using the computer as a machine that can provide sonic results otherwise unachievable by other means, towards the increasing use of the computer as some sort of musical companion with a musical behavior of its own in interaction with its users. Twenty years ago, the use of the computer as an interacting entity in musical performance could only be appreciated in specialized computer music concerts in certain (restricted) environments like universities or conferences. Nowadays it is not uncommon to carry an application on your smartphone that produces music interactively through tapping or swiping gestures on the phone's touchscreen.

This paper is comprised of four sections. This introduction, a brief section on the definition of RTC systems, their taxonomy, and anatomy; a section in which I discuss

M. Aramaki et al. (Eds.): CMMR 2017, LNCS 11265, pp. 445–453, 2018.
https://doi.org/10.1007/978-3-030-01692-0_29

a theoretical framework for RTC; and finally, a section where the fundamental differences between RTC and Improvisation are analyzed and explained.

2 RTC Systems: Definition, Taxonomy, and Anatomy

Real-time composition systems are interactive music systems [22] that enable composition in real time. These systems exist in the form of standalone applications, plug-ins, or even as libraries or programming environments that facilitate their creation. They can operate at the sub-symbolic or symbolic levels. The majority of existing RTC systems operate at the symbolic level.

Two levels of utilization of these systems can be identified: systems designed for common/lay users and systems for specialists.

Systems for common/lay users are easy and simple to operate and the processes inherent to music/sound generation are hidden from the users—e.g. *Bloom* [12]. Systems for specialists require specific knowledge for their operation. These can be programming environments, specialized libraries or even commercial software designed to be operated by users who have acquired specific knowledge for their operation—e.g. Karlheinz Essl's RTC Lib,[1] Max,[2] or Supercollider.[3]

A RTC system should possess at least two components: a musical search space that is defined by a generative algorithm, which provides the musical material that can be obtained and transformed by navigating that space, and parameter controls that provide access to that space or its features.

The work I have been involved with in the creation of RTC systems both for lay and specialized users [7, 13, 15, 25], follows the framework just described.

3 Discussion of a Theoretical Framework for RTC

The revolution computers operated on musical practices have created substantial breaches with the concepts and definitions of the pre-electronic/computer music practice. Notions of what constitutes a musical instrument, what is performing, composing, and improvising, have been shaken to a point that new definitions, re-definitions, and taxonomies are emerging to address these basic notions. Departing from an initial intimate relation to traditional music concepts to describe computer music constructs such as "score," "orchestra," "instrument," "player;" using interaction metaphors such as "soloist with accompaniment," "conductor with orchestra," "Jazz combo," the field of computer music has expanded in ways that originated different avenues of musical expression as well as new concepts. One of them is real-time composition.

Essentially, an RTC system is a peculiar combination between digital musical instrument design, algorithmic composition approaches, and interactive music systems. Digital musical instruments enable the creation of complex mediation spaces between physical

---

[1] http://www.essl.at/works/rtc.html.
[2] http://www.cycling74.com.
[3] http://supercollider.github.io.

gesture and sonic result. Generative algorithms occupy these spaces to mediate the inter-action [6]. Interactive music systems provide the possibility of modifying the behavior of these algorithms in real time and enable a metalevel approach to composition through the possibility of interactive and real-time control of the musical generation [22, 23].

3.1   On Digital Musical Instruments

The notion of what is a musical instrument and what types of class of instrument are there has been dramatically challenged with the advent of electronic and computer-based instruments (cf. [18]). On one side, there is the question if a musical instrument can (still) be considered a single sound-producing body as nowadays—especially with the use of distributed sensing, processing, computational and streaming technologies—this may not be always the case. On the other side, the emergence of what Chadabe [6] has termed interactive instruments, or indeterministic electronic instruments, blurs the notion of what a musical instrument performance is in the traditional sense. In a recently-published paper [21], Thor Magnusson proposes a taxonomic approach, which he calls "Musical Organics," to the analysis and classification of both traditional and new musical instruments that, according to him, "suits the rhizomatic nature of their material design and technical origins" (p. 286). In an earlier paper [20] He advances the idea that many digital instruments could be seen as extensions of the mind rather than of the body (as in the case of traditional instruments). This is precisely because of the possibility they afford of using computational music systems to build expressive intelligent sonic outputs.

In his comparison between acoustic and digital instruments [20], Magnusson states that the "primary body of the digital instrument is that of symbolic instructions written for the meta-machine, the computer. As opposed to the body of the acoustic instrument, the digital instrument does not resonate." (p. 168) The use of computational techniques such as generative algorithms "and their theoretical implications unavoidably involve an explicit systemic representation of music as a rule-based field or a creative search space" ([3] qtd. In [20], p. 169).

3.2   On Algorithmic Composition

Perhaps the most important characteristic that frames RTC within the realm of musical composition is the use of algorithms which provide creative search spaces to be explored interactively. Dodgde and Jerse [8] acknowledged two broad categories in which algo-rithmic composition with computers fall into: stochastic music, in which events are generated based on some statistical representation; and music in which the computer is used to calculate permutations of predetermined conditions. In both situations the computer is providing musical, navigable spaces that bear the characteristics defined by, and implemented in the algorithm.

This navigable space is typical of algorithmic composition with computers, and was identified by Xenakis [28] on his famous account of his first experience with the computer in 1962. The control/alteration of parameters in algorithmic computer music provides the possibilities for navigation of a musical space whose limits are defined by the ranges of values in the parameters.

Taube [26] considers the metalevel as a representation of the composition of the composition in algorithmic music: "A metalevel representation of music is concerned with representing the activity, or process, of musical composition as opposed to its artifact or score" (p. 3). He makes a pertinent distinction between computer-assisted, automatic, and computer-based composition as three different possible ways to engage with algorithmic composition. In short, he considers computer-assisted composition a situation where the computer facilitates compositional tasks such as computing pre-compositional data, and as a simulation tool; automatic composition relates to systems that compose music independently (e.g. David Cope's EMI). Finally, computer-based composition,

> [M]eans to use the computer to explicitly represent compositional ideas at a level higher than the performance score. An explicit metalevel representation means that the relationships and processes that constitute a composition (the composition of the composition) are represented inside the machine apart from the composer thinking about them. (p. 5)

Taube does not consider the temporal scale at which computer-based music can occur. Although he may not even be considering the real-time application of these concepts the properties of computer-based music he mentions can certainly be found in RTC systems.

3.3   On Interactive Music Systems

Interactive music systems constitute a possible way of designing the contact between gestural interfaces and compositional algorithms in digital musical instruments. Chabade [6] calls these type of instrument "interactive instruments." Drummond [9] rightly and succinctly asserts that "[i]nteractive systems blur these traditional distinctions between composing, instrument building, systems design and performance." (p. 124). The complexities of relations that can be established with interactive music systems challenge the traditional paradigms in music performance, composition, and instrument design.

Brown et al. [4] criticize the acoustic paradigm often used as a metaphor to describe the types of relationship that can be established between the users and these systems (see for example [22, 27]), and suggest new paradigms for addressing the new interconnections that can be established between software systems in these new situations.

The reality is that interactive music systems contribute to blur these distinctions, which are often imperceptible when one watches a performance. The performers of a certain system may even not grasp what the system is doing while they're performing it such as in the case of certain games or applications. This makes it hard to really understand where does one establish the boundary between digital instruments that simulate traditional instruments and RTC systems, or other interactive instruments that are not RTC systems. Moreover, if whatever one is doing while interacting with the system should be considered performing, improvising, or composing.

4   Improvisation vs. Composition, Composing with Improvisation, and Improvising Composition

The practice of improvisation is certainly as old as music itself. The interaction between improvisation and composition—especially with the advent and evolution of jazz and the emergence of other types of improvised instrumental music in the second half of the 20th century in the West—has created tensions that entail quality judgements about "composed" vs. "improvised" music: "composed" music generally tends to be taken "more seriously" than "improvised" music.

Yet, paradoxically, as pointed out by Iyer [17] one "recurrent conceit among classical musicians, critics and listeners is that the best performances of composed works are those that 'sound improvised'" (p. 172). Even though the performer is executing with utter precision the indications given by the composer, the "improvisatory character" denotes a fluency in performance that is commonly appreciated. Conversely, and not uncommonly, one of the praised qualities of "good" improvised music is that it sounds like written, "composed" music [17, 24].

Iyer [17] notes that it is hard to aurally identify the "improvised" passages in music. It is perhaps easier to identify those that sound "composed." Sequential motivic manipulations or points of synchronicity between musicians actually may lead the listener to infer that there is some sort of script supporting the music being performed.

In the world of music that combines improvisation with written/scripted sections it is even harder to distinguish where "composed" and "improvised" sections begin and end. But then, why make (and insist) on this distinction as a quality judgement?

Iyer notes that this brings us to a central paradox: "the drama of improvised music involves the understanding that those sounds were chosen and deployed at that moment by those people. And yet, you cannot tell this to be true just by listening: you have to already know that this is happening. It follows that you only really know by referring to something beyond the sound." (p. 174).

Being a musician who had an education both in the "classical" European tradition and in Jazz, who increasingly introduced improvised sections in his music, and who has never done any special value distinction between music from improvised traditions or music from the European erudite tradition, I feel a strong empathy with Iyer's views. For me, it is more important to understand the different ways in which improvisation can work in music, interact with composed/scripted sections, as well as the ways in which can be articulated.

In the case of computer music, what is the relationship between Real Time Composition and improvisation?; or how can the approach proposed by my definition be ported to improvised instrumental performance?

The tension surrounding the composition-improvisation dialectic has permeated into the computer music world too. Eigenfeldt [10, 11] and Lewis [19] are two authors who have largely discussed the distinctions between RTC and improvisation, and the ontology of RTC itself. I take a slightly different approach that resonates more with Chadabe [5] by acknowledging RTC as an inherently improvisatory practice that is fundamentally different from improvisation with musical instruments. Real-time composition allows *improvising while composing*. This is something fairly new in the musical landscape and only possible because of this particular combination between interactive music systems and generative algorithmic composition in the context of digital musical instrument design. What are then the fundamental differences between improvising while performing an instrument and improvising while composing?

In his analysis of Improvisation from a psychological perspective, Ashley [1], provides interesting insights that may help distinguish the differences between improvisation with musical instruments and improvisation with compositional algorithms. He distinguishes three constraints that operate on the processes of musical (instrumental) improvisation: (1) The body; (2) Real time; and (3) Limits on what we know.

In instrumental performance, the musicians work with their hands, feet and voices to produce the music. The physical capabilities of the body, and the training the body has obtained impose limits on what can be produced musically during the improvisation. The real-time aspect also constitutes an important constraint as there is a complex process of decision-making going on for determining what gets played, and how, as well as its consequences on establishing the musical narrative on the immediate future. Finally, perhaps the most important constraint in this characterization, is the limit of what the performer knows while improvising (cf. [2]). Ashley asserts that in the case of improvisation, the knowledge one uses is/should be encoded in procedural (know-how-to) form rather than in declarative (know about) form.

The perspective presented above is perhaps the one that so far provides a potential distinction between instrumental improvisation and RTC. When one is composing in real time, constraints 1 and 3, respectively the limits of the body and of what we know are substantially extended, if not abolished:

- One is operating an algorithm (or set of algorithms) that can produce musical results that go beyond the limitations of the body.
- One can rely more on declarative knowledge for the musical generation— i.e. know about the effects certain algorithms produce rather than having to know how to produce them— and perform with algorithms that can provide unexpected results.

Based on the above assertions, one could revisit the above definition and redefine real-time composition simply as *improvised composition with computers*.

4.1 Can RTC Exist Outside of Computer Music?

The short answer is yes, of course. One can work with a group of musicians as if they were "generative algorithms" and try to "manipulate" their content generation by interacting with them through specific instructions. (e.g. in the case of Soundpainting). However, this situation is substantially different from the traditional improvisation that occurs in Jazz, which is sometimes also called "real-time composition." For RTC to exist as a practice of improvisation with composition, some sort of metalevel needs to be established.

The piece I composed for this conference, "On the resolution of regional tensions," for big band and live electronics, a commission from Orquestra Jazz de Matosinhos explores the nuances and tensions between real-time composition, non-real-time composition, and improvisation. This piece has sections that are composed in real time by the conductor, who gives instructions and interacts with the musicians as if they were generative algorithms with a certain musical behavior (Fig. 1). These sections are oriented towards other sections that are fully notated, and in which the musicians may improvise in ways that are more traditional in Jazz performance (Fig. 2). In these latter sections, no matter how much the musicians try to move away from the music being executed, there is a structure that creates an unavoidable referential pole around which the music being performed orbits. In the sections that are composed in real time, this structure is fluid and built as time passes even though there are specific points in the music (the notated sections) to be reached.

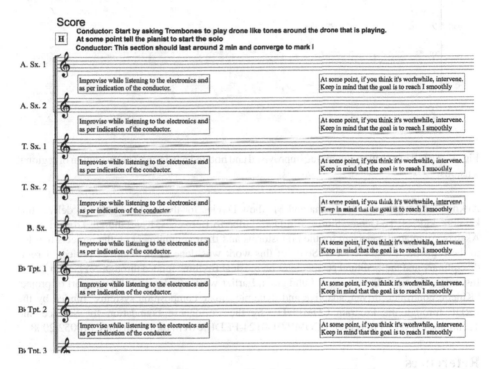

Fig. 1. Detail of a section of real-time composition in the score of "On the resolution of region tensions" with algorithmic-like indications to musicians and to the conductor.

This piece tries to highlight yet another qualitative difference between RTC and improvisation. In improvisation, there is a referential point (harmonic structure, vamps, texture, other referential elements that bind the musical discourse) around which the music moves. Improvisation could then be seen as a concentric structure. RTC could be seen as a swarm structure that moves fluidly as a consequence of the interaction between the different elements that is controlled externally by another entity.

Fig. 2. Detail of a section combining improvised and notated music on "The resolution of regional tensions."

Acknowledgments. To Rui Penha and Matthew Davies for the kind invitation to deliver this keynote address. To George Sioros, Rui Dias, Gilberto Bernardes, Konstantinos Trochidis, and Akshay Anantapadmanabhan for the brainstorms and their commitment on the projects that led to the refinement of these ideas. Some of this work was done in the realm of project "Cross-disciplinary and multicultural perspectives on musical rhythm" funded through NYU Abu Dhabi Institute's Research Enhancement Fund grant. Earlier work of mine on RTC was part of project "Kinetic controller, driven, adaptive and dynamic music composition systems" funded by the ERDF through the Program COMPETE, by the Portuguese Foundation for Science and Technology (FCT), Project ref. FCOMP-01-0124-FEDER-011414, UTAustin/CD/0052/2008.

References

1. Ashley, R.: Musical improvisation. In: Hallam, S., Cross, I., Thaut, M. (eds.) The Oxford Handbook of Music Psychology, 2nd edn, pp. 667–680. (2016)
2. Berliner, P.: Thinking in Jazz: The Infinite Art of Improvisation. University of Chicago Press, Chicago (1994)
3. Boden, M.A.: The Creative Mind: Myths and Mechanisms. Wiedenfeld & Nicolson, London (1990)
4. Brown, O., Eldridge, A., McCormack, J.: Understanding interaction in contemporary digital music: from instruments to behavioral objects. Organised Sound **14**(2), 188–196 (2009)
5. Chadabe. J.: Interactive composing. Comput. Music J. **8**(1), 22–27 (1984)
6. Chabade, J.: The limitations of mapping as a structural descriptive in electronic instruments. In: Proceedings of the New Instruments for Musical Expression Conference, Dublin (2002)

7. Dias, R., Marques, T., Sioros, G., Guedes, C.: GimmeDaBlues: An intelligent Jazz/Blues player and comping generator for iOS. In: Proceedings of the Conference on Computer Music Modeling and Retrieval, London (2012)
8. Dodge, C., Jerse, T.A.: Computer Music: Synthesis, Composition and Performance. Macmillan Library Reference (1985)
9. Drummond, J.: Understanding interactive systems. Organised Sound **14**, 2 (2009)
10. Eigenfeldt, A.: Real-time composition or computer improvisation? A Composer's search for intelligent tools in interactive computer music. In: Proceedings of the Electronic Music Studies 2007 (2007)
11. Eigenfeldt, A.: Real-time composition as performance ecosystem. Organised Sound **16**(2), 145–153 (2011)
12. Eno, B., Chilvers, P.: Bloom. [Generative music application for iOS devices]. Opal Inc (2008)
13. Guedes, C.: Mapping movement to musical rhythm: a study in interactive dance. Unpublished dissertation, NYU (2005)
14. Guedes, C.: Composição em tempo real. Unpublished typescript. Text submitted for support of public lesson for promotion to Associate Professor at the Polytechnic Institute of Porto, Portugal (2008)
15. Guedes, C., Trochidis, K., Anantapadmanabhan, A.: CAMeL: carnatic percussion music generation using N-gram and clustering approaches. In: Abstract of Presentation at the 16th Rhythm Production and Perception Workshop, Birmingham (2017)
16. Guedes, C.: Real-time composition, why it still matters?: a look at recent developments and potentially new and interesting applications. In: Proceedings of the 2017 International Computer Music Conference. ICMA, Shanghai (2017)
17. Iyer, V.: Improvisation: terms and conditions. In: Zorn, J. (ed.) Arcana IV: Musicians on Music, pp. 171–175 (2009)
18. Kvifte, T.: What is a musical instrument? Svensk tidskrift för musikforskning **90**(1), 45–56 (2008)
19. Lewis, G.E.: Too many notes: Computers, complexity and culture in *Voyager*. Leonardo Music J. **10**, 33–39 (2000)
20. Magnusson, T.: Of epistemic tools: musical instruments as cognitive extensions. Organised Sound **14**(2), 168–176 (2009)
21. Magnusson, T.: Musical organics: a heterarchical approach to digital organology. J. New Music Res. **46**(3), 286–303 (2017)
22. Rowe, R.: Interactive Music Systems: Machine Listening and Composing. MIT Press, Cambridge (1993)
23. Rowe, R.: Machine Musicianship. MIT Press, Cambridge (2001)
24. Santos Silva, S.: Quando a música improvisada é boa, soa a música escrita. In: Jornal de Negócios, August, 4, 2017 (2017)
25. Sioros, G., Guedes, C.: Automatic rhythmic performance in Max/MSP: the kin.rhythmicator. In: Proceedings of the 11th International Conference on New Interfaces for Musical Expression, Oslo (2011)
26. Taube, H.K.: Notes from the Metalevel: Introduction to Algorithmic Music Composition. Taylor & Francis, London (2004)
27. Winkler, T.: Composing Interactive Music: Techniques and Ideas Using Max. MIT Press, Cambridge (1998)
28. Xenakis, I.: Formalized Music: Thought and Mathematics in Music. Indiana University Press, Indianapolis (1992)

bf-pd: Enabling Mediated Communication and Cooperation in Improvised Digital Orchestras

Luke Dahl[1]([✉]), Florent Berthaut[2], Antoine Nau[2], and Patricia Plenacoste[2]

[1] McIntire Department of Music, University of Virginia, 112 Old Cabell Hall,
P.O. Box 400176, Charlottesville, VA 22904-4176, USA
lukedahl@virginia.edu
[2] Université de Lille, 42 rue Paul Duez, 59000 Lille, France
{florent.berthaut,patricia.plenacoste}@univ-lille1.fr,
antoine.nau@etu.univ-lille3.fr

Abstract. Digital musical instruments enable new musical collaboration possibilities, extending those of acoustic ensembles. However, the use of these new possibilities remains constrained due to a lack of a common terminology and technical framework for implementing them. Bf-pd is a new software library built in the PureData (Pd) language which enables communication and cooperation between digital instruments. It is based on the BOEUF conceptual framework which consists of a classification of modes of collaboration used in collective music performance, and a set of components which affords them. Bf-pd can be integrated into any digital instrument built in Pd, and provides a "collaboration window" from which musicians can easily view each others' activity and share control of instrument parameters and other musical data. We evaluate the implementation and design of bf-pd through workshops and a preliminary study and discuss its impact on collaboration within improvised ensembles of digital instruments.

Keywords: Digital orchestras · Laptop orchestra
Digital musical instruments · Collaboration · BOEUF · bf-pd
PureData

1 Introduction

Musical instruments based on electronic and digital technologies enable interactions between musicians that acoustic instruments do not typically afford. Control of a single instrument can be shared between multiple musicians, or a musical output from one instrument can be used as a control or input to another instrument. Ensembles such as the League of Automatic Composers and The Hub have been exploring the collaborative potential of digital technologies since at least the 1970's [8].

© Springer Nature Switzerland AG 2018
M. Aramaki et al. (Eds.): CMMR 2017, LNCS 11265, pp. 454–467, 2018.
https://doi.org/10.1007/978-3-030-01692-0_30

Contemporary ensembles, such as laptop orchestras, continue to use and extend these collaborative possibilities. However, composers and musicians who do utilize new modes of collaboration often build their own bespoke system for each composition or ensemble, thus re-implementing common functions and capabilities. We believe this is due to two factors. First, there is not a common language or terminology for labelling and discussing the ways in which musicians collaborate. Second, there is not a common widespread technical infrastructure for implementing these various modes of collaboration. This situation is especially problematic for spontaneously formed ensembles of heterogeneous instruments, where the lack of a quickly integrated system for sharing data between instruments leads to these interactions being neglected. New technologies may also impede interactions that were simple or easily available in acoustic ensembles. For example, a musician in a digital orchestra may find it difficult to discern which of their fellow musicians is generating a specific sound [12], which in turn might reduce the mutual engagement felt by musicians [5]. Thus, systems for musical collaboration may need to also enable digitally-mediated communication for activities that were previously unmediated.

1.1 Contribution

In [2] we presented BOEUF, a conceptual framework and set of components for describing digital orchestras and classifying the *modes of collaboration* they make possible. We developed this classification after conducting a survey of digital ensembles, collaborative instruments, and other frameworks and surveys such as [4,5,9,15].

In this paper we present bf-pd, an implementation of the BOEUF components in the PureData (Pd) language which aims at facilitating collaboration especially in the case of spontaneous orchestras (e.g. jam sessions). Musicians working in Pd can integrate components of bf-pd into their instruments, and thus gain access to a subset of the BOEUF collaboration modes, operated through a generic graphic interface. Specifically, bf-pd is designed to facilitate cooperation and sharing of control data between musicians, and to increase awareness by making musicians' activity visible to each other. Bf-pd is the first implementation of the BOEUF components, and the first system to explicitly support the BOEUF modes of collaboration. It allows us to test the usability of the components and the design of the protocol before going on to implement these in other software or hardware systems. It also allows us to evaluate how the use of these components affects musical collaborations. Bf-pd relies on a protocol of Open Sound Control (OSC) messages to communicate between instruments. This protocol can be used by future implementations of the BOEUF components on other platforms.

First we review the BOEUF conceptual framework. Then we describe the components currently supported by bf-pd, their interfaces and how to integrate them into a Pd instrument, and the details of the communication protocol. We also present the 'collaboration window', a graphical interface for controlling and displaying communication and cooperation between instruments. Lastly, we discuss preliminary results from a series of workshops and a pilot study we conducted.

1.2 Related Work

Monad [7] is an example of a recent networked musical collaboration, with game-like interaction and scoring, and a graphical UI for displaying user activity. Several protocols and software tools have been created to deal with the sharing of musical data for both single instruments and within networked orchestras. For example, Jamoma [14] and libMapper [11] both give access to the structure and parameters of networked instruments, sometimes with features for watching and grabbing parameters. An interesting example is the Digital Orchestra Toolbox [10] which simplifies the collaborative creation and mapping of digital musical instruments (DMI). Finally, Bridges [16], Diamouses [1] and NRCI [6] all provide features similar to bf-pd, in that they allow for the exchange of streams of data between instruments in a networked orchestra.

Like bf-pd, most of these tools rely on the OSC protocol for network communication. However, while they provide the generic sharing and mapping features required for networked musical control, these tools do not specifically cover all the modes of collaboration used in digital orchestras, and thus fail to provide a common basis for creating orchestras of mixed DMIs, especially in the case of spontaneous jam sessions. For example, with the exception of NRCI, these tools do not define standardised messages that would provide awareness of other musicians' activity. Nor do they allow musicians to send indications of gestures or control changes. Unlike these other software frameworks, bf-pd is based on a conceptual framework which is intended to cover the range of known collaboration possibilities. We used this framework to guide the design of bf-pd, and to evaluate its success.

2 The Boeuf Framework

BOEUF is a conceptual framework for modelling and building orchestras of DMIs. It consists of a classification of *modes of collaboration*, as well as a set of *components* which can be used to enable these modes in DMIs. Here we briefly summarize the framework, which is presented in more detail in [2], with a focus on the bf-pd implementation.

2.1 Modes of Collaboration

After conducting a survey of ways in which musicians in both acoustic and digital ensembles work together during a musical performance, we formulated three categories of modes of collaboration to describe these activities.

Cooperation. The three cooperation modes describe the coordination of musicians' actions with respect to their instruments. *Independent* cooperation occurs when each musician controls their own instrument while playing together. *Complementary* cooperation occurs when two or more musicians can affect different aspects of the same musical output. For example, in a digital orchestra one musician might change the pitch of an instrument while another controls the timbre. *Concurrent* cooperation occurs when multiple musicians can affect the same musical output at the same level, i.e. when they modify the same parameter on a single instrument. This mode is highlighted as an important component of mutual engagement, called mutual modifiability [5].

Communication. The communication modes are ways in which musicians exchange information which may then influence their actions. This communication may or may not directly impact the production of sound. *Awareness* includes all non-intentional communication, such as the means by which musicians keep track of each others' activities. In acoustic ensembles awareness is usually non-mediated and is facilitated by musicians' ability to see each other's movements and to distinguish each other's sounds.

However in digital ensembles, one's instrument may be unfamiliar to the other musicians and sound may not originate from the performer's location. These impediments to awareness can be addressed by creating digital channels by which awareness can be mediated. Brian-Kinns and Hamilton for example identify mutual awareness [5] as a key for mutual engagement in digital orchestras.

Indications are intentional communicative acts. These include commands, such as a conductor cuing an entrance, and suggestions, such as a nod or glance near the end of a solo. In digital ensembles indication can be mediated in the form of symbolic messages between musicians, such as the annotations in Daisyphone [5]. *Exchange* refers to the communication of musical data between musicians. These too can be mediated, such as sending MIDI or OSC data between devices, or non-mediated, as when an improviser riffs on a motif introduced by another musician.

Organisation. Organisation modes do not have any effect on the music produced, but rather impact the communication and cooperation modes. *Nomination* consists of defining the roles of musicians within the orchestra, e.g. who is the leader. *Grouping* defines a hierarchy of groups of instruments. *Selection* is the act of choosing a single instrument or a group in the context of cooperation or communication, e.g. selecting which musician to send an indication to. In the work described in this paper we focus on enabling the cooperation and communication modes of collaboration. The bf-pd library does not currently address organisation explicitly.

2.2 Components

The BOEUF components comprise a generic model of a digital orchestra, and are designed to enable the BOEUF modes of collaboration described above. In bf-pd, each of these components is implemented as an external object that integrates with the musician's instrument.

A **session** represents an instance of a collaborative music-making ensemble or event. A piece for laptop orchestra, or a spontaneous jam session of digital musicians would each take place within a session. A session contains instruments, and the network of possible interactions between them.

An **instrument** represents a bounded set of music-generating processes and a user interface (UI). An instrument may contain modules, parameters, and outputs, and it can send and receive messages. We presume that each musician in the orchestra is in control of at least one instrument. Thus, an instrument often acts as a proxy for the musician.

A **module** is a component of an instrument that produces musical data (either audio or control data), and can contain parameters, outputs, and meters. A module can have a type, which defines a set of parameters and outputs. For example all modules of type 'LowPassFilter' would have parameters for cutoff frequency and resonance. This would allow the state of entire modules to be exchanged between instruments.

Furthermore, in the case of instruments with multiple audio output streams, where the contribution may be too complex to be visualised in a single display (see the *meter* component below), decomposing an instrument into modules, each with its own meter, could help increase awareness. Modules are not implemented in the initial release of bf-pd.

A **parameter** is an attribute of a module or instrument that influences its musical production, and which can be controlled through the instrument's UI. Parameters can be of various types, and in bf-pd these types are: *cont* (a floating point number between 0.0 and 1.0), *midi* (a number between 0 and 127), *bang* (which can trigger an event), and *bool* (on or off). In bf-pd a parameter can also be a multiple of these types, e.g. a '4 cont' is 4-dimensional parameter, e.g. composed of four floating point values. Various actions can be performed on a parameter. A parameter can be:

- *Set* to a new value, either through the instrument's UI, or by other instruments (if the owner has granted access to do so).
- *Watched*, where the parameter value is sent to other instruments every time it is changed. (This functions as a means of both *awareness* and *exchange*.) In bf-pd all parameters are watched by all other instruments, and appear in the collaboration window (see 3.2).
- *Indicated*, where another instrument may propose but not set a new value for the parameter. In bf-pd this is done through the 'ask' functionality in the collaboration window.
- *Retrieved*, where the current value is returned once. This feature is not in the initial release of bf-pd.
- *Grabbed*, where a parameter can be set only by the instrument which has grabbed it. This is a strategy to deal with concurrent access to parameters, but is not implemented in the initial release of bf-pd.

An **output** is a musical attribute that is produced by a module or instrument. They can have the same types as parameters. Outputs can be retrieved and watched by other instruments, and function as a means for both *awareness* and *exchange*.

A **meter** is a component of an instrument that is not used in the actual sound production, but rather indicates the activity of the instrument. In bf-pd each instrument has an overall activity meter which is visible to other instruments through the collaboration window.

A **group** is a set of instruments or other groups, and is used for organisation modes. For example, the parameters common to all instruments in a group could be set simultaneously, or a message could be sent to all instruments in a group. Groups, like the other organisation modes, are not implemented in the initial release of bf-pd.

A **message** can be a text, image, or video sent from one instrument to another instrument or group. Messages are not currently implemented in bf-pd.

3   bf-pd

Bf-pd allows musicians to access the modes of collaboration described in the BOEUF framework within instruments developed in PureData. This is done by integrating into their instruments the bf-pd abstractions which implement the BOEUF components.

3.1   Integrating the Components

The first abstraction to add is *bf-instrument*, with the name of the instrument as an argument. As seen in Fig. 1a, this object displays an activity meter and manages the collaboration window (see Sect. 3.2). The 'collab' toggle allows for displaying or hiding the collaboration window.

Then for each parameter a musician wants to share with other musicians, they must create a *bf-param*. Arguments of this object are the instrument name, the parameter name, the number of values it has, and its type. Once created, a GUI is generated for the parameter, with widgets to control it directly, and with inlets and outlets for setting the values and retrieving them, as shown in Fig. 1(b and c).

For any musical output that the musician wants to share, they can add a bf-output. This object has the same arguments and possible types as bf-parameter, but has only inputs.

Finally, there must be at least one *bf-session* object instantiated at the same time as the bf-instrument. Bf-session has a single argument which is the name of the session. There can be one per bf-instrument (i.e. in the same patch) or a common one for multiple instruments. This object handles connecting with other instruments on the network, through OSC messages. (This is used to filter OSC messages so that multiple sessions can take place on the same network).

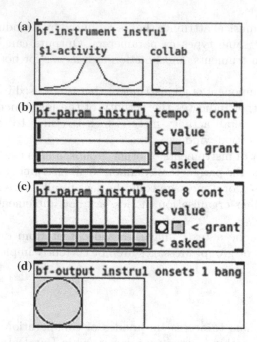

Fig. 1. Some bf-pd components: (a) bf-instrument and activity meter, (b) bf-parameter of type *cont*, (c) bf-parameters of type *8 cont*, (d) bf-output of type *bang*.

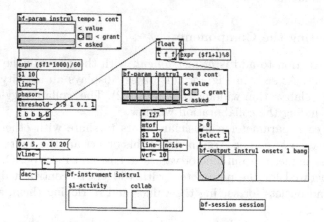

Fig. 2. The Pd patch for an instrument using bf-pd, with the components from Fig. 1.

Figure 2 shows an example patch of an instrument with two parameters, one with a single continuous value and the other with eight continuous values, and one output with a bang type which is used to share onsets with other musicians.

3.2   Collaboration Window

Bf-pd creates a *collaboration window* for each instrument (see Fig. 3), which functions as the primary UI for digitally mediated modes of cooperation and communication. The leftmost column displays the activity meter and all bf-parameters and bf-outputs of the musician's own instrument. The activity meters display each instrument's audio output as the energy in twelve bark-spaced frequency bands. The meters are intended to improve the ability to tell who is making which sound, and thus increase *awareness*[12].

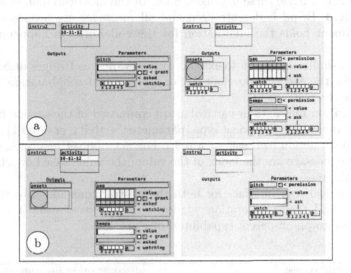

Fig. 3. Collaboration windows of bf-pd: (a) for instrument "instru1", (b) for instrument "instru2". In the left columns are the activity, parameters and outputs of one's own instrument, in the right columns are those of the other instrument in the session.

The collaboration window UI for each parameter affords a number of communication and cooperation modes, therefore allowing for mutual engagement as described by [5].

For parameters belonging to other instruments, the user can see a parameter's value as its owner changes it (*awareness*). The user may also 'ask' for a new value (*indication*), and the parameter's owner will see the asked value in their collaboration window. If the owner grants permission, asking for a new value will change the parameter (thus enabling both *concurrent* and *complementary* cooperation). *Exchange* can be enabled in two ways. The user can 'watch' another's parameter by selecting a *watch-bus* with the radial button on the parameter's UI. If the user selects that same bus with the 'watching' selector on one of their own parameters, their parameter will now be controlled by the other's parameter. Like parameters, the outputs of other instruments can also be watched. To send information from one's own instrument to another's parameter, one can send data to an *ask-bus* through a bf-ask object in one's own instrument. Then select this same bus in the 'ask' selector of the other instrument's parameter. The UI for all of the actions described here can be seen in Fig. 3.

3.3 Implementation

All communication between instruments is done through OpenSoundControl messages. This ensures that the implementation of BOEUF is not limited to PureData, but can be later extended to other software instruments through plug-ins that will parse these messages. Some of the most common messages are listed in Fig. 4. Bf-pd is decentralized and all messages are broadcast so that each instrument holds the information for the collaboration happening in the session.

This is a similar approach to existing systems such as Bridges or NRCI, and will allow for the eventual development of externalized collaboration interfaces (i.e. outside the instrument).

Collaboration messages in particular are composed of the session name, the instrument name, the component type (parameter, activity, or output) and name and the type of action (set, ask, or watch). For ask and set messages, the arguments of the message are the index of the value, the value asked or set, and the emitter of the message.

The graphical user interface for both the abstractions added to the instrument patch and the collaboration window are generated using the dynamic patching and graph-on-parent capabilities of PureData.

/boeuf/session/request	discover other instruments
/boeuf/session/hello ip_address	inform others of our ip address
/boeuf/session/instru/parameters/param/declare nb-values type	provide information on parameter
/boeuf/session/instru/parameters/param/set index value set-by-name	set the value for a parameter
/boeuf/session/instru/outputs/out/set index value set-by-name	set the value for an output
/boeuf/session/instru/parameters/param/ask index value asked-by-name	ask a value for a parameter

Fig. 4. Main Open Sound Control messages for bf-pd.

4   Evaluation

In this section, we present some preliminary results from a series of evaluations of bf-pd and its impact on improvised digital orchestras.

4.1   Workshops and Iterations

We conducted three workshops with both non-musicians and musicians. Each began with a PureData tutorial to ensure that all participants were familiar with the interface and concepts. We then asked musicians to play in groups of three for five-minute improvisation sessions using an instrument that we provided. Each group played a session for each of three conditions: (a) without bf-pd, (b) with only the communication part of bf-pd (i.e. watching others' activity in the collaboration window without interacting with them) and (c) with both the communication and cooperation possibilities of bf-pd (i.e. interacting using the collaboration window). We also used these same conditions in the study presented below.

We filmed each session and subsequent discussions to get feedback on each condition.

We used this feedback to iterate on the implementation of bf-pd and on the design of the collaboration window. At the time of the first session, musicians could control their own parameters only in the instrument patch, and could view and access others' parameters in the collaboration window. Some participants commented on the difficulty caused by frequently switching between the two windows. As a result, we added to the collaboration window a dedicated column to display and control one's own parameters and outputs. Now musicians can both play their instrument and collaborate without leaving the collaboration window.

At the time of the second workshop, the routing of watched parameters and outputs had to be done by modifying one's instrument patch, and was not possible from the collaboration window. Participants told us they wanted to experiment with different routings while playing. We then added the ability to connect watched parameters and outputs to one's own parameters without leaving the collaboration window (through the *watch-bus*). We also expanded the OSC protocol so that messages provide more information on cooperation, e.g. who is asking a parameter, who is watching someone's parameter, and so on. This allows us to analyse more precisely the impact of various bf-pd design choices.

4.2   Preliminary Study

After integrating the feedback from the workshops we conducted a preliminary study to investigate the effects of using bf-pd on musicians' interactions. Our study participants were 7 electronic musicians with an average 8.6 years of experience (sd = 5.5).

Our study was structured the same way as the workshop sessions: a Pd tutorial, followed by three sessions of improvisation of at least 5 min with an instrument we provided. The interface for this instrument was composed of one output and five parameters, including a repeating pattern of eight values driven by a tempo parameter. Musicians were randomly assigned into groups of three for each session. Unfortunately, due to technical issues we were only able to measure one group in all three conditions.

We compared the same three conditions as in the workshops: In Condition *NO* the musicians played only their own instrument. In Condition *COM* they could see the other instruments in the group via the collaboration window, but were instructed to control only their own instrument. In Condition *COOP* they were encouraged to cooperate by controlling others' parameters and granting access to their own parameters. All interactions took place in the collaboration window. This allowed us to analyse the separate impact of *communication* (visualising others' activity) and *cooperation* (actually interacting with others' instruments).

4.3   Analysis

During the study we recorded each time a musician changed one of their own parameters. We recorded video of all sessions. And we asked participants to fill out a questionnaire after each condition. A five-level Likert scale was used to evaluate different aspects of the participants' experience.

Parameter Analysis. From the recorded data we found that participants changed the values of their own parameters more frequently in *COM* (1.17 times per second on average) and *COOP* (1.0) compared to *NO* (0.61). This suggests that participants were more engaged with the interface when communication was enabled. The fact that changing one's own parameters was less frequent with cooperation may suggest that some attention was on other players' parameters instead of their own.

We also calculated to what degree participants manipulated one parameter versus manipulating all the parameters available to them. The results show that as participants moved from *NO* to *COM* to *COOP* they focused on fewer and fewer of their own parameters.

This is interesting because it may suggest that participants were more engaged and focused on how their actions affected and interacted with the actions of the other musicians (as opposed to haphazardly changing parameters). These two results could also be due to the increasing complexity of the interaction and higher cognitive load when moving from one condition to the next.

Video Analysis. From the recorded video we notice that participants seem to look at each other less often in Conditions *COM* (13) and *COOP* (11), compared to *NO* (19). We also saw that digitally mediated actions could effect non-mediated interactions. For example, occasionally participants would spontaneously laugh or move at the same time in response to something happening in their instruments. And we noticed that in *COOP* there was more verbal communication between participants, as they discussed strategies for synchronizing their tempo or provided explanations to each other.

Questionnaire Analysis. Our questionnaire results come from two groups: one from the third workshop and the other from the preliminary study. We found that musicians in *COM* (score = 4) could better distinguish between the activities of the other musicians than they could in *NO* (3.8). The question was not asked for *COOP*. We asked to what degree participants felt like they were making music together with the other musicians. Musicians felt equally together in Conditions *NO* and *COOP* (4.3), but less together in *COM* (3.5). We asked whether each condition was a better shared experience than the former, and found that *COM* was not better than Condition *NO* (2.6 out of 5), while *COOP* was better than *COM* (4.1/5).

5   Discussion

We note that our workshop and study results are "preliminary" in the sense that we do not have enough participants to generate statistically significant results.

However, they did generate valuable feedback which we used to improve bf-pd and which suggests directions for further investigation.

It is difficult to interpret some of the results. Did participants look at each other less in Conditions *COM* and *COOP* because they could view others' activity and cooperate with them through the UI? Or was it because each subsequent condition demanded more attention? Or perhaps this was due to the way collaboration information is displayed. An improved study design may help answer these questions. So might further research into how to better display collaboration information.

Another limitation of our study is that the order of conditions is not randomized between groups. As the participants pass through each condition they may become more comfortable with their instrument and with the other musicians. This may have an effect on the measured variables. Having multiple groups with a counterbalanced order of the conditions would remove this effect.

The study does suggest that bf-pd is succeeding at enabling and encouraging communication and cooperation. Participants can more easily distinguish others' activities when using bf-pd, and so *awareness* is increased. A recurring comment was that participants felt like they were "sharing their instrument with each other", or even that they were "all playing the same instrument". This may be due in part to the common interface, where all instruments appear and can be controlled at once. It is also a demonstration of what can happen when musicians use bf-pd to move from *independent cooperation* to *complementary* and *concurrent cooperation*.

There are a few components from the BOEUF framework which are missing in the initial release of bf-pd. Adding these might further enrich the experience of cooperative music-making. Messages could facilitate textual communication through the collaboration window. And, the ability to define groups and roles would facilitate organization within the orchestra. For example, one could take the role of "tempo master", so that others will watch their tempo parameter.

6 Conclusion

Bf-pd is a software framework that makes it easy for digital musicians working in PureData to access and change parameters on each others' instruments, to share data between instruments, and to perceive the actions of other musicians in the ensemble. One of the most challenging aspects of designing bf-pd was to create user interfaces in Pd that quickly convey awareness information, and which make it easy to access the various modes of cooperation. Future work will focus on refining the UI, especially by investigating visualisations of musicians' activity, whether inside Pd, or through network connected applications. Interaction design becomes even more challenging when we consider integrating bf-pd into embedded hardware platforms such as Bela [13] which lack GUIs. One solution might be to use augmented reality interfaces and allow musicians to modify the collaboration window and overlap it with their own unique physical interface [3], thus merging mediated and non-mediated communication. Lastly, we currently have limited information on musicians' experience of integrating bf-pd into their own music-making process, and so further user studies are needed.

A video of bf-pd can be seen at https://vimeo.com/214380530. Bf-pd will be released at https://gitlab.cristal.univ-lille.fr/boeuf/bf-pd We invite you to use it and we look forward to your feedback.

References

1. Alexandraki, C., et al.: Towards the implementation of a generic platform for networked music performance: the diamouses approach. In: ICMC, pp. 251–258 (2008)
2. Berthaut, F., Dahl, L.: BOEUF: a unified framework for modeling and designing digital orchestras. In: Kronland-Martinet, R., Aramaki, M., Ystad, S. (eds.) CMMR 2015. LNCS, vol. 9617, pp. 153–166. Springer, Cham (2016). https://doi.org/10.1007/978-3-319-46282-0_10
3. Berthaut, F., Jones, A.: Controllar: appropriation of visual feedback on control surfaces. In: Proceedings of the 2016 ACM on Interactive Surfaces and Spaces, ISS 2016, pp. 271–277. ACM, New York (2016)
4. Blaine, T., Fels, S.: Contexts of collaborative musical experiences. In: Proceedings of NIME 2003, Singapore, Singapore, pp. 129–134 (2003)
5. Bryan-Kinns, N., Hamilton, F.: Identifying mutual engagement. Behav. Inf. Technol. 31(2), 101–125 (2012)
6. Burns, C., Surges, G.: NRCI: software tools for laptop ensemble. In: ICMC (2008)
7. Cakmak, C., Camci, A., Forbes, A.: Networked virtual environments as collaborative music spaces. In: Proceedings of the International Conference on New Interfaces for Musical Expression, volume 16 of 2220–4806, pp. 106–111. Queensland Conservatorium Griffith University, Brisbane (2016)
8. Gresham-Lancaster, S.: The aesthetics and history of the hub: the effects of changing technology on network computer music. Leonardo Music J. 8, 39–44 (1998)
9. Hattwick, I., Wanderley, M.M.: A dimension space for evaluating collaborative musical performance systems (2012)

10. Malloch, J., Sinclair, S., Wanderley, M.M.: A network-based framework for collaborative development and performance of digital musical instruments. In: Kronland-Martinet, R., Ystad, S., Jensen, K. (eds.) CMMR 2007. LNCS, vol. 4969, pp. 401–425. Springer, Heidelberg (2008). https://doi.org/10.1007/978-3-540-85035-9_28

11. Malloch, J., Sinclair, S., Wanderley, M.M.: Libmapper: (a library for connecting things). In: CHI 2013 Extended Abstracts on Human Factors in Computing Systems, pp. 3087–3090. ACM (2013)

12. Merritt, T., Kow, W., Ng, C., McGee, K., Wyse, L.: Who makes what sound? Supporting real-time musical improvisations of electroacoustic ensembles. In: Proceedings of the 22nd Conference of the Computer-human Interaction Special Interest Group of Australia on Computer-Human Interaction, pp. 112–119. ACM (2010)

13. Moro, G., et al.: Making high-performance embedded instruments with Bela and pure data. In: International Conference on Live Interfaces (2016)

14. Place, T., Lossius, T.: Jamoma: a modular standard for structuring patches in max. In: Proceedings of the International Computer Music Conference, pp. 143–146 (2006)

15. Weinberg, G.: Interconnected musical networks: toward a theoretical framework. Comput. Music J. 29(2), 23–39 (2005)

16. Wyse, L., Mitani, N.: Bridges for networked musical ensembles. In: ICMC (2009)

Visual Representations for Music Understanding Improvement

Leandro Cruz[1](✉), Vitor Rolla[2], Juliano Kestenberg[3], and Luiz Velho[2]

[1] Institute of Systems and Robotics,
Department of Electrical and Computer Engineering, University of Coimbra,
Rua Silvio Lima, Polo II, 3030-290 Coimbra, Portugal
lmvcruz@isr.uc.pt
[2] Instituto Nacional de Matematica Pura e Aplicada,
Estr. Dona Castorina, 110, Jardim Botânico, Rio de Janeiro, RJ 22460-320, Brazil
{vitorgr,lvelho}@impa.br
[3] Universidade Federal do Rio de Janeiro,
Av. Pedro Calmon, 550, Cidade Universitária, Rio de Janeiro, RJ 21941-901, Brazil
info@julianokestenberg.com

Abstract. Classical music appreciation is non trivial. Visual representation can aid music teaching and learning processes. In this sense, we propose a set of visual representations based on musical notes features, such as: note type, octave, velocity and timbre. In our system, the visual elements appear along with their corresponding musical elements, in order to improve the perception of musical structures. The visual representations we use to enhance the comprehension of a composition could be extended to performing arts scenarios. It could be adopted as motion graphics during live musical performances. We have developed several videos to illustrate our method. We have also developed an ear training quiz and a research questionnaire. This material is available at http://www.impa.br/~vitorgr/VLMU/home.html.

Keywords: Music visualization · Geometric shapes
Pedagogy and music education

1 Introduction

Visual representations of music have been studied since 1938, when Oskar Fischinger presented the film "An Optical Poem". It is based on the 2nd Hungarian Rhapsody (by Franz Liszt). The movie associates movements of geometric shapes and musical elements. The definition of shapes is not clear, but the video is completely synchronized with musical elements. Two years later, in 1940, Disney's movie "Fantasy" featured eight cartoon segments in which the characters movement is also synchronized with excerpts from classical pieces of music.

Both films give evidence of the relationship between visual and musical elements. This is the main fundamental path of this research. We define visual

© Springer Nature Switzerland AG 2018
M. Aramaki et al. (Eds.): CMMR 2017, LNCS 11265, pp. 468–476, 2018.
https://doi.org/10.1007/978-3-030-01692-0_31

representations which are clearly associated with musical elements in order to improve their perception. It facilitates the understanding of musical phenomena. This pedagogical goal is the main objective of this research. Ordinarily, the full appreciation of classical music demands a substantial amount of time to learn the basics of music theory, as well as training the ear to be able to understand and identify the contrivances utilized by the composer.

We will present an approach for enhancing the perception of a note and its properties like tonal pitch, octave and volume. The proposed visual representation is based on polygons, and they are related to the notes through an appropriate association of visual properties like color and shape.

Our intention is to create a visual language that is able to represent complex musical phenomena, like rhythm, harmony, and melody. However, in this first step, we are proposing the basis of this language with the analysis of the most essential element for musical studies: the note. From our visualization approach, we can then highlight the occurrence of chords and also timbre. Furthermore, we can observe the relationship between dominance and accompaniment.

The music visualization can be an image (a global representation) or a video (a temporal representation). In the image, we will represent global phenomena providing a big picture of the composition. The local approach is a video with the same duration of the music, where the visual representations are synchronized with the respective musical elements. In our case, for each note in the music, we will show a corresponding polygon with the respective color and shape during the time the note is being played.

In Sect. 2, we describe other music visualizations types, and compare them to our approach. In Sect. 3, we present the association of colors and tonal pitch. We demonstrate how this association can be used to observe the dominance and accompaniment phenomena. In Sect. 4, we present our approach. Finally, in Sect. 5, we conclude with final considerations and future work.

2 Related Work

Coloppy (2000) proposed a conceptualization for music visualizations. In this work, the author presents a complete study on how to represent colors and how they can be related to elements of a song. In addition to colors, he presented a conceptualization about the use of shapes, such as points, lines, curves, polygons and free shapes, and how to associate them with musical elements such as rhythm and harmony. Finally, it also highlights the use of movements and shapes to create a relationship between the representations which are displayed. The conceptualization presented by Collopy is quite broad, and very associated with the use of procedural methods to control elements of a song. Our work goes in another direction, because we use visual elements that are more simple and can be used as a pedagogical tool in music learning environments.

Chan et al. (2010) propose an innovative representation to reveal the semantic structure of classical compositions. They propose an analogy of weaving in textile art to construct pictures. Such pictures demonstrate correlations and occurrences of the music *motif* within different sets of instruments. Sapp (2003) proposes two types of diagrams to view the harmonic structure and relationships between key regions in a musical composition. A discrete mapping of sound tones into color tones is proposed. Miyazaki et al. (2003) propose a method to create a 3D interactive picture from Musical Instrument Digital Interface (MIDI) files. Pitch, volume, and tempo of a note are encoded as height, diameter, and color saturation in the interactive illustration. The users can take advantage of 3D perspective view and illumination to navigate within the MIDI file data. These works present a global music visualization approach.

Fonteles et al. (2013) introduce a particle system to generate real-time animated particle emitter fountains choreographed by classical music. The authors describe music as highly organized sounds which exhibit time-varying structures in pitch and time domains. Their main goal was to visualize the music *motif* by analyzing such time-varying structures. Bergstrom et al. (2007) propose a method called Isochords, for visualizing the chord progression structure of musical compositions. A triangular isometric grid called Tonnetz (Cohn 1997), which was invented by Euler, is utilized to make the quality of chords and intervals more salient to the audience. The authors claim that their proposal shows harmony as it changes overtime and they believe it is possible to visually detect familiar *motif* patterns with Isochords. Ciuha et al. (2010) present a different color mapping for visualizing a group of concurrent tones. The authors propose a continuous color wheel for mapping. Their method is different from most sound tones to color tones mapping which are commonly discrete. Dissonance is represented with low color saturation, while consonance is represented with high color saturation. These works present a local music visualization approach.

Most of the related work is mainly concerned with: harmonic analysis, chord progression structure, *motif* identification, or 3D interactive illustration. The only exception is the paper published by Chan et al. (2010). In such paper, the authors are concerned with the role of instruments inside an orchestra. An orchestra is a large instrumental ensemble. Thus, the visual language proposed by Chan et al. (2010) is highly complex, turning out to be inadequate to pedagogical purposes. The visual representation proposed in this paper is designed to evince specific characteristics of music, such as: timbre, chord, note tone, and volume. Although the proposed visual language can also help the user to grasp some information about chord progression and *motif* identification, the focus is to apply the visual language on small ensembles, i.e., on compositions arranged for chamber music. The proposed visual language can be utilized to create global and local views of music.

3   Colors

Commonly, it is easier to recognize colors in a high contrast palette compared to distinguishing musical notes. In this way, we use an appropriate coloration of our visual representations to highlight the occurrence of each type of note played. In this section, we present a very simple association between colors and

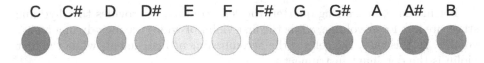

Fig. 1. Sound tones to color tones according to Louis Bertrand Castel. (Color figure online)

notes. We also show an example of how it is easy to extend a perception of the relationship between instrument dominance and accompaniment.

In this work, we are using an association between the tonal pitch of a note with a specific color from a palette. The construction of this palette is arbitrary, i.e., it is possible to use several types of palettes for specific purposes. But note that the colors of this palette should be easily distinguishable.

In our experiments, we used the colors palette proposed by Louis Bertrand Castel which presents a continuous chromatic transition, maintaining sufficient contrast between the tones adopted. In this way, the colors have a coherent flow, being easily recognized and facilitating learning processes. There are studies that show how the relationship between this colors palette and musical notes is intuitively perceived by the human brain (Brougher et al. 2005).

From the combination of colors and notes, we can create global visual representations of music. In particular, we will present two very simple visual representations that can be used to perceive dominance and accompaniment in a song. We will compare this approach with the temporal process of listening to a musical piece, or looking at a diagram containing the precise distribution of the notes for each timbre, showing how the colors make a great contribution to the perception of the dominance and accompaniment relationship. The Fig. 2 illustrates the diagram with the distributions of the notes and the two proposed visual representations.

This study was performed with chamber music, which is a type of classical music commonly played by a small group of musicians, which could be positioned in the chamber of a palace. In particular, we will analyze two interpretations of classical music played by string quartets.

Classical music composers usually build a piece of music with a principal theme, which is repeated along the piece by different instruments. Variations on volume, rhythm, and melody are utilized to introduce form and interest to the musical piece. Thus, the instruments may have different roles in a music composition. When the instrument has the accompaniment role, its composition part supports the dominant instrument.

Accompaniment instruments usually provide harmonic background and/or rhythmic structure to dominant instruments. Often, the harmonic background is a chord progression related to the song theme, while the rhythmic structure is a regular recurrence in time of a small set of notes. Instrument dominance can be characterized by higher volumes, higher variance of notes, and complex melodies.

For instance, in a string quartet, the cello commonly provides the rhythmic structure in a lower volume, while the first violin provides the melody in a higher volume. In this case, the cello is the accompaniment instrument, while the first violin is the dominant instrument.

The Fig. 2(a) shows a table with the number of notes played by each instrument in a song. This is a fairly accurate representation, objectively presenting such quantities. That way, with careful analysis, we can see which instruments play only a small set of notes (which indicates that they perform an accompaniment role) and which play a larger variety of notes (which indicates that they perform a dominant role). However, careful reading of several numbers is necessary to realize the existence of this pattern.

Although it is possible to observe the instrument accompaniment and dominance relationship based on the table, it is not as intuitive as color-based representations. For example, Fig. 2(b) shows two bars with the proportion of occurrence of each note played by different instruments (timbre: T4 and T1). This visual property quickly shows us the variety of notes played by each instrument, allowing us to easily define which is the dominant (T1) and which performs the accompaniment (T4).

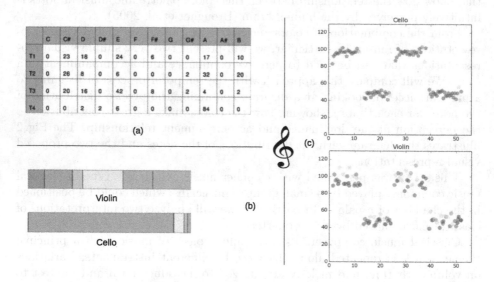

Fig. 2. Color Analysis: Dominance vs. Accompaniment. (Color figure online)

The volume of a note is associated with the intensity in which a note is played by the instrumentalist. Figure 2(c) shows a complete view of a song. It simultaneously represents a small geometric shape for each note played. The shape position is determined according to the moment in which the note was touched (x-axis) and also to its volume (y-axis).

In Fig. 2(c), it is not easy to notice the proportions of the notes like in the bar chart, because in the representation of a song with a reasonable amount of notes we will have an superposition of colors throughout the graph. However, we can still have a general perception of whether or not there is a variety of colors, as well as perceiving the velocities (volume) of notes. In this way, we can also perceive the dominance (more colors with varying velocities) and accompaniment (few colors with continuous velocities).

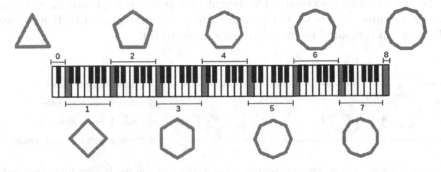

Fig. 3. Octaves visual representation.

4 Shapes

In this section, we will present the relationship between shapes and musical elements. The simultaneous occurrence of the visual representation and its respective musical element creates a synesthetic effect.

4.1 Note Perception

A note is the most fundamental musical element in a song. Therefore, we focus our approach on it. In addition to the association of note tones and specific colors, we will also show how other note properties can be highlighted.

Whenever a note is played, it must be visually represented by a geometric shape, in our case a polygon. As mentioned above, the pitch of the note is represented in accordance with a color palette already presented in Fig. 1. We will represent the octaves according to the number of sides of a polygon, as shown in Fig. 3. Higher octaves mean treble sounds and more polygon sides. Lower octaves mean bass sounds and less polygon sides. In addition, the note velocity is associated with the size of a polygon. The larger the velocity, the larger the size of the polygon in the visual representation.

4.2 Chord Perception

Chords are sets of notes played at the same time. They are represented by a group of polygons associated with the respective color notes. For example, representations may be nested or shifted, as illustrated in Fig. 4.

For instance, an instrument playing chord (a) would be playing notes "C", "E", and "G" at the third octave (hexagon). An instrument playing chord (b) would be playing notes "C", "E", "G", and "B" at the fifth octave (octagon). An instrument playing chord (c) would be playing notes "D", "G", "B", and "F#" at the second octave (pentagon). An instrument playing chord (d) would be playing notes "D", "G", and "B" at the fifth octave (octagon), and also "F#" at the third octave (hexagon). The height of a polygon is proportional to the velocity (volume) of a note. For instance, the green note in chord (d) has lower volume when compared to the green note in chord (c).

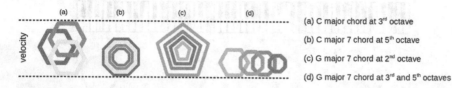

(a) C major chord at 3rd octave

(b) C major 7 chord at 5th octave

(c) G major 7 chord at 2nd octave

(d) G major 7 chord at 3rd and 5th octaves

Fig. 4. Chords are represented by nested or shifted polygons. (Color figure online)

4.3 Timbre Perception

The timbre of a musical instrument enables a listener to judge that two non-identical sounds, similarly presented and having the same loudness and pitch, are dissimilar. An approach that can be used to represent different timbres in a composition is to draw the polygons in different areas of the image accordingly. Figure 5 is a picture of a musical piece played by four instruments: a cello, two violins and a viola. The visual representation of each timbre is placed in a quadrant of the frame.

4.4 Motion and Blurring

In this paper, we kept the focus on the visual properties like color and shape. These features are easily observed, and thus, they produce a more efficient synesthetic effect. In this section, we will talk about two simple behaviors and their meaning for music visualization. These behaviors are motion and blurring.

When a note (or chord) is played, its corresponding polygon appears on the screen and grows reaching its maximum size at half of the note duration. For this purpose, we have observed that an appropriate use of the scaling (an arising and disappearing of the representation) has highlighted the musical note occurrence.

The other effect that we apply is blurring. After a note (or chord) is played, it disappears slowly blurred. The following notes are then shown in the front. This effect lets us perceive notes that have been played recently. Although we do not approach rotations and translations, we believe that they can be used further to represent rhythm or harmony.

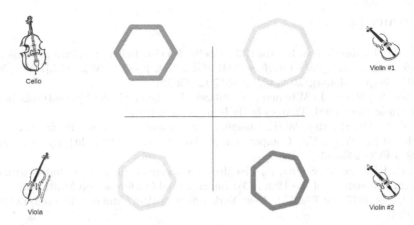

Fig. 5. Four timbres of a String quartet.

5 Conclusion and Future Work

This work demonstrates the potential of using visual representations to improve the understanding of musical elements. We present a method on how to use colors, shapes, movements, and blurring associated with musical notes and their respective properties. With our visual representations we show examples of dominance and accompaniment between different musical instruments.

Currently, we have made available an ear training quiz and a research questionnaire at the project website: http://www.impa.br/~vitorgr/VLMU/home. html. Our goals with this evaluation are (i) to understand the level of expertise necessary to use the system; and (ii) to receive feedback from users with different background experiences that might help us improve our method.

We intend to expand the set of visually represented musical elements. In this way, we can create more complex visual representations based on the analysis of rhythm and harmony. A research direction with great potential is to explore polygon positioning and movements, and also appearance and disappearance effects. Another extension is to work on instruments grouping in a way that would let us represent a whole orchestra.

A visual language for music understanding is proposed to facilitate common listeners and music students to understand and visualize important structures of classical music. The presence of *motifs* and instrument roles were visually identified in the music illustrated videos. MIDI music visualization has the potential to become a powerful pedagogical tool for teaching and learning classical music.

Acknowledgments. The authors would like to thank the following institutions for their support: Coordenação de Aperfeiçoamento de Pessoal de Nível Superior (CAPES), and finally Instituto Nacional Casa da Moeda (Portugal).

References

Bergstrom, T., Karahalios, K., Hart, J.: Isochords: visualizing structure in music. In: Proceedings of Graphics Interface 2007 (GI 2007), pp. 297–304. ACM, New York (2007). https://doi.org/10.1145/1268517.1268565

Brougher, K., Strick, J., Wiseman, A., Zilczer, J.: Visual Music: Synaesthesia in Art and Music Since 1900. Thames & Hudson, London (2005)

Chan, W.Y., Qu, H., Mak, W.H.: Visualizing the semantic structure in classical music works. IEEE Trans. Vis. Comput. Graph **16**, 161–173 (2010). https://doi.org/10.1109/TVCG.2009.63

Ciuha, P., Klemenc, B., Solina, F.: Visualization of concurrent tones in music with colors. In: Proceedings of the 18th ACM International Conference on Multimedia (MM 2010), pp. 1677–1680. ACM, New York (2010). https://doi.org/10.1145/1873951.1874320

Cohn, R.: Neo-Riemannian Operations, Parsimonious Trichords, and their Tonnetz Representations. J. Music. Theory **41**(1), 1–66 (1997)

Collopy, F.: Color, form, and motion: dimensions of a musical art of light. J. Leonardo **33**(5), 355–360 (2000)

Dannenberg, R.: A brief survey of music representation issues. Comput. Music J. **17**, 20–30 (1993)

Fonteles, J.H., Rodrigues, M.A.F., Basso, V.E.D.: Creating and evaluating a particle system for music visualization. J. Vis. Lang. Comput. **24**, 472–482 (2013). https://doi.org/10.1016/j.jvlc.2013.10.002

Gardner, R.: Music Notation: A Manual of Modern Practice. Allyn & Bacon, Boston (1964)

Gareth, L.: Musicians make a standard: the MIDI phenomenon. Comput. Music J. **9**, 8–26 (1985). https://doi.org/10.2307/3679619

Miyazaki, R., Fujishiro, I., Hiraga, R.: Exploring MIDI datasets. In: ACM SIGGRAPH 2003 Sketches & Applications (SIGGRAPH 2003), p. 1. ACM, New York (2003). https://doi.org/10.1145/965400.965453

Ohmi, K.: Music visualization in style and structure. J. Vis. **10**(3), 257–258 (2007). https://doi.org/10.1007/BF03181691

Sapp, C.: Harmonic visualizations of tonal music. In: Proceedings of International Computer Music Conference, Havana, Cuba, pp. 423–430 (2003)

Zhu, J., Wang, Y.: Complexity-scalable beat detection with MP3 audio bitstreams. Comput. Music. J. **32**(1), 71–87 (2008). https://doi.org/10.1162/comj.2008.32.1.71. Spring 2008

Melody Transformation with Semiotic Patterns

Izaro Goienetxea[1] and Darrell Conklin[1,2(✉)]

[1] Department of Computer Science and Artificial Intelligence,
University of the Basque Country UPV/EHU, San Sebastian, Spain
{izaro.goienetxea,darrell.conklin}@ehu.eus
[2] IKERBASQUE, Basque Foundation for Science, Bilbao, Spain

Abstract. This paper presents a music generation method based on the extraction of a semiotic structure from a template piece followed by generation into this semiotic structure using a statistical model of a corpus. To describe the semiotic structure of a template piece, a pattern discovery method is applied, covering the template piece with significant patterns using melodic viewpoints at varying levels of abstraction. Melodies are generated into this structure using a stochastic optimization method. A selection of melodies was performed in a public concert, and audience evaluation results show that the method generates good coherent melodies.

1 Introduction

In recent years the topic of computational music generation has experienced a dynamic renewal of interest, though automation of music composition has intrigued people for hundreds of years. Even before the age of computers the idea of automatic music composition existed. A classical example of the automatic composition idea is the *Musikalisches Würfelspiel* or musical dice game, like the one published in 1792 that was attributed to Mozart [16].

Statistical models of symbolic music have been prevalent in computational modelling of musical style, since they can easily capture local musical features by training on large corpora rather than hand coding of stylistic rules [1,7,12,15]. The lasting impact of statistical models on the topic of music generation spans from the earliest Markov models [5] to new variants of statistical models based on deep learning [4] and grammatical methods [21].

An issue faced by all methods for music generation is the *coherence problem:* ensuring that music material repeats or recalls in a more abstract sense material presented earlier in the piece. Nearly all forms of music involve repetition [18], either at the surface or deeper structural levels, and repetition imparts meaning to music [19]. Though early knowledge-based methods [13] explicitly considered repetition, the problem of achieving coherence in music generated from machine learning models remains largely unsolved.

A natural way to describe the coherence of a piece of music is by constructing a *semiotic structure*, defined as a representation of similar segments by a

© Springer Nature Switzerland AG 2018
M. Aramaki et al. (Eds.): CMMR 2017, LNCS 11265, pp. 477–488, 2018.
https://doi.org/10.1007/978-3-030-01692-0_32

limited set of arbitrary symbols, each symbol representing an equivalence class of segments [3]. A key observation is that a semiotic structure can be "inverted", generating new music by instantiating the symbols and retaining the abstract equivalence structure though having completely new music material [9]. The procedure can therefore be seen as *generation by transformation*: retaining abstract aspects of a template piece while modifying specific material.

Progress on the coherence problem was made recently in the music generation method of Collins et al. [6], where similar segments are identified by patterns indicating transposed repetitions in Chopin mazurkas. These "geometric" patterns are only suitable for carefully selected examples, because repetition in music need not be restricted to rigid transpositions. Consider, as an illustration, the simple melodic fragment of Fig. 1. Though the two indicated phrases are clearly related, apparent in the score and to any listener, this is not by sharing an interval sequence, but rather an abstract contour sequence. The method described in this paper is able to naturally handle such musical phenomena with heterogeneous patterns discovered automatically using various viewpoints.

Fig. 1. First two phrases of the melody *Begiztatua nuen* (http://bdb.bertsozale.eus/en/web/doinutegia/view/137-begiztatua-nuen-euskaldun-makila). The two phrases are related by an abstract melodic contour relation and there is no transposition that carries one into the other.

The style chosen to model is the folk style of *bertsos*. These are improvised Basque songs, sung by *bertsolaris*, that respect various melodic and rhyming patterns and have fixed rhythmic structures. They can be classified into traditional folk melodies, new melodies, and melodies that are specifically composed. Bertso melodies usually have repeated and similar phrases, making them a challenge for statistical models and a good style for exploring the coherence problem. In this paper rhythmic aspects are conserved, so that generated melodies can be used with lyrics created for the original melody.

The corpus used for this study is the *Bertso Doinutegia*, a collection of bertso melodies compiled by Joanito Dorronsoro and published for the first time in 1995 [14]. It currently contains 2379 melodies and is maintained and updated every year by Xenpelar Dokumentazio Zentroa[1] with new melodies that were used in competitions and exhibitions. Scores in the collection were encoded in Finale and exported to MIDI. Metadata associated with each song includes the melody name, the name or type of the strophe, type of the melody, composer, bertsolari who has used it, name and location of the person who has collected the melody,

---

[1] http://bdb.bertsozale.eus/es/.

and year of the collection. Some of the melodies in the collection have links to recordings of exhibitions or competitions where those melodies were used.

2   Methods

The transformation process presented in this paper has five main components: viewpoint representation; pattern discovery applied to a template piece to identify similar segments; pattern ranking and covering to form the semiotic structure; statistical model construction; and generation from the statistical model.

2.1   Viewpoint Representation

To describe the template piece on different levels of abstraction a multiple viewpoint representation [9,12] is used. A *viewpoint* τ is a function that maps an event sequence $e_1, \ldots, e_\ell$ to a more abstract derived sequence $\tau(e_1), \ldots, \tau(e_\ell)$, comprising elements in the codomain of the function τ.

Table 1. Viewpoints used in this study.

Viewpoint	Codomain
pitch	$\{50, 52, 53, \ldots, 83\}$
dur	$\{1, 2, 3, \ldots\}$
onset	$\{0, 1, 2, \ldots\}$
intpc	$\{0, \ldots, 11\}$
int	$\{-14, -12, -11, \ldots, 14, 15, 17\}$
3pc	$\{d, eq, u\}$
5pc	$\{ld, sd, eq, su, lu\}$
d3pc	$\{d, eq, u\}$

Table 1 presents five melodic viewpoints pitch, int, intpc, 3pc and 5pc, and three rhythmic viewpoints dur, onset, and d3pc. The viewpoint pitch represents the MIDI number of each event; the viewpoint int computes the interval between an event and the preceding one; the viewpoint intpc computes the pitch class interval (interval modulo 12) between an event and the previous one. The three-point contour viewpoint 3pc computes the melodic contour between two events: upward (u), downward (d) or equal (eq); and the five-point contour viewpoint 5pc computes whether the contour between two contiguous events is more than a scale step down (ld), is one scale step down (sd), is more than a scale step up (lu), is one scale step up (su), or stays equal (eq). The three-point duration contour viewpoint d3pc computes if the duration of a note is shorter (d) than the previous one, longer (u) or equal (eq). The viewpoint representation of an example segment, using several viewpoints of Table 1, is shown in Fig. 2.

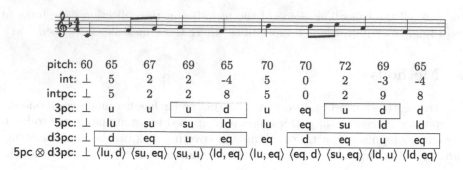

Fig. 2. A fragment from the melody *Abiatu da bere bidean* (http://bdb.bertsozale. eus/en/web/doinutegia/view/2627-abiatu-da-bere-bidean) and its viewpoint representation. Two patterns are highlighted.

To represent the interaction between melodic and rhythmic viewpoints, melodic viewpoints are *linked* with the rhythmic viewpoint d3pc. A linked viewpoint $\tau_1 \otimes \tau_2$ represents events as pairs of values from its constituent viewpoints τ_1 and τ_2. Each new linked viewpoint is used to represent the template piece independently; using the four melodic viewpoints of Table 1 we get four different linked viewpoints: pitch $\otimes$ d3pc, intpc $\otimes$ d3pc, 3pc $\otimes$ d3pc, and 5pc $\otimes$ d3pc. An example representation of one of these (5pc $\otimes$ d3pc) can be seen in Fig. 2. To establish the semiotic structure, pattern discovery is performed on the template piece for each linked viewpoint independently.

2.2 Patterns and Semiotic Structure

To construct a semiotic structure of a template piece it is necessary to identify interesting repeated patterns which provide a dense covering of the template piece. Patterns are defined as sequences of event features described using viewpoints, and an event sequence instantiates a pattern if the components of the pattern are instantiated by successive events in the sequence. More precisely, a pattern of length m is a structure $\tau:(v_1, \ldots, v_m)$, where τ is a viewpoint and the v_i are elements of the codomain of τ. For example, in Fig. 2 two simple patterns, each instantiated twice, are highlighted; 3pc:(u, d) and d3pc:(d, eq, u, eq).

Patterns in a template piece can be found by applying a sequential pattern discovery method [2,8] to each viewpoint representation of the template piece, identifying all patterns occurring more than once. This resulting list is then sorted according to an interestingness measure of patterns, and the ones that will form the coherence structure are chosen using a covering algorithm. These steps are described in the remainder of this section.

Pattern Distinctiveness and Ranking. Pattern interestingness is very important: in a given piece many patterns may exist but not all patterns are statistically or perceptually significant to a listener. For example, the 3pc pattern shown in Fig. 2 would likely be instantiated many times in any template piece, but its occurrences (simply three notes with an up-down contour motion) are probably not structurally related or distinctive to the template piece, while the d3pc pattern is more interesting. In order to build a good semiotic structure of the template piece, distinctive and interesting repetitions can be identified using a statistical method which provides the probability of seeing an indicated pattern at least the observed number of times in a template piece. Then a pattern is interesting if it occurs more frequently than expected. This is a standard model for assessing discovered motifs in music informatics [11] and bioinformatics [17].

More precisely, we derive a function $\mathbb{I}$ measuring the interest of a pattern. First, we note that the background probability p of finding a pattern $P = \tau$: $(v_1, \ldots, v_m)$ in a segment of exactly m events can be computed using a zero-order model of the corpus:

$$p = \prod_{i=1}^{m} \frac{c(v_i)}{c},$$

where $c(v_i)$ is the total number of occurrences of v_i (for viewpoint τ) in the corpus, and c is the total number of places in the corpus where the viewpoint τ is defined. Then the binomial distribution $\mathbb{B}(k; n, p)$ gives the probability of finding the pattern exactly k times in n events, and therefore interest of the pattern increases with the negative log probability of finding k or more occurrences of the pattern in a template piece:

$$\mathbb{I}(P) = -\ln \mathbb{B}_{\geq}(k; n, p), \tag{1}$$

where $\mathbb{B}_{\geq}$ is the upper tail of the binomial distribution, with $n = \ell - m + 1$ being the maximum number of positions where the pattern could possibly occur in the template piece.

Template Covering. Following pattern discovery, the template piece is covered by patterns, trying to use the most interesting patterns but also striving for a dense covering. Though finding a covering jointly optimal in those requirements is intractable, a greedy method can be used to rapidly find a reasonable semiotic structure. In the greedy covering method used in this study, discovered patterns are sorted from most to least interesting using Eq. 1, then this sorted list is processed to choose the patterns that fit into the positions of the template piece that have not yet been covered by any pattern, not allowing overlap between pattern instances.

Example. Figure 3 shows the pattern structure of the template *Erletxoak lorean*[2] after the covering process is shown, with patterns represented by the viewpoints pitch $\otimes$ d3pc and 3pc $\otimes$ d3pc. Above each pattern is the viewpoint name, the pattern label, and the $\mathbb{I}$ value in brackets.

---

[2] http://bdb.bertsozale.eus/en/web/doinutegia/view/241-erletxoak-lorean-orain-kantatuko-det-ii.

The template is a short piece with four phrases, having two sections in an overall $ABA'B$ structure. The music is syllabic with each phrase having 13 notes, in the key of Gm, briefly visiting B♭M in the third phrase (established at the high F♮). The B phrase is perfectly captured by a discovered pitch pattern, and though a few notes at the beginning of A and A' have not been covered by patterns, the discovered three-point contour pattern successfully captures the similarity between the second and fourth phrases. Note that there is no rigid transposition that relates these two phrases, but they have similar melodic contours that are related by more abstract viewpoint patterns.

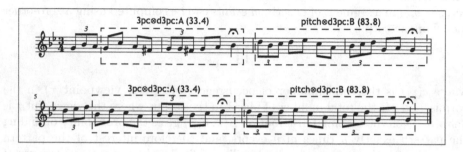

Fig. 3. Schema of a semiotic structure for the template piece *Erletxoak lorean*.

2.3 Statistical Model

The semiotic structure defines the structural coherence within the template piece that will be conserved. To generate into the structure, surface material is generated using a statistical model of the bertso corpus. In this work a trigram statistical model is built from a corpus to generate musical material into a template described by a semiotic structure. The exact probability of a piece using a trigram viewpoint model can be computed as described in [9]. Letting $v_i = \tau(e_i|e_{i-1})$ be the viewpoint τ value of event e_i in the context of its preceding event e_{i-1}, the probability of a piece $\mathbf{e} = e_1, \ldots, e_\ell$ is computed as:

$$\mathbb{P}(\mathbf{e}) = \prod_{i=3}^{\ell} \mathbb{P}(v_i|v_{i-1}, v_{i-2}) \times \mathbb{P}(e_i|v_i, e_{i-1}). \tag{2}$$

To elaborate, the product of all features in the sequence according to a trigram model is represented by the first term. Trigram probabilities of the viewpoint τ are computed from the entire corpus. The second term is the probability of the particular event given the feature, defined as a uniform distribution over events having the property v_i:

$$\mathbb{P}(e_i|v_i, e_{i-1}) = |\{x \in \xi : \tau(x|e_{i-1}) = v_i\}|^{-1},$$

where ξ is the set of possible pitches (see Table 1).

The model above can be applied for any viewpoint. To select a viewpoint for modelling stylistic aspects of the bertso corpus in this study, every melodic viewpoint presented in Sect. 2.1 was evaluated with leave-one-out cross validation. Probabilities of every piece, according to Eq. 2, were computed. Applied to the entire corpus of 2379 melodies, the product of all these probabilities gives a measure of the fit of the model to the corpus. The negative base-2 logarithm of this product is called the *cross-entropy* and lower cross-entropies are preferred. Every melodic viewpoint was tested, as were two linked melodic viewpoints intpc ⊗ 5pc and intpc ⊗ 3pc. The results of this procedure are shown in Table 2, which shows that the interval viewpoint int has the lowest cross-entropy on the corpus and is a good viewpoint to use for generation.

Table 2. Cross-entropy of different viewpoints, determined by leave-one-out cross validation on the corpus.

Viewpoint	Trigram model
3pc	4.45
pitch	2.62
int	2.55
intpc	3.83
5pc	3.38
intpc ⊗ 5pc	2.71
intpc ⊗ 3pc	3.13

2.4 Generation

To generate new pieces, a semiotic structure is used along with the trigram statistical model to generate new melodies. Generated sequences having high probability are assumed to retain more aspects of the music style under consideration than sequences with low probability. The process of *optimization* is concerned with drawing high probability sequences from statistical models.

A stochastic hill climbing optimization method is used to obtain high probability melodies. The method starts with a random piece that respects the coherence structure extracted from the template piece, using pitches from a pitch set ξ' that defines the admissible pitches for the generated piece. This set is typically the scale defined by the desired tonality of the generated piece and will be a subset of the complete pitch domain ξ. This initial piece is created with a left-to-right random walk, which samples a new note in every position of the template, and every time a complete pattern is instantiated, all of the future locations of the pattern are also instantiated, in this way conserving the original relation between them. The piece is then iteratively modified: in each iteration of the process a random location i in the current piece $\mathbf{e}$ is chosen. A pitch e_i is uniformly sampled from ξ' and is substituted into that position, producing a new piece $\mathbf{e}'$ with an updated probability $\mathbb{P}(\mathbf{e}')$. If $\mathbb{P}(\mathbf{e}') > \mathbb{P}(\mathbf{e})$, then $\mathbf{e}'$ is taken as the new current piece. Every time a position is changed, the pattern to which that note belongs is identified, and all other instances of that pattern are also updated. Thus at every iteration the generated piece conserves the semiotic structure. The optimization process is iterated up to 10^4 times, and after each update the probability of the new piece is computed using Eq. 2. If the new probability is higher than the last saved one the change is retained.

3   Results

To illustrate the generality of the method, new melodies are generated using two different templates, and properties of generated melodies are discussed. For the second template, two songs were performed and evaluated by an audience in a live concert setting in a jazz club in London.

3.1   Illustration on a Full Piece

The template used is *Erletxoak lorean*, which was discussed earlier in Fig. 3. The pitch vocabulary used is $\xi' = \{66, 67, 69, 70, 72, 74, 75, 77\}$ and two different viewpoints were used for the statistical model (Eq. 2): 5pc and int. The three transformations shown in Fig. 4 conserve the semiotic structure shown in Fig. 3. The first transformation contains within the B phrase a leap down by a diminished seventh, which though perhaps difficult to sing is interesting and is resolved properly by a step up. The A and A' phrases are somewhat reserved in their ambitus, though A contains an interesting ascending broken triad. The second transformation follows an overall smooth melodic contour and is a singable melody with internal coherence. Its shortcoming might be identified within the A' phrase which has a non-idiomatic leap which further exposes an F♯ and F♮ together in close proximity. This could be corrected by including another segmental viewpoint to ensure that the scale of each phrase is internally coherent. The final transformation of Fig. 4, generated with the int viewpoint as the statistical model, corrects to some extent the problems with excessive leaps of the general 5pc model, but is confined to a rather small ambitus.

3.2   London Concert and Listener Evaluation

A small suite of pieces was performed live in a public concert named "Meet the Computer Composer" at the Vortex Jazz Club in London on September 28, 2016. A bertso melody *Txoriak eta txoriburuak* was sung (by the first author IG) along with two generations that used the original as a template. The full scores of all three melodies can be seen in Fig. 5. Following the bertso tradition of new lyrics to existing melodies, the three melodies were sung each with the same new lyrics that were specially written for the concert.

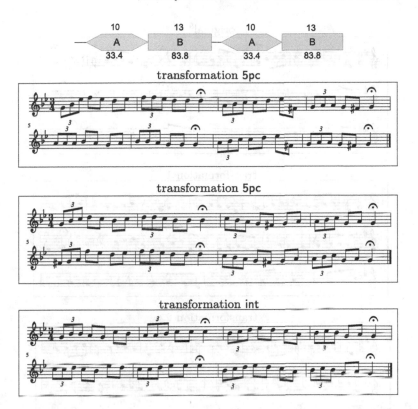

Fig. 4. Three transformations of the template piece *Erletxoak lorean*. Top: its semiotic structure with the number of notes in each pattern and their Ⅱ value. The first two transformations use a 5pc statistical model and the bottom one uses an int model.

An audience questionnaire (Table 3, top) was given at the beginning of the concert to all the members of the audience, where they would note which one of the three melodies they thought was the original, and how confident they were in their decision. A total of 52 questionnaires (from approximately 100 distributed) was returned. In Table 3 the results obtained from the questionnaires can be seen. The majority (55%) of respondents incorrectly identified one of the two transformations as the original piece, though the 44% identifying correctly the original had overall higher confidence in their decision. Regarding transformation 1, it must be noted that this was the first of three pieces performed, and the singer had not yet achieved perfect intonation: this no doubt affected the lower (15%, with 37.5% not confident in their response) audience result for that transformation.

Fig. 5. Three pieces performed at the London concert (http://bdb.bertsozale.eus/en/web/doinutegia/view/1564-txoriak-eta-txoriburuak).

Table 3. Top: the audience questionnaire distributed at the London concert. Bottom: results obtained. The original piece was the third melody sung.

> Which piece is the original?
> □1   □2   □3
>
> How confident are you on a scale of 1 to 5? (1=not confident, 5=very confident)
> □1   □2   □3   □4   □5

	transformation 1					transformation 2					original				
is original?	8 (15%)					21 (40%)					23 (44%)				
confidence	1	2	3	4	5	1	2	3	4	5	1	2	3	4	5
%	37.5	50	0	12.5	0	38	28.6	23.8	4.8	4.8	26	23.8	23.8	23.8	8.7

4   Conclusions and Future Work

In this paper a method for transforming bertso melodies conserving the internal coherence of a template piece is presented. The basis of the method is a trigram statistical model combined with the strong constraints provided by a semiotic structure, which is identified using a sequential pattern discovery algorithm followed by a pattern ranking and covering method. New musical content is created using the statistical model which iteratively changes a template piece to improve the final result.

The generation method presented in this paper extends the method of Collins et al. [6] in some important ways. Not restricted to patterns conserving exact intervals, the method here allows a heterogeneous semiotic structure comprising a variety of abstract viewpoints. The generated pieces are not single random walks from a model, rather some effort is made to generate high probability solutions which are expected to be more stylistically valid. The method can be extended to polyphony and some initial work in those directions has been completed for counterpoint generation in the style of Palestrina [20] and multilayer textures in electronic dance music [10].

Acknowledgments. This research was supported by the project Lrn2Cre8 (2013–2016) which was funded by the Future and Emerging Technologies (FET) programme within the Seventh Framework Programme for Research of the European Commission, under FET grant number 610859. The authors thank the Xenpelar Dokumentazio Zentroa for their enthusiasm in the project and for sharing the Bertso Doinutegia. Thanks to Kerstin Neubarth for valuable discussions on the research and the manuscript.

References

1. Allan, M., Williams, C.K.I.: Harmonising chorales by probabilistic inference. In: Neural Information Processing Systems, NIPS 2004, Vancouver, British Columbia, Canada, pp. 25–32 (2004)
2. Ayres, J., Flannick, J., Gehrke, J., Yiu, T.: Sequential PAttern Mining using a bitmap representation. In: Proceedings of the 8th ACM SIGKDD International Conference on Knowledge Discovery and Data Mining, KDD 2002, Edmonton, Alberta, Canada, pp. 429–435 (2002)
3. Bimbot, F., Deruty, E., Sargent, G., Vincent, E.: Semiotic structure labeling of music pieces: concepts, methods and annotation conventions. In: Proceedings of the 13th International Society for Music Information Retrieval Conference (ISMIR), Porto, Portugal, pp. 235–240 (2012). https://hal.inria.fr/hal-00758648
4. Boulanger-Lewandowski, N., Bengio, Y., Vincent, P.: Modeling temporal dependencies in high-dimensional sequences: application to polyphonic music generation and transcription. In: International Conference on Machine Learning, Edinburgh, Scotland (2012)
5. Brooks, F.P., Hopkins, Jr., A.L., Neumann, P.G., Wright, W.V.: An experiment in musical composition. IRE Trans. Electron. Comput. **EC-5**, 175–182 (1956)
6. Collins, T., Laney, R., Willis, A., Garthwaite, P.H.: Developing and evaluating computational models of musical style. Artif. Intell. Eng. Des. Anal. Manuf. **30**, 16–43 (2016). http://journals.cambridge.org/article_S0890060414000687

7. Conklin, D.: Music generation from statistical models. In: Proceedings of the AISB 2003 Symposium on Artificial Intelligence and Creativity in the Arts and Sciences, Aberystwyth, Wales, pp. 30–35 (2003)
8. Conklin, D.: Discovery of distinctive patterns in music. Intell. Data Anal. **14**(5), 547–554 (2010)
9. Conklin, D.: Chord sequence generation with semiotic patterns. J. Math. Music. **10**(2), 92–106 (2016)
10. Conklin, D., Bigo, L.: Trance generation by transformation. In: Proceedings of the 8th International Workshop on Music and Machine Learning, at the 21st International Symposium on Electronic Art, Vancouver, Canada, pp. 4–6 (2015)
11. Conklin, D., Weisser, S.: Pattern and antipattern discovery in Ethiopian Bagana songs. In: Meredith, D. (ed.) Computational Music Analysis, pp. 425–443. Springer, Cham (2016). https://doi.org/10.1007/978-3-319-25931-4_16
12. Conklin, D., Witten, I.H.: Multiple viewpoint systems for music prediction. J. New Music. Res. **24**(1), 51–73 (1995)
13. Cope, D.: An expert system for computer-assisted composition. Comput. Music. J. **11**(4), 30–46 (1987)
14. Dorronsoro, J.: Bertso Doinutegia. Euskal Herriko Bertsolari Elkartea (1995)
15. Dubnov, S., Assayag, G., Lartillot, O., Bejerano, G.: Using machine-learning methods for musical style modeling. Computer **36**(10), 73–80 (2003)
16. Hedges, S.A.: Dice music in the eighteenth century. Music Lett. **59**(2), 180–187 (1978). http://www.jstor.org/stable/734136
17. van Helden, J., André, B., Collado-Vides, J.: Extracting regulatory sites from the upstream region of yeast genes by computational analysis of oligonucleotide frequencies. J. Mol. Biol. **281**(5), 827–842 (1998)
18. Leach, J., Fitch, J.: Nature, music, and algorithmic composition. Comput. Music. J. **19**(2), 23–33 (1995). https://doi.org/10.2307/3680598
19. Meyer, L.B.: Meaning in music and information theory. J. Aesthet. Art Crit. **15**, 412–424 (1957)
20. Padilla, V., Conklin, D.: Statistical generation of two-voice florid counterpoint. In: Proceedings of the Sound and Music Computing Conference (SMC 2016), Hamburg, Germany, pp. 380–387 (2016)
21. Quick, D., Hudak, P.: Grammar-based automated music composition in Haskell. In: Proceedings of the 1st ACM SIGPLAN Workshop on Functional Art, Music, Modeling & Design, FARM 2013, Boston, Massachusetts, USA, pp. 59–70 (2013)

The Comprovisador's Real-Time Notation Interface (Extended Version)

Pedro Louzeiro[1,2,3]([✉])

[1] Universidade de Évora, Évora, Portugal
pedrolouzeiro@gmail.com
[2] Centro de Estudos de Sociologia e Estética Musical (CESEM), Lisbon, Portugal
[3] Fundação para a Ciência e a Tecnologia (FCT), Lisbon, Portugal

Abstract. Comprovisador is a system designed to enable real-time mediated soloist-ensemble interaction, through machine listening, algorithmic procedures and dynamic staff-based notation. It uses multiple networked computers – one host and several clients – to perform algorithmic compositional procedures with the music material improvised by a soloist and to coordinate the musical response of an ensemble. Algorithmic parameters are manipulated by a conductor/composer who mediates the interaction between soloist and ensemble, making compositional decisions in real-time. The present text, an extended version of a paper presented at CMMR 2018, in Matosinhos, focuses on the notation interface of this system, after overviewing its concept and structure. A discussion is made on how rehearsals and live performances impacted the development of the interface.

Keywords: Comprovisation · Dynamic notation
Performance mediation · Musical improvisation
Real-time algorithmic composition · Network musical performance
Graphical interface

1 Introduction

The musical motivations that drove the development of Comprovisador are discussed by the author in a recently published paper [21] which focuses on the compositional procedures in place. In short, the goal was to enable soloist-ensemble interaction expressed as a coordinated (composed) ensemble response to an improvisation as a way to join the broad concepts of improvisation and composition. Additional levels of interactivity were envisaged through mediation – manipulation of algorithmic parameters – and a feedback loop – the soloist's reaction to the ensemble's response.

1.1 Concept

In broad terms, Comprovisador is able to listen to an improvisation, decoding pitches, intervals and durations, and facilitate the creation of different musical

© Springer Nature Switzerland AG 2018
M. Aramaki et al. (Eds.): CMMR 2017, LNCS 11265, pp. 489–508, 2018.
https://doi.org/10.1007/978-3-030-01692-0_33

responses through algorithmic compositional procedures. These procedures are controlled in real-time, performed from a hardware terminal. The outcome of such procedures is displayed to players in the form of an animated staff-based score, viewed in a computer screen. Wireless connectivity, which allows real-time communication of score data, also makes it possible to place computers – and, therefore, musicians – apart from each other, allowing non-standard spacial settings.

1.2   Background

This system can be framed in four different areas of computer music: (1) computer-assisted composition, (2) improvised music with human-machine interaction, (3) dynamic musical notation and (4) networked music performance.

With examples from as far back as the 1950's, computer-assisted composition (CAC) consists of a compositional practice that uses algorithmic procedures performed by a computer, typically in deferred-time [9].

Regarding human-machine interaction systems, the main difference in relation to Comprovisador lies in the type of output: in most of these systems, the computer interacts directly with the musician, outputting electro-acoustic sounds[1]. In the case of Comprovisador, the computer coordinates the musical response by an ensemble of musicians who sight-read a generated score.

Since the late 90's, dynamic musical notation has been increasingly used in real-time music systems enabling various kinds of new interactive features [12]. Recent technological developments (such as tablets, laptops or video projectors) facilitate its implementation. Regarding software, advancements have been made which allow the use of staff-based notation in real-time applications. Among these we find MaxScore [8], INScore [11] and bach: automated composer's helper [2]. Still, many approaches to dynamic notation tend to use animated graphic scores [12,16,23] and other kinds of non-staff notation[2]. Such approaches have a visual level that can be in itself an aesthetic goal, since it is common to have the animated notation projected for audiences to see. Also, these approaches rely on the improvisational skills of all performers to make their own interpretation of the score whereas Comprovisador – apart from the soloist (or soloists) – requires more traditional sight-reading skills from the ensemble performers, since it is based on staff notation. This concertino-ripieno kind of function separation – one of the key aspects of Comprovisador – seems to be uncommon among other real-time notation work.

Networked music performance is another practice that has emerged in the recent decades thanks to the development of computer network technologies and the creativity of musicians [15]. It consists on performance situations where a

---

[1] Such is the case of "OMax", a computer program capable of learning in real-time the typical characteristics of a musician's improvisational style, as well as to play with him, in an interactive way [3].

[2] For example, Jason Freeman used colored LED light tubes to convey pitch and dynamics information to performers, in his work "Glimmer" [12].

group of musicians interact over a local or wide area network. This interaction can be achieved, for example, by audio streaming, score rendering or strategies for graphical direction. Among systems that use the latter, the main strategies consist on scrolling the score from right to left under a fixed vertical line, or having a fixed score and a cursor which moves horizontally [17]. For Comprovisador, a new strategy was developed in which a bouncing ball is responsible for synchronizing attacks and/or conveying a pulse (see Sect. 4).

On an aesthetic level, besides the four areas mentioned above, the development of Comprovisador has drawn inspiration from gesture languages for real-time composition and conducted group improvisation (with no computers involved) such as Walter Thompson's "Soundpainting" [25] and Lawrence "Butch" Morris's "Conduction"[3]. In fact, the author's personal experience as a performer[4] in this field has motivated the conceptualization of some of the system's features. The advantages of using a computer system in this type of practice are in terms of control over pitch (thanks to staff notation) and space distribution (thanks to wireless network connectivity).

2   System Structure

2.1   Hardware

To be fully operational, Comprovisador needs the following hardware equipment (see Fig. 1):

① a [number of] microphone(s) – to capture the improvisation of the soloist(s) (only necessary for non-MIDI instruments);
② an audio/MIDI interface – to convert the analog signal of the microphone(s) into digital signal and/or to input raw MIDI data;
③ a host computer – which receives input from the interface and performs compositional procedures;
④ a control surface – through which algorithm parameters are manipulated;
⑤ a wireless router – which establishes communication between computers; and
⑥ a number of client computers – to render and display the animated score to the musicians in the ensemble.

Optionally, a tablet may be used by the mediator to control a messenger module – via Miraweb [4]. Also, the soloist can use a web browser enabled device to receive messages (e.g.: messages related to musical form). Ensemble members will view messages in their respective client computers.

---

[3] Before coining the term "Conduction", Morris had used the term "Comprovisation" to define his performance practice [24]. This term (to which "Comprovisador" is a Portuguese derivative) was later used by authors such as Richard Dudas [10] and Sandeep Bhagwati [5] in other contexts but nonetheless referring to musical performance practices where both composed and improvised elements coexist.

[4] Pedro Louzeiro is a member of the Lisbon Soundpainting Orchestra.

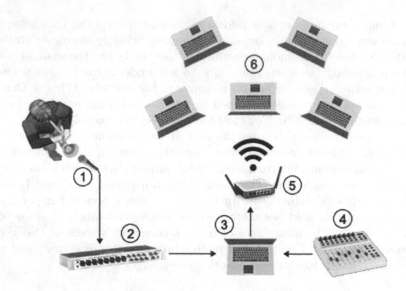

Fig. 1. Comprovisador: hardware setup.

Typically, one client computer is used for every two performers. In some cases, though, it is convenient to use one computer for each performer (see Sect. 4). For intonation purposes, there is a feature for singers that enables them cue sounds through a set of earphones. This feature requires one computer for every singer.

The system is fully reconfigurable regarding instrumentation of the ensemble, in regards to number, transposition and range, as will be seen in Sect. 2.2. According to our testing in real-world conditions, it is compatible with Mac OSX and Windows systems. Machines with 64-bit processors, dedicated graphics processors (for optimal OpenGL rendering) and 13″ or greater displays are recommended.

2.2 Software

Software for this system is being developed in Max 7 [22], with extensive use of Bach library [2] for its notation features, CAC tools and Max integration. The system consists of two applications: one which runs on the host computer and another which is instantiated on each of the client computers.

The host application is responsible for receiving and analyzing the input from the soloist(s), calculating the compositional procedures and responding to commands from the conductor/composer. The client application is in charge of rendering the generated score and displaying it to the musicians.

Host Application. It consists of multiple modules (see Fig. 2), namely:

pitch tracker – here, musical notes played by the soloist are deciphered in real-time from the digital audio signal input;

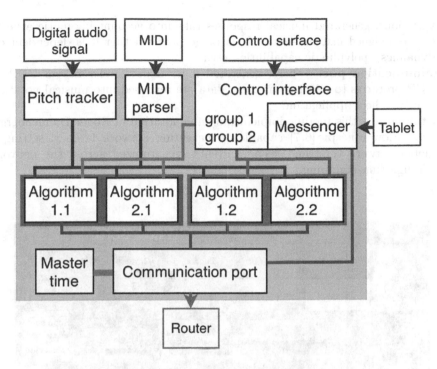

Fig. 2. Comprovisador: host application overview.

MIDI parser – in the case of MIDI enabled instruments, a MIDI parsing module is used instead of the pitch tracker; both polyphonic and multi-channel input are accepted;

control interface[5] – this module consists of two control groups containing a total of four slots for algorithms; algorithmic parameters are manipulated in real-time by the conductor/composer; the control interface provides graphical feedback for all commands performed on the external control surface (mirroring) and it is possible to store and recall parameter presets; it also provides information to its operator about ongoing algorithmic procedures;

messenger – inside the control interface lies a Miraweb [4] enabled submodule through which messages (both predefined and written on-the-fly) can be sent to players; with just one click (or tap, if a tablet is used), message recipients can be selected according to their family or group assignment (see Fig. 3);

compositional algorithms – there are two distinct algorithms – Harmony and Contour – which are instantiated in all four slots of the control groups (each slot can host any of the two algorithms); instruments can be assigned to any of these four instances, which work in parallel; each algorithm generates different musical responses (broadly, chords and melodic contours) when receiving pitch and parametric data; furthermore, each algorithm has two main

---

[5] A paper discussing the control interface module and its application in mediating a comprovisation performance was presented at ICMC 2017 [20].

variations; generated musical responses take into account idiomatic aspects of the assigned instruments such as range (and whether it is dependent on dynamics), polyphonic capabilities, etc.;

communication port – here, generated musical data are sent via UDP or TCP protocols to client computers; data are rendered into musical notation in every client application;

master time – this module implements an adaptation of Roger Dannenberg's Time-Flow concept [6,7] capable of measuring network latency, setting a global network time and keeping events synchronized across the network through time-stamping.

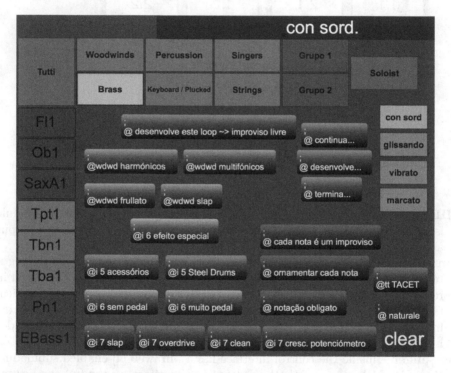

Fig. 3. Comprovisador: messenger window (Miraweb enabled). Tapping/clicking a family or group (e.g.: Brass) selects all relevant instruments. Tapping/clicking a predefined message (e.g.: "con sord") sends it to selected instruments.

Many aspects of the host application – communication port as well as parts of algorithms and control interface – are automatically configured on startup. This is done by means of a script that looks up an instrumentation list in crossed-reference to an instrumentation dictionary, both stored in text files. The former consists of a simple list of the instruments to be used in a session while the latter contains a large set of information pertaining to each instrument (family, range, transposition, clef, dynamic range mapping, strings tuning, initial IP port number, etc.).

Client Application. In addition to notation rendering, the client application also carries out some algorithmic tasks that could in theory be performed by the host application. Examples of such tasks include the quantization used in the Quantum Loop mode (see Sect. 4.2) and the transposition required for all transposing instruments. The goal of this task decentralization is to unburden the host computer's CPU and to keep the wireless data traffic as lightweight as possible.

Another important feature of the client application is the Practice Tool. Initially, this tool was developed in order to enable performers to get acquainted with the system's notation interface and its idiosyncrasies. This way, even before the first rehearsal, performers are able to experience sight-reading in a simulated performance context, being subject to unpredictable note patterns (thanks to a random walk algorithm) and to a specific cuing strategy – the bouncing ball. Moreover, this tool can play a significant role in a new way of improving sight-reading skills[6], in a broader educational context.

The client application is structured as follows (see Fig. 4):

UDP/TCP parser – arriving network data gets appropriately parsed;

slave time – this module is the client counterpart of the host's **master time** module; it enables local prediction of global time between global time updates;

message renderer – arriving messages are displayed in the notation interface;

transposer – pitch information is separated from other score data and transposed, if required, before being rendered as notation;

practice mode interface – an interface that lets the user manipulate algorithmic parameters for the practice mode; with this tool, the user can customize the level of difficulty of the generated score, for practice purposes;

generative algorithms – the stochastic behavior of these algorithms intends to emulate performance situations;

notation renderers – notes and their durations are set in place, according to rules of the active algorithm; these modules also control the audio renderer and the behavior of the bouncing ball;

quantizer – whenever a musical phrase needs to be quantized (in order to be presented in standard rhythmic notation) this module is activated;

audio renderer – for singers or for general practice, this module renders to sound the notation generated in real-time; provided there is enough time between notes, singers may listen in advance to sounds as cues for upcoming notes;

notation interface – see Sect. 4.

---

[6] A paper entitled "Improving Sight-Reading Skills through Dynamic Notation – the Case of Comprovisador" exploring this issue shall be presented at TENOR 2018 conference, taking place in Montreal, Canada.

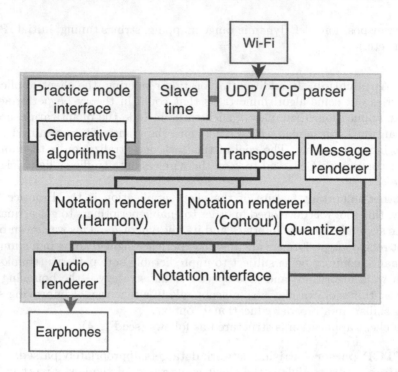

Fig. 4. Comprovisador: client application overview.

3   Real-World Testing

Since 2015, Comprovisador has been used in public performances in eight different occasions, involving close to 100 musicians. A/V recordings of most of these performances can be accessed through the project's website: https://comprovisador.wordpress.com/ [18].

Each performance has been preceded by development stages and short periods of rehearsal. Development choices and feature enhancement were only possible thanks to the feedback of musicians who tested the system in these real-world situations. In "Comprovisação nº 5" (see below), the rehearsal stage spanned over a four-month period of weekly rehearsals with an ensemble consisting of 12 students from the Lisbon College of Music (ESML) (flute, oboe, alto saxophone, tenor trombone, bass trombone, tuba, electric bass, marimba, piano, two singers – soprano and mezzo – and violin) and served as a test field for ongoing development with frequent discussion over musician experience.

It is fair to say that every public performance has served as a developmental milestone, every time leading the system towards its maturity. Following bellow are a few examples of such milestones as well as problems that were identified and opportunities they created for further development.

"Comprovisação nᵒ 1"

May 2015, Composition Week, ESML. This first performance was important for demonstrating proof of concept. Five composition algorithms were designed, among which 'Harmony' and 'Contour'. The other three were later deemed unnecessary, as these two were further developed. The system was initially designed for a fixed, "hardcoded" instrumentation and featured limited control over algorithmic parameters.

The notation interface contained two side-by-side notation viewers (serving a pair of musicians from each laptop) which were found to be too narrow to accommodate longer musical gestures (see Fig. 5). Also, a note scrolling approach was used but came to be uncomfortable for reading due to jitter – musicians reported.

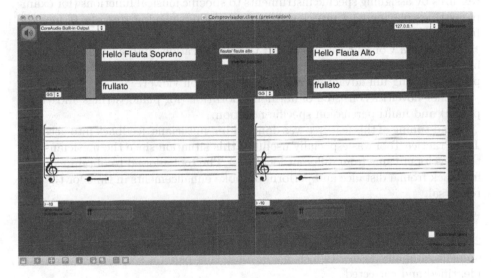

Fig. 5. Comprovisador.client: old notation interface (as of "Comprovisação nᵒ 1").

"Comprovisação nᵒ 2"

May 2016, Composition Week, ESML. The longest period of time between two performances ran between the first and the second, during which a great deal of changes to the system took place. Those changes enabled flexible instrumentation through auto-configuration features (see Sect. 2) and increased control over algorithmic parameters. Wide notation viewers (on top of each other) were implemented and the note scrolling approach was replaced by one where the notes wrap around to the beginning of the staff. A visual synchronization strategy consisting of a bouncing ball (further discussed in Sect. 4) was implemented using the `drawsprite` feature of Max object `lcd`.

During the performance, some stability issues were brought out by the large number of participating musicians (30) and client computers (16). The causes were discovered later. The lack of a preset mechanism to help in coping with the increase of controllable parameters was also felt.

"Comprovisação nᵒ 3"

2016, Festival Música Viva, O'Culto, Lisbon. A rudimentary preset system and slightly better control over rhythm were set in place. This performance featured electro-acoustic manipulation of the sound of the solo instrument – xylophone – made by a dedicated performer through a discrete system.

"Comprovisação nᵒ 4"

2016, Sound and Music Computing Conference, Kampnagel, Hamburg. For this performance, parallel algorithm running and separated control groups were implemented. These features allowed for richer and better structured musical textures by assigning specific instruments to specific musical functions (for example, strings playing long *mp* chords and woodwinds playing *staccato ff* melodic fragments).

Algorithm Contour was upgraded to take durations into account and other improvements which made it possible to capture and display longer musical phrases, taking full advantage of the wide notation viewer.

Other novelties consisted of harmonic notation (for piano, strings and vibraphone) and multi-percussion specific notation.

Fine-tuning of this features was done taking musicians' feedback into account. The Practice Tool was especially useful in this situation since the musicians and the developer came from different locations. The tool allowed to obtain valuable feedback from a distance and perform bespoke enhancements in time for the first rehearsal.

"Comprovisação nᵒ 5"

2017, ESML. As a result of a longer period of rehearsals and ongoing development, stability issues (which go beyond this paper's scope) were properly identified and corrected.

New features include quantization/standard rhythmic notation and further enhancement of algorithms including cross-algorithm tempo synchronization. Algorithmically generated lyrics text was also implemented and used, granting all singers with the same phonemes for simultaneous notes. This has proven to be an interesting aesthetic feature as was assessed during rehearsals and performance. Multiple soloists and a non-standard spacial setting (musicians played in two stairways, over 50 m apart from each other) were two key features of this performance.

An especially important aspect consisted in the development of (1) an improved preset mechanism, as well as (2) a Miraweb [4] enabled messenger module. The former allowed musical form to be planed ahead which in turn enabled a greater level of readiness for interaction, from the mediator's standpoint. The latter made it possible to quickly choose a group of recipients (according to instrument family, for example, or to group assignment) and send them a message (usually a technique term or instruction).

Yet one problem remained to be solved: synchronization (which is never perfect in a real-time composition network environment based on sight-reading) was sometimes undermined by poor graphics processing in some of the available computers. This caused the bouncing ball to be rendered at a low frame rate which had a noticeable impact on the timing accuracy of players. As of "Comprovisação nº 4", the lcd approach had been replaced with a jsui object using MGraphics system [14], but was found not to have made a significant difference and, in some cases, performance seemed even worse.

"Comprovisação nº 6"

2017, II European Saxophone Congress (EurSax'17), Casa da Música, Porto. To improve synchronization, a complete reconstruction of the notation interface using OpenGL hardware acceleration – which will be detailed in Sect. 4 – was undertaken. It was home tested by a number of musicians who agreed to continue collaborating in the project after "Comprovisação nº 5" and used in performance since "Comprovisação nº 6". Reconstruction had to account for the fact that layering of different graphical Max objects with transparent background would no longer be possible. Thus, all graphical features (with exception of the notation objects) had to be integrated in OpenGL programming, which turned out to be beneficial towards all aspects of the interface (not just synchronization), according to musicians' reports.

The preset module was further improved, alongside the messenger module. Since "Comprovisação nº 6", it is possible to automatically send a set of individualized messages whenever a new preset is called. This is an effective tool for managing musical form, where instructions can be simultaneously sent to all performers (including the soloist) concerning their specific role in a given musical context.

"Comprovisação nº 7"

2017, IV Peças Frescas Açores Festival, Colégio Church, Ponta Delgada. This performance for nine singers, five instruments and solo saxophone used 14 client computers in a successful way. Singers sang from the choir loft and instrumentalists were positioned in different points of the altar and lateral naves.

Microtonal notation was used for singers, with the aid of earphones to ensure good intonation, enabling the use of spectral harmony (listen to minutes 11'12"–12'57" of the A/V recording: https://youtu.be/kJfqNoDQnPM?t=672).

"Comprovisação nº 8"

2017, Symposium on Computer Music Multidisciplinary Research (CMMR), Real Vinícola, Matosinhos. In this performance, seven musicians (four saxophones, piano, electric bass and steel drums) were positioned around the audience. All seven were sight-readers but four of them were also improvisers, alternating between the roles of soloist and regular ensemble member. Microtonality was also used with the saxophones.

4   Notation Interface

4.1   Overview

The notation interface was conceived in order to have one client computer for every two instruments, regardless of range or transposition of the instruments used. In some cases it is preferable to use a single instrument per computer configuration.

Graphical objects of the interface adjust perfectly to every modern laptop computer screen, independently of the configuration used. This is achieved using JavaScript inside Max 7 to instantiate and position all graphical objects.

Fig. 6. Comprovisador.client: dual-instrument layout.

Video examples of the notation interface are provided via the following URL: https://comprovisador.wordpress.com/notation-examples/ [19].

Comparing layouts of the two different configurations (see video examples 1 and 2 from the page linked above and Figs. 6 and 7), we see that there are some advantages in single instrument layout. On one hand, multi-staves can be used, whereas on the other, both dynamics (under the staff) and direction (over the staff) bars can assume larger dimensions, ensuring faster information detectability and better legibility, being these good principles of graphical interface design [1]. This space optimization was motivated by musicians' suggestions and was found to have a positive impact in performance.

The notation objects consist of a combination of `bach.roll` and `bach.score` objects. While the former renders proportional durations, the latter renders standard rhythmic notation [2].

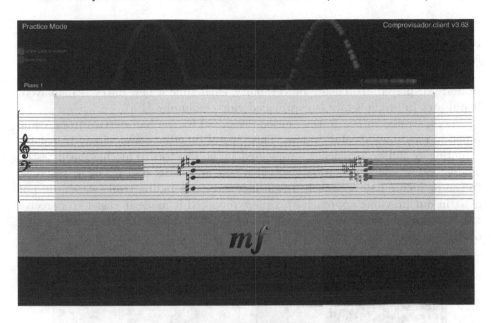

Fig. 7. Comprovisador.client: single-instrument layout.

The dynamics bar is a colored bar rendered in OpenGL over which dynamics text is displayed. Again, regarding good principles of graphical interface design, both background color and text size (3D space) change accordingly to the level of dynamics, in a reactive fashion. The color that symbolizes *pppp* is cyan and the one attributed to *ffff* is red. Any level in between will assume a proportional mixture of the two colors, maintaining the same perceived level of brightness.

Concerning text, whenever the level is being changed, the words *cresc.* or *dim.* appear and move forward or backward in a three-dimensional space (see Fig. 8). This feature is achieved using OpenGL (namely, Jitter object `jit.gl.text3d` [22].

These reactive features were highly valued by musicians who reported being able to easily identify the dynamic level while keeping full focus on the musical notes.

Fig. 8. Comprovisador.client: dynamics bar – text size (3D space) and background color. (Color figure online)

Regarding the direction bar, it also features OpenGL graphics in order to render at a high frame rate (around 60 fps) a small bouncing ball which allows for musicians to synchronize attacks and play in a given tempo.

Using the same OpenGL context, musical direction terms and other information are displayed. To ensure detectability, each time a new entry is displayed, it pulsates in bright white (see provided video examples [19]).

As illustrated in Fig. 9, the motion described by the ball derives from a sine function returning absolute values. This type of function convincingly translates a motion of fall and ricochet, often used by conductors. This has been tested against other synchronization strategies and musicians had a better response to the bouncing ball approach. Regarding the ball's fading trail (which did not exist in our previous approaches), testers reported it made it easier to perceive the bouncing motion (and the moment of impact) especially when not looking directly at the object.

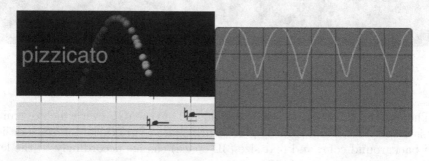

Fig. 9. Comprovisador.client: direction bar (left) Vs. "folded" sine wave (right).

4.2 Reading Modes

There are four different reading modes or directives, corresponding to the two variations of each of the algorithms. The modes and their characteristics are (see corresponding video examples from the provided link [19]):

In Sync with Green Ball – Harmony, Variation 1

- proportional notation;
- notes are written in real-time, from left to right;
- the player should begin each sound precisely as the ball aligns vertically with the note and changes direction (i.e. when it "hits" the note);
- a reading time window of about a second and a half is calculated so that the player has time to read and prepare each note on their instrument;
- when a note or its duration line stretches off the play region (a fixed darker rectangular area which represents a domain of 5 s), it reappears at the beginning of the same play region – this feature replaces traditional page turning;

Fig. 10. Comprovisador.client: orange ball (passive gesture) and grid (underlying tempo). (Color figure online)

- notes that have already been played are erased in order to free staff space for new notes to be written;
- the ball will move horizontally over a long note's duration line, stopping at its end or bouncing to the next note, if there is one.

In Sync with Green Ball (Grid) – Harmony, Variation 2

- the same as explained above except for the fact that there is an underlying metronomic tempo for all attacks;
- a grid representing the underlying tempo is shown in the staff (see Figs. 9 left and 10);
- during long notes or rests, instead of moving horizontally or disappearing, the ball continues to bounce in tempo assuming an orange color instead, while the vertical amplitude of its movement is reduced – thus, simulating a conductor's passive gesture of tempo keeping [13]; whenever a response from the player is demanded (active gesture) the ball becomes green again and bounces higher;

Loop (Non-Sync) – Contour, Variation 1

- proportional notation;
- melodic contours appears, all notes at once;
- the player should loop through the notes framed inside the play region which in this case can be dynamically adjusted to any arbitrary portion of the displayed melody (refer to Fig. 6);

– a vertical green line (play line) cycles through the play region so to give the player an idea of the intended playing rate, although to synchronize with the line is not mandatory;
– above all, the player should not attempt to synchronize with their fellow musicians; in fact, there is an intended rate discrepancy in each client's play line in order to help avoid synchronization between players.

Quantum Loop – Contour, Variation 2

– standard rhythmic notation;
– quantized melodic contours appears, all notes at once, fitted in two 4/4 measures[7];
– the player should play in tempo with the green ball, which in this case aims at the beginning of every beat of a measure (instead of at every note);
– instruments assigned to the same control group will always be in the same beat of the same measure and in the same tempo – hence, they should play in sync;
– when two instruments are assigned to different control groups[8], one of three possibilities may occur: (1) both instruments are in sync; (2) both instruments are in the same tempo but in different positions within the loop (which may differ in size) or (3) the two instruments are in different tempi.

5 Future Work

Currently, we are working on a number of improvements on the notation interface, most of which are already developed but need further testing. Such is the case of the Time-Flow adaptation mentioned in Sect. 2.2 which was implemented to further improve synchronization. Testing was carried out in two sessions with an ensemble and preliminary results were encouraging. Final results shall be published soon.

Regarding note appearance, after many requests from the musicians, the color of the duration line was changed to translucent green in order not to be mistaken for either staff lines or ledger lines (see Fig. 11). Also, we can now use breakpoints in the duration lines in order to represent glissando approximations.

In regards to rhythm, standard notation was enhanced at the quantizer level. Here, instead of writing two 4/4 measures, the algorithm writes eight 1/4 measures (see Figs. 12 and 13). This allows two things: (1) complex patterns are conveniently delineated by bar lines and thus easier to decipher; (2) long notes unfold into tied quarter notes, making it easier to count the beats – which is

---

[7] As a result of recent changes implemented in version 3.85 (explained in Sect. 5), quantization will now aim at eight 1/4 measures.

[8] See new video example of the score in action, made with versions 3.83 and 3.85 of Comprovisador.client (minutes 3'36"–4'09" – this section was made with version 3.83):
   https://youtu.be/MEMxpHCJa4s?t=216 [18].

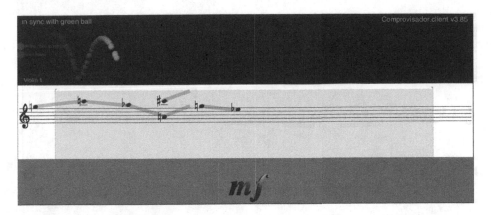

Fig. 11. Comprovisador.client: In Sync with Green Ball (v3.85) – translucent duration lines with breakpoints.

especially important when a loop is set in a way that a long note becomes truncated. In Fig. 13, we can see this happening: there are three tied quarter notes that would otherwise be written as a dotted half note. The loop region is truncating the 3rd quarter note. If it was written as two 4/4 measures, the loop region would end in an ambiguous, white portion of the measure, corresponding to the duration of the dot, which would be confusing for the reader.

Future developments shall include articulation signs and other features that will be made available in the upcoming Bach version. Among these features is an algorithm for respelling accidentals in a more musical way, in atonal contexts.

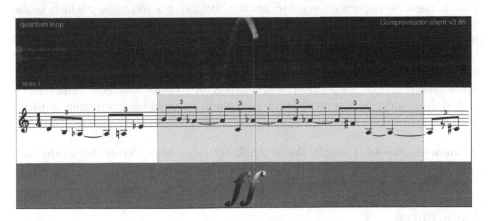

Fig. 12. Comprovisador.client: Quantum Loop (v3.85) – triplets.

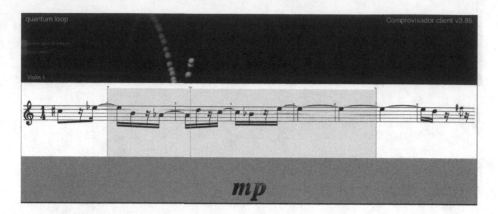

Fig. 13. Comprovisador.client: Quantum Loop (v3.85) – sixteenths.

6 Conclusions

We have been developing Comprovisador since 2015 and we are glad to begin to see in it signs of maturity. The performances that were carried out and the rehearsal stages that preceded them – in particular, the four-month stage at ESML – were crucial for identifying and correcting problems both on the technical and musical side. Throughout the latest performances, the system has proven to work in a reliable fashion with the available hardware and with a range of skills suitable for college level students up to professional musicians Furthermore, we find our musical goals are being achieved.

It has been found that poor graphics performance on slower machines could have a negative impact on synchronization. By using a technology which takes advantage of hardware acceleration (OpenGL) we were able to reverse those impacts and favor information detectability and legibility.

We hope that the latest improvements made to the notation interface – and the ones planned for the near future – will be welcomed by musicians and help make this real-time notation system a powerful tool for engaging improvisers and sight-readers in comprovisation performances yielding interesting musical outcomes.

Acknowledgments. I should like to thank my supervisors Christopher Bochmann and António de Sousa Dias for their advice and continued support. This research is supported by FCT by means of a PhD studentship (POCH/EU).

References

1. User Interface Design (2015). https://en.wikipedia.org/wiki/User_interface_design. Accessed 20 Aug 2015
2. Agostini, A., Ghisi, D.: A max library for musical notation and computer-aided composition. Comput. Music. J. **39**(2), 11–27 (2015). https://doi.org/10.1162/COMJ_a_00296

3. Assayag, G., Bloch, G., Chemillier, M., Lévy, B., Dubnov, S.: Omax (2015). http://repmus.ircam.fr/omax/home. Accessed 04 Apr 2017
4. Benson, A.: Content You Need: Miraweb (2016). https://cycling74.com/articles/content-you-need-miraweb. Accessed 13 Apr 2017
5. Bhagwati, S.: Notational perspective and comprovisation. In: de Assis, P., Brooks, W., Coessens, K. (eds.) Sound & Score: Essays on Sound, Score and Notation, pp. 165–177. Leuven University Press, Leuven (2013)
6. Brandt, E., Dannenberg, R.B.: Time in Distributed Real-time Systems. Carnegie Mellon University (1999). http://repository.cmu.edu/compsci/498/
7. Dannenberg, R.B.: Time-flow concepts and architectures for music and media synchronization. In: Proceedings of the 43rd International Computer Music Conference, Shanghai, pp. 104–109 (2017). https://www.cs.cmu.edu/~rbd/papers/timeflow2017.pdf
8. Didkovsky, N., Hajdu, G.: MaxScore: music notation in Max/MSP. In: Proceedings of the International Computer Music Conference, Belfast (2008)
9. Dodge, C., Jerse, T.: Computer Music: Synthesis, Composition, and Performance. Schirmer Books, New York (1997). https://books.google.pt/books?id=eY_BQgAACAAJ
10. Dudas, R.: Comprovisation: the various facets of composed improvisation within interactive performance systems. Leonardo Music J. **20**, 29–31 (2010)
11. Fober, D., Daudin, C., Letz, S., Orlarey, Y.: Partitions musicales augmentées. In: Actes des Journées d'Informatique Musicale, Rennes (2010)
12. Freeman, J.: Extreme sight-reading, mediated expression, and audience participation: real-time music notation in live performance. Comput. Music J. **32**(3), 25–41 (2008). http://www.jstor.org/stable/40072645
13. Green, E., Gibson, M.: The expressive gestures. In: The Modern Conductor, 7th edn. Pearson Prentice Hall, Upper Saddle River (2004)
14. Grosse, D.: JSUI-MGraphics Patch-A-Day (2011). https://cycling74.com/forums/jsui-mgraphics-patch-a-day. Accessed 23 Apr 2017
15. Hajdu, G., Didkovsky, N.: On the evolution of music notation in network music environments. Contemp. Music. Rev. **28**(4–5), 395–407 (2009). https://doi.org/10.1080/07494460903422313
16. Hope, C., Vickery, L.: The decibel scoreplayer – digital tool for reading graphic notation. In: International Conference on Technologies for Music Notation and Representation, Paris (2015)
17. James, S., et al.: Establishing connectivity between the existing networked music notation packages quintet.net, decibel scoreplayer and maxscore. In: International Conference on Technologies for Music Notation and Representation, A Coruña (2017)
18. Louzeiro, P.: Comprovisador – About (2017). https://comprovisador.wordpress.com/
19. Louzeiro, P.: Comprovisador.client – Notation Interface Video Examples (2017). https://comprovisador.wordpress.com/notation-examples/
20. Louzeiro, P.: Mediating a comprovisation performance: the comprovisador's control interface. In: Proceedings of the 43rd International Computer Music Conference, Shanghai, pp. 362–367 (2017). http://www.icmc2017.com/en/download.html
21. Louzeiro, P.: Real-time compositional procedures for mediated soloist-ensemble interaction: the comprovisador. In: Agustín-Aquino, O.A., Lluis-Puebla, E., Montiel, M. (eds.) MCM 2017. LNCS, vol. 10527, pp. 117–131. Springer, Cham (2017). https://doi.org/10.1007/978-3-319-71827-9_10

22. Puckette, M., et al.: Max 7: Documentation. https://docs.cycling74.com/max7/. Accessed 31 Jan 2017
23. Smith, R.R.: Animated Notation Dot Com (2014). http://animatednotation.com. Accessed 01 July 2017
24. Stanley, T.T.: Butch Morris and the art of conduction. Ph.D. thesis, University of Maryland (2009)
25. Thompson, W.: Soundpainting: The Art of Live Composition. Workbook, vol. 1. W. Thompson (2006). https://books.google.pt/books?id=m6BMnQEACAAJ

JamSketch: Improvisation Support System with GA-Based Melody Creation from User's Drawing

Tetsuro Kitahara[1]([✉]), Sergio Giraldo[2], and Rafael Ramírez[2]

[1] College of Humanities and Sciences, Nihon University, Tokyo, Japan
kitahara@chs.nihon-u.ac.jp
[2] Music Technology Group, Universitat Pompeu Fabra, Barcelona, Spain
{sergio.giraldo,rafael.ramirez}@upf.edu

Abstract. Improvisation is an enjoyable form of music performance but requires advanced skills and knowledge of music because the player has to create melodies immediately during the performance. To support improvisations by people without skills or knowledge of music, we have to develop (1) a human interface that can be used without skills or knowledge of music and (2) automatic melody generation from the user's input that may be musically abstract or incomplete. In this paper, we develop an improvisation support system based on *melodic outlines*, which represent the overall contour of melodies, with a function of melody generation using a genetic algorithm (GA). Once the user draws a melodic outline on the piano-roll display with the mouse or touch screen, the system immediately generates a melody using a GA with a fitness function based on the similarity to the outline, an N-gram probability, and entropy. The generated melody is performed expressively based on expression parameters calculated with an machine learning approach. The results of listening tests for comparing human performances and the system's performances suggest that generated melodies have quality similar to performances by non-expert human performers.

Keywords: Improvisation · Melodic outline · Melody generation
Algorithmic composition · Genetic algorithm

1 Introduction

Improvisation is one of the most enjoyable forms of music performance in which musicians create music compositions in real time combining communication of emotions, instrumental technique and spontaneous response to others. Hence, improvisation requires advanced skills and knowledge of music. Many people cannot improvise even if they have skills in playing an instrument. If computing technologies could enable these people to improvise without prior musical knowledge or skill, then they could enjoy music from a broader range of forms.

© Springer Nature Switzerland AG 2018
M. Aramaki et al. (Eds.): CMMR 2017, LNCS 11265, pp. 509–521, 2018.
https://doi.org/10.1007/978-3-030-01692-0_34

Thus, there have been several attempts to support non-musicians' improvisation. Parson [14] developed a system that composes improvisational melodies based on a chess game by the user. During a chess game, the user's behavior in the game are mapped into a musical structure, and are further transmitted to sound generation software. Amiot et al. [1] applied the Fourier transform to musical structures for computer-aided improvisation. Buchholz et al. [2] developed a collaborative improvisation support system called *coJIVE*, in which the width of each virtual key (a target to hit with the baton) varies according to its musical availability. Miyashita et al. [11] proposed a keyboard that presents the musical availability of each key by controlling its temperature; i.e., keys for dissonant notes are automatically hot. Ishida et al. [8] developed a system that identifies the musical appropriateness of each note in the user's improvisational performance using the N-gram model. If not appropriate, then it automatically corrects it to a musically appropriate note in real time. Fels et al. [5] developed an improvisation support system called *RhyMe* based on the fixed-function mapping, which is a key-to-note mapping method to maintain the harmonic function of each key. Pachet [13] proposed a system called *Continuator* that automatically generates stylistically consistent improvisations based on a Markov model. Keller [9] developed music notation software called *Impro-visor*, in which the user can compose jazz solo melodies using advices from the software.

One important issue in designing an improvisation support system is the design of the human interface for input of musical ideas. The human interface should be easy, intuitive, quickly inputable, and musically meaningful, but also should not require musical knowledge. Most systems described above [2,5,8, 11] are based on a traditional keyboard instrument, and they may be difficult for people who cannot play a keyboard instrument. Impro-visor [9] is based on traditional music notation software, so it may be difficult for people who are not familiar with the traditional music notation. The use of a chess game instead of playing an instrument [14] is a novel idea, but it is not easy to design reasonable mapping between situations in the game and musical semantics. If this mapping is not rationally designed, then the user cannot express his/her musical ideas as situations in the game.

In this paper, we propose an improvisation support system using a melodic outline that the user draws (Fig. 1). Use of drawing as the user's input is common in music systems for non-musicians. *Hyperscore* is a graphical music composition tool, in which different colors are assigned to different motives and the user can compose by drawing lines with various colors [4]. *Hand Composer* recognizes a gesture by the user using Leap Motion and creates music based on the gesture [10]. *InkSplorer* is a tool for composing contemporary music based on hand-written gestures [6]. *Music Sketcher* is also a drawing-based user interface for electroacoustic music [15]. *UPIC*, developed by Xenakis, is also an music composition tool based on drawing, in which the user draws on the built-in board and the system interprets the drawing as dynamic envelopes, scores in the time-pitch domain, or other musical parameters [17]. In addition, we also developed a melody editing system, in which the outline of a target melody is represented

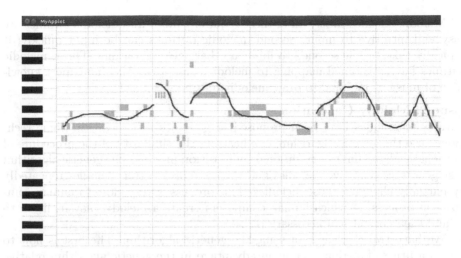

Fig. 1. An example of melodic outlines and screenshots of our system

as a curve and the user can edit the melody by redrawing the curve [16]. However, these systems do not focus on the support of improvisation. On the other hand, our system, called *JamSketch*, is capable of creating melodies in real time based on melodic outlines drawn by the user. Once the user draws outlines on the piano-roll display with the mouse or touch screen, the system immediately generates melodies that are along to the user's outline and musically appropriate using a genetic algorithm. With this melody generation feature, users can experience improvisational music performance.

2 Issues

Our goal is to develop a system in which non-musicians can enjoy improvisation with a simple operation. As discussed in Introduction, we have two issues:

Issue 1: Human Interface
We assume that our users have neither musical knowledge nor skills in playing an instrument. The system must allow users to input their musical ideas in an intuitive and easy way. Next, users should input them during musical accompaniment because our aim is to support improvisation, not off-line composition. The human interface should therefore be quickly inputable. Third, users have to realize a reasonable mapping between operators in the human interface and musical semantics in order to express their musical ideas with this interface. Of course, the human interface should not require users to have music knowledge.

We adopt *melodic outlines* as users' input data. Melodic outlines are a sub-symbolic representation of melodies in which note-level information (the onsets, durations, and pitch of each note) is hidden. An example of melodic outlines is shown in Fig. 1. By drawing a melodic outline, the user can specify the overall contour of the melody to be performed.

Melodic outlines satisfy all of these requirements. First, melodic outlines are easy and intuitive to input. Second, melodic outlines can be input quickly; it typically takes a few seconds to input a 4-bar melodic outline. Third, melodic outlines have a rational mapping to melodic semantics. Also, no expert knowledge of music is required to draw melodic outlines.

Issue 2: Melody Generation

Various techniques have been proposed to generate melodies [12]. Some techniques use the genetic algorithm, emphasizing the similarity of the procedure of the genetic algorithm to a traditional composition process. The genetic algorithm first generates tentative melodies and then explores better melodies repeatedly by partially changing those melodies. This process is very close to human composition process, in which human composers create a melody, play it, listen to it, and then correct it if necessary [12].

We have two challenges in using the genetic algorithm. The first is how to design a fitness function. The main advantage in the genetic algorithm relative to other techniques such as Markov models is the ability to use global features as well as local features such as N-gram probabilities. In fact, Ponce de León et al. [3] used global statistic descriptors such as the number of notes, the number of rests, average pitches, the largest pitch interval, etc. As a global feature, we introduce the similarity of a melody's entropy (how various note names appear) to those of existing melodies. By using this, we avoid excessively monotonous melodies such as C-D-C-D-C-D-...

The second is how to reduce the computation time. In general, the genetic algorithm is a technique that requires a computation cost. However, our system must generate melodies immediately because our aim is to support improvisation. We introduce two ideas to reduce the computation cost. One is to generate a melody individually for each measure to reduce the search space. The other is to generate initial chromosomes from existing melodies. A set of existing melodies are memorized as a prefix tree (called a *melody tree*). Initial chromosomes are generated by randomly proceeding in this prefix tree from the root. The initial chromosomes generated in this way are expected to be musically appropriate because they are generated from existing melodies, and the optimization of these chromosomes would quickly converge.

3   System Overview

Figure 1 shows a screenshot of our system. Once the system is launched, a piano-roll interface is displayed on the screen. During the playback of an accompaniment (given by a MIDI file with a chord transcription), the user can draw a melodic outline on the piano-roll screen with a computer mouse or touch pad as an input device. The melody is created individually for each measure. Once the mouse cursor enters the region of measure m and then moves out from that region (or the mouse button is released there), the creation of a melody for measure m starts. After the melody is created, the most likely expression parameters (the onset, duration, and energy for each note) are estimated. Generation of melody and expression parameters in the current implementation takes approximately 0.5 s and 0.2 s. Thus, users are required to draw their melodic outlines one bar in advance.

3.1   Drawing Melodic Outline

During playback, the user draws a melodic outline $\{y(t)\}$ on the piano-roll screen. Here, $y(t)$ represents the pitch of the outline (basically equal to a note number but it takes a continuous value) at time t. The time resolution is an eighth-note triplet in the current implementation.

3.2   Determining Rhythm of Melody

Melody generation for measure m initiates when the mouse cursor moves out from measure m in the piano roll (i.e. it moves to measure $m+1$) or the mouse button is released. First, the rhythm (i.e., the melody notes' durations) is determined. The key idea is to generate a note onset at time points of high-variability of $y(t)$. This is achieved through the following steps:

1. A set of note onset candidates, $\mathcal{R}$, is defined. Each element of $\mathcal{R}$ is a 12-dimensional binary vector, where 1 stands for an onset and 0 stands for a non-onset. For example, $(1, 0, 0, 0, 0, 0, 1, 0, 0, 0, 0, 0)$ represents a sequence of two half notes.
2. We decide a tentative rhythm R' from $\{y(t)\}$. The i-th element of R', denoted by $R'(i)$, is defined as follows:

$$R'(i) = \begin{cases} 1 \ (|y(t_m+i) - y(t_m+i-1)| > \delta) \\ 0 \ (\text{otherwise}) \end{cases}$$

   where t_m is the start time of m, and δ is a threshold.
3. We search for the closest candidate to R', that is,

$$\hat{R} = \operatorname*{argmin}_{R_k \in \mathcal{R}} ||R_k - R'||.$$

3.3   Determining Pitches

For each of the 1-value elements in $\hat{R}$, the pitch (MIDI note number) is determined. Let L be the number of 1-value elements in $\hat{R}$. What should be determined here is $N = (n_0, \cdots, n_{L-1})$, where n_i is a note name (i.e., the remainder of the division of a MIDI note number by 12). To determine these pitches, we use a genetic algorithm (GA), in which $N = (n_0, \cdots, n_{L-1})$ is regarded as a chromosome. To achieve a quick melody creation, the optimization through GA is limited to 0.5 s.

Initializing Chromosomes. Initial chromosomes are made from existing melodies. First, melodies taken from a melody corpus are memorized as a prefix tree (called a *melody tree* here). The basic concept of the melody tree is shown in Fig. 2. Each node represents a note name, and each edge has the transition probability from the note name associated with the parent node to the note name associated with the child node. Those transition probabilities are calculated based on the melodies to be memorized. After all melodies are memorized, edges with very low transition probabilities are pruned. When the system generates initial chromosomes, it randomly proceeds in this tree from the root.

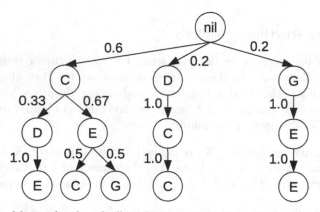

Memorized melodies: {C-D-E, C-E-C, C-E-G, D-C-C, G-E-E}

Fig. 2. Basic concept of a melody tree. Melodies are memorized in a prefix tree with transition probabilities.

Calculating Fitness Function. The melodies to be generated should satisfy both similarity to the melodic outline drawn by the user and musical appropriateness. A typical approach for measuring the musical appropriateness of a melody is to calculate its N-gram probability based on the N-gram model trained with existing melodies. However, this approach has two problems. First, to use a large number for N, a tremendous number of data are required because the model size becomes very large (this is known as the *data sparseness* problem). Because the musical availability of each note depends on the chord, ideally the N-gram model should be switched according to the chord, but this could enhance the data sparseness problem. Second, the N-gram model considers only local characteristics in a melody. If only local characteristics are considered, monotonous melodies where the same local note transition is repeated, such as C-C-C-C-... or C-D-C-D-C-D-..., may be generated. For the first problem, we approximate the N-gram model using lower-order models. Specifically, we approximate a per-chord trigram as a weighted sum of a bigram, a first-order derivative (so-called delta) bigram, and a per-chord unigram. For the second problem, we introduce the entropy of a melody as a global feature.

Thus, the fitness function $F(N)$ is defined as follows:

$$F(N) = w_0\mathrm{sim}(N) + w_1\mathrm{seq}_1(N) + w_2\mathrm{seq}_2(N) + w_3\mathrm{harm}(N) + w_4\mathrm{ent}(N),$$

where

– $\mathrm{sim}(N)$: Similarity to outline

$$\mathrm{sim}(N) = -\sum_{i=0}^{L-1} (n_i - y(t_i) \bmod 12)^2,$$

in which t_i is the onset time of note n_i, and mod is the modulo operator.
– $\mathrm{seq}_1(N)$: Bigram probability

$$\mathrm{seq}_1(N) = \sum_{i=1}^{L-1} \log P(n_i \mid n_{i-1}).$$

– $\mathrm{seq}_2(N)$: Delta bigram probability

$$\mathrm{seq}_2(N) = \sum_{i=2}^{L-1} \log P(n_i - n_{i-1} \mid n_{i-1} - n_{i-2}).$$

– $\mathrm{harm}(N)$: Per-chord unigram probability

$$\mathrm{harm}(N) = \sum_{i=0}^{L-1} \log P(n_i \mid c_i, b_i),$$

in which c_i is the chord name at time t_i, and b_i is the metrical position at t_i ($b_i \in \{\mathrm{head, on\text{-}beat, off\text{-}beat}\}$). We consider b_i because the acceptability of out-of-scale notes depends on their metrical positions.
– $\mathrm{ent}(N)$: Entropy

$$\mathrm{ent}(N) = -(H(N) - H_{\mathrm{mean}} - \varepsilon)^2,$$

in which $H(N)$ is the entropy of $\{n_0, \cdots, n_{L-1}\}$, and H_{mean} is the averaged entropy calculated from a melody corpus. Above, ε is usually zero, but setting this to more than zero will result in more complex melodies.

Above, $P(n_i \mid n_{i-1})$, $P(n_i - n_{i-1} \mid n_{i-1} - n_{i-2})$, $P(n_i \mid c_i, b_i)$, and H_{mean} are learned from a corpus, while $w_0, \cdots, w_4$ and ε are set manually.

3.4 Estimating Expression Parameters

The expression parameters, that is, the onset deviation, duration ratio, and energy (velocity) ratio for each note are estimated with Giraldo's method [7]. In this method, various features such as the pitch, duration, and Narmour structure description are extracted from each note, and the onset deviation, duration ratio, and energy ratio is estimated based on a machine learning model such as a k-nearest neighbor, a multi-layer perceptron, and a support vector machine. Here, we use the k-nearest neighbor estimator. The upper and lower bounds, if necessary, can be given to each parameter.

4   Implementation

We implemented this system on a touch-screen laptop PC. We used Groovy and CrestMuse Toolkit[1] as a programming language and an implementation framework, respectively. For GA, we used the Apache Commons Mathematics Library[2]. For feature extraction in estimating expression parameters, MIDI Toolbox[3] for Matlab is used through JavaOctave[4], i.e., a library binding Java and Octave.

As a melody corpus, we used 53 melodies with the tonality of Blues taken from Weimar Jazz Database[5]. The total number of the measures and notes are 3,533 and 23,142, respectively.

The default accompaniment is a 12-bar blues chord progression in the key of C, i.e., | C7 F7 C7 C7   F7 F7 C7 C7   G7 F7 C7 G7 |. This 12-bar chord progression is repeated four times. The accompaniment and repeat time can be changed; any accompaniment can be used if presents as a standard MIDI file with a separate chord transcription.

5   Perceptual Melody Quality Test

We conducted a perceptual melody quality test based on a Turing-test-like approach. Specifically, we collected human performances and the system's performances and asked listeners to rate their quality. If the ratings for human performances and the system's performances have no significant differences, then the system can be considered to be capable of creating melodies that have equivalent quality to human performers.

5.1   Procedure and Participants

Collection of Improvisational Melodies. We asked participants to improvise with both our system and a normal MIDI keyboard. The procedure is as follows:

1. Receive instructions on how to use the system.
2. Try improvisation with the system.
3. Practice improvisation with the system freely.
4. Improvise with the system again. This improvisation data will be used in a later listening test.
5. Try improvisation with the normal MIDI keyboard.
6. Practice improvisation with the normal MIDI keyboard freely.
7. Improvise with the normal MIDI keyboard again. This improvisation data will be used in the listening test.

---

[1] http://cmx.osdn.jp/.
[2] http://commons.apache.org/proper/commons-math/.
[3] https://github.com/miditoolbox/.
[4] https://kenai.com/projects/javaoctave/pages/Home.
[5] http://jazzomat.hfm-weimar.de/dbformat/dboverview.html.

The participants are the following six persons:

- P_1: PostDoc researcher in sound/music computing, has a long experience in playing improvisation with the accordion,
- P_2: plays the piano for about 15 years, composes musical pieces on a computer as a hobby, has not improvised,
- P_3: plays the trumpet for 11 years, cannot improvise,
- P_4: has no experience in music,
- P_5: plays the Electone for 12 years, has composed only a little bit before, has not improvised,
- P_6: plays the piano for about 15 years, plays improvisation as a professional player.

Improvisation with the normal MIDI keyboard (Steps 5 to 7) was skipped in participants with no experience in playing an keyboard instrument (P_3 and P_4). For advanced performers (P_1 and P_6), improvisation with our system, Steps 1 to 4, were skipped because they were not our target users.

Eventually, we collected the following performances:

- System's performances: s_1 (by P_2), s_2 (by P_3), s_3 (by P_4), and s_4 (by P_5),
- Human performances: u_1 (by P_1), u_2 (by P_2), u_3 (by P_5), and u_4 (by P_6).

Listening Test. We asked 12 researchers and students in music-related fields to evaluate each performance from the following criteria on a scale of 0 to 10:

1. Overall quality
2. Pitch appropriateness
3. Rhythmic appropriateness
4. Melodic variation
5. Blues-likeness
6. Skillfulness
7. Human-likeness.

5.2   Example of Generated Melodies

The melodic outline and generated melody of the third loop in s_4 are shown in Fig. 3. The generated melody is along the melodic outline and uses some blue notes ($E\flat$ and $B\flat$).

5.3   Results

The maximum value, 3rd quartile, median, 1st quartile, and minimum value of the ratings by the 12 listeners for each performance with respect to each criterion are shown in Fig. 4. From these figures, we can see the following observations:

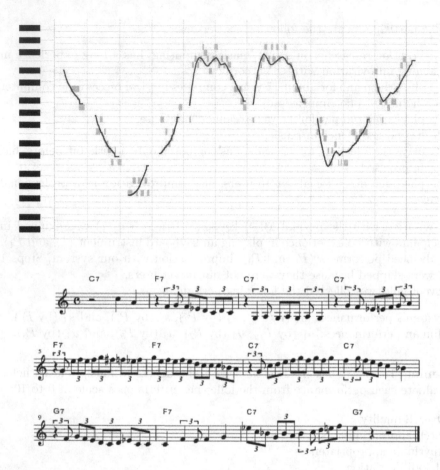

Fig. 3. The melodic outline and generated melody for 3rd loop in s_4. (Color figure online)

1. Overall quality

   The performance u_4 has the highest median score. The performances that have the second and third highest median scores are u_2 and u_1, respectively. For system performances (s_1 to s_4), the median scores are between 4 and 5, which is higher than that for u_3.

2. Pitch appropriateness

   The median scores for u_1, u_2, and u_4 are 7.5. Those for s_1 to s_4 are between 5 and 6, which is higher than that for u_3.

3. Rhythmic appropriateness

   In general, human performances (u_1 to u_4) have higher scores than the system's performances (s_1 to s_4).

4. Melodic variation

   The performance that has the highest median score is u_4. Other performances do not show clear differences in their scores.

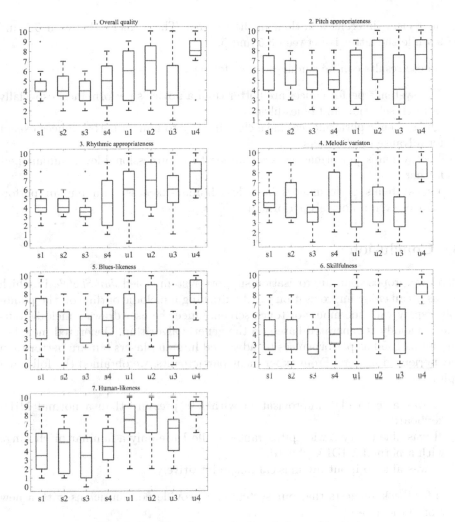

Fig. 4. Results of perceptual melody quality test

5. Blues-likeness

   Also for this criterion, u_4 has the highest median value. The performance with the second highest median score is u_2. The system's performances s_1 to s_4 have median scores between 4 and 5.5, which are almost equal to u_1 and definitely higher than that for u_3.

6. Skillfulness

   The performance u_4 has the highest median score. The performance with the next highest median score is u_2. Other performances do not have clear differences in their median scores, between 2.5 and 4.5.

7. Human-likeness

   The human performances u_1 to u_4 and the system's performances s_1 to s_4

have clear differences in their median scores. The former is between 6.5 and 9 while the latter is between 3.5 and 5.

These results can be summarized as follows:

- The system's performances are better than a novice's performance, especially in pitch selection and blues-likeness.
- The system's performances have close quality to human performances except for advanced performers.
- The system's performances are inferior to a professional-level human performer.
- The system's performances have less human-likeness than human performances even a novice's performance.

6 Conclusion

Here, we proposed an improvisation support system called *JamSketch*, in which the user can enjoy improvisation just by drawing a melodic outline on the piano-roll display with the mouse or touch screen. Once the user draws a melodic outline, a melody is generated based on the genetic algorithm. Generated melodies are not as good as performances by advanced human players but are better than inexperienced players. From experiment participants, we obtained the following opinions:

- "I was able to play improvisation with less pressure than a normal MIDI keyboard."
- "I was able to try a wide pitch range, while I use only a familiar pitch range with a normal MIDI keyboard."
- "I was able to input my musical image intuitively."

This feedback suggests that our system can provide non-musicians with a new way of music activity.

The main problem in the current melody generation method lies in the rhythmic aspect. Because the rhythm is determined by a simple rule, generated melodies often keep similar rhythms from beginning to end. In the future, we will improve the rhythm determination method using machine learning techniques, considering the dependency between the pitch and rhythm.

Acknowledgments. The listening tests were conducted at University of Tsukuba in collaboration with Dr. Masaki Matsubara. We appreciate him for his great effort to arrange the listening tests. We also appreciate Dr. Eita Nakamura for his fruitful advice.

This work was supported by JSPS KAKENHI Grant Numbers 26240025, 26280089, 16K16180, 16H01744, 16KT0136, and 17H00749 as well as by the Spanish TIMuL Project (TIN2013-48152-C2-2-R), and the TELMI Project of the Horizon 2020 Research and Innovation Programme (grant agreement No. 688269).

References

1. Amiot, E., Noll, T., Andretta, M., Agon, C.: Fourier oracles for computer-aided improvisation. In: Proceedings International Computer Music Conference (2006)
2. Buchholz, J., Lee, E., Klein, J., Borchers, J.: coJIVE: a system to support collaborative jazz improvisation. Technical report, Aachener Informatik-Berichte RWTH Aachen, Department of Computer Science (2007)
3. de León, P.J.P., Inesta, J.M., Calvo-Zaragoza, J., Rizo, D.: Data-based melody generation through multi-objective evolutionary computation. J. Math. Music **10**(2), 173–192 (2016)
4. Farbood, M.M., Pasztor, E., Jennings, K.: Hyperscore: a graphical sketchpad for novice composers. IEEE Comput. Graph. Appl. **24**(1), 50–54 (2004)
5. Fels, S., Nishimoto, K., Mase, K.: MusiKalscope: a graphical musical instrument. IEEE Multimedia **5**(3), 26–35 (1998)
6. Garcia, J., Tsandilas, T., Agon, C., Mackay, W.: InkSplorer: exploring musical ideas on paper and computer. In: Proceedings of International Conference on New Interfaces for Musical Expression (2011)
7. Giraldo, S., Ramírez, R.: A machine learning approach to ornamentation modeling and synthesis in jazz guitar. J. Math. Music **10**(2), 107–126 (2016)
8. Ishida, K., Kitahara, T., Takeda, M.: ism: improvisation supporting system based on melody correction. In: Proceedings of International Conference on New Interfaces for Musical Expression, pp. 177–180, June 2004
9. Keller, R.M.: Welcome to Impro-visor: Jazz Improvisation Advisor for the Improviser. https://www.cs.hmc.edu/~keller/jazz/improvisor/
10. Mandanici, M., Canazza, S.: The "Hand Composer": gesture-driven music composition machines. In: Proceedings of 13th Conference on Intelligent Autonomous Systems, pp. 553–560 (2014)
11. Miyashita, H., Nishimoto, K.: Theremoscore: a new-type musical score with temperature sensation. In: International conference on New Interface for Musical Expression (2004)
12. Nierhaus, G.: Algorithmic Composition. Springer, Vienna (2009). https://doi.org/10.1007/978-3-211-75540-2
13. Pachet, F.: The Continuator: musical interaction with style. In: Proceedings of International Computer Music Conference (2002)
14. Parson, D.E.: Chess-based composition and improvisation for non-musicians. In: Proceedings of International Conference on New Interfaces for Musical Expression (2009)
15. Thiebaut, J.-B., Healey, P.G., Kinns, N.B.: Drawing electroacoustic music. In: Proceedings of International Computer Music Conference (2008)
16. Tsuchiya, Y., Kitahara, T.: Melodic outline extraction method for non-note-level melody editing. In: Proceedings of Sound and Music Computing Conference, pp. 762–767 (2013)
17. Xenakis, I.: Music composition tracks. In: Roads, C. (ed.) Composers and the Computer (1985)

Virtual and Augmented Reality

Mobile Devices as Musical Instruments - State of the Art and Future Prospects

Georg Essl[1]([✉]) and Sang Won Lee[2]

[1] University of Wisconsin – Milwaukee, P.O. Box 413, Milwaukee, WI 53201, USA
essl@uwm.edu
[2] University of Michigan, 500 S. State Street, Ann Arbor, MI 48109, USA
snaglee@umich.edu

Abstract. Mobile music making has established itself as a maturing field of inquiry, scholarship, and artistic practice. While mobile devices were used before the advent of the iPhone, its introduction no doubt drastically accelerated the field. We take a look at the current state of the art of mobile devices as musical instruments, and explore future prospects for research in the field.

Keywords: Mobile music technology · State-of-the-art · Survey Prospects

1 Introduction

Mobile devices have been used for artistic performance for since 1998 at least, when Oliver Wittchow turned a gameboy into a looping instrument called nano-loop [20]. Smartphones predating the iPhone also drew research attention, but it is certainly true that the iPhone provided a substantial shift in the mobile smarthphone paradigm that firmly established the essence of the practice and research activities today. A review of the research developments of mobile devices, such as smart phones and tablets, as musical instruments, which is both current and thorough, is lacking and the purpose of this paper is to fill this void. The aim of the paper is to provide the working researcher a rapid entry into all the technological developments of the field and be able to identify knowledge gaps. Furthermore we seek to contextualize the current state of the field with respect to technological trend that should inform new research directions. The intent is to provide a thorough review of technical developments that support the use of commodity smart devices for musical purposes, with a strong emphasis on research activities. For this purpose we will not review literature that engages with performance practice, or with research that does not specifically look to address the mobile smart-device platform or exploit its specific benefits.

Previous surveys have addressed various aspects of mobile music. For pointers into the literature predating this review see [24]. John surveyed the literature

© Springer Nature Switzerland AG 2018
M. Aramaki et al. (Eds.): CMMR 2017, LNCS 11265, pp. 525–539, 2018.
https://doi.org/10.1007/978-3-030-01692-0_35

with a view to the broader context of mobile music and provided broad classification of the research activities with respect to technological, social, and geo-
graphical characteristics [31]. Our survey's aim is to review the state-of-the art of
technological aspects of mobile devices with sufficient detail to allow the reader
to get a solid overview of the research activities and identify possible future
directions. A large number of iOS music apps have appeared and have been cat-
alogued [3]. A more taxonomic review of the android offerings was conducted by
Dubus and co-workers [14]. Numerous apps have sprung from a research context
such as ZooZbeat [75] or the catalogue of Smule apps [71]. It is surprisingly
rare that existing hardware-based musical instruments are translated onto the
mobile platform. A rare example is Crackle [56] which realizes a mobile version
of the STEIM CrackleBox. Another is the mobile app Reactable which mimics
the tabletop instrument with the same name[1]. More frequent is imitation and
virtual augmentation of traditional instruments (see for example [72]). Games
are a form of interactive performance, and offer incentives as part of the interactive design. Musical games or musical instruments with game elements have been
explored in various projects [4] and discussed as strategy in detail [73]. Another
sizable class of research is concerned with creating new instruments that are the
result of software realization on the mobile device. For example, they make use
of the compass in mobile phones to facilitate performance [33].

This paper is organized into five main parts. First we situate mobile devices
as musical instruments in the context of music instrument research (Sect. 2).
Then we review the state of the art of research on mobile musical instruments
over the last ten years (Sect. 3). Then we review the landscape of substrate technological changes relevant for mobile musical instruments and their implications
for grounding future mobile music research (Sect. 5). Finally, Sect. 6 discusses
ongoing challenges facing mobile music research.

2   Mobile Devices as NIMEs

It is instructive to situate mobile devices as New Interfaces for Musical Expression (NIMEs) in comparison to other development in the NIME field. For this
purpose we provide the following definitions: A NIME is called *custom* if it is
built from various hardware components. A NIME is called *commodity-based* if it
uses a commercially available commodity device as hardware foundation. Many
NIMEs have historically been custom. Mobile devices are commodity devices and
hence mobile NIMEs are commodity-based NIMEs. Table 1 reviews the different
properties of these two approaches. The main advantage of custom NIMEs is the
ability to design them to specific ideas on all levels, including form factor, haptic
response, and even individual ergonomic needs. Commodity devices come with
a limited selection of form factors and hence a largely fixed set of opportunities
to create interactions. However commodity devices provide a number of advantages: (1) the ease of delivering NIMEs, as NIME solutions are completely or
predominantly software, which is easy to distribute, (2) great accessibility and

---

[1] http://reactable.com/mobile/.

musical participation, due to the wide availability of commodity devices. The main differentiating forces between the two approaches seem to be access, distribution paradigm, and flexibility. Commodity devices trade off some flexibility for substantial gains in access and distribution.

However it is important to remember the benefits of custom NIMEs and their specific research and artistic opportunities. Custom NIMEs can offer performance interfaces that are unthinkable on current commodity platforms and hence should not be overlooked. Finally it is worthwhile noting that with any taxonomy, it is also possible here to mix categories. In our case this can happen to augmentation and hybridization. We will discuss research efforts using these strategies in Sect. 3.4

Table 1. Custom versus commodity-based NIMEs

	Custom	Commodity-based
Access	Difficult	Easy
Availability	Limited	Ubiquitous
Distribution	Hardware	Software
Flexibility	Open	Limited

3 State of the Art of Mobile Musical Instrument Research

Research into the technology of mobile musical instruments can be categorized into proposals of a methodological nature, software support for the design of mobile music, augmentations or hybridizations, and mobile musical instruments for specific performance practice.

3.1 Methodologies

Various taxonomies to understand mobile possibilities for music performance have been proposed, including the use of multi-dimension design spaces [20] and drawing on taxonomies of embodiment and the classification of mapping approaches [65]. More recently multi-touch interactions in a number of existing platforms was categorized by type of interaction elements and processing [25]. Surveys and thematic analysis was used to study user's preferences in mobile performance GUIs [66]. The use of iterative prototyping and user study cycles has been advanced as methodology [5]. Strategies to augment social engagement in mobile music collaboration was studied using survey and Modified Stimulated Retrospective Think-Aloud methodologies for qualitative assessment [55].

Yang employed controlled user studies and timed tasks to study performance differences in mobile music programming representations [77]. Ouzounian and co-workers employed speculative strategies to investigate music making in a social media context with a particular emphasis on exploring potential notions of a musical selfie using both mobile and custom-build hardware artifacts [52]. Le Vaillant and co-workers study latency of touch-to-audio using latency measurements of impact to response recordings [70].

3.2   Musical Interface Software on Mobile Devices

Mobile devices are primarily made musical through software. Hence the support of mobile music through different software approaches takes a central role in the research of mobile music instruments.

Embeddable Software Libraries: Embeddable software libraries offer simplified solutions to important aspects of the software development mobile musical instruments. One of the most widely covered aspect is sound playback, recording, and synthesis. Typically these are either compilable C or C++ level wrapper and helper functions, or packaged libraries. MoMu is a set of C++ level functions that wrap important sound, networking, threading, and sensor interaction functionality into more easily accessible and higher level API calls to more rapidly create prototypes [7]. Ports of well-established synthesis environments are also available. In this category, Libpd is an embeddable version of puredata's synthesis engine [6]. Also an embeddable mobile port of CSound has been developed [38]. Experiences in developing audio apps using embeddable libraries was reported by Erkut and co-workers [15]. An alternative to C++ level mobile programming is cross-compilation of synthesis patches from desktop or laptop software environments. MobileFaust is such as cross-compiling solution for the Faust sound synthesis language and environment [49]. Some embeddable solutions were created to service full-fledged high level mobile music environments. UrSound, developed as part of the urMus project, is such a synthesis engine [17]. It differentiates itself from legacy ports by offering patching paradigms that seek to support rapid on-the-fly patching and improved CPU utilization by employing a multi-rate patching pipeline.

Multi-touch GUI and Interaction Design: Multi-touch displays and interaction play an important new role for mobile devices, as these are their canonical forms of interaction. Substantial effort has been exerted developing approaches to design graphical interactions for multi-touch as well as to support the rapid development of flexible new solutions. Multi-touch interaction design is one of the design features of urMus [21] allowing the creating of arbitrary dynamic graphical and interactive content in the Lua programming language. The efficacy of various graphical interaction paradigms (icon-based, menu-based, and gesture-based) was studied extensively using this framework [78]. Control [58] is an OSC and Midi remote controller with customizable interface through a set of extendable graphical interaction widget elements. Extensions to Control offer OSC-induced interface changes that can be executed on the fly, automated lay-outing of widgets, and integration with MAX/MSP, LuaAV, and SuperCollider [59]. NexusUI is javascript based widget library for web programming meant to along mobile and non-mobile control interface design [69] taking advantage of the web's cross-platform character. Mira is a Max/MSP mobile interface that uses the idea of GUI mirroring [67]. A remote Max patcher offers interface ele-ments that are mirrored and as needed dynamically updated as needed on the table display and that also can be interacted with. Controls are returned to the remote Max patcher. An alternative approach uses handwriting and drawing to sketch MAX/MSP style patches [60].

Mobile-Based Music Environments: urMus is an environment to support mobile music on the mobile device itself [16]. It offers the ability to create arbi-trary graphical representations and interactions, and provides a signal patching infrastructure. It supports access to a wide range of sensors and actuators, on-device as well as collaborative live-coding, networking, and machine learning. Rather than being distributed through mobile market places, it is available on an open source basis.

3.3   Machine Learning

Machine Learning approaches were incorporated into mobile music systems in various ways. Derbinsky and co-workers incorporated the Soar cognitive archi-tecture into urMus, which offers a range of common machine learning techniques in the context of a broader cognitive framework [12]. This system was utilized to create a collaborative mobile drum circle solution where machine learning can learn and then improvise from given live human performances [13]. Moodifier-live is a collaborative mobile performance platform that uses the KTH rule-based system to control expressivity in MIDI files on multiple mobile devices. The rule-based system is driven from the sensors [23].

3.4   Hybridization and Augmentation

Augmentation in instrument design refers to the extension of an existing musical instrument with some new capability [50]. We consider hybridization when two existing musical instruments are combined to form a joint new instrument.

There are different types of augmentations and hybridization. In Miranda and Wanderley's definition augmentation refers to an existing traditional musical instrument being augmented through technological means to change or enhance its musical capabilities. For the purpose of this paper we will consider a com-modity mobile device to be comparable to a traditional musical instrument, in that it is an easily available commercial artifact that is subject to extensions and modifications. In this view, augmentation and hybridization carries over to mobile devices (see for example [19]) allowing an instrument designer to create novel and more custom aspects in the context of a commodity technology.

Hybrid Instruments: An example of a traditional musical instrument being hybridized with a mobile device was introduced by Martin for vibraphones [46]. Another example of hybridization combines traditional turntable performance of scratching with mobile devices [8]. The mobile device is placed on top of the turntable and senses motion, but can access arbitrary sounds hence liberating the interaction from the need of having a fixed vinyl disk to perform. Another example of (internal) hybridization is Tok! It proposes that a mobile device can be viewed as an acoustic instrument when it is tapped against a surface [44]. Michon and co-workers introduced various examples of hybridized instruments using the iPad, a sensor-augmented electric guitar and 3D-printed acoustical horn augmentations around the iPad [48].

Augmentation of Mobile Devices: Commodity mobile devices come with a certain set of capabilities. These may not be sufficient for some musical performances. Augmentation can be used to overcome this limitation. The surface of a commercial multi-touch phone offers no discernible haptic features to orient a user of interaction elements. Allison and co-workers have proposed passive haptic overlays to improve on this problem [64]. A particular area of attention has been added force or pressure sensing [22,54]. While iOS devices only offer binary touch information (contact or no contact), Android devices offer information about the contact size. This can be exploited for touch interactions beyond binary, and can also be used as heuristic measures of pressure, where increased contact size is assumed to correspond to increased contact pressure. Another approach to hybridization is to give mobile devices physical characteristic by passive augmentation [47]. This approach uses 3-D printing to create attachments and extensions that can give mobile devices horns, mouth-pieces and other physical extensions that relate to how they can be performed. MobileMuse is a platform for biometric emotion sensing that combines galvanic skin response, pulse oximetry, temperature and accelerometer sensing on custom hardware that communicates with a mobile devices for data analysis [36].

4   Support of Mobile Muisc Performance Practices

Numerous mobile music instruments have been developed to support existing traditional performance practices. For example, apps to support spatialization [53] or choir artificial voice performance [11] have emerged.

Networked Mobile NIMEs, Audience Involvement and Participation: The ability to use numerous mobile NIMEs in a networked ensemble offers rich opportunities for artistic expression. Much of the work on networked mobile instruments has focused on audience participation. However, some research also involves generic support of network features. For example, Essl [18] proposed the use of ZeroConf network discovery to semantically organize networked mobile performances. Central to traditional notions of mobile music, geo-location was developed in a networked mobile music project by Allison and co-workers [2]. The commercial API Ableton Link provides network synchronization to support the Ableton music ecosystem and allows cross-linking of mobile apps[2].

We distinguish between audience involvement, in which the audience can respond to musical performances but is not participating in the music-making activities, and audience participation, where the audience is part of the musical performance. Examples of networked distributed audience involvement are many apps by Smule [71], in particular in the context of what Wang and co-authors call World Stage [74]. Social networking is a central part of World Stage in which a distributed audience and feedback mechanism is generated by listening to and liking the performance. An alternative classification was suggested by Liu and van der Heide where involvement is termed "passive" and participation is termed "active" [45]. They further use diagram structures to taxonomize different forms of audience participation performance.

While musicians can use audience's mobile devices as a speaker array over the network, (for example, [63] and also [68] for a historic review), they can distribute mobile music application where audience can directly and indirectly participate in the music making process. Mobile audience participation with mobile phones has a long history following the pioneering work of Golan Levin on Dialtones in 2001 and is perhaps the most active area of research for mobile music instrument technologies. Numerous technological approaches to supporting them have appeared. Oh and Wang explored a wide range of audience participation techniques and demonstrated them on a number of examples [51]. Challenges for audience participation in a concert space include the need to distribute the participation software or interface to participants. Numerous projects have tackled this problem. One approach exploits the captive web portal approach to ease the distribution problem. Captive portals are forced http redirects that allow the delivery of web pages without the need to specify web addresses. If the mobile performance interface is web-based, this solution solves both cross-platform issues and software download needs [28]. Another approach seeks to exploit cloud computing infrastructure for audience participation pieces. Pusher services allow massive distribution of data through the cloud. Using this approach, large numbers of participating audience members can receive vital performance data [9]. MassMobile environment that support large scale audience participation including mobile devices by taking a cloud-based database approach [76]. Network protocols for discovery and distribution in a concert hall network itself was explored in detail by Lee and co-workers [42]. A.bel is a multi-platform environment for rapid development of PD-based networked performances [10]. The echobo project provides detailed taxonomies of audience participation, design principles for mobile audience participation projects and demonstrates these principle in a concrete concert realization [43]. Another example of applications of mobile audience participation include the control the stereo output of a lead guitarist as part of a live rock concert [30].

---

[2] https://www.ableton.com/en/link/.

Web based composition interface to enable distributed composition for guided mobile music instruments [27]. The emergence of Web Audi API simplifies the realization of audience participation music performances [39]. Soundworks is a frameworks supporting collaborative mobile performances through the web [57].

Live Coding: Live Coding paradigms have entered mobile music instruments in various ways. One is in the design of mobile music environments. The patching interface of urMus was designed to allow live interactions [16,21]. Lee and co-workers introduced the idea of live-coding mobile instruments as part of a performance [40]. One or more live coders program on laptops and submit their code interactively to a mobile phone where changes are immediately enacted to create new performance interface capabilities and sound patches. Follow-up research investigated the support of collaboration between mobile and laptop performers through the a live-coding environment [41]. MiniAudicle is an iPad version of Chuck's Audicle editor that was designed to allow live-coding performance [61].

5   Future Prospects Through Technological Evolution

Technological changes create a changing environment of opportunity for musical expression. Many aspects of the mobile platform have seen improvements and additions over the past ten years. It is instructive to review these changes as well as to project some expected future capabilities to understand opportunities for future mobile music instruments.

Computational Performance: Computational performance is critical in setting barrier on the complexity of computation that can be completed under real-time constraints. For audio these real-time constraints are particularly tight as an audio sample only received 1/playbackrate seconds time. For typical rates (44.1 kHz–48 kHz) this leads to hard time limits of 22.67 µs. For visual updates (30–60 Hz) the real-time limits are substantially more generous at 16.66 ms.

Mobile smartphone CPUs have seen considerable gains over the last ten years. These gains have enabled more and more complex real-time software to be realized on mobile devices. However, it is important to note that mobile phones never experienced Moore's law-like gains in performance [26] and that already since 2013 power consumption of CPUs has plateaued [26]. This means that it is unclear that one can anticipate healthy performance gains for future architectures and that there might be a power-ceiling impacting CPU performance for mobile devices. Given that battery size, and hence screen size is the main limiter on power, we can anticipate that larger tablets will remain computationally more powerful than smaller devices.

Sensors and Actuators: Interaction is facilitated through sensors and actuators. The set of actuators in mobile devices has remained largely constant, and consists of audio display (speakers), visual display (touch-screen), and vibro-tactile display (motor). Most quality improvements have focused on visual displays, where screen resolution has changed from 320×480 for the original iPhone, to 1080×1920 for the iPhone 6s [35]. These improvements improve fidelity rather than enable new possibilities.

In contrast, new sensing technologies have been added especially in the early years of the design evolution of mobile devices. The original iPhone offered multi-touch, microphone, accelerometer, magnetometer, GPS, and distance sensing accessible to the programmer [20]. Since then, gyroscopes and video cameras have been added. Gyroscopes are attractive as they help expand gesture recognition possibilities. Cameras are particularly rich sensors that can be used both literally (by reproducing the visual content it captures) or to detect information that can be extracted from the visual content [32]. An example of the former is MadPad [37], an iPad instrument that allows to record audio and video of short sequences that can then be interactively performed. An example of the latter is the use of the camera to perform visual ambiance detection [62].

The types of sensors available has not changed in recent years. However their fidelity has improved. While numerous extensions (such as pressure sensing, see Sect. 3.4) have been proposed it is unclear if and in what form such technologies will be integrated in commodity devices. This, however, suggests that continued work on augmenting mobile devices to make them more suitable for certain performance intentions will remain an important line of investigation.

Networking: Already the original iPhone offered three different networking capabilities: (1) bluetooth for short range networking, (2) mobile cellular networking, and (2) WIFI networking. The basic connectivity options have not changed since, though mobile cellular networking performance for data has improved over the last 10 years and prospects are promising that this trend will continue with future developments [1]. Wireless networking already today offers substantial bandwidth that is rarely fully exploited in mobile music instruments, indicating there is ample opportunity to expand the involvement of higher bandwidth demands to the network in their design.

Cloud Computing: A mobile device does not live in isolation, but rather is embedded in a technological ecology though networking. Computation in the cloud is a particular opportunity here. Given that network bandwidth is plentiful, utilizing networked resources offers itself as an opportunity. Numerous cloud-based solutions have already been proposed (see Sect. 4) in particular in the context of helping to scale audience participation. There are certainly opportunities to find further ways to include computation in the cloud. As mobile devices might cap in power, offloading computation, particularly aspects of computation that can be predicted within a sensible time frame (network round-trip time + computation time) can be offloaded. Hindle proposed an example of this nature [29].

6   Challenges and Opportunities

One of the important challenges for gesture sensing is the ability to recover absolute positions in space. While GPS does offer low-resolution sensing for position outdoors, it is unavailable in most indoor performance spaces. Sensors incorporated into mobile devices such as accelerometers or gyroscopes do not offer absolute position, and standard integration techniques are subject to drift problems [20]. One solution for the problem was offered by Herrera and co-workers by using audio triangulation to detect position [34], though this method has certain limitations imposed by the sounding environment. Hence providing solutions to position sensing for indoor performances remain an important research topic with few avenues explored. Emerging performance practices frame numerous opportunities for mobile music instruments. Ease of access through the App store can enable rapid dissemination and participation, but further support for structure performance practices in ensembles and building of reproducibility and repertoire pose a persistent challenge.

7   Conclusions

Mobile music based on multi-touch mobile devices has developed into a vibrant area of research in the ten years since the iPhone was released. We documented a wide range of research activities on mobile music instruments and their underlying technologies and investigated technological trends that will impact future prospects in the field. Audience participation is perhaps the most active area of research so far, while topics such as machine learning in mobile music instruments remain underdeveloped. A range of software support for developing mobile music instruments have emerged from convenient embeddable libraries to full-fledged mobile music environments. Crowd and cloud computing have found their way into mobile music instruments pointing the way to the possibility of very large scale mobile music performances.

Acknowledgments. We are grateful for helpful comments by the reviewers, which helped improve the manuscript.

References

1. Agiwal, M., Roy, A., Saxena, N.: Next generation 5g wireless networks: a comprehensive survey. IEEE Commun. Surveys Tuts. **18**(3), 1617–1655 (2016)
2. Allison, J., Dell, C.: AuRal: a mobile interactive system for geo-locative audio synthesis. In: Proceedings of the International Conference on New Interfaces for Musical Expression (2012)
3. Axford, E.C.: Music Apps for Musicians and Music Teachers. Rowman & Littlefield (2015)
4. Baldan, S., Götzen, A.D., Serafin, S.: Sonic tennis: a rhythmic interaction game for mobile devices. In: Proceedings of the International Conference on New Interfaces for Musical Expression (2013)

5. Barraclough, T., Carnegie, D., Kapur, A.: Musical instrument design process for mobile technology. In: Proceedings of the International Conference on New Interfaces for Musical Expression (2015)
6. Brinkmann, P., et al.: Embedding pure data with libpd. In: Proceedings of the Pure Data Convention (2011)
7. Bryan, N.J., Herrera, J., Oh, J., Wang, G.: MoMu: a mobile music toolkit. In: Proceedings of the International Conference on New Interfaces for Musical Expression (2010)
8. Bryan, N.J., Wang, G.: Two turntables and a mobile phone. In: Proceedings of the International Conference on New Interfaces for Musical Expression (2011)
9. de Carvalho Junior, A.D., Lee, S.W., Essl, G.: Understanding cloud support for the audience participation concert performance of crowd in c[loud]. In: Proceedings of the International Conference on New Interfaces for Musical Expression (2016)
10. Clément, A.R., Ribeiro, F., Penha, R.: Bridging the gap between performers and the audience using networked smartphones: the a.bel system. In: Proceedings of the International Conference on Live Interfaces (2016)
11. d'Alessandro, N., et al.: A digital mobile choir: joining two interfaces towards composing and performing collaborative mobile music. In: Proceedings of the International Conference on New Interfaces for Musical Expression (2012)
12. Derbinsky, N., Essl, G.: Cognitive architecture in mobile music interactions. In: Proceedings of the International Conference on New Interfaces for Musical Expression (2011)
13. Derbinsky, N., Essl, G.: Exploring reinforcement learning for mobile percussive collaboration. In: Proceedings of the International Conference on New Interfaces for Musical Expression (2012)
14. Dubus, G., Hansen, K.F., Bresin, R.: An overview of sound and music applications for android available on the market. In: Proceedings of the 9th Sound and Music Computing Conference (2012)
15. Erkut, C., Jylhä, A., Serafin, S.: (and sound) of simpe: Showcasing outcomes of a mobile audio programming seminar. In: Workshop on Speech and Sound in Mobile and Pervasive Environments (2013)
16. Essl, G.: UrMus - an environment for mobile instrument design and performance. In: Proceedings of the International Computer Music Conference (2010)
17. Essl, G.: UrSound - live patching of audio and multimedia using a multi-rate normed single-stream data-flow engine. In: Proceedings of the International Computer Music Conference (2010)
18. Essl, G.: Automated ad hoc networking for mobile and hybrid music performance. In: Proceedings of the International Computer Music Conference (2011)
19. Essl, G., Rohs, M., Kratz, S.: Use the force (or something) - pressure and pressure-like input for mobile music performance. In: Proceedings of the International Conference on New Interfaces for Musical Expression (2010)
20. Essl, G., Rohs, M.: Interactivity for Mobile Music Making. Organ. Sound 14(2) (2009)
21. Essl, G., Müller, A.: Designing mobile musical instruments and environments with urMus. In: Proceedings of the International Conference on New Interfaces for Musical Expression (2010)
22. Essl, G., Rohs, M., Kratz, S.: Use the force (or something) - pressure and pressure - like input for mobile music performance. In: Proceedings of the International Conference on New Interfaces for Musical Expression (2010)

23. Fabiani, M., Dubus, G., Bresin, R.: MoodifierLive: interactive and collaborative expressive music performance on mobile devices. In: Proceedings of the International Conference on New Interfaces for Musical Expression (2011)

24. Gaye, L., Holmquist, L.E., Behrendt, F., Tanaka, A.: Mobile music technology: report on an emerging community. In: Proceedings of the International Conference on New Interfaces for Musical Expression (2006)

25. Gonzalez-Inostroza, M., Sylleros, A., Cádiz, R.F.: Understanding interaction in musical multi-touch surfaces. In: Proceedings of the International Computer Music Conference (2017)

26. Halpern, M., Zhu, Y., Reddi, V.J.: Mobile CPU's rise to power: quantifying the impact of generational mobile CPU design trends on performance, energy, and user satisfaction. In: IEEE Symposium on High Performance Computer Architecture (2016)

27. Hamilton, R., Smith, J., Wang, G.: Social composition: musical data systems for expressive mobile music. Leonardo Music J. **21**, 57–64 (2011)

28. Hindle, A.: SWARMED: captive portals, mobile devices, and audience participation in multi-user music performance. In: Proceedings of the International Conference on New Interfaces for Musical Expression (2013)

29. Hindle, A.: CloudOrch: a portable soundcard in the cloud. In: Proceedings of the International Conference on New Interfaces for Musical Expression (2014)

30. Hödl, O., Kayali, F., Fitzpatrick, G.: Designing interactive audience participation using smart phones in a musical performance. In: Proceedings of the International Computer Music Conference (2012)

31. John, D.: Updating the classifications of mobile music projects. In: Proceedings of the International Conference on New Interfaces for Musical Expression (2013)

32. Keefe, P.O., Essl, G.: The visual in mobile music performance. In: Proceedings of the International Conference on New Interfaces for Musical Expression (2011)

33. Kim, B., Yeo, W.S.: Interactive mobile music performance with digital compass. In: Proceedings of the International Conference on New Interfaces for Musical Expression (2012)

34. Kim, H.S., Herrera, J., Wang, G.: Ping-pong: Musically discovering locations. In: Proceedings of the International Conference on New Interfaces for Musical Expression (2014)

35. Kimmel, J.: Introduction to mobile and wearable displays. In: Chen, J., Cranton, W., Fihn, M. (eds.) Handbook of Visual Display Technology, pp. 1–12. Springer, Heidelberg (2016). https://doi.org/10.1007/978-3-642-35947-7_120-2

36. Knapp, B., Bortz, B.: MobileMuse: integral music control goes mobile. In: Proceedings of the International Conference on New Interfaces for Musical Expression (2011)

37. Kruge, N., Wang, G.: MadPad: a crowdsourcing system for audiovisual sampling. In: Proceedings of the International Conference on New Interfaces for Musical Expression (2011)

38. Lazzarini, V., Yi, S., Timoney, J., Keller, D., Pimenta, M.S.: The mobile Csound platform. In: Proceedings of the International Computer Music Conference (2012)

39. Lee, S.W., de Carvalho Jr, A.D., Essl, G.: Crowd in c[loud]: audience participation music with online dating metaphor using cloud service. In: Proceedings of the Web Audio Conference (2016)

40. Lee, S.W., Essl, G.: Live coding the mobile music instrument. In: Proceedings of the International Conference on New Interfaces for Musical Expression (2013)

41. Lee, S.W., Essl, G.: Communication, control, and state sharing in collaborative live coding. In: Proceedings of the International Conference on New Interfaces for Musical Expression (2014)
42. Lee, S.W., Essl, G., Mao, Z.M.: Distributing mobile music applications for audience participation using mobile ad-hoc network (MANET). In: Proceedings of the International Conference on New Interfaces for Musical Expression (2014)
43. Lee, S.W., Freeman, J.: echobo: audience participation using the mobile music instrument. In: Proceedings of the International Conference on New Interfaces for Musical Expression (2013)
44. Lee, S.W., Srinivasamurthy, A., Tronel, G., Shen, W., Freeman, J.: TOK!: a collaborative acoustic instrument using mobile phones. In: Proceedings of the International Conference on New Interfaces for Musical Expression (2012)
45. Liu, D., van der Heide, E.: Interaction models for real-time participatory musical performance using mobile devices. In: Proceedings of the International Computer Music Conference (2017)
46. Martin, C.: Performing with a mobile computer system for vibraphone. In: Proceedings of the International Conference on New Interfaces for Musical Expression (2013)
47. Michon, R., Smith, J.O., Wright, M., Chafe, C., Granzow, J., Wang, G.: Passively augmenting mobile devices towards hybrid musical instrument design. In: Proceedings of the International Conference on New Interfaces for Musical Expression, pp. 19–24 (2017)
48. Michon, R., Smith, J.O.I., Wright, M., Chafe, C.: Augmenting the iPad: the BladeAxe. In: Proceedings of the International Conference on New Interfaces for Musical Expression (2016)
49. Michon, R., Smith III, J., Orlarey, Y.: MobileFaust: a set of tools to make musical mobile applications with the faust programming language. In: Proceedings of the International Conference on New Interfaces for Musical Expression (2015)
50. Miranda, E.R., Wanderley, M.M.: New Digital Musical Instruments: Control and Interaction Beyond the Keyboard. A-R Editions (2006)
51. Oh, J., Wang, G.: Audience-participation techniques based on social mobile computing. In: Proceedings of the International Computer Music Conference (2011)
52. Ouzounian, G., Haworth, C., Bennett, P.: Speculative designs: towards a social music. In: Proceedings of the International Computer Music Conference (2017)
53. Park, S., Ban, S., Hong, D.R., Yeo, W.S.: Sound surfing network (SSN): mobile phone-based sound spatialization with audience collaboration. In: Proceedings of the International Conference on New Interfaces for Musical Expression (2013)
54. Park, T.H., Nieto, O.: Fortissimo: force-feedback for mobile devices. In: Proceedings of the International Conference on New Interfaces for Musical Expression (2013)
55. Pugliese, R., Tahiroglu, K., Goddard, C., Nesfield, J.: Augmenting human-human interaction in mobile group improvisation. In: Proceedings of the International Conference on New Interfaces for Musical Expression (2012)
56. Reus, J.: Crackle: a dynamic mobile multitouch topology for exploratory sound interaction. In: Proceedings of the International Conference on New Interfaces for Musical Expression (2011)
57. Robaszkiewicz, S., Schnell, N.: Soundworks a playground for artists and developers to create collaborative mobile web performances (2015)
58. Roberts, C.: Control: aoftware for end-user interface programming and interactive performance. In: Proceedings of the International Computer Music Conference (2011)

59. Roberts, C., Wakefield, G., Wright, M.: Mobile controls On-The-Fly: an abstraction for distributed nimes. In: Proceedings of the International Conference on New Interfaces for Musical Expression (2012)
60. Salazar, S., Wang, G.: Auraglyph: Handwritten computer music composition and design. In: Proceedings of the International Conference on New Interfaces for Musical Expression (2014)
61. Salazar, S., Wang, G.: miniAudicle for iPad: touchscreen-based music software programming. In: Proceedings of the International Computer Music Conference (2014)
62. Savage, N.S., Ali, S.R., Chavez, N.E.: Mmmmm: a multi-modal mobile music mixer. In: Proceedings of the International Conference on New Interfaces for Musical Expression (2010)
63. Shaw, T., Piquemal, S., Bowers, J.: Fields: an exploration into the use of mobile devices as a medium for sound diffusion. In: Proceedings of the International Conference on New Interfaces for Musical Expression (2015)
64. Strylowski, B., Allison, J., Guessford, J.: Pitch Canvas: Touchscreen based mobile music instrument. In: Proceedings of the International Conference on New Interfaces for Musical Expression (2014)
65. Tanaka, A.: Mapping out instruments, affordances, and mobiles. In: Proceedings of the International Conference on New Interfaces for Musical Expression (2010)
66. Tanaka, A., Parkinson, A., Settel, Z., Tahiroglu, K.: A survey and thematic analysis approach as input to the design of mobile music GUIs. In: Proceedings of the International Conference on New Interfaces for Musical Expression (2012)
67. Tarakajian, S., Zicarelli, D., Clayton, J.: Mira: Liveness in iPad controllers for Max/Msp. In: Proceedings of the International Conference on New Interfaces for Musical Expression (2013)
68. Taylor, B.: A history of the audience as a speaker array. In: Proceedings of the International Conference on New Interfaces for Musical Expression, pp. 481–486 (2017)
69. Taylor, B., et al.: Simplified expressive mobile development with nexusui, nexusup, and nexusdrop. In: Proceedings of the International Conference on New Interfaces for Musical Expression (2014)
70. Vaillant, G.L., Villée, G., Dutoit, T.: Portable C++ framework for low-latency musical touch interaction with geometrical shapes. In: Proceedings of the International Computer Music Conference (2017)
71. Wang, G., et al.: Smule = sonic media: an intersection of the mobile, musical, and social. In: Proceedings of the International Computer Music Conference (2009)
72. Wang, G.: Ocarina: designing the iphone's magic flute. Comput. Music. J. **38**(2), 8–21 (2014)
73. Wang, G.: Game design for expressive mobile music. In: Proceedings of the International Conference on New Interfaces for Musical Expression, vol. 16 (2016)
74. Wang, G., Salazar, S., Oh, J., Hamilton, R.: World stage: crowdsourcing paradigm for expressive social mobile music. J. New Music. Res. **44**(2) (2015)
75. Weinberg, G., Beck, A., Godfrey, M.: ZooZBeat: a gesture-based mobile music studio. In: Proceedings of the International Conference on New Interfaces for Musical Expression (2009)

76. Weitzner, N., Freeman, J., Chen, Y.L., Garrett, S.: massMobile: towards a flexible framework for large-scale participatory collaborations in live performances. Organ. Sound **18**(1), 30–42 (2013)
77. Yang, Q.: Not all gestures are created equal: gesture and visual feedback in interaction spaces. Ph.D. thesis, University of Michigan (2015)
78. Yang, Q., Essl, G.: Representation-plurality in multi-touch mobile visual programming for music. In: Proceedings of the International Conference on New Interfaces for Musical Expression (2015)

Augmenting Virtuality with a Synchronized Dynamic Musical Instrument: A User Evaluation of a Mixed Reality MIDI Keyboard

John Desnoyers-Stewart[1]([⊠]) [iD], David Gerhard[2] [iD], and Megan L. Smith[1]

[1] Faculty of Media, Art, and Performance, University of Regina,
Regina, SK S4S 0A2, Canada
{desnoyej,megan.smith}@uregina.ca

[2] Department of Computer Science, University of Regina,
Regina, SK S4S 0A2, Canada

Abstract. As virtual reality gains popularity, technology which better integrates the user's physical experience in the virtual environment is needed. Researchers have shown that by including real physical objects to interact with, the experience can be made significantly more convincing and user-friendly. To explore physically connecting the user to the virtual environment, we designed and developed a mixed reality MIDI keyboard. This project explores maintaining the user's physical connection to the real world in order to align their senses with their true state of *augmented virtuality*. A user study of the keyboard was performed which verified its ability to improve the VR experience and identified areas for further research. In addition to producing a mixed reality MIDI keyboard, this project serves as a roadmap and foundation for future developments and investigations in integrating physical and virtual environments to improve immersion and presence.

Keywords: Virtual reality · Mixed reality · Augmented virtuality MIDI · Interface · HTC Vive · Unity · Leap Motion · Arduino

1 Introduction

Although the technology has existed for decades, recent advances in *Virtual Reality* (VR) have led to a resurgence in interest, and with it the development and marketing of numerous consumer-oriented devices, from Head Mounted Displays (HMD) such as the HTC Vive and Oculus Rift, to 3D-tracking devices such as the Leap Motion and Microsoft Kinect. Additionally, haptic technologies such as gloves, tools, and body suits have experienced a re-emergence and application to this new interaction modality. While head-tracking combined with binocular display provides an immersive simulated virtual environment, the user remains necessarily fixed in a real physical environment—A user virtually floating in

© Springer Nature Switzerland AG 2018
M. Aramaki et al. (Eds.): CMMR 2017, LNCS 11265, pp. 540–557, 2018.
https://doi.org/10.1007/978-3-030-01692-0_36

orbit still experiences gravity. Indeed, it is often these disconnects between the physical world and the virtual environment that can lead to VR sickness (via vestibular miscommunication) [5]. As such, any virtual experience is, to a varying degree, a *Mixed Reality* (MR) experience and exists somewhere on the Virtuality Continuum proposed by Milgram and Kishino [6]. The position of a virtual environment on this continuum is related to the degree of physical interaction involved, with the pure real environment at one end, and the pure virtual environment at the other. An experience which is not properly aligned with its level of virtuality reduces the user's immersion.

The controllers used by the HTC Vive and Oculus Rift VR systems are designed to mimic the physical objects that the user might interact with. In this way, they seek to minimize the disparity between the experience and expectations; however, in more complex environments with objects that don't conform to the controller's gun-like shape, the immersion once again falls away. Hand tracking systems, such as the Leap Motion controller, enable the potential for a higher level of interaction with a broader variety of objects. This type of interaction feels far more natural until interacting with virtual objects, which require the user to grasp at empty space.

Integrating real objects into the experience is an effective way to create a physical connection, improve immersion, and create a sense that virtual objects belong to the user's reality [7]. According to Sra and Schmandt, few VR environments include touch, yet a closer connection between the user's real and virtual representation enhances presence [12,14]. To improve the immersion and interactivity of a virtual experience, this project aims to explore methods of physical interaction that better align with the user's level of virtuality, with a testbed of a real-world application that requires physical interaction: playing a musical instrument. Using a customized MIDI keyboard as a prototyping interface in conjunction with a number of emergent VR technologies, this project explores maintaining the user's physical connection to the real world in order to align with their true state of Augmented Virtuality [6].

2   Background and Related Work

There are numerous examples which integrate a MIDI keyboard with different levels of Augmented Reality (AR) including, VR Piano [2], AR Piano [8], and Music Education using Augmented Reality with a Head Mounted Display [3]. All of these systems project some kind of visual overlay onto a real keyboard with the goal of improving the user's piano learning experience. There are also a number of applications which enable the user to play virtual instruments including Music Room VR [10] and Sound Stage VR [13].

Unlike those works, the focus of this project is not to project visuals onto a real keyboard, nor to create entirely virtual instruments, but to produce a mixed reality interface which is physically present, yet corresponds directly to real-time virtual imagery. The addition of this physical presence to a virtual experience enables augmented *virtuality* as opposed to the augmented reality of other examples of MIDI keyboard integration. Furthermore, rather than simply building conventional engagement with a piano as instrument, this project seeks to enhance this familiar metaphor with extended physical interface interactions. The keyboard's presence forms a convenient hub around which other physical and virtual interfaces can be added.

3   Methodology

This project employs a number of readily available VR and AR technologies to produce a system which seamlessly forms the interface between the user and simulation. As illustrated in Fig. 1, an HTC Vive is used as the headset and the Leap Motion controller is used for hand tracking, working in conjunction with the Arduino based MIDI keyboard. All three components communicate via USB with the Unity game engine which integrates the data and handles the simulation.

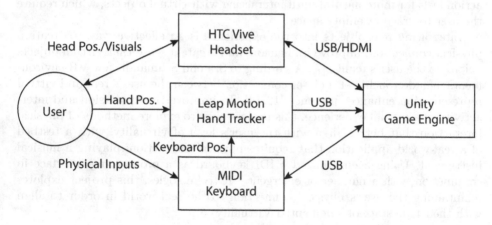

Fig. 1. Interaction model of the Mixed Reality MIDI Keyboard system.

3.1   MIDI Keyboard Design

While many off-the-shelf MIDI keyboards could work with this system, a specialized platform was developed for the project to allow for added flexibility as well as to enable rapid prototyping and experimentation with various real and virtual interfaces. As the keyboard is intended for use in an interactive public art installation this also allowed for greater control over the aesthetic design. We have made the design and code used for the keyboard and associated electronics open-source, and these are available on GitHub.[1]

The keyboard, shown in Fig. 2, consists of a reused key bed mounted to a black acrylic and wood frame. The electronics are easily modifiable while the

---

[1] https://github.com/jdesnoyers/Mixed-Reality-MIDI-Keyboard.

upper surface of the frame is used as a space to test various inputs which can be quickly added or removed. The keyboard surfaces were CNC milled from acrylic sheet to ensure precise placement of components and adherence to design tolerances.

Fig. 2. Mixed Reality MIDI Keyboard prototype.

The electronics center around an Arduino Mega 2560 microcontroller. A protoshield is used for more permanent fixtures, such as pull-down resistors for the key bed matrix, while a number of miniature breadboards are used to connect temporary components. Examples of components used in testing include capacitive sensors, IR proximity sensors, linear potentiometers, and optical encoders. An LED strip lines the top of the key bed to provide simple and direct feedback for observers and when the HMD is not in use. The microcontroller communicates using the MIDI protocol via both a hardware MIDI DIN connection and over USB. The MIDI standard is used for its ubiquity in digital music devices, and for its expandability to easily assign interfaces to both standard note or control messages as well as extensions using additional channels or SysEx messages.

Concurrent Design of Virtual and Physical Components. In order to rapidly develop a keyboard which exists in both the virtual and real environments, a detailed design was first produced for the physical production, while a simplified virtual version (with hidden elements and details such as screw holes removed) was created as a secondary branch in OnShape[2] CAD software. This method facilitates the application of any subsequent changes to both the physical

---

[2] https://www.onshape.com.

and virtual designs with minimal intervention. The physical design was produced using CNC milling, 3D printing, and woodworking tools and assembled within a maximum tolerance of ±1 mm on all exposed surfaces. The CAD model was exported as a COLLADA 1.4.1 interchange file, which was then imported into Blender for texture mapping, and subsequently transferred into Unity. This process ensures that the physical and virtual keyboards align with minimal effort.

While this was the most direct approach available, the loss of kinematic data in the interchange file means a duplication of effort in defining physical relations, especially those of the keyboard keys. The work-flow would benefit greatly from a direct conversion of kinematic data such as that supported by COLLADA 1.5 or as described by Lorenz et al. [9].

Special Considerations. Hand tracking via the Leap Motion assumes the hands are in open space, but the reflective white keys of the keyboard can lead to errors in hand tracking. To improve contrast in the infrared range between the hands and their surroundings, a matte black paint coating is applied to the keys (see Fig. 3). The upper surface uses matte black acrylic to minimize infrared reflectivity and visibility to improve the infrared tracking methods employed by the HTC Vive and Leap Motion.

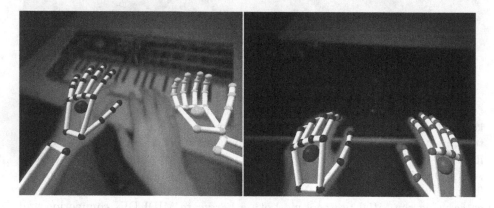

Fig. 3. Screenshots of IR data. Left: ordinary keyboard; Right: MR MIDI Keyboard.

3.2 Position Tracking

There are numerous methods available to locate the physical keyboard and accurately render that location in virtual space. There are trade-offs between accuracy, form factor, and portability between systems.

HTC Vive Tracker. This device easily integrates directly into the existing Vive virtual coordinate system; however, the form factor and cost ($ 100 USD) are problematic. In testing the Tracker can precisely locate the keyboard, but can lose tracking if obscured by the user or their hands. Since the physical keyboard does not (usually) move during a session, one-time location registration is sufficient, so the Vive Tracker is only used to initially align the keyboard and to correct noticeable misalignments. The original prototype used clear acrylic which seemed to reduce tracking reliability causing some jitter and more frequent loss of tracking. The second iteration's use of matte black acrylic has greatly improved the tracking accuracy and reliability, suggesting that the reflection and refraction of infrared light off of the clear acrylic interfered with the tracking.

Steam VR HDK. The Steam VR HDK makes the technology used in the HTC Vive available for developers to integrate into their own devices [16]. This system offers an ideal solution for large scale production but is very expensive for initial prototyping ($ 595 USD).

Co-Located Hand Tracking. It is possible to use the existing Leap Motion hand tracking and MIDI interface to locate the keyboard. The physical location can be determined using co-location between button and key presses on the MIDI controller and the hand location and gesture determined by the Leap Motion. This could provide sufficient data for location in two axes (X, Z). To fully constrain the device and locate it in the Y axis, the high contrast between the black key bed and its surroundings is used to find the edge of the keyboard, or, alternatively, specific buttons could be used to locate the device, such as a pair of capacitive touch sensors at its edges. The current implementation of the Leap Motion hand tracker does not sufficiently replicate the complicated gestures used in playing the keyboard so it must only be implemented for reliable and predictable gestures.

Infrared LEDs. The co-location technique relies on the accurate tracking of the user's hands near the keyboard. Alternatively, the Leap Motion's infrared camera could be used to detect the location of infrared LEDs strategically placed on the keyboard frame. This will provide more accuracy and reliability than the hand tracking option, although the two may be used in conjunction. This method provides less precise tracking than the Vive Tracker, but reliably positions the keyboard relative to the Leap Motion tracked hands.

Visible Markers. Finally, visible markers, such as those used by Chow et al. [3] could be used. These markers could be tracked by either the Leap Motion's infrared camera, or an additional depth sensing camera such as a Microsoft Kinect could be used. This system is expected to have similar accuracy to the Infrared LED solution at a slightly reduced cost, but at the expense of the aesthetic of the end product. Unlike the infrared solutions, which are invisible and can be hidden behind IR transparent materials, visible markers are necessarily prominent on the surface of the device.

Our prototype primarily uses the HTC Vive Tracker for tracking. Infrared LEDs were also used successfully and provided consistent alignment with the Leap Motion hands. Future versions will use the Steam VR HDK to improve reliability and accuracy. Tracking using co-location has been suspended due to issues of tracking and gestural accuracy with the Leap Motion; however, with continued improvement of the Leap Motion hand tracking system's accuracy it is expected to once again become a viable option in the future.

3.3 Virtual Environment Synchronization

The data from all interfaces is integrated and processed in the Unity game engine, which forms the hub of the system. Unity was chosen for its ease of use and ubiquity in current VR development. The SteamVR (HTC Vive) and Leap Motion SDKs along with K. Takahashi's MidiJack plug-in [15] are used to connect with each of the devices. The MIDI data is used to translate the keys and inputs proportionally to their physical components, as well as to control variables in the virtual environment. The movements are constrained to the physical object's location and data. In the virtual environment the keyboard appears identical in form, but with modified textures which are changed to suit the needs and aesthetics of the particular application.

This synchronization with the real environment not only allows for a true virtual representation, but also for the inclusion of virtual interfaces such as those shown in Fig. 4. These can be divided into two categories: simulated, and augmented. The simulated interfaces are ones which could exist in reality, but are instead replicated in the virtual environment. For example, IR proximity and capacitive touch sensors can be simulated by capturing the transform of the virtual hand while it is within specified bounds. By using virtual versions of these sensors, their presence, shape, location, sensitivity, etc. can all be modified in real-time and beyond physical limitations and constraints. The augmented interfaces are ones which could not exist in the real world—for example a three-dimensional position input could be controlled by moving a sphere's location within a cube. Further to this, other virtual instruments and components can be attached to the virtual keyboard, creating a modular virtual instrument. While these virtual components lack the tactility of the physical keyboard, they offer significant capacity for expansion and alteration to the device, with few constraints. These simulated and augmented interfaces offer the primary advantages over a conventional keyboard, giving the user the opportunity to interact in ways which otherwise would not be possible.

3.4 Prototype Interfaces

A number of real and virtual interfaces have been implemented on and around the Mixed Reality MIDI Keyboard. For physical controls in addition to the keys the keyboard has 3 buttons, 2 rotary potentiometer knobs, 1 rotary encoder knob, 1 slide potentiometer and 1 infrared (IR) sensor. The keyboard is also equipped with a number of capacitive proximity and touch sensors; however, these were disabled for the user evaluation.

Fig. 4. Screenshot of the keyboard and virtual interfaces as seen in the VR HMD.

The keyboard's surface is covered with virtual controls including 3 virtual 2D buttons, 9 virtual 3D buttons, 6 virtual rotary potentiometer knobs, and 6 virtual slide potentiometers. Sets of virtual controls can be changed between using a swipe gesture above the keyboard.

In addition, the keyboard is surrounded by 5 volumetric virtual interfaces including a real IR sensor, virtual IR sensor, 3-axis spindle control, virtual ball control, and a sphere in which a gun gesture can be used.

The real interfaces also send MIDI commands to a digital audio workstation, allowing for control of the audio parameters of a synthesizer or other instrument. The prototype virtual interfaces only affect visuals within the VR environment, such as turning on and off a light, adjusting its brightness, or changing the colour of the room. Further details of the design process and user evaluation of the individual virtual controls are presented in [4].

4   User Evaluation

4.1   Participants

11 participants were recruited through a number of methods to ensure a diverse sample. The study was announced in 5 undergraduate classes and advertised

through the University's Creative Technologies Facebook page. Some professional musicians were invited directly by email to ensure that musicians needs were well represented in the study. The user study was conducted in the University of Regina's Maker Space, following approval by the University of Regina's Research Ethics Board, with all participants' informed consent.

The age of participants ranged from 19 to 58, with an average age of 32. Participants' levels of education ranged from some undergraduate studies (63.6%) to PhD (18.2%), and participants had a wide range of musical experience, from 0 to 52 years with 54.5% of participants claiming to have some level of formal music training. Of those only 2 participants claimed to be expert musicians. 54.5% of participants rated themselves as highly experienced in playing video games, only one of which had formal music training. All but two of the participants had previous experience with some kind of VR system with 36.4% having used HTC Vive, 36.4% PlayStation VR, and 27.3% having used an Oculus Rift.

4.2 Procedure

The user evaluation followed a consistent procedure for all participants. None of the participants had previously used the Mixed Reality MIDI Keyboard system and were not briefed on its function or purpose other than as a "mixed reality keyboard interface" prior to the evaluation. With the participant's consent video of the study and interview along with a screen capture of their view in VR were recorded as shown in Fig. 5. Each session lasted approximately 30 min, with participants spending 15–20 min in VR and the remainder being interviewed.

Fig. 5. User study recordings. Left: screen capture view, Right: camera view

Each session began with a brief series of demographic questions after which participants were instructed to put on the VR headset. Participants were then asked to place their hands on the keyboard so that the alignment could be verified and adjusted if needed. They were then allowed to freely explore the keyboard for 5 min without any instruction from the researcher. After 5 min the researcher asked the participant to perform any tasks which the user had not elected to try previously, ensuring that all facets of the keyboard were fully interacted with. During these interactive phases the researcher observed the participant's discovery and mastery of each available control, noting the ease in which controls were discovered and to what extent they were mastered during the study. After all interfaces were tried at least once, the participant was given the option to continue using the system as long as they like, and to take off the headset when complete. Their choice and the amount of extra time was recorded up to a maximum of 5 min, after which the participant was asked to remove the headset. The researcher then asked the participant about their experience through a series of Likert Scale, rating, and open ended questions.

5   Results

5.1   Observed Interactions

All participants successfully engaged with the keyboard for the full duration of the study. Participants were able to use most of the interfaces with minimal interference from the researcher. Typically, instructions such as "move one of the sliders on the right side of the keyboard" were all that was required for successful interaction. As a measure of learnability, the timing and intervention required by the researcher were recorded on a 4 point scale as shown in Table 1. 65.4% of observed initial interactions were rated as "Immediately," 23.5% were successful after trial and error by the user, 10.5% required guidance by the researcher. The only unsuccessful interaction was a swipe gesture which one participant could not successfully use. The swipe gesture required detailed instruction as the researcher had to communicate the gesture verbally.

Table 1. Summary of user experience observational learnability

Interface type	Immediately	After trial & error	After guidance	Unsuccessful
Keyboard keys	100%	0%	0%	0%
Pure real	45.5%	42.4%	12.1%	0%
Mixed surface	77.3%	13.6%	9.1%	0%
Pure virtual	75.0%	23.1%	1.9%	0%
Gestural	31.8%	27.3%	36.4%	4.5%
Overall	65.4%	23.5%	10.5%	0.6%

5.2   Comparison to Previous VR Experiences and Immersiveness

All participants opted to continue in VR after being given the option with 54.5% playing up to the maximum additional time of 5 min. 62.5% of participants with previous experience in VR rated the Mixed Reality MIDI Keyboard as "much better" than their previous experiences. When asked about what made the MR MIDI Keyboard better or worse, Participant #3 stated, "I like this way more - much more engaged - the other ones you're walking through and can have limited interaction." Participant #4 commented that, "[the keyboard is] very unique - being able to actually touch things and have my hands mapped was very cool. It was very different in a good way." One participant found the experience to be worse than others due to misalignment between the keyboard and hands, stating that, "In terms of the immersive experience its every bit as good as fully developed things I've done. The misalignment made it worse."

When asked "did the keyboard make you feel more immersed than other virtual reality interfaces?" all of the participants agreed that the presence of the keyboard made them feel more immersed, with 66.7% reporting feeling much more immersed. Commenting on how it felt to see their hands in VR, participant # 1 stated "It was pretty cool. Almost otherworldly. Definitely different. With this you aren't holding anything. The hands definitely helped with the immersiveness." Participant #8 stated, "It is interesting not having to have a remote. You can place yourself much better. I like when you can see your hands." 3 participants reported that the hand tracking was weird, but improved as they got used to it. Another 3 participants stated that the hand tracking was clumsy or confusing as the visual representation of the hands sometimes did not reflect their actual gesture. Participant #9 stated "It was cool and its perfect as long as the hands are doing the same thing as I'm doing. If it shows me something different then it makes me confused."

When asked how it felt to touch something in VR, Participant # 4 stated, "It makes it more interactive. It felt like touching something in real life." 4 participants noted that it takes some getting used to. 3 participants stated that they were confused as to which objects could be touched and which could not, with participant #5 stating, "It was hard to tell what you could touch." 2 users stated that misalignment between the hands and keyboard made the touch problematic or confusing.

5.3   Experience Ratings

During the interview participants were asked to rate their agreement with several statements regarding the MR MIDI Keyboard on a 5-point Likert Scale. The results are shown in Fig. 6.

Augmenting Virtuality and Enhancing Reality. 90.9% of participants strongly agreed that the keyboard's presence made it feel as though virtual objects were more real, suggesting that the goal of augmenting the virtual environment with a real object was successful. 63.6% strongly agreed that touching

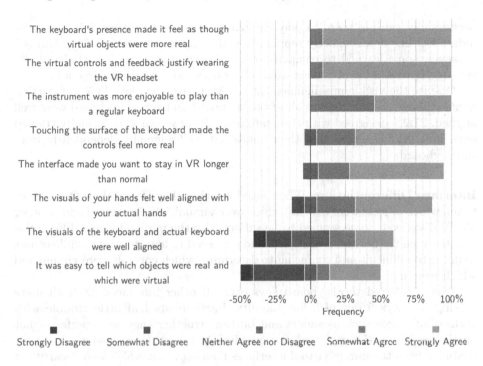

The keyboard's presence made it feel as though
virtual objects were more real

The virtual controls and feedback justify wearing
the VR headset

The instrument was more enjoyable to play than
a regular keyboard

Touching the surface of the keyboard made the
controls feel more real

The interface made you want to stay in VR longer
than normal

The visuals of your hands felt well aligned with
your actual hands

The visuals of the keyboard and actual keyboard
were well aligned

It was easy to tell which objects were real and
which were virtual

-50%   -25%   0%   25%   50%   75%   100%
Frequency

Strongly Disagree   Somewhat Disagree   Neither Agree nor Disagree   Somewhat Agree   Strongly Agree

Fig. 6. User experience interview Likert Scale responses

the surface of the keyboard made the controls feel more real. By providing tactile feedback and maintaining the user's physical connection to the real world, user presence was enhanced and the acceptance of virtual objects was improved.

90.9% of participants strongly agreed that the virtual controls and feedback justify wearing the VR headset. All participants agreed that the instrument was more enjoyable to play than a regular keyboard, with 54.5% strongly agreeing with this statement. 66.7% of those who had previously tried VR strongly agreed that the interface made them want to stay in VR longer than normal, with only 1 participant stating that they neither agreed nor disagreed.

Misalignment. All of the participants were observed to have noticed some misalignment between their hands and the keyboard, specifically when trying to interact with the physical keys or buttons at the far ends of the keyboard. At this distance the hands were typically misaligned by approximately 2 cm, roughly equal to the width of the key and buttons. This misalignment caused some confusion in attempting to push physical buttons, where users often pressed directly in-between two buttons, and occasionally pressed the wrong one.

Misalignment affected some more significantly than others. All of the musicians with formal training noted a discrepancy between their hand gesture and the one displayed. The leap motion seemed to struggle with some of the more complex hand gestures typical of experienced keyboardists and pianists, occasionally causing them to play the wrong notes. Participant #7 stated, "it didn't feel like it was exactly representing the angle and motion of my hands." However, some learned to compensate for the alignment, with participant #3 stating "It took a bit of getting used to - you would have to practice a bit."

Despite the visible misalignment at the keyboard's extents 45.5% of participants still agreed that the visuals of the keyboard and actual keyboard were well aligned. 27.2% disagreed with this statement, all of whom were formally trained musicians. 81.8% agreed that their hands felt well aligned independently from the keyboard.

Interface Differentiation. When asked whether they agreed that "it was easy to tell which objects were real and which were virtual," 45.5% agreed and another 45.5% disagreed. Some seemed to be satisfied by the minimal visual differentiation between virtual and real objects and expected to have to adapt, while others found it too difficult and confusing to determine which controls were virtual and which were not.

Users preferred the keyboard keys over all other interfaces, with all users scoring the keys 5 out of 5 for usability. Participants had little trouble with surface interfaces such as sliders and buttons whether they were perfectly flat on the surface of the keyboard or were slightly raised. Users also got excellent usability from the purely virtual interfaces floating in air which were clearly not a part of the keyboard, rating these higher than everything but the keys.

At the end of the interview 80% of participants strongly agreed and 20% somewhat agreed with the statement "This experience has improved your impression of the potential impact of virtual reality."

6   Discussion

The ability of this experience to improve the outlook of both experienced and inexperienced VR users, young and old, and with various degrees of technical and musical ability, suggests that devices which augment virtuality such as the Mixed Reality MIDI Keyboard could be an integral part of the near future of VR and MR development. The MR MIDI Keyboard was very successful at improving users' sense of presence and the potential usability and usefulness of VR interfaces. By maintaining the user's physical connection to the real world, the keyboard was able to improve their connection to the virtual environment. Aligning the user's tactile and proprioceptive senses through a dynamic interface provides an opportunity for a longer, more enjoyable, and believable interaction. Onto the physical foundation of the MR MIDI Keyboard, virtual interfaces and experiences can be built which increase the flexibility and utility of the keyboard beyond an ordinary one.

Despite the simple nature of the testing environment, the keyboard's presence improved the experience and made users want to spend more time in VR. The utility provided by the possibility of augmenting the keyboard with versatile, flexible controls in the virtual space, and the potential to control and adjust the visuals was sufficient to justify putting on the VR headset.

The results of this user study suggest that it is worthwhile continuing to pursue the development of the MR MIDI Keyboard and similar tactile interfaces. The study highlighted the most significant problems which need to be addressed to ensure the success of such interfaces: alignment between tracking systems and interface differentiation.

The keyboard itself was aligned as accurately as possible to the VR system by using the HTC Vive Tracker for positioning and using an HTC Vive Controller to calibrate it in the virtual space. The hands were then calibrated to the keyboard by playing a single note with both hands close to the center of the body. The version of the Leap Motion Core Assets used, 4.2.1 suffered from alignment which varied with distance from the headset and a "swimming" effect in which stationary hands would appear to move when the user rotated their head. Leap Motion claims to have resolved this problem in versions since 4.3.3.[3]. While this misalignment caused some problems for users during the study, it provided some valuable insight into how important accurate alignment is to users. Being off even slightly caused errors and frustration which have the potential to severely limit the usability of such an interface.

While participants were split as to whether the keyboard was well aligned, almost all users stated that their hands appeared to be in the correct location. This contradiction with the actual state of the system provided an interesting insight into user's trust of their representative body in VR. Although it was the hands that were misaligned, the user perceived the resulting discrepancy as an error in the keyboard's position.

VR is still a very new mode of interaction which requires some getting used to for users. Adding real objects into the space complicates this process. This system used a variety of untested experimental interfaces which the researcher expected to be sufficiently differentiated for the purpose of this study; however, as the results make clear interface differentiation is a problem which requires considerable investigation. It had been expected that participants might initially expect real controls but instead, the opposite seemed to be true. Despite the physical interaction with the keyboard, many users did not expect the presence of other physical controls on the keyboard. Particularly confusing were the real knobs. Users would grab at empty space above the real knobs without correcting when the knob was not found, seemingly expecting that the knob was not really there and attempting to adjust what they thought was a virtual object.

Improved alignment would subsequently improve the user's ability to differentiate between real and virtual. While the appearance of the object can give an indication of whether it is virtual or not, the user must confirm which it is through interaction, and upon grasping at empty space the user is led towards the expectation that the object is virtual. Another solution is simply designing the interfaces so that they conform closely to the keyboard's physical shape so that users are required to touch the surface to interact. By ensuring all interactions

---

[3] https://developer.leapmotion.com/releases.

provide tactile feedback users might more readily expect to interact with real knobs and buttons in addition to virtual ones. Alternately the real interfaces other than the keyboard keys could be removed entirely to provide consistency and reduce the significance of alignment. Interactions in the virtual space are aligned with the visual representation of the user's hands regardless of any misalignment between the actual hands and keyboard, providing an increased tolerance for misalignment. To ensure clear distinction, purely virtual controls should be placed at a distance from the keyboard similarly to some of the volumetric controls placed around the keyboard in this user study.

6.1 Applications

The Mixed Reality MIDI Keyboard has numerous applications. The platform can be applied for educational purposes as often considered by others [2,3,8], or as an integrated real and virtual instrument. The keyboard hardware and software can be directly interfaced with popular digital audio workstations to produce extraordinary instrument controls and compositional experiences. The techniques used for this virtual reality based system can also be applied to augmented reality systems such as the Microsoft Hololens to further retain connection to the real world, enabling the technology to be used by musicians in live performances. In addition to these direct applications, the discoveries made through this experimentation will enable a better understanding of mixed reality interfaces in general, and may be applied to the development of similar interfaces beyond the keyboard.

One such application is already in development concurrently with the Mixed Reality MIDI keyboard. The techniques being explored for this keyboard project are being applied to object tracking for the Royal Canadian Mounted Police (RCMP) VR and Simulation project. A number of virtual weapons are being designed and prototyped for use in a simulation which assists police in learning to make the best possible decisions in high-pressure situations. The immersion of the trainee and realism of the simulated interfaces is crucial in creating an environment which accurately reproduces the stresses of such a difficult situation. By integrating real objects into the simulation, the virtual experience is aligned more closely with the reality the trainee will face, and as such enables reactions that better match the desired real world outcomes.

6.2 Future Work

With the construction of the described prototype, we have confirmed the possibility and viability of such an interface. The user experience evaluation has provided valuable insight into the potential viability of mixed reality instruments such as this one and suggested research areas in need of focus for continued development. We will continue to improve the interface and to test other mixed reality interfaces, adding functionality for professional musicians, amateurs, and learners.

Further Evaluation. Further evaluation is required with a more developed prototype. While this user study verified the keyboard's utility and ability to improve immersion, problems with misalignment and reliability prevented a full understanding of the interface's potential as instrument and mixed reality interface. Further iteration of the prototype with improved tracking in the form of the Steam VR HDK and improved hand tracking will allow for further research into mixed reality as a platform for instruments which improve the virtual experience.

Detailed Interface Design. With the keyboard successfully providing a foundation for immersive interaction the interfaces to be used on such a device are now in need of refinement and detailed testing. The development and testing of individual virtual controls is a significant research challenge which will require considerable further investigation separately from the complexity of the MR MIDI Keyboard.

Experience Design. An immersive experience will be developed to explore the value and capabilities of a mixed reality interface compared to ones which are solely real or virtual. The experience will be designed for public consumption through an art installation with interaction for both the active user and any spectators in the space. The keyboard platform will be used in an unconventional way that defies expectations and encourages participants to experiment.

Streamlining of Design and Fabrication. Further streamlining of the process from design to operation is also needed to facilitate more experimentation and enable the use of other real-world keyboards and devices in the system. Enabling spectator participation (outside of the HMD) is a major challenge which will also be addressed to encourage interaction with the system.

Perceptual Alignment. Perhaps the most significant problem is the accurate alignment of the perceived real and virtual worlds as outlined by Ponto et al. [1,11,17]. At present, the focus is on aligning the virtual and real environments relative to the existing platforms; however, there is a noticeable difference between perceived distances and sizes in the real and virtual environments, as well as between the Leap Motion and HTC Vive tracking systems. The body's proprioception seems to be able to sufficiently manage and account for the discrepancy through visual and tactile feedback, but refining the calibration would further improve the user's presence, while reducing the time required to adjust to the virtual environment. The methods described by Ponto et al. will be explored for this purpose [11].

7   Conclusion

The Mixed Reality MIDI Keyboard enables experimentation with a wide variety of real and virtual interfaces. By integrating a real, interactive component the user becomes physically connected to the experience, creating a sense of presence and improving immersion. By exploring the potential of this interface, virtual reality experiences which better reflect the user's true mixed reality state, will be achievable. Augmenting the virtual environment with real interfaces will enable a heightened sense of connection and improved perceptual resonance. In addition, the virtual interface augments the keyboard itself, allowing for the implementation of novel controls that enable creativity beyond the constraints of a purely physical instrument. The user study verified initial expectations that such a dynamic real object could enhance the virtual experience, and has highlighted research areas in need of further focus. The success of this project will not only result in the development of a mixed reality MIDI keyboard, but will influence future developments and investigations in integrating real and virtual environments into a more cohesive, convincing experience.

Acknowledgments. Much of the research involved in this project has been made possible by the ongoing RCMP VR and Simulation Research led by Dr. Megan Smith.

References

1. Chen, K., Kimmel, R., Bartholomew, A., Ponto, K., Gleicher, M., Radwin, G.: Manually locating physical and virtual reality objects. Hum. Factors **56**(6), 1163–1176 (2014). https://doi.org/10.1177/0018720814523067
2. Cheng, S.-F.: VR Piano. https://vrpiano.tumblr.com/
3. Chow, J., Feng, H., Amor, R., Wünsche, B.: Music education using augmented reality with a head mounted display. In: 14th Australasian User Interface Conference (AUIC 2013), pp. 73–79 (2013)
4. Desnoyers-Stewart, J., Gerhard, D., Smith, M.L.: Augmenting a MIDI Keyboard Using Virtual Interfaces. J. Audio Eng. Soc. **66**(6), 439–447 (2018)
5. Kolanski, E.M.: Simulator sickness in virtual environments. Technical report 1027, (ARTI-TR-1027). Army Research Institute for the Behavioral and Social Sciences, Alexandria, VA (1995)
6. Milgram, P., Kishino, F.: A taxonomy of mixed reality visual displays. IEICE Trans. Inf. Syst. **E77–D**(12), 1321–1329 (1994)
7. Hoffman, H.G.: Physically touching virtual objects using tactile augmentation enhances the realism of virtual environments. In: IEEE Virtual Reality Annual International Symposium 1998, Los Alamitos, CA, pp. 59–63. IEEE (1998). https://doi.org/10.1109/VRAIS.1998.658423
8. Huang, F., Zhou, Y., Yu, Y., Wang, Z., Du, S.: Piano AR: a markerless augmented reality based piano teaching system. In: 2011 Third International Conference on Intelligent Human-Machine Systems and Cybernetics, Zhejiang, pp. 47–52 (2011). https://doi.org/10.1109/IHMSC.2011.82
9. Lorenz, M., Spranger, M., Riedel, T., Pürzel, F., Wittstock, V., Klimant, P.: CAD to VR - a methodology for the automated conversion of kinematic CAD models to virtual reality. Procedia CIRP **41**, 358–363 (2016). https://doi.org/10.1016/j.procir.2015.12.115
10. Music Room VR. http://www.musicroomvr.com/
11. Ponto, K., Gleicher, M., Radwin, R.: Perceptual calibration for immersive display environments. IEEE Trans. Vis. Comput. Graph. **19**(4), 691–700 (2013). https://doi.org/10.1109/TVCG.2013.36

12. Slater, M., Steed, A., Usoh, M.: Being there together: experiments on presence in virtual environments (1990s). Technical report, Department of Computer Science, University College London, UK (2013)
13. Sound Stage VR. http://www.soundstagevr.com/
14. Sra, M., Schmandt, C.: Bringing real objects, spaces, actions, and interactions into social VR. In: 2016 IEEE Third VR International Workshop on Collaborative Virtual Environments (3DCVE), Greenville, SC, pp. 16–17. IEEE (2016). https://doi.org/10.1109/3DCVE.2016.7563561
15. Takahashi, K.: MidiJack. https://github.com/keijiro/MidiJack
16. Triad Semiconductor Steam VR HDK. https://www.triadsemi.com/product/steamvr-tracking-hdk/
17. Wann, J., Rushton, S., Mon-Williams, M.: Natural problems for stereoscopic depth perception in virtual environments. Vis. Res. **35**(19), 2731–2736 (1995). https://doi.org/10.1016/0042-6989(95)00018-U

Toward Augmented Familiarity of the Audience with Digital Musical Instruments

Olivier Capra[✉], Florent Berthaut, and Laurent Grisoni

Univ. Lille, INRIA, CRIStAL, Lille, France
olivier.capra@etu.univ-lille1.fr,
{florent.berthaut,laurent.grisoni}@univ-lille1.fr

Abstract. The diversity and complexity of Digital Musical Instruments often lead to a reduced appreciation of live performances by the audience. This can be linked to the lack of familiarity they have with the instruments. We propose to increase this familiarity thanks to a transdisciplinary approach in which signals from both the musician and the audience are extracted, familiarity analyzed, and augmentations dynamically added to the instruments. We introduce a new decomposition of familiarity and the concept of *correspondences* between musical gestures and results. This paper is both a review of research that paves the way for the realization of a pipeline for augmented familiarity, and a call for future research on the identified challenges that remain before it can be implemented.

Keywords: Digital musical instrument · Performance · Familiarity Causality · Augmentations · Correspondences

1 Introduction

Whether as a musician or as a spectator, the experience of live music has very particular characteristics. It is often immersive, as intimate as collective and implies different modalities with both low and high level cognitive engagements. Moreover, a musical experience is often a corporeal, aesthetic as well as emotional commitment and is therefore difficult to define. Despite their great diversity and the parallel treatments they require, we assimilate all these aspects without any apparent effort. We naturally build this intense feeling that we all have experienced by attending a concert. Beyond the unfathomable subjective part of this musical experience (i.e. tastes and colors), we can identify objective characteristics that influence how we perceive live music, and among these, the way musicians interact with their instrument and how we perceive and integrate these interactions.

On the one hand, in the production of music with acoustic instruments, gestures and sounds are intrinsically linked by the laws of physics or at least by

© Springer Nature Switzerland AG 2018
M. Aramaki et al. (Eds.): CMMR 2017, LNCS 11265, pp. 558–573, 2018.
https://doi.org/10.1007/978-3-030-01692-0_37

intuitive connections that do not need any prior explanation. Beside the music they produce, every interaction is visible. Thereby the expressive intentions, as well as the intensity of emotions, are particularly vivid and underline the role of a multimodal integration [42]. Along this line, the degree of perceived control, influenced by the additional information usually extracted from the musician's interactions, participates in the emergence of the liveness of the performance.

On the other hand, the experience of live music produced by digital musical instruments (DMIs) may suffer from a deterioration of this intuitive link between the behavior of the musician, the inner mechanisms of the instrument and the sounds actually produced. When what we hear is not directly linked to what we see or what we may infer from a given gestural behavior, when music is not the direct and causal consequence of the specific gestures of the musician, then we may loose the multimodal integration that contributes to the immersive experience of live music.

These considerations have led to an increasing amount of recent researches on measuring the audience experience [2,3,11,12,17–19,26], sometimes used as a way to evaluate the instruments themselves [44]. The less familiar we are with an instrument, the less we are able to perceive the fine relationship musicians build with their instrument. This lack of coherence in multimodal information might downgrade the attributed agency [7], that is the perception of how much the musician is controlling their performance. Thus the knowledge we have about a DMI or its obvious behavior are crucial features to understand and integrate the interactions and thus fully experience live music. How do we ensure familiarity with DMIs?

1.1 Improving Familiarity with Digital Musical Instruments

Familiarity is the feeling of knowing about the behavior and the possibilities of an instrument. It can be associated with other concepts in the literature as *mental model* [18] or as an extension of *transparency* [16]. We believe that familiarity is a strong component of the live music experience as it provides the spectator the ability to detect the intentions and the virtuosity of the performance of the musicians as well as their errors. Several attempts have been made at improving the familiarity. In this section, we propose a quick review of these solutions and their limitations.

Building a Repertoire. Quite naturally, a first way to increase the familiarity of people with a particular instrument is to promote its use and dissemination by building a repertoire of compositions around it. Once a majority of spectators have seen the instrument played by many musicians in different contexts, or even practiced it themselves, they are aware of its potential for musical expression and of its behavior. Thereby, the familiarity issue does not exist anymore. This kind of "natural familiarity" is definitely effective but requires a large amount of time and energy to be achieved. Moreover, this method is not compatible with the very idea behind DMIs and the exponential creativity they embed. Whether a musician wants to evolve its instrument or let other musicians modify it, as soon as the instrument changes, the whole process of natural familiarity needs to start all over again.

Explaining the Instruments. When the problem of familiarity lies partially in the understanding of the operations of an instrument, demonstrating the behavior of the instrument can be a valuable solution. Building the familiarity with a pedagogical method is a simple way to make an audience understand what is going on stage. Before, after and even in breaks during the performance, the musicians can explain how their instrument works. Prior hands-on demos, where the audience can actually play the instrument, are also a good way to increase the familiarity. However, both these methods trigger some reservations as the technical understanding of an instrument is not necessarily linked to a better appreciation of the performance. For example, Bin et al. [10] demonstrate that explanations before the performance do improve the understanding of the instruments and its mechanisms but do not increase either the appreciation or interest. Besides these results, the audience may forget or unconsciously misreport important details from the performance [29] and the demos may not be possible when dealing with a large audience.

Designing for Transparency. Another strategy to increase the experience of spectators watching a musician playing an instrument they have never seen before lies in the design of the instrument itself. The idea is to expose a clear link between the gestures and the sound modifications operated by these gestures, what is called the *mapping* of an instrument. The fluency of perception of these mappings is often called "transparency", and is defined by Fels et al. [16] as follows:

> For the lay audience, this understanding is derived from cultural knowledge, including percepts of physical causality relationships.

Aiming for transparency from the very first steps of the design of a musical device can lead to "easier to perceive" instruments [31]. Following that lead, an interesting way to increase the transparency is the use of metaphors [16]. In that case, the common background of inexperienced audience, their general knowledge, are used as a mold to grow new knowledge about an instrument mapping. For instance, the timbre of a sound can be modified as the shape of an associated graphical representation that is getting sculpted. However, the instruments designed according to these specifications tend to maintain the familiarity we have with acoustic instruments and physical laws. Thus, despite the gain in transparency, this method may narrow the design possibilities usually available for DMIs.

Visually Augmenting the Instruments. Berthaut et al. [7,8] proposed to increase the familiarity by recreating a link of causality through visual augmentations of the instruments. Based on the attribution of causality by spectators (attributed agency) to a music performance, the visual augmentations provide insights on the musician's interactions with its instrument. Animated 3D objects overlapping the device reveal the relationship between the gestures and the musical result to the audience. These augmentations are based on Wegner's criteria of apparent mental causation [43] (See Sect. 2.1). By exposing the details of the interactions, the setup contributes to re-link the gestures of the artist to their intentions and expressiveness. Besides, the augmentations enable the distinction between automated part and actual live music production. Such a discrimination between live and pre-recorded music appears to be crucial in the experience of live music precisely because it is supposed to be a live performance. However, these augmentations do not take into account the audience reaction or their expertise. Indeed, the familiarity with an instrument is a personal characteristic that cannot be generalized. A concert in front of specialists or naive people does not imply the same requirement of explanations or augmentations (Fig. 1).

Fig. 1. Visual augmentations of DMIS for the increase of familiarity. The inner mechanisms of the instrument are dynamically revealed to the audience. (From Berthaut et al. [8])

Toward a New Method. These different methods offer a rather effective way to increase the understanding of the behavior of DMIs. However they don't fully cover a major aspect of the music experience which is the real time multimodal integration of visual and auditory cues. Furthermore, while the visual augmentations gave good results they do not take into account the audience expertise that may appeal for specific levels of details in the augmentations. Moreover, in some cases, non-visual augmentations may be more relevant. Thereby, we propose new insights to improve the familiarity in a more adaptable and reliable way.

1.2 Contribution

Our contribution is two-fold. First, we propose a conceptual pipeline to improve the familiarity of the audience with DMIs in real-time by analyzing spectators' reactions, musicians' actions, musical outputs and by augmenting the instrument. To do so, we introduce the concept of *correspondences*. Second, for each module of this pipeline, we briefly review relevant knowledge in computer and cognitive sciences. We also identify interdisciplinary challenges that need to be solved to reach a functional software implementation of the pipeline.

2   Toward Augmented Familiarity

In this section we propose a novel approach for improving familiarity, formalized by a software pipeline. While it remains conceptual, it was designed so that it could be implemented by addressing the challenges described in Sect. 2.2.

Here is a scenario that we envision with our pipeline:

Patricia attends an electronic music concert. At the entrance, she is given a small device equipped with physiological sensors (a choice of either a bracelet or a special glass that she holds). During the concert, she has trouble understanding what is happening, in particular what the musician's action on the sound is. The device senses a change in a set of physiological signals, that corresponds to a loss in familiarity, and sends the data to a server. Patricia may also directly indicate her loss in familiarity with a graphical slider on an app on her smartphone. Simultaneously, this server has been analyzing the musician's gestures, the flow of data inside the instrument and the musical output. When it receives Patricia's familiarity signals, the server, with settings defined by the musician, selects the adequate augmentations to be displayed. They aim at compensating for the familiarity disruption caused by the musical interaction context. Consequently, visual augmentations are displayed around the musician either for Patricia alone when she watches the performance through her smartphone (e.g. with video augmented-reality), or for the group of people around her using a mixed-reality display. They provide information that improve her degree of familiarity, allowing her for example to perceive the link between the musician's gesture and the resulting sound, and to enjoy the performance to a larger extent.

2.1 General Approach

To improve the liveness of music performances with DMIs, we suggest increasing the familiarity thanks to a trans-disciplinary approach in which both human and technological signals are analyzed. To achieve this goal, we first clarify the notion of familiarity. We then propose the concept of *correspondences*, which describes musical interactions and the way they are perceived. Finally we present a potential pipeline that would extract and process signals from the musician and from the audience to compose augmentations.

Familiarity Dimensions. As other high-level cognitive abilities, familiarity is not a unitary notion. It can be decomposed into components that differ by their nature, their inner rules as well as the type of information they convey. Besides, familiarity relates to expertise or attention and thus impacts on brain and motor system activities. We will describe in Sect. 2.2 how previous research show that these activities can be detected in more detail. Familiarity may also relates to various parts of the musical interaction that is perceived. Spectators can be more or less familiar with: musical gestures, relations between gestures and sound, instruments capabilities or musical genres. All these factors contribute to the general familiarity one has with an instrument. Following research by Fyans et al. [18,19] and Belloti et al. [5], Barbosa et al. [2] evaluate the audience experience through their comprehension of cause, effect, error, intention and mapping. However, measuring the familiarity might not be sufficient to inform the design of instruments or to augment performances if the origin of this familiarity is not understood correctly. For example, the perception of expertise, skill, error or intention of the performer, are consequences of the familiarity one has with a musical interaction rather than dimensions of the familiarity itself. For instance, the more familiar we are with an instrument, with the way the sound is produced and with the context of the performance, the better we can assess the quality of the performance and perceive the errors and the intention of the musician. Therefore while they can help measure the familiarity, to which they are correlated, these features do not provide insights on the reasons for this familiarity. One must therefore investigate the features which, when changed, have an impact on the overall familiarity, and in turn on the perception of expertise, skill, error or intention.

Taking this into account, our approach is to decompose familiarity into dimensions that we can both evaluate and improve. Based on results in HCI, NIME, and cognitive sciences that have explored various aspects of familiarity, we propose to decompose it into five components: *Causality, Instrumentality, Instrument expertise, Musical culture* and *Musical genre expertise.*

These in turn contain dimensions that can be evaluated independently:

Causality relates to the apparent mental causation, e.g. the judgment of causality of one's action, defined by Wegner et al. [43], where each of the three following dimensions are required to establish a judgment of causality of one's action:

– *Priority* - The thought should precede the action at a proper interval
– *Consistency* - The thought should be compatible with the action
– *Exclusivity* - The thought should be the only apparent cause of action

The consistency aspect is also closely related to the notion of naive physics, that is a set of innate or common knowledge about the physical world like gravity or friction that can also be used in digital interfaces as physical metaphors [21].

As proposed in [7], we transpose this model from the perception of one's own intentions/actions to the perception of others' actions. By doing so, we extend the concept of agency to the rather recent concept of *attributed agency.*

Instrumentality relates to common knowledge that allows one to predict the range of sound possibilities of a musical instrument from its appearance. It is composed of two dimensions: the *composition*, i.e. shape and material, and *behavior*, i.e. mechanisms and degree of autonomy from the musician's actions.

Instrument expertise relates to the exposure the spectator has had to the instrument, from a first-time observer to an expert player.

Musical culture corresponds to a basic knowledge of musical theory, that can for example be used to represent pitch as vertical position of a graphical element, i.e. mimicking a staff.

Musical genre expertise is composed of dimensions that correspond to the familiarity with the specifics of a genre, such as of *structure* and *constraints*. The effect of this category is obvious in the study by Bin et al. [10], where the same instrument played in two genres has a different impact on familiarity.

Notice that each component has a specific weight on the overall process. Furthermore, this model is consistent with the partial results that previous strategies have achieved. *Culture and expertise* for the "building a repertoire" and the "prior explanations" strategies, *Instrumentality* and *Culture* for "the design for transparency" and *Causality* for the augmentation strategy. This decomposition might evolve according to findings from the implementation phase. Some dimensions could prove harder to evaluate or others may emerge.

Finally, the complete decomposition of familiarity that we propose includes the following dimensions:

$$
\begin{aligned}
Familiarity = \ & C_{exclusivity} + C_{priority} + C_{consistency} \\
& + I_{composition} + I_{behavior} \\
& + E_{expertise} \\
& + M_{culture} \\
& + G_{structure} + G_{rules}
\end{aligned}
\tag{1}
$$

Correspondences. In order to handle the heterogeneous data (physiological, behavioral, musical, visual, mechanical) associated with the dimensions of familiarity, we introduce the notion of **correspondence**: a conceptual object that stands as a digital multidimensional representation of a musical interaction. This object associates several *properties*: musical output (audio), gesture data (time series of 3D coordinates), visual data (video of the movement), control data (time series of sensor values) and the *source* of the interaction. This last property specifies the author of the interaction. Indeed, interactions are not only produced by one musician but can be triggered and mastered by another one in a collaborative performance or, more usually, by autonomous prepared processes, e.g. automations or playlists.

Each property is subdivided in three elements: a *raw format element*, a *semantic element*, and a *classification element*.

The *raw format element* is a pointer to a collection of related files. For instance, the raw element of the visual property of a clap correspondence is a pointer to a collection of short videos showing a clap from different angles and velocities and the raw element of the audio property a pointer to a collection of short audio recordings of a clap.

The *semantic element* is composed of annotated descriptors of the property. For our clap example, the semantic element of the visual property could list obvious descriptors as "hands", "clap", "applause", "brief" but also more precise descriptors relative to specific taxonomies developed in the different analysis of gesture and sound.

The descriptors can be freely provided by the audience or taken from refined existing models such as [13] or [22]. For instance, "excitation gesture" or "effective gesture" could be used to populate the semantic element of the gesture property of a correspondence. Interestingly, by holding descriptors for each property of a unique interaction (aka correspondence), the semantic element offers the possibility to analyze the links between descriptors from different properties by the analysis of their co-occurrence. Finally, looking forward to the implementation, the processing of meaningful descriptors can rely on the strong foundation of web semantics [6].

The *classification element* is dedicated to the classification of the raw elements through machine learning methods and thus allows for the pairing of close correspondences with respect to their different properties. To compute such a distance between correspondences, multidimensional vectors can be used alongside more specific techniques as neural networks, informed by an efficient semantic analysis thanks to the semantic element of a given property.

In addition, correspondences hold a *score* for each of the familiarity dimensions described earlier (causality, instrumentality, ...). For example, two correspondences with the same musical result, e.g. the fade-in of an audio loop, can have different gesture and control properties depending on the mapping chosen for the DMI. While a continuous gesture on a fader would have a high score (meaning, the most natural way to fade) for the *consistency* dimension, a discrete tap on a pad would have a low one, since the effect would no be consistent with the cause for a spectator, e.g. discrete input and continuous output. This score of familiarity held by each correspondence plays a central role in our approach for an increase of familiarity as it allows for sorting correspondences from obvious to abstruse for a given audience.

Finally, as an interaction may be more complex and decomposed in a sequence of more basic interactions, a correspondence can also be linked to other, simpler correspondences.

Pipeline. Our envisioned pipeline (Fig. 2) is composed of five modules that handle the extraction of the data from the musician and their instrument (EXT_M), the extraction of physiological and subjective data from the audience (EXT_A), the processing of the data (IA) and the selection of fitting augmentations (AUG) based on a database of correspondences (DB_C). The pipeline is used at three different moments: before, during and after a performance.

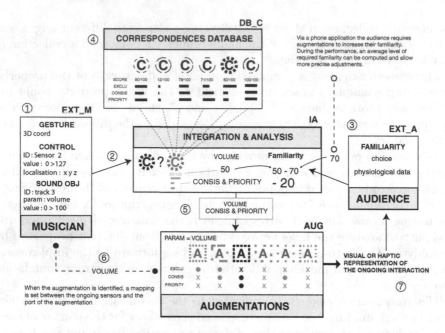

Fig. 2. The proposed pipeline with its main modules and data flows

Before the performance, correspondences, coming from a shared online database, or recorded specifically for the instrument, are saved in the *DB_C* module. ① During the performance, *IA* receives musical interaction data extracted by *EXT_M*. This data consists of both dynamic values such as gestural parameters, audio features and control values which will be used directly by *IA*, and of physical (position of gestures and sensors), logical (tracks, effects, synthesizers, ...) and structural information about the musical interaction, which will be used by *AUG*. ② *IA* builds and manages a set of ongoing correspondences from these signals. ③ Simultaneously, *IA* receives the familiarity evaluation (with the identification of the sensed individual or group) from *EXT_A*. If the familiarity evaluation is low, ④ *IA* finds in *DB_C* correspondences similar to the ongoing one, and select the familiarity dimensions that need to be compensated depending on their scores in these. *IA* then sends *AUG* the data required for the augmentation: live correspondences, associated signals from *EXT_M* with dynamic and structural data and identification of the source of the familiarity evaluation (in order to display the augmentations only to the correct person or group). ⑤ *AUG* creates (or selects if it already exists) the augmentation that matches the received structural data, for example a visual augmented-reality link between the physical position of a sensor and a virtual representation of an audio track. ⑥ Augmentations are then connected to *EXT_M* and listen to the signals required to update the augmentation, e.g. control values for the sensor, loudness of the track. After the performance, the familiarity extracted from the audience can be reused to refine the scores for the familiarity dimensions in each detected correspondence of DB_C.

2.2   Modules

Database of Correspondences (DB_C). DB_C manages all pre-existing correspondences. These can be generic, or specific to an instrument or performance. It receives queries from IA to select correspondences matching the ones detected during the performance. A very promising approach in dealing with heterogeneous data is the use of databases. Even if the efficiency of machine learning and analysis tools is still evolving, a numerous amount of initiatives, especially in analysis of emotion (DEAP [24], RECOLA [35], EATMINT [15]) but also in music-related actions [20], contribute to shared databases that compile multimodal and synchronized experimental data. The main goal of these databases is to predict complex and abstract states, e.g. the emotional state of an individual, thanks to the analysis of their physiological and behavioral signals such as face expression, electrodermal activity or heart rate variation. Most of the existing databases are composed of 15 to 30 entries referencing data of diversified nature. To allow the gathering of a more relevant amount of cross data, we first need to facilitate the indexing thanks to the more and more intuitive and effective front-end technologies of the web. We propose to develop a web interface that could provide the specific tools to aggregate the data required to constitute the properties of a correspondence. A typical correspondence would require a short video footage of a gesture, the motion capture of this gesture, sensor value and audio output of the instrument. Tags could also be manually added for each of these properties. The interface could be accessible from an open web platform where artists as well as researchers could populate the database, to constitute their own correspondences and therefore optimize their pipeline with more personal choices of gestures, mappings or sound processes. The same online platform can then be used for crowdsourced online evaluation sessions in which correspondences are exposed to participants with different levels of expertise. Their task is to indicate their understanding, using a questionnaire along the familiarity dimensions, and tag the correspondences.

Extraction of the Musician's Interactions (EXT_M). As explained in Sect. 2.1, EXT_M extracts data from the instrument and musician's gesture which is then sent to IA in order to be aggregated into *live correspondences*. At the instrument level, EXT_M extracts sensors states, mapping values as well as musical result of the musician interactions. At the musician level, EXT_M extracts the control gestures, the body movements and physiological signals. In addition to these signals, structural information needs to be provided for further use in the augmentations, such as the position of the physical sensors of the DMI and the position of the musician's hands, the list of tracks, effects or other sound processes with their names, or the mappings between sensors and sound parameters. While some of these obviously need to be defined by the musician manually, or sensed by devices external to the instrument, others can be extracted through a trans-disciplinary approach. Regarding the instrument input, research on gesture recognition, especially concerning hand gestures as demonstrated by Rautaray and Agrawal [34], can be used to identify the performed musical gestures. Regarding the instrument output, research in music information retrieval (MIR) provides tools for segmenting music from the audio signal only [32] using spectral, tonal, rhythmical descriptors and methods. Finally, the extraction can be facilitated by a multimodal approach, similarly to techniques developed for video indexing [40], as some events might appear clearer on one channel than on others. For example, control data might inform on the temporal boundaries of a change in the sound that can then be analysed.

We identify two main challenges for the implementation of this module. The first is the access to the data from the DMIs. In fact, while extraction from the audio signal provides many features that can be used to detect correspondences, it might not be enough for precise analysis. In order to access pre-mappings and post-mappings data, to differentiate between manual and automated changes and to analyze the output of individual tracks or other sound processes, one can not rely solely on the DMIs inputs and outputs, i.e. additional software components will need to be integrated. In most DMIs, plug-ins can be added at various stages of the instrument. However, the API might not provide enough information on the instrument to a single plugin. For example, one plugin per track might be needed to access and send the audio output features for each separately. The integration of EXT_M will be simpler if DMIs are built using patching environments such as PureData or Max/MSP, where the musician has more control over the architecture of the instruments. The second challenge is to combine detailed but costly and slow analysis of features for the detection of correspondences with maximum accuracy, and fast but less accurate analysis of features for the update of augmentations in AUG.

Extraction of the Audience Familiarity (EXT_A). The role of this module is to extract the audience subjective and objective information in order to inform IA.

It is now commonly accepted that the live music experience engages multiple complementary processes of low level perception, en-action and embodiment ([17], see Leman and Maes for a review [28]), processing of hierarchical and sequential information [25,30], as well as strong affective and social aspects. This perspective of complementarity is also included in recent studies relative to music produced with DMIs [37] The evaluation of such a rich experience triggers multiple methodological difficulties. Subjective assessment is therefore a common method that can be conducted through post-performance questionnaires [12,27, 44], emotion rating during the concerts [12,38] or when viewing an audio-video recording of a performance [4].

Post-performance questionnaires are a good source of information but may be less precise than live subjective reports. In addition, there are initiatives that do not require the participants to directly communicate their introspective evaluation. These more objective measurements require very specific equipment as eye trackers [4] and, to date, suffer from a lack of out-of-the-lab physiological measurements. Familiarity is one of the key aspects of the experience of live music and, as its other dimensions, relies on multiple underlying mechanisms. Therefore, as the mentioned studies above, and to initiate ecological (i.e. out of the lab, in "real life") measurements of physiological signals, we propose a dual methodology to extract the familiarity of the audience. First, we base the subjective assessment on a familiarity application for mobile phone. Its main purpose is to supply IA with data about the ongoing familiarity of the audience, from a graphical familiarity slider that spectators activate.

As other authors [3,12], we believe this continuous survey could be a good methodological answer to the reservations we exposed about questionnaires after the performance. The second part of the extraction relies on physiological signals. Neuroscience studies show that the expertise, a key component of familiarity, influences the perception of action [14]. Those findings, applied to music expertise, may lead to a better understanding of its role in the live music experience. By measuring the peripheral signals, we aim at discovering potential patterns that could correlate with the subjective data we extract. Widely used in the emotion studies, and rather suitable to extract in natural condition, four signals are particularly interesting in our musical context: Heart rate variability [36], electrodermal activity [39] and oculometry (eye tracking + pupillometry). The complementary analysis of extracted features of these signals already gave interesting result in the emotion classification by machine learning algorithms [23] and need to be further extended in music experience studies. Moreover, these signals can already be acquired by wearable devices and the quantified self movement [41] will surely provide more accurate and affordable devices in the near future.

Integration and Analysis (IA). IA is the central hub that connects to all the other modules. Its role is to: (1) compute the live correspondences with the data extracted from the musician and their instrument; (2) match the computed live correspondence with a correspondence from the database to calculate the familiarity dimensions that need to be augmented; (3) supply the AUG module with the information needed for the relevant augmentation selection. To fulfill these tasks, the module can rely on the classification element of each property of correspondences. Alongside the raw and the semantic parts, the classification element is a machine learning model dedicated to the classification of raw data. This model is pre-computed with the raw files registered in the correspondence. Its goal is to discriminate new stimuli and detect those who match with the recorded one. Considering the heterogeneity of the modalities, each property might require a specific machine learning model and specific extracted features. For example, MIR descriptors for a sound element and a deep convolutional network for picture classification. The main idea is to use the set of models as a global digital representation of the correspondence that can either be projected, depending of the context, on a single and more easy to handle property or be represented as a multidimensional vector that allows similarity comparison of whole correspondences (the matching process). Considering the variety of data and processes it has to handle, this module needs to be regularly updated with recent findings in signal processing, machine learning or movement models. Without a strongly modular structure of the available tools that the pipeline has at its disposal, the framework may not be able to evolve and thereby join a long list of deprecated initiatives.

Augmentation (AUG). This module manages both a database of available augmentations and a set of active ones. When a correspondence needs to be augmented, AUG receives the data required to create a new or select an existing augmentation, such as the physical position of the gesture and sensors and logical components of the instruments, the familiarity dimensions that need to be compensated, the destination of the augmentation (individual or group) and the data from EXT_M that the augmentation should listen to. The augmentations are selected from a database of augmentations designed to compensate the various dimensions of familiarity.

A number of research have shown the opportunities opened by augmentations to provide information on DMIs to the audience. For example, Perrotin et al. [33] used visualizations, projected on a screen behind an ensemble of DMIs, to help the audience understand better the contribution of each musician. In previous work, we proposed an augmented-reality (AR) approach where the visualizations are perceptually consistent with the physical instrument, e.g. visual links attached to the physical sensors. We designed a display where multiple spectators can reveal the augmentations [9] and all perceive them consistently. Finally, we proved the effect of 3D visual augmentations on the causality aspect of familiarity [7], i.e. the degree of control perceived by the audience. On the haptic side Armitage [1] has experimented with using haptic feedback to provide information on musician's interaction during a live-coding performance. We believe that the first challenge is the creation of a framework that allows one to design augmentations according to the specific dimensions of familiarity that they compensate. Rules will need to be defined so that one can adapt an augmentation to the artistic specificity of a particular performance. A second challenge is the design of augmentations that provide just enough content to fill the multimodal gap without distracting the audience from the musical performance because of a too heavy cognitive load.

3   Conclusion

In this paper, we presented a novel approach for augmenting familiarity of the audience with Digital Musical Instruments and reviewed associated research results and challenges.

Among the perspectives, our first future work will be the construction of the initial database of correspondences that will help refining our familiarity decomposition.

The first ones will therefore be generated through a systematical process, i.e. by recording unitary interactions (e.g. one gesture one change in the sound) with variations on each dimension perceived by the audience, e.g. gesture type and amplitude, mapping, sound parameter, point of view, and so on.

In addition, we plan on investigating the impact of familiarity variations on electrophysiological signals from the audience, with the aim of finding real-time measurements that could be used to assess familiarity during performances and guide the choice of augmentations. This transdisciplinary approach could reveal significant research avenues especially with the democratization of wearable devices. We hope that this paper will trigger exciting new research in NIMEs, and both cognitive and computer sciences.

References

1. Armitage, J.: Revealing timelines: live coding and its gestures. In: Proceedings of ICLC (2016)
2. Barbosa, J., Calegario, F., Teichrieb, V., Ramalho, G., McGlynn, P.: Considering Audience's view towards an evaluation methodology for digital musical instruments. In: Proceedings of NIME (2012)
3. Baytas, M.A., Göksun, T., Özcan, O.: The perception of live-sequenced electronic music via hearing and sight. In: Proceedings of the International Conference on New Interfaces for Musical Expression, 2220–4806, vol. 16, pp. 194–199. Queensland Conservatorium Griffith University, Brisbane, Australia (2016). http://www.nime.org/proceedings/2016/nime2016_paper0040.pdf
4. Baytas, M.A., Göksun, T., Özcan, O.: The perception of live-sequenced electronic music via hearing and sight. In: Proceedings of NIME (2016)
5. Bellotti, V., Back, M., Edwards, W.K., Grinter, R.E., Henderson, A., Lopes, C.: Making sense of sensing systems: five questions for designers and researchers. In: Proceedings of the SIGCHI Conference on Human Factors in Computing Systems, pp. 415–422. ACM (2002)
6. Berners-Lee, T., Hendler, J., Lassila, O., et al.: The semantic web. Sci. Am. **284**(5), 28–37 (2001)
7. Berthaut, F., Coyle, D., Moore, J., Limerick, H.: Liveness through the lens of agency and causality. In: Proceedings of NIME (2015)
8. Berthaut, F., Marshall, M.T., Subramanian, S., Hachet, M.: Rouages: revealing the mechanisms of digital musical instruments to the audience. In: Proceedings of NIME (2013)
9. Berthaut, F., Martinez Plasencia, D., Hachet, M., Subramanian, S.: Reflets: combining and revealing spaces for musical performances. In: Proceedings of NIME (2015). https://hal.inria.fr/hal-01136857
10. Bin, S.A., Bryan-Kinns, N., McPherson, A.P.: Skip the pre-concert demo: how technical familiarity and musical style affect audience response. In: Proceedings of NIME (2016)
11. Bin, S.A., Bryan-Kinns, N., McPherson, A., et al.: Hands where we can see them! investigating the impact of gesture size on audience perception. International Computer Music Conference (2017)
12. Astrid Bin, S.M., Morreale, F., Bryan-Kinns, N., McPherson, A.P.: In-the-moment and beyond: combining post-hoc and real-time data for the study of audience perception of electronic music performance. In: Bernhaupt, R., Dalvi, G., Joshi, A., Balkrishan, D.K., O'Neill, J., Winckler, M. (eds.) INTERACT 2017. LNCS, vol. 10513, pp. 263–281. Springer, Cham (2017). https://doi.org/10.1007/978-3-319-67744-6_18
13. Cadoz, C., Wanderley, M.M.: Gesture-music (2000)

14. Calvo-Merino, B., Glaser, D.E., Grèzes, J., Passingham, R.E., Haggard, P.: Action observation and acquired motor skills: an fmRI study with expert dancers. Cereb. Cortex **15**(8), 1243–1249 (2005)
15. Chanel, G., Bétrancourt, M., Pun, T., Cereghetti, D., Molinari, G.: Assessment of computer-supported collaborative processes using interpersonal physiological and eye-movement coupling. In: 2013 Humaine Association Conference on Affective Computing and Intelligent Interaction (ACII), pp. 116–122. IEEE (2013)
16. Fels, S., Gadd, A., Mulder, A.: Mapping transparency through metaphor: towards more expressive musical instruments. Organ. Sound **7**(2), 109–126 (2002)
17. Fyans, A.C., Gurevich, M.: Perceptions of skill in performances with acoustic and electronic instruments. In: Proceedings of the International Conference on New Interfaces for Musical Expression, Oslo, Norway, pp. 495–498 (2011). http://www.nime.org/proceedings/2011/nime2011_495.pdf
18. Fyans, A.C., Gurevich, M., Stapleton, P.: Where did it all go wrong? A model of error from the spectator's perspective. In: Proceedings of the International Conference on New Interfaces for Musical Expression, Pittsburgh, PA, United States, pp. 171–172 (2009). http://www.nime.org/proceedings/2009/nime2009_171.pdf
19. Fyans, A.C., Gurevich, M., Stapleton, P.: Examining the spectator experience. In: Proceedings of the International Conference on New Interfaces for Musical Expression, Sydney, Australia, pp. 451–454 (2010). http://www.nime.org/proceedings/2010/nime2010_451.pdf
20. Godøy, R.I., et al.: Classifying music-related actions (2012)
21. Jacob, R.J., et al.: Reality-based interaction: a framework for post-wimp interfaces. In: Proceedings of the SIGCHI Conference on Human Factors in Computing Systems, CHI 2008, pp. 201–210. ACM, New York (2008). https://doi.org/10.1145/1357054.1357089
22. Jensenius, A.R., Wanderley, M.M., Godøy, R.I., Leman, M.: Musical gestures. In: Musical Gestures: Sound, Movement, and Meaning, December 2009
23. Kim, J., André, E.: Emotion recognition based on physiological changes in music listening. IEEE Trans. Pattern Anal. Mach. Intell. **30**(12), 2067–2083 (2008)
24. Koelstra, S., et al.: Deap: a database for emotion analysis; using physiological signals. IEEE Trans. Affect. Comput. **3**(1), 18–31 (2012)
25. Kohler, E., Keysers, C., Umiltà, M.A., Fogassi, L., Gallese, V., Rizzolatti, G.: Hearing sounds, understanding actions: action representation in mirror neurons. Science **297**(5582), 846–8 (2002). http://www.ncbi.nlm.nih.gov/pubmed/12161656
26. Lai, C.H., Bovermann, T.: Audience experience in sound performance. In: Proceedings of NIME (2013)
27. Lai, C.H., Bovermann, T.: Audience experience in sound performance. In: NIME, pp. 170–173 (2013). http://www.nime.org/2013/program/papers/day2/paper4/197/197_Paper.pdf
28. Leman, M., Maes, P.J.: The role of embodiment in the perception of music. Empir. Music. Rev. **9**(3–4), 236–246 (2014)
29. Loftus, E.F., Palmer, J.C.: Reconstruction of automobile destruction: an example of the interaction between language and memory. J. Verbal Learn. Verbal Behav. **13**(5), 585–589 (1974)
30. Molnar-Szakacs, I., Overy, K.: Music and mirror neurons: from motion to 'e'motion. Soc. Cogn. Affect. Neurosci. **1**(3), 235–241 (2006)
31. Murray-Browne, T., Mainstone, D., Bryan-Kinns, N., Plumbley, M.D.: The medium is the message: composing instruments and performing mappings. In: Proceedings of the International Conference on New Interfaces for Musical Expression, pp. 56–59 (2011)

32. Paulus, J., Müller, M., Klapuri, A.: State of the art report: audio-based music structure analysis. In: Proceedings of ISMIR (2010)
33. Perrotin, O., d'Alessandro, C.: Visualizing gestures in the control of a digital musical instrument. In: Proceedings of the International Conference on New Interfaces for Musical Expression, pp. 605–608. Goldsmiths, University of London, London (2014). http://www.nime.org/proceedings/2014/nime2014_406.pdf
34. Rautaray, S.S., Agrawal, A.: Vision based hand gesture recognition for human computer interaction: a survey. Artif. Intell. Rev. **43**(1), 1–54 (2015)
35. Ringeval, F., Sonderegger, A., Sauer, J., Lalanne, D.: Introducing the RECOLA multimodal corpus of remote collaborative and affective interactions. In: 2013 10th IEEE International Conference and Workshops on Automatic Face and Gesture Recognition (FG), pp. 1–8. IEEE (2013)
36. Sammler, D., Grigutsch, M., Fritz, T., Koelsch, S.: Music and emotion: electrophysiological correlates of the processing of pleasant and unpleasant music. Psychophysiology **44**(2), 293–304 (2007)
37. Schacher, J.C., Neff, P.: Skill development and stabilisation of expertise for electronic music performance. In: Kronland-Martinet, R., Aramaki, M., Ystad, S. (eds.) CMMR 2015. LNCS, vol. 9617, pp. 111–131. Springer, Cham (2016). https://doi.org/10.1007/978-3-319-46282-0_7
38. Schubert, E., Ferguson, S., Farrar, N., Taylor, D., McPherson, G.E.: The six emotion-face clock as a tool for continuously rating discrete emotional responses to music. In: Aramaki, M., Barthet, M., Kronland-Martinet, R., Ystad, S. (eds.) CMMR 2012. LNCS, vol. 7900, pp. 1–18. Springer, Heidelberg (2013). https://doi.org/10.1007/978-3-642-41248-6_1
39. Sequeira, H., Hot, P., Silvert, L., Delplanque, S.: Electrical autonomic correlates of emotion. Int. J. Psychophysiol. **71**(1), 50–56 (2009)
40. Snoek, C.G., Worring, M.: Multimodal video indexing: a review of the state-of-the-art. Multimed. Tools Appl. **25**(1), 5–35 (2005)
41. Swan, M.: The quantified self: fundamental disruption in big data science and biological discovery. Big Data **1**(2), 85–99 (2013)
42. Vines, B.W., Krumhansl, C.L., Wanderley, M.M., Dalca, I.M., Levitin, D.J.: Music to my eyes: cross-modal interactions in the perception of emotions in musical performance. Cognition **118**(2), 157–170 (2011)
43. Wegner, D.M., Wheatley, T.: Apparent mental causation: sources of the experience of will. Am. Psychol. **54**(7), 480 (1999)
44. Wu, J.C., Huberth, M., Yeh, Y.H., Wright, M.: Evaluating the audience's perception of real-time gestural control and mapping mechanisms in electroacoustic vocal performance. In: Proceedings NIME (2016)

Use the Force: Incorporating Touch Force Sensors into Mobile Music Interaction

Edward Jangwon Lee[1], Sangeon Yong[1], Soonbeom Choi[1], Liwei Chan[2], Roshan Peiris[3], and Juhan Nam[1(✉)]

[1] KAIST, Daejeon, Korea
{noshel,koragon2,cjb3549,juhannam}@kaist.ac.kr
[2] NCTU, Hsinchu, Taiwan
liwei.name@gmail.com
[3] Keio University, Yokohama, Japan
roshan82@gmail.com

Abstract. The musical possibilities of force sensors on touchscreen devices are explored, using Apple's 3D Touch. Three functions are selected to be controlled by force: (a) excitation, (b) modification (aftertouch), and (c) mode change. Excitation starts a note, modification alters a playing note, and mode change controls binary on/off sound parameters. Four instruments are designed using different combinations of force-sound mapping strategies. ForceKlick is a single button instrument that plays consecutive notes within one touch by altering touch force, by detecting force down-peaks. The iPhone 6s/7 Ocarina features force-sensitive fingerholes that heightens octaves upon high force. Force Trombone continuously controls gain by force. Force Synth is a trigger pad array featuring all functions in one button: start note by touch, control vibrato with force, and toggle octaves upon abrupt burst of force. A simple user test suggests that adding force features to well-known instruments are more friendly and usable.

Keywords: Mobile music · Force touch · 3D touch · Touch gestures
Relative force

1 Introduction

Recently, Apple's iPhone featured *3D Touch*[1], which captures the finger pressure of a touch on the screen. Although mobile musicians always have enjoyed designing instruments using new sensors on smart devices [4,8], only a handful of commercial musical applications adopt the new technology after more than a year since 3D Touch's debut. It seems that the current force sensing feature is just not enough: while force mapped to aftertouch is considered to work perfectly, its relatively slow update rate[2] alongside with noisy data at the beginning

---

[1] 3D Touch by Apple, on models after iPhone 6s:
https://developer.apple.com/ios/3d-touch/.
[2] Although Apple does not disclose 3D Touch's sample rate, our preliminary experiments indicate it to be approximately between 10 and 15 ms (67–100Hz).

© Springer Nature Switzerland AG 2018
M. Aramaki et al. (Eds.): CMMR 2017, LNCS 11265, pp. 574–585, 2018.
https://doi.org/10.1007/978-3-030-01692-0_38

of a strongly struck touch acts as a hurdle for this technology being used for note velocity control [5]. However, we believe that force sensors will surely open a new possibility for more expressiveness on touchscreen music, and therefore deserve more attention by computer music researchers.

This paper aims to discuss on how force sensors on touchscreen devices can be used as a musical input gesture, and presents a compilation of simple mobile instruments each differing in musical mapping of force. Usage of force sensors on music is categorized into three categories: (a) excitation (note triggering), (b) sound modification (aftertouch), and (c) mode change, an on/off switch similar to electric guitar effects pedals. Each instrument is implemented with a different combination of the three functions, and two among them employ relative force – using the first and second time derivatives of force data for capturing peaks in force and generate discrete events using them.

1.1 Related Work

Lack of force sensing has been considered a loss of gestural information, which in turn leads to restrictions in musical expressiveness. In this sense, several workarounds are found throughout the computer music literature. Tanaka attached an external device with force-sensing resistors (FSRs) on a PDA device [7]. Park and Oriol also addressed this issue by attaching deformable foam blocks beneath an iPad and measuring accelerometer data change during touch [6], and Apple also uses accelerometer data in iOS GarageBand for note velocity control[3]. Recently, to overcome the restriction that accelerometer data can only measure force from a single touch, Michon et al. attached several FSRs beneath an iPad and measured multi-touch force [5].

In addition to these two approaches, FSRs and accelerometers, Essl et al. takes touch radius into consideration and presents three prototypes using different force sensing approaches [3]. Now that a force sensor has been included in smart devices, in addition to exploring how to be able to "use the force", this paper discusses how to "use the force" and presents several examples of various force-sound mappings and force data parsing methods.

Recently, mobile music applications also began to feature 3D Touch functions, mostly mapped to aftertouch controls, where such examples include ROLI's Noise[4], Miditure[5], Aftertouch[6], and Apple's GarageBand. ROLI's Seaboard 5D supports advanced 3D Touch features such as velocity control and finger lift speed. However, the velocity value seems to be zoned into only a few levels, rather than 128, which is the standard MIDI velocity range. This restriction may have been set due to the unreliable behavior of initial touch force measurements, as discussed above. In this paper, we propose alternative mappings of force, including mappings using relative force over time, rather than the absolute measurement.

---

[3] Apple's GarageBand: http://apple.com/ios/garageband/.
[4] http://roli.com/products/noise.
[5] http://facebook.com/Miditure.
[6] http://aftertouchapp.com.

2   Mapping Touch Force to Sound

Borrowing real instrument metaphors that require force and applying them to force-sound mapping would be advantageous in terms of intuitiveness and usability. First, for blown instruments, pitch and timbre differ greatly depending on embouchure, lip tension, and air pressure. As mobile devices do not have the ability to recognize such input, mapping those to force sensors might be a meaningful alternate. That is, force sensors can be used for deciding pitch and timbre, which are usually a part of *excitation*. Second, in stringed instruments such as the guitar, a player may alter pitch during a note playing by pushing a vibrating string orthogonally to the neck (bending or vibrato, depending on the speed and style of push). These techniques can be categorized as *aftertouch*, and be used as a metaphor in force-sound mapping. Finally, guitar effects pedals such as distortion and chorus can be turned on and off anytime during playing. This metaphor is also taken into consideration, and is categorized as *mode change*. Each of the three mapping categories is described in detail in the following subsections.

2.1   Excitation

Although 3D Touch in the current state is inappropriate for note velocity control, force sensors can improve the excitation process, and two possibilities are presented in this paper.

First, *adaptive gain control* is for non-percussive instruments with continuous sound, such as blown and bowed instruments. Such instruments accept force in a continuous fashion, starting from zero and gradually increasing. As touch force theoretically begins at zero and gradually increases as well, mapping force measurement to output gain is an intuitive idea. However, due to the slow sample rate of 3D Touch, initial force readings tend to be non-zero when touch begins with large force, which lead to an unpleasant abrupt change in gain: therefore the gain envelope must *adapt* to the force curve over time. For this purpose, a gain control model similar to time constant models is designed:

$$g = g_{fixed}(e^{-\frac{t+\alpha}{2\alpha}}) + \frac{f}{f_{max}}(1 - (e^{-\frac{t+\alpha}{2\alpha}})) \tag{1}$$

where g: output gain (0.0 to 1.0), g_{fixed}: a fixed gain value, t: time, f/f_{max}: force value normalized from 0.0 to 1.0, and α: the time constant. 2α, rather than α, is used to produce a more natural adaptation curve.

Figure 1 depicts the input-output gain of the model. Although initial force readings exhibit unstable values, the model smooths the output gain to a continuous curve, eventually adapting into real force readings.

Another model, *down peak detection*, focuses on the *timing* of excitation. This model uses relative force (time derivatives of force data) over a single touch and a note is played on every down-to-up peak. Although velocity control is not available, this technique produces notes quickly upon user intention and enables the user to play consecutive notes by controlling touch force, without

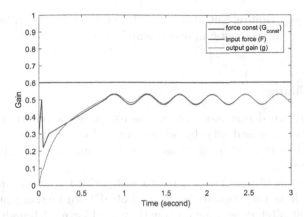

Fig. 1. Adaptive gain control. The green curve indicates normalized real force values input, blue is the fixed gain value, and red is the result of adaptive gain control. (Color figure online)

lifting the touching finger [9]. This model is suitable for percussive instruments such as drums, where timing is crucial and normally do not require additional sound modification (aftertouch) after a note is played. Figure 2 illustrates the excitation process with down peak detection.

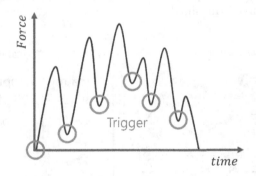

Fig. 2. Excitation with down peak detection. Notes are generated at the start of touch, and upon detecting down-to-up peaks – an increase in force is regarded as the user's intention of playing a note.

2.2   Sound Modification

In contrast to note excitation, sound modification does not require as much as frequent force value updates, therefore implementation is straightforward. Apple's GarageBand 2.1 for iOS has aftertouch implemented into some of its instruments using 3D Touch. As described in the previous section, force is used to control not only timbre, but also gain. This concept has been borrowed from blown and bowed instruments, in which amplitude envelope follows the force of blowing.

2.3   Mode Change

In this research, we define *mode change* as extending a button's function set to more than two (on and off), by adding touch force features to an ordinary button. Two different implementations of mode change are introduced: *toggling* and *tri-state* buttons.

Tri-state button utilizes touch force to add a third state to ordinary touch buttons, which have only two states: on and off. Blown instruments are able to produce different pitch depending on how they are blown, although the fingering is identical. Woodwinds feature *overblowing*, which usually causes the instrument to shift to a higher octave. Tri-state buttons can be used to emulate overblowing, by mapping force on octave control.

The implementation of tri-state buttons is illustrated in the left panel of Fig. 3. In addition to the two original states, *on* and *off*, the third state is denoted *on2*. The red line depicts the user's change of touch force, and the blue line is the first derivation of force over time. The button switches between the three states upon the following conditions: (a) *off* when the button is not touched, (b) *on* when button is touched but does not fulfill the conditions of *on2*, and (c) *on2* when absolute force applied is above a certain threshold *or* relative force (dF/dt) exceeds a fixed threshold.

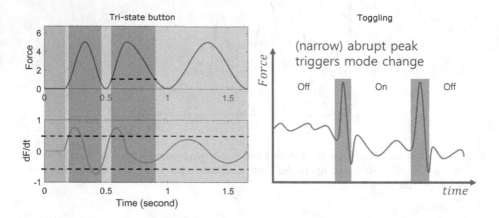

Fig. 3. Mode change. *(Left panel)* Tri-state button. The button is idle *(off)* when there is no touch (green area). The first function is activated *(on)* upon detecting force beneath a fixed threshold or a steep decrease in force (blue area). The third function *(on2)* is triggered by applying force higher than a fixed threshold or rapidly increasing force (orange area). *(Right panel)* Toggling. Within a single touch, the button's function can be toggled by applying high force during a short period. (Color figure online)

Toggling is another mode change method that borrows metaphors from guitar effects pedals, which can be turned on and off anytime during play by stepping on them. By recognizing an *abrupt, narrow and steep peak* in force, sound parameters can be toggled on and off, while steady changes of force are mapped to other continuously changing sound parameters such as amount of vibrato. The concept of toggling is illustrated in the right panel of Fig. 3. In order to detect narrow peaks of force, relative force over time is used and a recognition model is devised: by analyzing first and second derivatives from 200 collected samples of narrow up-slopes of force generated by 10 different subjects, a linear regression model is obtained. Afterwards, during testing the research team added restrictions and refinements to further filter unintended mode changes.

3   Instrument Prototypes

Based on the discussion above, four instruments are implemented on iPhone 6s, using STK [2] and MoMu [1] as the sound engine. User interface is built using UIKit, the basic GUI library for iOS. Each instrument differs in usage of force sensors and the combinations of usages. All rectangular and circular buttons are named *force buttons*, which are designed to accept a single touch and constantly monitor the amount of force applied. As iOS reports touch data only upon change in position or force, for constant monitoring a function that calculates the change of force over time is called every 1/60 s.

Rather than assessing the usability and playability of each touch force mapping strategy introduced in Sect. 2, each instrument is designed to exhibit the extended expressiveness of existing musical interfaces by utilizing touch force. Therefore, depending on the instrument, more than one of the mapping methods may be applied. The mappings used on each instrument are introduced in Table 1, and the screenshots and summaries of how each instrument's touch force mappings operate are illustrated in Fig. 4. The following subsections describe each instrument in detail.

Table 1. Selected mapping strategies for the four instrument prototypes.

Instrument	Excitation	Modification	Mode change
ForceKlick	down-peak detection		
Ocarina			tri-state button
Force Trombone	adaptive gain control	gain control	
Force Synth		vibrato control	toggling button

3.1   ForceKlick

Force mapping: excitation (down-peak detection). ForceKlick is a very simple instrument for testing force buttons, with only one force button that can play

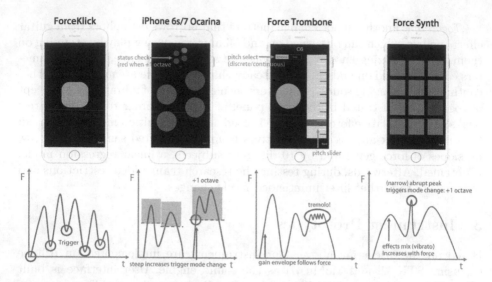

Fig. 4. Instrument screenshots and their force-sound mapping strategies.

consecutive notes with fixed pitch and gain within a single touch, using down peak detection (Sect. 2.1). A new note is played whenever a down-to-up peak is detected. That is, note excitation occurs shortly after force begins to increase. This is efficient in a sense that an increase of touch force is one of the first signals of the user's intention of playing a new note.

3.2 The iPhone 6s/7 Ocarina

Force mapping: mode change (tri-state button) – octave. The original iPhone Ocarina [8] has four buttons (holes), accepting sixteen (2^4) combinations of fingerings. Excitation is done by blowing breath into the microphone: stronger blowing increases the amplitude of sound. The iPhone 6s/7 Ocarina extends the original by implementing the buttons as tri-state buttons Sect. 2.3.

Each button is implemented as force sensitive buttons, and their color changes corresponding to applied force. The instrument's octave can be heightened by activating the third state of any button by satisfying one of the following conditions: (a) the first time derivative of force is higher than a fixed threshold – a rapid increase in force, or (b) the absolute amount of force is higher than a fixed threshold. The original octave is restored upon detecting either a steep decrease of force or force below an absolute threshold. This transposition feature extends the number of playable pitches to 31.[7]

---

[7] Not $2^4 \times 2 = 32$, as "all holes open" does not have any fingers on screen to apply force.

3.3 Force Trombone

Force mapping: excitation (adaptive gain control), modification – gain control.
Rather than blowing, the force trombone is excitated by pressing the circular
force button. Amplitude is increased by applying stronger force on the button.
By controlling force, players can not only change gain but also execute tremolos
and other amplitude-based techniques, without lifting the touching finger. The
slider on the right is mapped to pitch, and it can be toggled between continuous
and discrete pitch mode. For initial gain control, the model in Eq. 1 is used,
and the g_{fixed} and α value is manually tuned to 0.6 and 0.3, respectively for
acceptable outcomes.

3.4 Force Synth

*Force mapping: modification – vibrato control, mode change (toggling button) –
octave.* The Force Synth is an example that implements sound modification and
mode change into one button. The instrument consists of twelve force buttons,
each assigned to a note following pentatonic scale. Touching a button triggers
the corresponding note with a fixed amplitude, and controlling force during
touch decides the amount of vibrato (modification). Additionally, a narrow peak
in force immediately toggles the button's pitch to a higher or original octave
(mode change). The toggled higher octave is indicated by the button's color
changing from purple to red, and vibrato amount can be noticed by darker hue
of colors.

4 Evaluation

4.1 Test Design

As mentioned above, the objective of this research is to explore the possibilities
of touch force on mobile music by presenting a compilation of ideas, rather than
designing a single gesture and assess its usability and playability. The instruments introduced above are not complete instruments: they are designed to
provide ideas on how the suggested touch force mappings can be used on music.
Therefore, rather than conducting a quantitative test on each instrument, an
overall simple qualitative test is more suitable.

To evaluate the experimental use of force sensors, a simple user test has been
conducted. The four instruments have been evaluated by 9 participants, all in
their twenties and using smartphones as if they were a part of their bodies. 8
participants had musical experience, mostly in guitar and piano.

Before handing out the instrument to participants, a demo and training session was conducted. The demos included playing performance by the research
team. As force change cannot be easily noticed by watching others play, the test
conductors had to hold the participants' finger and help them control force and
explain how the force-sound mappings were designed. Afterwards, a free-play

session was given, and the device was taken back after completing the online survey.

The questionnaire consisted of three or four questions for each instrument. The forth question is applied to ForceKlick and Force Synth only, as only these two employ relative force methods. Each question was answered in a 5-point Likert scale. The questions are as follows:

Q1. Is the force-sound mapping intuitive?
Q2. Does the instrument follow the player's intention?
Q3. Is it easy to use force sensors under this mapping?
Q4. (for ForceKlick and Force Synth) Is relative force mapping easy to use?

Questions on overall preference were also included, "Which instrument did you like (and dislike) the most, and why?" Finally, users were asked to optionally provide written feedback.

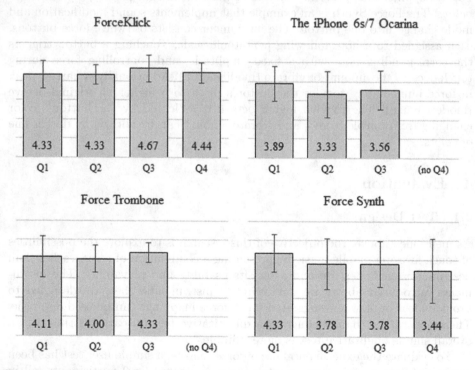

Fig. 5. Survey results for each instrument. Average and standard deviation of the corresponding question.

4.2   Results and Discussion

Figure 5 displays the test results for each instrument. ForceKlicks received high points for all items with low variance, notably 4.44 points for Q4: relative force mapping usability. Alongside with high ratings in other questions, this suggests that users felt comfortable and satisfied with note triggering via down-to-up peak detection.

The iPhone 6s/7 Ocarina received the lowest ratings in all items, with a rather high variance in Q2 and Q3 (playability and force sensor usability). The high variance in responds were explained in the comments, "Difficult to control force while holding the phone and blowing into it".

Force Trombone recorded all items higher than 4 points, suggesting that gain control by touch force is intuitive, playable, and usable to users. One participant that gave low points remarked that "The pitch slider is too sensitive, I can't stop sliding at the right pitch", which implies that low points were caused by the slider rather than the force mapping.

Force Synth received high points in Q1: intuitive force-sound mapping. This is surprising, as this instrument has the most complex mapping design: all three force features – note triggering, aftertouch, and mode change – are included in one force button. Moreover, mode changing by creating narrow peaks of force was rather experimental and not expected to be easily accepted. The guitar effects pedal metaphor behind this mapping might have been convincing. However, although users perceived the mapping as intuitive, other questions in terms of playability, force mapping usability, and relative force usability (mode change) received low points. This discrepancy suggests that although participants agree in how the force button works, they feel rather challenged in actually generating narrow force peaks to activate mode change. One participant commented that he wanted a different action mapped to mode change.

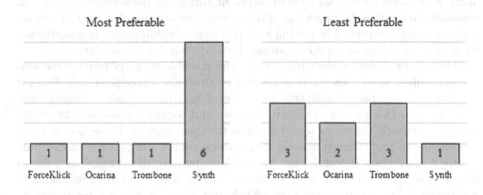

Fig. 6. Preference survey results.

The overall preference results are presented in Fig. 6. Force Synth has received the most votes as best instrument, and votes were evenly spread out for the least preferable, from Force Synth (one vote) to ForceKlick and Trombone (three votes). Both votes required a reason, and notable comments are presented in Table 2. In contrary to the individual instrument survey where ForceKlick received the highest ratings, in preference polls users tended to focus on the instrument itself, rather than the force-sound mapping strategies: the simplicity of ForceKlick was the main complaint. Force Synth was most preferred mostly for its familiarity with prior trigger pad instruments and convincing addition of force sensors, alongside with its polyphonic capabilities.

Table 2. Selected comments for the most and least preferable instrument.

ForceKlick	Worst	"Too simple"
Ocarina	Worst	"Difficult to hold phone while controlling force"
	Best	"Works well and interesting"
Trombone	Best	"Good use of trombone metaphor"
Synth	Best	"Impressive force features added on usual trigger pad UI"
		"Intuitive, all features work well"
		"Easy to use and behaves as my expectation"

5   Future Work and Conclusion

Although mode change feature in Force Synth works well after a certain time of training, a better method to satisfy all users is being devised. Various methods are being tested such as support vector machines (SVMs) to fit the needs of as many as possible. Personal customization of threshold parameters are also in consideration, either by providing option screens or machine learning. The user test can also be improved by setting a control case – building similar instruments without force mappings and comparing them to their force counterpart.

This paper discusses the current state and possible usage of touch force sensors on mobile music. Several new musical gestures are introduced including (a) two types of excitation: adaptive gain control and down peak detection, and two types of mode change of button: tri-state and toggling. Alongside to simple mapping of force values to sound modification parameters, these gestures are combined into four different mobile instruments, each having their own mapping strategy. User tests revealed that rather than defining new mappings such as blowing the trombone with a force button, adding additional force functions to conventional button mappings (ForceKlick and Force Synth) are more acceptable to participants, although the added functions used relative force data and were not expected to be easily convincing.

6   Demo Video

A demonstration video of the four instruments introduced in this paper can be found at the following link: https://youtu.be/quxAEBEp97Q.

References

1. Bryan, N.J., Herrera, J., Oh, J., Wang, G.: MoMu: a mobile music toolkit. In: Proceedings of the 2010 International Conference on New Interfaces for Musical Expression, pp. 174–177. Sydney, Australia (2010)
2. Cook, P., Scavone, G.P.: The synthesis toolkit (STK). In: Proceedings of the 1999 International Computer Music Conference, pp. 164–166. Beijing, China (1999)
3. Essl, G., Rohs, M., Kratz, S.: Use the force (or something) - pressure and pressure-like input for mobile music performance. In: Proceedings of the 2010 International Conference on New Interfaces for Musical Expression, pp. 182–185. Sydney, Australia (2010)
4. Kim, B., Yeo, W.S.: Interactive music performance with digital compass. In: Proceedings of the 2012 International Conference on New Interfaces for Musical Expression. Ann Arbor, Michigan (2012)
5. Michon, R., Smith, J.O., Chafe, C., Wright, M., Wang, G.: NUANCE: adding multitouch force detection to the iPad. In: Proceedings of the 2016 Sound and Music Computing Conference. Hamburg, Denmark (2016)
6. Park, T.H., Oriol, N.: Fortissimo: force-feedback for mobile devices. In: Proceedings of the 2013 International Conference on New Interfaces for Musical Expression, pp. 291–294. Daejeon, Korea (2013)
7. Tanaka, A.: Mobile music making. In: Proceedings of the 2004 International Conference on New Interfaces for Musical Expression, pp. 154–156. Singapore (2004)
8. Wang, Ge.: Designing smule's iPhone ocarina: the iPhone's magic flute. In: Proceedings of the 2009 International Conference on New Interfaces for Musical Expression, pp. 303–307. Pittsburgh, Pennsylvania (2009)
9. Yong, S., Lee, E.J., Peiris, R., Chan, L., Nam, J.: ForceClicks: enabling efficient button interaction with singer finger touch. In: Proceedings of the TEI 2017: Eleventh International Conference on Tangible, Embedded, and Embodied Interaction. Yokohama, Japan (2017)

Sonifying Twitter's Emotions
Through Music

Mariana Seiça[1]([✉]), Rui (Buga) Lopes[2], Pedro Martins[1],
and F. Amílcar Cardoso[1]

[1] CISUC, Informatics Engineering Department, University of Coimbra,
DEI, Polo 2, Pinhal de Marrocos, 3030-290 Coimbra, Portugal
`marianac@student.dei.uc.pt`, {`pjmm,amilcar`}`@dei.uc.pt`
[2] Coimbra, Portugal

Abstract. Sonification is a scientific field that seeks to explore the
potential of sound as an instrument to convey and interpret data. Its
techniques have been developing significantly with the growth of technology and supporting hardware and software, which have spread in our
daily environment. This allowed the establishment of new communication tools to share information, opinion and feelings as part of our daily
routine.

The aim of this project was to unite the social media phenomena with
sonification, using Twitter data to extract user's emotions and translate
them into musical compositions. The focus was to explore the potential
of music in translating data as personal and subjective as human emotions, developing a musically complex and captivating mapping based
on the rules of Western Music. The music is accompanied by a simple
visualization, which results in emotions being heard and seen with the
corresponding tweets, in a multimodal experience that represents Twitter's emotional reality. The mapping was tested through an online survey,
and despite a few misunderstandings, the results were generally positive,
expressing the efficiency and impact of the developed system.

Keywords: Musical sonification · Emotion detection · Twitter
Algorithmic composition · Sound design

1 Introduction

Sonification, defined by Kramer et al. [12] as "the use of nonspeech audio to
convey information", has been establishing its place as a new field of communication, exploring new techniques to represent complex data through sound [8].
Since the birth of the International Community of Auditory Display (ICAD) in
1992, where the study of auditory displays was proposed as a scientific field, sonification techniques have been developed significantly, with applications in areas

---

R. (Buga) Lopes—Independent Researcher.

M. Aramaki et al. (Eds.): CMMR 2017, LNCS 11265, pp. 586–608, 2018.
https://doi.org/10.1007/978-3-030-01692-0_39

such as Medicine or Seismology, and concepts from multiple areas, from Human Perception to Design and Engineering that form its interdisciplinary nature [8].

The development of the sonification field is directly connected to the significant growth that technology experienced in the last decade, with personal computers containing the hardware and software needed to manipulate sound [8], and auditory displays becoming a presence in everyday life. This technological growth and accessibility to the main population also allowed the establishment of new communication media as a daily routine: the social media. Facebook and Twitter are examples of these social tools that became the new mass media, not only for the common citizen, but also for companies, news industry and important figures. The study of social media data has gained new potential in several areas, such as marketing for extracting consumer's opinions, or social studies for understanding the user's moods and views about events. The field of sentiment analysis emerges from this potential, with the focus of studying computational analysis to extract opinion and sentiment from text, interacting with affective computing to explore the computer's ability in recognizing emotions [19].

This paper presents a project that handles with these three fields: sonification as the core, with data retrieved from social media, specifically Twitter, and analysed through sentiment analysis. The main goal is to explore new ways to read, through sound, data as personal and complex as human emotions. This study is primarily motivated by the potential of music in conveying emotions, and lies to this potential, exploring ways to transmit information through a melodic and harmonic composition. It involves two major challenges: the emotion extraction, implementing a system that properly analyses the tweets and classifies their emotions; and the musical mapping, choosing a set of parameters that can distinguish and embody the emotions. The main focus of this paper is on the musical mapping. However, we also briefly describe how the process of extracting emotional information from the tweets is implemented.

This paper starts with an overview of Sonification works and projects that used social media data, which influenced and inspired this work. Section 3 discusses the model of the emotions chosen, and the process for emotion classification. Section 4 presents the musical mapping and its structure. Section 5 details the implemented system and visualization. Section 6 presents the evaluation process and the analysis of the results. Section 7 lists possible improvements.

2   Related Work

There are many studies of sonifications developed in a vast number of areas, proven successful in practical and scientific terms [12].

The first two examples show the potential of sonification in scientific data. The work of Vicinanza, specifically his *Voyager 1 & 2 Spacecraft Duet* is a sonification of data gathered by the Voyager 1 & 2 NASA probes during 37 years of spatial exploration. It consists of two melodies in different frequencies, with the measurements made at the same times, but billions of kilometers apart [25]. The second example is *The Climate Symphony* by Quinn [21], where he used data from the chemical composition of an ice block in Greenland to translate into music the climatic changes endured by the great continental ice sheets.

In the poetry field, Coelho, Martins and Cardoso [3] created a *A Musical Sonification of the Portuguese Epopee*, specifically of The Lusiads, by Luís de Camões. It is an interactive sonification where the user can explore the poem by choosing different levels of "zooming", listening to it as a whole, as a canto/subnarrative or a specific episode and therefore customising the experience.

Bulley and Jones developed *Living Symphonies*, a sound installation based on the fauna and flora of four ecosystems in the United Kingdom. The authors built a model that reflected the behavior, movement and daily patterns of every being in the wild, translating a network of interactions that formed the ecosystem [2].

Rhapsody In Grey, developed by Brian Foo in 2016, is a real-time visual sonification that uses data from an EEG of a patient with epilepsy to generate a musical composition. The goal of this project is to give an empathic and intuitive view over the brain activity during a seizure [4].

Using Twitter as the main data source, *TwitterRadio* is an audio-only interactive installation that seeks "to convey public opinions on the world trending topics through suitable musical forms" [18]. Developed by Morreale, Miniukovich and De Angeli, it takes the concept of a traditional radio, where the users can tune to a station and listen to a musical translation of the polarity retrieved from tweets with a certain hashtag.

#tweetscapes is the most similar project to this study, consisting in the sonification of German tweets in real-time. Developed by Hermann, Nehls, Eitel, Barri and Gammel, the goal was to create "a new sense of media awareness" [9]. Tweets were mapped according to the hashtags, replies and location, adding a visual geographic distribution that accompanied the sonification.

#Emotional Imaging Composer is an experience conducted in the Input Devices and Music Interaction Lab (IDMIL) at the McGill University, that aims to create a real-time audio expression of emotions, extracted from a vocal performance [28]. This interactive sonification is based on Russell's Arousal/Valence circumplex [23], positioning musical parameters over the two axis.

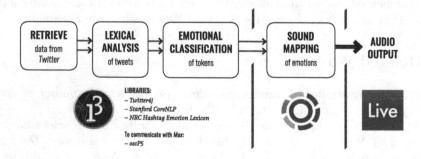

Fig. 1. Process flow diagram

The last example is a website created by Harris and Kamvar, named *We Feel Fine* [7]. It is a visualization that collects human emotions from a vast number of blogs, searching for entries that contain the expression "I feel" or "I am feeling" and providing a social and demographic study.

3   Processing Data

The process implemented in our system comprises four steps (Fig. 1) and uses three software tools to produce the sonification: Processing, to get and classify tweets, Max, to generate the musical composition, and Ableton Live, to play the composition using VST's plugins. The current section describes how the three first steps were implemented. The sound mapping step will be presented in detail in Sect. 4. The sonification system will be explained with more detail in Sect. 5, which includes the developed visualization. Section 6 describes the evaluation process, and the discussion of the obtained outcomes. The last section lists possible future developments and improvements based on the results.

3.1   Data Gathering

The emotional content of a tweet lies in two elements that will form the dataset: the hashtags, metadata tags that establish the subject and mood of a tweet, and the main text, that elaborates the subject and expresses the user's opinion.

To retrieve the tweets, we are using the *Twitter4j* Java library. The data is filtered by language, receiving only tweets in English. To ensure data with some relevance, the tweets are also filtered by the number of followers of each author: only tweets whose author has more than 1000 followers are considered.

3.2   Emotion Lexicon

We implemented a system based on a lexicon of words composed of associations of emotions to each word using a lexicon developed by Mohammad, the *NRC Hashtag-Emotion Lexicon* [17], with the aim of maintaining a simpler and more open approach. It is based on a model of emotions created by Plutchik [20] (Fig. 2) that comprises eight primary emotions: joy, trust, fear, surprise, sadness, disgust, anger and anticipation.

3.3   Lexical and Emotional Analysis

The next task was to implement a set of natural language processing (NLP) tools to parse the tweets, establishing the structure of sentences, word dependencies and "Part-Of-Speech Tagging", classifying each word with its root form, called lemma, and its grammatical category. Working in a Java environment, we have chosen the *Stanford CoreNLP* tool [15], developed by the Stanford NLP group.

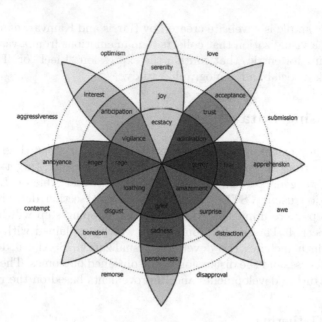

Fig. 2. Robert Plutchik's model of emotions

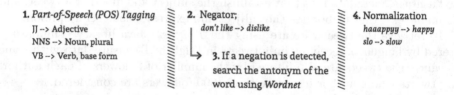

Fig. 3. Steps of the lexical analysis

The analysis of the receiving tweets comprises three steps (Fig. 3):

1. Tweet's parsing and tagging: to define the main structure of the sentences and the words classes. Words classified as nouns, verbs, adverbs or adjectives are stored, due to these classes describing usually the emotion and intensity of a sentence.
2. Identify negations: find the antonyms of negated words using *Wordnet* [16].
3. Submit the remaining words to a combination of two normalisation lexicons [6,14], converting the terms and abbreviations of the texting language to its correct writing form (example of the word "happy" in Fig. 3).

The emotional classification is then applied to the resulting list of words. First, we search the existence of each word in the *NRC Hashtag-Emotion Lexicon*. If it is not found, a search for the lemma of the word is made. Without results, *Wordnet* is used to find a synonym of the word, repeating the first and second steps if a result is found. For the hashtags, the process is more simplified: as the

NRC Hashtag-Emotion Lexicon contains a considerable amount of hashtags and their emotional associations, we search the hashtags directly in the lexicon.

TEXT: @SgtBigC Thank you for your service! I look forward to your tweets !

TOKENS / LEMMAS / TAGS: [@sgtbigc/@sgtbigc/NN, thank/thank/VBP, you/you/ PRP, for/for/IN, your/you/PRP$, service/service/NN, I/I/., i/i/FW, look/look/VBP, forward/forward/RB, to/to/TO, your/you/PRP$, tweets/tweet/NNS]
NEGATED, FILTERED & NORMALISED: [@sgtbigc/@sgtbigc/NN, thank/thank/VBP, service/service/NN, look/look/VBP, forward/forward/RB, tweets/tweet/NNS]

SYNONYMS OF @sgtbigc:
thank: surprise (0.1104075), joy (0.8362264),
service: anticipation (0.048728146), anger (0.3141353), joy (1.4751366), disgust (0.104729064),
look: trust (2.5172772), surprise (0.08125829), disgust (0.2233381),
forward: anticipation (0.8324527), fear (0.38292524), joy (0.14821284),
tweets: anticipation (0.16105315), anger (0.27538794),

HASHTAGS: []

--- **Emotional Classification** ---
Anger - 0.58952326
Anticipation - 1.0422341
Disgust - 0.32806715
Fear - 0.38292524
Joy - 2.459576
Sadness - 0.0
Surprise - 0.1916658
Trust - 2.5172772

Fig. 4. Example of a tweet's emotional classification

3.4   Intermediate Results

All the steps were saved in a text file for evaluation, including the parsing (with each word, correspondent lemma and tag), the lexical analysis' resulting list, the emotions extracted from each word and the sum of every word's emotion, providing the tweet's classification. In the example shown in Fig. 4, *Trust* and *Joy* have the highest and similar values. The majority of the words obtain a classification, allowing a more complete and differentiating categorisation of each tweet. This process takes an average time of 1.6 tweets per second, ensuring a consistent set of variables to sonify and establishing emotional tendencies.

4   Mapping Twitter's Emotions to Music

In 1936, Hevner [10] conducted a series of studies of the expressive elements in music, associating a list of adjectives to musical parameters, such as major/minor mode, dissonant/consonant harmonies and firm/flowing rhythms. The results determined a tendency in the associations, achieving an universal affective nature in musical forms. The main challenge of this project is to explore this expressive dimension to map emotions. Gabrielsson and Lindström [5] gathered over 100 studies made in the last century on this subject, which served as an initial foundation for this sonification. The majority focused on evaluating simple parameters, like tone quality, melody direction, loudness or tempo. Studies of more complex parameters, such as harmonic progressions or chords natures are very limited, exploring only differences in consonant/dissonant harmonies. The authors concluded that although each parameter can influence the emotional expression, it is rarely determined by one factor, but a combination of several.

In our project, we decided to organize the mapping into three main musical aspects: melody, rhythm and harmony, associating probabilities with each parameter for each emotion. At the start of the program, the root note is defined, which provides the tonic for the harmonic progressions and the melody scale.

For the melody, each note is raffled from the current scale, the current chord, or as a chromatism, following probabilities that change according to each emotion (Fig. 5). Chromatic notes are dissonant notes that occur half-step above or below one of the chord's pitches. They travel outside a given scale and are generally used as transition notes to create tension before returning to consonance, releasing the tension. In our system, they are played on weak beats, lasting only half a beat, to keep a subtle dissonant and a tonal feeling. *Fear*, for example, has a higher chance of occuring a chromatic note (50%) than *Joy*, with only 5%.

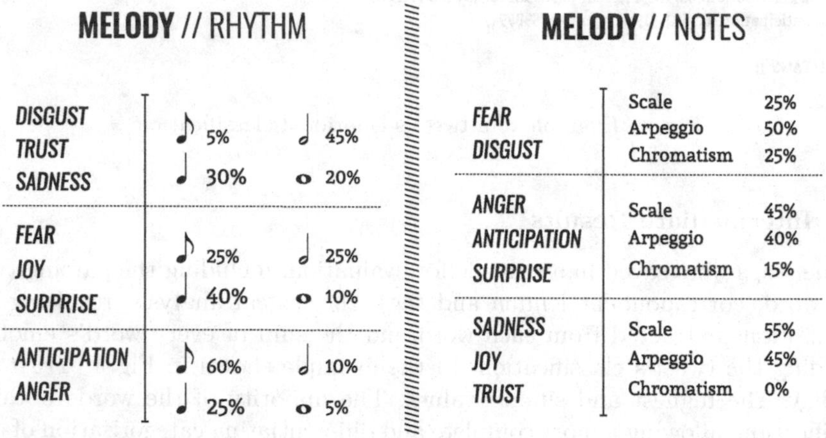

MELODY // RHYTHM   **MELODY // NOTES**

	♪	♩			Scale	
DISGUST	5%	45%	FEAR	Scale	25%
TRUST			DISGUST	Arpeggio	50%
SADNESS	♩ 30%	○ 20%		Chromatism	25%

	♪	♩			
FEAR	25%	25%	ANGER	Scale	45%
JOY			ANTICIPATION	Arpeggio	40%
SURPRISE	♩ 40%	○ 10%	SURPRISE	Chromatism	15%

	♪	♩			
ANTICIPATION	60%	10%	SADNESS	Scale	55%
ANGER			JOY	Arpeggio	45%
	♩ 25%	○ 5%	TRUST	Chromatism	0%

Fig. 5. Melody probabilities on notes and rhythm figures

Hevner also concluded that a slow tempo was associated with more solemn, sad or gentle sounds, whereas happy, exciting and vigorous sounds where likely translated by a fast tempo [5]. Translating this structure to rhythm figures, the duration of the melody notes were associated through probabilities for each emotion, using four rhythm figures: whole, half, quarter and eighth notes (Fig. 5). *Anticipation, Anger* and *Surprise* have higher changes of producing quarter notes, ensuring a more rapid and tense melody. In opposition, for *Trust* and *Disgust* there is a higher tendency to play longer notes.

The melodic interval between two consecutive notes is also raffled according to the emotion being conveyed (Fig. 6). *Joy* and *Sadness* have a higher chance of producing a stepwise motion, using seconds and thirds to provide a more stable and comfortable flow. On the other hand, *Surprise* has a higher probability of sixths and sevenths in order to create sudden jumps that bring an unexpected feeling. An emotion like *Trust* has then a higher probability of producing a consonant sound, in opposition to *Disgust*, that produces a heavily dissonant sound.

MELODY // INTERVALS

	ANTICIPATION / FEAR	ANGER	JOY / TRUST / SADNESS	SURPRISE	DISGUST
Tonic	0%	5%	5%	5%	20%
2nd	25%	30%	35%	10%	10%
3rd	25%	15%	30%	15%	10%
4th	10%	5%	5%	10%	10%
5th	25%	10%	10%	15%	10%
6h	5%	15%	5%	20%	15%
7th	5%	15%	5%	15%	15%
8th	5%	5%	5%	10%	10%

Fig. 6. Melody probabilities on intervals

The melody is built over a certain set of scales (Fig. 7), that were defined according to their association with the harmonic progressions and the constituent chords. They are commonly known to reflect certain emotional contexts. Some examples include the major scale (Ionian mode) the "one with which most people will be familiar" [13], very embedded in Western Music and considered happy and joyous; the minor scale (Aeolian mode), considered negative and sad; the Lydian mode, with a dreamy, mysterious nature; the minor harmonic, with a tone and half interval between the 6th and the 7th that breaks the melodic flow [1]; or the whole tone scale, without a tonal center that originates an unstable, floating quality [26].

MELODY // POSSIBLE SCALES

Ionian	1 2 3 4 5 6 7
Dorian	1 2 b3 4 5 6 b7
Phrygian	1 b2 b3 4 5 b6 b7
Lydian	1 2 3 #4 5 6 7
Mixolydian	1 2 3 4 5 6 b7
Aeolian	1 2 b3 4 5 b6 b7
Locrian	1 b2 b3 4 b5 b6 b7

Major Pentatonic	1 2 3 5 6
Minor Pentatonic	1 3 4 5 7
Major Harmonic	1 2 3 4 #5 6 7
Minor Harmonic	1 2 b3 4 5 b6 7
Phrygian Dominant	1 b2 3 4 5 b6 b7
Mixolydian Augmented	1 2 3 4 5 b6 b7
Diminished	1 2 b3 4 b5 b6 6 7
Whole Tone	1 2 3 b5 b6 b7

Fig. 7. List of melody scales

HARMONY // CHORDS

TRIADS		
X	*Major*	1 3 5
X⁻	*Minor*	1 b3 5
X DIM	*Diminished*	1 b3 b5
X AUG	*Augmented*	1 3 #5
X SUS4	*Suspended4*	1 4 5
X SUS2	*Suspended2*	1 2 5

TETRACHORDS		
X Δ	*Major 7*	1 3 5 7
X 7	*Dominant (7)*	1 3 5 b7
X -7	*Minor 7*	1 b3 5 b7
X ø	*Half-Diminished*	1 b3 b5 b7
X o	*Diminished*	1 b3 b5 bb7(6)
X Δ#5	*Augmented Major 7*	1 3 #5 7
X ALT	*Augmented 7 (Altered)*	1 3 #5 b7
X Δ#11	*Major 7#11 (Lydian chord)*	1 3 #4 7
X 7#11	*Lydian Dominant*	1 3 #4 b7
X 7SUS4	*7 Suspended4 add 9*	1 4 b7 9
X 6/9	*Major Six-Nine*	1 3 6 9
X -Δ	*Minor Major 7*	1 b3 5 7
X -6	*Minor 6*	1 b3 5 6
X -Δ#11	*Minor Major 7#11*	1 b3 #4 7

Fig. 8. List of chords

Music is built over tension and release moments that define the harmonic sequence, which have an impact on the conveyed emotions. Our approach for distinguishing each emotion harmonically was based on Hevner's studies, Gabrielsson and Lindström's analysis, comparing major to minor modes and consonant to dissonant harmonies. Hevner concluded that "it is apparent that the use of the major or minor mode is of the most clear-cut significance in the expression of four different mood effects" [10], with the major mode strongly associated with happiness, gaiety and playfulness, and the minor with sadness, agitation and disgust". A simple/consonant harmony is defined as happy, graceful, serene and dreamy, connected to joy and tenderness, and a complex/dissonant harmony as vigorous and sad, connected to agitation, fear and unpleasantness. These two notions serve as the basis for exploring the progressions and correspondent chords. Due the complexity associated with harmony, we decided to define a set of 20 chords with different natures (Fig. 8). These chords would serve as the structure for a series of progressions that translate each emotion (Fig. 10), ensuring the coherence of the sequence and the affective nature associated.

The chords may be played in three possible voicings (Fig. 9), chosen randomly: in the root position, with an added tonic in the bass (an octave lower), with the tonic and the fifth in the bass, or with the tonic and the seventh (third if triad) in the bass.

For each emotion, a progression is chosen from the list, all with equal probability. Each progression is associated with a number of scales from which the

HARMONY // CHORD VOICINGS

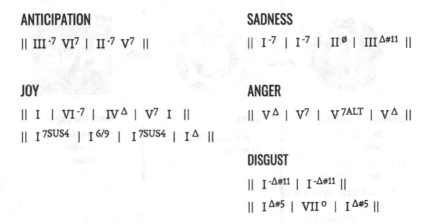

Fig. 9. List of voicings for the chords

HARMONY // EXAMPLES

ANTICIPATION

|| III⁻⁷ VI⁷ | II⁻⁷ V⁷ ||

SADNESS

|| I⁻⁷ | I⁻⁷ | II ∅ | III^(Δ#11) ||

JOY

|| I | VI⁻⁷ | IV^Δ | V⁷ I ||

|| I⁷ˢᵁˢ⁴ | I⁶/⁹ | I⁷ˢᵁˢ⁴ | I^Δ ||

ANGER

|| V^Δ | V⁷ | V⁷ᴬᴸᵀ | V^Δ ||

DISGUST

|| I⁻^(Δ#11) | I⁻^(Δ#11) ||

|| I^(Δ#5) | VII° | I^(Δ#5) ||

Fig. 10. Examples of progressions

melody is created. The scales are either built over the modes of the major scale, or the pentatonic scale, or harmonic and melodic scales.

The harmonic structure explores known progressions (Fig. 10), such as the major *I (Major) - VI (Minor) - IV (Major) - V (Dominant)* or the minor *I (Minor) - I (Minor) - II (Half-Diminished) - III (Major)*, and combinations of different chord natures, building sequences that relate them with the tension associated with each degree. For example, the progression *I (Suspended4) - I (Six-Nine) - I (Suspended4) - I (Major)* combines different major chords with a suspended chord, always built on the first degree. The major chords maintain the stability, and the suspended chord adds tension and a more open sound, establishing the possible set of association with *Joy*.

The tone quality is adapted to each emotion, with associations of certain sounds and technical aspects to each musical context provided by the harmony.

For example, sounds with higher distortions were more connected to emotions like *Anger* and *Disgust*, with more reverb and sustain to *Fear* or *Joy*, or with a fast attack to *Anticipation*, *Surprise* or *Anger*. The overall tone quality resembles the ambient music genre, which evokes a more atmospheric and open sound.

5   Implemented System

The system that was developed implements the sonification in two stages: the first for reception, analysis and emotional classification of tweets, and the second for musical mapping and composition of the audio outcome. A visualization was also made, as a complement to the sound that shows the revised tweets.

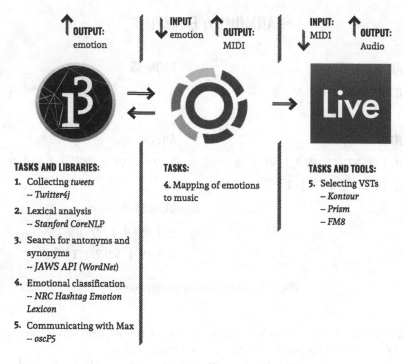

Fig. 11. System diagram

The system was developed over the dynamic communication of three modules (Fig. 11): a Processing sketch, a Max patcher, and an Ableton live set. The first two communicate using the Open Sound Control.

The Processing sketch begins by collecting and classifying tweets, task that runs in the background throughout the entire process. It also saves the values of the emotions extracted from each tweet and their sum. After the first 10 s of the program, the sketch sends to the Max patcher the most prominent emotion of the collected tweets. This begins the composition relative to that emotion, choosing the melody's starting note and a possible harmonic progression.

The progression chosen is repeated a random number of times, with the system choosing a progression again randomly at the end of the loop, ensuring a more dynamic, continuous and flowing composition. At the end of each progression's loop, the Max patcher sends a message to the Processing sketch requesting the next emotion with the highest value, which represents the emotional tendency of the tweets during that previous cycle.

For each progression loop and the correspondent emotion, one of the possible instruments is chosen for the melody and the harmony, which defines the channel and the VST that the Ableton Live Set will use to interpret the MIDI data. It can use three VSTs from the framework Reaktor 6, from Native Instruments: Kountour and Prism for the harmony, and FM8 for the melody.

Some of the resulting sounds produced so far are available at: https:// soundcloud.com/mariana-seica/sets/music-emotions-sonification

5.1 Visualization

The main goal of the sonification is to be capable of transmitting emotions independently, relying only in the potential of sound to communicate information, and of music to convey the emotional qualities. However, a simple visualization was implemented to show the correlations between the composition and the analysed tweets.

The visualization (Fig. 12) is based on the flocking paradigm [22], implemented in Processing by Daniel Shiffman, which simulates the behavior of birds in groups and their movement. It is comprised of a set of agents that move according to three forces: separation, that keeps a certain distance between agents to avoid collision; cohesion, that steers the movement towards the center of the

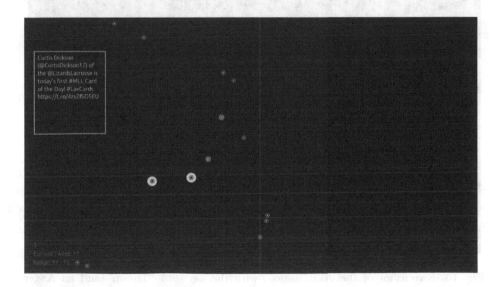

Fig. 12. Screenshot of the visualization

group; and alignment, that keeps the agents moving in the same direction as its neighbors.

Each tweet is an agent, represented by a circle belonging to a group. Eight groups were implemented, relative to Plutchik's eight emotions and represented by the correspondent colors. The tweets are collected and added to the group that represents its highest-scoring emotion.

For each progression cycle, the tweets classified with the current emotion, either its highest or not, are highlighted with an increase in their circle's size and stroke, with the rest disappearing. The text of each tweet is successively shown, with an animation that morphs the circle into a window. The change of progression triggers the death of the circles from the previous loop, that begin an erratic and frenetic movement until their size decreases and they disappear.

6 Evaluation

For the evaluation of the results, a survey was conducted online to understand how the emotions were being perceived.

The survey was comprised of 18 questions, which were divided in two sets of questions. In the first set, the participants were asked to listen to a composition, and evaluate its association with a given emotion, or chose the associated emotions from Plutchik's eight emotions list. In the second one, they were asked to listen to two compositions, and select the most plausible answer.

The chosen pairs of emotions to be tested were chosen from the Plutchik's Wheel of Emotions (Fig. 14), by selecting two opposite pairs and two neighbor-

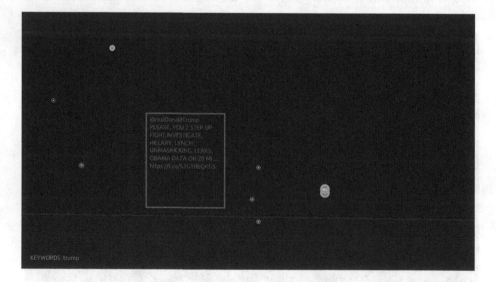

Fig. 13. Screenshot of the visualization, with the keyword "Trump" and an Anger tweet pointed out

Fig. 14. Chosen pairs of emotions for the survey

ing pairs. They were also chosen due to the implemented mapping, which originated emotions with similar sounds and thus more likely to produce incorrect
associations.

The participants were also asked to evaluate their musical knowledge, which
could give us a general insight on how the musical background could influence
the perception of the sounds. The evaluation was made from 1 to 5, in which 1
means someone who has never had any class or training of a musical instrument,
and considers himself "tone deaf", and 5 means professionals in the music area,
as teachers, artists or technicians. In the end of the survey, a comment section
was added to allow the participants to share some insights and suggestions.

The survey was built using the *Jotform* platform, which allows the creation
of a survey within a web environment with integration with Soundcloud, where
the sounds were published.

6.1   Analysis of the Survey Results

The survey was shared among members of the Cognitive and Media Systems group (CMS) of the Centre for Informatics and Systems of the University of Coimbra (CISUC), people associated with music schools in Coimbra (teachers and students), and others from mixed backgrounds, collected on social networks. One hundred answers were obtained, which allowed to draw some conclusions.

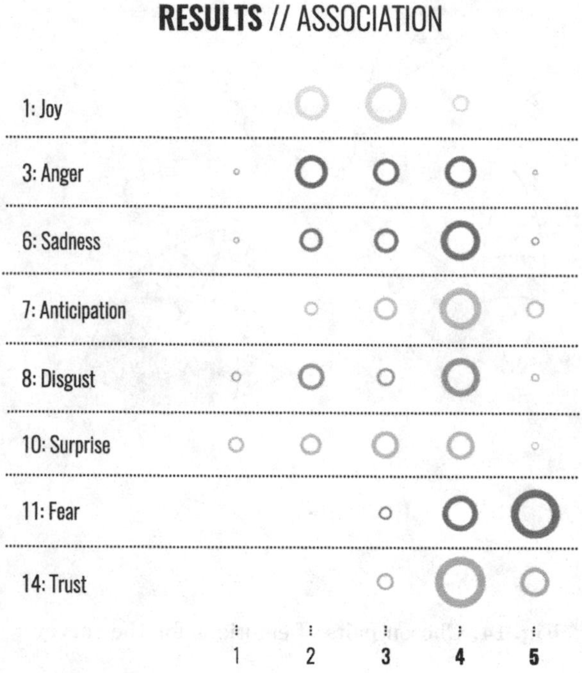

RESULTS // ASSOCIATION

Fig. 15. Results of the association questions

For the eight questions regarding direct association with emotions (Fig. 15), some revealed an incorrect perception. *Joy*, for example, had the highest score in the most neutral value (3), with 41 participants, and the second highest in the previous score (2), with 34 participants, which revealed that more than 75% did not find a clear association. *Anger* is distributed by the three central values. *Sadness* and *Anticipation*, although they had a few scores in the values 2 and 3, the association was mainly positive, with 39 participants scoring *Sadness* and 41 scoring *Anticipation* with the second highest value (4). Therefore, 50% of the participants scored *Sadness*, and 60% *Anticipation*, with the two highest scores (4 and 5). *Disgust* also had a similar distribution, with 38 participants scoring the second highest score (4), with almost 50% of the participants distributed in the two highest scores. *Surprise* had less positive results, with 64 participants distributed in the three lowest scores, with 16 participants considering the lowest score of 1. *Fear* and *Trust* achieved the best results, with almost 85% participants scoring the first with the two highest values, and 80% scoring the second.

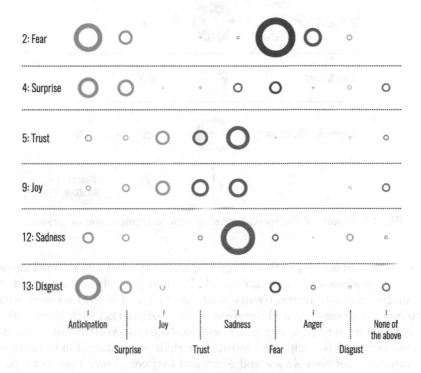

Fig. 16. Results of the selection questions

For the eight selection questions – choosing possible associations from a list with the 8 emotions (Fig. 16) – the results revealed more disagreement. *Joy* and *Trust* were perceived mainly for *Sadness*, emotion that got the highest score in both examples. They were also mistaken by each other, with almost 30 answers. *Surprise* also had a distributed set of associations, with 25 participants choosing *Fear*, almost 20 *Sadness* and the option *None from the list*, and 41 *Anticipation*, with only 34 choosing the correct emotion. *Disgust* produced the less positive results, with only 7 participants perceived it correctly. It was mainly mistaken by *Anticipation*, option chosen by half of the participants. *Sadness* revealed the highest agreement, chosen by almost 70 participants with a small distribution in the remaining options. On the contrary, *Fear*, although achieving a high value of association, with almost 80 participants, generated a higher distribution, with associations with *Anticipation* by 57 participants, *Surprise* by almost 30 and *Anger* by 37.

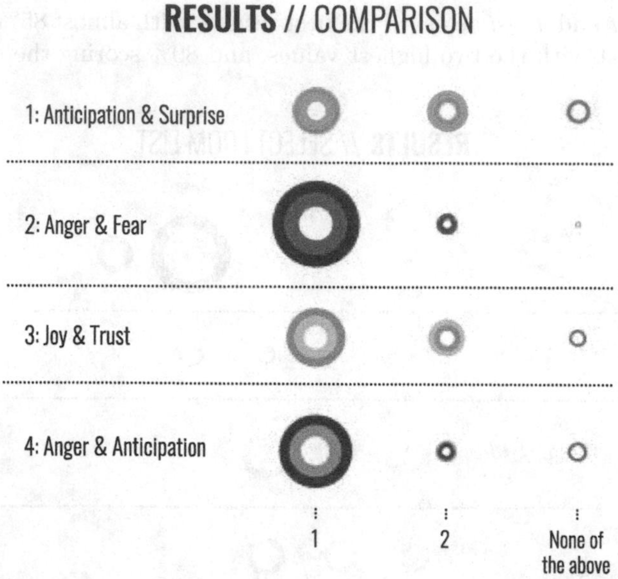

RESULTS // COMPARISON

	1	2	None of the above
1: Anticipation & Surprise	◎	◎	○
2: Anger & Fear	◉	○	·
3: Joy & Trust	◎	○	○
4: Anger & Anticipation	◉	○	○

Fig. 17. Results of the second set of questions (comparison questions)

For the second set of questions (Fig. 17), some expected misconceptions were revealed in emotions with a similar sound. The first pair, *Anticipation* and *Surprise*, originated more mixed results, with the first and second answers with a similar amount of answers, and the *None of the above* option with almost 20% of the answers. The third pair, *Joy* and *Trust*, produced the worst results of the four sets, with only 33% participants choosing the right association. On the contrary, the comparison between *Anger* and *Fear*, and between *Anger* and *Anticipation* achieved a positive differentiation, with around 75% of the participants choosing the right answer in the first set, and 65% in the second.

MUSICAL KNOWLEDGE

Fig. 18. Participants' level of musical knowledge

Regarding the musical knowledge of the participants (Fig. 18), the biggest portion considered themselves at an intermediate level, with 42 participants.

AVERAGE // MUSICAL KNOWLEDGE // ANSWERS

	Mean & Median	Mean & Standard Deviation	**Mean // Standard Deviation // Median**	
1: Joy			4.00 ± 0.894	4
2: Fear			2.59 ± 1.097	3
3: Anger			2.20 ± 1.6	1
4: Surprise			2.79 ± 1.051	3
5: Trust			2.61 ± 1.037	3
6: Sadness			2.50 ± 1.323	3
7: Anticipation			2.56 ± 1.165	3
8: Disgust			3.13 ± 1.053	3
9: Joy			2.43 ± 1.202	2
10: Surprise			3.00 ± 0.866	3
11: Fear			2.50 ± 1.19	3
12: Sadness			2.61 ± 1.157	3
13: Disgust			2.86 ± 1.125	3
14: Trust			2.55 ± 1.162	3
15: Anticipation & Surprise			2.64 ± 1.042	3
16: Anger & Fear			2.45 ± 1.129	3
17: Joy & Trust			2.48 ± 1.131	3
18: Anger & Anticipation			2.34 ± 1.064	2

Fig. 19. Table comparing statistical measures between the musical knowledge of the participants and the results

The lowest scores achieved the highest distribution, with 23 and 20 participants in the values 1 and 2, respectively. The highest scores only had 15% of the participants, with just 5 selecting the highest level.

The correlations between the musical knowledge and the correct perception of the emotions revealed a balanced result (Fig. 19). We chose to calculate the mean, median and standard deviation for the participants who, in each question, selected the right answer, so we could have a general view on how the musical knowledge could improve the perception. In the selection questions, we picked the participants who chose the correspondent emotion, even if they had also chosen multiple options. In the association questions, we used only the participants that chose the highest score (5). In the second set of questions, we used the participants that opted for the correct answer.

The three values were calculated so we could understand the distribution of the data and compare some discrepancy caused by extremely large or small values. In general, the mean of the level of participants that chose the right answer is at the intermediate level (3). The only value that stands from this scenario is in the first question, were the mean of the five participants that scored the highest value reached the second highest level of musical knowledge (4). The values tend to be symmetrically distributed around the mean, with the median reaching an equal value to the rounded mean in almost every answer. The only exception is the third question of the first set, with the median decreasing a value relative to the mean, and the standard deviation with the highest score of the 18 questions, which shows a higher distribution between the levels of musical knowledge.

The general conclusion points out that the level of musical knowledge is not directly connected with the correct perception of the emotions. Nevertheless, only 15% of the participants had the two highest values of musical knowledge, so it could be beneficial to test the results with a a larger music community, to withdraw more concrete conclusions.

6.2 Discussion and Reflection

The submitted answers, along with suggestions and appreciations left in the comments section, allow us to understand the necessary revisions and future experimentations to improve the perception of certain emotions.

The subjectivity of emotions is an underlying topic to consider, for the characterization of Plutchik's eight emotions, and the number of emotional realities that could be associated with each one. This scenario may have influenced the larger discrepancy of the results in the selection questions: by giving the participant the freedom of choice from a list, one gives her the opportunity to think and associate several realities, which contribute to a selection of more options.

Trust was one of the most commented emotions, as being hard to describe and ambiguous, easily mistaken by *Calm* and *Peace* and even associated with choir music by one participant. Another one associated *Trust* with *Love*, as a feeling of safety, or "someone in a good mood on a calm Spring Day". These metaphors with daily realities were curious to observe, as emotions are lived in these contexts.

Joy was one of the most questioned emotions, and the one that demands more exploration, as it was characterized by sounding too calm and passive to represent *Joy*. However, it should be noted that, in the association question relative to *Joy*, the mean of the musical knowledge reach the value 4, which may represent a better perception by the ones with a musical background. It may be one of the emotions that could benefit more from a strong rhythmic element, which could convey a more vivid and cheerful *Joy*.

Fear, although it produced some misconceptions with *Anticipation* and *Anger* in the selection questions, was one of the emotions that revealed the best results, connected to *Distrust*, *Suspense* and an upsetting sound, "as if something bad was about to happen".

Sadness also had positive results, characterized as *Melancholy*. It originated some misconceptions in the selection questions, probably due to the calmer nature of *Joy*, which even using chords with different natures, had a similar rhythm and tone quality that could influence these doubts.

Anger, although it produced mixed results in the direct association, it was correctly distinguished when compared to other emotions as *Anticipation* and *Fear*. Characterized as "evil, as if someone was planning something bad, does not show anger directly". Therefore, like *Joy*, it could also gain with a more structured and present rhythmic element.

Disgust, also it produced positive results in the association questions, it produced several misunderstandings in the selection question, chosen only by seven people and characterized as "not disgust, but when someone is starting to get mad". The mapping of this emotion was thought to be simultaneously upsetting and boring, with unusual chord natures that produce high levels of discomfort, which may have produced confusing compositions that were hard to understand.

Anticipation and *Surprise*, emotions in a neutral spectrum (which can be either positive or negative), also lead to mixed results. The first still obtained a positive association, with 60% participants, and was correctly distinguished between *Anger* when compared directly. However, it was still confused with *Disgust* and *Fear*, characterized as "when someone is planning something malicious". *Surprise* had worse results, with a weak association and misconceptions with varied emotions, especially *Anticipation*.

Although the results produced a few misconceptions, we can say they were generally positive, with several comments from participants stating this study as "interesting", "challenging", that made them "think about emotions and the influence of music", and that "even if the emotions were not the intended, the compositions really show emotions".

7   Future Developments

The complexity of several fields addressed in this project demands a series of improvements, which could enhance the main two steps of this sonification: the emotional classification of text and the musical mapping.

The emotional analysis, as it is being made by classifying each filtered word through the chosen lexicon, becomes a fallible method, prone to errors due to the limited number of lexicon words and lack of analysis of phrase structure. Besides, the personal language used in social media has usually underlying intentions, with sarcasm and irony changing the emotional tone and creating a higher complexity. One possible solution is to adapt the lexical and emotional analysis to *Python* language, which offers a larger set of possible tools for linguistic review. It would also be interest to adapt the analysis to multiple languages, which could allow a classification of the almost 30 languages that the Twitter API offers, and a global view of the emotional scenario. To expand the emotional spectrum, it would be a possibility to expand the Plutchik's model to the 24 emotions, that could provide a higher set of emotional realities. Another hypothesis is to change the emotional model, using Russell's circumplex model of affect and its two-axis numerical graph to explore more emotional states.

The musical mapping can be expanded in several ways. Winters and Gresham-Lancaster [27] suggest that the focus and complexity of the musical forms should be, instead of the orchestral level (tone quality), in terms of rhythm, tempo and intensity, combined with the sound envelope, mainly the speed of the attack, decay and articulation. The rhythm was revealed through the results as being one of the main parameters to explore with more detail, from tempo variations (BPM) to time signatures. The melodic rhythm can be improved through the addition of rests and the exploration of upbeats, to refine the system of chromatisms. Loudness will also be a priority parameter to explore, to distinguish more energetic emotions like *Joy*, *Anticipation* and *Fear*.

The visualization, as it was a relatively simple experimentation to complement the sonification, can be largely improved, exploring other visual styles and objects that could enhance the communication of tweets, and how the musical parameters could influence the object's movements.

8   Conclusion

With this project, we proposed a structured and musically complex mapping that could translate emotions through a musically captivating sonification. Its implementation produced a sonification of the eight main emotions of Plucthik's model [20], extracted from Twitter in real-time and accompanied by a visualization of the collected tweets and emotional classification.

Underlying problems of the Sonification field are kept unsolved, namely the cultural issues. The implemented mapping, as it was built over the rules of Western Music, does not produce the same results in different regions. Winters e Gresham-Lancaster [27] discuss this problematic, stating that harmonic and melodic artefacts can be highly effective for western listeners, but may not work with others. It is then clear the cultural limitation these sound objects represent.

The cultural matters heighten the emotion subjectivity, whose study is still "one of the most confused (and still open) chapters in the history of psychology" [20]. This scenario comes not only from the difficulty in defining emotions, but also from the musical expression, and its ability in not only conveying emotions, but also induce them [24]. These two types of emotions (perceived and induced) rise from the interaction between the user and the sound object in a given context [24], which is dependent by several individual factors as personality, mood, cultural and musical background.

The relationship between emotions and music is a field that demands a profound study and understanding, due to the complexity of the data and the chosen channel for transmission. This project was an effort to tackle this relationship in the Sonification area, exploring its multidisciplinary nature. The results, although they produced a few misconceptions, were generally positive, expressing the effectiveness and impact of the musical mapping. Several issues that arise focused on the context and musical preferences, which change between listeners and influence the understanding of musical parameters.

The proposed intentions were achieved, with the development of a structured and thought sonification process that transmits the emotional nature of the data in an effective and comprehensible way to the user. We sought to explore how could the use of sound contribute in understanding data, demonstrating the sound potential as a tool to communicate, building a sound object that could be relevant not only in the Sonification field, but for Design as well, usually focused on visual communication. The resulting sound object is another proof, from the increasing number of Sonification projects, of the chance to elevate sound from a supporting communication element to a lead element, expanding the auditory and musical universe.

References

1. Aldwell, E., Schachter, C.: Harmony & Voice Leading. Thomson-Schirmer, Belmont (2003)
2. Bulley, J., Jones, D.: Living Symphonies (2014). http://www.livingsymphonies.com/
3. Coelho, A., Martins, P., Cardoso, A.: A Portuguese Epopee seen through sound. In: 5th Conference on Computation, Communication, Aesthetics & X (2017)
4. Foo, B.: Rhapsody in grey (2016). https://datadrivendj.com/tracks/brain
5. Gabrielsson, A., Lindström, E.: The role of structure in the musical expression of emotions. In: Juslin, P.N., Sloboda, J. (eds.) Handbook of Music and Emotion: Theory, Research, Applications. Oxford University Press, New York (2010)
6. Han, B., Cook, P., Baldwin, T.: Automatically constructing a normalisation dictionary for microblogs. In: Proceedings of the 2012 Joint Conference on Empirical Methods in Natural Language Processing and Computational Natural Language Learning, Jeju Island, Korea (2012)
7. Harris, J., Kamvar, S.: We Feel Fine (2006). http://number27.org/wefeelfine
8. Hermann, T., Hunt, A., Neuhoff, J.G.: The Sonification Handbook. Logos Verlag, Berlin (2011)
9. Hermann, T., Nehls, A.V., Eitel, F., Barri, T., Gammenl, M.: Tweetscapes - Real-time sonification of Twitter data stream for radio broadcasting. In: Proceedings of the 18th International Conference on Auditory Display, Atlanta, GA, USA (2012)
10. Hevner, K.: Experimental studies of the elements of expression in music. Am. J. Psychol. **48**(2), 246–268 (1936)
11. Juslin, P., Västfjäll, D.: Emotional responses to music: the need to consider underlying mechanisms. Behav. Brain Sci. **31**, 559–621 (2008)
12. Kramer, G., et al.: Sonification report: status of the field and research agenda. Faculty Publications, Department of Psychology. Paper 444 (2010). http://digitalcommons.unl.edu/psychfacpub/444

13. Ligon, B.: Jazz Theory Resources: Tonal, Harmonic, Melodic and Rhythmic Organization of Jazz. Houston Publishing (2003)
14. Liu, F., Weng, F., Jiang, X.: A broad-coverage normalization system for social media language. In: Proceedings of the 50th Annual Meeting of the Association for Computational Linguistics, pp. 1035–1044 (2012)
15. Manning, C.D., Surdeanu, M., Bauer, J., Finkel, J., Bethard, S.J., McClosky, D.: The Stanford CoreNLP natural language processing toolkit. In: Proceedings of the 52nd Annual Meeting of the Association for Computational Linguistics: System Demonstrations, pp. 55–60 (2014)
16. Miller, G.M.: WordNet: a lexical database for English. Commun. ACM **38**(11), 39–41 (1995)
17. Mohammad, S.M., Kiritchenjko, S.: Using hashtags to capture fine emotion categories from tweets. Comput. Intell. **31**(2), 301–326 (2013)
18. Morreale, F., Miniukovich, A., De Angeli, A.: TwitterRadio: Translating Tweets into Music. In: Proceedings of the SIGCHI Conference on Human Factors in Computing Systems, Toronto, ON, Canada (2014)
19. Pang, B., Lee, L.: Opinion mining and sentiment analysis. Found. Trends Inf. Retr. **2**(1–2), 1–135 (2008)
20. Plutchik, R.: The nature of emotions. Am. Scientist. **89**, 344–350 (2001)
21. Quinn, M.: Research set to music: the climate symphony and other sonifications of ice core, radar, DNA, seismic and solar wind data. In: Proceedings of the International Conference on Auditory Display, Espoo, Finland (2001)
22. Reynolds, C.W.: Flocks, herds and schools: a distributed behavioral model. In: Proceedings of the 14th Annual Conference on Computer Graphics and Interactive Techniques (SIGGRAPH), pp. 25–34 (1987)
23. Russell, J.: A circumplex model of affect. J. Pers. Soc. Psychology. **39**(6), 1161–1178 (1980)
24. Song, Y., Dixon, S., Pearce, M.T., Halpern, A.R.: Perceived and induced emotion responses to popular music: categorical and dimensional models. Music. Percept.: Interdiscip. J. **33**(4), 472–492 (2016)
25. Vicinanza, D.: Voyager 1 & 2 Spacecraft Duet (2014). http://www.geant.net/MediaCentreEvents/news/Pages/The-sound-of-space-discovery.aspx
26. Waite, B.: Modern jazz piano: a study in harmony and improvisation. Wise-Publications (Book Sales Limited) (1987)
27. Winters, R.M., Gresham-Lancaster, S.: Sonification of Emotion (2015). https://creativedisturbance.org/podcast/mike-winters-sonification-of-emotion/
28. Winters, R.M., Hattwick, I., Wanderley, M.M.: Emotional data in music performance: two environments for the emotional imaging composer. In: Proceedings of the 3rd International Conference of Music & Emotion (ICM3), Jyväskylä, Finalnd (2013)

Research and Creation: Spaces and Modalities

Reflections on the Use of Musical Software in Compositional Processes for Light Art

Charlotte Beaufort[✉]

University of Picardie Jules Verne, Amiens, France
charlotte.beaufort@u-picardie.fr

Abstract. Music and the visual arts are both temporal and spatial arts. My artistic research focuses on the use of light as a medium and in this respect my interests are both spatial and temporal and revolve around phenomenological questions related to the perception of volume and space, but also to the problems of how temporal sequences may be arranged and written into a score. After a short presentation of my artistic production and of my theoretical (and phenomenological) interests, I will try to explain and show how and why musical software is better designed for my light installations, especially because they presuppose the activity of autonomous composition in time.

Keywords: Light installation · Light art · Software · Composition · Music Visual arts · Phenomenology · Perception · Space · Time · Body · Score Notation

1 Introduction

First, let me say that I am neither a musician nor a composer. My contribution will be that of a visual artist and a researcher in the visual arts. I will briefly present my visual productions in order to set the frame of my reflections. This will allow me to show how my reflection and my visual experimentation derived from traditional pictorial questions—such as simultaneous color contrasts—but also from a phenomenological approach focussed on the production of visual phenomena and on the global question of perception, which, as far as my visual productions are concerned, is not limited to visual perception. Indeed, the environments I make, with or without natural light, seemlessly push the beholders to fell space and time and to become aware of their perception, of how their body acts and reacts as it experiences the environment. My research is about how to enhance perception awareness.

This talk will also be about the specificities of light as artistic medium. I will try to describe the problems and the questions raised by the use of its specific technological tools. In particular, I will show how and why technological tools developed for musicians may allow me to attempt to compose and write light scores, although this still is the source of many interrogations for me.

© Springer Nature Switzerland AG 2018
M. Aramaki et al. (Eds.): CMMR 2017, LNCS 11265, pp. 611–624, 2018.
https://doi.org/10.1007/978-3-030-01692-0_40

2 A Visual Form for a Spatial and Temporal Experience

Recent artistic productions and experiments show that the temporal dimension is not exclusively musical and that the spatial dimension is not limited to the visual arts. Music and the visual arts are both temporal and spatial.

My visual research is fundamentally temporal and spatial. I build three-dimensional objects designed to enhance our perception of light and color and whose perception is modified by a light score. When I come to think of it, I believe I have never produced a work that was not designed to be experienced in time. The reason for this is that what interests me is change and the phenomenon—as appearance and disappearance— whence my interest in programming tools. This is also the reason why I find many converging points of interest with the vocabulary, the methods, the concepts and the tools used in the musical field—especially since the second half of the XXth century.

To make things clear I will need to describe how time and the phenomenon are related to my artistic practice of light and color-light. I will describe a few light installations I made in the past ten years. The pictures and short films I will present are excerpts of site-specific light installations in which the spatial and temporal dimensions are essential and intertwined in producing a complex aesthetic experience. Needless to say that these images should be seen as utterly imperfect representations of phenomena created for the human eye and not for cameras…

2.1 Moving Light

First, here are two site-specific installations made for the Moving Light exhibition in 2008. Untitled 1 & 2 lasted (Figs. 1 and 2) approximately 20 min each. The light score was set in a loop with no perceptible beginning and end. The exhibition was open all day long, and visitors could come in, walk around and go out of this immersive environment at any time.

The two 100 m^2 rooms had one massive central pillar which was the main element I had to take into account. I used it to stress the spatial dimension of the installation, but also to focus on the beholder as a moving subject. This led me to focus on the formal, sculptural or scenographic organization of space, but also on the temporal dimension of perception—which in this case is not only visual, but also tactile, bodily and auditory. For instance, in U1 the beholder could never see the three apertures at the same time. The installation was made so that it was necessary to walk around to get a notion of the whole. The constraint of the pillar had been transformed into the incentive to move around, although the visitors were not aware of this. There is something very phenomenological in this insistence on perception as action which reminds me of the Japanese zen garden in the Ryoanji Temple where the fifteen stones can never all be seen at once, there being always one that remains hidden, whatever one's viewpoint on the garden.

Fig. 1. Charlotte Beaufort, *Untitled 1*, 2008 (Fish-eye lens view)

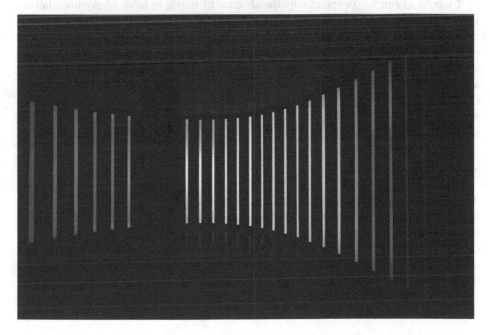

Fig. 2. Charlotte Beaufort, *Untitled 2*, 2008 (partial view)

Concerning this installation, I wish to stress two things: firstly, there was no music; secondly, the 20-min light score was very slow. I will later explain why most of my light scores can be described as odes to slowness—although they are not without effects of rupture and rhythm. Actually, here again a technical constraint became a central aesthetic object and I transformed the constraint into an object for research. Let me also briefly note here that I deliberately chose not to introduce music in my light scores for reasons I will evoke later.

In brief, U1 and U2 proposed an aesthetic experience based on three elements: slowness, ambient sound, perambulation. The square rooms in this old slaughterhouse turned into an art center had thick sound-proof walls with clear acoustics. The visitors entered the room through an entry light-lock. In U1 the visitors entered a dark, silent space barely animated by the slow evolution of the light score thus calling for more intense attention to light and ambient sounds and forcing visitors to hush or whisper as they walked around the central pillar to experience the full scope of the installation. A friend of mine who is a musician and a musicologist told me how she realized that the extreme slowness of the light score led her to unconsciously slow down her own moves around the room and significantly altered her whole perception, thus showing that indeed the aesthetic and perceptual conditions of the installation (its immersive quality, a clear acoustics, no music, extreme slowness of the light score) were able to make the beholder think about and reflect upon the aesthetic conditions of his perception and to create an atmosphere for a more focused attention to the environment.

I would like now to explain why the absence of music in most of my installations was a deliberate choice. There is this idea that one of the senses always supersedes the others and that my medium is light and not sound. The absence of music avoids an excess of information to the senses that would lead to the beholder becoming more passive in his experience. My idea was to allow and even push the beholder to be perceptually active. In this respect, I find it very significant that someone who saw my soundless installations in 2008, after she experienced the light and musical score of *Eos* in 2016, mentioned that she had always remembered the *Moving Light* installations as being accompanied by music.

2.2   Diaphanies

The second example I wish to mention here is a series called Diaphanies (Figs. 3 and 4), which etymologically evokes what appears through something else. The Diaphanies are based on the interaction of preprogrammed light and the unpredictable changes of daylight in order to multiply the instances and interplays of appearing-disappearing phenomena—thus continuously producing the ongoing phenomenon that is the work proper.

Fig. 3. Charlotte Beaufort, *Diaphanies* Series, 2012

Fig. 4. Charlotte Beaufort, *Diaphanies* Series, 2012

I will single out two characteristics of this series: The first one is that here again there is no music, but that the work uses two types of light (one is artificial and programmed, the other natural and random) so that one could describe it as a mixed lightscore—much as one would speak of mixed music. Although I had not then thought of the musical experimentations with randomness, it seems to me now that this convergence with mixed music and John Cage's experiments with randomness tends to show that there is indeed something in common between musical experimentation and my own experiments with light as a medium.

The second point I wish to make concerns the motifs in the Diaphanies. Their being figurative or not, or uncertain, is not the point. They only point to an interrogation about what Cage has stated as «Life without a structure is not visible». In a similar way, such horizon or formal choice, such lightscore serves as a leverage point or structure to make better visible our relation to the world, to life, to extension and duration.

2.3   Light and Music Scores: Eos (2016), Leucosia (2016), Sirius (2017)

I wish now to describe a next field of research I began to explore in 2016 based on the combination of light scores with electroacoustic music specifically composed by Mark Lockett. Mark and I have thus produced three light and musical scores in 2016 and 2017: Eos, Leucosia and Sirius. These works are plastically based on an initially musicless series of mine called Photospheres (Fig. 5) which I started in 2015.

Fig. 5. Charlotte Beaufort, *Photospheres* Series, 2015

The Photospheres are approximately 1 m by 1 m by 1 m. They are composed of three (or more) panels with perfectly circular apertures of varying sizes perceived as so many concentric rings, and of a translucent hemisphere in the back with a contrasting irregular surface. The composition is both spatial and temporal. The formal choice of the circular shape and of the rings' width and proportions make up the structure—it is specific to each photosphere. Each of these pieces has a looped light score of approximately 10 min which combines various effects—color combinations, varying intensities, simultaneous contrasts, rhythmic effects, etc.—which may form a narrative sequence and are meant to create sensorial and emotional intensity.

In 2016 and 2017, I created two new works, EOS and SIRIUS. Apart from the hemisphere which I gave up, they are similar to the photospheres but much larger (2.50 m × 2.50 m) and deeper (1 m and 3 m) for a more powerful phenomenological impact. One has seven rings, the other has ten.

Based on these installations, Mark Lockett and I created three light and electroacoustic scores—*Eos* (2016 - 16'24), *Leucosia* (2016 - 17'50), *Sirius* (2017 - 14'57) (Figs. 6 and 7) based on a common reflection on the combination of different sensorial experiences, in order to produce three coherent polysensorial works.

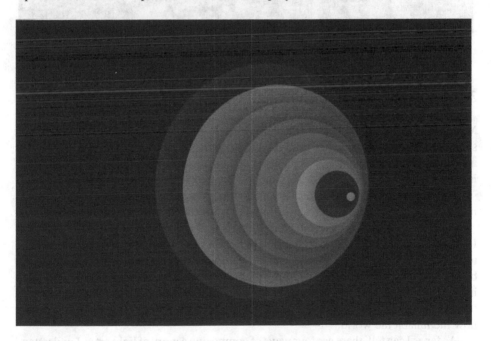

Fig. 6. Charlotte Beaufort, *Sirius* (14'57), *Photospheres* Series, 2017. Music Mark Lockett

I would like now to deal with the specificity of light as a medium and a few questions about light composition which were raised in the course of my collaboration with Mark.

Fig. 7. Charlotte Beaufort, *Sirius* (14'57), *Photospheres* Series, 2017. Music Mark Lockett

3   Reflections of the Writing and Composition of Light Scores

My conception of light as a plastic medium which must be considered as a phenomenon in space and time no doubt comes from my past experience as a light designer. Light, color and change are the fundamental elements of my artistic research, along with form—which is a receptacle, a structure and an instrument—, content and temporal evolution.

Form is important because it is very much linked to content. Content, as I understand it, is not a figurative image but results from the arrangement of form, color and evolution.

An important specificity of my work is that it is not made of a videoprojected image. I work with the omnidirectional emission of light, I try to fashion it in three dimensions, to give it a bodily presence, what I call *voluminosity*. Another specificity, which is yet barely developed in the visual arts, is my focus on writing a score for a work that unfolds in time. An important point for me is how my work may create the conditions for a temporal aesthetic experience that foregrounds our relationship to space and time and how the inhabit the world.

As far as I can tell, there are four ways of composing a work of light art as I understand it:

– The first one, inspired by painting, consists in creating «chromatic objects» through the arrangement of colors;
– The second one, inspired by music, puts the stress on syntax, temporal and rhythmic organization;

- The third one relies on the integration of randomness: this was the case in the Diaphanies that involved different «instruments»: the artificial light played its own pre-written, pre-programmed line, while the second instrument, the natural light, kept changing in intensity, color and rhythm in a totally unpredictable way, thus making the interaction between both lights unpredictable.
- The fourth way, which I have yet never wished to adopt, consists in using computer technology in order to compose pieces based on mathematical, algorithmic or geometric formulas, or else by relying on databases. Once the parameters have been selected the composition is an automatic self-making process.

These four methods may be used individually or in combination. In my case, they are closely linked to the software I use. I began to address these questions about composition when I quit the performing arts to become an autonomous visual artist using light as a medium. My work was not collective anymore, I was not determined by the conceptions of a stage director, nor constrained by a text or by predetermined scenographic choices, and the question of writing became central. I had to give up some of my professional techniques and habits and I then realized how much the tools we use determine and often limit our compositional work.

Paradoxically, when I began to collaborate with Mark Lockett I had once more to deal with the parameters of the performing arts. Mark seemed to think of our collaboration in terms of the performing arts. He was excited by the idea of playing his music live and of improvizing with my light compositions. Nothing could have been further away from my intentions. We then had to discuss all sorts of questions about how the work should be presented, how long it should be, about its linear or looped structure, whether it should have a beginning and an end, narrative content and should it be open to interpretation.

All these questions led to fruitful exchanges. They were essential to me because I wanted the final piece, made of sound and music, to make one integrated work. It was capital, in my view, to reflect upon how we should write our two scores so that no medium would gain the upper hand over the other or become the illustration of the other.

These questions lead me now to my next point about compositional tools.

4   Reflections About Technological and Compositional Tools

During my research, I became interested in the question of simultaneous contrasts (especially in painting), of gradation (harmonization), and then in the question of how colors bleed into one another—in space or time. Indeed, I rapidly realized that these questions covered two distinct objects: what happens in a fixed arrangement of colors, and what happens as movement in the succession of colored states. The temporal arrangement of colors creating change or movement in time or duration led me to the notion of the interval and to develop a conception of the intervallary nature of color phenomena. This explains how my research interests, initially close to pictorial questions raised by the fixed image, also led me to questions usually associated with music.

Until now, the tools used to command and record the evolution of several light sources are light design software used in the performing arts (theatre, dance, concerts).

The digital protocol used for light is called DMX 512 (Digital Multiplexing), it is different from the MIDI protocol used for sound.

Despite their differences, all light softwares are based on the same principle. They all allow you to record a fixed light state as a cue. This cue is recorded under a number, but it is quite significantly referred to as either an «image» or a «tableau» (or picture). So that when I work on my photospheres, my work consists in creating a number of light states much like a painter composing his picture with a brush on a canvas. And indeed, I may choose to exhibit such a fixed light composition, for every single light state in my compositions has been carefully composed and recorded with precise aims in mind and could constitute a work in itself.

Once several such light states have been created, with the various values of each source determined from 0 to 100%, it is possible to create movement or change from one state to the other—cue 1 to cue 2—by ascribing a given time to the transfer. The simplest example would be when I choose how long it will take for a source to go from a 0% to a 100% intensity. Doing this in one second or ten minutes produces a very different effect. Things become very complex when dealing with dozens of multicolored sources on different planes which constantly and instantly interact and modify our experience of color.

Here are a few examples of the commands on one of these softwares (Fig. 8):

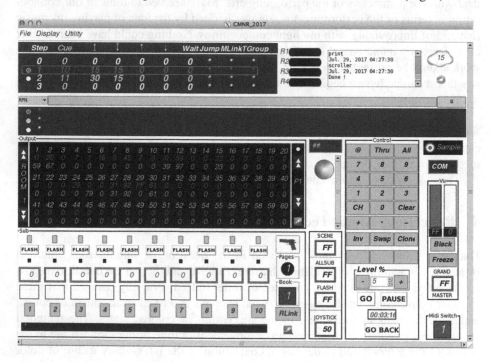

Fig. 8.   Screen capture, Dlight Software

- Here are my light sources represented by numbers
- I can choose an intensity from 0 to 100
- I then record a cue (as number 10, for example)
- This cue is automatically recorded in a sequential series
- I then record a second cue (number 11, for example)
- I then ascribe a time for ascent or descent
- I then hit «Go» to see what happens on stage

Fixed image 10 ⇔ Transfer - temporisation ⇔ Fixed image 11.

The software I use is Dlight[1]. It's an open source software. One should note that all the vocabulary used on this kind of software comes from the theater.

This short presentation shows that this kind of software is conceived in order to compose fixed states or images and only as a secondary function allow to work on a temporal evolution of light. Some sophisticated software allow to command the moves of motorized projectors but this is totally different from my problems with the composition of light and color in time, because these softwares are not conceived for the purpose of composing in time. This is logical for generally the lighting of plays changes from one scene to the other—from one tableau to the other—or from one moment to another in order to follow what happens on stage. For in the theater, light does not lead, it does not show itself for itself, it contributes to a show whose goals are defined elsewhere. Lighting does sometimes evolve in a continuous move—but frenetically and with no discernible aesthetic plan, in rock or pop concerts.

I want to stress that such a tool very rapidly becomes a severe limitation when one wishes to work with light in the temporal dimension—and light keeps changing in my installations, even when we may have the feeling that it has stopped.

Basically this kind of software is useful to compose luminous states, they can be relatively useful to work on the transfer between states and on the interval, but they are very burdensome if one wishes to focus on rhythm or the temporal structure of a piece.

Among the limitations, I would note:

- A very linear form of writing
- The necessity to compose successive states which forbids to think of composing otherwise
- A very abstract and unintuitive interface. Each light source must be programmed individually and is represented by a number.
- Writing thus becomes time-consuming (and leaves no room for improvisation, as one would do with a musical instrument—for my installations are like so many light instruments, after all)
- The software limits creativity. For instance, there is no copy/paste function.

Apart from that, the absence of a timeline and composing with a succession of fixed images also pose problems:

---

[1] https://www.nicole-banana.com/.

– When working on a collaborative piece, I need to play the whole piece in order to check that light and sound are still synchronized;
– I would need to have a common timeline for light and sound

The problem is that light-designing software was not able to benefit from the research that was made in the musical field under the impulse of John Cage in the 50s or with the strong institutional support of Pierre Boulez and the IRCAM in France since the 70s. Lighting software remains limited to the performing arts and does not allow to rethink light art from a more global perspective—and the most sophisticated tools on the market are meant for strictly professional use and are far too expensive for individual researchers and artists.

This is the reason why to this day I developed my compositions within the limits of the software's constraints, trying to overcome these constraints or to transform them into objects of research—which revealed itself to be stimulating. Since I could not really work on the temporal or rhythmic structure, I focused on the questions of flux and slowness, composing complex chromatic evolutions through the succession of tableaux, and thus concentrating on the intervallary nature of color and the stretching of temporal experience. I sometimes use rhythmic effects to compose dynamic moments of rupture or combined after-image effects to create absent colors. For indeed, chromatic compositions and temporal evolutions are composed to produce in duration the appearance-disappearance of phenomena, and to provide sensorial, emotional and physical experiences. To a large extent these compositions may be described as odes to slowness[2]. This mode of composition may remind us of spectral music, and the concepts of spectromorphology developed by Denis Smalley may be relevant to what I do as a light artist.

As I struggled with my light designing software, I tried to find new better-adapted tools. I thought of checking the tools developed by musicians hoping to adapt them to my technical and compositional needs.

In 2014, I tried MAX software. MAX could allow me to develop my own software and to create non-linear evolutions but it was not well suited to my compositional needs. I felt I could not control many parameters and that the compositional means were too often based on loops, randomness and self-writing processes. Moreover, my command of MAX—which, I must admit, is very limited—was insufficient for many of my purposes: for instance, create a timeline, composing a fixed image, creating a more intuitive graphic interface. The tool's complexity kept me away from a more free creative process. I found MAX could be essentially used as an ancillary interface between softwares and could serve my purposes to integrate a composed page or a patch within a composition.

This year, I was able to use new composition software.

Iannix[3] is an open source graphic sequencer for the digital arts and specifically adapted to music and to musical spatialization (Fig. 9). As its name indicates, it was inspired by Iannis Xenakis and the UPIC, an electronic instrument he created in 1977

---

[2]   *Cf.* Beaufort, Charlotte. «Color in the Interval», *JAIC – Journal of the International Colour Association*, Volume 17 (2017). Special Issue: «Colour and Light» . http://www.aic-color.org/journal/current.htm.

[3]   https://www.iannix.org/fr/.

in order to compose music graphically by drawing on an architect's drawing table, after he was inspired in the 50s by his architectural collaboration with Le Corbusier. The main goal was to reach a form of compositional immediacy. Iannix software, which has been developed since the early 2000s by Thierry Coduys and Guillaume Jacquemin, aims to develop non-linear writing beyond the western linear left-to-right reading model. It also questions the one-slider model and favors polytemporality, and it allows to compose graphically (in two or three dimensions), to have a dynamic score that can be modified in real time.

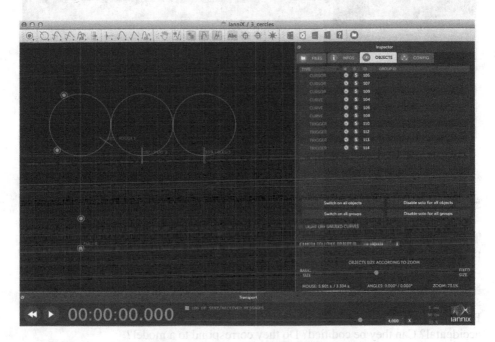

Fig. 9. Screen capture, IanniX Software

Although it was not meant to control light, Iannix opens experimental possibilities for me. I can use it to compose light scores with a graphic interface, from a different perspective and with non-linear writing processes. However, like MAX, Iannix does not do fixed images and has no general timeline, which for me is a severe limitation.

The second software I experimented this year is a kind of hybrid called Vezér[4] (Fig. 10). It allows to create compositions that integrate MIDI, OSC, DMX or Audio tracks based on a common timeline. Vezér is the first software that allows me to have a timeline that may be shared with the sound timeline. When I compose a light score in collaboration with Mark Lockett, this allows me to perfectly synchronize light and sound but also to work precisely with the information of the soundtrack. However, like MAX and Iannix, Vezér does not do fixed images and this considerably modifies the approach to composition—and its outcome.

---

[4] https://imimot.com/vezer/.

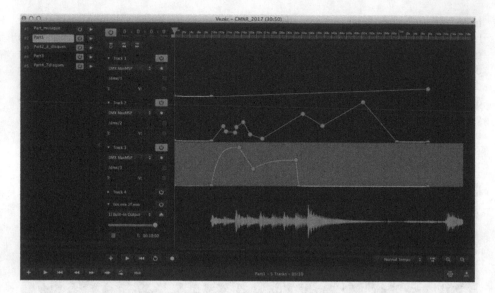

Fig. 10. Screen capture, Vezér Software

5   Conclusion

To conclude, I would say that if software developed for—or derived from—musical purposes allow me, as a light artist, to better approach the temporal dimension of compositional work, they still raise major structural problems concerning the composition of light scores. From the moment the compositional structure is not based on a succession of fixed images anymore, it must rely on a rhythmic and temporal structure. But what is the nature of these rhythmic and temporal elements? Are they random or accidental? Can they be codified? Do they correspond to a model?

   These questions raised by my experimentation with various softwares seem to indicate that my research as a visual artist confronts two radically different compositional methods: one is pictorial and the other is musical. If the software I used allowed me to measure how different these compositional methods are, the question raised now for me, is perhaps not whether I can find or create the magical software that would allow me to compose both statically and temporally, but whether it is merely thinkable to do so…

SELFHOOD: An Evolutionary and Interactive Experience Synthesizing Images and Sounds

Jonatas Manzolli[1], Artemis Moroni[2(✉)], and Guilherme A. Valarini[2]

[1] IA, NICS/University of Campinas – UNICAMP, Campinas, SP 13083-970, Brazil
jonatas@nics.unicamp.br
[2] CTI Renato Archer, Dom Pedro Highway (SP-65), Km 143.6 – Amarais-Campinas, Campinas,
SP 13069-901, Brazil
artemis.moroni@cti.gov.br, guilherme.a.valarini@gmail.com

Abstract. The SELFHOOD installation was conceived aiming to instigate a
reflection on the self through a practical and interactive experience. A representation of each participant is created in a form of a cloud of points and a sound
drone, suggesting their selves. The dynamics of the visitors' movements is sonified in such way that colours and sound textures are fused in a surrounding hexaphonic system. CromaCrono≈, the system for immersive improvisation that
produces digitally synthesized sounds in real time, is described. Philosophical
concepts concerning notions of the Self are presented. We propose that the notion
of Presence can be induced by virtual and/or physical sources of stimulation
governed by a number of principles that underlie human experience, creativity,
and discovery. The methodological point of view is that the notion of Presence
indicates that there are essential inputs for the construction of self-referral agents.

Keywords: Evolutionary systems · Interactivity · Multimodal installation
Presence · Self · Sound synthesis

1 Introduction

In the development of new music interactive technologies, a mixed reality environment
[1] can function as a laboratory to evaluate interactive behaviour [2, 3]. With the advent
of new technologies that have emphasized interaction and novel interfaces, alternative
forms and modes of interactive media have been realized [4]. These developments raise
fundamental questions on the role of the embodiment as well as the environment and
interaction in the understanding of the man-machine interplay. In addition, it places
emphasis on a more situated and externalist view. Moreover, body's perception, cognitive and motor responses have to be reconfigured to the needs and constraints concerning
action and perception in these new domains. Thus the man-machine interface interaction
can now be optimized [5–7].

In line with these recent developments, we present here the SELFHOOD installation
as an interdisciplinary research framework. SELFHOOD is an evolutionary and interactive installation in which particle systems and Boids algorithm [8] are used to synthe-
size images and sounds digitally. The sonification of the installation is done by the

© Springer Nature Switzerland AG 2018
M. Aramaki et al. (Eds.): CMMR 2017, LNCS 11265, pp. 625–636, 2018.
https://doi.org/10.1007/978-3-030-01692-0_41

CromaCrono≈ system that operates with a "Composition Curve" with 10 sections containing 14 parameters. Genetic algorithms were applied in order to control the whole generative engine. The reduced set of parameters and of operations allow to evolve and share compositions and improvisations in real time.

Our research is anchored in a multimodal laboratory where we study human cognition and musical creativity supported by digital interfaces, computer graphics, and motion capture. This laboratory is an interactive environment with a large 3D screen and a six-channel sound diffusion system. The key points discussed here are:

- investigation of new paradigms of human cognition mediated by interactive technologies that attempt to describe how creativity operates [9–12];
- development of new technologies that incorporate interactive techniques based on the integration of multimodal signals [13];
- the creation of new art forms based on interactive narratives, digital music instruments, virtual soundscapes and synthetic visualization [14].

These systems can be evaluated from the perspective of the interaction between agents and devices, generating sounds, video, and 3D graphics.

The next section presents notions of the Self, of Presence, and how behaviour and meaning are affected in virtual reality and in interactive environments. In the third section, the SELFHOOD installation and its technical aspects are described. The fourth section introduces the development of interactive sonification. Finally, the conclusions are presented.

2 Theoretical Viewpoint

Many are the attempts to describe the self.
Prescott [15, 16] enrols some of them:

- I know that I exist; the question is, what is this "I" that I know [17]?
- The soul, so far as we can conceive it, is nothing but a system or train of different perceptions [18];
- What was I before I came to self-consciousness? ... I did not exist at all, for I was not an I. The I exists only insofar as it is conscious of itself. ... The "Self" posits itself, and by virtue of this mere self-assertion, it exists [19];
- The "Self" ..., when carefully examined, is found to consist mainly of ... peculiar motions in the head or between the head and throat [20, 21];
- The ego continuously constitutes itself as existing [22];
- Any fixed categorization of the Self is a big goof [23];
- The self which is reflexively referred to is synthesized in that very act of reflexive self-reference [24];
- The self ... is a mythical entity. ... It is a philosophical muddle to allow the space which differentiates "my self" from "myself" to generate the illusion of a mysterious entity distinct from ... the human being [25];
- A self ... is ... an abstraction ..., [a] the centre of narrative gravity [26].

Returning to Descartes [17]: what is this "I" that I know? What constitutes a "self" [25]?

All the semiotic signs that compose our knowledge were defined over time, by successive generations, so that people could communicate, define concepts, elaborate, construct. There are common, universal signs and concepts; there are other signs and concepts that are specific, differentiated, associated with an individual, a culture or a region. Is the self the set of signs associated with each person's knowledge? Removing the signs (concepts, habits, beliefs, strategies, etc.), *does the self cease to exist*? But if the signs were elaborated through generations, how to define *individuality*, perhaps the *individual combination of signs*? How do we modify and are modified by each other?

2.1 Presence and Virtual Reality

Recently, the literature suggests that the notion of Presence results from the interplay of central and peripheral factors and that it should be accessed through a series of convergent measures that include estimates of the subjective, physiological and behavioural state of the user. Body and space refer to vital and interrelated dimensions in the experience of sounds and music. Sounds have an overwhelming impact on feelings of bodily presence and inform us about the space we experience. Even in situations where visual information is artificial or blurred, such as in virtual environments or certain genres of film and computer games, sounds may shape our perceptions and lead to surprising new experiences [27]. In the approach presented here, we propose that the Presence can be induced by virtual and/or physical sources of stimulation governed by a number of principles that underlie human experience, creativity and discovery [9, 12, 28].

Presence has long been a key concept in teleoperation and virtual reality (VR) and has been defined as the *sense of being in a virtual environment* [29]. It is not clear, however, how this "sense" is generated and it is not uncommon to see it explained by the notion of "the suspension of disbelief" coined by in the early 19th century by the poet and philosopher Coleridge. Since the inception of the field in the early 80s, a large research effort in this area focuses on establishing the constraints governing the emergence of Presence in virtual environments. For example, it has been found that detailed visual scenes are not very important, whereas multisensory convergence, body representations themselves and active environmental engagement, all increase the reported Presence. Currently, the research on Presence is facing two fundamental and interrelated questions: (a) an ontological question on whether Presence is a central phenomenon that is "in the head", or whether it is peripherally defined by action in the world and (b) epistemological question of how Presence can be measured. These two questions are reminiscent of the fundamental challenges the science of psychology was facing at the beginning of the 20th century with the debate between the centralism of continental structuralism and the peripheralism of the functionalism in the US that led to the rise of behaviourism.

The methodological point of view is that the notion of Presence indicates that there are essential inputs for the construction of *self*-referral agents [13]. Thus, we will employ methodological efforts focusing on interactive media within a mixed reality environment in order to study the constructions of the meaningful relationship between agents and environmental stimuli in a virtual space. The assumption is that the interaction of an organism/agent or group of agents within an immersive space, using various interactive devices, indicates how these processes affect their behaviour and the meaning that is constructed by them. The notion of interaction with which we work goes beyond the textual and analytical dimensions only and it will be linked to several perceptual modalities. In the specific case study on scientific sonification and visualization, an interactive narrative is seen as a result of emergent processes, more specifically from the interaction with soundscapes, interactive video, animation, and 3D-graphics digitally generated.

3   The SELFHOOD Installation

The new approach to cognition focuses attention on the fact that most real-world thinking occurs in very particular (and often very complex) environments, and exploits the possibility of interaction with and manipulation of external props. It thereby foregrounds the fact that cognition is a highly embodied or situated activity and suggests that thinking beings ought to, therefore, be considered first and foremost as acting beings. This shift in focus from Descartes' "thinking thing", and the picture of human being and subjectivity it suggests, to a more Heideggerian approach to being in the world, in which agency and interactive coping occupy centre stage, is an extremely important development, the implications of which are only just beginning to be comprehended [30].

In the SELFHOOD installation (Fig. 1), a vision system identifies the body of the visitors and creates a visual representation of each one, suggesting their selves. Since

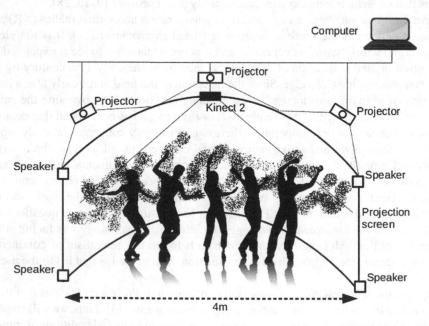

Fig. 1. The layout of the SELFHOOD installation, with three projectors, a Kinect2 sensor, a computer, and loudspeakers.

the self is still something misunderstood, a cloud of points and a sound drone with grains were first used to represent it. Different colours are assigned to the points of each participant. The clouds are displayed on a curved screen, following the movement of their owners. Depending on the spatial distance between visitors, they influence each other: a set of points from a visitor's cloud is displayed with the colour of the cloud of the neighbour. The closer people are the greater the influence on each other and the greater the number of coloured dots with the other person's *self* representation. Figure 1 shows the layout of the SELFHOOD installation. Three projectors, a Kinect2 sensor, a computer and six loudspeakers were used in the first setup. The dynamics of visitors' movement in the installation is sonified in such way that colours and sound textures are fused in a surround hexaphonic system. Therefore, not only the uniqueness of each one is represented as well as how they modify each other. A video showing people playing at the SELFHOOD installation can be seen at [31].

3.1 The Particle System

In order to create a representation of the visitors, three main components were applied: (1) a physical sensor capable of tracking the visitor's body, (2) a programming environment/language focused on visual effects and (3) a screen. The first component is the Microsoft Kinect v2 sensor, which utilizes a set of two sensors (a coloured camera and an infrared sensor) to track up to 6 bodies (at 30 Hz) from 0.5 to 4.5 m away. Each body is represented as a set of 25 joints with real space coordinates relative to the sensor's position, depicted in Fig. 2, and a colour ID (identifier). This ID is used to differentiate one body from another. The sensor data can be acquired through the Microsoft API or through distributed libraries. The KinectPV2 library was used to allow the communication between the Processing environment and the Kinect v2 sensor. With this library, it is possible to detect the bodies and their joints. It is also possible to get the visual input

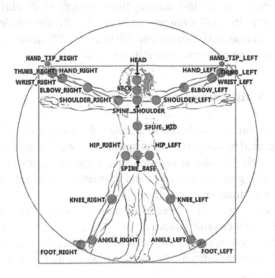

Fig. 2. The skeleton made up of the main joints of the human body.

from the coloured camera and the infrared sensor. The second component is the Processing graphic programming environment, and the third one consists of a three hall immersive display with (5760 × 1080) pixels of resolution.

By using these tools, the SELFHOOD environment creates a representation of each participant in a form of a set of particle systems. Each body contains 25 particle emitters, each one located in a joint. These emitters create coloured particles that match the colour of the ID of their bodies. Figure 3 shows the representation of the selves through particle systems.

Fig. 3. An interactive experience at the SELFHOOD installation. A performance video demonstration can be found in the link https://youtu.be/9F-s3Cafhc4 [32].

The particles are created with random initial velocities and directions, affected by a gravitational force present in the simulation. Depending on the distances between the bodies, their self-representations interfere with each other, by *sharing and acquiring particles* of different colours. The closer the participants are, the more particles they share.

Once created, the participant's representation is showed on a screen. Aiming to improve his immersion in the installation, three projectors display the particles on screens aligned in a "coliseum" arrangement in order to fill the whole field of vision of the human eye. The coliseum is also big enough to create a "mirror" effect of the participants' bodies, improving even more their immersion.

4   Interactive Sonification

Furthermore, our research is anchored in a series of artworks described as interactive narratives and supported by digital music instruments, virtual soundscapes and synthetic visualization [1, 33–39]. We also study how virtual spaces, augmented with interactive soundscapes, digitally generated sounds and animations, and interactive video clips contribute to the understanding of creativity [40].

SELFHOOD sonification has been implemented with a system for immersive improvisation that produces synthesized sounds in real time, called CromaCrono≈ [41]. Departing from observations on the way sensory processes are integrated into the environment, CromaCrono≈ explores the interaction of space and time from the perspective of the human agent.

In CromaCrono≈, simple geometric shapes and computer-synthesized sounds support an audio-visual textural architecture (Fig. 4). The Boids [35, 43] are used to control several parallel processes generating sounds and animating graphics in real time. Therefore, trajectories generated by the Boids algorithm are used to control the display of hundreds of primitive geometric shapes that vary in shape, colour, speed, and dispersion in space. All these variations produce the audio-visual texture which is coupled with generative rules for controlling sounds and interactions with local and remote agents.

Fig. 4. Presents the visual display of CromaCrono≈ (on the left) and a visual pattern generated by the system (on the right). A demonstration video can be found at [42] https://vimeo.com/145326063

Sounds are generated in real time by four different standard synthesis methods: Additive Synthesis, FM Synthesis, Waveshaping, and Karplus-Strong Algorithm [44]. A granular synthesis engine post-process is applied to the initial synthesized signal according to the spatial projection of two colour-voices: the bluish and reddish ones. In order to emphasize the visual discrimination of two independent interwoven textures, the opposition in the colour spectrum defined these starting colours. Therefore, the whole system works as a unified generative process (see Fig. 5).

The small set of parameters and of compositional operations make possible to evolve and share real time compositions/improvisations. Sound and images are synthesized in local machines while agents exchange the parameters that produce a texture of musical times. These features, still to be explored in the SELFHOOD installation, raise questions such as:

– how do close people influence us and are affected by us?
– who affects the other the most: geographically close people or the people with whom we are virtually connected?

The shapes in the complex visual textures (see Fig. 4) are associated with sound synthesis engines: spheres with additive synthesis, squared frames with FM, planes with Waveshaping and triangular frames with Karplus-Strong.

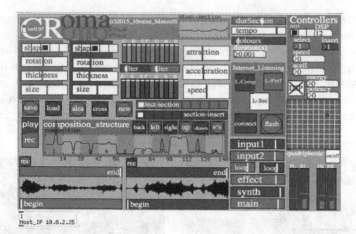

Fig. 5. GUI of CromaCrono≈ showing all the integrated control parameters of the system (top), and, in detail, the "Composition Curve" and the buttons to apply genetic and structural operations on the curve.

4.1 Experiments Around the SELFHOOD

The SELFHOOD installation aims to verify how dynamic representations of the visitors' bodies coupled with real-time granular synthesis sonification of their movements endorse their notion of selves. Explicit actions and gestures, associated with a cloud of points and sounds, induce an implicit cognitive state. Different behaviours were observed in the persons who experienced the SELFHOOD installation. Those unfamiliar with art installations felt uncomfortable. A member from the research group who is an artist, a musician and a performer, already very familiar with such environments, was invited to try the installation. She explored the environment, experiencing it with large and restrained, slow and fast gestures. The student-developer who was observing the performance understood then the application of his work, and began to follow the researcher with similar gestures. Subsequently, when performing technical tests in the environment, he performed some choreography himself.

A skilful dance teacher, unfamiliar with interactive installations, pleasantly experienced the environment for a long time. Finally, the music students who tried the different possibilities of the installation remained all the time intrigued about how the system behaved as a whole, performing movements in front of the Kinect sensor in order to find out what a particular gesture would result in the sound produced, or in the characteristics extracted from it.

5   Next Steps

At the moment, the SELFHOOD installation is only reactive but it is being re-designed to *surprise* [45] the participants and *register their emotions*. After some experimentation reacting to people's interaction it will change the visual representation and sound responses and its behaviour from being responsive to being pro-active. Figure 6 depicts some visual representations that are being included in the SELFHOOD installation.

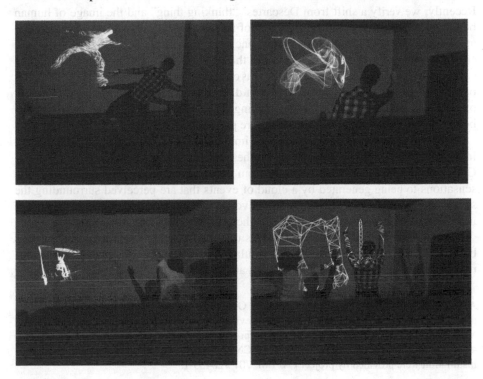

Fig. 6. New visual representations that are being developed for the SELFHOOD installation.

As the system becomes more pro-active, a question arises: can an installation have a self? Schemes aiming to generate some awareness in an artificial system are only beginning to emerge [46, 47]. Specific components are devised for the computational treatment of human processes such as attention, perception, sensation, emotion, learning, language, consciousness, imagination and planning, behaviour and motor, as well as episodic, perceptive, sensorial, working, semantic, episodic buffer, just to enumerate some of them.

Based on Dourish [48], many of the assumptions as to what should be supported and what should be inhibited in an interactive installation are hidden or implicit in the craft of the system design, which reflects the way that it is not just the external devices for input and the output devices that affect a person's use and interpretation of a computer system. The internal digital components are designed to support some activities and interpretations while inhibiting others, stimulating designers to be more aware of the communicative significance of their systems.

6 Conclusions

Recently, we verify a shift from Descartes' "thinking thing" and the image of human being, with the notion of subjectivity and of an inner self it suggests, to an interactive approach to being in the world, where agency and interactive coupling occupy centre stage. In order to instigate a reflection on the self through a practical and interactive experience, the SELFHOOD installation was conceived wherein a representation of each participant is created in the form of a set of different colour particle systems. Different participants interact with each other sharing particles as a function of the distances between them. The closer they are, the more particles they share.

The sonification of SELFHOOD was implemented with a system for immersive improvisation that produces digitally synthesized sounds in real time, called Croma-Crono≈. It expands the sound texture from being generated by physical and tactile sensations to being generated by a cloud of events that are perceived surrounding the subject. Subsequently, the sound texture evolves to a sound mass with the density of interwoven processes, which increases as the processes get interconnected.

The approach presented here reinforces that the sense of Presence can be induced by virtual and/or physical sources of stimulation governed by a number of principles that underlie human experience, creativity, and discovery.

Acknowledgments. We thank Thomas Taichi Okubo for his commitment and dedication. We thank Georges Schwarzstein for his careful review and appropriate suggestions. Okubo and Valarini were supported by the PIBIC/CNPq program and Manzolli is supported by projects 470358/2014-9 and 305065/2014-9 also from CNPq. The sensory devices used on SELHOOD installation were provided by project FAPESP 2013/26453-1.

References

1. Mura, A., Manzolli, J., Verschure, P. F., Rezazadeh, B., Groux, S. L., Wierenga, S.: re(PER)curso: a mixed reality chronicle. In: Proceedings of the 2008 ACM SIGGRAPH Conference (2008)
2. Inderbitzin, M., Wierenga, S., Väljama, A., Bernardet, U., Verschure, P.F.M.J.: Social cooperation and competition in the mixed reality space eXperience Induction Machine (XIM). Virtual Reality **13**, 153–158 (2009)
3. Papachristodoulou, P., Betella, A., Manzolli, J., Verschure, P.F.M.J.: Augmenting the navigation of complex data sets using sonification: a case study with BrainX3. In: Virtual Reality (VR), IEEE (2015)
4. Miranda, E.R., Wanderley, M.M.: New Digital Musical Instruments: Control and Interaction Beyond the Keyboard. A-R Editions, Middleton (2006)
5. Bernhardt, D., Robinson, P.: Detecting affect from non-stylised body motions. In: Paiva, A.C.R., Prada, R., Picard, R.W. (eds.) ACII 2007. LNCS, vol. 4738, pp. 59–70. Springer, Heidelberg (2007). https://doi.org/10.1007/978-3-540-74889-2_6
6. Bernhardt, D., Robinson, P.: Interactive control of music using emotional body expressions. In: Human Factors in Computing Systems, pp. 3117—3122 (2008)

7. Castelli, F., Happé, F., Frith, U., Frith, C.: Movement and mind: a functional imaging study of perception and interpretation of complex intentional movement patterns. NeuroImage **12**(3), 314–325 (2000)
8. Reynolds, C.W.: Flocks, herds, and schools: a distributed behavioral model. In: SIGGRAPH Conference Proceedings, vol. 21, pp. 25–34 (1987)
9. Colton, S., Wiggins G.A.: Computational creativity: the final frontier? In: 20th European Conference on Artificial Intelligence (2012)
10. Sternberg, R.S. (ed.): Handbook of Creativity. Cambridge University Press, Cambridge (1999)
11. Pope, R.: Creativity: Theory, History, Practice. Routledge, New York (2005)
12. Boden, M.: What is creativity? In: Boden, M. (ed.) Dimensions of Creativity, pp. 75—117. MIT Press, Cambridge (2005)
13. Bernardet, U.: The eXperience induction machine: a new paradigm for mixed-reality interaction design and psychological experimentation. In: Dubois, M., Gray, P., Nigay, L. (eds.) The Engineering of Mixed Reality Systems. HCIS, pp. 357–379. Springer, London (2010). https://doi.org/10.1007/978-1-84882-733-2_18
14. Wasserman, K., Manzolli, J., Eng, K., Verschure, P.F.M.J.: Live soundscape composition based on synthetic emotions: using music to communicate between an interactive exhibition and its visitors. IEEE Multimedia **10**, 82–90 (2003)
15. Prescott, T.J., Verschure, P.F.M.J., Lepora, N.: A Handbook of Research in Biomimetic and Biohybrid Systems. Oxford University Press, Oxford, In Press (To appear)
16. Strawson, G.: The self. J. Conscious. Stud. **4**, 405–428 (1997)
17. Descartes, R.: The Philosophical Writings of Descartes, vols. 1 and 2, translated by J. Cottingham et al. Cambridge University Press, Cambridge (1985)
18. Hume, D.: Dialogues Concerning Natural Religion. In: Smith, N.K. (ed.). Nelson, Edinburgh (1947)
19. Fichte, J.G.: The Science of Knowledge, translated by Heath P. and Lachs, J. CUP, Cambridge (1982)
20. James, W.: The Principles of Psychology. Dover, New York (1950)
21. James, W.: Psychology: Briefer Course. Harvard University Press, Cambridge (1984)
22. Husserl, E.: Cartesian Meditations, translated by D. Cairns. Nijhoff, The Hague (1973)
23. Ginsberg, A.: Statement to the Burning Bush. Burning Bush II, San Francisco (1963)
24. Nozick, R.: Philosophical Explanations. Clarendon Press, Oxford (1981)
25. Kenny, A.: The Self. Marquette University Press, Marquette (1988)
26. Dennett, D.: Consciousness Explained. Little, Brown, Boston (1991)
27. Wöllner, C. (ed.): Body, Sound and Space in Music and Beyond: Multimodal Explorations. Routledge, New York (2017)
28. Krausz, M., Dutton, D., Bardsley, K.: The Idea of Creativity. Brill Academic Publishers, Leiden (2009)
29. Sanchez-Vives, M.V., Slater, M.: From presence to consciousness through virtual reality. Nat. Rev. Neurosci. **6**(4), 332–339 (2005)
30. Anderson, M.L.: Embodied cognition: a field guide. Artif. Intell. **149**(1), 91–130 (2003)
31. Moroni, A., Manzolli, J., Valarini, G.: SELFHOOD Installation. https://www.youtube.com/watch?v=lavHYLFXL8w&feature=youtu.be
32. Moroni, A., Manzolli, J.: SELFHOOD—cloudiness of the selves. https://www.youtube.com/watch?v=9F-s3Cafhc4&feature=youtu.be

33. Castellano, G., Villalba, S.D., Camurri, A.: Recognising human emotions from body movement and gesture dynamics. In: Paiva, A.C.R., Prada, R., Picard, R.W. (eds.) ACII 2007. LNCS, vol. 4738, pp. 71–82. Springer, Heidelberg (2007). https://doi.org/10.1007/978-3-540-74889-2_7

34. Le Groux, S., Manzolli, J., Verschure, P.F.M.J.: Disembodied and collaborative musical interaction in the Multimodal Brain Orchestra. In: Proceedings of NIME, pp. 309–314 (2010)

35. Heppner, F.H.: Avian flight formations. Bird-Banding **45**(2), 160–169 (1974)

36. Manzolli, J.: continuaMENTE: Integrating percussion, audiovisual and improvisation. In: Proceedings of the International Computer Music Conference, Belfast, Ireland, (2008)

37. Moroni, A., Manzolli, J.: From evolutionary composition to robotic sonification. In: Di Chio, C., et al. (eds.) EvoApplications 2010. LNCS, vol. 6025, pp. 401–410. Springer, Heidelberg (2010). https://doi.org/10.1007/978-3-642-12242-2_41

38. Moroni, A., Von Zuben, F., Manzolli, J.: ArTbitration: human-machine interaction in artistic domains. Leonardo (Oxford) **35**, 185–188 (2002)

39. Wassermann, K.C., Manzolli, J., Eng, K., Verschure, P.: Live soundscape composition based on synthetic emotions: using music to communicate between an interactive exhibition and its visitors. IEEE Multimedia **10**, 82–90 (2003)

40. Verschure, P., Manzolli, J.: Computational modeling of mind and music. In: Language, Music, and the Brain. ESF Reports, MIT Press (2013)

41. Manzolli, J.: Multimodal generative installations and the creation of new art form based on interactive narratives. In: GA2015—XVIII Generative Art Conference, (2015). http://www.generativeart.com/ga2015_WEB/Multimodal-Installation_Manzolli.pdf

42. Manzolli, J.: CromaCrono ≈ . https://vimeo.com/145326063

43. Reynolds, C.W.: Flocks, herds and schools: a distributed behavioral model. ACM SIGGRAPH Comput. Graph. **21**(4), 25–34 (1987)

44. Karplus, K., Strong, A.: Digital synthesis of plucked string and drum timbres. Comput. Music J. **7**(2), 43–55 (1983)

45. Macedo, L., Cardoso, A., Reisenzein, R., Lorini, E., Castelfranchi C.: Artificial surprise. In: Handbook of Research on Synthetic Emotions Sociable Robotics New Applications in Affective Computing Artificial Intelligence. IGI Global, Hershey, USA (2009)

46. Paraense, A.L.O., et al.: The cognitive systems toolkit and the CST reference cognitive architecture. Biol. Inspired Cogn. Archit. J. **17**, 32–48 (2016)

47. Gudwin, R., Paraense, A., de Paula, S.M., Fróes, E., Gibaut, W., Castro, E., Raizer, K.: The multipurpose enhanced cognitive architecture (MECA). Biol. Inspired Cogn. Archit. J. **22**, 20–34 (2017)

48. Dourish, P.: Where the Action Is: Foundations of Embodied Interaction. MIT Press, Cambridge (2001)

Music(s), Musicology and Science: Towards an Interscience Network

The Example of the Deaf Musical Experience

Sylvain Brétéché[✉] and Christine Esclapez

Aix Marseille University, CNRS, PRISM, 31 Chemin J. Aiguier, CS 70071,
13402 Marseille cedex 09, France
{sylvain.breteche, christine.esclapez}@univ-amu.fr

Abstract. This contribution traces the history of musicology in order to set its object. The history of the discipline is clear: born as historical musicology, it flourished as an interdisciplinary discipline over the second half of the 20th century, with the development of new musicology and critical musicology. Defining the scope of musicology, however, is challenging, since it encompasses various aspects of music: music as sound, as a historical fact, as text. Music, therefore, oscillates between natural sciences, humanities, philosophy, and aesthetics, shifting of identity, between a quantifiable sound, the meaningful object of miscellaneous debates, and the purpose of boundless interpretations. These observations induce contemporary musicologists to elaborate an intersciences project which is exposed in the present paper. To concretize our remarks, we will take as an interscientific musicological object a specific situation: the Deaf musical experience.

Keywords: Musicology · Intersciences · Interdisciplinarity · Musical reality
Deaf musical experience

1 Introduction

Since the beginning of the 21st century, the development of digital technologies, *open source* strategies, free access and democratization of softwares has given rise to a new sort of dialogue between artistic creation, science, and technology. This rapprochement is also the subject of numerous works and academic events[1].

The relationship between music and science arose early compared to other arts, in the 1950s, with the emergence of concrete and electroacoustic music, and a generation of composers-scientists such as Pierre Schaeffer, Karlheinz Stockhausen, and Iannis Xenakis. At the same time, musicology, leaving the historical field, widened its scope

---

[1] For instance, a symposium entitled "Arts and Sciences: intersecting views" will take place on October, 26th and 27th, 2017, in Liege (Belgium), http://www.gaphe.ulg.ac.be/ArtCol2017/index.html [accessed: 07/2016].

© Springer Nature Switzerland AG 2018
M. Aramaki et al. (Eds.): CMMR 2017, LNCS 11265, pp. 637–657, 2018.
https://doi.org/10.1007/978-3-030-01692-0_42

to human and social sciences. The composer Tod Machover emphasized in 1985 that the study of the relations between music and sciences:

> "[...] implies a musical reflection that can be oriented towards two directions: firstly towards other disciplines that may offer tools, models or materials (literally or by analogy), useful for musical expression; secondly, towards a reflection on purely musical materials, forms, processes and notations that can be directly applied to the works themselves."[2] [1, p. 13]

In the present paper, we will consider more specifically the first direction proposed by Machover, namely the opening of musicology to other disciplines. Primarily, we will consider the bases and specificities of an interdisciplinary musicological thought; an interscience model is subsequently presented in that respect, which will be based on a singular musicological situation, the musical experience of the Deaf persons; we will examine in conclusion the epistemological foundations and contributions of such an orientation.

There is no science, however, without delimitation of its object of investigation. We shall, therefore, begin with a simple question: *what is music?*

2 Did You Say "Music(s)"?

> [...] it is not just the fact that music could be the subject of a scientific activity which disturbs. It is also the great diversity of the sound facts which may be described with the word "music" which surprises, and the large number of fields who are studied by the musicology to better understand how the music works, sorry, musics.[3] [2, p. 9]

In his article («Les conceptions de l'histoire de la musique», Philippe Vendrix underlines a major difficulty of musicology, namely, "the definition of its object of study" [3, pp. 644–645]. Indeed, the history of the discipline, examined in great detail in several meta-musicological works, is rather clear: musicology was first strictly historical, and subsequently diversified into interdisciplinarity, "new musicology" and critical musicology over the second half of the 20th century. Because, a priori, "musicology does not have a specific object" [4, p. 121]. This will remain only an *a priori*, who finds in the deployment of more than a century of musicological practices, the culmination *a posteriori* of objective considerations. However, the very object of the discipline seems difficult to determine. Following the integration into the field of musicology of disciplines such as psychology, linguistics or cognitive sciences and especially in view of their recent evolutions (mediationist and/or interactionist

---

[2] By respect for the authors and their words, we will systematically propose the original text of the quotation. Original text: «[...] implique une réflexion musicale qui peut être orientée dans deux directions: premièrement vers d'autres disciplines qui semblent offrir des outils, des modèles ou des matériaux (soit littéralement, soit par analogie), utiles à l'expression musicale; deuxièmement vers une réflexion sur des matériaux, des formes, des procédés et des notations purement musicaux qui peut être directement mise en pratique dans des œuvres.».

[3] Original text: «[...] ce n'est pas seulement le fait que la musique puisse faire l'objet d'une activité scientifique qui dérange. C'est aussi la grande diversité des faits sonores que l'on désigne par le mot «musique» qui étonne, et le grand nombre de domaines que la musicologie étudie pour mieux comprendre comment fonctionne la musique, pardon, les musiques.».

approaches), the very term of *object* does not seem perfectly adequate, for it is too closely related to exact sciences, or philosophical determinism. Yet we will venture here to question the object of musicology again, to find out possibly what constitutes its subject of study.

Margaret Bent recalls us that "music is, in fact, the only fine art that has adopted, in English, as in most European languages, the suffix *-logy* to designate the knowledge associated with it [...]"[4] [5, p. 612]. Musicology would, therefore, be the discourse on music. Music is then its object and musicology, the scientific study of this object, reintroducing here the long-standing idea of a *musica pratica* who would interest a *musica speculativa* [6].

This first distinction seems very simple, and yet it does not take into account the very complexity of the *object-music*, fundamentally paradoxical, straddling at least three "domains":

– **Music as "sound"**: physical and acoustic object, which is the subject of research in Music Theory, Acoustics or Psychology of perception.
– **Music as a "historical fact" ("context")**: works, styles, and methods of composition which, as of the end of the 18th century, were the subject of comparative, stylistic or historical research.
– **Music as "text" (in the sense of Roland Barthes)**: the interaction between works, practices, intentions, and situations: anthropological fact, expression and meaning that is the subject of interdisciplinary research: semiotics, sociology, anthropology, philosophy or aesthetics (Fig. 1).

The first branch – the earliest – characterizes a musicology which draws its roots from Pythagorean theories, cosmology, and ancient cosmogonies, alike the natural sciences. In the Middle Ages, let us recall that music was part of the Quadrivium (arithmetic, music, geometry, astronomy). The second approach is based on the model of the historical and literary sciences, while the third is more recent, following the *linguistic turn* of the 1960s and the profound change in the human and social sciences.

These above-mentioned domains constitute, at present, the main branches of musicology as a contemporary science of music. In 1885, the musicologist Guido Adler proposed moreover, in his demarcation project of the dimensions of the *musikwissenschaft*, to make a clear distinction between historical musicology and so-called systematic musicology [7]. Adler was starting notably his founding article "The Scope, Method, and Aim of Musicology"[5] with: "Musicology originated simultaneously with the art of organising tones"[6] [7, p. 5]. Poetical wording which was already making of the *object-music* - the sounding aspect of music – the source of musicological

---

[4] Original text: «*musique est en fait le seul des beaux-arts qui ait adopté, en anglais, comme dans la plupart des langues européennes, le suffixe – logie pour désigner les savoirs qui lui sont associés [...]*».

[5] Original text: "Umfang, Methode und Ziel der Musikwissenschaft", translated and commented by Erica Mugglestone, in "Yearbook for Traditional Music", Vol. 13 (1981), pp. 1–21. Bibliographic references mentioned in this text correspond to the original article of Guido Adler. English translations in text are borrowed, unless specified, from Erica Mugglestone.

[6] Original text: "*Die Musikwissenschaft entstand gleichzeitig mit der Tonkunst*".

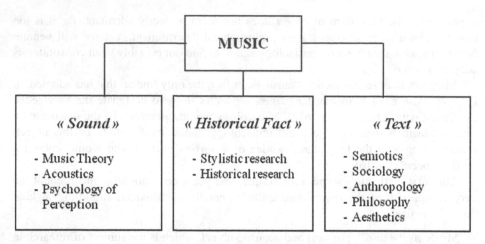

Fig. 1. 3 "domains" of musicology

investigation, not only object but also subject of musicology, understood with Adler that "The methodology of musicological research depends on the nature of the subject under investigation"[7] [7, p. 15]. We will come back to this, however, we can already specify that, of the distinction proposed by Adler, persists in the English vocabulary - and more particularly in American musicology - two orientations: the term "musicology" remains mainly associated with historical approaches, whereas the prospects strictly systematic are mostly brought together under the global denomination "music theory". This distinction disappears in French language (but also in other languages), where *musicology* is sometimes "Historic" or sometimes "Analytic" but maintains nevertheless in its general consideration a real form of unicity and remains still in its exclusive designation: "musicology". It is in this sense that we will talk more specially in the continuation of this text of "musicological science", in order to overcome the possible confusion inherent in term "musicology" and in its translation - but also to consider more specifically the Germanic origins of the discipline: *Musikwissenschaft* literally "science of music". (Furthermore, Adler used in his text the term "Musikologie" to describe what he calls "comparative musicology, which envisages to compare the sound products, in particular the popular songs of various peoples, countries, and territories, with an ethnographic purpose, to group and put them in order according to their different qualities"[8] [7, p. 14]).

Thus, as in natural sciences, the first theories and philosophies of music sought to establish common, permanent and universal laws, inserting sound into the world order (modes, scales, resonances of sound bodies). As early as 1949, Swiss musicologist

---

[7] Original text: *"Die Methode der musikwissenschaftlichen Forschung richtet sich nach der Art des zu Erforschenden"*.

[8] Original text: *"[...] die Musikologie, d.i. die vergleichende Mussikwissenschaft, die sich zur Aufgabe macht, die Tonproducte, insbesondere die Volksgesänge verschiedener Völker, Länder and Territorien behufs ethnographischer Zwecke zu vergleichen und nach der Verschiedenheit ihrer Beschaffenheit zu gruppiren und sondern."*

Jacques Handschin suggests, however, that this analogy between the natural sciences and musicology is based on a certain vision of music which tends to reduce in an abstract way the musical reality [8]. In 2001, Hubert Reeves responds to Handschin, arguing that, undeniably – and whatever one thinks about it – music and its representation played a crucial role in the birth of science: "By studying the relationships between sounds and the length of strings, Pythagoras had the intuition of the importance of numbers in the explanation of the real world"[9] [9, p. 8].

There was never a clear line, therefore, defining the object of musicology, and music has always oscillated between natural, human, philosophical and aesthetic sciences. Music can be observed as a measurable, quantifiable sound or as a signifying entity, leaving the door open to multiple debates and interpretations. Music appears as versatile art, diversified by contemporary practices and means of productions, whether written, historically informed, traditional, from an oral tradition, popular, modern, improvised and more recently, inter/multi-media. In this sense, we can consider with Jean-Marc Warszawski, that:

> "Music is not a natural object, it is not even an object. It is produced by members of a humanity in progress. Everything, in music, emerges of human decisions. Today, the inventory which can be done of the diversity with which "music" is inserted into social practices, with which it is produced, broadcast, received, from the point of view of personnel and technical means, institutions, reproductions, does not determine, out of social context, a matter sufficiently homogeneous and autonomous for objectify a positive specific science, but summons many fields of knowledge [...]."[10] [4, p. 129]

These forms of creation widen the scope of traditional musicological knowledge and require the musicologist to cope with polymorphous realities.

3 For a Musicological Science

The object of musicological science, as we see, overows on every side and cannot be defined as a fixed instance insofar as any diversification of knowledge objects leads to a diversification of this knowledge [10, 11]. These observations reveal the complex territory of musicology and its main actors (historians, analysts, composers, interpreters, but also physicists, acousticians, psychologists, historians, analysts, hermeneuticists, aestheticians, philosophers, sociologists, semioticians, doctors, neuroscientists, etc.), and orientate contemporary musicological research towards the development of a true intersciences project [10].

---

[9] French version of this text: «En étudiant les relations entre les sons et la longueur des cordes vibrantes, Pythagore a eu l'intuition de l'importance des nombres dans l'explication du monde réel».

[10] Original text: «La musique n'est pas un objet naturel, elle n'est pas même un objet. Elle est produite par les membres d'une humanité en devenir. Tout, en musique, ressort de décisions humaines. L'inventaire qu'on peut faire aujourd'hui de la diversité avec laquelle «la musique» s'insère dans les pratiques sociales, avec laquelle elle est produite, diffusée, reçue, tant du point de vue des personnels que des moyens techniques, des institutions, de la reproduction, ne permet pas de cerner une matière suffisamment homogène, autonome, hors contexte social, pour objectiver une science spécifique positive, mais, convoque de nombreux champs de connaissances, [...]».

3.1 Of a Systematic Musicology [...]

Previously, we mentioned the initiative of one of the founders of musicology as scientific discipline, that of Guido Adler, who proposed to differentiate in the studies of music the historical perspectives of those that he qualifies of systematic musicology, based on the principle that "the laws of art which have emerged from the historical development as the highest [...] are systematically organized"[11] [7, p. 11]. For Adler, the musicological enterprise had to interrogate (historical) contexts, but also to focus on a critical and speculative study of music. In his presentation of the new-found *Mussikwissenschaft*, the Austrian musicologist proposed a theoretical organization of the discipline based on two main lines which he considered essentials for a real and global determination of scientific characteristics of the musicological project. He proposed in his article of 1885 a schematic representation which specified the different dimensions and perspectives of the musicological science (Fig. 2).

By distinguishing the historic and systematic considerations, Adler integrated in this latter musicological posture a complex of "auxiliary sciences" [7, p. 14] which unified already our first and third branches previously evoked into an unique orientation: acoustics, music theory, pedagogy, sociology, psychology,... so many analytic perspectives which gave to think the plurality of the real object of the musicological science and its profoundly interscientific nature. Because if the musicological object is complicate to define, its epistemological foundations appear in a multidisciplinary network which formalizes the scientific posture of the musicologist. Thus, music presents itself at the intersection of sciences, disciplines and technologies, and its objectal nature reveals in this sense a multitude of facets which form as many potential ways forward for its specific study.

If this duality inherent in the musicological science finds its meaning in the contextual dimension given to the music itself – origin or product of context? - it remains true that domains which compose it formalize the unity of our discipline. This one, in its various methods, technics and ambitions to approach the *object-music* like a context or the *context-music* like object, draws on comprehensive strategies requiring diversified and expanded prospects which find fundamentally a place in both principal orientations which constitute the vast field of musicology.

3.2 [...] to an Intersciences Project

It is according to this perspective that, as early as 1992, the French musicologist Bernard Vecchione developed an intersciences project where sciences and music technologies formed a network of collaborative points of view, structured as an open space (Fig. 3).

This project implies the participation of critical, historical, semiotic, computer and cognitive sciences in the mutual understanding of music. The contribution of critical sciences (mainly hermeneutics) is central. Through their overarching eye, they help overcoming with diversity, or even scientific dispersion, to which the interdisciplinary

---

[11] Original text: *"Hier warden die Kunstgesetze, die sich aus der geschichtlichen Entwicklung als zu höchst stehend [...] ergeben, systematisch geordnet"* [we translate].

I. HISTORICAL
(History of music according to epochs, peoples, empires, nations, regions, cities, schools of art, artists).

A. Musical palaeography (notations).	B. Basic historical categories (Grouping of musical forms).	C. Historical sequence of laws. 1. As they are presented in the works of art of every epoch. 2. As taught by the theoreticians of the age in question. 3. Ways of practising art.	D. History of musical instruments.

Auxiliary sciences: General History with Palaeography, Chronology, Diplomatics, Bibliography, Library and Archival Science.
History of Literature and Philology.
Liturgical History.
History of Mimetic Arts and Dance.
Biographies of composers, Statistics of musical associations, institutes and performances.

II. SYSTEMATIC
(Establishing of the highest laws in the individual branches of tonal art).

A. Investigation and founding of these laws in: 1. Harmony (tonal). 2. Rhythm (temporal). 3. Melody Coherence[25] of tonal & temporal.	B. Aesthetics of tonal art. 1. Comparison and evaluation of these laws and their relation to the perceiving subjects, with respect to the ascertaining of the criteria of the musically beautiful. 2. The complex of directly and indirectly related questions.	C. Musical paedagogics and didactics (The compilation of these laws with respect to teaching purposes). 1. Scales. 2. Theory of harmony. 3. Counterpoint. 4. Theory of composition. 5. Orchestration. 6. Vocal & instrumental teaching methods.	D. "Musicology" (Examination and comparison for ethnographic purposes).

Auxiliary sciences: Acoustics and mathematics.
Physiology (tone sensation).
Psychology (tone perception, tone-judgement, tone-feeling).
Logic (musical thinking).
Grammar, metrics, and poetry.
Paedagogics.
Aesthetics, etc.

Fig. 2. Adler's domains of the musicological science [12, p. 14–15]

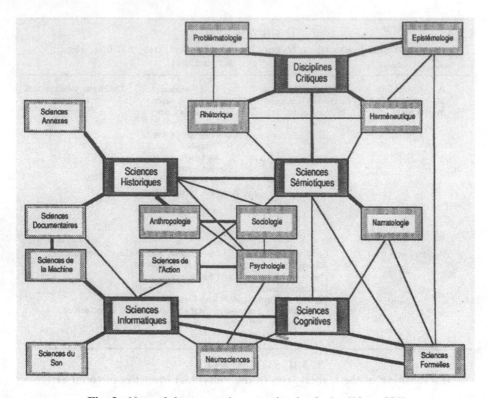

Fig. 3. Network between sciences and technologies [10, p. 294]

study of music may lead. The hermeneutical approach allows articulating inter-scientific relations simultaneously involved in each of the two planes of musical reality and musicological reality [10]. This network between sciences constitutes an open model, its integration of other disciplines is imposed by the evolution of our discourse about the world and about music, but also by the evolution of musical practices. Its challenge is "the preservation of local fields of research"[12] [10, p. 281] but also the desire to understand the problem of the functional articulation which, since the 1970s, forms our musical horizons.

In view of these explorations, and as Vecchione emphasizes, musicology is considered on its most general level, that is to say, from an anthropologic point of view:

"as a discipline concerned with all aspects of knowledge about music (intellectual, practical, sensitive), regardless of their type (scientific, technological, philosophical) and regardless of the aspects of music studied (works or practice, sound or spectrogram, existing music or music to come, in project, in progress, in process...). This definition goes in the direction of the history

---

[12] Original text: «*la préservation des champs de recherche locaux*».

of the discipline and matches, if not with the classical meanings of the term, at least with the nature of the object on which musicology questions itself: the reality of music in civilizations, its nature, its function."[13] [10, pp. 281–282]

The theorization of the musicological field and the acknowledgment of its fundamental diversity, as proposed by Vecchione, lead to the reformulation of the musical object, or even to its total reconsideration. Vecchione will use the term "musical reality"[14] to consider this weaving to which refers the fundamentally anthropological nature of musical works and activities. Vecchione writes:

"As subject of musicology, musical reality is to be considered as a complex anthropological reality, made up of works and activities, all marked historically but also socially, culturally, psychologically and not only within civilizations where these activities take place, but also relatively to the social groups, and to the individuals who played within these groups a key role in the establishment of this reality: production, interpretation (updating, perenniality, etc.), perception..."[15] [10, p. 282]

To conceive "musical reality" as the object of musicology allows an ecological approach, exempt from all forms of reductionism, and allows embracing its main components, namely works and activities (currently known as practices). For Bernard Vecchione, it is the music itself that guides the research and silently accomplishes its power to relate, in the light of its own sonorous and temporal deployment, connected with bodies in action and musical gestures. It will be noted that this proposal is related to the deep mutations that experienced the cognitive sciences since the end of the last century, with, for example, the deployment of works of Francisco Varela on cognition (action/knowledge polarity, enactment, embodied knowledge), or interaction and mediation research on language. These approaches postulate a more interleaved relationship between cognition and language, action and knowledge and, more generally, revisit the porosity between subject and object. The musicology proposed by Bernard Vecchione is a territory fundamentally crossed by cooperative modes of action and

---

[13] Original text: «comme discipline que concerne l'ensemble de la question de l'élaboration des connaissances sur la musique, quelles que soient ces connaissances (intellectuelles, pratiques, sensibles), quels que soient leurs types (scientifiques, technologiques, philosophiques) et quels que soient les aspects de la musique étudiés (œuvres ou activités, son ou partitogrammes, musiques déjà existantes ou musiques virtuelles, en projet, en progrès, en procès,...). Cette définition va dans le sens même de l'histoire de la discipline et se trouve tout à fait conforme, sinon aux acceptions plus classiques du terme, du moins à la nature de l'objet sur lequel la musicologie s'interroge: la réalité de la musique dans les civilisations, sa nature, sa fonction».

[14] This term was also used in 1927 by Boris de Schloezer in his Introduction à Jean-Sébastien Bach. Essai d'esthétique musicale (1947), reissue presented and established by Pierre-Henry Frangne, Rennes, Presses Universitaires de Rennes, 2009. The term "réalité musicale" (musical reality) conceived by Bernard Vecchione, however, is based on works of Pierre Francastel imported to the field of music. La réalité figurative thus surpasses Schloezer's objectivism.

[15] Original text: «Comme objet de la musicologie, la réalité musicale est à considérer comme une réalité complexe d'ordre anthropologique, faite d'œuvres et d'activités, toutes marquées historiquement mais aussi socialement, culturellement, psychologiquement et ce non seulement au sein des civilisations où les activités musicales s'instituent et se développent, mais relativement aussi aux groupes sociaux, et aux individus qui jouent ou ont joué au sein de ces groupes un rôle déterminant dans l'instauration de cette réalité: production, interprétation (actualisations, pérennisations...), appréhension...».

reflection: between the sciences themselves, but also between scientists and artists. Interdisciplinarity is understood in a new manner: not only as a game between disciplines, but also as a game between practices, know-how, and knowledge.

3.3   Towards an Epistemology of Practices (in Arts)

In an article published in the proceedings of an international seminar held at IRCAM in 1983, entitled «*Quoi, quand, comment la recherche musicale*» [13], the musicologist Célestin Deliège tried to identify the similarities between musical research and scientific research, although he recognized their profound differences:

> "In scientific research, if intuition can create a new theory, it is put to the test by '…a long series of deductive operations which fortify the axiomatic bases and create the conditions for possible extension'. The process of artistic research, on the other hand, is invoked by a capacity for invention. In our society, the artist is, - or at least endeavors to be - an innovator, or else his action is secondary. His intuition, like that of the scientific researcher, leads him to inductive inferences, but they lead not to a theory but to a new practice."[16] [13, pp. 38–39]

…he was already trying to bring them closer together:

> "The scientist, at best, sees his research as an aesthetic experience; his discoveries bring him a pleasure of a comparable nature; He perceives in the course of his activity a quality which tends towards completion. On the other hand, the artist aims like the scientist to constantly overcome what he has achieved, to encounter the new, the unprecedented, the unheard."[17] [13, p. 38]

Deliège will nevertheless retain in both processes the experience of the same temporality due to the autonomy of the experimental phase: "the time of the quasi-autonomous experiment, postulating a long-term discovery, most often indeterminate"[18] [13, p. 37]. Scientists and artists will have to negotiate with their own experience with tools and technologies of which they cannot foresee the outcome. It is to this rapprochement that also responds Bernard Vecchione's musicological conception. The field of research of the musicologist presents two different aspects:

– **Works of Arts**: The works as fictional and critical regimes of the world which do not merely illustrate, but which interpret it, that say it, denounce it and experience it sensibly, as can be seen, for instance, in the work of the HeHe collective, between sonic and visual arts. The installation/*Champs d'ozone* (2007)/(see Fig. 4) exploits

---

[16] Original text: «*Si l'intuition peut créer une théorie nouvelle, celle-ci est mise à l'épreuve par «(…) une longue suite d'opérations déductives qui en fortifient les bases axiomatiques et créent les conditions d'extension possible», à l'inverse, le processus de la recherche artistique est mis «en jeu par une capacité d'invention. L'artiste, dans notre société est, tout au moins, doit être un novateur, sans quoi son action est secondaire. Son intuition, comme celle du chercheur scientifique l'amène à des inférences inductives mais, en périodes normales, celles-ci débouchent, non sur une théorie, mais sur une pratique nouvelle.*».

[17] Original text: «*Le scientifique, dans le meilleur des cas, vit sa recherche comme une expérience esthétique; ses découvertes lui apportent un plaisir d'une nature comparable; il perçoit dans le déroulement de son activité une qualité qui tend vers un achèvement. D'autre part, l'artiste vise comme le scientifique à dépasser constamment son acquis antérieur, à édifier l'inédit, l'inouï*».

[18] Original text: «*le temps de l'expérience quasi autonome ne postulant la découverte qu'à échéance lointaine, le plus souvent indéterminée*».

air quality analysis data in Paris, provided in "near real time" by Airparif (Association for the monitoring of air quality in Ile-de-France), and transposes them into a sonic and visual space-time continuum. Air quality information is here freed from its usual cartographic representation; It is diffused through its constituent element: air. A simulated cloud, generated from digital data, is suspended on the city's horizon. The concentration of polluted air - nitrogen dioxide (NO_2), ozone (O_3), dust particles (PM10) and sulfur dioxide (SO_2) - are thus made perceptible on the surface of the projection by colors ranging from bright red to celestial blue. The possible interpretations of the visual codes inherent to the cloud are at the discretion of the viewer.

Would a red cloud be more toxic than an orange cloud? Would level zero (i.e.: silence) indicate a total lack of pollution?[19]

- **Musical Practices**: Musical practices (and not just "written texts") become aware of the observer's point of view. Thus, research is always an encounter between different approaches (scientific and artistic), different sensibilities and insights on the world. This encounter involves researchers and artists in an equidistant sharing of their knowledge. As in quantum physics, where representation of space and time cannot be considered simultaneously, the asynchronous approach between different domains leads to a situation where not yet fully master the effects on the epistemology of the sciences and the arts.

This musicology can be qualified of "situated" and, as such, resembles in some ways the anthropological approach that has gradually become one of the strong models of the humanities since the beginning of the 21th century. The practical turn of the epistemology of sciences has become a paradigm henceforth unavoidable of our modern world [14, 15], revealing a profound mutation of the sciences as proposed by the philosopher of sciences Michel Bitbol in his article "About the blind spot of science" [16]. For Michel Bitbol, if science aims for objectiveness, there is a distinction between "**utopian objectivity**" and "**topological objectivity**" that allows us to accept two complementary but also opposing aims of science.

- "**Utopian objectivity**" aims for the elaboration of general laws, explaining reality from a distant point of view, neutralizing individual consciousness, and without taking into account the instruments (tools and methods) used in the experience.
- "**Topological objectivity**" accepts, on the other hand, the limited (not to say reductive) scope of the knowledge which it is capable of transforming or producing. These limitations are mainly related to the situation of the knowledgeable individual (his tools, methods, theoretical and epistemological presuppositions...). Topological objectivity should be understood as in a permanent relationship with the world

---

[19] https://vimeo.com/1745381. "The HeHe collective's works, which always place the viewer at the center of his preoccupations, pass through several fields of experimentation: questions related to perception or chromatic games, to wider questions concerning social or ecological phenomena. But with a true sense of performance, and with humor, we will always be able to visualize some of our daily concerns (pollution, consumption ...) in which we are all involved." Collective created in 1999 and composed of Helen Evans (born in 1972) and Heiko Hansen (born in 1970) who live and work in Paris.

Fig. 4. Champs d'ozone (http://hehe.org.free.fr/hehe/champsdozone/) (Color figure online)

as it is lived and shared. It thus offers a special formulation of a reduced form of knowledge can be shared by "all knowing subjects, embodied and situated, and on which everyone can agree"[20] [16, p. 15]. Indeed, for Michel Bitbol, the act of knowing would gain in abandoning the utopia of an objective and restricted science by accepting to be thought intersubjectively. Situated objectivity (topical) is generally regarded as weak in comparison with the utopian (i.e. aiming for universality) objectivity of science as it has developed since the 18th century. "Thus, always with Michel Bitbol's words, at the most accomplished endpoint of the objectification research, it has become clear that objectivity in the strong sense of complete detachment from the action to know, in the strong sense of complete indifference to

---

[20] Original text: «*tous les sujets connaissants, incarnés et situés, et sur laquelle chacun peut s'accorder*».

instruments, methods, and situation of the knowing subject, is proving to in principle impossible"[21] [16, p. 14]. Indeed, topical objectivity is based on two prerequisites: that of the integration of the blind point (the researcher cannot observe everything, and what he sees is determined by his situation, his point of view - epistemological, theoretical and methodological - and the acceptance of its finitude.

In that context, the researcher recognizes and assumes his situation or even his subjectivity as well as his limits. As Hilary Putnam, a philosopher of science and professor at Harvard University writes:

"What we call "truth" depends both on what exists (the way things happen) and on the participation of the thinker (the mind). There is a human input, a conceptual input, in what we call truth. Scientific theories are not simply dictated by facts."[22] [1, p. 14]

4 One Interscientific Musicological Context: The Deaf Musical Experience

To illustrate our proposal and to concretize the prospect of an interscientific vision of a musical context, we would like to expand our thinking with a specific musicological situation which seems to echo the words of Bernard Vecchione and Michel Bitbol, by proposing at the same time a fundamentally transdisciplinary research posture and a decompartmentalization of the musicological knowledge: the Deaf musical experience [17].

Initially a priori paradoxical, the musical experience of the Deaf allows nevertheless to beyond ordinaries considerations of music and to envisage it in its deep complexity with a careful and specialized analysis.

Thus, this situation requests a systematic musicology, by making music the real context of the scientific observation. Beyond the historical and cultural standards which characterize it currently, music become in itself the main source of study, the true object of its own study. Because deafnesses suppose other relations to music and other musical practices, to consider the Deaf musical experience disrupts the common sense, accepted notions and even more, the conventional musicological reasonings. Beyond any paradox, the Deaf make music and only their experience can explain that. And maybe more...

---

[21] Original text: «Ainsi, à l'extrémité la plus accomplie de la recherche d'objectivation, on s'est aperçu que l'objectivité au sens fort de détachement complet vis-à-vis de l'acte de connaître, au sens fort d'indifférence complète aux instruments, aux méthodes, et à la situation du sujet connaissant, s'avère principiellement impossible».

[22] Original text: «Ce que nous appelons «la vérité» dépend à la fois de ce qui existe (la manière dont les choses se passent) et de la participation du penseur (l'esprit). Il y a un apport humain, un apport conceptuel, dans ce que nous appelons «la vérité». Les théories scientifiques ne nous sont pas simplement dictées par les faits».

Because, like Charles Gaucher has written:

"Strange and attractive, the deaf difference speaks the language of the radical otherness, that which monopolizes, but for minor details, what must be thought by contemporary social sciences"[23] [18, p. 356]

4.1 "Being Deaf" and "Deafnesses": Anthropological Context

To develop a musicological study of the Deaf musical experience, it is necessary, in the first instance, to take interest in deafness which determines a particular anthropological context. Because fundamentally, deafness induces and involves in itself a singular experience. Experience of the otherness, experience of the difference, experience of the abnormality, as many life situation features which seems to pose itself as an uncommon space, little known and reduced to the first representation that one usually associates with it: the "handicap".

Deafness is a "handicap", since the individual is carrying a substantial deterioration of his auditive functions. But beyond the handicap, which assesses experienced situations relative to the share of alteration they imply and not to their share of "otherness", beyond the impairment can we see deafness as a significant anthropological context, and a singular cultural affiliation.

The Deaf constitute a community in its own rights, integrated into the ordinary world, community which carries its identity, its values, history and culture. This dimension of the deafness is the one we are interested in; and more particularly the situation "of being Deaf". "Being Deaf" is in a general consideration, a singular situation coming under particular physiological provisions that we could call "extraordinary". "Extraordinary" because deafness conditions are detached from those whose the hearing is "ordinary". "Extraordinary" because deafness conditions are detached from the "ordinary" ones of the hearing person. Here, we choose to speak of "ordinary" rather than "normality", because the standard carries coherent values, only for the individual who agrees with it; and in the words of Claude Hamonet: "We are all normal, proceeding from the same humanity with functional characteristics, and thus performances, which are different"[24] [19, p. 375]. Thus, "being Deaf" implies a differential determination regarding the ordinary condition; the deficiency transforms the usual vision of realities and the world representations. In that sense, "being Deaf" means apprehending the world in a non-normalized way, beyond the ordained normality. For that, "being Deaf" means living in the world, in a particular place, inaccessible to those who do not share the requirement to seize the world following this point of view.

There is not just one deafness situation but a multitude of deafnesses, since "being Deaf" necessarily corresponds to the individual experience of a singular situation. This categorization of the deafness levels is not enough to demonstrate the diversity of

---

[23] Original text: «*Étrange et attractive, la différence sourde parle le langage de l'altérité radicale, celle qui monopolise, à peu de chose près, ce qui se doit d'être pensé par les sciences sociales contemporaines*».

[24] Original text: «*Nous sommes tous normaux, procédant de la même humanité avec des caractéristiques fonctionnelles, et donc des performances, différentes*».

situations. If it allows considering the situation from Hearing standards, it does consider the individual and social situations of the subject who carries the auditive deficiency. Deafness is above all a life situation, and if one considers it from the phenomenological point of view, the question of the standard seems to disappear. The experience of a Deaf person is fundamentally an experience of the world, of the same world shared by every individual. The world does not differ, it's apprehended in a singular way and appears to the individual according to what seems standard to him. In this, the deafness situation needs to be thought as an individual and cultural reality. Individual because the subject lives the reality; cultural since every individual carries its very own culture.

The Deaf people constitute a multitude of social categories, sharing certain conditions but being united in various ways to the hearing community. The importance of the deficiency will influence this reunion to the standard, as well as the efficacy of a possible technical treatment with an auditive aid. But what seems to determine the relationship with at the ordinary community appears to be firstly the linguistic choice. The question of the language is in the center of the individual construction of the Deaf person. The communication is in essence the social vector and the possibility of using the vocal communication facilitates coming together with the ordinary community. However, the natural language of Deaf people, the Sign Language, is very often an obstacle to the union of the individual to the ordinary community. But the sign language represents the language of the Deaf community, and underlines at the same time the integration of the subject in a linguistic and cultural minority. This is precisely what we aim at studying and in particular the group of Deaf persons, with a capital D, which designates the persons who claim for an identity and a particular culture, the Deaf culture. In this situation, deafness is the place of affiliation and cohesion of an entirety of representations and singular creations, including music in various ways.

4.2   "Deaf Musical Receptions": Physiological Context

What seems a priori paradoxical in the Deaf musical experience is the loss of hearing: "how the Deaf, who don't hear, can make or listen music?"

To answer – quickly – this question, we rely on au sociological investigation [17, 20] realized among the French-speaking Deaf persons, in order to determine the specifics which appear in the singular relation they have with music. This investigation allows us to contextualize the reality of this special connection to music, allowing us to exceed the initial paradox involved in the relation between music and deafness. This survey comprises all deafnesses in order to determine the possible differences of musical and sound apprehension depending on the various experienced situations.

Without detail here all the results, we can still specify that, in the two hundred responses obtained:

– 50% of respondents declare "not hearing any sound with their ears" and 55% declare "not hearing music".

However, regarding the musical practice:

– 69.7% of respondents declare *"listening to music"*; 36.3% say they *"practice music"*, and 36.4% of the not-practitioners *"wishes to do it"*.

Moreover:

– 70.9% concede that *"music occupies a particular place in their everyday life"*.

However, the music reception does not lie on the usual elements being used to determine it:

– 82.3% confess *"not make a distinction between music notes"*; 51.2% do *"not differentiate rhythms"*; 65.6% do *"not recognize a musical style"*; and 77% do *"not differentiate musical instruments"*.

Thus, the musical experience seems to move from the ear to the body:

– 60.8% declare *"feeling corporeally the sounds"*, including 3% *"without any auditive perception"*. 66.4% *"perceive music in their bodies"*; and 59.3% say that *"the sight helps to perceive sounds"*.

Can one observe that music seizes the body, and that it touches a certain number of very specific zones. From obtained responses, we can propose a classification of the bodily perception which approximates the categorization of bodily types of sound perceptions elaborated by Maïté Le Moël [21]: (1) the "cutaneous perception", on surface with in priority the hands, the arms and the face; (2) the bones, "in-depth perception", which relates to the hands, the feet, the legs, or the cranium/skull; and (3) the "visceral perception", which touches the belly, the heart, the lungs.

Thus, when we asked how the sound elements were perceived, the vibrating dimension of sounds is designated. The sound is mainly experienced via the vibrations which it produces, in the air, but also with the elements and the present objects (soil, walls, chair…). Vibrations are perceived by the body and are described like *"pressures which come from the outside"*, *"tickles"*, *"stirrings"* and *"buzzes"*, or *"discharges"*. One can thus point out that for the Deaf people, the body offers itself as the privileged space of the musical realization or according to one of the answers: *"the music expresses a certain harmony that all the body accepts and feeds from"*.

Therefore, as Pierre Schmitt wrote in his article "The music and the Deaf"

"This relationship of deaf persons to the music recalls us that it is much more than one sensory experience, it is a social and cultural fact where the ear does not necessarily have a role to play. With regard to the direct music experience, since it is only vibrations, deafness, even profound, does not prohibit the sound contact but it shifts the privileged spot from the ear to the body."[25] [22, p. 221]

---

[25] Original text: «*Ce rapport des sourds à la musique nous rappelle qu'elle est bien plus qu'une expérience sensorielle, elle est un fait social et culturel où l'oreille n'a pas forcément de rôle à jouer. En ce qui concerne l'expérience directe de la musique, puisqu'elle est vibration, la surdité, y compris profonde, n'interdit pas le contact sonore mais elle en déplace le lieu privilégié de l'oreille au corps*».

4.3 "Deaf Music": Musical Context

The music exists really within the Deaf community and has a particular role: at the same time meeting and cultural exchange spot with the hearing community, but also a space for the creation of a specific music, a denormalized music, carrying culturally singularities. Considered as a cultural space, music can be seen in the Deaf world like a place of esthetic creation detached from ordinary goals and impregnated of a strong cultural identity. But it is also a bridge between the Deaf and hearing cultures, in particular via the Sign Language.

From the point of view of a cultural and artistic opening, the hearing musical community is interested in the Deaf community and more particularly in its language, the Sign language. The gestural communication attracts and intrigues hearing persons, and a certain number of artists sought to integrate it into their musical productions. This musical incorporation of the Sign Language will have a significant evolution and will carry various values.

In a more thorough musical perspective, since few years Sign Language songs are being developed. The "sign-singing" (or "signsing") aims at being a musical expression of one text, musical but not sounding, the body carrying the melody and rhythmic values specific to the song, with a "choreographed Sign language, abstract and poetic"[26] [22, p. 222]. Here we may observe the progress of a real Deaf musical experience, where the melodicity seizes the body as the space of production of the musicality. The sign-singing belongs to Deaf world, but also acts like a bridge between the Deaf and hearing community. Various musical projects seek to intertwine vocal language and Sign Language, in particular in the hip-hop movements where the Deaf create their own musical style: the "Dip-hop" for "Deaf hip-hop".

But the Deaf musical reality exceeds the simple collaboration between sign-singers and hearing artists, with the existence of a real Deaf musical scene. From an identity prospect, since the early years of 2000 a singular artistic and cultural scene exists, specific to the Deaf community, like Pierre Schmitt describes it, some "contemporary networks of young dynamic and mobile deaf persons, protagonists of a kind of *underground* deaf culture"[27] [22, p. 222]. We indeed witness musical activities but also visual events, organized by the Deaf themselves and bound to the Deaf. They are in particular the "Signs and Vibrations" evenings, "Laser Sign" or the "deafraves". We can observe that the musical space for creation is here completely hogged by the Deaf and even diverted to become a specific cultural object. The image is integrated into the music so that Deaf persons speak then of "Vusic", contraction of *Visual* and *music*. The "Vusic" describes what music reality is for a Deaf person: at the same time of the images and vibrations, two constitutive elements of a singular esthetic object.

---

[26] Original text: «*une langue des signes chorégraphiée, abstraite et poétique*».

[27] Original text: «*des réseaux contemporains de jeunes sourds dynamiques et mobiles, protagonistes d'une sorte de culture sourde* underground».

Thus, to consider the music of the Deaf is both to study the Deaf creative abilities and also the music itself, in its depth and in what constitutes it in itself. And as Pierre Schmitt writes:

"If the claiming of a particular musical experience [...] represents a contemporary expression of this shared culture resulting from deafness, it imposes at the same time the assessment of a plural deaf culture, where the limits between the deaf and hearing worlds are permeable. These worlds thus seem like categories to be deconstructed"[28] [22, p. 232]

If music brings together the Deaf and hearing worlds, it seems that the Deaf musical experience can to expand the musical world and its common comprehension. Because the musical experience of Deaf reveals one part of the ordinary experience of music, the neglected part due to "ear's domination": the place of the body in the musical existence.

4.4 "Musical Experience": Phenomenological Context

Common sense approaches music as a *product* of listening, subsequently making the ear its crucial auxiliary for realization; the musical experience is very often thought to be the privileged field of the *audible*, where the sound matter organizes itself so that it be sieges, through the ear, the subject's mind. However, the individual inscription as a *body* within the musical space implies a true physical investigation, essential feature of the musical experience. Although apparently secondary, this body experience of music seems fundamentally engraved in the heart of the *sensible* share of the sound world, featuring a unique representation of human existentiality, specific to each musical experience. Entirely projected in the heart of the latter, the body offers itself as the interface binding the man to music; at the root of its perception and mental outlook, it establishes a unique relationship with the sound world.

From a phenomenological point of view, the music arises as an event appearing in the world. As an object or phenomenon, the music proposes to an individual a specific spatio-temporal context which constitutes the world's musical appropriation. The music is thus primarily a context, which becomes an event when the individual takes part in its realization. Music's evenemential dimension finds its place in the necessary inscription of the individual in the heart of the context given to be lived. Moreover, the concretization of the musical existence is carried out primarily in the instant of its realization, which is no other than that of the presentation to the individual. In this way, music is very often regarded as *the art of the present*, taking into account its ability to exist materially only in its time of presentation. The present offers itself as time of existence, that of the being-there, and necessarily implies a presentation to an

---

[28] Original text: «*Si la revendication d'une expérience particulière de la musique [...] représente une expression contemporaine de cette culture partagée issue de la surdité, elle impose en même temps le constat d'une culture sourde plurielle, où les limites entre les mondes «sourd» et «entendant» sont perméables. Ces mondes apparaissent ainsi comme des catégories à déconstruire*».

individual in presence, who achieves it. However, the sound event being fundamentally temporal, the music imposes its materiality and its own temporality on the individual who lives it. From this point of view the music is transposed in *art for presences* [23]: individual presence and sound space's presence. The individual becomes the central point of the instantaneous musical achievement, his presence inducing the event's realization.

The encounter of the individual and the sound event is at the foundation of the musical experience. For the music to exist as an event and to match a reality, it is necessary that the individual experiences it, in being in the presence of the musical event's spatio-temporal context. However, the experientiality principle implies necessarily another principle, that of "incarnation", since the individual is invested consciously and corporally in the experience. To live an experience is to penetrate the existence of something, and to be penetrated by this something. It is via my body, as it frames my existence and my inscription in the world that I understand this world and that I feel belonging to it.

Generally, musical situations have the individual falling in line with a material and temporal context, a singular context within which the body dispositions reveal two essential aspects: it places itself both as realization "medium" of the musical event, but is also offered as the instantaneous "center" of the experiences. So, may we observe that the body firstly fashions the music, offering itself as the support of its existence and the pedestal of its achievement, and also that music has an essential impact on the body, commanding a specific time and space from which it cannot be separated. The musical event given to *be lived* is embodied in us within the time of the experience.

To approach as close as possible to the bodily dimension of music and finding the essence of the musical incarnation, deafness offers a very singular perspective. It allows to exceed the permanent presence of the ear and to focus only on the body experience. Thus, the Deaf musical experience contributes to develop the musicological research by giving it new orientations and at the same time offering it an opening to itself.

To summarize the interscientific nature inherent in our musicological consideration of the Deaf musical experience, we can propose the schematic representation below which incorporates and expands – in the view of Bernard Vecchione – the fundamental domains of our analytic enterprise (Fig. 5).

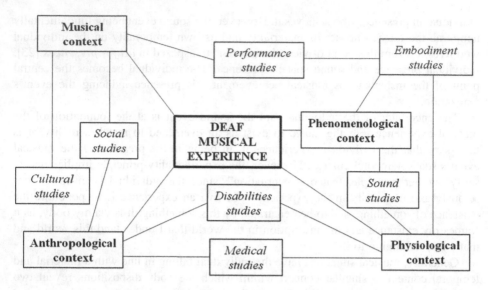

Fig. 5. Deaf musical experience – intersciences network

5   To Conclude

The current musicology looks up its objects in all contemporary realities – historical, cultural, social… - and music appears today more than ever at the basis of a profound study of what it is in its most various forms. Thinking the interscientific aspects of the musicological project, it is to aim for the scientific nature of our discipline, considering the true subject of all its study objects, music, on the basis of what it produces as practices, contexts or realities – starting from social, historical, analytic or praxeologic orientations. Not music like a product of all these domains, but like the only one domain. The intersciences project, if it finds a sense to the musicological enterprise, it is necessarily in this way: of the object-music to music as subject. Of the musicological science towards an interscientific musicology.

References

1. Machover, T.: Introduction. In: Machover, T. (ed.) Quoi, Quand, Comment. La recherche musicale. Bourgois/IRCAM, Paris (1985)
2. Nattiez, J.-J.: Profession musicologue. Presses Universitaires de Montréal, Montréal (2007)
3. Vendrix, P.: Les conceptions de l'histoire de la musique. In: Nattiez, J-J. (ed.) Musiques. Une encyclopédie pour le XXIᵉ siècle, vol. 2. Les savoirs musicaux. pp. 628–648. Actes Sud/Cité de la musique, Arles-Paris (2004)
4. Warzawsky, J.-M.: La musicologie et le mystère du logos. In: Itamar, Revista de investigación musical: territorios para el arte. pp. 121–130. Rivera Editores Universitat de València (2008)

5. Bent, M.: Le métier de musicologue. In: Nattiez, J.-J. (ed.) Musiques. Une encyclopédie pour le XXIᵉ siècle, vol. 2. Les savoirs musicaux. pp. 611–627. Actes Sud/Cité de la musique, Arles-Paris (2004)
6. De Murs, J.: Musica speculativa (1323); Compendium musicae practicae (1325)
7. Adler, G.: Umfang, Methode und Ziel der Musikwissenschaft. Vierteljahresschrift für Musikwissenschaft 1, 5–20 (1885)
8. Handschin, J.: Musicologie et Musique (1949). http://www.musicologie.org/theses/. Accessed July 2017
9. Reeves, H.: Préface. In: Proust, D.: L'Harmonie des sphères. pp. 7–9 (2001)
10. Vecchione, B.: La recherche musicologique aujourd'hui: Questionnements, intersciences, métamusicologie. Interface 21(3–4), 281–312 (1992)
11. Nattiez, J.-J.: Présentation générale. In: Nattiez, J.-J. (ed.) Musiques. Une encyclopédie pour le XXIe siècle, vol. 1. Musiques du XXe siècle. pp. 23–37. Actes Sud/Cité de la musique, Arles-Paris (2003)
12. Muggletone, E.: Guido Adler's "The Scope, Method, and Aim of Musicology" (1885): an english translation with an Historico-Analytical Commentary. In: Yearbook for Traditional Music, vol. 13. pp. 1–21 (1981)
13. Deliège, C.: Variables historiques du concept de recherche musicale. In: Machover, T. (ed.) Quoi, Quand, Comment. La recherche musicale. pp. 25–61. Bourgois/IRCAM, Paris (1985)
14. Hacking, I.: Concevoir et expérimenter, thèmes introductifs à la philosophie des sciences expérimentales (1983). Bourgeois éd., Paris (1989)
15. Latour, B.: Nous n'avons jamais été modernes. Essai d'anthropologie symétrique. La découverte éd., Paris (1991)
16. Bitbol, M.: À propos du point aveugle de la science. In: Hess, G., Bourg, D. (eds.) Science, conscience et environnement. Presses Universitaires de France, Paris (2016)
17. Brétéché, S.: L'incarnation musicale. L'expérience musicale sourde. Thèse de doctorat en musicologie. Esclapez, C., Vion-Dury, J., (dir.). Aix-Marseille Université (2015)
18. Gaucher, C.: L'indiscutable différence des Sourds: intégration et pluralisme au sein des mondes occidentaux. In Vibert, S. (ed.) Le pluralisme dans les sociétés modernes: culture, droit et politique. pp. 354–392. Québec-Amérique, Montréal (2007)
19. Hamonet, C.: Handicapologie et anthropologie. Thèse de doctorat en anthropologie sociale, Thomas, L-V. (dir.). Université René Descartes-Paris IV (1992)
20. Brétéché, S.: Du corps en-Lieu. Phénoménologie et "expérience musicale Sourde". In ESCLAPEZ, C. (dir.): Ontologies de la création en musique, volume III: des Lieux en Musique. L'Harmattan, Paris (2014)
21. Le Moël, M.: L'univers musical de l'enfant sourd. In: Marsyas n 39/40, Dossiers Pédagogies et Handicaps. pp. 51–58 (1996)
22. Schmitt, P.: De la musique et des sourds. Approche ethnographique du rapport à la musique de jeunes sourds européens. In: Bachir-Loopuyt, T., Iglesias, S., Langenbruch, A., Zur Nieden, G.. et al. (eds.) Musik – Kontext – Wissenschaft. Interdisziplinäre Forschung zu Musik/ Musiques – contextes – savoirs. Perspectives interdisciplinaires sur la musique. pp. 221–233. Peter Lang, Frankfurt am Main (2012)
23. Brétéché, S.: Au cœur de l'expérience musicale : l'incarnation comme principe existentiel. In Maeder, C., Rebrouck, M. (dir.) Sémiotique et vécu musical. Du sens à l'expérience, de l'expérience au sens. Leuven University Press, Leuven (2016)

Reading Early Music Today: Between Reenactment and New Technologies

Julien Ferrando[✉]

CNRS, PRISM "Perception, Représentations, Image, Son, Musique, Aix Marseille University,
31 Chemin J. Aiguier, 70071 13402 Marseille Cedex 09, France
julien.ferrando@univ-amu.fr

Abstract. Since the revival of *Historically Informed Performance* in the 1960s, the interpretation of Early Music has continuously raised questions many of which remain unanswered. Nevertheless, understanding of earlier practice continues to grow and performers have long surpassed the strict historical *urtext* approach that initially prevailed, largely due to the growing body of evidence that instrumentalists of earlier times relied heavily on aurally transmitted improvised musical traditions, which can only be re-imagined today. The modern musician must also improvise in order to reconstitute or re-invent missing elements belonging to a long-forgotten tradition. From a philosophical point of view, therefore, the performance of early music today is closely related to hermeneutics, and the multiple questions involved in the interpretative process.

Keywords: Early music · Re-enactment · Re-creation · Interpretation
Binaural listening

1 Introduction

I propose here to discuss issues concerning the performance of Early Music today, in order to present the dialectic that lies between *historically informed performance* (HIP) and *re-creation*, or between a faithful reconstruction and a creative act. These considerations will lead to the presentation of *Musical Performance in Historical Soundscape* (MPHS) that is today realizable with the help of new technologies (binaural restitution in particular). To do so, I will first observe how the concept of musical heritage has evolved in our century, and then present an approach where a new insight on this heritage can foster creative musical ideas. I will talk here as a musicologist, but also as a practitioner specialized in early keyboards (organetto, clavicytherium and harpsichord).

2 The Necessity to Rebuild History

The problem of re-interpreting the past was addressed in particular in the first half of the 19th century. Productions inherited from History were named antique or primitive and, most of the time, were considered at best as interesting curiosities. With the exception of Gregorian chant (from the Solesme school), Music of the Middle Ages, similarly,

© Springer Nature Switzerland AG 2018
M. Aramaki et al. (Eds.): CMMR 2017, LNCS 11265, pp. 658–665, 2018.
https://doi.org/10.1007/978-3-030-01692-0_43

was considered as exotic. Major academic institutions such as Paris Conservatoire or Schola Cantorum had a strong influence on musical aesthetic values. Tonal harmony, with its strict rules, constituted the foundations of any apprenticeship of musical composition. Amédée Gastoué is a perfect example. Organist and well-known teacher at the *Schola Cantorum*, he occupied a prominent role in the exhumation of medieval musical sources, and was also a vitriolic critic towards contrapuntal techniques used in the 14th Century in Avignon. Here are few examples extract from an academic article about the music of the Apt Manuscript (one of the major sources of Fourteenth Century Polyphonic music), published in 1904 in the Rivista Musicale Italiana:

> It would be vain to transcribe the rest of the piece since it would sound too primitive to our refined ears (…). This might seem laborious but I believe it is good to display few extracts of this crude style, that will later find its accomplishment in Josquin. [1, p. 275–276]

This quote present history as a goal oriented process, implicitly founded upon a theory of a linear progression in the arts, or simplistic social and artistic evolutionist principals. Such views presuppose that archaic societies were governed by superstitious thinking, and evolved towards an implicit progress guided by modern scientific laws. An influence of philosophical positivism can be perceived in this approach to musical research. These judgments betray advanced forms of ethnocentrism, as well as an anthropologic view based on simplified classifications, presupposing value judgments, and an arbitrary superiority of the new over former societies. Chronology is therefore profoundly misread in such conceptions, and hijacked as a means to classify works of art in successive and coherent periods of History. Unfortunately, such chronologic classification often let down the anthropologic reality of the works themselves.

3   Re-writing as a Means to Re-interpret the Past

At the end of the 19th Century, in spite of increasing interest in Baroque and Renaissance music, the concept of historically informed performance or replacing a repertoire in its context is not yet considered a legitimate approach. Vincent D'Indy exhumes and rewrites Monteverdi's operas (among which the Orfeo). Around 1904, Debussy and Ravel found French baroque music a major source of inspiration. The *Tombeau de Couperin*, for instance, is a stylistic hommage to the court of Louis XIV, with clear references to dance suites (Prelude, Menuet, Rigaudon, Forlane…). However, beyond those references to ancient form, he could only use a parodic tone in order to make his own a language that was far too remote from his time, since very little was known about the organology of harpsichord at that time. Ravel therefore adapts and uses as a major source of inspiration what he imagines characteristic of Couperin's style [2, p. 54, 106, 246]. In this process of adaptation, Ravel recombines elements of a remote era with his own compositional taste and techniques. He uses ornaments in his own way, adopts the flow of baroque phrasing with a harmonic language which will become characteristic of his style. With his singular relationship towards tradition, Ravel opens new perspectives for the *Groupe des Six*. Among them, Poulenc is perhaps the main instigator of this tendency[1] [4]. Around the same time, Wanda Landowska [5] starts pioneer research works on instruments that initiated a whole rediscovery of Baroque keyboard music, and her collaboration with Pleyel makes the reconstitution of the first harpsichords possible [6, p. 425]. Such instruments were already well-known at that time, however, harpsichords were conceived as plucked-stringed pianos rather than copies of historical instruments. The goal here was to adapt modern instrument rather than reproduce replicas of the historical models. In this sense it is reminiscent of the way Ravel absorbs a music of the past that he imagines in order to create something new: Baroque music is in this case readjusted so as to become a major source of inspiration, thus provoking experimentation and creation. The work of Wanda Landowska even prompted composers of the time to write for modern harpsichord [7], and this is how the Polish-French keyboard player initiated the composition of Francis Poulenc's Concerto Champêtre, the first harpsichord concerto of modern times.

4   Re-reading Early Music as a Neoclassic Act?

The works of Poulenc, Ravel, and all composers using materials inspired by modal Gregorian Chant, were classified as Neo-Classical in their time. This term, when used by a progressivist such as Varèse, was derogatory [8, pp. 178–180]. Nevertheless I propose here that such an issue was not addressed correctly at that time. Beyond a mere taxonomy by time period and style, writing in a language inspired from the past should not always be understood as a regressive act, but rather as a means to integrate references from the past, engage with tradition, in order to place them in a contemporary perspective. Meschonnic [9] proposes to speak of a *modern unity*, and shows that elements can resemble each other in such a way that they all can be conceived as related to one unique kernel. A modern unity, with a sense of a one-way History, endeavors to find, in avant-gardes, structural resemblances, so as to group them around few types, and extract meaning from them. The notion of convergence is here of particular relevance: reject of difference are classified as one further category of the whole: Compulsion of convergence, compulsion of unity, wordplay of the singular, a stance of universality [8, pp. 56–58]. This linear conception of time also reveals a conception of music as a vertical construction, or purely architectural, in which History would therefore not anymore be understood as filtered by religious thought. Michel Faure says:

> "Designation such as gothic, baroque, rococo, impressionist, cubist, applied to certain forms of art, were initially highly pejorative, but later acquired their dignified signification" [8, p. 180].

Novelty is often observed with fear. The notion of Neoclassicism itself denotes the insight of a composer for understanding music as necessarily overstepping tradition. Under this assertion Neoclassicism can only be pejorative. However, beyond progressivist considerations, a growing interest in Early Music will entail a desire for the discovery of an exhaustive unknown heritage [10]. Such aspirations for rediscovery of

---

[1]   The CD "Poulenc au Moyen Âge", by the French ensembles Mescolanza and Les Zippoventilés illustrates this tendency [3].

the past see their first peak in the 1950s, which musicians such as Nicolaus Harnoncourt, Ralph Kirkpatrick and Gustav Leohnardt.

5 Rebuilding the Musical Gesture: An Attempt to Magnify Heritage?

Approaching an ancient musical document requires several steps in order to surpass the mere historical framework. The interpreter should aim for a re-creation, a philological approach that involves a return to the source, itself a transcription of an expunged and re-interpreted reality[2]. The interpreter also seeks a hermeneutical approach, understanding the work as a document, eventually leading to the elaboration of musical gestures and sounds. The same applies to the reconstructed musical instrument: a "monument" which is necessarily derived from an interpretation of the factor and his practices. Thus every single aspect of an interpretation participate to the elaboration of the work: recording techniques, organology and performance all contribute to the co-authorship of the work [11, pp. 31–32]. Since the beginning of the 21st century, economic realities have led early music artists not to produce only "historical" programs, but also performances that offer singularity and originality in their contemporary rereading. Encounters and interactions between artists enable new redeployment of the work. Another major aspect in this reflection concerns the techniques of sound and image taking. A very special experience developed in the late eighties, with the arrival of digital. Labels such as *Astrée Auvidis, Arcana*, or *Harmonia Mundi* have developed an editorial singularity in the way to capture the musical reality of the performers and in the choice of microphones. Today multi-micro systems, multitrack editing, high-resolution recording and artificial sound environments open the way to a new way of conceiving the capture and publication of these productions. Discoveries in art history and iconography made possible the (re)production of genuine instruments from representation engraved on stones or manuscripts. These crucial research works and practices enabled reflexions on sound or sonic material-, timbre, and opened new fields in organology. For instance, bowed vielas of first medieval ensembles resembled fiddle-violins, but during the 1980s, French luthier Christian Rault called into question the presence of the soundpost (*âme* in French) in the resonance chamber of the instrument. Playing techniques were subsequently deduced from gut strings, bows adjustments, and representations of musicians playing (The recording Mille Bonjours (Alpha [15]), by the

---

[2] I refer here to the interpretation of Le Bourgeois Gentilhomme staged by Benjamin Lazar and interpreted by Le Poème Harmonique. In search of a form of reenactment, the piece is reconstituted in all its dimensions, which also implies for instance the lightings of the time, made of candles. The artists played with shadows and light in an expressive way, which has only been possible through their to attempt to reconstruct and understand the work. The Reconstitution of the diction by Eugene Green also, according to the director Benjamin Lazar, proposed new forms of interpretations, and La Comédie franse. The work as a whole cannot be fully grasped when omitting the musical part, which is crucial to its integrity (http://fresques.ina.fr/en-scenes/fiche-media/Scenes00285/le-bourgeois-gentilhomme-mis-en-scene-par-benjamin-lazar-au-theatre-l-apostrophe-de-pontoise.html).

French ensemble *Diabolus in Musica* is a good exemple of such creative research processes). In this sense, an interpreter like Nicolaus Harnoncourt becomes much more than a mere executant. The skills of the musician in his case encompass knowledge in history, a philology, and music anthropology. His aim consists in recontextualizing the work, with rebuilt instruments which increasingly resemble to the ones present in museum collections [12, pp. 42–60]. Harnoncourt therefore addresses the complex issue of interpretation through an understanding of the contextual environment of the work. It is a form of historical truth that is at stake in this case. Working on original manuscripts inevitably draws attention to the concept of faithfulness when interpreting a piece of music. This stage of the research process has the great advantage to guide a creative interpretation with essential notions of organology, notation, and improvisation, thus avoiding misreading in transcriptions, or giving access for instance to the reenactment of improvisatory skills through the study of rules expounded in the treatises. This practice became little by little characteristic of early music studies. Oral tradition takes an important role in this domain, since any many cases, the score is only a canvas into which musical practices can be inserted [12, p. 159].

6   Is Early Music a Space for Creation?

If we consider that the problem is not to put ourselves in the timeline of a tradition, but rather to consider productions of the past as a way of being in History constantly rebuilt by interpretation [13, pp. 127–128], Early Music becomes an object of creation. Then, it does not have a truth-in-itself, but gives to each interpreter a range of possibilities to explore. Contribution of Early Music performers has opened minds regarding the need of a re-contextualized work. However, nowadays, the historical context can be surpassed, beyond a simple reconstitution on old instruments. For example, we can see some pianists playing today Bach, Couperin, or Rameau's music, acknowledging proposals of interpreters such as Scott Ross, Gustav Leonhardt, Tom Koopman, Muray Perahia or Alexandre Tharaud, who have changed interpretation, ornamental quality and tone color. The idea is not to sound like a harpsichord, but simply to take into account this tradition of interpretation, in order to re-create a work on their instrument. The purpose of this re-creation is to cultivate some awareness about the gap that lays in each musical work, between its historical reality and its contemporary interpretative reality. Consequently, today, for a performer, two conceptions of Early Music coexist and complement each other:

– Decrypting the sources, collecting data, and interpret them in order to gather a maximum of evidences informing about the context of the work, in order to attempt a re-creation or re-enactment.
– Considering this first step as preliminary research, or as a basis for a creation, an important part of the work still remains hypothetic, and requires creative imagination, to write, improvise, perform, and adapt results to the adequate production context.

This concept of re-enactment what was described above as the first step emerges from the 1960s, but it presents a keen interest in the context of medieval festivals since the last ten years, with the emergence of multiple reconstructions of historical events or past traditions. Today, many of these festivals involve a sort of popular collective construction of lost traditions. As Aline Caillet says, living and reincarnating History, reenacting helps to build collective History in individual stories, by re-engaging them in present time. Whether for re-enactors or artists, it is an attempt to make present an experience of past. As a contemporary scene, its *presence here and now* is also a way of affirming that History is never gone or resolved. Beyond the mere cliché of a troubadour in a costume, this definition perfectly fits with my approach to Early Music interpretation today, which goes hand in hand with notions of philology, organology, repertoire reconstitution, and perspectives with Art History [14]. This interpretation is nevertheless always conceived as an experience taking place in the present, and therefore as a contemporary artistic attempt. As an example illustrating this idea, I will mention a project I was involved in with the French ensemble *Diabolus in Musica*. In 2004, the harpsichord maker David Boinnard was asked to recreate a keyboard instrument of the fifteenth century, whose original is in the collection of the Royal College of Music in London. The project was a musical program consisting of Guillaume Dufay songs combined with the projection of a collection of paintings by Jean Fouquet. This project led to a series of concerts and a CD produced in 2007 by Alpha [15]. This program was therefore the pretext to attribute a particular repertoire to this instrument. I have now acquired a great familiarity with this instrument, and experimented with the size of feathers that suits me, so as to facilitate the dexterity shown in the keyboard repertoire of that time. However, because of the string arrangement, the instrument can be seen as a sort of keyboard harp. I have therefore proposed a string pinching technique, as an alternative to the plucked strings of the keyboard. This attempt led to a rewriting of a keyboard piece of the 15th century: *Ein vroulein edel von nature*[3]. The piece opens with an improvisation in the mode that is not necessarily historic but rather deduced or felt. This interpretation therefore allowed a form of rewriting, or recycling of an existing material. For the second concept, which consists in using existing repertoires for recreation and emergence of new musical languages, we will give two examples:

- A medieval chant of Martin Codax (A Galician troubadour) revisited by two musicians of the French ensemble *Le Poème Harmonique*: Claire Lefilliâtre et Joel Grare (of which the recording is unavailable).
- An improvisation/encounter between prepared piano and medieval portative organ by Nathalie Negro and myself[4].

7   Avignon 3D: The Reconstruction of Ancient Musical Practices

I would like to conclude by evoking a final point linked to the notion of *sounding space*. It is clear that sound technology and its spatial representation have recently made huge progress with respect to digital technologies. More recently binaural perception has, thanks to the works made at IRCAM and also at PRISM (AMU-CNRS), enabled

---

[3]   https://www.youtube.com/watch?v=JdfkxOzTc.

[4]   http://www.pianoandco.fr/spip.php?page=mediaidarticle=137iddocument=392.

to open a research field that we would like to take into account in order to provide new ways of listening to ancient music in a 3D real-time environment:

- Virtually reconstitute both sensory and sonic characteristics of a historical monument, hotspot of musical creation.
- Enable artists to confront, while practicing in a recording studio, their musical repertoire with the original acoustics associated to a chosen edifice (St. Mark's Basilica, or a specific concert hall…) in real-time and to choose the localization of their listener's point of view.

This setup would constitute an invaluable tool for recreation of artistic and innovating practices. I am for instance referring to the project Ars musica 3D (Papal Palace of Avignon), which aims at restoring the conditions of creation in the pontifical chapel of Avignon during the XIV century: a way to link the ancient to the modern. The project will seek above all to recreate an environmental soundscape in order to stimulate the interpreter and provide him/her with the means to reveal the possible deployment of their musical gestures, or to grasp for instance what the ear of the cantor would perceive at the time of its execution. Placing a musical work in its "eco-logical" context undoubtedly implies research as well as interpretation, and, therefore, a part of creation. From an epistemological point of view indeed, trust in artistic taste (over a desire for an imagined authenticity) seems today a valid approach in many ways.

The setup should therefore serve musicians and researchers in two different ways:

- **Avignon's *Palais des Papes* as a museum**: To reconstitute the sound space of the pontifical chapel, and recreating an extract from an office of polyphonic mass in the time of Clement VI (c. 1352), with the help of binaural 3D acoustic emulation techniques, and to simulate, inside the *Palais des Papes*, a historically informed performance to be diffused by an audio system (binaural 3D helmet) adapting to the situation of the visitor in space.
- **Interpretive: MPHS (Musical Performance in Historical Soundscape**: To enable artists to confront, while practicing in a recoding studio, their musical repertoire with the original acoustics associated to a chosen edifice (St. Mark's Basilica, or any specific concert hall…) in real-time and to choose the localization of their listener's point of view. The acoustic simulation becomes here a recording/rehearsal tool, as a recording device in the studio that allows for the total immersion of the musicians in a real-time virtual 3D sound space.

For a plausible result, the recording of musicians must be realized in silence, in a neutral studio, with as little reflections as possible (as in an anechoic chamber). Each singer must be equipped with helmet headphones that instantly returns the digital processing, in order to feel immersed in the virtual space. However, we will surely find ourselves faced with a cultural and technical problem: wearing helmet headphones disturbs the way the singers traditionally listen to each other and to their own voice, in a repertoire that was not conceived for amplification. The "singing body"5 has a crucial impact on the way the singer projects his voice, and the simulation of virtual space could be of tremendous help for guiding his interpretation. The objective is to allow any musician or ensemble to be able to test, evaluate the conditions of performance of a musical production in its original sonic environment. This setup could inform early music musicians as well as open wide range of experiments for contemporary artists. The project is interdisciplinary in essence, and proposes to interrogate the above-mentioned repertoires in an original way. In line with the work undertaken since Schafer, but also on reconstructed soundscapes (ReViSMartin, Cubiculum Musicae, Bretez Project), we propose to exploit the possibilities offered by new sound technologies to recreate an immersive virtual space in three dimensions. The notion of increased perception is at the heart of this approach, in which the reconstitution of musical gestures is be prompted by virtual acoustic spaces of a new kind. Our approach seeks above all to give the performers the means to experiment with the multiple possible realisations of their own musical gestures, in order to perceive for instance which type of aural feedback the medieval cantor was interacting with, but also to place a musical work in its *eco-logical* context of origin, and thus stimulate new and original forms of research-creation.

Acknowledgments. We are grateful to Jonathan Bell for his French-English translation.

References

1. Gastoue, A.: La Musique en Avignon et dans le comtat du XIVe au XVIIIe siécle, R. M. Italiana, Ed., Roma, vol. XI (1904)
2. Zinc, S.: Irony and Sound: The Music Maurice Ravel. University Rochester Press, New Haven (2009)
3. Poulenc, F., Poulenc au Moyen Age, Paris, P. E. (CD), Ed., Cucuron, France, no. PAR 69 (2015)
4. Poulenc, F.: J'écris ce qui me chante: Textes et entretiens réunis, présents et annotés par Nicolas Southons. fayard, Paris (2011)
5. Landowska, W.: Musique ancienne: le mépris pour les anciens - la force de la sonorité - le style - l'interprétation - les virtuoses - les Mécènes et la Musique, ivrea-édition. M. Senart, Paris (1996)
6. Kottock, E.: A History of the Harpsichord, vol. 1. Indiana University Press, Bloomington (2016)
7. Eigeldinger: Wanda Landowska et la renaissance de la musique ancienne. actes sud, Arles (2010)
8. Faure, M.: Le néoclassicisme musical, une esthétique de crise? L'influence de la socitie sur la musique. l'harmattan, Paris (2008)
9. Meschonnic, H.: Modernité-Modernité. folio essais, Paris (2005)
10. Harnoncourt, N.: Le discours musical. Gallimard, Paris (1984)
11. Escal, F.: Espaces sociaux, espaces musicaux. Payot, Paris (1979)
12. Lawson, C.: The Historical Performance of Music: An Introduction. In: Stowell, R., (ed.) Cambridge University Press, Cambridge (1999)
13. Najarro, J.-P.: Jean-Sébastien Bach: deux œuvres au fil du temps. Inharmoniques: musique et authenticités (1991)
14. Vecchione, B.: Une poétique du motet médiéval: Textes, hypotextes et niveaux de discours dans l'Ave regina celorum/Tenor [Joseph]/Mater innocencie de Marchetto da Padova, lim. ed., F. d. Actes du Colloque de Certaldo Ziino, A. Zimei, Ed., Lucca (2009) (2013)
15. Guerber, A.: Mille Bonjours, chansons de Guillaume Dufay. Alpha, Ensemble Diabolus in Musica (CD), no. 116 (2007)

ArtDoc - An Experimental Archive and a Tool for Artistic Research

Henrik Frisk(✉)

Royal College of Music, Stockholm, Sweden
henrik.frisk@kmh.se

Abstract. ArtDoc is an experimental archive primarily for document-ing artistic practice. One of the ambitions is to address the question of how artistic practice may be documented in a manner that makes visi-ble the processes in action. ArtDoc has its roots in research and artistic practice that began over ten years ago and preliminary tests shows it to be a useful complement to other means to document musical works and artistic processes. The particular case of open form works, works that in some respect are negotiated between the different agents involved, such as composers, musicians and members of the audience was a point of departure and has guided the development to a significant degree. The underlying structure of documentation classes is presented and some of the design choices are discussed. ArtDoc is still under construction but a working proof of concept will be released in 2018.

Keywords: Electro acoustic music · Artistic research
Music representation · Cooperative music networks

1 Introduction

What is it to document a musical work? Perhaps the most obvious way is to record the performance, but what is gained, or lost, in the transformation from the work's material reality to its recorded representation? In this paper I will attempt to approach this question indirectly by presenting a method for doc-umenting the both the result as well as the processes behind the creation of a musical work. These thoughts have developed through my work in electro acous-tic music with and without live parts in the sense that some of the particular challenges in these genres have guided the choices made.

The assumption that the process that leads up to a finished version of a work of music contains information that is valuable both for the musician performing the work and the listener that approaches the result as well as for any research activity that attempts to understand the artistic process at large, has been a guiding principle in much of the developments of artistic research in the last couple of decades [3]. This supposition has likewise guided much of the research in the current project and, as a consequence, whether the work is a composition, a performed improvisation or an interpretation of a musical work is less important.

© Springer Nature Switzerland AG 2018
M. Aramaki et al. (Eds.): CMMR 2017, LNCS 11265, pp. 666–676, 2018.
https://doi.org/10.1007/978-3-030-01692-0_44

But however relevant the question of how to document artistic processes in music is, there is still a lack of stable solutions and tools for the requirements seen in the current project. However, several interesting and useful examples exist. One of the notable attempts to create a framework for documenting and sharing artistic research is the Research Catalogue [1]. Different in scope, the CASPAR project is a large scale system for archiving digital data [2,8,9,18]. These are only two out of many examples and given the impact of the process of digitization this is an area in which many new initiatives will be taken.

To add to the complexity of the question of documenting artistic practice, due to the novelty of the field of artistic research it is not always self evident what artistic research data actually consits of. Hence, even if a useful tool for documenting artistic research practice were to be developed, there is still the question of *what* should be documented remains. In any research context there is a need to collect material necessary for a systematic investigation. In addition, to research processes of creation there is a need to develop a suitable method that surfaces and makes visible the activities that relate to the work creation. The issue may be divided into several subtopics but first and foremost it is important to distinguish between the gathering of research data, and the documentation of the result. As was pointed oput above, even if the result may be easily documented, the data, the processes that lead to the result, is commonly of central importance to the artistic research process. How can the integrity of the data be preserved in an artistic research project that may contain a number of different kinds of data, as well as raw material from the artistic process?

The current research has its roots in events that started more than ten years ago, and my piece for guitar and electronics that was premiered in Beijing in 2006, *Repetition Repeats all other Repetitions* [16], has played an important role. Another related project that has contributed to the research to a significant degree is the *Integra* project [19]. *Integra* was a project hosted by Birmingham Conservatoire and funded by the EU, and one of its initial ambitions was to document electronic musical works in a sustainable manner addressing the issue that musical works that rely on technology, such as live electronic music or interactive music, may be difficult to preserve when the technology the works depend on becomes obsolete. In some cases works may become impossible to perform unless an effort is made to migrate these works to newer technologies [4,5,7]. Such processes of migration are often complicated and costly and this was an experience made in the *Integra* project. The overarching ambition was to collect works involving live electronics from the project partner countries and create robust and somewhat generic and technology independent descriptions of these pieces. In addition, the works adapted in the *Integra* project should be documented in ways that would make it easy for musicians and music ensembles to rehearse and perform them without the composer present. It was an original ambition that all data relating to supported musical works, including scores, electronic parts, information about different versions and renderings of these works, biographical data, etc., should be stored on a web-accessible database, and that it should be possible to transfer the data to a variety of usable target applications.

ArtDoc has developed out of the work done in *Integra*, in particular the research that Jamie Bullock and I did concerning a hierarchy of documentation classes [6, 7]. These were to some extent influenced by the work done in the large European MUSTICA project [2]. Whereas *Integra* to a some degree had a work-centered view on the musical work, a view based on the idea that each musical work has an identity that any performer and interpreter should adhere to, the current project has the ambition to also include the processes that lead up to a performance. As such it focuses on the elements of the processes that are essential to the creation of the work and regards each instance of the work as a new configuration with new possibilities. These two models, the work-centered view and the process oriented view, obviously have very different needs when it comes to documentation, but they also overlap in interesting ways. The main empirical data is taken from my experiences with the way *Repetition Repeats all other Repetitions* evolved from a strictly notated piece of music for guitar and electronics to an open form composition that has taken many shapes since its first performance.

The main difference between these two models is that in a traditional view of documentation, in which the work as it was conceived of by its originator, the performed result is actually a fairly decent means for communicating the intended result, given that the result is in line with the original intentions, and provided that there is a cultural, and perhaps social, context in which the performance took place. A good recording of a solid interpretation of a work in a known performance tradition can provide a good point of entry in the attempt to unpack its significance. However, as soon as the work questions conventional aesthetics and departs from expected traditions there is different need for contextual information in order for the work to make sense.

This is also true in the case of a electro acoustic music where the lack of a physical performer further detaches the sonic result from the material reality of the activities that gave rise to the work. For a work for which the process of creation plays a conceptually important part, the situation is not only aesthetically substantially different, it is also philosophically different. The work's authenticity lies no longer in the intentions of the originator, but rather in the ears of the listener, or in the hands of the interpreter.[1] How is such a work best documented?

ArtDoc has evolved out of this background to provide a preliminary solution to the question of how to document artistic practice in a way that allows it to be communicated to others. An important aspect of the documentation strategy discussed here is that it should also serve methodological needs of an associated artistic research effort. In order to successfully attempt to research one's own artistic practice there is a constant need to both archive the intermediary results

---

[1] This discussion could be expanded significantly and it may well be argued that also traditional music is molded by the listener as well as the originator. See [15] for an introduction.

and make connections between these and the final results. In a relatively early study in the development of creative technologies for music production Folkestad, Lindström and Hargreaves showed the importance of mapping the changes in the ongoing creative process as a method for researching processes of computer-based composition [11]. By collecting consecutive versions of the developing work by young composers they could effectively analyze the compositional strategies employed by the participants of the study.

For the rest of this short paper I will mainly discuss ArtDoc from the point of view of my own artistic work, but it nonetheless rests on the experiences and comparative discussions in the *Integra* project with its many different types of works.

2   Background

One of the strong aesthetic tendencies since the 1960s has been the move towards a more open work definition. An open work allows for the final construction to take place during, or in preparation for, the performance. This is not to say that all works that are not open are fixated, but rather that the actual openness in itself is an important aspect of the open work. Furthermore, there has been a great interest in expanded collaborations between composers and interpreters which has had an impact on the way that the limits of the musical work is recognized [17].

In his seminal book *Open Work* Umberto Eco analyzed a number of musical works that "are linked by a common feature: the considerable autonomy left to the individual performer in the way he chooses to play the work" [10]. In his analysis of the Belgian composer Henri Pousseur's piece *Scambi* he identifies a more radical version of openness that he refers to as "work in movement". Such works "invites us to identify inside the category of 'open' works a further, more restricted classification of works which can be defined as 'works in movement', because they characteristically consist of unplanned or physically incomplete structural units" [10]. The *work-in-movement* is a latent, or prospective, possibility rather than a defined and notated creation. For such a work, composing consists of supplying material for a work, delivering a potential work rather than a finished one. In *Repetition Repeats all other Repetitions* we found an interesting parallel in Umberto Eco's reasoning and developed an artistic method that leaned strongly on the idea of the work as a continuously developing field of possibilities. What started as a fairly standard composition for guitar and electronics soon developed into a *work-in-movement* whose identity as a work was located in change rather than fixity [10,12]. The development of the process in the beginning of the project is discussed in more detail in two articles on the topic of the negotiation of the musical work [14,15].

The early work on *Repetition Repeats all other Repetitions* coincided with the development of the documentation database for the *Integra* project. The idea of creating a work that invited interpreters to design their own version out of an assembly of segments that could be combined in a number of different manners surfaced and became one of the goals for the development of the project. Had these segments only consisted of written instructions in musical notation the challenge of creating this particular work's documentation may have been easier. However, a meaningful documentation for this piece will have to contain all the different electronic parts – software for interaction, DSP processes for altering the acoustic sounds, etc. – and sound files, but also previous versions and their modes of construction should be documented. If not, there will be a risk that each version repeats previous versions rather than keep moving the work in new directions. The idea of building a documentation database for the piece appeared as a sensible solution. Although the database developed in the *Integra* project was mainly designed for the preservation of works, its basic structure turned out to be apt also for the current context.

The ruling principle for *Repetition Repeats all other Repetitions* is that there is no such thing as an ultimate and defining performance. The work is not a conclusive end product but a conceptually organized process, and each instance of it may overthrow decisions made in earlier versions. Hence, each performance of the work makes possible a new work, and this development is the true nature of the work identity. Making an exact repetition of a prior performance is impossible for any work of music, but here the change from performance to performance is the very essence of this work. How can this incremental process be documented to allow the *work-in-movement* to continue to move and not just repeat itself? Will not the act of archiving then defeat the purpose of the goal to perpetuate change? Is an archive that archives in order to allow for change possible, or even desirable? Considering the fact that most archives are constructed to preserve a state that may otherwise be lost in ongoing developments, this is a relevant question.

3 Method

One preliminary, however inconclusive, way to understand the question of the nature of the archive in the context of artistic research is that the material basis of the artistic practice may be both data and result. The way in which either could be represented in the research is however a challenge, particularly in the context of performative arts and music. One point of departure for the project presented here is that it is necessary to critically examine the relations between artistic practice in music and its possible representations in various forms for archives. This, and the more general question of the tendency of any archive to, in a manner of speaking, write itself, is discussed in an forthcoming article in a thematic issue on digitization in *The Swedish Journal of Music Research* [13].

An archive of musical material most often archives representations of musical content, and to be meaningful such archives have to go beyond a mere collection of the resources. An archived score is relatively easy to represent accurately, but is a poor or difficult to access representation of the actual music. A recording of a performance is an accurate representation of the sonic trace, but a poor representation of the material performance. Furthermore, within the category of musical recordings, there are a number of different methods to record and archive performances, most, if not all, of which become reductions of the materiality of the performance when they are adapted to the archivable documentation format. How, then, may a sustainable archive for artistic research and artistic practice be structured such that it avoids the risk that the archiving force hides important aspects of the data?

Conveniently, in the case of *Repetition Repeats all other Repetitions* the nature of the research data and the elements of the artistic practice coincided to a significant degree. In other words, the method that was developed for exploring efficient means for archiving the data overlapped with the artistic methods used in the creation and the development of the piece. In this particular case the development of the work provided us with answers to the question of what was required of the archive. Departing from this methodological framework, and from the work previously done in the *Integra* project, a model for a database that could live up to the needs for documentation of this particular project was developed. It should also be noted that *Repetition Repeats all other Repetitions* explores a number of non-conventional playing techniques that are difficult to describe in notation. Hence, not only was it our ambition to develop an expanded score that would allow for continuous recreation of the work, there was also an interest in embedding video documentation of the various playing techniques used.

The question of sustainability needs to be addressed in connection with any kind of archiving effort [7], and in the case of digital storage of a wide variety of kinds of data it is crucial to consider the aspect of durability. The choice to use Extensible Markup Language (XML) as the main format for encoding data in ArtDoc was informed by the fact that XML is human readable. It is a design choice to regard the data, the technology to order it, and the user interface as three somewhat independent layers of the system. It should be possible to read the data without the database and the interface, and this fact supports the potential sustainability of the system.

4   The Archive

The structure of the archive is a set of classes that represent different kinds of resources and it is a feature of the system that classes can easily be added and extend the basic classes. There are a number of general, abstract, classes that serve as templates for further specialized classes. For example, the two base classes that most other classes inherit from are the *Class* and *Document* classes (see Fig. 1). As a consequence a reference of the type *Document* can point to almost any kind of resource in the archive, and all instances of any type that are children of these classes will have the same basic set of attributes. Similarly, an *OrganizationalUnit* is the base class for all kinds of references to *Persons*, *Users* or *Authors*. A *Collection* is a means for grouping resources together, for example as a convenience when several users collaborate on a project, and a *View* is a presentation of a list of one or more such collections.

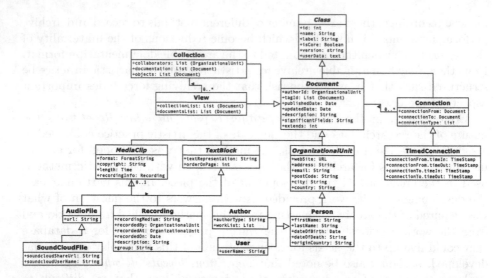

Fig. 1. A part of the diagram for the latest version of the class hierarchy for the documentation system ArtDoc. All classes extend the base class *Class* and most classes also extend the *Document* class. This allows for new and more specialized classes to be easily added.

One of the fundamental properties of this experimental documentation archive is the *Connection* class. It defines a connection between two instances and the principle is that it should be possible to connect anything to anything – that is any *Document* may be connected to any other *Document*. In this way connected objects can create a semantic web where the kinds of connections, as well as the number of connections, gives the user information about the documented data. Hence, connections give meaning to instances, and instances can further be understood through the number of connections they have. In this way, even after the raw data has been entered and connections have been made, the archive becomes a method in its own right. Furthermore, connections of the type *TimedConnection* can point to a specific point in time, or a range, in an instance that documents some kind of time based data such as an audio or video file.

All classes are defined in an XML description which acts as a template for all instances of that particular type, adding in the attributes of all parent classes. Below is an example of the definition of the *Connection* class (some information is stripped out for legibility). The instance attributes are defined within the *attributes* tag.

Example of a class definition

```
<Class xmlns:xsi="http://www.w3.org/2001/XMLSchema-instance">
    <class-name>Connection</class-name>
    <parent>Class</parent>
    <class-description>A child class to Class describing a
```

```
    connection between two nodes within the system. The id of the
    connected classes are the references.
  </class-description>
  <documentation/>
  <attributes>
      <connection-from type="Ref" ref-class="Document"
                       desc="Connection from" edit="1"
                       required="1" doc="The reference to the
                       document that connects another document. />
      <connection-to type="Ref" ref-class="Document"
                     desc="Connection to" edit="1"
                     required="1" doc="The reference to the
                     document that is connected."/>
      <connection-type type="String" desc="Type of connection"
                       edit="1" required="0"/>
  </attributes>
</Class>
```

(Example class definition for the *Connection* class. As can be seen the definition contains documentation strings for both the class and for each of the attributes. The 'type' and 'required' parameters of each attribute allows for basic validation of an instance.)

The design principle has been to keep classes small and particular, and as mentioned above, it should be possible to add new classes to the system simply by adding new class definitions that inherit existing classes. However, more complicated and specialized classes may obviously require additional definitions on either the client or the server, or both. For example, a video class that allows the user to add a video through an external service may depend on a particular API for which support needs to be added.

Using abstract classes as basic types for the data allows the implementation of simple and generic widgets in the user interface. For example, the *MediaClip* class serves any sub-classes with basic functionality for playing back an audio or video file with a generic set of playback functions. Implementing support for a class that extends this base class, such as YouTube or similar, may then be limited to supplying a wrapper that maps the base class functionality to the extended class' API. Though the system could easily be made to support that routines needed for a particular class be added in the class definition, this may introduce security issues that needs to be considered.

The development of an implementation of ArtDoc is currently progressing using eXist db [20] as the backend using XQuery for the server side scripts, and a web client as front end (see Fig. 2). Apart from the goal to document *Repetition Repeats all other Repetitions* ArtDoc will be tested as a documentation database for works performed in the *Klangdome* at the Royal College of Music in Stockholm. The *Klangdome*, situated in one of the concert halls is a flexible system of up to 49 loudspeakers in a dome like configuration that affords a platform for a wide variety of scientific and artistic projects. The attempt to document the works performed offers a challenging task for ArtDoc that will guide its future development.

Finally, ArtDoc will be used in a newly initiated research project under the headline of *Musical Transformations*. *Musical Transformations* brings researchers in ethnomusicology and artistic research in music together in order to develop new knowledge and deepened understanding of processes of renewal of musical practices in intercultural and transnational contexts. Musical traditions in Vietnam and in Sweden will be documented and new interdisciplinary methods for research into creative processes in music will be developed in which ArtDoc will play an important role.

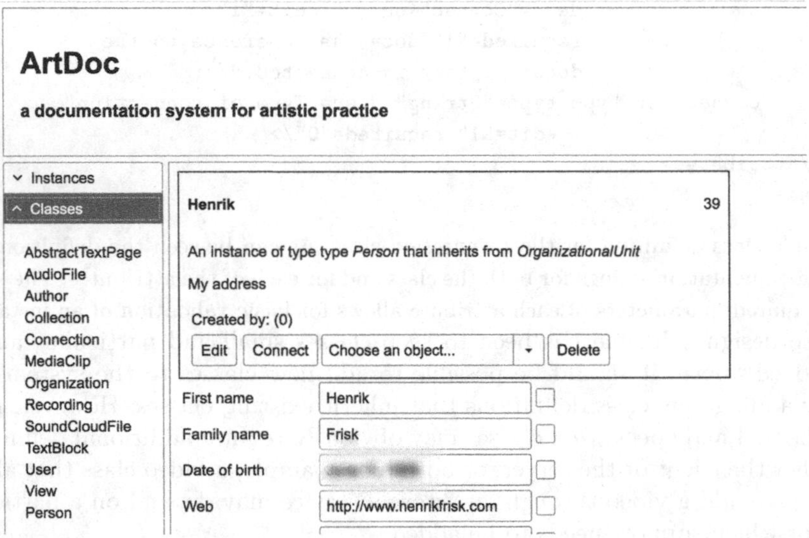

Fig. 2. A screen dump from an early and preliminary version of the interface to ArtDoc. To the right are a list of instantiable classes and in the main view is an item of the type *Person* open for editing.

5   Discussion

The question of how to best document the creative forces that digital technology allows for is without doubt one of the important challenges in the near future. Though this is a question that has bearing on almost all aspects of social life in the 21st century, in the case of artistic practice in music there are a few important considerations that are of particular interest. First, there is the risk that the nearly ubiquitous digital domain negatively influences the willingness to invest in an active listening process. Though there is little that actually points in this direction, if anything listening to live music appears to have increased in urban areas, the convenience of online music services that delivers exactly the music it thinks we want to hear is intimidating at times. The materiality of music production in the widest sense is not necessarily encoded into the digital representation of music. Secondly, the incredible digital tools that we have at hand may make visible aspects of musical composition and performance in new and interesting ways. Collecting audio and video documentation, for example, has never been easier, but the massive amounts of data that it generates can be daunting without a structured method. These are only two of many facets of the changes that digitization affords, but if these are addressed in a way that bring forth the conditions of musical practice they may provide interesting opportunities for the development of artistic practices. When the focus moves from the result to the processes prior to the result, the view on the musical work is likely to also change.

If it proves effective there are a number of ways in which it can be expanded. For example, currently ArtDoc is largely a single user application that offers musicians and composers to document their own work. However, its real strength will show when users can interact on projects together. The driving force in the development has been my own need for a tool to both document my work, but also to allow for a more efficient way to interact with my colleagues on projects. The basic ability to control access to individual items in the archive through permissions is already in place. Furthermore, the functionality that the classes *Collection* and *View* offer can with some modification turn the archive into a proper presentation tool, or even a tool for performance, in its own right.

In this short overview I have tried to argue for the need for new strategies for the documentation of artistic practice, as well as presented an experimental tool to meet these demands. A modular system with a hierarchy of documentation classes, an archive and a user client to enter and access data is under development and preliminary tests have been carried out. The primary purpose of ArtDoc, however, is to explore the various ways in which a documentation of an artistic practice can be carried out that provides meaningful information to both the artist and the listener.

Acknowledgments. With acknowledgments to my colleague Jamie Bullock and the other contributors of the Integra project.

References

1. About the research catalogue web resource (2017). https://www.researchcatalogue.net/portal/about. Accessed 15 May 2017
2. Bachimont, B., et al.: Preserving interactive digital music: a report on the MUS-TICA research initiative. In: Proceedings of Third International Conference on Web Delivering of Music. Web Delivering of Music. WEDELMUSIC (2003)
3. Biggs, M., Karlsson, H., (eds).: The Routledge Companion to Research in the Arts. Routledge, London (2010)
4. Bullock, J., Coccioli, C.: Modernising musical works involving yamaha DX-based synthesis: a case study. Organised Sound **11**(3), 221–227 (2006)
5. Bullock, J., Frisk, H.: libIntegra: a system for software-independent multimedia module description and storage. In: Proceedings of the International Computer Music Conference 2007, Copenhagen, Denmark (2007)

6. Bullock, J., Frisk, H.: An object oriented model for the representation of temporal data in the integra framework. In: Proceedings of the International Computer Music Conference 2009. ICMA (2009)
7. Bullock, J., Frisk, H., Coccioli, L.: Sustainability of 'live electronic' music in the integra project. In: The 14th IEEE Mediterranean Electrotechnical Conference Proceedings, Ajaccio, Corsica (2008)
8. Cuervo, A.P.: Preserving the electroacoustic music legacy: a case study of the salmar construction at the university of illinois. Notes **68**(1), 33–47 (2011)
9. Douglas, J.: General Study 03 Final Report : Preserving Interactive Digital Music. Technical report, The MUSTICA Initiative (2007)
10. Eco, U.: The Open Work. Hutchinson Radius, London (1968). (English translation published in 1989)
11. Folkestad, G., Lindström, B., Hargreaves, D.J.: Young people's music in the digital age: a study of computer based creative music making. Res. Stud. Music Educ. **9**(1), 1–12 (1997)
12. Frisk, H.: Improvisation, Computers and Interaction: Rethinking Human-Computer Interaction Through Music. Ph.D. thesis, Faculty of Fine and Performing Arts, Lund University (2008)
13. Frisk, H.: The Archive that Writes Itself. SMC (2018, in print)
14. Frisk, H., Östersjö, S.: Negotiating the musical work. an empirical study. In: Proceedings of the International Computer Music Conference 2006, pp. 242–249. ICMA, San Francisco, California. Computer Music Association (2006)
15. Frisk, H., Östersjö, S.: Negotiating the musical work. an empirical study on the inter-relation between composition, interpretation and performance. In: Proceedings of EMS -06, Beijing. Terminology and Translation. Electroacoustic Music Studies, EMS (2006)
16. Frisk, H., Coessens, C., Östersjö, S.: Repetition, resonance and discernment. In: Crispin, D., Gilmore, B. (Eds.) Artistic Experimentation in Music: Orpheus Institute Series, Gent (2014)
17. Östersjö, S.: SHUT UP 'N' PLAY! Negotiating the Musical Work. Ph.D. thesis, Malmö Academy of Music, Lund University (2008)
18. Roeder, J.: Authenticity of Digital Music: Key Insights from Interviews in the MUSTICA Project. Technical report, The MUSTICA Initiative (2006)
19. IntegraLab. http://integra.io/
20. eXist db. http://exist-db.org

Author Index

Printed in the United States
By Bookmasters